This study was inspired by the dramatic shift that occurred between 1976 and 1980 in China's education policies and the outside world's perception of them. In 1976, China's "education revolution" was being hailed by foreign observers as an inspiration for all low-income countries and many others as well, whether communist or otherwise. By 1980, the Chinese themselves had disavowed the experience, declaring it devoid of even a single redeeming virtue.

The author's search for clues to explain this sudden change ultimately spanned most of the 20th century. The study of both pre- and post-1949 China provided the historical perspective necessary to distinguish continuities from innovations and to trace communist educational decisions back to their pre-communist antecedents. Rather than the epitome of good or evil, China's 1970s educational experience emerged instead as only the most tumultuous episode in a long and contentious struggle to adapt Western ways for use in a non-Western society.

The story of the rise and fall of China's education revolution unfolds along three dimensions: first, from the perspective of the international development community, to suggest why the Chinese experience found so receptive an audience there; second, from the vantage point of China's own educational history, in a search for the origins of radical education reform; and finally, from the perspective of those who actually participated in the 1966–1976 experience.

Radicalism and education reform in 20th-century China

Radicalism and education reform in 20th-century China

The search for an ideal development model

SUZANNE PEPPER

CAMBRIDGE
UNIVERSITY PRESS

PUBLISHED BY THE PRESS SYNDICATE OF THE UNIVERSITY OF CAMBRIDGE
The Pitt Building, Trumpington Street, Cambridge, United Kingdom

CAMBRIDGE UNIVERSITY PRESS
The Edinburgh Building, Cambridge CB2 2RU, UK   http://www.cup.cam.ac.uk
40 West 20th Street, New York, NY 10011-4211, USA   http://www.cup.org
10 Stamford Road, Oakleigh, Melbourne 3166, Australia
Ruiz de Alarcón 13, 28014 Madrid, Spain

First published 1996
First paperback edition 2000

Printed in the United States of America

Typeset in Times Roman in FrameMaker [au]

A catalog record for this book is available from the British Library

Library of Congress Cataloging in Publication data
Pepper, Suzanne.
Radicalism and education reform in 20th-century China : the search
for an ideal development model / Suzanne Pepper.
p.   cm.
Includes bibliographical references and index.
ISBN 0-521-49669-1 (hardback)
ISBN 0-521-77860-3 (paperback)
1. Education – China – History – 20th century. 2. Educational
change – China – History – 20th century. 3. Communism and education –
China – History – 20th century. 4. China – History – Cultural
Revolution, 1966–1969. 5. School management and organization –
LA1131.82.P47   1996
370'.951'09047 – dc20   95–24843
CIP

ISBN 0 521 49669 1 hardback
ISBN 0 521 77860 3 paperback

Contents

Contents

Acknowledgments

Because this study has been "in progress" for almost two decades, the debts of gratitude and inspiration are similarly extensive. In fact, the project grew incrementally: first from curiosity over the substance of Chinese education development, which was attracting considerably more attention 20 years ago than it does today; and then from frustration at the difficulties of researching the subject in China itself. Once the sum total of the 1966 to 1976 period was rechristened a decade of disaster, all the new opportunities for foreign scholars generally did not apply to the study of all its aspects. The official periodization and selective access thus determined both the parameters of this study and the research method. Accordingly, I tried to make the best of both worlds – using the new opportunities to work on the post-Mao period, while simultaneously falling back on the "old" Hong Kong émigré interview alternative as the only means of studying its immediate predecessor. The publications that resulted on the post-Mao period are listed in the Bibliography; the Appendix explains the Hong Kong interviews which are the main focus of this book.

The interviews themselves concentrated on the educational component of the 1966–1976 Cultural Revolution, known in contemporary parlance as the education revolution. They concluded, as does this book, with the backlash against it in the late 1970s and early 1980s. So dramatic were those events, however, that they inevitably raised another set of important questions about where the extreme radicalism of the 1966–1976 years might have come from. Such questions also paralleled the general reassessment of all aspects of the Chinese revolution that began after Mao's death. In this manner the book finally assumed its present outline, as a history of radical education reform in 20th-century China culminating with the Cultural Revolution experience.

The sequence of research "events" that promoted the above course of intellectual development involved far more people than can be thanked individually. Nor are the events any less significant for including the negative as well as positive. First and most definitive was the long-awaited 1980 research trip. This was sponsored by the Committee on Scholarly Communication with the People's Republic of China and, through no fault of the sponsor, was limited to the post-1976 period. On the contrary, the then CSC/PRC Beijing representative, John

vii

Jamieson, and the Washington staff smoothed over many difficulties to make the opportunity an otherwise rewarding one.

The changing intellectual concerns of the 1980s were registered specifically in the form of two research assignments, together with the accompanying critical input by editors and conference participants. Those assignments produced the education chapters in *The Cambridge History of China*, volumes 14 and 15, edited by Professors John K. Fairbank and Roderick MacFarquhar; and the century-spanning essay demanded for the June 1984 conference on reforming the Chinese political order, led by Professor Michel Oksenberg. But for those two assignments, I would no doubt have left mostly unexplored questions about the origins of radical education reform which added many years to the writing and many insights to the years.

Additionally, I would like to thank Christine Wong for insisting that the cumulative record of the 1980s deserved another separate publication; and also Joyce Kallgren for her assistance in publishing that manuscript. The resulting monograph, *China's Education Reform in the 1980s* (1990), allowed me to concentrate thereafter on the earlier years, and readers of the present volume interested in following its themes through 1989 can refer to that study. Before, during, and after its publication, critical comments by Wong, Kallgren, Deborah Davis, and Ronald Price contributed to the progress of the work that followed.

My greatest debt, however, is to the Hong Kong interviewees without whom my continuing study of the Cultural Revolution decade would not have been possible. The exercise was not an easy one and all were aware of the unusual step they had taken in agreeing to be interviewed by a foreign researcher. Yet a majority also accepted at face value the aim of providing "raw material" for scholarly research. And while most would undoubtedly argue over the resulting interpretations – because it was a time and topic about which everyone was always arguing about something – I hope I have satisfied their trust in my use of the data they provided.

Also, but for those who had gone before me in researching contemporary China by means of such interviews, I might not have been inclined to follow that course myself. Many scholars did so to good advantage in the 1960s and 1970s, but I should acknowledge especially the work of Anita Chan, Stanley Rosen, and Jonathan Unger. Here again, interpretations sometimes differ. But my own questions and understanding benefited greatly from their prior interview-based work, especially on the complicated issues of social class and factional alignments in Chinese schools before and during the Cultural Revolution.

Small grants from the Ford Foundation in 1979 and the American Association of University Women in 1982 helped defray expenses. I was also aided by a fellowship from the An Wang Foundation in 1987. But most importantly, this book could not have been written without the library facilities and staff support provided by the Universities Service Centre, which has sustained my research in Hong Kong for many years. Since it is not possible to name everyone who contributed assistance, I would like to take this opportunity to thank them collectively. The interviews themselves were conducted at the "old" location while the library research was done both there and at the new venue on the Chinese University campus.

Special acknowledgment is due John Dolfin, who did much to keep the USC going under difficult conditions in the 1980s, as well as to Professor Kuan Hsin-chi and Jean Hung, who have maintained it since at the Chinese University. All three facilitated my research in many ways. Among other things they, together with former USC librarian Lau Yee-fui, activated the various arrangements necessary to use the Union Research Institute materials as well as the University of Hong Kong and Chinese University main libraries. The university collections contain most of the pre-1949 publications on Chinese education listed in the Bibliography. Wu Yeen-mei at the East Asia Library, University of Washington, Seattle, helped locate other similar hard-to-find titles.

At the USC, four individuals in particular helped me during various phases of this study: in order of their appearance, Liu Zicheng, Jean Hung (Xiong Jingming), Liu Huiling, and Wen Yanxia. At different times and in different ways, they introduced me to the unfamiliar routines of interviewing and assisted my search for corroborating documentation. But most important, they demonstrated a rare tolerance for arguing the pros and cons of a multitude of contradictions that had to be unraveled as the research progressed, and it is for this contribution that I am most grateful. There are many disadvantages to remaining forever "in the field" and far from home base. Among the benefits, however, has been the presence of these and other Hong Kong friends who talked me through countless follow-up questions. The technology remained happily pre-modern from start to finish, and USC veteran Moni Tai typed the completed manuscript.

Finally, I thank the editors at Cambridge University Press for their reception of this book. Elizabeth Neal and Janis Bolster guided it smoothly through the last steps toward publication and Pamela Bruton deserves special mention for her skill in making presentable so ungainly a manuscript. It goes without saying, however, that no one but myself should be held responsible for the end result, including especially all matters of emphasis and interpretation.

1

Educational development and the Chinese experience

By the mid-1970s, China's experience was being heralded within the international development community as a new model worthy of praise and emulation. Leftist radicalism inspired by events in China and elsewhere during the 1960s was already beginning to fade. But as China opened its doors to the outside world after the chaotic inaugural years (1966–1968) of the Cultural Revolution, political pilgrims were followed by a growing assortment of development professionals, academics, and others. They usually arrived asking what might be learned from the Chinese experience and left in general agreement that, while revolution might be a heavy price to pay, its achievements deserved to be acknowledged as such. Educational development ranked high on the list of benefits.

Admiration grew so great that China was soon being hailed as an example, virtually unique among low-income countries, in following the spirit of the World Bank's 1974 education sector recommendations – even though China was at that time still beyond the pale of the bank's lending and advisory operations.[1] Economist John Simmons reiterated the new consensus when he wrote at the end of the decade that China's education system "comes closest to the World Bank's model program for a developing country." The essential features of the Chinese system in this respect were a curriculum designed to meet the needs of a mass clientele; the widely promoted goal of 10-year universal schooling; decentralized local administration; and tertiary-level selection aimed at minimizing discrimination against the poor. These achievements were, moreover, being sustained at low cost within an economy where per capita yearly income was estimated at only U.S.$250. This placed China within the lowest-income category, where levels of educational development were generally least impressive.[2]

[1] Hans N. Weiler, "Education and Development: From the Age of Innocence to the Age of Scepticism," *Comparative Education*, vol. 14, no. 3 (Oct. 1978), p. 189. For the recommendations themselves, see *Education: Sector Working Paper* (Washington, D.C.: World Bank, 1974); for a contemporary critique of the 1974 working paper, see Peter Williams, ed., *Prescription for Progress? A Commentary on the Education Policy of the World Bank* (London: University of London, Institute of Education, 1976).
[2] John Simmons, "Introduction and Summary," in John Simmons, ed., *The Education Dilemma: Policy Issues for Developing Countries in the 1980s* (New York: Pergamon Press, 1980), pp. 9–

Many others, including both practitioners and researchers, were similarly forthright in lauding China's education policies during the early 1970s. British sociologist Ronald Dore heralded them as the first antidote to be administered on a nationwide basis for the "diploma disease," which he held responsible for the troubles besetting education generally. Like many others, he saw problems which originated in the West grow more virulent when developing education systems tried to adapt Western models to non-Western societies and low-income economies.[3] Dore also, like many others, cited Tanzania. Building on its education for self-reliance doctrine, the Tanzanian government announced additional measures in the mid-1970s inspired by the Chinese example.[4]

That such measures were part of larger socialist experiments in both countries, China and Tanzania, failed to dampen enthusiasm even among those not usually so inclined. "There was," said Kenneth King of Canada's International Development Research Centre, "a considerable readiness to leave to one side the explicitly political side of the reforms, and to concentrate on the elements that seemed in themselves to be eminently sensible approaches to educational improvement in low income countries."[5]

Yet even as this consensus of international approval was still growing, the Chinese were already dismantling the model that inspired it. The Cultural Revolution was declared officially ended shortly after Mao Zedong's death in 1976, and by 1980, the new official line decreed that "not one good thing" could be said of developments in education (or anything else) throughout the entire 1966–1976 Cultural Revolution decade. The new line refused to distinguish between the inaugural Red Guard rebellion of 1966–1968; the subsequent intensified application of political and social criteria after schools reopened in 1968–1969; and the specific policies introduced. All alike were redefined as manifestations of the "10-year turmoil" and as unworthy of anything but historical oblivion. Educators throughout the country professed themselves incredulous in 1980 that the outside world could have sought to learn from the

10. John Simmons was at this time with the Word Bank's Policy Planning Division. He prepared or coordinated a number of internal working papers which reflected the international development community's changing concerns during the 1970s.
[3] Ronald Dore, *The Diploma Disease: Education, Qualification, and Development* (London: George Allen and Unwin, 1976), chap. 14.
[4] On Tanzania's education for self-reliance doctrine, which actually predated China as a focus of international interest, see, e.g., J. K. Nyerere, *Education for Self-Reliance* (Dar-es-Salaam: Government Printer, 1967); Robert McCormick, ed., *Tanzania: Education for Self-Reliance*, rev. ed. (Milton Keynes: Open University Press, 1979); Bill Williamson, *Education, Social Structure and Development: A Comparative Analysis* (London: Macmillan, 1979), pp. 153–177.
[5] Kenneth King, "The Chinese Model and Developing Countries," p. 2, presentation to the International Development Research Centre's China Education Seminar, Toronto, June 1980. For the interest generated by the early 1970s Chinese model, see also Robert D. Barendsen, *Education in the People's Republic of China: A Selective Annotated Bibliography of Materials Published in the English Language, 1971–1976* (Washington, D.C.: U.S. Department of Education, 1981).

Chinese experience of the early 1970s. Indeed, they were unwilling to identify even one feature that deserved to be retained or remembered from the educational model that was still being lauded internationally as the best of all possible solutions for the dilemmas of educational development.[6]

The present study was inspired by this dramatic shift that occurred between 1976 and 1980 in China's education policies and the outside world's perception of them. The questions that emerged then have now become part of China's educational history and are the central focus of this inquiry. How could so sharp a discretionary and so swift a change be explained? Was there any substance to the earlier claims? Or were they all part of some grand illusion created by the impact of Mao's aging political ego on a naive foreign audience? Had the international development community been collectively overcome by Potemkin Village syndrome, to which earlier visitors in communist countries had also sometimes succumbed? Or, following an even older tradition among foreign observers, were they perhaps using China for purposes of their own, reflecting images more of themselves and of what they wanted China to be than of Chinese realities? And if there was substance to the earlier claims, why were the Chinese so insistently denying them? Still "too sensitive" to research in China itself at the time, these questions guided the interviews conducted with Chinese émigré schoolteachers in Hong Kong during the late 1970s and early 1980s (see Appendix). Their answers are presented in the final chapters of this study.

Assuming the validity of those answers, however, raised a second set of important questions about the past and future, or whether the suddenly discredited "education revolution" of the 1966–1976 era had either. Ironically, such questions were underlined by the polemical excesses of the immediate post-1976 years. Where, in other words, did the 1966–1976 episode come from? If it was, as the post-1976 rhetoric suggested, just another of the mistakes Mao committed in his dotage, then the episode might indeed be successfully erased from the pages of history and the memories of its participants. But if the education revolution was something more, as interviewees suggested, then the experience must have had antecedents and roots of its own, which might not be so easily extracted.

---

[6] The reference is to three months of interviews conducted by the author in China in 1980, under the U.S.–China exchange program administered by the Committee on Scholarly Communication with the People's Republic of China (Washington, D.C.). Not one administrator at any of the 15 universities and 8 secondary schools visited was willing to offer even one qualification to the new line that the Cultural Revolution was a 10-year disaster. On the 1980 research, see Suzanne Pepper, "China's Universities: New Experiments in Socialist Democracy and Administrative Reform – A Research Report," *Modern China*, vol. 8, no. 2 (Apr. 1982), pp. 147–204; Suzanne Pepper, *China's Universities: Post-Mao Enrollment Policies and Their Impact on the Structure of Secondary Education: A Research Report*, Monographs in Chinese Studies, no. 46 (Ann Arbor: University of Michigan, 1984).

In fact, this historical line of inquiry yielded an unexpected bonus by revealing the long-standing nature of the educational "development dilemmas" that received so much international publicity during the 1960s and 1970s. The dilemmas themselves or at least their clearly identifiable predecessors, the international development community's understanding of them, and their articulation within the Chinese context by Chinese and foreign activists and educators, all predated Mao's Cultural Revolution by about half a century.

Pursuing the historical inquiry thus had the further result of reducing China's educational experience of the 1970s to more manageable proportions. Rather than the epitome of good or evil, that experience emerged instead as part of China's long struggle to adapt Western ways for use in a non-Western society. The struggle was at least as traumatic as those dramatized for development purposes in the 1970s. And beyond the specific solutions posited for development, there was revealed the example of an ancient society still unreconstructed after nearly a century's concerted effort to modernize in the image of the Western world. Hence it was only by tracing their roots backward in time that questions about the substance of the education revolution and causes of its downfall could be properly addressed.

We will therefore explore these questions along three dimensions: first, from the perspective of the international development community itself, to suggest why the Chinese experience found so receptive an audience there (chapter 1); second, against the backdrop of China's 20th-century educational history, in a search for the origins of radical reform (Parts I and II); and finally, in terms of the cultural revolution experience itself (Part III).

Changing perceptions of education and development

If the dilemmas associated with educational development were not new in the 1970s, they were at least being reproduced on a scale unknown in earlier decades due to the quantum leap in educational growth that occurred internationally during the first quarter century after World War II. Education was officially declared a human right by the new United Nations organization, and expansion everywhere seemed to be based on two related assumptions. Trained personnel were essential for economic development; and economics and education together would promote the general wellbeing, including equality of opportunity for all. In Western Europe and America, tertiary-level enrollments expanded rapidly while traditional barriers in Europe separating elite from non-elite education at the secondary level began to weaken.

Elsewhere, the impetus for growth was further strengthened by the self-conscious efforts at nation building and economic modernization that accompanied the ending of the colonial era, especially during the first 25 years after

World War II. These efforts came to be symbolized in a new concept, known as the "Third World," which evolved from the early cold war division of capitalist and communist nations. That original usage soon fell out of fashion and was replaced by a new formulation defining the U.S. and the Soviet Union together as the First World; the other developed nations of Europe and North America as the Second World; and the Third World as everyone else. By definition, the chief characteristic shared by all Third World nations was their relative poverty. "Development" referred to the effort to close the gap between rich and poor.

According to development's credo, wealth derived from industrialization, which occurred first in the West during its long history of scientific discovery and technological innovation. Accordingly, the Third World's poverty was paralleled by a low level of industrialization together with scientific and technological backwardness. Related to economics and technology, but maintaining a certain independent life of its own, was the social dimension of development, which included education. Despite a variety of permutations in this sector as in others, the poverty and backwardness of the Third World usually translated into a small educated elite concentrated in urban centers and a large poorly educated mass predominating in rural areas, where a majority of the population lived.

The exact nature of the relationship between intellectual and economic poverty had not been conclusively demonstrated. But it was accepted almost as an article of faith that the two were related. Education was therefore valued, both for the individual and for the larger society, not only as a basic human right and a measure of progress but also as a prerequisite for economic advancement and its concomitant benefits. Expectations were initially such that education was imbued with all the attributes of an independent force – capable in itself of promoting economic development, modernization, national integration, independence, and reduced population growth, as well as a more equitable distribution of opportunity and income. Similarly, for the individual, education would provide the socialization and skills necessary to increase productivity, enhance earning power, promote upward social mobility, and allow fuller participation in political life. It was an "age of innocence" when optimism grew from the seemingly limitless possibilities of a new postcolonial beginning.[7]

Hence the main educational objective of the United Nations First Development Decade (1960–1970) was to provide schooling for all children. Quantitative goals dominated work in the early 1960s. The goals for Asia specified that the rate of educational expansion achieved during the 1950s should be doubled

---

[7] The much-quoted "age of innocence" phrase is from the Ford Foundation's F. Champion Ward in his Introduction to F. Champion Ward, ed., *Education and Development Reconsidered: The Bellagio Conference Papers* (New York: Praeger, 1974), p. xv.

and that every country in the region should provide universal, compulsory, and free education of seven years or more by 1980 at the latest.[8]

Formal education systems in pre-independence Asia and Africa were typically modeled on those in the Western colonizing countries. These same patterns were retained in the immediate post-independence years, when educational change was largely quantitative in nature. This strategy of superimposing quantitative goals on the inherited systems was paralleled in the economic sector by an emulation of Western-inspired models of industrial and urban growth. The strategy persisted more or less unchallenged into the late 1960s and produced some impressive growth rates. The First Development Decade's goal of an annual 5 percent increase in national incomes was ultimately achieved. Enrollments doubled and tripled, and investment in education rose accordingly.

By the early 1970s, however, innocence was long gone. It had begun to die, wrote modernization theorist Lucian Pye, "soon after the first ex-colonial people began to experience frustrations and disappointment in their efforts to become modern nations."[9] Chief among the new concerns were the continuing disparities, both international and internal, between industrial rich and agrarian poor. Beneath the aggregated growth statistics, conditions of poverty and underdevelopment remained seemingly unchanged. There were actually more hungry and illiterate people in the world in 1970 than two decades earlier, during which time the "revolution of rising expectations" had given way to a "revolution of rising frustrations."[10]

Most of the Second Development Decade (1970–1980) was consequently devoted to the search for more refined definitions and strategies aimed at solving the "dysfunctions of development." Priorities began shifting: from urban to rural, from industry to agriculture, and from the growth of the gross national product to essential human needs. New goals focused more directly on the poor and landless, or those whose needs were greatest, and on ways to guarantee employment, income, nutrition, health care, and of course schooling.[11] But these concerns, in the absence of any certainty about how best to proceed, eventually produced a "new" perspective. According to this view, a more equitable sharing of present and future benefits, as anticipated by the new priorities, could not be achieved without a redistribution of existing economic and political power. By the early 1970s, the weight of opinion was

---

[8] C. E. Beeby, *The Quality of Education in Developing Countries* (Cambridge: Harvard University Press, 1966), pp. 7–8 n. 2; Edgar Faure et al., *Learning to Be: The World of Education Today and Tomorrow* (Paris: United Nations Educational, Scientific, and Cultural Organization, 1972), p. 53.

[9] Lucian W. Pye, Introduction to Lucian W. Pye, ed., *Communications and Political Development* (Princeton: Princeton University Press, 1963), p. 12.

[10] The phrase is from Daniel Lerner, "Toward a Communications Theory of Modernization," in Pye, *Communications and Political Development*, pp. 327–350.

[11] E.g., H. M. Phillips, *Planning Educational Assistance for the Second Development Decade* (Paris: Unesco, International Institute for Educational Planning, 1973).

clearly shifting within the international development community as socialist-like prescriptions began emanating from even the most unlikely quarters.

"Increases in national income ... will not benefit the poor unless they reach the poor," declared former U.S. Defense Secretary Robert McNamara in his new capacity as World Bank president. Yet policies always favored urban and better-off areas, he said, in part because of the "greater participation of the highly privileged in the political process." He recommended direct government intervention on several points, including income growth targets for the poor and institutional changes to redistribute economic power.[12]

In education, a similar reordering of priorities occurred. The new concerns did not, of course, emerge full blown in 1970. Rather they appeared in piecemeal fashion throughout the 1960s, as the consequences of the development effort began to make themselves felt. During that time, scholars were also chipping away at the optimistic assumptions even as these were still inspiring the work of advocates and practitioners. Thus, early statistical explorations revealed only a moderate relationship between education and economic development. Research findings did not uphold the assumption that education in whatever form – basic literacy, primary, or postprimary – was a direct cause of development. Complicating the search was the dual nature of the subject matter. Education could be analytically distinguished as both means and ends, that is, as a means of production and an object of consumption, which people and communities were more likely to "buy" as incomes rose. But in practice researchers had difficulty determining when education was a cause of development and when its result.[13]

Research findings also did not uphold the assumption that education, by itself, could promote equality or upward mobility. Studies were inconclusive, arguments flourished, and the experts could not agree.[14] By the mid-20th century, tertiary education had become a virtual prerequisite for the technical, managerial, and intellectual skills necessary to sustain economics at the upper end of the development scale. Yet C. Arnold Anderson discovered that even in the U.S., inequality of opportunity remained a "widespread and stubborn characteristic" of access to higher learning.[15]

---

[12] Robert S. McNamara, *One Hundred Countries, Two Billion People: The Dimensions of Development* (New York: Praeger, 1973), pp. 102, 114–116, and chap. 6 passim.

[13] See esp. Mary Jean Bowman and C. Arnold Anderson, "Concerning the Role of Education in Development," in Clifford Geertz, ed., *Old Societies and New States: The Quest for Modernity in Asia and Africa* (New York: Free Press, 1963), pp. 247–279; and a critique of the research in Mark Blaug, *An Introduction to the Economics of Education* (London: Allen Lane, Penguin, 1970), chap. 3.

[14] E.g., Seymour Martin Lipset, "Research Problems in the Comparative Analysis of Mobility and Development," *International Social Science Journal*, vol. 16, no. 1 (1964), pp. 35–48.

[15] C. Arnold Anderson, "Access to Higher Education and Economic Development," in A. H. Halsey, Jean Floud, and C. Arnold Anderson, eds., *Education, Economy, and Society: A Reader in the Sociology of Education* (New York: Free Press, 1961), pp. 252–265; see also C. Arnold Anderson, "A Skeptical Note on Education and Mobility," in ibid., pp. 164–179.

Adding to the disillusionment over education's inability to guarantee the anticipated benefits, moreover, was the discovery that it could actually work toward negative ends. Education's two irreducible functions both for individuals and for their communities were (1) socialization, or the transmission of a society's cultural heritage from one generation to the next; and (2) training, both general and specialized, as a requisite for allocating talent within the social division of labor. Education under some conditions might fulfill these functions smoothly, but under others, it might obstruct these functions and create conflict, dislocations, or stagnation.

Among the most problematic conditions were those in developing Third World countries where values and skills were changing rapidly because of the introduction of First World ways and means. Third World education systems, even more than others, could serve as both initiators and inhibitors of modernization and development. Their chief problems, argued one social scientist elaborating the lessons of communications theory, were usually associated with the growth through education of aspirations and demands that could not be met.[16]

Political scientists focused more specifically on the political dimensions of education's functions, namely, political socialization, recruitment, and integration. But their conclusions paralleled those of everyone else. The precise ways whereby education contributed to political socialization, or attitudes and feelings about a given political system, were difficult to pin down. And given the typical combination of rising expectations plus differential access to educational resources, the consequences of development for integration and recruitment were problematic at best. As for negative results, experience was already demonstrating that educational development could perpetuate and even intensify the "elite–mass gap" characteristic of Third World societies, as well as the divisions among different ethnic, regional, and local groups.

James Coleman explained this latter phenomenon in terms of the seemingly universal "law of unequal development advantage." Everywhere, children of upper-class parents had greater access to higher education, and regions with more development potential tended to attract more investment. Groups with greater skills and educational resources enjoyed a differential advantage in further development. Similarly, the ability of a government to sustain its development programs was enhanced by concentrating scarce resources in a few existing "centers of strength." Exploiting these centers allowed the preferential recruitment of people having the necessary skills and preferential investment to maximize returns. In this way, however, the circle of uneven and unequal development perpetuated itself indefinitely unless countervailing measures were

[16] S. N. Eisenstadt, "Education and Political Development," in Don C. Piper and Taylor Cole, eds., *Post-primary Education and Political and Economic Development* (Durham, N.C.: Duke University Press; London: Cambridge University Press, 1964), pp. 27–47.

implemented, which usually brought negative consequences for the more advantaged. Indeed, an excessive or premature effort to achieve equality might stretch resources so thinly as to actually jeopardize results. Yet popular pressure for such expanded educational and economic development was a feature of Third World environments evident almost everywhere. Heightened political tensions therefore had to be calculated among the likely costs of educational development as policymakers were forced to make choices from among the competing demands for scarce resources.[17]

Samuel Huntington went further and argued that education could have directly destabilizing consequences within the political realm. He argued that increasing levels of literacy, education, and communications led to increased levels of mass mobilization and participation, which were in turn among the most dangerous components of modernization. Concerned as he was primarily with political development and with institution building as a critical element thereof, Huntington saw education as a potential destabilizer given its capacity to raise aspirations faster than developing political institutions could satisfy them. He cited Korea, Ceylon, Burma, Cuba, and the Indian state of Kerala as examples of societies with relatively high rates of literacy and highly volatile polities. "In general," he concluded, "the higher the level of education of the unemployed, alienated, or otherwise dissatisfied person, the more extreme the destabilizing behavior which results." Nor was literacy any guarantee of democracy if Cuba and Kerala were any indication. Kerala, with the highest literacy rate in the country, was the first Indian state to elect a communist government. Political participation by illiterates was more likely to remain limited than participation by literates, which tended to escalate with "potentially disastrous effects on political stability."[18]

Within the political realm as for the society as a whole, then, education was both actor and acted upon, both independent and dependent variable. Education's determinant functions were at least matched by its dependence upon governments, political decisions, public funds, and popular demands. And when developing Third World education systems performed their functions directly, the consequences could be as costly as they were beneficial. The attention of Western scholars doubling as occasional advisors in the 1960s therefore began to focus explicitly on ways of containing the disruptive potential of educational development. Given his concerns about the relationship between social mobilization and institution building, Huntington looked for ways to reduce the former, among which limiting "communications" was one. He therefore recommended a reduction in the number of university graduates,

---

[17] James S[moot] Coleman, Introduction to James S. Coleman, ed., *Education and Political Development* (Princeton: Princeton University Press, 1965), pp. 31–32.
[18] Samuel P. Huntington, *Political Order in Changing Societies* (New Haven: Yale University Press, 1968), pp. 47–49.

especially those with skills not in great demand. He also suggested that governments not concern themselves unduly with eradicating illiteracy.[19]

Given the uncertain relationship between education and economic development, Anderson too suggested that countries might want to limit initial targets to estimated critical thresholds: perhaps 40 percent adult literacy, 30 percent of all school-aged children in elementary schools, and 2 percent of the total population at the secondary level or above. Economic, political, and social costs should always be weighed against benefits. Schools also needed to calculate society's relevant needs in terms of the jobs available for graduates and the occupations needed for economic development, criteria that were not necessarily identical. Education should be linked with the world of work but not, argued Anderson, via the wasteful strategy of substituting narrow practical training for regular schooling or adapting curricula to local ways of life. He viewed the lack of adult extension courses and of on-the-job training as typical of the Third World educational milieu. Hence, the temptation in their absence to use schools "to prepare children for jobs instead of preparing them to be trained for a job." But cultural transfer was essential for rapid economic development, including both study abroad and the substitution of expatriate expertise for that of the departing colonial service officials.[20]

Toward the end of the 1960s, however, a shift began to occur in First World perceptions of Third World realities. Idealistic assumptions had been effectively laid to rest. Arguments raged over causes and solutions. Consensus seemed beyond reach. Yet if American-influenced thinking about development in the 1960s was dominated by the cost–benefit rationale of modernization theory, its critics had taken center stage by the early 1970s. Different ways of calculating costs and benefits yielded different conclusions for economic development generally and for education.

Instead of contributing to individual growth and by extension to economic development and social equality as he had initially assumed, wrote Adam Curle of Harvard University in 1973, formal education seemed to be chaining people to the "values and aspirations of a middle class which many of them are unlikely to join."[21] Curle recorded his disillusionment in a personal memoir that reflected the changing concerns of that time. He had initially assumed that development was a function of economic growth; that the latter could be achieved by following the example and accepting the aid of rich nations; and that education would play a key role in economic development. But by the early 1970s, he was ready to disavow all these assumptions, which had guided

[19] Samuel P. Huntington, "Political Development and Political Decay," *World Politics*, no. 3 (Apr. 1965), pp. 418–420.
[20] C. Arnold Anderson, "Economic Development and Post-primary Education," in Piper and Cole, *Post-primary Education*, pp. 1–26. Anderson was at this time professor of education and sociology, University of Chicago, and director of its Comparative Education Center.
[21] Adam Curle, *Education for Liberation* (London: Tavistock, 1973), p. 1.

his work for nearly two decades. Rich nations he now perceived as wasteful, dangerous, and exploitative; their economic development model was dominated by the single aim of consumption; their aid was self-serving; and formal education systems were benefiting only Third World elites adept primarily in the emulation of their rich Western mentors.[22]

In this manner, the center was moving leftward, the president of the World Bank seemed to have converted to socialism, and the weight of opinion within the international development community shifted toward the "political-economy" approach. Long neglected at least by Americans, this orientation led its adherents to conclude that development was serving the interests of the already advantaged. Nor was this phenomenon an unintended consequence of the development process. The new arguments of the 1970s held that the interests of existing elites, by reason of their influence within the political system, could often be identified as the chief obstacle to progress. Policymakers regularly sacrificed the twin goals of growth and equity for the population as a whole in the interests of political stability or of the middle-class and elite support necessary to maintain it. Meaningful development could not occur in education systems, therefore, without changes in the structure of economic and political power as well. The power balance between different groups and classes would have to be changed as the prerequisite for breaking through the dilemmas of development in all sectors.

Those who adopted this orientation came to it largely by force of circumstances since most were probably not committed beforehand either intellectually or politically to its basic premises. They were in effect acknowledging the Marxist view that a society's institutions were interrelated and that control of the economy was fundamental to that relationship.[23] Few were as straightforward as Harvard sociologist Christopher Jencks, whose massive study of inequality in the U.S. confirmed the thrust of Anderson's preliminary explorations. Jencks's statistical findings indicated that education reform could not bring about economic or social equality and that school quality had little effect either on achievement or on economic success. He therefore concluded in 1972 that so long as social reformers skirted the main issue and proceeded "by ingenious manipulations of marginal institutions like the schools, progress will remain glacial. If we want to move beyond this tradition, we will have to establish

[22] Ibid., esp. chap. 9. Curle's earlier work included *Educational Strategy for Developing Societies: A Study of Educational and Social Factors in Relation to Economic Growth* (London: Tavistock, 1963). In the mid-1960s, Curle was director of the Center for Studies in Education and Development, Graduate School of Education, Harvard University.

[23] John Simmons provides a policy-oriented survey of the education development field leading to the political-economy conclusion in "An Overview of the Policy Issues in the 1980s," in Simmons, *The Education Dilemma*, pp. 19–66; for a research-oriented survey, see Jerome Karabel and A. H. Halsey, "Educational Research: A Review and an Interpretation," in Jerome Karabel and A. H. Halsey, eds., *Power and Ideology in Education* (New York: Oxford University Press, 1977), pp. 1–85.

political control over the economic institutions that shape our society. This is what other countries usually call socialism. Anything less will end in the same disappointment as the reforms of the 1960s."[24] Having thus infuriated many people, he reassessed the data but reached the same conclusion. "If we want to redistribute income," he wrote a few years later, "the most effective strategy is probably still to redistribute income."[25]

It was at this point – in the early 1970s – that China began to reopen to the outside world following the onset of the Cultural Revolution. The new school system that was taking shape incorporated, as a matter of national policy, solutions to the same development dilemmas that were confounding reformers everywhere. Yet China was an economically poor country with a large population predominantly rural and preponderantly illiterate as of 1949. For over a decade since the departure of the Russians, it had been without foreign aid or investment. Its level of industrialization was not high by Western standards, nor was its technology advanced. But it had carried out a social revolution, expropriated the former privileged classes, redistributed economic and political power, and was now directing that power among other things toward the economic and social development of all its people. China exemplified the principle of self-reliance both internationally and internally. Evidently by a coincidence of simultaneous development, China had devised solutions similar to those preoccupying everyone else. The difference was that in most other countries, the planners and academics were still struggling to gain acceptance for their ideas, whereas in China the leadership had accepted the solutions and was in the process of trying to translate them into reality.

Such were the circumstances that created the "Chinese model" of the early 1970s. It provided a real-life example that seemed to corroborate a range of findings derived from other countries' failures. It seemed clear that the Chinese were able to make and implement policy decisions that others could only hypothesize about because the Chinese had overthrown the old class structure and the political elites whose power derived therefrom. Specific issues associated with educational development indicate further why the various components of the Chinese model seemed so relevant and how they served to reinforce the political-economy conclusion.

Mass education

The first and most basic goal of educational development was to create systems of mass education where none had previously existed. The professed objective

---

[24] Christopher Jencks et al., *Inequality: A Reassessment of the Effect of Family and Schooling in America* (New York: Basic Books, 1972), p. 265.

[25] Christopher Jencks et al., *Who Gets Ahead?: The Determinants of Economic Success in America* (New York: Basic Books, 1979), p. 311.

of most Third World governments, advice to the contrary notwithstanding, was to eradicate the stigma of illiteracy and provide everyone with at least a primary school education. As a result, aggregate enrollment ratios in Third World elementary schools increased by over 200 percent between 1950 and 1970. The likelihood of impending trouble, however, began to command attention in the mid-1960s. Major policy reviews then commenced. Four influential documents chronicled the shift from the First Development Decade's "age of innocence" to the emerging concerns of the 1970s.[26] The last of these documents was the World Bank's 1974 education sector working paper.

Dilemmas were said to be of historic dimensions. They were created by an ever-increasing demand for education, seen as an irreversible 20th-century trend; the population explosion; escalating costs; scarce resources; and the inefficient use of existing educational facilities as demonstrated by high dropout rates, low quality, and graduates with unmarketable skills. The supply of even most basic education was still insufficient to meet demand. As of 1970, more than half the total population of the developing countries had never been to school.[27] For Asia alone, despite an unprecedented decrease in the percentage of adult illiterates in the population, their absolute number had increased from 307 million in 1955 to 355 million in 1970.[28] Calculating only the elementary school age-group, estimates varied between 45 and 55 percent of Asia's children still not enrolled in 1968.[29]

One reason why educational development seemed to be running while standing still was, of course, the population explosion. The school-age population in Third World countries generally was growing at a rate faster than the population as a whole, for which, by the early 1970s, the median age was approximately 16. It was estimated that by 1985, there would be half again as many school-age children in these countries as there were in 1965.[30] Meanwhile, the costs of education were escalating everywhere. Even if demand remained constant, expenditure would continue to rise. Philip Coombs concluded, moreover, that

[26] The first three documents were the working paper prepared by Philip Coombs for the International Conference on the World Crisis in Education, 1967 (Philip H. Coombs, *The World Educational Crisis: A Systems Analysis* [New York: Oxford University Press, 1968]); the report of the International Commission on the Development of Education sponsored by the United Nations Educational, Scientific, and Cultural Organization (Unesco) and led by Edgar Faure (Edgar Faure et al., *Learning to Be*); and the proceedings of the Bellagio conferences in 1972 and 1973, sponsored by the Ford and Rockefeller Foundations (Ward, *Education and Development Reconsidered*).

[27] Edgar Faure et al., *Learning to Be*, p. 34. China was not included in this estimate or in any of the aggregate figures reviewed in this section.

[28] Economic and Social Commission for Asia and the Pacific, Secretariat, *Economic and Social Survey of Asia and the Pacific, 1978: Biennial Review and Appraisal at the Regional Level of the International Development Strategy for the Second United Nations Development Decade* (draft) (Manila: United Nations Economic and Social Council, 1979), p. 273.

[29] Edgar Faure et al., *Learning to Be*, pp. 38, 54; Ward, Introduction, p. xvii.

[30] Ward, Introduction, p. xvii; Coombs, *World Educational Crisis*, pp. 26–27.

developing countries had probably already exhausted the usual cost-cutting measures. And he warned that public expenditures could not continue at the same sharply rising rates that had characterized their growth since the early 1950s. Education budgets would have to be kept more closely in line with the growth rates of economies and public revenues.[31]

Nor did public expenditures for education represent the total costs of schooling even in state-financed systems. Family expenditure for the child's school supplies, clothing, and transport had to be calculated as costs, together with earnings forgone while studying. In Third World countries, there were sectors of the population where the labor of every family member was necessary to sustain the economic well-being of the unit as a whole. In such situations, the "demand" for education was therefore moderated by the poor family's cost–benefit calculations with respect to educating all or some of its children. These individual family calculations, like those of governments, seemed to be based on considerations at once more subjective and complex than the economists' rate-of-return criteria (calculated as costs versus likely long-term benefits). If nothing else, the need or desire for immediate returns might outweigh the anticipation of a future higher income. Similarly, the calculation that a girl would marry into someone else's family whereas in the short run she could provide needed household labor resulted in lower enrollment ratios among girls. Thus, it was not always perceived among those in the lowest income brackets that elementary schooling was an investment which represented good value for money. The attitude of poor parents – themselves uneducated – was also often detrimental to academic achievement. So too were malnutrition and poor health. In addition, a lack of sufficient school places made it necessary to "fail" the lowest achievers rather than permit their automatic promotion as in compulsory education systems.

Such considerations appeared to explain the high "wastage" rates characteristic of Third World schools. Approximately half of all their students enrolled at the elementary level did not complete the fourth grade. The dropout and failure rates were typically lower overall in East Asia (statistics for the 1960s did not include China) than in South Asia and Latin America, and lower in the cities than in the countryside. Within cities, they were lower for children from white-collar families than for working-class children, and lower overall for boys than for girls. Such dropout and failure rates represented a significant waste of scarce resources since functional literacy and numeracy are usually not achieved with fewer than four years of schooling.[32]

Confronted with the pressures of population growth and rising costs, and

[31] Coombs, *World Educational Crisis*, pp. 45–63 passim.

[32] Ibid., pp. 71–73; Simmons, "An Overview of the Policy Issues in the 1980s," pp. 45–52; see also John Simmons, "Retention of Cognitive Skills Acquired in Primary School," *Comparative Education Review*, vol. 20, no. 1 (Feb. 1976), pp. 79–93.

calculating the ambiguous nature of the "demand," Third World governments began quietly scaling back their quantitative goals. Elementary school enrollments increased at a decreasing rate during the early 1960s; by the latter half of the decade, the trend was evident at all levels. Increases in public educational expenditure also began to decline. Governments nevertheless seemed more inclined to invest in secondary and tertiary education than in elementary schooling or basic literacy training. The higher levels, which usually had no more than 20 percent of a country's total enrollment, often accounted for more than half its annual education expenditure.[33]

For their part, however, development experts were concluding that the overall initial strategy of quantitative growth superimposed upon inherited systems had probably been a mistake. Within the education sector specifically, millions were still without schooling; existing institutions could not accommodate them; and existing Third World economies could not afford the added expenditure necessary to fill the gap. After 20 years of effort, the most basic problem of educational development – how to achieve universal elementary schooling – remained unsolved. The experts also concluded, therefore, that new ways and means would have to be found, including new ways of thinking about education and new means of providing it.

No sooner had these conclusions been reached in the late 1960s than China emerged in the early 1970s as one of the few low-income countries continuing to promote universal elementary schooling. According to its own official statistics, the goal was actually close to being achieved, despite the large predominantly rural population and the apparently modest level of educational investment. Little was known about the dynamics of this achievement, but it was thought to be a function of national government resolve translated into action through the collective support network at commune and village levels. Aside from the Western industrialized countries, it was said, only socialists seemed capable of meeting their quantitative growth targets, and even the least developed among them were evidently no exception.

Education and employment

A second major issue associated with educational development concerned the inability of Third World economies to absorb the output of Third World schools. We have already noted the emphasis placed by modernization theorists on the potentially destabilizing consequences of educational development because of the unrealistic aspirations it might arouse. The most concrete and immediate manifestation of this danger appeared in the form of the "educated unemployed" – large numbers of young people unable to find the jobs and

---

[33] *Education: Sector Working Paper*, p. 13; Edgar Faure et al., *Learning to Be*, p. 45.

salaries they had been led to expect given their academic qualifications. Even though the demand for education tended to outstrip its supply, educational systems still typically produced more graduates and school leavers than job markets could accommodate.[34] The popular response took many forms, ranging from passive alienation to active protest. These in turn raised serious questions within governments about wasting scarce resources on education that might have been better invested directly in the economy.

Strictly speaking, schools were not to blame. Too many people were chasing too few jobs, and education was powerless to create them. The cause of the problem seemed to lie more specifically in poor coordination between expanding school systems and several other components of development, the rate of economic growth being only the most obvious. For example, educated unemployment, if not underemployment, was primarily an urban phenomenon. At least it was in the cities where the largest proportion of the student-age population was actually attending school, where the largest numbers of unemployed school leavers and graduates tended to congregate, and where the political and social pressures they created were most intense. But one of the reasons there were too many people looking for work in cities and towns was the rapid increase in the urban population. The reasons for this in turn divided about evenly between natural population growth and rural–urban migration. Still, the evidence seemed to indicate that the more education rural children received, the more likely they were to migrate townward.[35]

Conventional wisdom held that education in Third World countries contributed to the demand for modern urban sector jobs because education generally imitated conventional academic models, with the specific aim of urban application. Before independence, efforts by colonial administrators to adapt schooling more closely to "local," that is, rural and vocational, needs were resisted by local people as an attempt to inflict an inferior kind of education on them. But whoever was to blame within the colonial context, curricula and values were oriented toward the metropolitan country and/or the modern sector, a pattern that continued into the postcolonial era. Yet the populations of most Third World countries were still predominantly rural in the 1960s. This meant that only a minority of the total labor force could be absorbed into the urban

---

[34] For more refined definitions see Coombs, *World Educational Crisis*, pp. 64–97; David Turnham and Ingelies Jaeger, *The Employment Problem in Less Developed Countries: A Review of Evidence* (Paris: Development Centre of the Organisation for Economic Cooperation and Development, 1971); Paul Bairoch, *Urban Unemployment in Developing Countries* (Geneva: International Labour Office, 1973); Mark Blaug, *Education and the Employment Problem in Developing Countries* (Geneva: International Labour Office, 1973).

[35] Bairoch, *Urban Unemployment*, pp. 33–43; Michael P. Todaro, "The Influence of Education on Migration and Fertility," in Simmons, *The Education Dilemma*, pp. 180–182; Michael P. Todaro, *Internal Migration in Developing Countries: A Review of Theory, Evidence, Methodology and Research Priorities* (Geneva: International Labour Office, 1976), chap. 5.

economy. Hence rural youngsters, if they attended school, were receiving an education that at least did nothing to prevent them from migrating townward and ill-prepared the majority for the lives they would continue to lead in the countryside.

Even this poor coordination between education and the rural community was not the only variable at work, however, or probably even the most important. In the end, the most basic reason for rural–urban migration was the great disparity between rural and urban incomes, opportunities, and living standards, a gap that economic development itself tended to exacerbate at least in the short term.

At the same time, disparities within the urban sector itself also contributed to the seeming imbalance between education and employment opportunities. Most significant were those created by the structure of remuneration for urban jobs. Societies typically attached higher rewards – income and prestige – to positions filled by college graduates than to those occupied by secondary school leavers, and so on down the line. The average lifetime earnings of people with more education remained substantially higher than others, even with an extended period of postgraduation unemployment. Popular demands for more education were made on such calculations, despite all the "rate-of-return" equations showing greater value for money at the elementary level. The demand for more education was thus not "irrational" from the individual's standpoint, however frustrated the accompanying aspirations might be and however negative the consequences for society as a whole.[36] Contributing further to the demand for more education was the influence of educated middle- and upper-income sectors of the population. Because of that influence, Third World governments usually found it difficult to implement measures designed to suppress demands for higher education.[37]

Finally, traditional attitudes about formal schooling, status, upward mobility, and manual labor also combined to intensify the problem. Unlike societies where elementary and secondary education had long been universal, expanding educational opportunities at those levels tended not to be taken for granted. Parents and pupils were more likely to regard the new opportunities as an investment calculated to enhance the family's prospects. Peasants illiterate for generations did not necessarily appreciate the value of education for a son if it led to a life no better than that of his unschooled father before him. This

---

[36] George Psacharopoulos and Keith Hinchliffe, *Returns to Education: An International Comparison* (San Francisco: Jossey-Bass, 1973), chap. 8; Blaug, *Introduction to the Economics of Education*, esp. chap. 8; Simmons summarizes the varying rate-of-return calculations in "An Overview of the Policy Issues in the 1980s," pp. 55–61.

[37] For one such set of recommendations, see Edgar O. Edwards and Michael P. Todaro, "Education and Employment in Developing Countries," in Ward, *Education and Development Reconsidered*, pp. 3–22. Blaug offers a critical review of the options in *Education and the Employment Problem in Developing Countries*, pp. 41–89.

attitude was enhanced by the clear distinction which persisted in most developing societies between mental and manual labor, and the antipathy for the latter that seemed to be acquired along with even the most basic rudiments of education.

The ensuing pressures could influence educational development in one of two ways. Where opportunities for advancement were clearly lacking, the old attitudes could serve to inhibit interest in sending children to school. Where opportunities were not lacking, however, such views had the opposite effect, contributing to upward pressures for more education. Elementary school graduates tended to demand either "appropriate" work or access to the next level. The traditional prejudice of the educated against manual labor only seemed to break down as schooling approached universality first at the elementary level and then at the secondary. It is still retained everywhere for those who progress further. Meanwhile, the process whereby more highly educated people finally resigned themselves to the saturated job market and accepted lower-paying lower-status jobs appeared to be a lengthy and painful one for all concerned.

Again there were no easy answers since the educated unemployment problem obviously derived from a wide range of pressures. After a decade of intense scholarly scrutiny, education had emerged as the intervening variable, sometimes mediating but powerless to overcome the economic, demographic, social, and cultural constraints of its environment. Given existing rates of economic growth, any attempt to solve the unemployment problem by reforming school systems could not succeed so long as population growth rates remained unchanged, urban–rural disparities persisted, migration from the countryside to the cities continued, and income patterns were not realigned to reduce disparities between those with higher and lower academic qualifications.

Yet again China emerged as unique in providing solutions. Concerning unemployment per se, China had long been regarded as a special case by reason of its socialist system, which guaranteed employment to everyone whatever the costs and inefficiencies. In addition, the Chinese system contained features that seemed to be designed specifically to cope with many of the above pressures. The onset of a declining birthrate from the early 1970s, as published statistics later revealed, was not generally known at this time. But what could be observed were the effective curbs on rural–urban migration, the effort to minimize rural–urban disparities, and modifications in the wage structure within the state sector aimed at reducing income differences between mental and manual labor categories, along with political efforts to reverse the order of popular prestige between the two.

Additionally, unified enrollment and work assignment plans coordinated the supply of college graduates with the numbers and kinds of jobs available. At the secondary level, "excess" urban youth were being mobilized to work in the countryside. A revolutionary government that overtly identified itself with the "poor and lower-middle peasants" was not obliged to make undue concessions to the existing educated elite. Indeed, the educated elite became an express target for transformation and status reversal rather than a source of political power and support. The foreign observers noted, finally, that however reprehensible its means, the Chinese government at least had the organization and will to carry out intentions and implement policies.

Content and quality

The difficulty of trying to match academic qualifications with existing job opportunities pointed to a third major area of concern associated with educational development, namely, content and quality. Ronald Dore hypothesized in three related propositions that the later development started in a given country, (1) the more school certificates and degrees were likely to be used as the main criteria for occupational selection, (2) the faster the rate of educational inflation, and (3), as a consequence of the foregoing, the more examination-ridden schooling would become. He reasoned that late-developing countries tended to adopt the latest methods and skills from the developed countries, where the practice of using educational degrees and credentials as the main requirement for job selection was ever more in vogue. Escalating enrollments or ever more educated people chasing too few modern sector jobs made a bad situation worse, aggravating long-standing inflationary pressures set in motion everywhere by the 20th-century demand for more schooling.

The third proposition followed logically from the preceding but bore directly on the quality issue. Given the relative scarcity of jobs and the intense competition for them, the all-important certificate examinations dominated schooling. The entire system came to revolve around them. Primary schools prepared children to enter secondary schools – although a majority of the students never reached them – and secondary schools prepared children for their final examinations. Schools and teachers were judged in accordance with the examination results. School curricula were geared toward these exams, as were teaching methods. Ritualized drills, rote memorization, and pre-exam cramming had proven the surest quickest means of obtaining the desired results and were therefore the preferred means of instruction. The content of what had thus been inculcated was usually forgotten shortly after the examinations ordeal had been completed. Meanwhile, a majority of the children entering these school systems left them either as dropouts or as failures.[38]

Whether Dore's "late development effect" was a reality, or whether he was simply describing education systems that looked the worse to Western eyes for having expanded quantitatively without first undergoing the qualitative impact

---

[38] Dore, *The Diploma Disease*, esp. chap. 6.

of John Dewey's "education for life" revolution, remained to be verified. By contrast, the familiar characteristics of Third World schools led New Zealand educator Clarence Beeby to theorize, in a much-quoted study, that education probably had to pass through several qualitative stages of development. This line of reasoning was inspired by his mid-1940s discovery of educational practices in Western Samoa's elementary schools that were similar to those in the West nearly a century before. Beeby concluded that the transitional stages from traditional and formalistic to modern and progressive probably could not be skipped by any wholesale borrowing of skills and techniques from the modern classrooms of the West. The chief reason: teachers found the old-fashioned methods more congenial and seemed to adhere instinctively to them.[39]

The teaching force therefore emerged as a key ingredient necessary for change which often played exactly the opposite role. Meanwhile, the prerequisites for removing the obstacles of pedagogical conservatism included money, will, and a considerable length of time before teachers throughout a school system could be adequately trained or retrained. Thus, while Western academics worried most about the regressive nature of Third World schooling, the first concern of Third World educators themselves was the dilution of *existing* standards. Preoccupied as they were in the early 1960s with the quantitative dimensions of development, Asian education ministers expressed this concern as a simple trade-off at a United Nations Educational, Scientific, and Cultural Organization (Unesco) meeting in 1962. Seeing themselves faced with the "unhappy choice" of quantitative growth as required by the right of all to education or of restricting that right in order to maintain "quality," the ministers acknowledged their fear that a "dilution of standards" was likely in the short run especially at the elementary level.[40]

Such fears were not without foundation for small select systems designed to approximate international academic standards. But the quantity–quality equation represented only the simplest of the choices that would have to be made when such a system was transformed into one with a mass base. Nor were those choices confined only to the elementary level. Previously, in Europe as in its colonies, the chief aim of a secondary education was to prepare a small minority for university. Even in the West, the expansion of secondary schooling beyond this aim was a relatively recent phenomenon. But as the number of secondary school students grew beyond the fraction who could continue their studies, the futility of preparing the majority for such a future became obvious – hence the search for secondary school curricula that could at once be college preparatory for some and terminal for the majority. Such questions injected the concept of relativity into the definition of quality. Assumptions about universal international standards, inherited with the transfer of Western models

[39] Beeby, *Quality of Education*, esp. chap. 4.
[40] Quoted in ibid., p. 8.

to the Third World, were falling into disfavor. They were being challenged by a growing recognition that the content and quality of education should be "relative to the particular purpose, place, and time of the student clientele."[41]

To say that new definitions were emerging within the international development community does not, of course, mean there was consensus on specific operational aims and priorities, much less that they were being translated into reality by Third World educators. Nevertheless, it was a time for challenging old assumptions. Just as parents and students had to confront the changing realities of education and work, so educators had to devise new ways of preparing young people for both. What was initially seen as a simple matter of quantitative growth ultimately necessitated systemic redefinitions of quality, relevance, and international standards, including the relationship between Third World education systems and their Western counterparts. And yet again, China emerged as the front-runner in accepting these challenges. Hence Dore's declaration that China was the first country actually to attempt reforms along the lines he advocated.

Equality, equity, and dependency

Also inherent in the simple matter of quantitative growth, or building mass education systems where they had never before existed, was the most complex of all the issues associated with educational development, namely, equality. Quantitative expansion derived among other things from the mid–20th century's new definition of education as a basic human right, meaning it was no longer the prerogative of the elite few. But having proclaimed that right as universal, the challenge was to find ways whereby it could be universally claimed by all.

Definitions

Our purpose here is not to explain how or why this challenge emerged seemingly at the confluence of Western democracy and international socialism. We need only note that by the latter half of the 20th century, the ideal of equality had become a "universal norm" and promoting it a "major objective" in all Western countries. By extension, therefore, inequality was still the prevailing condition. The close connection between measured ability and social background was called "one of the major social discoveries of the 20th century."[42] Everywhere, people who lived in cities were better educated than people in rural areas, as were children from white-collar families by comparison with those of working-class parents.

---

[41] Coombs, *World Educational Crisis*, p. 106.
[42] John Vaizey, *Education in the Modern World* (London: Weidenfeld and Nicolson, 1975), p. 116.

We should also note that Western definitions of social equality (in contrast to its political counterpart as in equality under the law) were changing under the glare of public scrutiny and scholarly dissection. The more intensely the goal was pursued, the more elusive it became. Nowhere was the effort greater than in education, due to the widespread assumption that schooling was a key to equalizing life's chances. Yet data from developed countries indicated that expanding economies and enrollments, time, and the "filter-down effect" were not sufficient in themselves to correct educational inequalities, although they did appear to reduce them somewhat. While higher education translated on everyone's statistical tables into higher incomes, education could not guarantee such an outcome for any given individual, and more education certainly did not mean more equal outcomes in terms of achievement, income, or status.

French sociologist Raymond Boudon analyzed school attendance rates in relation to family income and socioeconomic status for selected developed countries. The results showed inequality of educational opportunity to be declining generally but still high, although relatively lower in the U.S., Eastern Europe, and Scandinavia. He attributed the lower inequality to much higher attendance rates in the U.S. and to deliberate egalitarian policies, "hard" and "soft," in the other two regions respectively. As a measure of inequality in the U.S., using 1960 data, he calculated that a young person whose father had a college education and an annual income of more than $10,000 was about six times more likely to attend college than a young person whose father earned less than $5,000 per year and had not graduated from high school.[43]

When Americans scrutinized such continuing inequalities, however, the causes were difficult to ascertain. James Coleman and Christopher Jencks led two benchmark investigations. Coleman was commissioned by the U.S. government to investigate unequal educational opportunities in U.S. public institutions with the aim of devising remedial measures. He found instead that the distribution of material resources was surprisingly equal and could not be the reason for differences in achievement, especially between black and white students. He concluded that family background was more important than schools in explaining educational inequality and was consequently credited with redefining the concern in U.S. educational thinking from equality of opportunity to equality of result. Inspired by the ensuing controversy, Jencks and a team of Harvard researchers reassessed Coleman's data and reached the conclusions cited above, namely, that school quality had little effect on either educational achievement or subsequent economic success, that "native ability" also had relatively little effect on success in later life, and that education could not bring about social or economic equality.[44]

---

[43] Raymond Boudon, *Education, Opportunity, and Social Inequality: Changing Prospects in Western Society* (New York: John Wiley and Sons, 1974), chap. 3.

[44] James S[amuel] Coleman et al., *Equality of Educational Opportunity* (Washington, D.C.: U.S. Government Printing Office, 1966); Jencks et al., *Inequality*. These studies were widely

Jencks and his associates found, for example, that the inputs assumed to influence student performance actually had little impact in U.S. schools. Money and the things it could buy for a school, beyond a certain minimal unspecified threshold, apparently made little difference in the end result.[45] Instead, the factors found to influence student output were those, more difficult to measure, which promoted motivation. And the most important of these were not even school related: parental income, occupation, and education; together with other related variables, including nutrition, health, occupational expectations, and, more specifically, the clearly apparent link between present achievement and future benefit such as the realistic possibility of going on to college. "Native ability" was found to explain perhaps 50 percent of the inequality on student test scores. But these in turn affected only modestly the amount of education received. In other words, someone born into "advantaged" circumstances was more likely to receive more education than a disadvantaged person with the same intelligence quotient.[46]

The amount of education distributed in U.S. society was more "equal" than in earlier decades because the percentage going on to college had not expanded as fast as that at the lower levels. Elementary schooling through the eighth grade was universal and compulsory, having finally been extended to all previously excluded minority groups. By the 1960s, 99.2 percent of all children aged 6 to 13 were in school. The percentage of the age-group entering secondary school had risen from 40 percent in 1914 to 94 percent in the mid-1960s. Yet the relationship between family economic status and the amount of schooling a child received had remained essentially unchanged.[47]

The inescapable conclusion was that schools were powerless to reduce significantly the unequal characteristics with which children entered the classroom and that schooling could not significantly influence economic inequality among its recipients thereafter. The root cause of social inequality lay in the unequal structures of occupations and especially incomes. Boudon, relying primarily on Western European data, reached essentially the same conclusion. He pointed to economic inequality as the key variable defining social stratification or class distinctions. He also concluded that economic inequality must be changed if the twin "malfunctions" of educational and social inequality were to be effectively challenged.[48]

In this manner, the 1960s search for the causes of educational inequality led from equal opportunities, to results, and finally to equalizing life's chances

discussed; see, e.g., Karabel and Halsey, "Educational Research," pp. 16–28, and the references they cite; Daniel Bell, *The Coming of Post-industrial Society: A Venture in Social Forecasting*, 2d ed. (New York: Basic Books, 1976), pp. 427–433.

[45] Jencks et al., *Inequality*, pp. 93–97, 146–151.

[46] Ibid., pp. 64–81, 109–110, 138–146.

[47] Ibid., pp. 18–23, 138.

[48] Boudon, *Education, Opportunity, and Social Inequality*, esp. chaps. 6 and 10.

altogether. By the early 1970s, American social philosophy was developing a concept of equality as equity or the just and fair distribution of all social advantages. Describing the work of John Rawls in this respect as "the most comprehensive effort in modern philosophy to justify a socialist ethic," another Harvard sociologist, Daniel Bell, predicted that it would "go far to shape the last part of the 20th century, just as the doctrines of Locke and Smith molded the 19th."[49] Bell criticized the threat to individual merit and achievement implicit in contemporary egalitarian efforts to realize the distributive principle Rawls championed. But Bell nevertheless advocated "basic social equality," meaning not just an end to discrimination but instead the positive "priority of the disadvantaged" in social policy and the right of every person to "a basic set of services and income."[50]

Third World pressures for parity

Such were the evolving liberal-to-left definitions of equality in the West that inevitably colored the West's perceptions of Third World development. "The ever-growing gap between industrialized and developing countries has produced the fundamental drama of the contemporary world," intoned the 1972 Unesco report.[51] Enthusiasm for this international dimension of the struggle to redress the balance between rich and poor was more than shared by the leaders of the latter. Their demands for a "new world order" would grow increasingly determined and effective on many fronts.

By contrast, the internal application of the same principle within individual countries drew a more mixed response. The Unesco report was consistent on both dimensions but acknowledged "political and financial obstacles, psychological resistance and, above all, the rigid stratification of society" that would complicate the quest for "democratic" and "non-discriminatory" models of education. The authors of the report were clearly committed to the emerging liberal–left norms. The universal right to education was often refused, they wrote, to the underprivileged. By a "complete reversal of justice," the underprivileged were the "first to be denied their right in poor societies; the only ones deprived in the rich." But equal access to education was only a necessary, not a sufficient, condition for justice, which required an "equal chance of success." Such justice was a possibility, however, only in societies trying to achieve integration through an overall "dismantling of their social barriers." Education alone was powerless to surmount those barriers but should at least not reinforce them by an unfair distribution of its resources.[52]

[49] Bell, *The Coming of Post-industrial Society*, p. 444; see also John Rawls, *A Theory of Justice* (London and New York: Oxford University Press, 1972).
[50] Bell, *The Coming of Post-industrial Society*, pp. 452–454.
[51] Edgar Faure et al., *Learning to Be*, p. 49.
[52] Ibid., chap. 5.

The challenge was possible to accept but virtually impossible to surmount, and everyone listed the reasons why. Regional disparities in educational development of over 50 percent were not uncommon within individual Third World countries. Everywhere, educational facilities were concentrated in cities and towns, and in the richer neighborhoods within them. Everywhere certain racial, ethnic, and social groups, sectors, and classes were favored over others. Everywhere, too, school systems were designed to select and exclude, leaving no alternatives for those factored out of the system at different points along the way.

The question of how the evolving norms of the West and the international development community were and were not transplanted into different Third World environments is a complicated one and has not been subjected to the same scrutiny as others. But developing education systems seemed to have little difficulty in generating and articulating countervailing tendencies both for and against equality.

We have already mentioned some of the factors militating against equality. The development process itself often began by increasing, rather than decreasing, existing social inequalities. When educational facilities were introduced into a region that had none, the event could be hailed as an important step forward. Yet so long as such facilities remained limited and incapable of serving everyone, they increased the inequalities between the educated few and the unschooled majority. Where facilities were limited and communications poor, the boarding school might represent the only possible means of making education available to children from different regions or ethnic groups. Yet the necessity of living at school added to educational costs, restricted attendance to those children whose families could afford to have them live away from home, and removed young people from their local communities, all of which contributed to the elitist nature of the student body. The same boarding school might therefore be viewed as a means of promoting equality and integration at the elite level and at the same time as an institution which enhanced the disparities between that level and the uneducated mass of the population.

All societies felt the strains imposed by the competing claims for scarce educational resources. The education budgets of even the richest were not unlimited. In Third World countries, scarcities were greater and so too the claims that could not be met because of them – although this did not necessarily produce a relatively greater degree of tension or dissent among the less advantaged. Where expectations had not yet been widely aroused, resignation might be more common than resentment – hence the possibility of concentrating resources in a few key "centers of strength." This was the development strategy designed to maximize efficiency by preventing a dispersal of meager resources on "premature and excessive" efforts to realize equality.[53]

[53] James S[moot] Coleman's discussion on "centers of strength" is cited above; see also Coombs, *World Educational Crisis*, pp. 31–33; Louis Malassis, *The Rural World: Education and Development* (London and Paris: Croom Helm and Unesco, 1976), pp. 80–82.

The tendency in developing societies, then, was to perpetuate, if not exacerbate, existing inequalities. Coleman's principle of comparative unequal advantage, with all its attendant cost–benefit calculations, could be observed everywhere at work in official development plans and investments. The principle could also be seen working informally through the combined weight of individual decisions and cultural inheritance, as existing educated elites bequeathed their privileges to their children.

Conversely, we have also seen how Western standards of quantitative development were ultimately adopted everywhere as a universal goal. And just as progress in realizing it necessitated new ways of thinking about quality and content, so quantitative growth also generated the imperatives for an ever wider distribution of scarce educational resources. Suddenly, the field was crowded with competing demands, and as these continued to multiply, decisions had to be made about priorities: how much education, of what kind, for whom, how quickly.

Frustrated aspirations were inevitable, but the potential for "dysfunction" seemed to be reduced when decisions could at least be seen by the parties directly concerned to have been fairly made. Internal pressures for an equitable response to rising demands were therefore inherent in developing education systems and did not need to be inspired by or articulated specifically in terms of the new 1960s definitions of equality. For example, colonial officials had earlier encountered local resistance everywhere when they tried to introduce vocational education. Economists would subsequently "discover" sound reasons for such resistance. Income and prestige attached to modern sector jobs were typically higher. And the most abundant modern sector jobs were in administration and commerce, which typically maintained formal academic requirements. Modernization theorists would explain the resistance further in terms of the "revolution of rising expectations." Additionally, however, it seemed to represent an instinctive demand to share – among those who could reasonably aspire to do so – the best of the opportunities available. Philip Foster referred to this demand as the "pressure for parity" which developed when "colonial peoples were involved in unequal competition with resident Europeans for a limited number of high-status jobs."[54]

Colonial administrators promoting "practical" education therefore had to show cause why local elites should be deprived of access to a future that all alike regarded as superior to the alternative offered. Clarence Beeby recalled his days as an administrator responsible for a remote corner of New Zealand in the 1940s. Maori chiefs and elders confounded his efforts to sell them the idea of a technical school as more appropriate for their district than the classical

---

[54] Philip J. Foster, "The Vocational School Fallacy in Development Planning," in C. Arnold Anderson and Mary Bowman, eds., *Education and Economic Development* (Chicago: Aldine, 1965), pp. 146–147.

college-preparatory course on which they had set their hearts. They argued that since he himself had studied Latin to such successful advantage, they wanted the same for their young people as well.[55] In Uganda, British administrator H. M. Grace struggled similarly with local Baganda chiefs to prevent the introduction of Latin into a local college and to establish an experimental school farm.[56] Writing of Ghana under British rule in the 1920s and 1930s, Philip Foster noted the "paradoxical situation" wherein European thought favored "African" curricula while African chiefs and the local educated elite were strongly opposed. They were demanding instead a continuation of the standard academic course initially introduced.[57]

Everywhere, efforts to adapt schooling to local needs were resented as an attempt to subject colonial peoples to second-rate forms of education which reduced their competitive advantage. In later years, the controversy was reborn as independent Third World countries tried to resolve the dilemma created by the continuing desire to approximate "advanced world standards" and the growing numbers of school leavers increasingly ill-prepared to embark upon life in their local communities. Academically and otherwise, the principle of equality – as manifested in the general desire for education systems able to compete internationally – might have been possible to achieve in small colonial-style education systems with uniform academic curricula. But such systems were much more difficult to maintain once the 20th-century demands for mass education gained general acceptance, necessitating locally relevant schooling. The contradictions seemed impossible of solution for Third World countries. They could not have it both ways, and the balance of international opinion on the issue was, in the 1970s as in earlier decades, leaning toward relativity.

Internally, the demand for relevance anticipated many more parity principle contradictions, all equally difficult of solution. Typically most troublesome were the old academic–vocational tensions and the urban–rural divide. The academic bias of education and traditional attitudes about the separation of mental and manual labor were initially diagnosed as causes of unemployment among urban school leavers. Vocational training and technical education were prescribed as the cure. But it rarely succeeded due to the difficulty of matching vocational curricula with the particular jobs available. It also did not succeed because vocational education was regarded by all (i.e., by the more economically secure, who were the main beneficiaries of expanding school systems) as offering less attractive prospects than the academic stream. Where the two

---

[55] Beeby, *Quality of Education*, p. 30.
[56] E. B. Castle, *Education for Self-Help* (New York and London: Oxford University Press, 1972), pp. 72–73.
[57] Philip Foster, *Education and Social Change in Ghana* (London: Routledge and Kegan Paul, 1965), p. 167. See also J. S. Furnivall, *Colonial Policy and Practice: A Comparative Study of Burma and Netherlands India*, 2d ed. (New York: New York University Press, 1956), pp. 381–387.

stood in competition for students, funds, and popularity, the academic stream usually continued to thrive and the vocational alternative foundered.[58] At the secondary level, then, the controversy centered on the search for forms of schooling that would be at once academic or college preparatory for some students and vocational or terminal for others, without creating a rigid hierarchy of opportunity and status between them.

In the 1960s, attention also began to focus specifically on the failures of rural education. But it was soon realized that "where the public image of farming is that of a poor, old-fashioned, and brutish way of life, the schools are in general powerless to supply a solution."[59] Obviously, the problems of rural education did not rest primarily with education. Not content to await the solution of so fundamental a matter as the modernization of agriculture, educational planners began searching for ways to adapt schooling to rural areas. "Nonformal" education was one way. "Ruralized" education was another.[60]

The difficulty with all such solutions, however, was that they confined the students who might suffer them to a ghetto of their own making. Those who received elementary schooling designed to be "a complete education in itself" preparing them for life in the countryside would have little chance of ever participating anywhere else. They therefore found little incentive to patronize and support the local school that offered such a curriculum, while local elites who could most easily afford to do so sought other more promising alternatives for their children. A curriculum that catered to the needs of the rural areas would not be able to meet the demands of urban life. Hence, the call for relevance logically assumed at least two different educational tracks. Yet until the means could be found to make rural life as attractive as urban, such dualities would inevitably be viewed as a means for perpetuating the inequalities inherent in the existing division of labor.

Just as education could not create jobs or determine the differential rewards attached thereto, so schooling was not to blame for the disparities between town and countryside. But to the extent that people perceived education as an avenue of social mobility, they tended to make such demands upon it and resent forms of schooling that clearly obstructed the route, particularly when the way was blocked for some people's children more than for others. Thus, new insights derived from the study of education systems everywhere were raising some difficult questions about the most effective means of responding fairly to the competing imperatives of development.

[58] Foster's essay "The Vocational School Fallacy" became the acknowledged "classic" statement of this dilemma. The essay summarizes findings from his larger study of Ghana, cited above.

[59] V. L. Griffiths, *The Problems of Rural Education* (Paris: Unesco, International Institute for Educational Planning, 1968), p. 20.

[60] E.g., ibid.; Castle, *Education for Self-Help*; Philip H. Coombs and Manzoor Ahmed, *Attacking Rural Poverty: How Nonformal Education Can Help* (Baltimore and London: Johns Hopkins University Press, 1974); Tim Simkins, *Non-formal Education and Development: Some Critical Issues*, Manchester Monographs, no. 8 (Manchester: University of Manchester, 1976).

The emerging socialist persuasion

Adherents of the "new" perspective argued that although formal schooling might not be particularly reliable in terms of either cognitive or economic outcomes, it did play an important role in reproducing the social order. According to this revision of earlier functionalist insights, certain characteristics often previously deplored as dysfunctional were actually just the opposite – given the nature of capitalist systems. Schools were embedded in them, corresponded to them, and performed important functions for them. Schools did not develop talent as much as they performed a sorting, labeling, and certification function that was, by reason of the education inflation also under way, more than sufficient to meet the cognitive requirements of most jobs that most school leavers would fill. Through meritocratic values – with grades allocated for performance and promotion for grades – schools were therefore legitimating the present and future status of all who passed through them.

According to this interpretation, schooling was essentially an authoritative mechanism for resigning young people to their respective fates or socializing them to accept *as fair* their more or less predetermined slots in society. Youth could thus be confined to their appropriate station in life without separate academic and vocational curricula. Failing and dropping out produced the same result, conditioning those who did so to accept precisely the kind of lives they would have to live at the bottom of the socioeconomic hierarchy. They could accept failure and nonpromotion in school and afterward because they had not met the grade and deserved no better. By inhibiting the growth of potentially disruptive conflicts over the unequal distribution of wealth, prestige, power, etc., education played an important role in helping the social order reproduce itself. Education served, in other words, to legitimize the class structure of capitalism and produce forms of consciousness compatible with its perpetuation.[61]

In Third World countries, education performed the same functions, albeit in more economically complex environments characterized by dual modes of

---

[61] Among the foremost proponents of this argument in the 1970s were Samuel Bowles and Herbert Gintis. E.g., see their *Schooling in Capitalist America: Educational Reform and the Contradictions of Economic Life* (New York: Basic Books, 1976), which is discussed in Karabel and Halsey, "Educational Research," pp. 33–44. See also Gintis, "Towards a Political Economy of Education," *Harvard Educational Review*, vol. 42, no. 1 (1972), pp. 70–96, reprinted in Roger Dale et al., eds., *School and Capitalism: A Sociological Reader* (London: Routledge and Kegan Paul; Henley: Open University Press, 1976), pp. 8–20; Bowles, "Education, Class Conflict, and Uneven Development," in Simmons, *The Education Dilemma*, pp. 205–231. Stanford University professor Martin Carnoy was another prolific contributor. See e.g., Martin Carnoy, *Education as Cultural Imperialism* (New York: David McKay, 1974); Martin Carnoy and Henry M. Levin, *The Limits of Educational Reform* (New York: David McKay, 1976); Martin Carnoy, *Education and Employment: A Critical Appraisal* (Paris: Unesco, International Institute for Educational Planning, 1977). For a different style with similar conclusions, see the work of historian Michael B. Katz: *The Irony of Early School Reform: Educational Innovation in Mid–19th Century Massachusetts* (Cambridge: Harvard University Press, 1968), and *Class, Bureaucracy, and Schools: The Illusion of Educational Change in America*, expanded ed. (New York: Praeger, 1975).

production (i.e., combining both modern/urban/capitalist and traditional/rural). These were typically economies and societies "in transition" where the old order was in decline while the processes of capital accumulation, production, and reproduction were not yet strongly developed. Formal Third World education systems usually provided the socialization and skills necessary to prepare people for life and work in the modern sector, where wages and living standards were higher.

In such societies, universal education or equal education for all could create serious disorders, including those arising both from material costs and from frustrated aspirations. Hence the tendency was to restrict educational development in accordance with the "centers of strength" investment strategy. Hence also dual education systems often characterized Third World countries: expensive formal urban schools providing recruits for the offices and factories of the modern sector and separate, lower-quality, lower-cost education providing practical training or nothing at all for everyone else.

Martin Carnoy combined these neo-Marxist insights with dependency theory to elaborate the idea of "education as cultural imperialism." Dependency theory sought to explain the nature of the postcolonial relationship between the former colonies and the dominant nations of the capitalist West. But he portrayed the relationship as one between people as well as nations. The dependency relationship could occur anywhere and was characterized by subjugation and clearly defined hierarchies. Thus, "a school that colonizes students and is rooted in inequality has its counterpart in a school system that provides one type of schooling for the wealthy and another for the poor."[62]

Third World elites played a central role in the transmission process, identifying their interests with the colonizers while internalizing their ways and means as well. Few Third World leaders chose to break their countries' political and economic ties with the West after independence. Economic systems continued to adjust to the needs of international capitalism while social stratification remained intact. Accordingly, education systems in the ex-colonies also remained largely unchanged after independence. Dependency theory defined the result as "cultural alienation," or "the need to copy everything from the developed metropoles," including values, norms, technology, art forms, etc. Foreign nationals continued to serve as teachers; foreign examiners continued to determine standards; those who succeeded within the modern sector school system at home continued to seek their fortunes in the best universities abroad since the former was in all respects an extension of the latter.[63]

The great difficulty with this line of reasoning was how far beyond the education sector its adherents had to look for solutions. Their concerns led them from a growing awareness of the political and economic constraints on

[62] Carnoy, *Education as Cultural Imperialism*, p. 27.
[63] Ibid., pp. 69–72.

education into a realm where the policy-oriented aims of their research could only assume revolutionary proportions. The logic of this argument left them with no choice but to call for the overthrow of the middle-class, consumer-oriented values of the Western world and ultimately the overthrow of capitalism itself. Such logic produced Jencks's conclusion that American reformers should redirect their attention away from marginal institutions like schools and indirect goals such as equalizing opportunities in favor of a direct assault on the true sources of inequality.

Bowles and Gintis elaborated further on the political mechanisms for change in their influential *Schooling in Capitalist America*, funded, ironically, by the Ford Foundation. Crucial changes had occurred in U.S. education when production relations themselves had changed, as with the growth of wage labor and the factory system in the mid–19th century or the subsequent growth of corporate capital and organized labor. The existing school system had to adjust in order to continue performing its function of socializing and sorting the work force within the context of a changing economy. This functional relationship between education and the economy produced the basic deterministic element in educational change. It tended to occur naturally as local and national governments, school boards, curriculum developers, and parents all adjusted in "free-market" fashion to the changing demands from the economy.

When free market adjustments and compromises were not sufficient to realign disjunctures between the school system and the economy, however, conflict and purposeful political struggle emerged. At such times, argued Bowles and Gintis, it was possible to articulate demands against the interests of the dominant capitalist power structure. The capitalist class, through its domination of values, information, and foundation money, usually retained its dominant role in deciding the substance of economic reforms. Still, capitalism's opponents had won some victories. For example, American labor had waged a successful battle in the early decades of the 20th century against the attempt to establish separate vocational and academic streams in the form of a dual school system.

Bowles and Gintis nevertheless concluded that the best means for creating an education system that could promote personal development and social equality – instead of helping to reproduce the existing class structure – was the "revolutionary transformation of economic life." The economic control, domination, and subordination characteristic of capitalism, with its pursuit of profit and class privilege, would have to give way to a form of socialism based on economic democracy, egalitarianism, and participatory power relationships.[64]

In Third World countries, a deliberate political movement to challenge the class structure and uneven development could include educational programs

[64] Bowles and Gintis, *Schooling in Capitalist America*, pp. 265–266.

designed to promote social equality and a more rational growth process. But to promote such educational ends alone, "in the absence of rebellion against the capitalist order," was a futile gesture, the only outcome of which would be to obscure the inequality and economic irrationality inherent in capitalist systems. The prerequisite for a more equal and rational distribution of economic rewards was not to be sought in educational policy but in the redistribution of economic and political power.[65]

China as Third World model of the 1970s

The path that led via practical experience, empirical research, and theoretical argument from the undifferentiated optimism of the 1950s to the perceived crises of the 1960s and the conclusions of the 1970s should now be clear. A quarter century of concerted effort had not brought commensurate rewards, and expectations remained unfulfilled. Rapid educational development was initially thought to promote economic growth, but it was discovered that historically the latter usually preceded the former rather than vice versa. Education had also been thought to promote equality and social mobility; instead, its contribution to those aims seemed negligible at best. Insights deriving from this experience produced a new emerging consensus: the dysfunctions of educational development could not be solved without changes in the structure of economic and political power. Not everyone jumped on this bandwagon, to be sure. But it was no longer the preserve of a few fringe radicals.

The path that led similarly to such widespread interest in the Chinese model of educational development should also be apparent. China itself had remained outside and separate from the experience which led to the conclusions of the 1970s. None of these had been based on in-depth studies of Chinese data. But the practical lessons and theoretical implications drawn from the experience of developed and developing countries alike seemed to have general validity. Meanwhile, China – following its own course of development – appeared at first glance and by reason of its policy pronouncements not only to have reached similar conclusions but to have begun implementing concrete solutions based upon them as well. China had also achieved the newly discovered prerequisite by carrying out a revolution that abolished the pursuit of profit and the accumulation of wealth as a basis for social stratification. Even Bowles and Gintis, in their book on education in the U.S., held up the Chinese revolution as the sine qua non for China's subsequent successes. "Often the best social policy," they concluded, "is a revolutionary policy."[66]

It was also a commonplace that the Soviet Union and Eastern European

---

[65] Bowles, "Education, Class Conflict, and Uneven Development," p. 226.

[66] Bowles and Gintis, *Schooling in Capitalist America*, p. 264.

countries had long since forfeited their claim to revolutionary purity.[67] Bowles and Gintis noted that even though private ownership had been abolished in those countries, their hierarchical control of production was similar to that of corporate capitalism. "Revolutionary" elites perpetuated their power through the centralized Communist Party organization and a centralized control structure in the workplace based on relationships of domination and subordination. Socialist systems per se could not guarantee the "revolutionary socialist" reforms the authors championed. Indeed, there was no absolute model for the kind of economic democracy or egalitarian and participatory power relationships they had in mind. But one area from which they were prepared to derive inspiration was the "substantial degree of worker control of production" reportedly achieved in some factories in China, Cuba, and Chile.[68]

China's new Cultural Revolution policies thus appeared as a deliberate attempt to change certain features of its system that China shared with the other socialist states and now deplored as "revisionist." "China," wrote Karabel and Halsey in the mid-1970s, "presents a strikingly different situation in that it is self-consciously trying to avoid establishing a Russian-style 'bourgeois' educational system whose hierarchical character would lend itself to analysis based on the theoretical framework neo-Marxists use to criticize inegalitarian systems under capitalism."[69]

Internationally, China had cut its ties with the dominant powers of both the capitalist West and the communist East. Free of external obligations, the Chinese now appeared set on an independent course of their own, beholden to and dependent upon no one. They seemed to have emerged from the Red Guard inaugural phase of the Cultural Revolution bent on reviving the promises of an almost forgotten socialist tradition and verifying the all-or-nothing case being made for a redistribution of economic and political power. Measures to equalize incomes further were being promoted in both industry and agriculture. The same course was being followed in other areas of social policy, including health care, housing, and welfare. And especially in education, the dominant thrust of the 1970s was in the direction of a more egalitarian distribution of resources and outcomes.

It was this experience, evaluated from the intellectual and political perspectives of the 1960s and 1970s, which the international community lauded as coming closest to its own model program for educational development in

---

[67] E.g., Boudon, *Education, Opportunity, and Social Inequality*, p. 114; Karabel and Halsey, "Educational Research," p. 40; Richard B. Dobson, "Social Status and Inequality of Access to Higher Education in the USSR," in Karabel and Halsey, *Power and Ideology in Education*, pp. 254–275.

[68] Bowles and Gintis, *Schooling in Capitalist America*, pp. 81, 266.

[69] Karabel and Halsey, "Educational Research," p. 40 n. 54, citing Marianne Bastid, "Economic Necessity and Political Ideals in Educational Reform during the Cultural Revolution," *China Quarterly*, no. 42 (Apr.–June 1970), pp. 16–45; and Victor Nee, *The Cultural Revolution at Peking University* (New York: Monthly Review Press, 1969).

Third World countries. China became the main empirical reference point, a real-life example used to reinforce the hypotheses emerging from decades of frustrations with other countries' failures. So close was the correspondence, in fact, between the Chinese experience and those hypotheses that had the former not existed, someone might have wanted to invent it, which raises the next question to which we must turn.

Having addressed the preliminary question of what the Chinese model meant to the outside world, we must now take up the more difficult task of trying to assess what it meant to the Chinese themselves. Ultimately, the model both in external image and internal reality was an exercise in educational development. That endeavor is best defined as the attempt to create a formal education system, inspired by the prior Western example, within a historically and culturally different setting, constrained by a low-income economy. The radical Chinese effort of the 1970s was by no means foreordained when China began building its first modern school system around the turn of the 20th century. But the issues associated with educational development generally – the contradictions at the mass level, rising expectations, the gap between educational output and society's needs, scarce resources, unequal distribution, and the strains created by the Western example – were all evident in China almost from the start. Hence, our search for the origins of China's radical experience might best begin with the controversies those issues provoked during the early decades of the century.

Part I

The republican era:
origins of radical education reform

2

Development dilemmas in the
republican era: the League
of Nations report

The League of Nations 1932 report on Chinese education provides a direct link
between past and present development concerns. Terms of reference are not
always the same, but the issues elaborated in the report are clearly identifiable
as antecedents of those that defined the Third World's decades of development
between 1960 and 1980. A new Chinese government established in the late
1920s by the Nationalist Party (Guomindang) had invited the League of Nations to help prepare a plan for comprehensive education reform. This would
have been one of several such major revisions that marked the growth of
Western-style education in China after its widespread introduction around the
turn of the century. A mission of "experts" consequently spent three months
in China during 1931. Read more than half a century later, their report and
proposals not only reflect the early thinking of the international development
community but stand also as a benchmark against which to evaluate China's
precommunist education system.[1]

---

[1] The League of Nations Mission of Educational Experts, *The Reorganisation of Education in China*
(Paris: League of Nations Institute of Intellectual Co-operation, 1932) (cited hereafter as League
of Nations report). The four principal members of the mission were professors: C. H. Becker
(University of Berlin, former Prussian minister of education), M. Falski (director of the Primary
Education Department, Ministry of Education, Warsaw, Poland), P. Langevin (Collège de
France, Paris), and R. H. Tawney (London School of Economics and Political Science). The
authors claimed that their conclusions on "all the essential points" were reached unanimously
and not by compromise. Chapters were drafted by individual members, but the final version was
prepared by only one of their number, who, although not named, was reputed to have been
Tawney (personal communication, John K. Fairbank, 1983; also Guy S. Alitto, *The Last Confucian: Liang Shu-ming and the Chinese Dilemma of Modernity* [Berkeley: University of California
Press, 1979], p. 143). The tendency to dismiss the document as "Tawney's report" reflected
even many years later the indignation it originally aroused among interested Americans. They
were excluded from the project because the U.S. was not a League of Nations member. But
more important, the report was straightforward in its criticism of Chinese students educated at
Columbia University's Teachers College and their enthusiastic efforts during the 1920s to
emulate the American model. A German account of the contemporary controversies surrounding
the report is cited by Ruth Hayhoe, "Catholics and Socialists: The Paradox of French Educational Interaction with China," in Ruth Hayhoe and Marianne Bastid, eds., *China's Education
and the Industrialized World: Studies in Cultural Transfer* (Armonk, N.Y.: M. E. Sharpe, 1987),

The report was highly critical. It defined China's modern schools as "independent organisms modelled on the forms and ideology of private education instead of being included in an organised system of public education."[2] Reiterating the conventional wisdom of that time, the authors blamed this weakness on China's lack of public spirit and social organization. Specifically within the educational realm, the origins of the weakness were seen as twofold. It was rooted, first, in the tradition of family, clan, and village schools inevitably confined by the narrow interests and private financial sources which supported them. Traditionally, the state had been concerned not with education as such but with administering the civil service examinations, which controlled access to public office and political power. Yet the central role of the examinations and the Confucian learning they perpetuated provided a coherence to the system as a whole that ended with the 1911 revolution. Among the remains of that educational tradition two decades later was the now truncated custom of autonomous locally supported schools.

Second, reinforcing this traditional remnant was the new 20th-century compulsion to adopt foreign models. These in turn had their own diverse origins and consequences. The Christian mission schools provided one kind of foreign influence, but these too were disparately run and individually financed. Also, by the 1920s and 1930s, they were oriented toward providing an exclusive kind of education concentrated at the secondary and tertiary levels.[3] Equally important was the influence of Chinese returning home from overseas studies to introduce foreign models of life and learning, firm in the belief that this was the best means to the desired end. Unfortunately, the new generation of intellectuals equated their mission with the "mechanical imitation" of foreign educational institutions, including curricula, textbooks, and teaching methods. This tendency reflected the growing isolation of China's educated elite both from the contemporary concerns of the masses and from its own past: in the experts' view, two disjunctures with potentially dangerous consequences for all of Chinese society.

Thus, many richly endowed modern schools and colleges had been established without being integrated into a larger system of public education. These schools of higher standard were divorced from the country's basically unchanged economic conditions while mass education was neglected. The result was an "enormous abyss between the masses of the Chinese people, plunged in illiteracy, and not understanding the needs of their country, and the

p. 307 n. 99. See also John Cleverley, *The Schooling of China* (London: George Allen and Unwin, 1985), pp. 57–59.

[2] League of Nations report, p. 19.

[3] For a review of the late-19th-century missionary enterprise and its reorientation based on the new idea that the best way to influence China was through its educated upper classes rather than the poor, see Shirley S. Garrett, *Social Reformers in Urban China: The Chinese Y.M.C.A., 1895–1926* (Cambridge: Harvard University Press, 1970), esp. chap. 1.

intelligentsia educated in luxurious schools and indifferent to the wants of the masses."[4] Specific recommendations provided a profile of the education system's dimensions and defects from the outsiders' perspective.

Equity, efficiency, and mass education

In contrast with the inclination of their successors in later decades to focus on the trade-off between equity and efficiency, or the optimal use of scarce resources, the experts in 1931 emphasized efficiency as a precondition for more equitable distribution. Within the Chinese environment of that time, inefficiency was cast as a wasteful attribute of elitism and a consequent drag on development. Such elitism was evident generally in the emphasis on higher education, as well as in the management of individual schools.

Extending elementary schooling to all children should have been among the highest priorities. But it could be realistically promoted nationwide only with more efficient administration and resource use, necessary to ensure more adequate financing and rational distribution. Within the existing system of public education, the central government generally supported the tertiary level, provinces were primarily responsible for secondary schools, and elementary instruction was financed mainly by counties or subcounty districts. But public as well as private and foreign funds were drawn to the secondary and tertiary levels. Meanwhile, counties and villages lacked the resources to keep their end of the bargain because they were relying on unreformed inherited arrangements, which could not support the goals of modern mass education.

The mission also noted that children of well-off parents who could have afforded private schooling enjoyed preferential access to public education. Public kindergartens were frequently located in the wealthier neighborhoods. Enrollment was based on "entrance examinations" designed to select those demonstrating mental and physical superiority even at so young an age. These were usually the children of the more affluent, thereby excluding the youngsters who most needed such preschooling. Tuition fees were demanded from all alike, regardless of ability to pay. The same practices governed attendance at the public elementary schools as well, where children from poorer families were similarly denied access. Yet schools were regularly underutilized, and expensive facilities often bore no relationship to practical needs.

At the elementary level, the average student/teacher ratio was 20:1, whereas a ratio of 40:1 or more was typical in other countries. The ratio in China was said to be due to the large number of small village schools, the small size of classes everywhere, and the common practice of educating boys and girls separately. The pattern of overstaffed schools and underused buildings was

[4] League of Nations report, p. 21.

reproduced throughout the system. At the secondary level, the student/teacher ratio was 10:1. In higher education, there were one administrator and two teachers for every 10 students. As a result, teachers at both levels enjoyed lighter workloads than their counterparts in any other country at that time.

Given existing resources, the experts calculated that at least twice the number of students could have been accommodated in the existing schools at each level, that is, elementary, secondary, and tertiary. The number of elementary school students could have been increased immediately from the then current 8.8 million (about 21 percent of the age-group) to at least 17 million. Yet available statistics indicated an annual increase in elementary school enrollments during the 1920s of only about 5 percent. At that rate, 20–30 years would be needed to achieve universal schooling.[5]

Secondary schooling

China's secondary, or middle, schools inspired the experts to address all the major issues of educational development save one, namely, quantity. Otherwise, their assessment of secondary schooling swept the field, introducing in an early form the concerns about quality, content, equity, the schooling–employment relationship, and dependency. As with elementary schooling, demand at the secondary level was greater than supply: applicants were more numerous than school places. Nevertheless, "the urgent need of the moment is not to increase the quantity of secondary education, but to improve its quality."[6] Defects were similar in kind to those found in elementary schools but seemed greater in degree and with graver consequences. The qualitative defects included formalism, remoteness from practical life, reliance on talk and textbooks, overemphasis on cramming the memory rather than arousing curiosity, neglect of inductive and experimental methods, failure to cultivate initiative and a sense of responsibility.

Civics, or the teachings of Sun Yat-sen, the father of the Republic, and other state doctrines were presented from books and in abstract lectures in as formalistic a manner as the teaching of all the sciences, whether natural or social. Passive classroom lecturing was the norm at both the elementary and the secondary levels, with teachers sometimes reading their lectures directly from textbooks. There was little opportunity for individual student initiative or involvement, whether by way of independent study, classroom discussion, laboratory experiments, field study, practical application, or manual labor. Chinese students received virtually no introduction to the problems of public and collective life, the organization of work, or the practical use of scientific

---

[5] Ibid., pp. 45, 62–67, 76–79, 80–84, 90–92. For contemporary statistics, see chap. 4 tables, below.

[6] Ibid., p. 108.

knowledge. Secondary education was also constricted by examinations at every stage, with monthly tests, semester finals, year-end examinations, and additional entrance exams at each level.

Chinese secondary schools were by this time patterned on the U.S. model, which did not endear them to the Europeans. A uniform curriculum at the three-year junior middle level was followed by the three-year senior secondary course in an American-style comprehensive school. Senior-level students were theoretically given a choice of different majors: general (college preparatory), normal (teacher training), commerce, agriculture, and sometimes domestic science for girls. In practice, most students opted for the general academic course. With little interest in the others, programs and curricula were not even fully developed.

Discrepancies in the official statistics provided to the mission made enrollment figures impossible to estimate. But there were obviously many more students in secondary schools than could be accommodated at the tertiary level. Such imbalances were already causing alarm, and Chinese authorities were recommending the then standard solution: vocational education. A recent "rapid increase" in secondary schools had prompted the central government's Education Ministry to issue new "guiding principles" in 1931. Noting that many of the new graduates were neither financially able to attend college nor trained for any line of work, the ministry concluded that "the middle school is not only an educational failure, but also a troublesome social problem." The provinces were therefore instructed not to establish any new junior middle schools or college-preparatory sections at the senior middle level. All new secondary schools should henceforth be of the technical and vocational variety. All existing middle schools should at least offer vocational subjects and establish vocational courses if possible. All middle schools run by lower-level governments should eliminate their college-preparatory curriculum in favor of vocational and teacher training courses.[7] In another set of proposals issued specifically for vocational training, the ministry indicated that such schools should give preference to children from poor families.[8]

Curiously, given their critical stance and anti-elitist concerns, the experts approved these proposals while ignoring their implications (i.e., vocational training for the poor and college preparatory for the rich). Perhaps the official injunction to introduce vocational subjects in all schools seemed to indicate sufficient evidence of good intentions (which appear insignificant only with the benefit of hindsight). Nevertheless, in principle, the experts remained consistent and professed themselves adamantly against creating separate streams

[7] Chinese Education Ministry, "Guiding Principles for the Establishment of Secondary Schools," translated in ibid., pp. 115–116.
[8] Summarized in ibid., pp. 137–138.

or education catering to separate kinds of students. "It is to be feared," they warned, "that besides the schools for general education a completely separate system of professional and technical schools may arise, whereas there should only be one system."[9]

They chose to argue their case, however, in terms of content, quality, and intellectual equity rather than the social pressures for parity already evident within the system. In 1931, the experts defined terminal – in contrast with college preparatory – secondary schooling as that which trained the middle classes, including the majority of civil servants and businessmen. These students required a form of general education "complete in itself" rather than a disparate package of vocational courses. Such education should be uniform in quality and degree but differentiated in accordance with practical needs. Hence, China did not so much need more vocational schools as a reform of the curriculum for *all* secondary institutions at both junior and senior levels to orient them more closely to the realities of life and work. The assumption that practical work belonged only with vocational study was wrong. "The academic student requires ample opportunities for such work at school, precisely because his special interests tend later in life to divorce him from it. There is a scientific as well as a literary humanism."[10]

Curiously also, given their concerns, the experts could find little to praise in the American model. In the U.S., the effort to divide secondary education into two separate academic and vocational streams had only recently been defeated by a coalition of liberal educators, including John Dewey, and organized labor. They had argued, among other things, that such streaming would reinforce social divisions by ensuring that working-class children inherited the occupational status of their parents.[11] The experts acknowledged only that the American-style comprehensive high school which China had adopted represented a "middle course" between the German system, which was based on the two separate streams, and the Soviet Union, which offered a uniform secondary curriculum combining academic and practical training for all.

Instead, on the issue of foreign influence, the Europeans argued their case strongly against intellectual dependency, a concept obviously already well developed. They cited the consequences of "superficial Americanization" for China's secondary schools as a case in point. Secondary education should be "providing the foundation of a modern culture which is really Chinese," and the structure of the school should be determined by the actual requirements of that culture and the needs of the people. For China at that time, still in search

---

[9] Ibid., p. 129.
[10] Ibid., p. 110.
[11] Bowles and Gintis, *Schooling in Capitalist America*, chap. 7; Lawrence A. Cremin, *The Transformation of the School: Progressivism in American Education, 1876–1957* (New York: Alfred A. Knopf, 1962), chap. 2.

of a new national identity following the collapse of the old order, such a culture would have to be some new fusion of tradition and modernity. It would have to combine elements both Chinese and Western, including both European and American. But creating such a culture and maintaining an appropriate education system was a task for Chinese intellectual leaders, not their foreign advisors.

As for specific reasons why the American model was inappropriate, the European experts found it too fragmented and expensive. Its various subdivisions required a range of resources, both human and material, not yet available in China. Also, the American method of studying in return for "credits" led in Chinese schools to the "mechanical teaching of unrelated subjects." The Europeans were looking instead for a "unity of intellectual activity" and a curriculum linking academic subjects with the practical realities of life. Alas, they found "no trace of it in the secondary education scheme functioning in China."[12]

The mission was also critical of the American "science of teaching" so effectively promoted by prominent Chinese graduates from Columbia University's Teachers College. The consequence of emphasizing technique and teaching methods rather than mastery of particular subjects or branches of learning was especially unfortunate in China, where the most pressing need was still to replace the traditional literary learning with scientific modes of thinking and the acquisition of specialized knowledge. In any event, the Chinese were allowing themselves to be "dazzled" by the material manifestations of America's success story without adequately considering how to adapt its ways and means to China's very different economic and scientific environment.[13]

Higher education

Most of the issues found at the secondary level were also evident in higher education, leading the mission to conclude that the Chinese had not yet understood the function of a modern university. Its task should not be supplying knowledge to passive students but rather training individuals how to acquire it for themselves. Yet lectures predominated, and textbooks and lecture notes constituted the students' main reading matter. Seminars and independent study were rare. The majority of books used were in foreign languages, and most of the subject matter and examples given were of foreign origin. This reinforced natural tendencies to memorize the prepared texts and lessons in the traditional manner without questioning or application.

The experts also found much to criticize in the structure of higher education, which was then based on more than 50 institutions virtually all established

---

[12] League of Nations report, p. 105.
[13] Ibid., pp. 118–122.

within the preceding 25 years. Of the 59 recognized universities in 1931, about half were private and half run by national and provincial governments, with the total 33,847 students (90 percent male) also about evenly divided between the public and private institutions.[14] The points of criticism included haphazard geographical distribution; too many institutions concentrated in the same areas (Beijing and Shanghai) doing almost the same work without any rational division of labor between them; and the "hypertrophy of legal, political and literary studies" to the neglect of science and technology (see Table 4.5). Without actually acknowledging the ancient career pattern that was thus reproducing itself in modern guise, the report noted regretfully that "the ambition of most Chinese university students is a career in the public service, central or local, and, failing that, a post as a teacher."[15]

The mission nevertheless reserved harsh words for the elitist component of the same ancient tradition which was being perpetuated by teachers and students alike. The aura of the past, when scholars were exempt from manual labor and granted the privileges of official position, still surrounded them, heightened now by their possession of the new Western learning. In fact, the mission expressed skepticism about the general desire to go abroad for study since the objective was usually only the prestige of a foreign degree. The foreign-trained students' well-known problems of adjusting to work in China and the dislocations they were creating caused the mission to recommend that only advanced scholars be permitted to study abroad and only in fields for which there were no adequate facilities yet existing in China.[16]

The European experts were careful to note that most of their criticisms had already been formulated by Chinese educators themselves. But the experts' most basic reservations were directed against those same educators. For it was they who were perpetuating the prevailing and "fundamental misconception of the function of a university."[17] They also repeatedly advanced the "false argument" that modern Europe and America were the products of science and technology, instead of the other way around – hence the still widely prevailing belief that China had only to acquire Western science and technology in order to become similarly advanced. And Chinese educators equated modernization with the superficial imitation of foreign models. The experts counseled intellectual leaders to borrow instead that "spirit of originality with which Americans have succeeded in adapting the culture of Europe to American conditions."[18] The three misconceptions – about the function of a university, the autonomous

[14] Ibid., pp. 141–142.
[15] Ibid., p. 151 and pp. 139–158 passim.
[16] Ibid., pp. 173–174.
[17] Ibid., p. 161.
[18] Ibid., pp. 27–28.

role of science and technology, and the mechanical use of foreign models – lay at the heart of the system these intellectual leaders had created and were responsible for many of the defects they themselves acknowledged yet seemed powerless to correct.

The issues confounding the task of educational development generally in 1980 were thus already present and accounted for in China at least half a century earlier. But the experts in 1931 did not analyze the swift currents of change that had transformed Chinese intellectual life during the first three decades of the century. China's new school system, to which modern Western concepts and criteria could at least be applied, was scarely as old as the century itself. Nor did the experts adequately record the controversies and conflicting interests that had impelled the Chinese government to solicit their opinions in the first place.

3

The inheritance

Acceptance of modern Western learning did not come in China until successive military defeats and encroachment by the Western powers forced change upon the self-confident Chinese empire. But change, when it finally came, was systemic in scope, reflecting the close relationship between traditional learning and the imperial bureaucratic state. The two collapsed almost simultaneously, suggesting that neither could have long survived the other. Yet under the old regime, the state's direct involvement with learning was limited primarily to administering the examinations used for selecting government officials. The content of the examinations was limited in turn to the classical Confucian canon. This ensured the latter's propagation, however, not only as the main repository of learning and values but more concretely as the sole course of study leading to the most prestigious occupation in the land.

Education and the Confucian tradition

The examinations are traced by convention to certain nonhereditary values idealized by Confucian tradition as requisites for filling government posts in antiquity. Historically, this Chinese device for bureaucratic selection has been interpreted as a function of medieval dynastic struggles for control over central and local government posts. The civil service examinations, which survived until 1905, date from the Sui dynasty (A.D. 581–618) and were used to enhance its power by invoking the Confucian tradition of merit to legitimize imperial hegemony over administrative appointments. During the subsequent Tang and Song dynasties (618–906 and 960–1279, respectively), the examinations accordingly played a pivotal role in the development of an imperial bureaucratic state. They did so, first, by enforcing objective qualifications in addition to the ascriptive criterion of parentage; then by allowing commoners to qualify for office via the examinations; and ultimately by establishing the degrees earned individually but bestowed under imperial authority as the main route to official position.

The system expanded quantitatively during Song times, when increased economic productivity and accumulation of wealth, together with the development of printing and publishing, led to growing pools of candidates and degree holders. In this manner, a ruling class of literati–bureaucrats emerged. Meanwhile, families with dynastic aspirations continued to vie for the right to stand as the chief source of hereditary authority, personified by their emperors, who stood at the apex of the examination system and the state bureaucracy as a whole.[1]

These trends persisted over the centuries – despite foreign invasions, demographic pressures, and growing occupational diversity – to produce, in modern parlance, the first fully documented occurrence of diploma disease. The examinations grew increasingly formalistic, and the system itself was articulated with increasing degrees of refinement. This was the response of successive dynasties trying to accommodate not just population growth, territorial expansion, and supplies of candidates outstripping the need for more bureaucrats but also ancient "pressures for parity," or demands for fair access, dating back at least to Song times.[2]

Borne along by the hopes of candidates and their families from one generation to the next, the influence of the examinations ultimately pervaded the entire society. They became the chief mechanism for bestowing local and informal elite status as well as for choosing government officials. Confucian learning, imperial power, and bureaucratic authority were thus bound together in a mutually sustaining relationship that would dominate Chinese intellectual life until the examinations were abolished in 1905 and the imperial system was overthrown in the 1911 revolution. The League of Nations experts were referring to this relationship when they noted the coherence of the traditional order in contrast with its as yet unreconstructed successor. And it was the remnants of this tradition that played so important a role in the educational controversies of the 1920s and 1930s.

The hierarchical structure of the examinations achieved final form during the Ming dynasty (1368–1644) and remained basically unchanged for some 500 years of Ming and Qing (or Manchu; 1644–1911) rule. The system was centralized under the authority of the Board of Rites, with the emperor himself presiding at the highest level. The examinations were empirewide in scope, with quotas drawn to ensure an adequate supply and distribution of educated

[1] E.g., Ichisada Miyazaki, *China's Examination Hell: The Civil Service Examinations of Imperial China*, trans. Conrad Schirokauer (New Haven: Yale University Press, 1981); David S. Nivison, "Protest against Conventions and Conventions of Protest," in Arthur F. Wright, ed., *The Confucian Persuasion* (Stanford: Stanford University Press, 1960), pp. 177–201; John W. Chaffee, *The Thorny Gates of Learning in Sung China: A Social History of Examinations* (Cambridge: Cambridge University Press, 1985); Thomas H. C. Lee, *Government Education and Examinations in Sung China* (Hong Kong: Chinese University Press, 1985); Edward A. Kracke, Jr., *Civil Service in Early Sung China, 960–1067* (Cambridge: Harvard University Press, 1968).

[2] See chap. 13 on the parallels between the old principles for fixing examination quotas and the emerging key-point school system of the early 1960s.

men, albeit also in relation to a locality's existing cultural level, throughout the country.

To summarize what had become a highly complex system, during the Qing period the process began with a series of three examinations, the first administered by county government officials and the second by officials at the prefectural level. The third, administered by the provincial director of studies in each prefectural capital, was decisive, and central government quotas determined the number who could pass. Those who did so were advanced to the status of *shengyuan*, popularly known as *xiucai*, or "government student." This achievement qualified the "student" to join the ranks of the gentry (*shenshi*) class, although strictly speaking *shengyuan* was not a degree but only a title denoting the preliminary status qualifying an individual to sit for the degree examinations. Additional preliminaries then preceded provincial-level examinations supervised by a centrally appointed official and leading to the *zhuren* degree. Success at this level, too, was limited by quotas and represented the basic achievement necessary (with the inevitable exceptions) for holding government office. Finally, metropolitan and palace examinations, the latter with the emperor officiating, were held in the capital and led to the highest, or *jinshi*, degree.[3]

Newcomers or men from nonofficial families could enter the ranks of officialdom via the examinations; commoners could enter gentry ranks; and commoners could even become officials. In earlier centuries, formal restrictions denied eligibility to many, including merchants, artisans, and those in occupations regarded as demeaning. But except for the customary exclusion of women, most of the bans were not uniformly maintained for all proscribed categories over time. In practice however, the perpetual "examination life" imposed upon those who sought to achieve and retain even *shengyuan* status ensured that only families with a certain amount of surplus wealth could support such a pursuit by one or more of their male members. Literary achievement and official appointment were clearly dependent upon and facilitated by wealth.[4]

---

[3] In decades past, much controversy surrounded the use in the Chinese context of the English term "gentry." He Bingdi (Ho Ping-ti), for example, argued that the term was inappropriate since this Chinese class was not by definition "landed" but owed its status instead to office holding and examination performance. He also drew a claear line between the official ruling class, or degree-holdig scholar–officials, and the *shengyuan*, scholar–commoners. Zhang Zhongli (Chang Chung-li) differentiated the two categories as "upper gentry" and "lower gentry" respectively. See Chung-li Chang, *The Chinese Gentry: Studies on Their Role in Nineteenth-Century Chinese Society* (Seattle: University of Washington Press, 1955); Chung-li Chang, *The Income of the Chinese Gentry* (Seattle: University of Washington Press, 1962); Ping-ti Ho, *The Ladder of Success in Imperial China: Aspects of Social Mobility, 1368–1911* (New York: Columbia University Press, 1962). For a recent survey of the literature, see Benjamin A. Elman, "Political, Social, and Cultural Reproduction via Civil Service Examinations in Late Imperial China," *Journal of Asian Studies*, no. 1 (Feb. 1991), pp. 7–28.

[4] On mobility, see Kracke's "new men" in the Song bureaucracy, He Bingdi's "rags to riches" *jinshi* during the Ming and Qing dynasties, and Zhang Zhongli's "newcomers" in the 19th

In any event, the boundary between gentry and commoner once crossed was clearly drawn. That line, marked by the acquisition of *shengyuan* status, qualified the holder as a member of the gentry class whether or not he ever went on to hold public office. Regulations forbade him thereafter from engaging in the "lowly" occupations. Traditionally, the stigma was also attached to commerce. The sons of traders and artisans who passed the examinations did not normally engage in the family occupation thereafter, although the prejudice against commercial activity was breaking down in the 19th century. *Shengyuan* of modest means typically resigned themselves to the respectable but not highly esteemed occupations of teaching and medicine.

Yet gentry status brought with it automatic benefits substantial enough, and that could not be achieved otherwise, to induce hundreds of thousands to attempt the examinations. They did so knowing that the quotas would prevent all but 1–2 percent of the preliminary candidates from ever advancing even to the *shengyuan* level.[5] But if rate-of-return calculations could be made retroactively, they would surely reveal the reasons why so many continued to judge the potential benefits worthy of the cost. Among the economic, social, and legal privileges which set the lucky few apart was their exemption from the corvée service and its tax equivalent. They were also exempt from the corporal punishments administered for lesser offenses and treated differently from commoners for major ones. Similarly, infractions against them would be punished more severely than those against others. Sumptuary laws entitled them to wear special clothing and certain luxury items of apparel forbidden to commoners. Prescribed terms of address, etiquette, and ceremonial functions also set them apart. In terms of the local power structure, gentry and officials were of comparable status. The former had rights of access to the latter, while the commoners were clearly subordinate and inferior.

In addition to these formally authorized privileges, the gentry were regularly able to exploit their status to a variety of advantages growing out of their informal elite status. "Unemployed," or non-office-holding, gentry played an important role in Chinese society, serving as accessories to local government and intermediaries between officialdom and the mass of ordinary folk. The quotas for those allowed to pass each exam were actually calculated to ensure that each county produced neither too many nor too few given the needs of the empire for officials and of each locality for a supportable number of informal leaders. Higher-degree holders even when not in office tended to gravitate to

century in the following: Kracke, "Region, Family, and Individual in the Chinese Examination System," in John K. Fairbank, ed., *Chinese Thought and Institutions* (Chicago: University of Chicago Press, 1957), p. 259; Ping-ti Ho, *The Ladder of Success*, pp. 107–125, 189–190; Chung-li Chang, *The Chinese Gentry*, pp. 214–219. See also P'an Kuang-tan and Fei Hsiao-t'ung, "City and Village: The Inequality of Opportunity," in Johanna M. Menzel, ed., *The Chinese Civil Service: Career Open to Talent?* (Boston: D. C. Heath and Co., 1963), p. 15.

5 Chung-li Chang, *The Chinese Gentry*, p. 11.

provincial capitals or other important towns. But the lower gentry stayed home. The lowest government office was that of the county magistrate, whose staff was small and whose budget was limited. Local gentry therefore performed many of the public functions that would in a modern setting be the responsibility of local governments. Such functions included arbitrating disputes, organizing the local militia, assisting in tax collection, mobilizing private funds for local public works, and helping to maintain local cultural institutions, schools, examination halls, temples, etc. Together with teaching, these local leadership functions constituted the principal "professional" activity of most holders of titles and degrees who did not otherwise occupy public office.[6]

In the latter half of the 19th century, there were about 900,000 "regular" gentry members (i.e., those who had at least advanced to the *shengyuan* level via the examination route). The number of purchased ranks and degrees had risen substantially, reflecting the social disruptions of the period. The total figure for *shengyuan*, including those who had purchased equivalent status, was about 1.4 million. Of this total, around 200,000 (11–14 percent) had risen above the *shengyuan* level to qualify for bureaucratic appointments. Since only their immediate families (their children, wives, and concubines) enjoyed the privileges and protection of gentry status, this class was estimated at about 7.2 million overall, or close to 2 percent of the total population (approximately 377.5 million in the late 1800s).[7]

Ultimately, the examinations with their uniform Confucian ideology dominated not only elite selection but the entire structure of traditional education as well. By the end of the imperial era, educational institutions were oriented not toward teaching and learning but to inculcating the skills necessary to pass the civil service examinations. Each administrative district down to the county had its own "school" or school–temple ceremonial halls attached to the government offices. This institution no longer served any educational function, being instead the local center for conducting official Confucian ceremonies and administering the examinations. As these schools lost their original teaching function in earlier centuries, a new institution, the *shuyuan*, or academy, had grown up to fill that need. But it, too, was co-opted by the examinations.

Academies had developed during Song times as centers of learning, intellectual

---

[6] On the privileges and functions of local gentry, see ibid., pp. 32–70; T'ung-tsu Ch'ü, *Local Government in China under the Ch'ing* (Stanford: Stanford University Press, 1962), chap. 10. Zhang Zhongli estimated that in the latter half of the 19th century, the dominant portion of gentry income derived from the services they rendered as government officials, informal local leaders, and teachers. This service income amounted to 48 percent of the total; landholding accounted for another 34 percent; and commerce 17 percent. Gentry income as a whole accounted for about 24 percent of the total gross national product (Chung-li Chang, *The Income of the Chinese Gentry*, pp. 146, 197, 326–327).

[7] Chung-li Chang, *The Chinese Gentry*, pp. 97–113, 137–141; Elman, "Political, Social, and Cultural Reproduction," p. 16.

discourse, and contemplation, preferably situated in secluded natural settings. The ideal of learning as an end in itself remained and continued to be pursued. But by the Qing dynasty, the academies were oriented primarily to the content and schedules of the examinations. Education beyond the elementary level was thus dominated by the subjects and skills necessary for examination success. The subjects were the Confucian classics, history, and literature; the skills were essay and poetry writing and of course calligraphy; the specific focus was on past and future examination questions. Institutions acquired fame in direct relation to their students' skills in writing mock examination essays and the degrees they ultimately won.

By the end of the 19th century, some 4,000 *shuyuan* existed in an informal hierarchy from county (*xian*), to prefecture (*fu*), to provincial capital. But the most important and famous academies were located in the largest cities and specialized in preparing for the provincial and metropolitan examinations. The academies had become increasingly urban based, tied to the centers of bureaucratic power that dominated their reason for existence and the sources of wealth that sustained them. As with other civil endeavors, they were established, funded, and operated through the joint cooperation of local government officials and nonofficial local gentry. Financial support was both government and private, the latter including both gentry and merchant. Reflecting the two main sources of wealth – property and commercial capital – funding usually took the form of rent and interest derived from endowments of agricultural land, urban properties, and trust funds. The income was used to pay salaries, student stipends, and examination expenses.

Regardless of who founded and funded them, however, official supervision was a fact of academy life. By the mid-19th century, local officials were approving the appointments of academy headmasters, fixing academy regulations, and conducting regular assessment examinations of their students. Official supervision extended from the provincial to county levels. In Guangdong, the total number of academy students was fixed by official decision, and admission based on ranked performance in preliminary examinations.

Although the practice seems not to have been universally developed, the precedent also already existed, by the mid-1800s, of maximizing success with a kind of hierarchical ranking system for the academies themselves. Tilemann Grimm writes of an "atypically neat case" from Shaozhou Prefecture in Guangdong Province, where the single academy in a county seat was fed by 13 lower-level preparatory schools, one each in the 13 districts into which the county was subdivided. Similarly, the principal academy in the prefectural capital sent examiners each year, with official permission, down to the individual counties to assess and select their best students. A second school in the prefectural capital served as feeder and backup for the principal academy. In the provincial capital, Guangzhou, a few major academies selected top students from surrounding prefectures and eventually from throughout the province.[8]

At the elementary level, traditional schooling was almost uniformly private, and the most common institution, other than the household tutor, was the tutor school (*sishu*). These received neither public assistance nor supervision and were not even officially regarded as schools, being essentially private single-teacher classes. They existed everywhere in both urban and rural settings and took a variety of forms, including the family school, with a tutor hired by an individual family; communal schools, that is, the joint effort of an extended family, clan, or village; and fee-charging schools run by the teacher himself. Expenditures were not great, being confined largely to the teacher's salary, toward which parents contributed a negotiated sum. Supplies and furnishings were provided by the parents, who, when pupils were too numerous to be taught in a private home, might secure the use of spare rooms in a village temple or some other public building.[9]

Teachers were drawn from among the relatively large pool of advanced students and gentry that existed as an important cultural by-product of the examination system. As noted, only a small percentage of the county candidates achieved gentry status and only a small proportion of these ever qualified for public office. This left a substantial portion of "unemployed" gentry in addition to all the candidates who passed the first qualifying examinations but failed to attain formal gentry status. Overall, the number of such active and former candidates has been estimated at about 5 million commoners, or 5 percent of the adult male population in 1800.[10]

Regardless of the means by which basic instruction was conveyed, however, the average boy who received it studied for only two or three years, and content was essentially the same everywhere. Schooling at the elementary level

[8] Tilemann Grimm, "Academies and Urban Systems in Kwangtung," in G. William Skinner, ed., *The City in Late Imperial China* (Stanford: Stanford University Press, 1977), pp. 488–490, 493. Rankin argues that academies in Zhejiang Province did not function in so hierarchical a manner. While acknowledging that students were drawn to leading academies in the provincial capital and neighboring intellectual centers in southern Jiangsu, she suggests that county and prefectural academies did not maintain the custom Grimm describes for Guangdong of filtering students upward into the nearest next-level institution within a given administrative or de facto catchment area (Mary Backus Rankin, *Elite Activism and Political Transformation in China: Zhejiang Province, 1865–1911* [Stanford: Stanford University Press, 1986], pp. 49–50). Also on academies, see John Meskill, *Academies in Ming China: A Historical Essay* (Tucson: University of Arizona Press, 1982); Ping-ti Ho, *Ladder of Success*, pp. 168–209; Kung-chuan Hsiao, *Rural China: Imperial Control in the Nineteenth Century* (Seattle: University of Washington Press, 1960), pp. 235–254; Sally Borthwick, *Education and Social Change in China: The Beginnings of the Modern Era* (Stanford: Hoover Institution Press, 1983), pp. 6–13, 62.

[9] Borthwick, *Education and Social Change*, chap. 2.

[10] David Johnson, "Communication, Class, and Consciousness in Late Imperial China," in David Johnson, Andrew J. Nathan, and Evelyn S. Rawski, eds., *Popular Culture in Late Imperial China* (Berkeley: University of California Press, 1985), p. 59.

was intended to teach children to recognize and write several hundred characters and to transmit fundamental Confucian values. These were conveyed through textbooks and teaching materials based upon the classical works used in formal studies by those who went on to prepare for the examinations. But at the elementary level, which marked the beginning and the end for most of the boys who had access to such instruction, the objective was less ambitious. The end result for them was what might be called not so much functional as subsistence literacy. The pupil would also have been introduced through his primers to the Confucian concepts of morality, filial piety, and correct conduct in interpersonal relations, as well as to basic information about China's past.

Practical subjects, such as arithmetic and science, were not normally included in the curriculum. Calculation, account keeping, and the use of the abacus were treated as specialized knowledge and reserved for apprentices in commerce and trade. Rote memorization and recitation were the standard teaching methods. But the average student would probably have gained sufficient introduction to the skills of reading and writing to be able subsequently to teach himself, with the aid of popular illustrated character glossaries, enough practical-use vocabulary to master the simple written communications needed for daily life.[11]

Evelyn Rawski has made the most systematic effort to assess the diffusion of such learning. Her careful calculations of literacy rates at the end of the imperial era tend to confirm the conventional off-the-cuff "80 percent illiteracy" ratio for the population as a whole. She concluded that at most only 2–10 percent of all women, who made up something less than half the population, were literate. These would have been primarily women born into more affluent circumstances who benefited from the home tutor custom. Among males, between 30 and 45 percent had probably received enough schooling to claim literacy. These estimates are, however, based on a definition of literacy which included those with knowledge of only a few hundred characters, who would, in a modern context, be classified as only semiliterate.[12]

The educational inheritance with which China entered the 20th century was thus ancient, complex, and empirewide in scope. It was dominated first and foremost by the civil service examinations as the single most important mechanism for occupational and social elite selection. Despite a distinguished critical undercurrent maintained by the Ronald Dores of Chinese history, who lamented the link between education and bureaucratic career seeking, in reality that association was only challenged but never broken. On the contrary, from Song times the examinations and the role they played in Chinese society

---

[11] Evelyn Sakakida Rawski, *Education and Popular Literacy in Ch'ing China* (Ann Arbor: University of Michigan Press, 1979), pp. 43–53, 125–139; see also Alexander Woodside, "Some Mid-Qing Theorists of Popular Schools," *Modern China*, vol. 9, no. 1 (Jan. 1983), pp. 3–35.

[12] Rawski, *Education and Popular Literacy*, p. 23 and passim.

repeatedly defeated or co-opted innovations that might have weakened their hold over the educational realm.

Preparing for the examinations did create a reservoir of educated men who served as the formal transmitters of learning to a wider clientele. Chinese society also maintained a tradition of extensive private tutoring at the local level, both urban and rural. But teachers and teaching were regarded essentially as by-products of the bureaucratic enterprise rather than esteemed even as its essential building blocks, much less as alternative sources of intellectual inquiry, professional expertise, or social mobility. Hence family and neighborhood groupings assumed primary responsibility for the earliest years of schooling, beyond which education unrelated to preparing for the examinations remained essentially a gentry avocation bound even then by the conventions of Confucian classicism. The net result was a highly educated elite stratum, expanding, to be sure, but nevertheless superimposed upon a commoner population the vast majority of whom remained illiterate or semiliterate at best.

The Western intrusion: resistance, defeat, and conversion

China did not venture out in search of new learning, nor was it generated spontaneously from within. So strong was the self-confidence of Chinese tradition that more than half a century of direct contact and confrontation with the West would be needed to shake it. Active memories of the ensuing national humiliation would wax and wane, yet seemed likely to linger into the 21st century as China struggled through many political generations to free itself from foreign intervention and the fears of dependency it generated.

Western learning was initially promoted in China by Christian missionaries. But as one Chinese scholar noted in the early 1930s, it was natural that 19th-century mission schools did not develop rapidly, since that was a time "when the Chinese people looked down upon the missionaries as barbarians."[13] Chinese officialdom and the scholar class in general remained as antagonistic to the intellectual intrusion as to the military and political interventions that were making it possible. Missionaries were able to establish the first modern schools in China only after 1842, when its defeat in the First Opium War with Britain led to the first of the "unequal treaties," which forced China to cede the island of Hong Kong and open five ports to foreign trade and residence.[14] This same sequence of Western pressure, Chinese military defeat, and Western advance

---

[13] Lu-dzai Djung, *A History of Democratic Education in Modern China* (Shanghai: Commercial Press, 1934), p. 167.

[14] On antiforeign sentiment and the 19th-century missionary enterprise in China, see, e.g., Paul A. Cohen, *China and Christianity: The Missionary Movement and the Growth of Chinese Antiforeignism, 1860–1870* (Cambridge: Harvard University Press, 1963); Kenneth Scott Latourette, *A History of Christian Missions in China* (Taibei: Ch'eng-wen Publishing Co., 1966); Garrett, *Social Reformers in Urban China*; Jessie Gregory Lutz, *China and the Christian Colleges, 1850–1950* (Ithaca and London: Cornell University Press, 1971).

occurred repeatedly during the next six decades, after which Japan emerged as the most aggressive of the intruding powers.

Under these circumstances, Western learning remained peripheral to the traditional education system until the end of the century. During that time, official reforms followed a limited course promoted by a few individuals acting on their own tentative perceptions of China's changing needs. The latter were expressed almost exclusively in terms of China's military and diplomatic defense against the outside world.

To Feng Guifen (Feng Kuei-fen), one of these early modernizing officials, is attributed the famous quote of that time: "what we then have to learn from the barbarians is only the one thing, solid ships and effective guns." "Shamefully humiliated" by the treaties with England, Russia, America, and France, the Chinese were in a state of "unparalleled anger," he wrote. Feng was articulating a new awareness in the early 1860s that however superior its civilization, China could not compete with Western military technology. But he was decades ahead of his time in advocating that Western learning be integrated into the traditional examination system and rewarded with the same degrees. His target was the educated class as a whole, which would not deign to study foreign affairs.[15]

Feng also advanced the idea of "self-strengthening" (ziqiang), anticipating the efforts that would develop in succeeding decades to enhance China's power but preserve its traditional culture. The ideas used to promote those efforts were encapsulated in the motto of the era: "Chinese learning for fundamental principles; Western learning for use" (Zhongxue wei ti; xixue wei yong). According to its rationale, the Western nations were able to force themselves on China because they were rich and powerful. This superiority as manifested in their weapons of war was due to their superior technical learning. The career of another famous modernizing official, Zhang Zhidong (Chang Chih-tung), epitomized this line of reasoning. From ships, guns, and foreign languages, the interest had grown to include technology, technical learning, and Western education. These were the new means whereby the essence of China's tradition might be preserved while its power was rebuilt in a changing world.[16]

---

[15] Feng Kuei-fen, "On the Manufacture of Foreign Weapons" and "On the Adoption of Western Knowledge," both from his *Jiaobinlu kangyi* (Protests from Jiaobinlu), ca. 1860, originally published in 1898, trans. in Ssu-yü Teng and John K. Fairbank, eds., *China's Response to the West: A Documentary Survey, 1839–1923* (Cambridge: Harvard University Press, 1961), documents 8 and 9, pp. 51–53.

[16] William Ayers, *Chang Chih-tung and Educational Reform in China* (Cambridge: Harvard University Press, 1971), pp. 149–160; Daniel H. Bays, *China Enters the Twentieth Century: Chang Chih-Tung and the Issues of a New Age, 1895–1909* (Ann Arbor: University of Michigan Press, 1978); Luke S. K. Kwong, *A Mosaic of the Hundred Days: Personalities, Politics, and Ideas of 1898* (Cambridge: Harvard University Press, 1984); and Zhang Zhidong, *Zhang Wenxiang gong quanji* (The Complete Works of Zhang Zhidong), 6 vols., ed. Wang Shutong (Taibei: Wenhai chubanshe, 1963).

The self-strengtheners' argument was soon swept aside in the revolutionary haste of the coming decade. But the underlying logic was never forgotten. Especially within the educational realm, as noted by the League of Nations team in the 1930s, it was still a commonplace that China need only master the West's science and technology in order to achieve comparable wealth and power. The assumption of Chinese superiority and the preoccupation with armaments would evolve into the more conventional 20th-century concerns of nationalism and economic development. But whatever its faults, the idea of science, technology, and education as panaceas for China's ills seemed to take on a life of its own. The influence of that idea, like the associated sense of national humiliation itself, would still be visible, albeit much more dimly, even as the 20th century neared its end.

It would be tempting to conclude that such logic, focusing on the intellectual component of the West's advance, was natural within a ruling class whose status was based on scholastic achievement. A similar argument was, of course, made in Japan as well. But there it did not inhibit a range of options that bore immediate practical result, as Feng Guifen was already able to discern in the early 1860s. It would be equally tempting to conclude, therefore, that the "fault" for China's failure to respond similarly to the West's challenge lay with that same intellectual ruling class – whose commitment to its traditional source of power was so strong that many decades of dithering and military defeat would be necessary before any substantive change could occur. In fact, for more than half a century, resentment and disdain dominated the orientation of educated Chinese, both official and otherwise, to Western learning: because it came in the baggage train of the foreign invader; and also because that invasion represented so unprecedented a challenge to Chinese civilization's ancient claim to superiority; but most immediately, because Western learning represented a direct threat to the position, prestige, and power of China's ruling class.

Therefore, in contemplating the question that has preoccupied many since Feng Guifen's day as to why Japan was first off the mark despite Japan's traditional dependence on Chinese culture, responsibility inevitably fell upon that same culture and its guardians. Yet their "error" seemed less in overestimating the autonomous power of Western science and technology than in underestimating the importance of its application or, in effect, trying to force Western-style education into the social and intellectual molds vacated by traditional Confucian learning. This miscalculation was reflected many times over in the difficulties experienced by China's educated elite as it made the transition from Confucian scholar–bureaucrat to modern intellectual, and from guardians of an independent culture to one dependent upon the outside would much as Japan had traditionally been dependent upon China.

Education reforms thus remained disparate and unpopular among the literati establishment throughout the last half of the 1800s. Proposals to integrate the handful of new government schools into the civil service examination system were successfully resisted.[17] It was not until the Sino-Japanese War of 1894– 1895, that the wall of indifference and hostility was finally breached. China's defeat, not by a Western power but by a neighbor traditionally regarded as "inferior," was widely interpreted as an indication of failure for China's self-strengthening efforts. This final blow to the national honor ignited a sudden craze for Western learning. The emperor himself was said to be studying Western science, and even old men enrolled themselves in the hitherto despised missionary schools. Within a year, schools teaching Western subjects were reportedly overflowing with students.[18]

Events then followed in rapid succession. The court-sponsored Reforms of 1898, anticipating among other things radical changes in education, were aborted by the empress dowager leading the conservative reaction. Its force culminated in and collapsed after the 1898–1900 antiforeign Boxer Rebellion in north China, when modern schools were among the targets. The uprising provoked another round of foreign retaliation, but the die was cast and there was no turning back.

Between 1901 and 1905, the imperial government issued a series of reform decrees. The diverse array of academies were to be reorganized and upon their foundations would be built a three-tier system of elementary, secondary, and tertiary schools patterned on Western lines. The Japanese school system, which had in turn been modeled on that of Germany in the years immediately following the Meiji Restoration of 1868, was used as the primary reference point. Despite modifications, the examination route to public office allegedly continued to stifle the new schools, which could not compete for students, patrons, and funds. The examinations were therefore abolished in 1905, and the practical function of a classical Confucian education ceased to exist, breaking the direct link between learning and bureaucratic power that had dominated Chinese public life for a thousand years. Overseas study was officially promoted to fill the void. Japan became the destination of choice due to proximity, cultural similarities, the conservative nature of Meiji education, and Japan's

---

[17] E.g., Mary Clabaugh Wright, *The Last Stand of Chinese Conservatism: The T'ung-chih Restoration, 1862–1874* (Stanford: Stanford University Press, 1962), pp. 129–133, 241–248; Knight Biggerstaff, *The Earliest Modern Government Schools in China* (Ithaca: Cornell University Press, 1961); Kwang-ching Liu, "Politics, Intellectual Outlook, and Reform: The T'ung-wen Kuan Controversy of 1867," in Paul A. Cohen and John E. Schrecker, eds., *Reform in Nineteenth-Century China* (Cambridge: East Asian Research Center, Harvard University, 1976); Wolfgang Franke, *The Reform and Abolition of the Traditional Chinese Examination System* (Cambridge: East Asian Research Center, Harvard University, 1960), pp. 16–43; Yung Wing, *My Life in China and America* (New York: H. Holt, 1909); Thomas E. La Fargue, *China's First Hundred* (Pullman: State College of Washington, 1942).

[18] Ping Wen Kuo, *The Chinese System of Public Education* (New York: Teachers College, Columbia University, 1915), p. 69.

initial success in adapting Western education. Sources differ on numbers but according to one, some 15,000 Chinese students went to Japan in 1906, compared with only 1,300 in 1904, and 2,400 in 1905. A majority of the influx enrolled in short-term courses, officially sanctioned as a substitute for the examinations in qualifying candidates for public employment.[19]

The demise of the examinations preceded by only a few years that of the dynasty and the imperial system itself in 1911. The capitulation appeared complete. Efforts to preserve the essence of Chinese tradition soon became a target of derision. In an ironic end for so unyielding a tradition, the first deliberate attempt to create a synthesis between it and Western learning was unceremoniously jettisoned in the headlong rush to be rid of the past.

[19] Y. C. Wang, *Chinese Intellectuals and the West, 1872–1949* (Chapel Hill: University of North Carolina Press, 1966), p. 64. Much disagreement surrounds the number of Chinese students in Japan. Some of the discrepancies may be due to lack of clarity about different categories of students: officially sponsored, privately sponsored, nonsponsored, etc. Japanese sources indicate that only 7,000–8,000 Chinese students were in Japan during the peak year, 1906 (cited in Hiroshi Abe, "Borrowing from Japan: China's First Modern Educational System," in Hayhoe and Bastid, *China's Education and the Industrialized World*, pp. 74–78). See also Saneto Keishu, *Zhongguoren liuxue riben shi* (A History of Chinese Studying in Japan), trans. Tan Ruqian and Lin Qiyan (Beijing: Sanlian, 1983), pp. 35–40.

4

The modern school system

It was the sudden new demand for change, rather than the continuing pull of tradition, that struck veteran China watchers and made headlines during the decade between the Boxer Rebellion and the 1911 revolution.[1] In their delight over the reality of change, however, observers failed to gauge its depth, for no sooner had China's first modern school system received imperial approval in 1903 than "there arose a loud outcry for the preservation of the ancient classics." As a result, the classics dominated the approved curriculum at all levels.[2]

In fact, key trends were already evident during the first decade of the century that would have a lasting impact on the development of China's modern school system. Those trends were: the continuing undercurrent of conservative opposition; the assumption that Western learning would bring China wealth and power; the assumption that study abroad and foreign degrees could be substituted for classical learning and the examination system; a consequent voluntary dependence on foreign education systems as models for development; and the paradox of the reform mentality, or constant change as one of the few constants in a society struggling to reconstruct itself but unable to agree on what course to take.

With the unified structure of power and learning broken, diverse sectoral interests emerged to pull the society in a multiplicity of directions. As the empire disintegrated into the feuding politics of the warlord era, political, military, intellectual, and regional leaders went their separate ways, unable to find a consensus upon which to build a new order. Even within their own shrinking sphere of influence, intellectuals could not agree on how best to reconstitute the system of learning as they followed shifting "world trends" by introducing one foreign-inspired model after another.

---

[1] E.g., Mary Clabaugh Wright, "Introduction: The Rising Tide of Change," in Mary Clabaugh Wright, ed., *China in Revolution: The First Phase, 1900–1913* (New Haven: Yale University Press, 1968); W. A. P. Martin, *The Awakening of China* (New York: Doubleday, Page and Co., 1907).

[2] Ping Wen Kuo, *The Chinese System of Public Education*, p. 100.

National reform models for the new era

Japan was soon abandoned as the model of choice. The U.S. became the new most popular destination, although greater costs and difficulties associated with study there limited the numbers who did so. But their influence soon overshadowed all others.[3] The reform rationale was evolving as a variation on the original theme. China was poor because it had not yet industrialized. The solution was to develop modern education in the sciences and learn to use foreign capital. Hence, educational modernization was the "very pivot around which all other reforms turn, for it is to education that China is looking for the men to steer the ship of state into the haven of safety."[4] The education system was "not only dependent on the new order for its maintenance and expansion" but "must be the most potent agency in bringing the reconstruction to pass."[5] Education was both dependent and independent variable, and the force that would somehow make all things possible.

Yet the new education system was in such constant flux that no single generation of students between 1900 and the onset of the Japanese war (1937) would have found the system they entered as first-graders unchanged by the time they graduated from the secondary level. Thus, stability was one key attribute of the Japanese model that the Chinese chose to ignore. After a trial-and-error period (1871–1886), the modern Japanese system retained its basic structure throughout the pre–World War II years. By contrast, the new Chinese school system, like the society surrounding it, was in a state of perpetual motion as reform modes followed one another in endless succession. A selected survey illustrates the point.

Between 1904 when it was formally inaugurated and 1912, a number of modifications were made in the original Japanese-style public school system. Lower elementary was reduced from five to four years. English was permitted at the upper elementary level in treaty port schools. In 1907, separate elementary schools for girls were authorized within the public system (pioneered by missionary educators, private girls schools run by Chinese were opened prior to their formal authorization within the public school system). The original 1904 system, like its Japanese counterpart, comprised regular academic middle schools supplemented by two specialized variations in the form of normal (teacher training) schools and vocational schools. In 1909, the academic middle

---

[3] According to official statistics, in 1910 there were only 600 Chinese students in the U.S., including those supported by public and private funds. By 1924, there were about 2,200. Statistics cited in Theodore E. Hsiao, *The History of Modern Education in China* (Shanghai: Commercial Press, 1935), p. 102.

[4] Ping Wen Kuo, *The Chinese System of Public Education*, pp. 86, 149, 163–164.

[5] George Ransom Twiss, *Science and Education in China: A Survey of the Present Status and a Program for Progressive Improvement* (Shanghai: Commercial Press, 1925), p. 12.

schools were divided into two streams – industrial and liberal arts – inspired by German secondary education.[6]

In 1912, the new republican government decreed a major reorganization to create an education system more in tune with prevailing world trends, that is, with the "progressive ideas of modern education" being promoted by students returning from Western countries and especially the U.S. Elementary and secondary schooling was reduced (from a total of 14 years in the original 1904 system to 11 years). The Chinese classics were dropped from the curriculum. New emphasis was placed on "Western subjects" requiring laboratory work and experimentation. The new system also sought to adapt schoolwork to new social and industrial demands by including practical courses. Coeducation was allowed at the elementary level; middle schools for girls were also authorized. The two streams in regular middle schools were reintegrated into a single secondary curriculum, although the separate normal and technical schools were retained, including those specializing in commerce, agriculture, and various trades.[7] In the mid-1910s, educators concluded after further investigation that Germany was probably the best model after all. But contemplated revisions in that direction ended with Germany's defeat in World War I.[8]

In 1922, the influence of students returning from the U.S. was dominant although not exclusive. Accepting their demands with some reluctance, the Education Ministry of a national government weakened by the chaotic politics of the warlord era promulgated the 1922 school reform decree. Accordingly, the Chinese education system was reorganized along American lines.[9] Elementary

---

[6] On the similarity between the 1904 Chinese and Japanese systems, and the longevity of the latter, see Hiroshi Abe, "Borrowing from Japan," pp. 57, 63–64; Ping Wen Kuo, *The Chinese System of Public Education*, pp. 78–109. Relevant Chinese documents for 1903 (on the 1904 system), 1907, and 1909 are reprinted in Shu Xincheng, ed., *Zhongguo jindai jiaoyu shi ziliao* (Materials on the History of China's Modern Education) (Beijing: Renmin jiaoyu chubanshe, 1980), *shang*: 196–220; *zhong*: 416–443, 506–525, 750–785; *xia*: 800–818.

[7] Ping Wen Kuo, *The Chinese System of Public Education*, chap. 6; Mao Lirui, ed., *Zhongguo jiaoyu shi jianbian* (A Concise History of Chinese Education) (Beijing: Jiaoyu kexue chubanshe, 1984), pp. 453–464; Paul J. Bailey, *Reform the People: Changing Attitudes towards Popular Education in Early Twentieth-Century China* (Vancouver: University of British Columbia Press, 1990), chaps. 2 and 4; documents reprinted in Shu Xincheng, *Zhongguo jindai jiaoyu shi ziliao, shang*: 226–231; *zhong*: 449–463, 526–537.

[8] Cyrus H. Peake, *Nationalism and Education in Modern China* (New York: Howard Fertig, 1970), p. 81.

[9] The fullest descriptions of this reorganization are in the bulletins of the Chinese National Association for the Advancement of Education (CNAAE). This influential body was dominated by American-trained Chinese educators, who were the chief promoters of the 1922–1923 reforms. See esp. C. W. Luh, "China's New System of Education," *Bulletin*, no. 8 (1923), pp. 1–17; King Chu, "The Reorganization of the Middle School Curriculum," *Bulletin*, no. 13 (1923), pp. 1–8; and Cheng Tsung-hai, "Elementary Education in China," *Bulletin*, no. 14 (1923), pp. 1–40; all reprinted in CNAAE, *Bulletins on Chinese Education, 1923*, 2d ed. (Shanghai: Commercial Press, 1925). Also see Gao Qi, ed., *Zhongguo xiandai jiaoyu shi* (A History of China's Contemporary Education) (Beijing: Beijing shifan daxue chubanshe, 1985), pp. 26–

schooling was combined into one six-year course, although four-year junior elementary schools were allowed where the complete course could not be maintained. Separate vocational schools at the upper elementary level were to be abolished.

For general secondary education, the American-style comprehensive school with three years each at the junior and senior levels became the new norm, although Japanese-style separate normal and vocational schools were retained at the secondary level. In the comprehensive secondary schools, however, a differentiated curriculum was adapted from American practice. Besides general studies, each school was supposed to create industrial, commercial, agriculture, and teacher training departments, and students were allowed to choose a specialty at the senior level. In reality, most students opted for the general studies curriculum. The junior secondary level remained undifferentiated, with vocational courses optional as needed locally. The credit system and electives were also adapted from American practice at both secondary and tertiary levels. Intelligence testing was introduced.

During 1927–1928, the new government established by the Guomindang (GMD), or Nationalist Party, acquiesced to leading educator Cai Yuanpei's plan for a system based on the French model. This plan called for regionally independent education districts under university management. The Education Ministry was replaced by a national University Council (Daxueyuan) with Cai as chairman, but the experiment was short-lived, ostensibly due to administrative difficulties and the university-dominated bias. In addition, however, the principles upon which the experiment was based – educational independence combined with continuing overt dependence on a foreign model – ran counter to the GMD's new demands for education. These called for more nationalistic content and centralized control, reviving trends evident in the mid-1910s that were interrupted by the weakened central authority of the warlord period.[10] Ironically, it was within this climate that the new GMD government invited the League of Nations experts to render yet another authoritative foreign opinion on education reform.

A new curriculum, developed in the early 1930s, abolished the American-style comprehensive secondary school and formalized the separation of academic and vocational education. As noted, the restored Education Ministry

33. The 1922 school reform decree is reprinted in Zhongyang jiaoyu kexueyanjiusuo jiaoyu shi yanjiushi, ed., *Zhonghua minguo jiaoyu fagui xuanbian, 1912–1949* (A Selection of Laws and Regulations on Education from the Chinese Republic, 1912–1949) (Nanjing: Jiangsu jiaoyu chubanshe, 1990), pp. 41–45.

10 Allen B. Linden, "Politics and Education in Nationalist China: The Case of the University Council, 1927–1928," *Journal of Asian Studies*, vol. 27, no. 4 (Aug. 1968), pp. 763–776; William J. Duiker, *Ts'ai Yüan-p'ei: Educator of Modern China* (University Park: Pennsylvania State University Press, 1977); Chen Qingzhi, *Zhongguo jiaoyu shi* (A History of China's Education) (Taibei: Shangwu yinshuguan, 1978), pp. 754–762.

also issued an order of intent that academic secondary schooling should be restricted in favor of vocational (*zhiye*) education. Detailed prescriptions for assessment and grading culminated in a set of regulations issued by the Education Ministry in 1935, on unified secondary school graduation examinations (*biye huikao*).

These examinations were to be administered by local government education officials and unified on a city and district basis, in accordance with the nationally stipulated subjects and conditions. Controversy surrounded this means of enforcing the new curriculum because it resurrected the format of the traditional government-administered examinations and because it did so to promote GMD-sponsored political content against growing communist influence. Concurrently, the GMD government also enforced measures growing out of the 1920s anti-Christian movement to bring foreign-run and foreign-funded schools under Chinese leadership and official supervision.[11]

Perhaps more than any of the above, however, the new elementary school regulations deserve special attention because they formalized a developing "Chinese" style of education administration taking root even as one foreign model after another was being cast aside. The 1932 elementary school law and follow-up regulations issued in 1936 sought to standardize the haphazard hierarchy of institutions that had grown up, including the education they provided and the way they did so. Schools run directly by provincial- and county-level governments were to be designated by taking the place-name of the locality in question. When additional public schools were established in each locality, they were to be named in numbered sequence, as in "Zhongshan County Number Two Elementary School," and so on. Private schools had to use other names. The number of pupils per grade per school was stipulated at not less than 25. Each school was to follow the curriculum and weekly study plans issued by the national Education Ministry. Besides daily performance, grades were to depend on interim tests given at least three times per semester, plus semester finals and a graduation examination.

Elementary schools with five or more teachers were to organize an education research committee (*jiaoyu yanjiu hui*) to promote teacher training and improve schoolwork. This committee was to meet at least once per month under the leadership of the headmaster. Similarly, joint education research committees

[11] On the effort to bring Christian education under Chinese control and the curriculum changes, see, e.g., Djung, *A History of Democratic Education in Modern China*, pp. 160–183, 222, 228–230, 238–239; Chen Qingzhi, *Zhongguo jiaoyu shi*, pp. 763–777; Gao Qi, ed., *Zhongguo xiandai jiaoyu shi*, pp. 118–132. Columbia University Teachers College professor Paul Monroe provides a contemporary summary of the anti-Christian mood during the 1920s (Paul Monroe, *China: A Nation in Evolution* [New York: Macmillan, 1928], chap. 11). On the 1931 order of intent, see chap. 2, above. For many of the relevant documents on private, foreign, and religious schools, GMD-sponsored political education, and the unified exams (*hui kao*), as well as on the new elementary, secondary, and vocational school regulations, see *Zhonghua minguo jiaoyu fagui xuanbian, 1912–1949*, pp. 45–62, 119, 139–148, 237–265, 348–352, 527–537.

were to be formed among the elementary school teachers within each subcounty school district, and so on at each administrative level, where representative committees would function under the leadership of the county, provincial, and national government education authorities.

In addition, each provincial education department was to designate a central school (*zhongxin xiaoxue*) in each subprovincial administrative unit (*fenqu*) from among its provincially run elementary schools. Similarly, each city and county education office was also to designate one central elementary school within each school district under its jurisdiction. These central schools were to be promoted as leaders in education research and their experience shared for the benefit of others in their respective districts.[12]

Although the 1932 League of Nations report was not officially invoked in the manner of past sources of foreign inspiration, the new curriculum and other measures introduced in the early 1930s could be seen at a number of points to reflect recommendations included in the report.[13] Nevertheless, the failure to invoke directly the authority of foreign precedents was significant. The new government seemed intent on trying to minimize overt dependence on foreign models. In this respect, by the 1930s, the government had the support of many educators, for reasons that will be elaborated in the following chapter. All the new minutely detailed rules and regulations articulated a style that seemed to grow steadily as the attraction of foreign models moderated. That style would continue to evolve for better and for worse: for better, because it was the kind of genuine synthesis between Chinese and foreign that seemed necessary to create a viable modern school system; and for worse, because of the adverse reactions that system was also generating.

The "political economy" of transition

Their search for the ideal route to wealth and power seemed to make the creators of China's modern education system more sensitive to changing trends abroad than to the realities of educational life at home. This impression was reinforced by their failure to calculate the administrative and financial requisites for the declared aim of establishing a Western-style education system. Such a failure in turn gave credence to the charge of superficial or mechanical copying, which would become a favorite rallying cry for the new system's critics.

The national Board of Education was created, following Japan's example, in 1905. Official decrees complete with volumes of rules and regulations defined

[12] The 1932 law and the 1936 regulations are reprinted in *Zhonghua minguo jiaoyu fagui xuanbian, 1912–1949*, pp. 243–245, 271–282.
[13] On the apparent League of Nations influence, see Hayhoe, "Catholics and Socialists," pp. 117–118.

the new system. But unlike Japan, the national government was unable to centralize control of revenues, and the new regulations failed to specify how schools were to be financed, the assumption being that existing arrangements would suffice. As a result, the foundations of the new system were neither stable nor strong enough to permit effective emulation of its Japanese and Western models.

Although the professed objective was a system of universal education, early regulations for government schools were far more modest. They required a minimum of one postsecondary school in each provincial capital to be maintained by the province; one secondary school per prefecture; and one upper elementary school at the county level. This skeletal structure run by the various levels of government was typically created by converting academies into the standard hierarchy of a Western-style system. Lower elementary schools were advocated for every village, but no authority was assigned formal responsibility for them. Additionally, however, central regulations urged that the thin network of provincial, prefectural, and county government schools be supplemented by private schools and by ad hoc community arrangements following local custom. The latter were briefly distinguished as "public" schools by contrast with their formal government-run counterparts. By 1910, according to official national statistics, there were only 14,300 government schools of all kinds nationwide, augmented by 32,250 local public or community-funded (*gongli*) schools and 5,790 private (*sili*) schools.[14]

In practice, such distinctions were difficult to maintain, and local gentry played a pivotal role whatever the designation. Initiative might be taken by one side or the other – local government officials or local nonofficial community leaders – to convert an existing academy or establish a new school. When the rent and interest from old endowments of land and lending capital proved insufficient to support a modern school, however, local elites were largely responsible for mobilizing the necessary additional funds.[15]

As a rule, funds for both government and public schools, which were officially merged into a single category after 1911, came from a range of sources, including surcharges on the land tax, local taxes on a variety of goods and

[14] Statistics cited in Ping Wen Kuo, *The Chinese System of Public Education*, p. 108; see also Borthwick, *Education and Social Change in China*, p. 94. Early statistical compilations were usually incomplete and often varied widely. Compare those cited here with Marianne Bastid, *Educational Reform in Early Twentieth-Century China*, trans. Paul J. Bailey (Ann Arbor: Center for Chinese Studies, University of Michigan, 1988), table 4, pp. 68–69.

[15] E.g., Richard A. Orb, "Chihli Academies and Other Schools in the Late Ch'ing: An Institutional Survey," in Cohen and Schrecker, *Reform in Nineteenth-Century China*, pp. 231–240; Joseph W. Esherick, *Reform and Revolution in China: The 1911 Revolution in Hunan and Hubei* (Berkeley: University of California Press, 1976), pp. 40–45; David D. Buck, "Educational Modernization in Tsinan, 1899–1937," in Mark Elvin and G. William Skinner, eds., *The Chinese City between Two Worlds* (Stanford: Stanford University Press, 1974), pp. 171–212; Rankin, *Elite Activism and Political Transformation in China*, pp. 174–176, 211–227.

trading operations, compulsory and voluntary contributions, the takeover of temple properties, and the diversion of religious and entertainment funds. Even when gentry money was not contributed directly, gentry influence was, as in the past, usually necessary to mobilize local resources. Considerable resentment was also aroused in the process since it not only afforded added opportunities for graft but added directly to the financial burdens of local merchants, peasants, and the public at large. Nor were commensurate rewards necessarily provided in return since most levies were regressive, and funds were usually extracted from a far wider range of people than could benefit by sending their children to the new schools.[16]

The enthusiasm of local elites for fund-raising and school founding soon merged with their new demands for self-government as another new alternative for the old examination route to position and status. When government reform regulations were promulgated in the closing years of the dynasty, they stipulated for participation – as voters, assembly candidates, and election supervisors – qualifications which included one of the following: teaching experience; a secondary school education either in China or overseas; a traditional gentry degree; experience in public office; or a specified amount of capital or property. The disqualified included illiterates and women. Some 1.7 million men registered as voters for the first provincial elections of 1909, a figure very close to the 1.4 million estimate cited in chapter 3 for regular (qualified by examination) and irregular (qualified by wealth) gentry in the latter half of the 1800s. Accordingly, the majority of assembly members also qualified for gentry status of one kind or the other.[17]

Elementary and secondary schools were subsequently placed under the jurisdiction of subprovincial assemblies and corresponding self-government councils, which were given general fund-raising responsibilities as well. Anti-tax riots against the new governing bodies then merged with those against new

---

[16] Bastid, *Educational Reform*, p. 74; Borthwick, *Education and Social Change in China*, pp. 93–103; David Buck, "Educational Modernization in Tsinan," p. 188; Peter Buck, *American Science and Modern China, 1876–1936* (Cambridge: Cambridge University Press, 1980), p. 102; Stephen R. MacKinnon, *Power and Politics in Late Imperial China: Yuan Shi-kai in Beijing and Tianjin, 1901–1908* (Berkeley: University of California Press, 1980), pp. 149–150; R. Keith Schoppa, *Chinese Elites and Political Change: Zhejiang Province in the Early Twentieth Century* (Cambridge: Harvard University Press, 1982), pp. 121–122.

[17] John H. Fincher, *Chinese Democracy: Statist Reform, The Self-Government Movement, and Republican Revolution* (Tokyo: Institute for the Study of Languages and Cultures of Asia and Africa, 1989), pp. 108–112, 123–124. On the gentry status of provincial assemblymen in Shandong and Zhejiang, see David D. Buck, *Urban Change in China: Politics and Development in Tsinan, Shantung, 1890–1949* (Madison: University of Wisconsin Press, 1978), p. 64; and Rankin, *Elite Activism*, p. 233. Schoppa's data for county and subcounty self-government leaders in Zhejiang show much more varied origins, however, with the largest single category in most counties during 1911–1914 being nongentry, nonschool graduates, with no elite family ties and no leadership roles other than the self-government post itself (*Chinese Elites and Political Change*, esp. tables 5–8, pp. 42–46).

schools. During the 1911 revolution, schools were again looted and destroyed, having become – as symbols of authority, whether foreign, imperial, or local – familiar targets of mob violence. But through it all, local elites had managed to enlarge their traditional informal functions into formal government roles, using their traditional credentials and the new schools as stepping stones in the process.[18]

The search for administrative order

Gentry democracy was, of course, soon challenged by the first republican president's coup against the fledgling institutions of self-government, provoked among other things by the center's inability to compete with them in extracting tax revenues. The search then commenced for a new social contract that might replace the old divisions of power and responsibility between state and society, or between government officials and nonofficial elites. Rooted as it was in every locality, education administration inevitably reflected that search.

A common thread running throughout was the ongoing struggle to redefine the nature of control and autonomy along three dimensions: (1) within the government bureaucracy, between center and locality; (2) within the government bureaucracy, between the general authority and functionally specific educational authorities; and (3) between government and nonofficial elites, including both the general (gentry) and functionally specific (educators). This inconclusive struggle continued even as the nature of those waging it evolved from traditional or transitional officials and gentry to modernizing bureaucrats, militarists, and professional educators.

The first education exhortation bureaus (*quanxuesuo*) were local bodies established by imperial decree in 1906 to take charge of modern school development. They had independent fund-raising powers but were responsible to a provincial education commissioner. This represented centralization, albeit within the government education bureaucracy, in a pattern inherited from the imperial examinations administration. The exhortation bureau's functions were then supposed to be taken over by the self-governing bodies in a formula which emasculated the functional education bureaucracy and allowed increased local political interference. But as long as gentry-dominated self-government remained an important part of the local power equation, this arrangement also gave maximum leeway to local nonofficial education leaders.[19]

---

[18] E.g., Esherick, *Reform and Revolution*, pp. 113–142; Chuzo Ichiko, "The Role of the Gentry: An Hypothesis," in Mary Wright, *China in Revolution*, pp. 301–302; Ping Wen Kuo, *The Chinese System of Public Education*, p. 110; Schoppa, *Chinese Elites and Political Change*, pp. 32, 62, 83, 121.

[19] Hu Chang-ho Jiugow, "A General Outline on the Reorganization of the Chinese Educational System" (Doctor of Pedagogy diss., New York University, 1916), p. 170. On late Qing and early republican administration, see Miyazaki, *China's Examination Hell*, p. 26; Hsiao, *History of*

In 1914, however, President Yuan Shikai abolished all the self-governing bodies, including assemblies and councils from the provincial to the sub-county level. The exhortation bureaus were officially restored but in different form, now integrated within the local government administration. A provincial education department (*jiaoyu ting*) was established in 1917, organized as before 1911 under the direct control of the national education authority (reconstituted during the Republic as the Education Ministry) in an attempt to reassert functional bureaucratic power. County school "boards," which replaced the exhortation bureaus in 1923, were run much like their predecessors, that is, with a mix of local political interference and centralized bureaucratic control.

Education leaders, inspired by the American example of independent state and county school boards, tried to use that precedent to win formal functional autonomy throughout the system. According to the proposal, each board would be composed of professional educators who would act as an independent policymaking and fund-raising authority within the local government. The proposal was adopted but only in compromise form. Implementation at the provincial level lapsed. The new county education boards established in 1923 were appointed by the county government, and, except for the superintendent, professional status was not a prerequisite for other board members.[20]

Cai Yuanpei's abortive 1927–1928 plan tried to achieve the aim of autonomy in yet another way, by creating an independent national education authority under the University Council. Subordinate university districts were to have academic and administrative responsibility for all schools under their respective jurisdictions. The scheme did not leave the drawing board in most provinces, although its organizational antithesis was not introduced until the early 1930s, when local education administration was formally integrated into the county government bureaucracy. This indicated in turn the aim of the new GMD regime to recentralize and integrate political, bureaucratic, and educational authority. Whether educators found enough common cause with the centralizing bureaucracy or simply regarded it as a lesser evil is unclear. But educators in the 1930s complained far more about GMD political interference than about all the new centrally issued rules and regulations – which seemed to contradict the prevailing demands for professional autonomy during the 1920s.

Modern Education in China, chap. 5; Bastid, *Educational Reform*, pp. 62–63; and Helen R. Chauncey, *Schoolhouse Politicians: Locality and State during the Chinese Republic* (Honolulu: University of Hawaii Press, 1992), pp. 77–81.

[20] The conflicting proposals leading up to the 1923 reorganization are discussed in Djung, *A History of Democratic Education in Modern China*, pp. 31–40; and Luh, "China's New System of Education," pp. 15–17. The conventional translation used by contemporary American-educated writers to describe the new boards suggested their hybrid nature. After the 1923 reorganization, these writers continued to refer to "education boards" when a more appropriate translation both in name and in fact for *jiaoyu ju* would have been "education bureau," which was subsequently adopted.

Yet despite the constant motion, the administrative and economic roots of China's school system seemed remarkably constant. In the 1920s, qualifications for county school board members included a combination of educational and local leadership or fund-raising capabilities similar to those that defined original exhortation bureau members during the early 1900s. The regulations suggested a change not so much in who was running the schools or even how but rather in that local elites were increasingly the products of modern learning. It was probably not accidental, then, that educators dated the inauguration of their demand for autonomous professional control over education from 1915.[21] That date coincided with the demise of the self-governing movement and the relatively high degree of autonomy enjoyed by local elites and educators over their domains during the first years of the Republic. Evidently, what was seen in later years as a modern demand by the new corps of professional educators for protection against the political and financial vicissitudes of the 1910s and 1920s had originated in the transitional struggle to redefine the respective power of local government officials and nonofficial local elites, including but not exclusively those most immediately concerned with education.

Meanwhile, throughout the period, even as the local balance continued to shift around them and the source of their authority continued to change, the "gentry" maintained a dominant influence over educational affairs at the grassroots level. In 1914, Guo Bingwen (Kuo Ping-wen) noted that educational affairs within individual communities were in the hands of "local gentry."[22] Two decades later, the Education Ministry acknowledged that within each county's school district subdivisions, the "gentry" still usually raised money on their own for local schools.[23] Accordingly, an individual school's affairs were

---

[21] The demand was raised at the first conference of the National Federation of Education Associations, in 1915 (Ronald Yu Soong Cheng, *The Financing of Public Education in China: A Factual Analysis of Its Major Problems of Reconstruction* [Shanghai: Commercial Press, 1935], p. 5; Peake, *Nationalism and Education in Modern China*, p. 79).

[22] Ping Wen Kuo, *The Chinese System of Public Education*, p. 118.

[23] Cited in Cheng, *The Financing of Public Education in China*, p. 96. American researcher Sidney Gamble described the administrative and financial arrangements for Ding County, Hebei, in the late 1920s. The head of the county education bureau (or board), working under the chief appointed county administrative officer (magistrate), presided over a governing board of four other members, usually "leading gentry," who served without pay. Salaried staff included several inspectors, a treasurer, a business manager, and a clerk. Additionally, the county magistrate appointed an education administration committee of nine members, who also served without pay. The county itself was composed of 6 administrative districts, each divided into 2 school districts. Administration committee members were responsible for supervision and coordination between the 12 school districts and county-level authorities. The county bureau ran directly two normal schools, a vocational school, a regular middle school, and some upper elementary schools. The combined county budget for these schools, plus subsidies for some others run by local communities, amounted to less than one-quarter of the reported expenditure for all schools within the county. The bulk of that expenditure was met by the villages themselves and "other" sources (Sidney D. Gamble, *Ting Hsien: A North China Rural Community* [New York: Institute of Pacific Relations, 1954], pp. 188–190.

also still circumscribed by the same network of official and nonofficial authorities on whom its survival depended.

On paper, the school system appeared ever more centralized under a government education bureaucracy that, by the 1930s, extended neatly from top to bottom, that is, from the national Education Ministry, through the provincial education bureaus, to counties, and to subcounty school districts. But except for trying to follow the central regulations and curriculum recommendations, individual schools operated essentially as individual units. Schools were, in other words, always freer from central government control than from the traditional-style network of local relationships, against which they had little protection. The pattern prevailed at all levels because schools were generally located near the seat of government responsible for collecting or authorizing the collection of funds, making disbursements, and sanctioning or otherwise interfering in personnel appointments. Table 4.1 suggests the pattern of these relationships, with elementary school administration dominated by county-level interests and secondary schools by those in cities and provincial capitals.

The greatest resulting handicap to teaching, school management, and discipline, wrote American professor George Twiss in the 1920s, was from "political and military officials and influential gentry who are using the school system in countless and devious ways as agencies for the promotion of their own private ends and advantage." Inevitably, given the prevailing social disarray, even educators themselves were often found playing at politics and manipulating school funds for personal or political gain.[24]

The search for financial order

After the Yuan Shikai presidency failed to provide a functional substitute for imperial authority at the center, China's national government in effect retreated to the provincial level. There, military governors, with their mercenary armies feeding off local resources, emerged as the most powerful figures. Educators blamed in particular the excessive military expenditures of the warlord era (peak years: 1917–1927) for national and provincial allocations that were as inadequate as funds raised by counties and school districts. Estimates varied widely. Those of Columbia University Ph.D. Ronald Cheng were among the more conservative. He concluded that between 1928 and 1934, military expenditures amounted to about half the central government's budget, with debt service and foreign indemnity payments accounting for another one-third.

---

[24] Twiss, *Science and Education in China*, p. 86 and pp. 79–88 passim. For more on modern school development, focusing on the provincial and county levels, see Chauncey, *Schoolhouse Politicians*; Robert J. Culp, "Elite Association and Local Politics in Republican China: Educational Institutions in Jiashan and Lanqi Counties, Zhejiang, 1911–1937," *Modern China*, vol. 20, no. 4 (Oct. 1994), pp. 446–477.

Table 4.1. *Estimated proportional costs of education, 1930–1931*

| | Public (vs. private) (%) | Public and private, by school level (%) | Public only, by government level | | |
			National (%)	Provincial and city (%)	County (%)
Tertiary	58.1% (41.9)	18.1	61.6	38.4	nil
Secondary	64.2 (35.8)	26.2	2.6	63.0	34.4
Elementary	79.0 (21.0)	48.1	nil	8.0	92.0
Social (literacy, museums, libraries, parks, theaters, etc.)	47.4 (52.6)	7.6	nil	50.0	50.0
		100			

Source: Ronald Cheng, *The Financing of Public Education in China,* table 9 and pp. 32–35; table 10 and pp. 35–39.

Data on selected provincial budgets showed a decline in the proportion allocated for military purposes from about 60 percent to 20 percent of budgetary
expenditures between 1913 and 1930. Official GMD statistics showed an increase in educational outlays, with about 5 percent of the central government's
total budgetary expenditure being allocated to education in 1931–1932. Provinces and cities that year reported that about 18 percent of their budgets were
allocated for education.[25]

Yet disruptions in the flow of funds were so common that schools at all
levels and of all kinds often had to cease operations temporarily or even close
down altogether. In almost every province throughout the 1920s and into the
1930s, it was not unusual for teachers' salaries to be paid two or more months
late. Ronald Cheng's calculations provide a useful profile of China's educational finances after three decades of development and just before the Japanese
invasion reordered everyone's priorities. The root of the problem emerging
from his analysis was not warlord politics or even poverty but rather the
"antiquated and unjust" financial system, which demonstrated the inability of
old unreformed arrangements to support modern ends. By the 1930s, these
arrangements had deteriorated into "multifarious exorbitant taxes and miscellaneous levies," regressive in nature, inefficient to collect, and prone to abuse.
Conventional wisdom held that for every tax dollar reaching public treasuries,
at least three went into private pockets.[26]

According to Cheng's final aggregate figures for China's total educational
costs in 1930–1931, public and private proportions were about 71 percent and
29 percent respectively. Of the total revenue for publicly funded education
alone, only about 10 percent came from sources controlled by the central government; 27 percent was controlled by provincial and city governments; and 63
percent by local authorities.[27]

The central government's share was appropriated mainly from its general
tax revenues. These derived largely from customs duties, the salt tax, and other
commodity taxes. The provincial government's share of educational revenues
derived from the land tax, public loans, central aid, and various taxes. At the
county and school district levels, surtaxes on the provincial land tax were the
single most important sources of local school revenues. In fact, local tax rates
were determined locally and varied widely. But Cheng estimated that county
public school revenues were paid primarily by farmers due to the importance
of the various land taxes, which fell in turn primarily upon smallholders and
tenants. Sales and commodity taxes, another source of education funds, were
levied most commonly on necessities. As a result, perhaps 80 percent of the
burden was carried by the "poorer classes." Cheng also cited economist Ma

[25] Ronald Cheng, *The Financing of Public Education in China*, pp. 78–84, 91–93.
[26] Ibid., p. 202.
[27] Ibid., pp. 47, 105.

Yinchu to the effect that in foreign countries, the rich paid to educate the poor; only in China did the poor maintain schools for the rich.[28]

The solution, according to American advisors, lay in the American example: local voluntary or community-imposed taxes controlled by school boards safeguarded against outside interference. Europeans were more inclined to favor a greater role for the central government, albeit also with safeguards against political interference. Chinese could be found on both sides but were unable to devise effective solutions based on either. The pressure within the education sector for control of its own affairs included a demand for fiscal independence as well. One such proposal was that of education administrator S. C. Tai, who suggested that independent powers fix tax rates as well as collect, deposit, disburse, and audit educational tax revenues. The new GMD government committed itself to the principle of fiscal independence for education and Tai's proposal gained a hearing in official circles. But actual reform, when announced, aimed more at unifying the tax structure under government control than under conditions of independence for the education sector specifically.

Educational finance remained in any case "kaleidoscopic" in the early 1930s. Using Tai's criteria, Ronald Cheng concluded that only five or six provincial education departments could be considered more or less fiscally independent. Counties showed a more mixed record. No county education bureau enjoyed the power to determine tax rates independently, but bureaus in five provinces could collect their school taxes directly, and most provinces allowed education bureaus to control their own treasuries. That even localities with the maximum degree of independence did not enjoy adequate educational funding Cheng blamed on the lack of "complete" independence and control by the education authorities over their own finances.[29]

Shanxi and Jiangsu

Whether independence was really the prerequisite for success remained open to question, however, since educators could provide no evidence that public finances were better managed by them than by others. On the contrary, the performance of Shanxi and Jiangsu Provinces suggested just the opposite. Shanxi's educational finances were dominated by the provincial military government. Yet compulsory education was regarded in the early 1920s as one "among other notable things" that Military Governor Yan Xishan was "doing for good government in his province."[30] At the time, Shanxi led the nation with an estimated 69 percent of its school-age children enrolled in the four-year lower elementary course. In another measure, Shanxi's proportion of

[28] Ibid., pp. 117–136.
[29] Ibid., pp. 101–103.
[30] Twiss, *Science and Education in China*, p. 132.

elementary students to total population was calculated at 7.2 percent. Yan
Xishan was at least as interested in political indoctrination as literacy. But
whatever his motives, sources seemed to agree that his regime did successfully
promote mass education. The "people's schools" were administered and sub-
sidized by the provincial government although financed largely by a local
income tax.[31] The county school districts were generally seen as loosely organized and powerless, except in Shanxi. There, it was said, every village and
every street had responsible persons to look after education who were given
adequate power to do the job properly.[32]

By contrast, Jiangsu Province in China's intellectual heartland had one of
the highest rates of fiscal independence for education in the country. It also
enjoyed an impressive tradition of intellectual achievement, which was being
maintained in the contemporary era by prominent "returned students" (i.e.,
returned from overseas study) who were congregating in the Shanghai–Nanjing
region. From that base, they dominated the national movement for a "new
education," which culminated in the national school reforms of 1922–1923.
Organizationally, the influence of this educational establishment, both old
and new, was exerted through the powerful Jiangsu Education Association
(Jiangsusheng jiaoyu hui); the annual national conferences of the provincial
education associations which Jiangsu had helped promote and which were
organized loosely into the National Federation of Education Associations
(Quanguo jiaoyu hui lianshe hui); and the Chinese National Association for the
Advancement of Education (Zhonghua jiaoyu gaijin she). This last was organized in 1921–1922 to unify more effectively the lobbying efforts of the various
lower-level associations in the interests of promoting their reform proposals.[33]
Demands for professional autonomy were first raised in 1915, at the first
national conference of provincial education associations. The 1921 conference,

---

[31] Donald G. Gillin, *Warlord: Yen Hsi-shan in Shansi Province, 1911–1949* (Princeton: Princeton
University Press, 1967), p. 68 and chap. 5; League of Nations report, p. 78; Monroe, *China*,
chap. 12.

[32] H. G. W. Woodhead, ed., *The China Year Book, 1934* (Shanghai: North-China Daily News and
Herald, 1934), p. 313.

[33] The education associations were influential bodies dating from the last decade of the Qing
dynasty and founded to promote modern education. Financed by the typical mix of official
subsidies and private contributions, membership also at least initially included the typical mix
of local notables, whose concerns were not exclusively with education. According to Bastid,
teachers constituted only a minority of the Jiangsu association's early members. Such associations were formed in all the provinces and at the county level as well. Under Jiangsu's leadership, a joint conference was first held in 1911. The National Federation of Education Associations
was formed about the same time, with the annual national convention as its major activity. The
first national convention was held in 1915. See Bastid, *Educational Reform*, pp. 63–65; Barry
Keenan, *The Dewey Experiment in China: Educational Reform and Political Power in the Early
Republic* (Cambridge: Harvard University Press, 1977), pp. 61, 84; Bailey, *Reform the People*, pp.
100–102. On the intraprovincial work of the Jiangsu Education Association, see Chauncey,
Schoolhouse Politicians, esp. chap. 4.

which provided the basis for the government's 1922 school reform decree, also advocated independent American-style school boards.

The returned students' home base in Jiangsu was the Nanjing Higher Teachers Training School. This institution was elevated to university status in 1921 and named National Southeastern University, a mark of recognition for the growing prominence of its faculty, led by Guo Bingwen. Guo, president of the institution from 1919 to 1925, was the first Chinese student to earn a doctorate from Columbia University Teachers College. Thanks to Guo's recruiting policy, American-trained returned students (especially those from Columbia) dominated the education faculty. Its members were noted not just as activists in the national movement for a "new education," but also for running the best graduate program in the country and for their experiments with progressive American methods in Nanjing city schools.[34] The leading force in the education department of the provincial government as well, the returned students were undoubtedly responsible for the high degree of independence achieved in Jiangsu's educational financing. Yet the financing was neither sufficient nor stable and, with only 1.19 percent of its population enrolled in elementary schools, Jiangsu's development of mass education was poor compared with many other provinces besides Shanxi, the national pacesetter in that respect.[35]

Education as dependent variable

The new school system thus came into being under the leadership of a few modernizing imperial officials, the Qing court, the growing pool of modern intellectuals, and, later, local gentry who shifted allegiance from the old to the new learning after 1905. National leaders advocated the new learning to promote national wealth and power. Local leaders supported new schools, after 1905, as a substitute for the main traditional source of position and status.

---

[34] Keenan, *The Dewey Experiment*, pp. 56–57. The New Education Movement is discussed in chap. 5, below.

[35] The contrast between Shanxi and Jiangsu in mass education was noted by American advisor and professor George Twiss, who otherwise lauded the influential role being played by Jiangsu educators (*Science and Education in China*, pp. 132–133). Comparative educational development data are from Cheng Tsung-hai, "Elementary Education in China," *Bulletin*, no. 14 (1923), pp. 6–7, which also noted the Shanxi case; and "Statistical Summaries of Chinese Education," *Bulletin*, no. 16 (1923), p. 35; both reprinted in CNAAE, *Bulletins on Chinese Education, 1923.* CNAAE compilers claimed to base their elementary school statistics largely on data provided to them by the individual counties (*Bulletin*, no. 16 [1923] p. ii). According to an earlier compilation, Shanxi reported that 57 percent of its elementary school age-group were enrolled in elementary schools as of 1919. Its nearest competitors on the 1919 list of provincial achievements were Guangxi, with 28 percent, and Zhejiang, with 24 percent. By 1928, Shanxi was claiming 72 percent, or 90 percent for boys and 50 percent for girls (Djung, *A History of Democratic Education in Modern China*, pp. 82–83, esp. table IV). Financial arrangements in Jiangsu and Shanxi are noted in Ronald Cheng, *The Financing of Public Education in China*, pp. 100, 103.

Gradually, national leadership of education passed to those educated in Japan and the West, who sought to apply the ideals and models they had learned overseas. Within a few years, however, many of these leaders would conclude that their new education system was more dependent than independent; more the product of a partly traditional, partly modern society than a positive force for change in itself; and that, as leaders, they bore a certain measure of responsibility for many of the system's failures.

In the U.S. and England, for example, education systems had developed during the 19th century from a mix of altruistic and utilitarian motives aimed at producing law-abiding citizens and a disciplined work force. The Chinese system, however, grew from the spur of national humiliation and weakness. Political training in patriotism and physical education in the form of military drill were therefore early components of the new curriculum, and training advanced talent for national reconstruction took precedence over mass education. Yet the question remained as to which was more responsible for the similarity between old and new student bodies. Did the fault lie with the new statist goals, as was often suggested, or with the continuing influence of the old education on the decisions of leaders still committed to many of its ways and means?

The Japanese experience, then as now, provides a useful comparison. Japan was inspired by similar statist motives. Yet modern schools there grew rapidly into a mass-based system. According to official Japanese statistics, compulsory elementary schooling was launched in 1873, with only 28 percent of the age-group (including both girls and boys) in school. The proportion grew to 40 percent by the end of the decade, 80 percent by the end of the century, and 98 percent by 1909.[36]

In China, despite repeated declarations in favor of universal education, the new schools did not appear to enlarge dramatically nor to change the nature of the existing educated population. Reformers did address the need for literate workers and civil order. Early experiments with different kinds of schooling for the poor were also widespread. Yet the net results were not statistically impressive.[37] Schooling for girls, a major social innovation, yielded similarly slow growth. Their number rose from an estimated 0.07 percent of the total number of students in modern schools as of 1906 to 6.32 percent of the more than 6.5 million in 1922–1923. Of China's 1,843 counties in 1923, 1,328 had no girls studying above the lower elementary level; 582 counties had no female enrollment in elementary schools at all.[38]

[36] Japan, Ministry of Education, Science, and Culture, Minister's Secretariat, Research and Statistics Division, *Japan's Modern Educational System: A History of the First Hundred Years* (Tokyo: Ministry of Finance, 1980), p. 50 (tables 2–3) and p. 464 (table 4).
[37] See Bailey, *Reform the People*, esp. chap. 5.
[38] "Statistical Summaries of Chinese Education," *Bulletin*, no. 16 (1923), p. 5, reprinted in CNAAE, *Bulletins on Chinese Education, 1923*; Djung, *A History of Democratic Education in Modern China*,

Statistics from the period, although plentiful, should be regarded as approximations only, but they suggest the unremarkable nature of the achievement. For a selection of those available, based on contemporary Chinese sources, see Tables 4.2 through 4.5. As of 1930–1931, an estimated 22 percent of China's school-age children were enrolled at the lower elementary level, or 33.4 percent of the boys and 7.6 percent of the girls.[39]

Additionally, however, the traditional tutor schools (sishu) continued to flourish even after years of official discouragement and nonrecognition. Statistics, including those cited here, never included data on such schools.[40] They were synonymous with the Dark Ages for early modernizing intellectuals and ignored by the creators of the new school system. Subsequent efforts to reform them lapsed, and the sishu persisted in their own way using the old methods and materials. The compilers of the 1923 "Statistical Summaries," issued by the Chinese National Association for the Advancement of Education (CNAAE), cautioned that the number of students in sishu was probably at least equal to the number of those in modern schools. Perhaps the proportion of the former to the latter increased outside the big coastal cities. But in Jiangsu Province, Nanjing's population of about 400,000 within the city walls was still served by about 500 sishu. Guangzhou, with twice the population, maintained more than 1,000. And in Nanjing, a center of experimentation by prominent modern educators, the total sishu enrollment of 12,000 was said to be more than all the students in the city's modern schools combined.[41]

In the countryside, the continuing preference for traditional schooling was reflected in John Lossing Buck's early 1930s survey of rural China. Of the 87,000 persons surveyed on this question, 45.2 percent of the males and 2.2 percent of the females reported receiving some schooling. Of the males, 66.5 percent reported that the education they received had been in the traditional style, for an average of four years.[42]

These traditional tutor schools further underlined the similarities between China and Japan "at the start" and the differences that multiplied thereafter. The Japanese equivalent was the terakoya, wherein commoners learned to read

p. 157 (this source provides a detailed survey of female education through the 1920s; see pp. 128–130, 139–159). See also Borthwick, *Education and Social Change in China*, pp. 114–118.

[39] Ronald Cheng, *The Financing of Public Education in China*, p. 26.

[40] The exclusion of data on sishu is stated explicitly in ibid., p. 16, and by Tao Xingzhi in his foreword to the "Statistical Summaries of Chinese Education," *Bulletin*, no. 16 (1923), p. ii. The "Statistical Summaries" are also reprinted in *Tao Xingzhi quanji* (The Complete Works of Tao Xingzhi) (Changsha: Hunan jiaoyu chubanshe, 1983), 1:308–360.

[41] *Bulletin*, no. 16, p. ii; on the persistence of sishu, see Rawski, *Education and Popular Literacy*, pp. 162–167; Liao T'ai-ch'u, "Rural Education in Transition: A Study of Old-fashioned Schools (Szu Shu) in Shantung and Szechuan," *Yenching Journal of Social Studies*, no. 2 (1949), pp. 19–67.

[42] John Lossing Buck, *Land Utilization in China* (London: Oxford University Press, 1937), pp. 373–375.

Table 4.2. *Elementary schools and students, 1909–1931*

	1909			1922–1923			1930–1931		
	Schools	Students	Est. % of age-group	Schools	Students	Est. % of age-group	Schools	Students	Est. % of age-group
Upper	—	—	—	10,236	615,378	—	18,000	1,135,029	—
Lower	—	—	—	167,076	5,965,957	—	222,545	9,145,822	—
Vocational	—	—	—	439	20,467	—	676	30,223	—
Total	50,000	1,500,000	2–4	177,751	6,601,802	15	241,221	10,311,074	22

Sources: 1909 – Borthwick, *Education and Social Change in China*, pp. 109, 152; Ronald Cheng, *The Financing of Public Education in China*, pp. 22, 24.

1922–1923 – From data compiled by the Chinese National Association for the Advancement of Education in "Statistical Summaries of Chinese Education," *Bulletin*, no. 16 (1923), pp. 1, 2, 35, in CNAAE, *Bulletins on Chinese Education, 1923.*

1930–1931 – Ronald Cheng, *The Financing of Public Education in China*, pp. 15, 26 (using figures taken from the *Shun Pao Yearbook, 1934*, which contained unexplained discrepancies). Cheng also gives (p. 24) the figure 10,788,582 for elementary students in 1930–1931 from the Education Ministry's *First Education Yearbook of China, 1934*. A later source also cites this yearbook, giving a 1930 combined kindergarten and elementary enrollment figure of 10,948,949, with 22% of the age-group in elementary school (Zhongyang jiaoyu kexue yanjiusuo, *Zhongguo xiandai jiaoyu dashiji, 1919–1949*, p. 215).

and write. By the start of the modernizing Meiji era, these schools, which were common in both urban and rural areas, numbered in the "tens of thousands," although by modern standards relatively few children attended them. Japan's official education historians note on this point that, "generally speaking, the ordinary person saw almost no necessity for school education" to explain why so few boys spent only just long enough at their studies to acquire basic literacy.[43] Ronald Dore's "informed guess," as to the diffusion of such education in pre-Meiji Japan yielded much the same percentages as Rawski's calculations for Qing China. Dore estimated that *terakoya* education made schooling possible for "somewhat more" than 40 percent of all Japanese boys and about 10 percent of the girls.[44]

Nevertheless, the *terakoya* were used as the foundation upon which Japan's system for universalizing elementary schooling was rapidly built, albeit with a combination of central direction, uniform administration, local school district funding, and backup grants by the national treasury. Many of Japan's early elementary schools were indistinguishable from their predecessors, having no more than 40–50 students and only one or two teachers holding classes in temple compounds and other private buildings.[45]

In China, traditional demands and facilities for popular education were, by all accounts, very similar to those in Japan. Yet in China, such facilities were scorned by modernizing officials and gentry, while the demands were used to justify the slow growth of elementary schooling. Meanwhile, a dual system evolved to serve the dual interests of early-20th-century Chinese society. The division as reflected in education was not just regional, between the hinterland and the cities, but was more specifically social. By and large, elites sent their children to modern schools, and the masses continued much as before, with a few years of unreformed and unrecognized traditional instruction or nothing at all.

The failure to exploit the potential of the *sishu* tradition was often rationalized, like the call for educational autonomy, as deriving from the new sense of professionalism among Chinese educators. Initially, Chinese intellectuals themselves also advanced this rationale, which matched their self-perceptions as creators of a totally new society and an education system to go with it. But their failures and demands seemed to represent something besides the desire of professional educators to create a modern system. Influenced by the more self-critical mood that took hold in the 1920s, such professionalism would be reinterpreted as a superficial cloak of modernity covering the only partially reformed body of China's educated elite.

---

[43] Japan, Ministry of Education, Science, and Culture, *Japan's Modern Educational System*, p. 50.
[44] R. P. Dore, *Education in Tokugawa Japan* (Berkeley: University of California Press, 1965), p. 254 and chap. 8.
[45] Japan, Ministry of Education, Science, and Culture, *Japan's Modern Educational System*, pp. 6–10, 41–51.

Table 4.3. *Secondary schools and students, 1911–1931*

	1911		1922–1923		1930–1931	
	Schools	Students	Schools	Students	Schools	Students
General:	438	38,881	547	103,385	—	—
Senior	—	—	—	—	554	44,571
Junior	—	—	—	—	1,320	336,851
Vocational	—	—	164	20,360	272	39,647
Teacher training	—	—	394	43,846	846	93,540
Total	—	—	1,105	182,804	2,992	514,609

Sources: 1911 – S. C. Liao, "Middle School Education in China," *Bulletin*, no. 12 (1923), p. 5, in CNAAE, *Bulletins on Chinese Education, 1923*.

1922–1923 – "Statistical Summaries of Chinese Education," *Bulletin*, no. 16 (1923), in CNAAE, *Bulletins on Chinese Education, 1923*. Figures for "schools" do not include missionary schools (pp. 17, 21, 25, 29); figure for "students, total," includes all but Catholic missionary school students (p. 1); all other "students" figures do not include missionary school students (p. 16).

1930–1931 – Ronald Cheng, *The Financing of Public Education in China*, p. 15.

Modernizing officials in Japan made a deliberate decision to recycle its traditional elementary schools and established a stable structure combining central leadership and local support capable of achieving the declared aims. Chinese leaders proclaimed the same aims but apparently remained under the spell of their own much stronger intellectual–bureaucratic traditions and assumed that the new learning should be used as a formal substitute for the old. They therefore turned the old facilities used for preparing candidates to take the civil service examinations into modern schools, encouraging them to rely on the same administrative and financial formulas as their predecessors. Meanwhile, the mass base was left as before outside the scope of formal learning. And it was that traditional inheritance, or the assumptions deriving from it, as much as the added military and political obstacles of the early 20th century, that seemed responsible for the failure to create an effective system of mass education even in localities where the influence and autonomy of modern educators were greatest.

Study and career patterns also continued to reflect the influence of the past. Even in the 1930s, most students still aimed for a career in government or an official position and settled for teaching as the second-best alternative. The separate vocational schools established as part of the modern school system from its inception remained at best an auxiliary component. The proportion of teachers in the different streams indicates the nature of that bias. According to

Table 4.4. *Vocational schools, 1916–1922*

	Number	
Kind of school	1916	1922
Secondary agricultural	56	82
Elementary agricultural	269	345
Secondary industrial	30	38
Elementary industrial	38	82
Secondary commercial	31	45
Elementary commercial	80	129
Vocational (for men)	3	51
Vocational (for women)	21	158
Vocational continuation schools	—	250
Vocational teacher training courses	3	5
Philanthropic vocational	—	19

Source: Huang Yen-pei, "Vocational Education in China," *Bulletin*, no. 1 (1923), p. 12, in CNAAE, *Bulletins on Chinese Education, 1923*.

an official 1910 report, there were 89,766 teachers in modern schools, divided as follows: general academic, 84,755; technical and vocational, 2,712; teacher training, 2,299.[46]

New secondary schools had difficulty teaching the full curriculum recommended by the Education Ministry. The subjects most often not taught due to lack of teachers, equipment, interest, and demand were those in the sciences and physical education. In the early 1920s, even at the elementary level, the recommended curriculum was said to be largely hypothetical and seldom followed in practice. Especially in rural schools, instruction focused mainly on Chinese language and history.[47]

At the tertiary level, students concentrated overwhelmingly in the legal and liberal arts fields (see Table 4.5). Assuming that contemporary statistics at least approximated reality, however, an interesting anomaly appears between domestic and foreign study programs. Despite the concentration in liberal arts and legal studies at home, Y. C. Wang's calculations showed that the single most popular field among Chinese students in the U.S. was consistently engineering for every year from 1905 to 1952, for which statistics were available. The average total for all years in the fields of engineering (28.7 percent), science (12.3 percent), medicine (7.8 percent), and agriculture (3.3 percent) was 52 percent.[48]

[46] Cited in Ping Wen Kuo, *The Chinese System of Public Education*, p. 159.

[47] Twiss, *Science and Education in China*, p. 124.

[48] Y. C. Wang, *Chinese Intellectuals and the West, 1872–1949* (Chapel Hill: University of North Carolina Press, 1966), pp. 168–169 and table 10, pp. 510–511.

Table 4.5. *Distribution of students in tertiary institutions, by school and major, 1922–1937*

| | 1922–1923 | | | 1930–1931 | | | 1937 | |
Institutions	No. of institutions	No. of students (%)	Major subjects	No. of institutions	No. of students (%)	Major subjects	Major subjects	Students (Christian and secular) (%)
University	35	13,098 (37.55)	Liberal arts	—	6,462 (22.53)	Liberal arts	Liberal arts	19.0
Law college	33	10,864 (31.15)	Law	—	10,522 (36.70)	Law	Law	26.4
Teachers college	8	3,093 (8.87)	Education	—	1,789 (6.24)	Education	Education	9.7
Commercial college	8	1,890 (5.42)	Commerce	—	1,803 (6.29)	Commerce	Commerce	7.3
Technical college	13	2,026 (5.81)	Engineering	—	3,322 (11.58)	Engineering	Engineering	14.16
Agricultural college	7	1,271 (3.64)	Agriculture	—	908 (3.17)	Agriculture	Agriculture	4.39
Medical college	7	832 (2.39)	Medicine	—	1,079 (3.76)	Medicine	Medicine	6.31
Other	14	1,806 (5.18)	Natural science	—	2,792 (9.74)	Science	Science	12.75
Total	125	34,880	—	59	28,677			—

Note: The 1922–1923 figures include both colleges and universities; the 1930–1931 figures cover only students taking degree courses in the then existing universities, including national, provincial, and registered private.

Sources: 1922–1923 – Kuo Ping-wen, "Higher Education in China," *Bulletin,* no. 10 (1923), p. 22, in CNAAE, *Bulletins on Chinese Education, 1923.*

1930–1931 – League of Nations Mission of Educational Experts, *The Reorganisation of Education in China,* p. 151.

1937 – Lutz, *China and the Christian Colleges, 1850–1950,* p. 303.

A more detailed study of the data than is possible here is required to explain fully the apparent contradiction between the majors of Chinese students at home and those overseas.[49] But that contradiction seems to reflect the transitional phenomenon created by the ability of individuals to change faster than their societies as a whole, a process exacerbated by education abroad. In later years, the "brain drain" would become the most common indicator of this phenomenon everywhere. In China, during the 1920s and 1930s, the disorientation of the returned student became one of the major issues fueling the critique of Western learning discussed below. Engineers and scientists educated in the U.S. returned home to follow career patterns similar to those who had not studied overseas. Statistics for 1917–1937 show that government service and college teaching were the two main sources of employment for returned students from the U.S. Different surveys during those years show 50–75 percent of American-trained students working in those two general categories. Virtually all of those trained in agronomy and the sciences went into teaching or worked in fields other than those in which they had majored. Of the engineering graduates, about half went into teaching and government, while unemployment remained highest among them as a group.[50]

The educational interests of business and industry were said to be represented by the vocational education movement and the Chinese Association for Vocational Education (Zhonghua zhiye jiaoyu she). The association was founded in Shanghai by Jiangsu educator–official Huang Yanpei in 1917.[51] But the aim of training students for jobs in business, industry, and agriculture enjoyed only modest success (see Tables 4.3 and 4.4). Factors inhibiting the growth of vocational education in China, although evidently magnified by Chinese literary traditions, were typical of those associated with such training in general. Philip Foster could have used this early Chinese experience to reach many of the same conclusions he drew from the African example to produce his critique several decades later.[52] One contemporary Chinese source listed the drawbacks. Location needed to be convenient to work sites rather than to teachers and students. Equipment was more expensive than that needed for regular schooling. Leadership and teaching materials were inadequate; specialties, too narrow. But perhaps most difficult was the need to match education with

---

[49] Jessie Lutz suggests there was a simple division of labor, with those majoring in "Western" specialties more likely to study abroad. She notes that the Christian colleges in China had a significantly higher proportion of science majors than their secular counterparts and that the former were regarded as offering better preparation for overseas study (Jessie Gregory Lutz, *China and the Christian Colleges, 1850–1950*, p. 303).

[50] Wang, *Chinese Intellectuals and the West*, pp. 169–173 and table 13, pp. 514–515.

[51] Huang Yen-pei, "Vocational Education in China," *Bulletin*, no. 1 (1923), reprinted in CNAAE, *Bulletins on Chinese Education, 1923*; *Huang Yanpei Jiaoyu wenxuan* (Selections from Huang Yanpei on Education) (Shanghai: Shanghai jiaoyu chubanshe, 1985).

[52] Foster, "The Vocational School Fallacy in Development Planning."

employment. Such schools inevitably produced more students with particular skills than there were corresponding jobs for them to fill.[53]

Unlike Foster, however, the Chinese writer followed many of his professional contemporaries in supporting the idea of vocational training even while acknowledging its drawbacks: the typical contradiction that would inspire Foster's critique. Inevitably, early proponents of vocational education failed to draw the link between regular academic schooling and the vocational alternative. So long as the former set the standard both for learning and for subsequent employment opportunities, the intellectual and social competition it provided combined with the problems inherent in vocational education itself guaranteed the latter's failure as a viable alternative.

The modern education system had been promoted as an independent variable necessary for China's modern reconstruction. But as the League of Nations team noted, the system's founders seemed not to have appreciated that the education they were introducing into China was as much a product of Western industrial society as its creator. Hence, they did not anticipate the consequences of allowing the new system to be taken over by the very same educated class whose support had only been won by abolishing its main traditional source of authority and status. Despite the succession of foreign models upon which it was superficially based, the new system was therefore immediately co-opted and put to much the same use as the old, perpetuating many features which were actually detrimental to the professed aim of building a modern system. These features included a predominantly legal and liberal arts orientation, with career interests to match in government and academia. The pyramid of Western-style institutions was also, in effect, substituted for the old examinations hierarchy and managed in much the same way.

Attention was accordingly transferred from the examinations to the regular college-preparatory system, which continued to produce a relatively small educated elite, while the masses were left to fend for themselves as before. The regular system also inherited the customary formula for financing traditional education. And these ad hoc local arrangements were juxtaposed with a centralizing bureaucracy that sought to prescribe rules and regulations for school management, much as the imperial bureaucracy had orchestrated the traditional examination system, in minutest detail, from the imperial palace down to the most distant county examination hall.

Together with these marks from its past, however, the new system by the late 1910s already revealed at least two major anomalies foreshadowing a future that would be anything but static. One was Jiangsu's poor record in promoting mass education even though the province's leading educators stood in the vanguard of the national effort to emulate advanced world trends. Shanxi's

---

[53] Djung, *A History of Democratic Education in Modern China*, pp. 136–138, and chap. 6.

performance compounded the contradiction. With no illustrious intellectual tradition to speak of, the province's warlord government led the country in developing mass education.

The second anomaly, reinforcing the first, emerged at the elite level between students educated abroad and those at home. The former were evidently more inclined to select specialties in science and technology appropriate for the advanced Western countries from which China sought to learn. But such studies were so divorced from Chinese realities that students regularly returned to follow premodern career patterns, much like their counterparts at home who remained bound from the start by the old intellectual–bureaucratic traditions. Meanwhile, the need at all levels for technical and vocational training was evident, but educational leaders seemed unable to appreciate the basic conflict of interest between academic and vocational education, much less devise solutions for the latter's inherent weaknesses.

5

The critical backlash

Three characters from Lu Xun's short stories stand out as symbols of China's educational modernization in the early republican era. One was the pathetic remains of a traditional scholar; the second was a satirical caricature of the new; and third was Ah Q, the most famous of all Lu Xun's characters. The old scholar, Kong Yiji, was a failed *shengyuan* who died in direst poverty unable to abandon his scholarly airs or put his out-of-date learning to any use whatever. His successor was the "returned student," whose pretensions derived from half a year's study in Japan. He was immortalized as the "false foreign devil," a title bestowed upon him by Ah Q, in the role of illiterate Chinese Everyman. The returned student kept Ah Q from joining the 1911 revolution when it finally reached their village. And it was a coalition of such partly old, partly new officials and scholars – the revolutionaries – who finally brought about Ah Q's downfall.[1]

These characters were created some two decades after the shift to Western learning, and reflect the self-critical backlash that began to quicken against it around 1920. In real life, Ah Q was doubtless trading jibes with returned students long before then, but he could not have become a hero in that role until after 4 May 1919.

The reassessment sprang from diverse origins, including the firmly rooted strains of conservative dissent and modern liberal criticism. Guo Bingwen's *The Chinese System of Public Education*, completed as a doctoral dissertation in 1914, helps illustrate both the conservative and the liberal views of that time. It also serves as a standard against which to compare the critical changing mood of the 1920s. Guo listed the following major unsolved problems, in the following order:

- *Missionary education*: How to use missionary schools to supplement the national network while bringing them, like private institutions, under official supervision and control. This demand grew from ongoing resentment against the foreign missionary intrusion, the new influence of Christian education

---

[1] These characters appeared in two of Lu Xun's stories: "Kong Yiji" (1919) and "Ah Q zhengzhuan" (The True Story of Ah Q) (1921), in *Lu Xun quanji* (Complete Works of Lu Xun) (Beijing: Renmin wenxue chubanshe, 1981), 1:434–439 and 487–532.

after China adopted Western learning, and the perceived tendency of mission schools to turn out graduates who were "aliens" in their own land.

- *Ethics*: How to use education to develop moral character in the absence of the character-building Confucian curriculum, without restoring the latter as conservatives continued to demand.
- *Discipline*: How to govern schools so as to curb the "spirit of independence and unruliness" typical of Chinese student bodies.
- *Funding*: How to devise adequate sources of financing for the new schools.
- *Mass education*: How to overcome the initial bias in favor of higher learning and the neglect of universal elementary schooling.
- *Relating education to life*: How to transform book learning into more practical forms of education. Here Guo used the new arguments of progressive Western education reformers against old-fashioned teaching methods to counter the "loud cry" of conservative Chinese against the new schools. "The charge is made that from the moment a child enters school, he begins to alienate himself from the life of the family and that of the community, and by the time he graduates he is fit neither to be a farmer nor to be a merchant." The problem was not the new Western subjects, argued Guo, but the formalistic way in which they were being taught.
- *Education and government service*: How to eliminate "quickly and entirely" the idea that education was primarily a stepping stone for government office holding.
- *Teacher training*: How to transform the diverse collection of teachers into a professional teaching corps.
- *Centralization*: How to find the right mix of centralization (to achieve control, promote national consciousness over local identities, promote the national language over local dialects, prescribe national curricula, approve textbooks) and decentralization (to promote local initiative, mobilize local resources, adapt the approved curricula to local needs).[2]

A decade later, these problems, still unsolved, had acquired the more radical contours they would retain in one form or another for at least half a century. The critique of Western-style education in China had fused into a common denominator of key issues:

- The new schools, study abroad, and foreign-run missionary education at home had all combined to foster an urban-oriented elite divorced by its learning and lifestyle from the practical needs of Chinese society.
- The new intellectuals were estranged from the rest of society in part because they were inclined to accept uncritically and apply mechanically the Western ideas and educational models to which they were indebted for their new learning.

[2] Ping Wen Kuo, *The Chinese System of Public Education*, pp. 136–171.

- When transplanted into the alien Chinese environment, where many traditional values still held sway, the foreign models acquired an impractical and elitist nature that they did not necessarily have in their original settings. Chief among these traditional values were the social status and self-perceptions of the intellectuals, including their disdain for practical work and manual labor.
- New and more appropriate forms had to be designed, and the necessary sources of teachers and financing had to be found, in order (1) to promote mass education, especially rural mass education, since the great majority of China's people lived in the countryside; and (2) to promote at all levels learning that would be more relevant to China's most pressing needs.

The later formulation obviously had evolved from the earlier. Differences between them initially seemed more of degree than of kind. But the issues had acquired a more combative tone on specific points: foreign models, elitism, manual labor, practical learning, rural degeneration, and mass education. Also, along with the sharper focus, came the need to fix blame and a new self-critical inclination to look beyond the familiar villains – conservatives and militarists – to the products of modern learning itself.

The much-debated questions of who "discovered" these issues and when have yet to be definitively answered. All can be traced in some form to the first two decades of the century and seem to have grown along with the new education system itself. But how and why these issues took the particular form that they did in the early 1920s need not detain us here. It should suffice only to demonstrate that they did and that they were not the preserve of any individual, group, or party. On the contrary, the critique of modern schools became, like Chinese nationalism itself, one of those rare questions on which the full spectrum of opinion could find common ground.

Also as with Chinese nationalism, the well-known events of 1915–1919 emerged as a critical turning point. Politically, during those years, hopes for representative government disintegrated into Yuan Shikai's monarchical ambitions and the turmoil of the warlord era. Intellectually, the desire for change dating from the turn of the century intensified into the movement for a "new culture." Fed and inspired by foreign ideas and Chinese returning from abroad, the movement was sweeping in scope. It called for a literary revolution using the vernacular (*baihua*) rather than classical Chinese as the medium for literary discourse, and the events of everyday life as its subject matter. It advocated the promotion of Western science, democracy, philosophy, and literature and a skeptical attitude toward all traditional ideas, customs, and institutions. "Mr. Science" and "Mr. Democracy" became the code words of the new tide symbolizing the focus of its concerns.[3]

[3] Chow Tse-tsung, *The May Fourth Movement: Intellectual Revolution in Modern China* (Cambridge: Harvard University Press, 1960), p. 59 and passim.

Idealizing democracy in the abstract – as a subject for intellectual discussion but not participation – was perhaps the most unrealistic of all the movement's aims. Even while their careers and concerns kept them well within the scholar–official tradition of all their predecessors, the new generation of May Fourth intellectuals was distinguished, briefly, by its search for a new identity separate from government and politics. Seemingly repelled by the political chaos around them, this generation of intellectuals looked for solutions in Western distinctions between state and society and in the Western concept of education as a prerequisite not for office holding but for functionally specific intellectual and professional roles in modern society.

So seriously were these new ideas taken that vows were made and oaths declared against accepting public office under any circumstances. But one of the era's most influential figures, Hu Shi, revealed the underlying commitment in his famous ultimatum to refrain from talking politics for 20 years.[4] Politics was still the ultimate concern and never far from anyone's mind. The assumption that intellectual reform was an autonomous independent variable reached its apogee in this New Culture Movement of the late 1910s. Yet such reform was always advanced as the prerequisite for national and political renewal, not as an end in itself. And not surprisingly, the oaths and vows succumbed quickly to political temptation.

After World War I, the victorious Western democracies sanctioned the transfer to Japan of German interests in Shandong. Old grievances against foreign encroachment were reborn in more potent form as the new Chinese nationalism of the May Fourth period. The student protest on 4 May 1919 over the Shandong question gave its name to the new era of Chinese intellectual and political awakening. In fact, 1919 marked the culmination of the New Culture Movement. Before 1919 there had been an idealistic faith in the generalized power of Western science and democracy to reconstruct China on the basis of a cultural rebirth led by the returned students. Afterward, came the consequences of doubt and uncertainty. Adherents were forced to confront the failures of democracy both at home and abroad, as well as disillusionment with the achievements of Western civilization that emerged in the West itself after the world war.

Thus, under the influence still of "world trends," Chinese intellectuals embarked upon a critical reappraisal of their newfound devotion to all things foreign. A victorious revolution in Russia stimulated interest in Marxism, and the new Chinese mood created a receptive audience for this most self-critical of all Western perspectives. Yet the immediate post–4 May 1919 generation was united only in its search for answers. During the years 1919–1921, diverse conclusions began to harden into competing commitments reinforced by direct

[4] Jerome B. Grieder, *Hu Shih and the Chinese Renaissance: Liberalism in the Chinese Revolution, 1917–1937* (Cambridge: Harvard University Press, 1970), p. 175.

political action. Conservative arguments found new strength on the right; a fast-growing Communist Party emerged on the left; and doubts spread even among the previously most confident of American-trained centrists.[5]

The reappraisal of Western learning developed accordingly, drawing inspiration from the range of ideas that marked the era. Chinese educators and erstwhile education reformers from across the developing political spectrum now joined in rejecting the earlier uncritical imitation of Western ideas and models in China's schools. Students returning home with their prized foreign degrees were suddenly objects of satire. It was at this juncture that Lu Xun reversed the usual order of things to cast Ah Q as his leading man and the returned students as inconsequential villains.

Competing interests and inclinations were already taking the critics in many diverse directions. Nor did they necessarily agree on causes, consequences, and solutions. But by the mid-1920s, the common denominator of agreement had taken shape. Then, instead of dissipating like so many other intellectual fads and fashions of the time, this one strengthened during the following decade into a critical consensus against China's modern school system. The consensus was such in the 1920s that emergent Marxist Mao Zedong, cultural conservative Liang Shuming, and Columbia University graduates could all share it. By the 1930s, the critique was so popular that virtually everyone was at least paying lip service to it, including the new Guomindang government, League of Nations experts, American missionaries, and the Rockefeller Foundation.

The 1920s

The political and intellectual implications of the students' vanguard role in militant nationalism were not registered immediately within the adult establishment, at least in part because the students' activism contradicted a dominant theme of the movement their elders were leading for cultural reform before politics. The education sector, moreover, lagged somewhat behind, following its own agenda within the overall New Culture Movement. The leading New Culture journal, *New Youth* (*Xin qingnian*), was founded in 1915, but its educational equivalent, *New Education* (*Xin jiaoyu*), did not begin publication until February 1919.[6] Aims for a "new education" proclaimed at that time

---

[5] The Communist Party grew from Marxist study groups and cells formed between 1918 and 1920. Its formal founding was in 1921, and it had a membership of some 58,000 by April 1927 (James Pinckney Harrison, *The Long March to Power: A History of the Chinese Communist Party, 1921–72* [New York: Praeger, 1972], pp. 18–41, 99). Prominent representatives of the "conservative" backlash against the New Culture Movement at this time were Liang Qichao's articles written in 1919 upon his return from Europe; Liang Shuming's book *Eastern and Western Cultures*, published in 1921; and returned-student Zhang Junmai's (Carsun Chang) "Philosophy of Life" lecture in 1923 (Guy S. Alitto, *The Last Confucian: Liang Shu-ming and the Chinese Dilemma of Modernity* [Berkeley: University of California Press, 1979], pp. 77–81).

[6] On the New Education Movement, see Keenan, *The Dewey Experiment in China.*

paralleled those for a new culture. A Society for the Promotion of New Education (Xin jiaoyu gongjin she) was formed in early 1919. Its leaders intended to concentrate on education reform alone, albeit guided by the spirit of democracy and individualism. Their specific goal was to reorganize the country's school system in accordance with then prevailing ideals. The inauguration of their New Education Movement in 1919 therefore also marked the start of a concerted lobbying effort that resulted in the 1922 school reform decree.

The American-educated establishment

Original sponsors of the New Education Movement were the Jiangsu Education Association, the National Vocational Education Association, National Beijing University, and the Nanjing Higher Teachers Training School. Most prominent among the movement's leaders were Jiang Menglin, Guo Bingwen, Tao Xingzhi, and Hu Shi. Hu Shi was best known as an advocate of literary and cultural reform. Jiang Menglin became the first editor of *New Education* and the movement's *de facto* leader. Guo Bingwen, as noted, headed the Nanjing Higher Teachers Training School and its successor, National Southeastern University. Tao Xingzhi headed the Department of Education at the university, and when the Society for the Promotion of New Education was reorganized in 1921 as the Chinese National Association for the Advancement of Education (CNAAE), he became its first director. All four men were graduates of Columbia University. Guo and Jiang were the first Chinese students to earn doctorates from the Teachers College there, in 1914 and 1917, respectively. To further their cause, they organized the two-year visit (1919–1921) of John Dewey, their professor from Columbia and the foremost contemporary authority on progressive education. Dewey's visit was the centerpiece of the lobbying effort for the 1922 school reform decree.

American influence on Chinese education also culminated in that 1922 decree and the subsequent changes at the local level (see chap. 4). But these reforms represented a kind of symbolic high-water mark pointing to ideals and commitments which were already being eroded even as the mark itself was being drawn. Currents were running so swiftly that by the time the 1922–1923 reforms materialized, their sponsors were already beginning to disengage. Dewey himself, sensitized to the changing climate, cautioned against uniform prescriptions and detailed foreign borrowing before he left China in mid-1921, although he had not emphasized this theme during his stay.[7] Uncertainty was spreading rapidly even among those most receptive to foreign ideas. By late 1922, just one month after the school reform decree was promulgated, Jiang

---

[7] Ibid., pp. 29, 44, 86; see also *John Dewey: Lectures in China, 1919–1920*, trans. Robert W. Clopton and Tsuin-chen Ou (Honolulu: University Press of Hawaii, 1973).

Menglin, previously among the most committed of "internationalists," criticized Chinese educators for blindly imitating foreign ideas.[8] In 1923, Tao Xingzhi summarized the confused odyssey they were all embarked upon: "At first she [China] sacrificed everything old for the new. Gradually she came to a realization that the old is not necessarily bad and the new is not necessarily good. Thus our schoolmen have become much more critical than in former years."[9]

The year 1923 actually marked a great turning point in Tao's life. He wrote in the autumn of his own personal "moment of awakening" whereupon he decided to buy a set of cotton peasant clothes and "rushed back to the way of the common people."[10] His work with the CNAAE reflected this change. At its second annual meeting in August 1923, he, his new friend James Yen (Yan Yangchu), and others had established yet another organization: the Chinese Association for the Promotion of Popular Education (Zhonghua pingmin jiaoyu cujin hui). Although American-educated, James Yen was not part of the Columbia old-boy network that dominated the CNAAE. He was then developing his literacy training programs for the Young Men's Christian Association, a project that originated with his experience in France working among Chinese laborers recruited to support the Allied effort during World War I.[11]

Interest in popular (*pingmin*) or mass education was of course not new. In the mid-1910s, younger intellectuals, with their workers night schools, reading circles, and the like, seemed to pick up where the imperial government's first mass education programs had lapsed a few years earlier. The term of reference was education for ordinary people, or workers, peasants, and all others left out of the regular school system, which had hitherto been the chief preoccupation of those running the CNAAE. The typical program developed by Yen and others relied on volunteers, often middle school and college students, who

[8] Keenan, *The Dewey Experiment in China*, p. 78. Jiang was among those whose conception of culture and of the role of the state attracted him more to Germany than to the Anglo-Saxon democracies prior to the former's defeat in World War I. His easy shift from one dominant "world trend" to another illustrates how the charge of "superficial" infatuation with foreign models applied to individuals as well as to the collective policy decisions that kept the education system in a state of constant change. See Chiang Monlin (Jiang Menglin), *Chinese Culture and Education: A Historical and Comparative Survey* (Taipei: World Book Co., 1963), chap. 14.

[9] Keenan, *The Dewey Experiment in China*, p. 91, quoting from Tao's contribution to the *Educational Yearbook of the International Institute of Teachers College, Columbia University, 1924* (New York: Macmillan Co., 1925).

[10] From a much-quoted and reprinted letter to his sister in Nov. 1923; see, e.g., Philip A. Kuhn, *Tao Hsing-chih, 1891–1946, an Educational Reformer*, Papers on China, 13 (Cambridge, Harvard University, Dec. 1954), p. 170; Keenan, *The Dewey Experiment in China*, p. 90; *Tao Xingzhi nianpu gao* (Chronicle of the Life of Tao Xingzhi) (Beijing: Jiaoyu kexue chubanshe, 1982), p. 11; *Tao Xingzhi nianpu* (Chronicle of the Life of Tao Xingzhi) (Hefei: Anhui jiaoyu chubanshe, 1985), p. 60.

[11] Garrett, *Social Reformers in Urban China*, chap. 5; Charles W. Hayford, *To the People: James Yen and Village China* (New York: Columbia University Press, 1990), pp. 22–31.

tried to teach one thousand basic characters in a sequence of lessons lasting a few months. The new mood of the early 1920s provided a ready host for such an activity, which soon outgrew the limited aims and means of the YMCA. After 1923, when the Chinese Association for the Promotion of Popular Education was founded to coordinate work, the mass education movement reportedly "swept through China like wild fire." By the end of the decade, there were over 30 municipal associations and one in every province.[12] In the autumn of 1926, the national promotion association, following contemporary trends, set up an experimental project in Ding County, Hebei, to adapt the literacy program specifically for use in rural areas.[13]

After 1923, Tao Xingzhi devoted himself increasingly to nonformal learning and followed the mass education movement's progression from the cities into the countryside. Literacy training and especially peasant literacy became his chief preoccupation. Toward that end, he developed the idea of relay teaching, whereby semiliterates, or those who had learned only a few Chinese characters, would teach them to others. The idea led to his famous "little teacher" movement, with children first learning and then teaching characters to adults.

These views led Tao into the mid-1920s debate over the nature and role of Chinese intellectuals as one after another of their plans and projects came to nothing. Marxists were denouncing them as exploitative idealists. Tao was equally scathing but on different grounds. In his view, real knowledge could only derive from experience, and anyone could acquire it. By contrast, the status of intellectuals in imperial times was typically based on dead knowledge epitomized by the formalistic "eight-legged essay": dead knowledge from dead books for position, wealth, fame, and glory. "Eight legs" referred to the set form, with eight headings, adopted for writing examination essays during the Ming dynasty. Modern critics used the term to denounce the rigid conventions of the old learning. But Tao argued that the self-strengtheners were no better. They "copied the entire foreign education system," furnished it with beautiful imported equipment, substituted science books for the old classics, and ignored China's own characteristics – leading the new knowledge into the same trap as the old. Tao's aim was to break the cycle. Books were to be used, not learned, and everyone, not just scholars, should have access to them.[14]

His most innovative attempt to provide an answer was the Xiaozhuang Experimental Rural Normal (Teacher Training) School, which he established near Nanjing in 1927. His experiment, which briefly paralleled that of the

[12] Djung, *A History of Democratic Education in Modern China*, pp. 102–103 and chap. 5 passim; see also Chow, *The May Fourth Movement*, pp. 51, 191–194; McDonald, *The Urban Origins of Rural Revolution*, pp. 114–122.
[13] Gamble, *Ting Hsien*, pp. xix–xx; Hayford, *To the People*, pp. 67–68.
[14] "Wei zhishi jieji" (False Intelligentsia), 1928, in Tao Zhixing (Xingzhi), *Zhongguo jiaoyu gaizao* (China's Education Reform) (Shanghai: Yadong tushuguan, 1928), pp. 189–207, reprinted in *Tao Xingzhi quanji*, 2: 85–97.

Chinese Association for the Promotion of Popular Education in Ding County, aimed to combine his ideas for rural education and reconstruction. By then Tao was, of course, only one of many who had "discovered" the countryside, and his rationale was drafted in the spirit of the times. Any one of many others might have written it. "China's rural education has taken the wrong road," he declared. "It teaches people to leave the villages and run away to the cities. It teaches people to eat rice but not to grow it, to wear clothes but not to plant cotton, to build houses but not to maintain forests. It teaches people to admire extravagance and to look down on agriculture."[15]

The new GMD government closed down Tao's project within three years of its founding and he fled temporarily to Japan. He had moved with the leftward drift of the 1920s and did not follow the GMD's shift to the right after 1927.[16] So ended the direct influence of the New Education Movement. Jiang Menglin had already given it up as a lost cause in the early 1920s, when he claimed that the New Culture Movement's success had been limited to the years 1917–1920. Both he and Hu Shi would later blame the May Fourth upheaval for obstructing their educational and cultural reform goals.[17] Meanwhile, the CNAAE held its last annual meeting in 1925. *New Education* ceased publication after its October 1925 issue. At its final meeting, the CNAAE acknowledged the developing wave of nationalistic antiforeign demonstrations that the 4 May 1919 protest had set in motion. Tao Xingzhi led the convention in voting to support partriotic political education, greater centralized control, and military training for students. The last, originally copied from Japan, had been renounced by Chinese educators in 1919. Now that phase had been superseded by the rise of nationalism, communism, and the military strength of the GMD as ultimate unifier of the warlord era.

The next time China's leading educators met was for the First National Education Conference in 1928, held under the auspices of the new Nanjing regime established by the GMD following its victorious Northern Expedition and anticommunist purge. Cai Yuanpei convened the conference in his capacity

---

[15] "Zhongguo xiangcun jiaoyu zhi genben gaizao" (The Fundamental Reform of China's Rural Education), 1926, in Tao Zhixing, *Zhongguo jiaoyu gaizao*, p. 131, reprinted in *Tao Xingzhi quanji*, 1:653–655.

[16] Tao remained committed in a general way to Dewey's pragmatic philosophy and the principles of progressive education, including experimentation and the relationship of education to life. But these ultimately led in a logical progression to Tao's criticism of Chinese educators who applied too literally Dewey's ideas in conditions so far removed from the U.S. environment that had inspired them. For two surveys of Tao's work in the 1920s, see Keenan, *The Dewey Experiment in China*, chap. 4; and Hubert O. Brown, "American Progressivism in Chinese Education: The Case of Tao Xingzhi," in Hayhoe and Bastid, *China's Education and the Industrialized World*, pp. 120–138. Brown cites several new Chinese sources on Tao's life and work that appeared in the 1980s.

[17] Keenan, *The Dewey Experiment in China*, p. 74; Grieder, *Hu Shih and the Chinese Renaissance*, pp. 176–177.

as University Council president. This conference endorsed the principles of GMD leadership for education including military training and use of the party's political ideology.[18] Jiang Menglin convened the Second National Education Conference in his capacity as the GMD government's first conventional minister of education.[19]

The influence of Tao's post-1923 aims for popular education was, however, far from extinguished. Had he been their sole champion, the regular school system being created by the GMD-led bureaucracy might have emerged as unchallenged heir of all the earlier conflicting currents. The willingness of Cai and Jiang to accept official appointments, however briefly and despite their differences with the new political order, indicated the relative appeal of the GMD's nationalistic centralizing formula among Chinese educators of diverse inclinations. But the struggle had only just been joined. The school system was not allowed to develop unchallenged, because the aims Tao had adopted in the early 1920s were simultaneously taking root in many other corners of China's educational world as well.

The new left

Inspired by the example of earlier Russian populism, China's "first Marxist," Li Dazhao, formulated his demands for an "intellectual youth to the countryside" movement in early 1919. The "peasant problem" was already in the air at that time. But Li was apparently the first to project it into the limelight of intellectual discourse. Later in the year, he declared: "Those intellectuals who eat but do not work ought to be eliminated together with the capitalists. The condition of China today is that the cities and the villages have been made into two opposite poles and have almost become two different worlds."[20]

Founded in 1920, the Chinese Communist Party (CCP) would eventually appropriate as its own the issues of intellectuals and peasants. But the history of the 1920s indicates that those issues helped define the nature of Chinese Marxism as much as it defined them. Even if Marxism did provoke a somewhat earlier and sharper focus among its adherents, the contradictions identified and remedies attempted were no one's exclusive property. The same could not be said, of course, for theoretical explanations and final solutions. Growing disenchantment with idealistic assumptions about the priority of cultural and educational reform as prescriptions for "saving China" did give added credence to

[18] Barry C. Keenan, "Educational Reform and Politics in Early Republican China," *Journal of Asian Studies*, vol. 33, no. 2 (Feb. 1974), p. 236; Peake, *Nationalism and Education in Modern China*, pp. 90–92.

[19] *China Handbook, 1937–1944* (Chungking: Chinese Ministry of Information, 1944), p. 568; Djung, *A History of Democratic Education in Modern China*, p. 212.

[20] Quoted in Maurice Meisner, *Li Ta-chao and the Origins of Chinese Marxism* (Cambridge: Harvard University Press, 1967), pp. 87 and 80–89 passim.

the Marxist rationale. And that credence naturally contributed to the leftward drift of intellectuals in the 1920s. But the educational concerns of young leftists and of the CCP itself grew directly from the critical milieu of that time.

Because of Mao Zedong's later preeminence, his early interests and activities have been more carefully chronicled than would otherwise have been warranted since they were in no way atypical. Everyone seemed to be addressing the same questions and experimenting with similar kinds of remedies – all of which suffered the same dead-end results. The young Mao Zedong's interest in educational questions was actually a professional one, which helps explain his continuing close association with this issue area on and off throughout his life. He received his highest formal education at the First Hunan Provincial Normal School in Changsha, where he was a student from 1913 to 1918. This was a secondary-level institution that prepared young people for careers as elementary school teachers, then as now one of the few respectable ways out of agriculture for upwardly mobile rural youth of modest means. In 1920, he was appointed acting principal of the elementary school attached to the normal school, a position he held for three semesters.

Mao was appointed by Yi Peiji, director of the school complex and concurrently the highest education official in the provincial government. Yi was a leading progressive educator in the province, and Mao's appointment was one of many that he made to inaugurate his reform-minded administration at First Normal. By 1920, moreover, the school could already boast several reform experiments to its credit. A workers night school had been set up in 1916. But interest soon flagged among teachers and staff, so students took over the project. Student activist Mao Zedong was director of the night school for about a year during 1917–1918.[21]

Also in 1916, the normal school inaugurated a "labor association" designed to accustom students and teachers to manual labor. Among other things, they did janitorial duties and practiced farming on campus.[22] The novel idea that students should learn to work with their hands was another foreign import but not new. "Handwork" was included in the 1904 curriculum and remained so at both the elementary and secondary levels thereafter, perceived as a modern corrective for the premodern distinctions between mental and manual labor. But like popular education, the idea itself plus actual performance of manual labor by students appear not to have caught on until the mid-1910s.

Those who championed the new "dignity of labor" slogan included men

[21] *Hunan diyi shifan xiaoshi, 1903–1949*, (The History of the First Hunan Provincial Normal School, 1903–1949) (Shanghai: Shanghai Jiaoyu chubanshe, 1983), pp. 62–63; Li Rui, *Mao Zedong tongzhi de chuqi geming huodong* (The Early Revolutionary Activities of Comrade Mao Zedong) (Beijing: Zhongguo qingnian chubanshe, 1957), pp. 59–64; "Gongren yexue zhaoxue guanggao" (Enrollment Advertisement for the Workers Night School), 1917, in *Mao Zedong ji* (Collected Works of Mao Zedong) (Hong Kong: Jindai shiliao gongying she, 1975), 1:49–51.
[22] *Hunan diyi shifan xiaoshi*, pp. 66–69.

whose political proclivities would soon place them at opposite ends of the spectrum. One was Li Dazhao. Another was Cai Yuanpei, who set aside his anarchist scruples initially to return from Europe in 1916 and serve as head of Beijing University. A decade later, Li would be executed in the anticommunist pogrom of 1927, whereas Cai would support in varying degrees and capacities the anticommunist government that was established in its wake. But in the late 1910s, both men lent their prestige to the new concern about bridging the gulf between educated elites and unschooled masses. Teaching projects wherein educated youth taught workers and peasants was one practical result; another was manual labor for students.[23] First Normal in provincial Changsha was obviously very up-to-date in following these new trends with its workers night school and student labor program.

When Yi Peiji took over as headmaster at First Normal in September 1920, he thus entered on the crest of a reformist wave. He hired a number of new "progressive" teachers, recruiting them from as far away as Beijing and Shanghai. He even hired an American woman English instructor. The outsiders brought with them all the new ideas then sweeping China's intellectual world. Foremost among them and part of the new concern to popularize learning was the shift from classical Chinese to a simpler style closer to the spoken language. Previously, there had been little contact between teachers and students except in the formal atmosphere of the classroom. This began to change after most of the new teachers moved onto campus to live. Girls were enrolled in 1921, an "extraordinary" step in Changsha at the time and the first experiment in coeducation at the secondary level in the entire province. Mao took up his duties at the same time, in the fall of 1920, and followed the lead of his superior in reforming the elementary school.[24]

Given the context of the times, there was nothing very unusual about the changes introduced during the brief tenures of Yi Peiji and Mao Zedong. Both moved on to other things in 1922, due to the shifting currents of provincial politics. But the Changsha normal school's record is important in that it helps illustrate the range of reform concerns in the May Fourth period. Those concerns, like Guo Bingwen's list of unsolved problems, reflected the sum total of elite reform ideas and actual implementation *within* the developing education system. Then, in the immediate post-1919 years, a subtle change occurred. Those same problems and practices were reinterpreted in ever more negative terms, as an accusation *against* the system for failing to solve and absorb them.

Mao's activities in Changsha before and after 1920 reflected that same shift. His work, begun in 1920 as an elementary school reformer, was essentially an extension of his activities between 1916 and 1918 as a student activist. By 1921,

---

[23] Meisner, *Li Ta-chao and the Origins of Chinese Marxism*, pp. 86–89, 257–260; Duiker, *Ts'ai Yüan-pei: Educator of Modern China*, pp. 53, 63–64, 81–92.
[24] *Hunan diyi shifan xiaoshi*, pp. 150–165.

he had become a critic of the system itself. His metamorphosis was comparable
to that registered by Tao Xingzhi and was expressed in similar terms. The
occasion for Mao was the Self-Study University founded by him and a few
like-minded friends in Changsha in August 1921.

According to the formal announcement, which Mao wrote, this was to be a
new kind of institution combining the best of modern and traditional schools
while avoiding the defects of both. Mao noted that the old Confucian academies had been replaced by modern schools as everyone "rushed to condemn
the academies and praise the schools." "In fact," he continued, "both the
academies and the schools have things to censure and praise."

The academies' defects were well known. Their old eight-legged essays were
useful only for passing the civil service examinations. But the academies also
had some good features, and these were precisely what most modern schools
lacked. Mao then went into some detail in elaborating the faults of modern
schools. There was no feeling between teachers and students. The former were
interested only in money and the latter only in obtaining diplomas. The biggest
fault of the modern schools, however, was their mechanical, uniform teaching
and management methods. People naturally had different abilities and temperaments, but the schools cared nothing about this. They just poured the
same thing down everyone's throat. The curriculum was also too heavy, and
students had to spend all their time in class while gaining little knowledge of
the outside world. Their minds thus grew muddled and they could not think
things through or study on their own. As a result, "students become passive,
their individuality is ground down, their initiative extinguished, and they just
drift along complying with convention while their intelligence is bound and
fettered." Mao argued that the academies were superior in all of these respects:
human feelings were sincere; there was little supervised instruction, so students could study freely; and the curriculum was simple, so they could be
carefree and take time off to play.

The good points of modern schools, by contrast, lay primarily in the content
of what they taught: the new scientific subjects, scientific methods, and so on.
Hence the aim of the new Self-Study University was to combine the *form* of
the old academy with the *content* of modern learning, to create an institution
appropriate to human nature and convenient for study.

The social element of populism (*pingmin zhuyi*) was, however, absent in
both the old academies and the new schools. Both had strict requirements and
regulations, and those who did not meet them could not be admitted. As a
result, many young people were still deprived of a higher education. As a
further result, both the old Confucian academies and the new universities
treated learning as something mysterious, something for only "a few special
people" which the majority could not hope to share. Finally, there was the
problem of money. To graduate from a university cost 1,000–2,000 Chinese
dollars. Thus, for a poor person to go to a university was like "a stray cat

aspiring to eat the flesh of a swan." The Self-Study University would therefore strive to become an institution of truly popular learning.[25]

The Self-Study University passed quickly into history like most other experiments of its kind. This one was closed down by the military governor in late 1923 on grounds that it was promoting unorthodox ideas and threatening public order. Mao's ideas were, of course, seditious by this time. They not only placed him within the developing current of criticism against modern schools but were bringing him new insights into the futility of education reform alone, whether as an end in itself or as a means to larger social aims. Still, his insights were different from those of many of his contemporaries only in that Mao's were beginning to show the self-conscious influence of Marxism.

In 1920, when small communist cells were being formed in cities around the country, Mao took the lead in organizing one for Changsha as well, about the same time he took up his duties at the elementary school. Representatives from all these groups gathered in Shanghai in July 1921, the official founding date of the CCP. Mao returned to Changsha as secretary of the CCP for Hunan Province. When he wrote the inaugural declaration for the Self-Study University a month later, he had not progressed much beyond the contemporary intellectual criticism of the educated "class," which enslaved the uneducated. But however rudimentary his Marxism, Mao had already reached the stage where he saw education reform as only a place to begin – a part of the overall agenda and not even a leading one at that.

British philosopher Bertrand Russell was, like John Dewey, traveling and lecturing in China at this time. Russell had argued during his stay in Changsha in 1920 that socialism and even communism could be achieved without war or violent revolution or limitations on personal freedom. Instead, he advocated the use of education to change the consciousness of the propertied classes. Russell's view was good enough in theory, Mao wrote, but it would not work in practice. This was because education required money, people, and facilities. But all these resources, including most importantly the schools and the press, were already controlled by capitalists. In addition, they simultaneously controlled all the other institutions of society necessary for perpetuating their predominance. Hence, the nonpropertied class, despite its numerical superiority, would be helpless to turn education to its own ends. The only solution was for the communists to "seize political power." For similar reasons, Mao wrote off as well the anarchists' ideal of a society without power or organization: "My present viewpoint on absolute liberalism, anarchism, and even democracy is that these things are fine in theory, but not feasible in practice."[26]

---

[25] "Hunan zixiu daxue chuangli xuanyan" (The Founding Announcement of the Hunan Self-Study University), in *Mao Zedong ji*, 1:81–84.

[26] From two letters to Ts'ai Ho-shen (Cai Hesen) dated Nov. 1920 and Jan. 1921; trans. in Stuart R. Schram, *The Political Thought of Mao Tse-tung* (New York: Frederick A. Praeger, 1963), pp. 214–216.

Finally, Mao may have been two years ahead of Tao Xingzhi in articulating his criticism of modern schools, but rediscovering his peasant roots evidently took Mao some two years longer. He later wrote that it was not until 1925, after he had become a Marxist and returned to live for six months in the country-side, that he came to appreciate rural attitudes toward education. Actually, everyone was "discovering" the countryside in the mid-1920s. And again, because of his later preeminence as champion of a successful rural-based re-volution, Mao's 1927 "Report on an Investigation of the Peasant Movement in Hunan" became a landmark document on the CCP's shift from town to countryside.

In the post-Mao era, however, this report came under scrutiny, and the originality of Mao's much-quoted comments on rural education was chal-lenged. The report was allegedly written by Mao after he spent January 1927 investigating rural conditions in five Hunan counties. As it happened, Mao's investigation immediately followed the monthlong First Peasants Representa-tive Conference of Hunan Province in December 1926. The later challenge derived from similarities between conference resolutions on rural schools and the section in Mao's report on the same topic. Since Mao was only one of several people who attended the meetings during which the rural education resolutions were drafted, it was argued, he probably did not draft them alone. Yet they obviously constituted the basis of his subsequent report.[27]

That the report represents collective wisdom and not just the views of one communist provincial is, of course, even better for our purpose here, which is to demonstrate the diverse origins of the 1920s critique against modern schools. The three main points in the education section of Mao's report, which were all contained in the conference resolutions as well, were the following:

(1) On equity, the conference resolutions pointed out that direct and indirect costs of both urban and rural education in China were borne by the peas-ants, most of whom did not receive any education in the schools they were supporting. Yet the "special classes" who did used their superior knowl-edge to oppress the poor, while ridiculing them as "ignorant fools." Sim-ilarly, Mao wrote that "historically in China, only the landlords have had culture and the peasants have had none. Yet the landlords' culture is created by the peasants, and because it is the landlords' culture, that means it comes from the blood and sweat of the peasants' own bodies."

(2) On relevance, both the conference resolutions and the report emphasized that rural education should start from the realities and needs of rural life. The conference had noted that old-style private schools (*sishu*) were products

---

[27] Chen Guisheng, "Mao Zedong tongzhi zai diyici guonei geming zhanzheng shiqi dui jiaoyu de gongxian" (Comrade Mao Zedong's Contribution to Education during the First Revolutionary Civil War Period), *Jiaoyu yanjiu* (Education Research), no. 11 (1983), pp. 6–7.

of the village economy and not only were they still flourishing but they were still using the old Confucian primers as texts. Although this last was a great defect, the old-fashioned classes nevertheless seemed appropriate to the peasants' way of life, so they continued to support them. New schools were good in that they replaced the old "feudal" teaching materials with progressive modern ones. But the contemporary content seemed relevant only for city life and was not suitable for village needs. Also, in their attitude and manner, the teachers seemed completely cut off and distant from rural people. As a result, most of the latter had their doubts about the new schools. In his report, Mao noted that the peasants did not like the "foreign-style schools." When he was himself a student in such schools he identified with them and thought the peasants wrong. It was only later, in 1925, after he had become a Communist and returned to live in the countryside for half a year, that he relearned the peasants' perspective.

(3) Finally, both the resolutions and the report emphasized that to succeed in universalizing rural education, it would be necessary to rely on the resources of the rural people themselves. First relieve their economic oppression, then let them run their own schools in ways suitable to their needs, and their enthusiasm for education would grow accordingly.[28]

Regardless of who composed these passages, the underlying principles were also almost identical with those outlined for the Self-Study University that Mao and his friends had established in Changsha five years before – except that by 1927, some important socioeconomic prerequisites had been added. Those prerequisites aside, both versions were clearly rooted in the developing 1920s critique of modern schools.

Cultural conservative Liang Shuming

Like Tao Xingzhi, Liang Shuming sought solutions outside the regular school system and the official power structure, while also trying to use education to achieve larger social reforms. And like Tao, Liang's solution was similar in many ways to those the Communists would later introduce. But he reached his conclusions by traveling a route very different from that of either the Marxists or John Dewey's disciples.[29] Liang joined the faculty at Beijing University in the late 1910s as a young self-taught Buddhist scholar and philosopher who had neither attended college nor studied abroad. Nor is it recorded that he ever

---

[28] "Hunan nongmin yundong kaocha baogao" (Report on an Investigation of the Peasant Movement in Hunan), 28 Mar. 1927, in *Mao Zedong ji*, 1:246–247; "Hunansheng diyici nongmin daibiao dahui jueyian" (Resolutions of the First Peasants Representative Conference of Hunan Province), Dec. 1926, in *Diyici guonei geming zhanzheng shiqi de nongmin yundong ziliao* (Materials on the Peasant Movement during the Period of the First Revolutionary Civil War) (Beijing: Renmin chubanshe, 1983), pp. 427–429.

[29] The summary of Liang's ideas presented here is based on Alitto, *The Last Confucian*.

traded his scholar's gown for a peasant's cotton tunic. But by the early 1920s, he had begun to explore the causes of China's demoralization and ultimately concluded that it was due to Western influence.

According to Liang's line of argument, previous reform efforts had been led by intellectuals in imitation of the West to gain wealth and power. They failed to achieve that objective and had destroyed China's cultural roots in the process. Wealth and education were concentrating in the cities while the countryside was being destroyed. In particular, he blamed the new Western-style education system, which was "educating people for another society" but inadequate to meet China's own needs.[30]

In Liang's view, the new system actually contained the worst of both worlds since the defects of traditional education were still present while its good points had been jettisoned and those of the West lost somewhere in between. The authority of the old educated class had derived from its dual role of political leader and transmitter of moral values. The new education ignored the old morality, and intellectuals had become self-serving, luxury loving, and profit seeking as a result. They retained their privileged elite status, but without any sense of moral rectitude or responsibility. Unlike Western intellectuals, moreover, their Chinese counterparts still generally aspired to become officials. Also unlike their Western counterparts, they retained the old intellectuals' disdain for manual labor. Furthermore, Liang anticipated that Chinese society, like those in the West, would soon divide into two permanent hereditary classes since the new education was so costly that only the rich could afford it.

The new education was thus alienating the elite from the masses and the cities from the countryside. Even rural children once educated in the new primary schools in town were lost to the countryside thereafter, looking down on the life and work that continued there. Like the peasants in everyone's rural surveys, Liang therefore criticized the curriculum of the new schools for its urban orientation and irrelevance to practical needs, and also the impersonal style of the Westernized teachers.

Liang, however, went a step further, declaring that the new education was actually of no use to anyone. He criticized secondary schools and higher technical institutes as largely pointless since students in the former acquired no practical skills and those in the latter were not given the kind of education ostensibly intended. Even the agricultural schools produced urban-oriented graduates who rarely worked in the specialties for which they had been trained. Liang ultimately criticized all of China's higher education as "utterly irrelevant." He called for students to stop using foreign books that could not contribute to China's immediate needs, and for the reorientation of research to concentrate on the applied sciences.[31]

[30] Quoted in ibid., p. 143.
[31] Ibid., pp. 141–144, 150–151, 160–165, 200, 212.

By contrast, Liang was enthusiastic about Tao Xingzhi's experimental normal school project and turned similarly to rural reconstruction as the most suitable means of applying his ideas. These were most extensively implemented in Zouping (Tsou-p'ing) County, Shandong, between 1931 and 1937. At the heart of Liang's program was the Shandong Rural Reconstruction Institute, which trained his new-style rural administrators and managers. But he conceived of the school as an institution that would not just train personnel but replace local government and achieve the revitalization of society as well. This goal came closest to realization after 1933, when the central government – by then seeking alternatives to match the communists' success in their rural Jiangxi Soviet – granted administrative autonomy to experimental county reconstruction projects. The institute was thereafter given the power to make all personnel appointments at the county level. Subcounty government was also reorganized to conform to Liang's vision of the school center as the basic administrative organ at the rural district (*xiang*) and village levels.

Actual education programs offered by the school centers reflected Liang's critique of the regular school system. Rural elementary schools emphasized subjects relevant to village life and the particular vocational requirements of the locality. But despite the originality of his plan, Liang's rural reconstruction workers occupied a role not unlike the ideal-type scholar–officials of old, whose authority derived from learning and moral leadership as well as from their administrative positions.[32]

Like Tao Xingzhi's experiment in Jiangsu, however, Liang's also soon became more irrelevant than the education system he hoped to supplant. Both experiments seemed to fail primarily because of their ambivalent relationship with political power. Each reformer, for his own reasons, sought to avoid direct contact with it. Their aim was to reform government and politics indirectly through the diffuse social influence of reason and moral suasion, without touching power directly themselves. But they soon found that without it, to coin Mao's phrase, no one would listen to what they had to say. Hence they had to rely on the sufferance of a suspicious central government and whatever protection the local power holders might provide. Liang's experiment was initially set up under the sponsorship of Shandong's military governor, Han Fuqu, and was able to expand after 1933 only because higher-level tolerance was evidently encouraged by the combined threat of the communists and later the Japanese. Liang's experiment collapsed in 1937, after the Japanese invasion and Han's withdrawal from Shandong.

The 1930s

The rural reconstruction bandwagon continued to roll throughout the 1930s, however. But the critical themes from the 1920s were evolving in a curious

[32] Ibid., pp. 238–253.

way: so fashionable that seemingly everyone felt obliged at least to pay them lip service, yet so ineffective as to have virtually no impact on the education system itself, reinforcing in turn the subculture of dissent surrounding it.

Mass education in Ding County, Hebei

Among foreigners and Chinese government officials, James Yen was the most influential of the rural reformers and maintained the closest links with both. After his interests shifted to the countryside in the mid-1920s, the futility of promoting literacy alone soon became apparent. By the early 1930s, the Ding County experiment had grown into a program to counteract the four dimensions of China's "agrarian crisis," that is, ignorance, poverty, disease, and civic disintegration. Two additional experimental districts were created in Hunan and Sichuan before the Japanese war intervened. After the GMD government retreated into the Southwest, a rural reconstruction college was established in 1940 near Chongqing to train young people for rural service.[33]

The formula James Yen and his associates had worked out relied on enlightened intellectuals for initial leadership, on contributions from the wealthy and from government for seed money, on tolerance from provincial warlords and county magistrates, and on the cooperation of local notables. Programs eschewed "slavish copying" of foreign models in deference to adaptation, with the main emphasis on local needs and abilities.

In the early 1940s during a wartime trip to the U.S., James Yen discussed his work in an interview with the writer Pearl Buck. Despite his moderate stance Yen nevertheless betrayed the typical reformer's ambivalence for contemporary politicians and intellectuals. Of politics, his initial instinct had been to remain as detached as the need for subsidies would allow. He feared compromise, the loss of integrity, and also the loss of his freedom to experiment. But as his movement grew, and assuming as it did the fourth dimension of civil reintegration, that is, effective local government, participation in local, national, and ultimately even international politics became a prerequisite for continuing success.[34]

As for the other external threat to his work, Yen was, wrote Buck, "scorching in his condemnation of the intellectuals, old and new, who still hold

[33] See e.g., "Dingxian de xiangcun jianshe shiyan" (The Ding County Experiment in Rural Reconstruction), July 1934, "Zhonghua pingmin jiaoyu cujin hui Dingxian shiyan gongzuo baogao" (Chinese Association for the Promotion of Popular Education, Ding County Experiment Work Report), Oct. 1934, and "Shinianlai de Zhongguo xiangcun jianshe" (Rural Reconstruction in China during the Past Ten Years), 1937, in *Yan Yangchu quanji, 1919–1937* (Complete Works of Yan Yangchu, 1919–1937) (Changsha: Hunan jiaoyu chubanshe, 1989), 1:256–287, 307–347, and 559–571, respectively; and Hayford, *To the People*.

[34] Pearl S. Buck, *Tell the People: Talks with James Yen about the Mass Education Movement* (New York: International Institute of Rural Reconstruction, 1959), pp. 80–81, 95–104.

themselves aloof from the people." He had shared the common intellectual view until his own awakening in France, where, in an alien setting, he suddenly became aware of the "bitterness and distress of the people." Subsequently, he reached the conclusion that would govern all his life's work: "Those who have learning keep it for themselves. . . . They do not think of it as something which ought to be shared with all."[35] He also spoke of the practical difficulties when foreign-trained Ph.D.'s in agriculture and rural economics tried to turn their knowledge to simple ends like raising cabbages and running cooperatives. About one-third of the outside staff members at Ding County gave up and left.[36]

Nor had the League of Nations mission been particularly impressed in 1931. It criticized the individualistic tradition of uncoordinated and experimental projects the reformers were perpetuating and singled out Ding County to exemplify the wasteful use of scarce resources. The mission noted that "enormous sums" were being spent there while "in reality only very little work is achieved." With respect to education specifically, the main criticism did not concern the literacy programs run for the benefit of those outside the regular school system but concerned that system itself, which was ironically perpetuating illiteracy! Village elementary schools were not effectively dispersed, so that only 53 percent of the county's children of elementary school age were actually in attendance, by comparison with a much higher rate in Shanxi Province.[37]

Rural reconstruction in Jiangxi

The last rural education–reconstruction project was sponsored by the GMD government itself and was launched after its pacification campaigns finally succeeded in driving the communists from their Jiangxi base. In 1927, the same year that Chiang Kai-shek (Jiang Jieshi) led the victorious Northern Expedition into the Yangzi River valley and turned against his communist allies, he also married into a wealthy Chinese Christian family. The religious implications of the union were not immediately apparent because the anti-Christian movement of the 1920s was one force underlying its bid for power that the GMD did not repudiate in victory. On the contrary, the new government moved quickly to establish official control over foreign-run schools and religious institutions. The popularity of such moves was evident in the continuing antiforeign and anti-Christian agitation during the early 1930s.

In 1931, however, Generalissimo Chiang converted to Christianity. The Chiangs then surprised everyone two years later by asking Christian missionaries

---

[35] Ibid., pp. 21, 25.
[36] Ibid., pp. 55–59, 109.
[37] League of Nations report, pp. 64, 84, 90.

to pioneer rural rehabilitation in Jiangxi Province once the communist rebellion there was quelled. Evidently, nationalistic and political considerations intervened, because the government itself assumed responsibility in 1934 for an ambitious rehabilitation program coupled with the much-publicized New Life Movement.[38] The new official tolerance for Christianity continued, however, symbolized by the rural reconstruction pilot project led by New Zealand–American missionary George Shepherd in Lichuan County, Jiangxi. Yet as soon as the project was launched, all the familiar themes emerged.

Rural reconstruction in Jiangxi was inspired by the growing concern over China's agrarian problems, reinforced by the communists' success in exploiting them, both as the GMD's ally during the Northern Expedition and later as its enemy in Jiangxi. But foreigners seemed more impressed by the challenge than their GMD sponsors. Shepherd launched his experiment in 1934 under the assumption that "the only road for Christians to travel is the same one that the communists are traveling – love the poor." His major problem was to find Chinese rural reconstruction workers willing "to serve as the communists do – for living expenses only."[39]

Outside expertise was essential since virtually none existed locally. Shepherd was heartened by the initial response. He secured promises of cooperation from several Christian universities. Two years later his optimism was largely spent. Volunteers came but did not stay. Few college-educated young people were willing to commit themselves to labor in so backward an area. Here, too, the Western-trained intellectual appeared not as the vanguard but as the obstacle to reform. In 1931, he had deplored the urban prejudices which Christian schools were instilling in their students. Five years later, after his Lichuan experience, Shepherd endorsed the view of a League of Nations advisor who criticized the mission schools for "training an intellectual group of men and women, most of whom have refused to become a part of an agricultural civilization and to work and sacrifice for the uplift of the farmers."[40]

On the relationship with politics, Shepherd eventually accepted the need to work with government. Locally, school attendance could not be enforced or project funds protected against graft until an ally had been appointed to head the district government. Although private institutions did not have the authority to coordinate and implement a project so extensive as rural reconstruction,

---

[38] E.g., Stephen C. Averill, "The New Life in Action: The Nationalist Government in South Jiangxi, 1934–37," in *China Quarterly*, no. 88 (Dec. 1981), pp. 594–628; Arif Dirlik, "The Ideological Foundations of the New Life Movement: A Study in Counter-revolution," *Journal of Asian Studies*, vol. 34, no. 4 (Aug. 1975), pp. 945–980; James C. Thomson, Jr., *While China Faced West: American Reformers in Nationalist China, 1928–1937* (Cambridge: Harvard Unversity Press, 1969), esp. chap. 7; Lloyd Eastman, *The Abortive Revolution: China under Nationalist Rule, 1927–1937* (Cambridge: Harvard University Press, 1974), pp. 66–70.
[39] Quoted in Thomson, *While China Faced West*, pp. 94, 95.
[40] Quoted in ibid., pp. 116–117.

to identify with the government in Jiangxi was to risk being compromised by its failures. This risk had underlain the determination of May Fourth era intellectuals to avoid warlord-style politics, a determination that began to erode as the GMD's power grew. Its record in Jiangxi then redefined the risk as the communists became public enemy number one.

The GMD began its rehabilitation program seemingly with all the ingredients necessary for success. The dozen counties that originally were to have been given over to Christian rural reconstruction became the sites for 10 government-run rural welfare centers, each with staff trained in the four areas targeted for development: education, agriculture, rural cooperatives, and health care. Government funding seemed adequate, League of Nations advisors gave the necessary expert encouragement, and the Christian First Family generated the requisite publicity among both the local population and sympathetic foreigners. But within two years, the latter were noting regretfully that local elites seemed more interested in restoring the status quo ante and regaining their expropriated properties than in promoting rural reform.[41]

Many years later, a staff member from the Jiangxi Rural Welfare Service who had served as chief administrative officer in one of the centers published survey data from the region gathered in 1936–1937 and summarized the unsolved problems with specific reference to education. The survey included 10,129 households, or 46,210 people, in 214 villages selected from among all 10 counties in the rehabilitation program. A majority of households, 62 percent, were headed by farmers; 17 percent were headed by skilled and ordinary laborers; and 9 percent were headed by merchants. Only 22 percent (8,700 males and 1,100 females) of all persons surveyed were literate. But "literacy" was apparently defined only in terms of school attendance, and about 3,000 of the literate people reported receiving one year or less of schooling. Only 7.5 percent had more than six years of formal education.[42]

The 214 villages surveyed had 73 schools, 10 of which were designated central (*zhongxin*) schools, 1 in each of the 10 rural welfare centers. The budget for these central schools was seven times as large as that for ordinary village schools, and teachers in the former earned on the average twice as much as those in the latter.[43] The author nevertheless concluded with a familiar litany of unsolved rural education problems. The Education Ministry's recommended elementary school curriculum was too remote from rural life. Most educated people were urban and therefore unsuited for rural work, making it difficult to

[41] Ibid., pp. 114–115. Averill argued that it was not just the restoration of the old system, which meant returning land and property redistributed by the Communists and restoring tenancy, but the rise to power within that system of the worst elements of the old local elite that was most subversive of the GMD's program in Jiangxi ("The New Life in Action," pp. 620–628).

[42] Jen-chi Chang, *Pre-Communist China's Rural School and Community* (Boston: Christopher Publishing House, 1960), pp. 35–38, 71, 77–86.

[43] Ibid., p. 84.

staff rural schools with qualified people. In any case, modern teachers looked down on the peasants as illiterates and could not work effectively among them. Educational funding came largely from land taxes, placing an unfair burden on the farmers, who did not receive a proportionate share of the benefits.[44]

The Rockefeller Foundation

Responding to the contemporary mood, the Rockefeller Foundation invested close to 2 million (U.S.) dollars between 1935 and 1943, aimed specifically at trying to bridge the continuing gap between modern intellectual expertise and the rural objects of everyone's intentions. This new approach reflected the dominant concerns discovered in China in the early 1930s by Selskar Gunn, a foundation vice-president.[45] He found that skeptical questions raised a decade earlier had hardened into a critical consensus. The same contradictions remained and, if anything, were intensifying, while the critique had yet to produce any effective solutions. Gunn's dominant impression was one of conflict: between the obvious Westernizing tendencies then under way and the sharply critical attitude toward those same tendencies even among people educated in the West and obviously committed to them.

Reflecting the critical consensus he found in China, Gunn judged the standards of missionary schools mediocre and their significance declining. Equally harsh was his judgment of the Peking Union Medical College, which had received the bulk of Rockefeller investment in China since 1913. Despite the high standards of modern medicine it had introduced, Gunn declared that achievements were not commensurate with the investment since its conventional approach was incapable of addressing China's real medical and public health needs.

Gunn's most severe criticism, however, was reserved for education abroad and the returned students. Degrees from foreign universities were used as tickets to academic positions in China. Ability and productivity were secondary. Most of the Chinese Rockefeller fellowship recipients had become displaced persons upon their return to China. Being no longer wholly Chinese and not really Western, they could not reintegrate themselves into Chinese life and work. Nor could they make much of a contribution in the fields in which they had been trained. Yet despite widespread awareness of these faults, concerned Chinese were often either afraid to speak out or powerless to effect the necessary reforms. Basing itself on this critique, the foundation redirected its support away from missionary schools and study abroad. The new aim was to exploit the strengths of existing institutions in China while reorienting them

[44] Ibid., pp. 95–107.
[45] See esp. Thomson, *While China Faced West*, chap. 6.

toward practical application and especially toward the rural areas, where needs were greatest.[46]

Educational development and the legacy of the republican era

Such was the climate within which the League of Nations team had prepared its assessment. Our review confirms the team's disclaimer that most of its criticisms had already been voiced by Chinese educators themselves. But what the League report could not do, given its cross-sectional view from a single point in time, was to gauge the depth and significance of the Chinese critique itself. In fact, all manner of correctives had been tried: from the extracurricular activities of urban universities and middle schools to mass literacy programs and on to rural reconstruction. Yet despite the common denominator of agreement among the critics, their solutions were always disparate and uncoordinated. Nor did they ever progress much beyond the pilot project stage (except briefly in the communist border regions, as the following chapter will show). The aim always was to produce successful working models for emulation on a wider scale, but the experiments were typically set up outside the regular school system and had little influence within it. The piecemeal approach seemed to derive from China's tradition of private responsibility for educational funding and management – admirable in itself but totally insufficient for building a modern system of universal education.

Nevertheless, the Chinese controversies would belie the corresponding tradition that "reforms die with the reformer," since in this case the reforms died but the critique lived on. James Yen's remarks to Pearl Buck in the early 1940s would have been entirely acceptable to Tao Xingzhi in 1923. If anything, the agreement had hardened over two decades, perpetuated as a self-critical undercurrent of dissent by the failure of its adherents to produce any substantive changes in the regular education system. The reasons for their failure contributed to some of the key intellectual debates of the time. Immediate causes could usually be traced to a hostile or at best nonsupportive political environment. Those reformers who tried to retain their apolitical New Culture ideals soon discovered the futility of their cause. Having embarked upon a public undertaking, however small scale, local political sponsorship seemed the minimum requirement to ensure the cooperation and protection necessary for survival.

This was essentially the same lesson that did so much to undermine the credibility of the New Culture Movement as a whole. Best known in this

---

[46] See also Mary Brown Bullock, *An American Transplant: The Rockefeller Foundation and Peking Union Medical College* (Berkeley: University of California Press, 1980), chaps. 6–7; Lutz, *China and the Christian Colleges*, chap. 8.

regard was the debate between CCP founder Chen Duxiu and Hu Shi over the relationship between cultural and political reform. These two New Culture leaders would soon part company over this question because Chen, like Mao, had concluded that cultural reform could only be achieved in direct confrontation with hostile power holders, a view that predisposed both to Marxism. By contrast, Hu Shi continued to champion cultural reform as a prerequisite for building democratic attitudes and institutions until he saw his movement overwhelmed by the political currents of the time.[47]

Undermining further the pre–May Fourth assumptions of New Culture liberals, however, was the growing awareness among post–May Fourth education reformers that politicians and militarists were not their only adversaries. Warlords and the GMD government may have been immediately responsible for closing down individual reform projects and assassinating a few reformers, while the Education Ministry and its bureaucracy may have been responsible for the failure of the system as a whole to respond to the reformers' critique. But the system over which it presided was the creation of the intellectuals and returned students themselves. In fact, it was they who staffed the Education Ministry, enjoying as one of the rewards of power the political support necessary to build the system more or less as they wished. And it was they who sponsored the repeated reorganizations of the national education system, each reflecting the demands of successive waves of students returning from abroad. Yet each reproduced the same basic features, seemingly impervious to the controversies they provoked.

Throughout the 1920s and especially after 1927, men who had been educated abroad monopolized all the leading administrative and academic positions, including those in the Education Ministry, the provincial education bureaus, and tertiary education. Invariably, the most prestigious jobs, whether in government administration or academia, went to the returned students rather than graduates of the new Chinese colleges. The former, upon their return to China, tended to congregate near the centers of national power: in Beijing before 1927, and in the Shanghai–Nanjing area after the GMD government established its capital in Nanjing.[48]

That a "critical consensus" was developing throughout the 1920s, that the sharpest critics included some of the returned students themselves, and that the failure of individual reform projects could usually be traced to some immediate political–military cause should not therefore be allowed to obscure the full context of the controversy. Tao Xingzhi and James Yen were acclaimed because they were *exceptions* to the rule, not representatives of it. And they had to set up their experiments *outside* the formal education system created and

---

[47] Grieder, *Hu Shih and the Chinese Renaissance*, pp. 175–188; Meisner, *Li Ta-chao and the Origins of Chinese Marxism*, pp. 100–114.
[48] Y. C. Wang, *Chinese Intellectuals and the West*, pp. 366–367.

maintained by the returned students because there was no place for such innovations within it. Success was therefore undermined not only by obscurantist politicians and militarists but also by their own fellow intellectuals. Because of that resistance, they probably could not at that time have reformed the system as a whole in accordance with the prevailing critique, even had they been given a politics-free environment in which to proceed.

Indeed, anxious to deflect blame, the GMD government itself fell back upon this by then popular line of argument when, in 1936, it launched a special training program for college graduates in government service. The education system was blamed for the mismatch between its output and the needs of the economy. College graduates were left unemployed, while jobs went begging for lack of qualified people. And the government also blamed, along with the education system its intellectuals had created, the socially detached elitist pretensions of the young graduates that system was turning out.[49]

Hence, it is not sufficient to draw the line of distinction between reform-minded intellectuals outside the government bureaucracy and those within, although such "ideal types" undoubtedly existed in both places. The contradictions also persisted even within the former group, and the critique had adherents among those most firmly committed to the new learning. Some, like Tao Xingzhi and Liang Shuming, were aware of and consciously torn by the inability to reconcile in practice their conflicting interests and commitments. Others did not even trouble to acknowledge the contradictions within themselves, much less seek solutions for them.

What had emerged in pre-1949 China, then, was not simply a conflict between left and right or tradition and modernity or politicized amateurs and academic professionals or locally educated versus returned students. The conflict cut across all those dimensions and persisted as a highly ambivalent controversy among modernizing intellectuals over the flawed structure of the education system they had created but were incapable of correcting. This critique of China's education system seemed to draw its strength from the diverse inclinations of those contributing to it, and those inclinations in turn thrived upon the material and social contradictions that came with the early stages of modernization.

Exploiting further the benefits of hindsight and the intervening lessons of educational development, additional points can be drawn from the early Chinese experience. These derive especially from the "dependency" principle in both its non-Marxist and neo-Marxist formulations. Concerning the former, it is ironic, given China's importance to the international development community in the 1970s, that the country's earlier experience remained largely unknown. China therefore contributed nothing to the revival of the development

---

[49] Ibid., p. 374.

enterprise in the 1950s. It was as though the traumatic events of the mid-20th century – another world war, Third World independence movements, and the containment of communism – had wiped the slate clean, leaving everything to be recalibrated with the promise of a new beginning. Had the records of the 1920s been more carefully examined, they might at least have served to moderate the midcentury euphoria surrounding education as a solvent for all problems.

According to the assumptions of China's New Culture devotees in the late 1910s (which they skillfully nurtured by invoking the authority of John Dewey), intellectual, cultural, and educational reforms were prerequisites for effective political change. Like Dewey, these Chinese intellectuals assumed that culture and education would play a key role in society's overall regeneration.[50] And they willingly attached themselves to successive foreign cultural models firm in the belief that the right formula would guarantee China's salvation.

Adherents soon went their separate ways over this issue as the political realities of China in the 1920s wreaked havoc with their idealistic assumptions. Even those who tried to keep the faith could survive only by adjusting and compromising after every setback. For example, many of the rural reconstruction projects retained the earlier ideal of using education as the key to overall reform. But they also implicitly acknowledged that the promise of education could not be realized without simultaneous social and economic reforms of the kind that could only be attempted in the relative safety of experimental model districts. And even then, the lines of protection drawn around them were never adequate. Not only could cultural reform not change politics; it could not even succeed in its own sphere without political protection and the risk of co-optation that entailed.

Dewey himself ultimately acknowledged the limitations of his earlier ideals after a trip to the Soviet Union in 1928. He sympathized with socialist aims but opposed essential features of Maxism–Leninism. Nevertheless, Dewey admitted that if followed to their logical conclusion, the lessons he saw in Soviet education would turn upside down his earlier assumptions about the primacy of educational reform. He was referring especially to the aim of linking study with social life and "the fact that for the first time in history there is an educational system officially organized on the basis of this principle." He concluded that the socialist economic revolution had made the achievement possible by placing the authority of the state behind it.[51]

---

[50] Dewey articulated his beliefs during his China visit (e.g., "The Cultural Heritage and Social Reconstruction," in *John Dewey: Lectures in China*, pp. 210–216).

[51] *John Dewey's Impressions of Soviet Russia and the Revolutionary World: Mexico – China – Turkey, 1929* (New York: Bureau of Publications, Teachers College, Columbia University, 1964), pp. 88–89, 99.

Seemingly everywhere, the 20th century's early promises had not material-ized. Reformers had to adjust their ideals accordingly as education proved more dependent on the forces surrounding it than independently capable of changing them. And in a sequence that would be repeated in the 1960s and 1970s, once education was discredited as an independent force for social change, many of its champions were drawn instead to socialist alternatives.

Yet the later, neo-Marxist formulation seemed only marginally more suc-cessful in its ability to explain, retrospectively, China's early educational devel-opment. To reiterate, according to that formulation, schools in Third World countries existed in a relationship of cultural and economic dependency vis-à-vis the dominant Western nations; and a similar dependency relationship existed internally between a country's school system and the structures of economic and political power.

China, however, did not fit exactly into the requisite Third World category of "peripheral capitalist country," perhaps because it was never more than "semicolonial" to begin with. Chinese sovereignty over Chinese territory was only compromised, not lost. Nor was its economy directly dependent on that of any other country, despite its vulnerability and the existence of foreign-dominated treaty ports on Chinese soil. Cultural dependency existed, to be sure, but it was not directly tied to the political economies of the metropolitan powers. China's cultural dependency was instead always complicated by the peculiar circumstances of its history, producing a pattern of resistance, attrac-tion, and reaction that was unique even if as "dysfunctional" as any conven-tional colonial relationship.

Western learning was initially resisted as part of the unwelcome foreign intrusion. China's ruling educated class clung self-confidently to its traditional heritage close to forty years longer than did Japan. The Chinese then accepted foreign learning on the assumption that it was a prerequisite for overcoming China's weaknesses. But the ensuing intellectual and cultural dependency never rested easily on the shoulders of China's educated elite and even less so on those of anyone else. Released finally from the constraints of tradition, many embraced the Western world to become what they assumed to be "modern" intellectuals. Yet no sooner had the demands for a completely "new culture" inspired by Western models begun to rise than the reappraisal commenced.

The growth of Marxism, the most self-critical of all Western perspectives, dates from this period. It entered China as a foreign import, but its adherents soon learned that their survival would depend on their blending into that most Chinese of environments, the countryside. The educational history we have reviewed here indicated that the Western-educated intellectuals from at least the mid-1910s onward were placed on the defensive over their inclinations to import foreign learning "mechanically" and "slavishly" without adapting it to the Chinese environment. They continued to do just that, of course, since they believed it was the way to China's salvation. But sensitivities were such that they rarely failed at least to pay lip service to the opposition, which was always present in one form or another – inevitably producing a complex self-critical reaction.

Thus, the new concept of nationalism may have been a foreign import redefining the Middle Kingdom in modern Western terms, but its Chinese roots drew strength from the old conservative resistance and ongoing resentment against foreign political intrusion. Similarly, the new Western learning advocated popular institutions, one of which was universal mass education. It may only have been because his professor, Paul Monroe, so admonished that Guo Bingwen promoted the practical application of learning in 1914; or because James Yen worked in France as the representative of a foreign organization that he discovered the humanity in Chinese coolies in 1917; or because Li Dazhao had discovered Russian populism through the October Revolution that he advocated the unity of intellectuals and peasants in 1919; or because Mao had become a Marxist that he could appreciate the peasants' demands in 1925. But once those discoveries were made, they tied increasing numbers of Western-educated Chinese to new commitments that were as firmly rooted in Chinese soil as the new nationalism itself.

In this manner, Western learning both created a relationship of cultural dependency with the West and at the same time sowed the seeds of resistance to it. The result was a volatile combination of dependence, insecurity, and resentment – articulated by individuals, reflected in public policy, and evident in foreign cultural relations – that can still be seen even as the 20th century nears its end. This contradiction persisted apparently because China's intellectual leaders, having finally accepted the need to reconstruct China on modern lines, could not agree on how to do so. They could not agree upon a new pattern of ideas and institutions that would effectively combine the varying commitments they had acquired along the way. Uncertain over how to proceed, they tried to guarantee success by emulating the most successful example. Accordingly, they rushed to embrace one dominant foreign model after another, as reflected in the repeated reorganizations of the education system to accommodate, as they said, "changing world trends."

Yet despite overt initial enthusiasm, the copies were always selective and "superficial." And their promoters invariably retreated in a rush of mutual recrimination when world trends shifted or when the superimposed copy began to create more problems than it solved. In this manner, a pattern of attraction to and reaction against foreign models developed during the early decades of the century. Repetitive and extravagantly wasteful in terms of time, talent, and material resources, this pattern would then continue indefinitely in the absence of a successful breakthrough to a new consensus capable of replacing that lost with the collapse of the old inherited order.

For their part, foreigners, with differing mixes of altruism and self-interest, did try to promote dependency. But inevitably, the results were as ambivalent for them as for the Chinese. Life was never easy for the Christian missionary enterprise and it bore the brunt of the anti-imperialist upsurge during the 1920s. There were few sectors of Chinese public opinion which did not approve of the new GMD government's regulations bringing all missionary and private schools under Chinese government control and transferring leadership of foreign schools to Chinese churches and management bodies.[52] Diplomatic maneuverings to win influence in China by educating its students were deliberately pursued by the U.S., Japan, Great Britain, and France, in an exercise bearing great resemblance to that undertaken by many countries in the post-Mao era.[53] But dependency was not necessarily the other side of the foreign influence coin, particularly when so many foreign powers were competing so keenly for the privilege. Given the climate of opinion among the Chinese themselves, such competition suggested relationships productive more of compromised interests, mutual co-optation, and lost causes than of straightforward domination and dependency.

The revisionist insights of the 1970s require fewer qualifications when applied internally. Education policy did correspond to the structures of political and economic power, albeit within the particular transitional context of postimperial China. Initially, the dominant sector was neither an industrializing bourgeoisie nor a nascent middle class but the official–scholar–gentry establishment. Its goals were statist, promoted on that basis by a few government officials, and accepted as such by the educated elite when they finally embraced the new learning. But promoters of the new education system did not at first appreciate the extent to which that system and all the actors within it were prisoners of the larger society and its traditions.

This is not to suggest that the society and its authority structures remained static. On the contrary, significant changes were under way. The unified hierarchy of political power and learning had been broken; mastery of the latter no longer guaranteed a monopoly over the former. As a consequence, after 1911, military men began "usurping" Chinese government – a frequent lament of intellectuals in the China of warlords and Chiang Kai-shek's GMD.

---

[52] Hsiao, *History of Modern Education in China*, pp. 119–120; Kenneth Scott Latourette, *A History of Christian Missions in China* (Taipei: Ch'eng-wen Publishing Co., 1966), pp. 811–822; Ping Wen Kuo, *The Chinese System of Public Education*, pp. 136–140; Djung, *A History of Democratic Education in Modern China*, pp. 160–183; Garrett, *Social Reformers in Urban China*, pp. 164–183.
[53] On the earlier exercise, see Keenan, *The Dewey Experiment in China*, pp. 15–18, 96–98; Peter Buck, *American Science and Modern China*, pp. 88–90 and passim.

Meanwhile, education was being relegated to the less exalted status it occupied in Western countries, in a process largely unanticipated by early Chinese modernizers. Rather, they assumed that just as Confucian learning both epitomized the state and controlled access to the most prestigious occupations, so Western learning would guarantee both national and personal wealth and power. In reality, Western learning did neither, at least not in the manner anticipated. But decisions based on those assumptions continued to influence the new education for decades. Its clientele retained traditional attitudes toward education, regarding it as the equivalent of the old elite route to scholar–official status – hence the emphasis on building a college-preparatory system with a literary liberal arts orientation and career aspirations to match.

The products of the new learning, with their Ph.D.'s in political science and education, may therefore have been new-style intellectuals in the sense that their Western learning had prepared them for specialized occupations in the modern sector. And their demands for academic independence from the chaos of warlord politics may have represented the new differentiations of modernity. But these combined easily with the traditional scholar's assumptions about the nature of authority, the right to rule, and the functions of learning. Certainly, these men were not yet wholly modern professionals, as reflected in their interests and career aspirations, which persisted in many ways unchanged.

Industrialization remained in its infancy during the early decades of the 20th century and could not exert influence sufficient to break these inherited assumptions and aspirations. Vocational and practical training was so alien to this academic milieu that it could not survive even in the American-compromise comprehensive school format. The separate vocational school seemed the only solution, and Huang Yanpei exploited both his old and his new scholarly credentials to win support from his Jiangsu industrialist friends for this alternative. But it had little chance of success in the Chinese setting of that time.

Formal schooling continued to mark the route upward, and all who acquired such schooling hoped to use it toward that end. A secondary level education became the modern equivalent of elevation to *shengyuan* status under the old regime, allowing the recipient to move into the transitional, expectant status between commoner and elite. Neither the modernizing economic sector nor the changing structure of political power was yet strong enough to force major changes in old assumptions about the functions of learning.

Viewed from this perspective, traditional/transitional Chinese society had co-opted Western education. In the process, modern intellectuals were being projected into a potentially vulnerable position. Having lost their traditional status at the top of the social hierarchy, they were nevertheless using the new schools to retain and reproduce the old elite pretensions, even as the controversies surrounding their new learning intensified.

Thus, perhaps the most significant feature of the new education was not its discordant mix of old and new but the impetus for more radical change being generated within. This dynamic could be seen in the critical consensus that, by the 1930s, dominated all assessments of the education system. The critique was rooted in a growing awareness of the need for education that more appropriately reflected the contemporary condition and future aspirations of Chinese society. The demand was for an education system that would be technologically appropriate yet modern in form and content, but also China centered and mass based.

6

Early communist alternatives:
Jiangxi and Yan'an

Historians have yet to do justice to the GMD–CCP competition for hearts and minds in Jiangxi during the 1930s. The GMD government's rural reconstruction program there was clearly inspired by communist success in exploiting the widely perceived "agrarian crisis" to create CCP-led enclaves in Jiangxi and in many other provinces as well. Observers also concluded that the GMD's failure was the obverse of the CCP's success in overturning the status quo. Dispossessed local elites returning after the communist retreat in 1934 were more interested in restoring the old order than implementing idealistic schemes for rural regeneration. Yet the CCP was evidently not all that successful either. And if we accept at face value the implications of Mao's contemporary "rich-peasant line," at least one reason for the mixed record was disruption caused by excesses in overturning the status quo!

The CCP nevertheless did begin to reverse the "natural" order of communist revolution after Chiang Kai-shek ended his marriage of convenience with the communists in 1927 and destroyed their urban organization. Largest and most stable of the CCP's new rural base areas was that created by Mao and others in southern Jiangxi. But Mao's power eroded after national Party leaders began taking refuge in the region, about the same time a Chinese Soviet Republic was proclaimed there in 1931. Chiang Kai-shek's successive "bandit suppression campaigns" finally drove the communists from this base area in 1934.[1]

During the Soviet Republic's brief existence, agrarian revolution or land reform and military survival were the main preoccupations. Civilian administration in general and education in particular were not high on the list of

[1] The territory included all or part of at least 29 counties located on either side of the Jiangxi–Fujian border and in adjoining northern Guangdong as well. The population of the region is usually given as about 3 million. E.g., Trygve Lotveit, *Chinese Communism, 1931–1934: Experience in Civil Government*, Scandinavian Institute of Asian Studies, Monograph Series, no. 16 (1973), pp. 8–9, 156; Stuart Schram, *Mao Tse-tung* (Baltimore: Penguin Books, 1966), chaps. 6–7; Stephen C. Averill, "Party, Society, and Local Elite in the Jiangxi Communist Movement," *Journal of Asian Studies*, vol. 46, no. 2 (May 1987), pp. 279–303. For other well-known works on or containing accounts of the Jiangxi soviet period of CCP history, see the Select Bibliography for works by Otto Braun, Hsiao Tso-liang, Harold Isaacs, Ilpyong Kim, Warren Kuo, John Rue, Edgar Snow, and Derek Waller.

priorities. This was, however, the first area of any size to be ruled by a CCP-led government, and erstwhile education reformer Mao Zedong served as its chief administrator, or chairman of the Council of People's Commissars (the then standard translation for Zhongyang renmin weiyuanhui), from 1931 to early 1934. Most of the data on actual education work in Jiangxi comes from reports and investigations attributed to him. Two main concerns in this record link communist rule in southern Jiangxi with contemporary education reform efforts elsewhere: ambivalence toward intellectuals and commitment to rural mass education. Mao would, of course, never again approach the subject as an eclectic education reformer. His perspective was now that of a communist policymaker in assuming the CCP's revolutionary power as a precondition for educational development. The Jiangxi experience thus illustrates some preliminary CCP-sponsored solutions and suggests in turn some preliminary reasons for their failure.

Jiangxi: intellectuals as casualties of class warfare

Mao's so-called rich-peasant line refers to his differences with national Party leaders over land reform. The nature of these power relationships is a complicated story and has been the subject of many scholarly treatises.[2] But whatever Mao's actual role and ex post facto interpretations thereof, education concerns were involved in the argument and reflected one dilemma of educational development peculiar to communist rule. The communist solution, as Dewey finally realized, contained the ingredient of political will necessary to make genuine societywide reform possible. But the communist solution also created conditions which undermined that same goal. This was especially true at the outset when the revolutionary imperative decreed that existing class and power structures had to be overthrown, and especially so in China, where the "educated class" had until so recently been the "ruling class" as well.

The CCP also had its own variation of the returned-student problem. In this case it entailed not just voluntary infatuation with foreign models but direct political ties to the Communist International in Moscow. The CCP's central leadership passed at this time into the hands of the returned-students group, or the 28 Bolsheviks as they were also called. They had been studying in Moscow at Sun Yat-sen University, had sided with Stalin against Trotsky, had returned to China in 1930, and soon took control of the CCP's central apparatus, committed to following the line laid down by the Communist International. Shortly after that, they began moving from Shanghai to Jiangxi. What remains unclear is the relative influence of Moscow, the returned-students group, and Mao, respectively, over Jiangxi soviet affairs. For our purposes here, however,

---

[2] Most voluminous are those of Hsiao Tso-liang (see Select Bibliography); see also works by authors cited in n. 1, above.

the basic facts about which there is more or less general agreement should suffice.

All the participants – Moscow, other CCP leaders, and Mao – were in a relatively radical phase. But among them, Mao eventually emerged as the most moderate. Stalin, having recently vanquished Trotsky, had then turned against his "rightist" opposition. An anti-kulak (rich peasant) line began to dominate the Soviet Union's rural life from 1928, as the New Economic Policy (NEP) gave way to collectivization. Stalin was also in an anti-intellectual mood and was propelling his party through an episode which seems to have been the precursor of Mao's Cultural Revolution 40 years later.[3]

After the returned students began exerting their influence in Jiangxi, they promoted a radical new land reform law, promulgated by the first national soviet congress in November 1931. All landlords were to be totally expropriated without compensation. Farm laborers as well as poor and middle peasants were the beneficiaries and were to receive equal allotments of land and shares of other confiscated movable and immovable properties. Rich peasants also were to be expropriated, but in the subsequent redistribution they were to receive lesser shares of poor-quality land.[4]

Mao was subsequently accused of trying to moderate the impact of expropriation. Especially at issue was his "Decision on Some Problems in the Land Struggle," adopted by the council on 10 October 1933. With this document, he had tried to establish more precise (and less radical) guidelines for investigating land reform than had applied when the effort was at its height. His October decision had then allegedly been used by landlords and rich peasants to demand reversals of judgments made against them during the high tide of land investigation and led to a revival of their influence as well. Mao's "rich peasant line" was soon repudiated, however, and a more radical orientation on the land and class questions was resumed. He was replaced as chairman of the Council of People's Commissars by a member of the returned-students group, and they dominated all organizational power centers within the central soviet district for the remaining few months of its existence.

The section devoted specifically to intellectuals in his October 1933 decision reflected the dilemma of trying to carry out class warfare and lay the foundations for a "postrevolutionary" civilian administration at the same time. The immediate question was how to destroy the power of the classes to which most intellectuals belonged while simultaneously using them to build a system of mass education. Mao's October 1933 decision not only defined intellectuals in

---

[3] On the similarities between the Soviet Union in the late 1920s and China's Cultural Revolution 40 years later, see chap. 11, below.
[4] The various land reform laws and documents from the Jiangxi period are translated in Hsiao Tso-liang, *The Land Revolution in China, 1930–1934: A Study of Documents* (Seattle: University of Washington Press, 1969).

conventional Marxist terms, thereby separating them from automatic identification with the exploiting economic classes, but also ordered that intellectuals be hired and protected regardless of their class origins. The relevant points of the decision were as follows:

(1) Intellectuals did not make up a separate classification; their socioeconomic status depended on the class to which they belonged and not their occupations. In other words, intellectuals who came from landlord families were classed as landlords; but if they belonged to middle peasant families, they were still middle peasants.

(2) So long as they obeyed the soviet's laws, all intellectuals from landlord and capitalist families should be welcomed to work in its service.

(3) When intellectuals worked as teachers, editors, journalists, office clerks, writers, artists, or in any other nonexploiting occupation, they should be regarded as performing mental labor and protected under soviet law.

Elaborating these points, Mao noted that many places had sent their intellectuals away without cause, which was not correct. Using intellectuals of landlord and capitalist origins was beneficial for revolutionary policies, and their problems of livelihood should be properly resolved when they worked in the service of the soviet. On class designations, the decision noted, not only was it incorrect to give intellectuals an independent status. "Even more incorrect" was the practice of treating those peasant youths who had studied in school and managed to graduate as "some kind of bad-status elements."[5] The irony of this last was that the Soviet Republic was theoretically a "worker–peasant democratic dictatorship," with all educational institutions "in the hands of the worker–peasant laboring masses." The soviet constitution did not even guarantee an education to everyone. Rather, it specified that the right to an education would be guaranteed to the "worker–peasant laboring masses." Since they were the basis of the new society, their children enjoyed preferential access to education or "all possible political and material assistance."[6] This meant that they were supposed to be able to attend school free of charge and the schools might provide them with free books and supplies. It also meant that middle- and higher-level schools were supposed to give preference in enrollment to the children of workers and peasants.

Yet the identification between learning and elite status was so strong that radical Party cadres responsible for implementing the class line evidently

[5] "Guanyu tudi douzhengzhong yixie wenti de jueding" (Decision on Some Problems in the Land Struggle), 10 Oct. 1933, in *Mao Zedong ji*, 4:56–57.
[6] "Zhonghua suweiai gongheguo xianfa dagang" (Outline Constitution of the Chinese Soviet Republic), passed by the First National Representative Congress of the Chinese Soviet Republic, 7 Nov. 1931, reprinted in *Zhonghua suweiai gongheguo falu wenjian xuanbian* (Compilation of Legal Documents from the Chinese Soviet Republic), ed. the Xiamen University Law Department and Fujian Provincial Archives (Nanchang: Jiangxi renmin chubanshe, 1984), pp. 6–9.

retained the non-Marxist view of intellectuals per se as part of the ruling class. As soon as peasants began benefiting from the region's education system, the inclination was to place them automatically on the enemy side of the ledger, thereby defeating one of the regime's basic goals, which was to extend opportunities for education to those who had not previously enjoyed them. After Mao's demotion, the more radical course was resumed. A resolution issued in March 1934, with the approval of the central education commissariat, reflected that inclination, declaring that "the viewpoint of using landlord and rich peasant intellectuals unconditionally . . . must be most vigorously attacked."[7]

Understandable, then, was Mao's diatribe against the education department in a directive issued on 15 September 1933, when his conflict with the returned-students group was sharpening. Chiang Kai-shek's fifth and ultimately successful annihilation campaign was also just beginning, and Mao criticized those who allowed education work to fall behind as a result. Some comrades did not understand the importance of education for the war effort; others felt that education could not be pursued under wartime conditions. The situation, declared Mao, "absolutely must not be allowed to continue." Because of it, no clear education policy had been formulated, and the central education department had not yet created a system which could provide universal public schooling.

A system of universal mass education (for children) had to be created, continued the directive. An anti-illiteracy movement (for adults) had to be started immediately. Social education had to be developed as well, with drama groups, clubs, and libraries. Schools for teachers and cadres had to be established in order to train the necessary personnel. As for their class origins, the aim should be to train a large group of workers and peasants to become educators. But additionally, "some bourgeois intellectuals and experts who are enthusiastic in wanting to serve the soviet must also be used to participate in education work."[8]

---

7 "Jiangxisheng diyici jiaoyu huiyi de jueyian" (Resolution of the First Education Conference of Jiangxi Province), issued with the approval of the Central People's Commissariat of Education, Mar. 1934, reprinted in Chen Yuanhui, Qu Xingui, Zou Guangwei, eds., *Laojiefangqu jiaoyu ziliao: tudi geming zhanzheng shiqi* (Materials on Education in the Old Liberated Areas: The Period of the Agrarian Revolutionary War) (Beijing: Jiaoyu kexue chubanshe, 1981), 1:82.

8 "Guanyu jiaoyu gongzuo" (On Education Work), Zhongyang renmin weiyuanhui xunling di shiqi hao (Council of People's Commissars Directive Number 17), 15 Sept. 1933, in *Mao Zedong ji*, 4:29–31. This directive was apparently laying down guidelines for an education conference in October, which announced similar objectives. See "Muqian jiaoyu gongzuo de renwu de jueyian" (Resolution on the Present Tasks of Education Work), passed by the Central Culture and Education Construction Conference, 20 Oct. 1933, reprinted in Chen Yuanhui et al., *Laojiefangqu jiaoyu ziliao*, 1:60–62. The main conference report and summary were given by Communist Youth League Secretary Kai Feng (also known as He Kaifeng and He Kequan), one of the USSR-trained returned students who dominated leadership during the final year of the soviet's existence. But his reports also reiterate the themes of Mao's September statement. Kai Feng's two reports are reprinted in Chen Yuanhui et. al., *Laojiefangqu jiaoyu ziliao*, 1:39–59, and translated in *Chinese Education*, vol. 6, no. 3 (fall 1973), pp. 5–32.

The source of his evident frustration was reflected in the statistics Mao presented to the Second National Soviet Congress a few months later in January 1934. Whatever their accuracy, the figures suggested the uneven nature of the achievement. Mao's statistics claimed to cover over 2,930 *xiang* (townships) in the three-province border region of Jiangxi, Fujian, and Guangdong. At this time, the *xiang* was the basic-level administrative unit in the region. Rules stipulated that a *xiang* should contain from two to five villages and have a population of 1,000–2,000.[9]

Mao claimed there were 3,052 elementary schools (or Lenin primary schools as they were called), with a total of about 90,000 students. In addition, there were 6,462 night schools, with 94,500 students; and 32,300 literacy groups serving another 155,000 people. On the average, every township had an elementary school, and every village a night school or at least a literacy class. But of the 90,000 elementary school students, some 12,800 were from only one county, Xingguo. Xingguo was the soviet district's model county, and Mao himself had investigated conditions there at least twice. Of 20,969 school-age children (12,076 boys and 8,893 girls), only about 60 percent were enrolled (8,825 boys, 3,981 girls).[10]

The problem of educational financing also remained unsolved in the soviet district. Its schools rested on the same unstable foundations as those elsewhere. In principle, the local governments were supposed to guarantee, to the greatest extent possible, the expenditures necessary to maintain schools. But in practice, they relied heavily on the direct support of villagers themselves. This was an ad hoc affair, and no fixed or reliable formula appears to have been found.

One 1932 document lamented the lack of everything necessary to run the Lenin primary schools properly, including teachers, inspectors, books, materials, equipment, and especially funds. Some of the comrades doing education work could read only a few words. Others were *sishu* teachers who knew only the traditional curriculum and nothing of politics, science, or modern education. As for finances, because the soviet government itself had no fixed income,

[9] Lotveit, *Chinese Communism*, pp. 15–16.
[10] "Zhonghua suweiai gongheguo zhongyang zhixing weiyuanhui yu renmin weiyuanhui dui dierci quanguo suweiai daibiao dahui de baogao" (Report of the Chinese Soviet Republic's Central Executive Committee and the Council of People's Commissars to the Second National Soviet Representatives Congress), 24–25 Jan. 1934, in *Mao Zedong ji*, 4:261–264. These remain the standard education statistics for the Jiangxi soviet district. E.g., Lai Zhikui, "Guanyu suqu jiaoyu yanjiu zhong de jige lilun wenti" (Some Theoretical Problems in Research on Education in the Soviet District), *Jiaoyu yanjiu* (Education Research) (Oct. 1984), p. 59. Mao's two investigation reports from Xingguo County are "Zhanggang xiang diaocha" (Investigation of Zhanggang Township), 15 Dec. 1933, in *Mao Zedong ji*, 4:125–174; "Xingguo diaocha" (An Investigation of Xingguo), 26 Jan. 1931, in *Mao Zedong ji*, 2:185–252. For a similar report on two other townships in southwestern Fujian, see "Caixi xiang diaocha" (An Investigation of Townships in Caixi), 1933, in *Mao Zedong ji*, 4:175–198. All the investigation reports contained data on education.

there was as yet no unified budget or financial system. Still, more money could have been made available were it not for the prevailing tendency to disregard education. In any case, even the basic standard of providing each teacher with three dollars per month for food could not always be guaranteed. Naturally, few people wanted to become teachers when conditions were so spartan.[11]

Under the circumstances, however, the statistical achievement was probably not all that bad. The League of Nations team in 1931 cited an overall elementary school enrollment figure of 7.2 percent of the age-group for Jiangxi Province as a whole, among the lowest in the country and well below the estimated national average of 22 precent.[12] The team was using a then standard formula calculating 13 percent of the total population as constituting the elementary school age-group (6–11 years of age). The 90,000 enrollment figure within a total population of some 3 million suggested that the soviet district had at least achieved close to the national average proportion of the age-group in elementary school.

Foremost among the lessons for educational development from Jiangxi, however, was the paradox that quickly surrounded the communist solution. And whatever his motives at the time, that paradox was best illustrated by Mao himself. In his 1927 report on the Hunan peasant movement, Mao had presented the standard revolutionary rationale: mass education could develop only after local landlords and power holders were overthrown, leaving peasants free to run their own schools. He repeated himself at the height of the land investigation movement in June 1933, declaring the mobilization of people for that movement to be a prerequisite for cultural construction.[13]

The hitch in this logic, of course, was that illiteracy tended to be a condition of the impoverished masses and literacy a resource of the propertied elite. The land and valuables of the latter could be divided up and redistributed to the poor, as was done during land reform. Intellectual resources, however, could not be separated from their owners in quite the same way. Yet Mao and the CCP continued to declare their commitment to class warfare and to the proposition that rural mass education could only be developed fully after the power of the dominant class had been broken.

That the CCP's professed willingness to seek friends among the intellectuals should always be compromised in practice was thus not so much unintended as

[11] "Jiangxisheng gongnong diyici daibiao dahui wenhua jiaoyu gongzuo jueyi" (Resolution on Culture and Education Work by the First Workers and Peasants Representatives Conference for Jiangxi Province), May 1932, reprinted in *Zhongyang geming genjudi shiliao xuanbian* (A Selection of Historical Materials on the Central Revolutionary Base), comp. and ed. Jiangxi Provincial Archives and the Party History Teaching and Research Office of the Party School of the Jiangxi Provincial CCP Committee (Nanchang: Jiangxi renmin chubanshe, 1982), 3:582–586.
[12] League of Nations report, pp. 78–79.
[13] "Baxian quyishang suweiai fuze renyuan chatian yundong dahui suo tongguo de jielun" (Conclusion Passed by the Land Investigation Conference of Responsible Soviet Personnel from the District Level and above of Eight Counties), 21 June 1933, in *Mao Zedong ji*, 3:262.

unavoidable. The self-critical undercurrent that marked the intellectuals' descent from traditional ruling elite to modern intellectual at first merged easily with the Party's developing scenario of class warfare and was then overwhelmed by it. Inevitably, Chinese intellectuals by reason of their past status and present associations would become casualties of the CCP's struggles against the existing power structure. Within that revolutionary scenario, modernizing intellectuals inhabited their own sort of border region, along the demarcation line between the propertied classes, whose surplus wealth was necessary to educate them, and the masses, who could not rise above their untutored state without them. This dilemma also pointed to the cost of solving on Marxist terms the equity–efficiency conundrum that so bedeviled Western development experts.

In 1926 the young Mao, obviously still more of an intellectual than a Marxist revolutionary, thought he had found a way around the dilemma when he tried his hand at analyzing China's class structure. He fixed upon a three-level solution: enemies, friends, and people in between, with intellectuals scattered throughout. Enemies included warlords, big landlords, and "reactionaries within the intellectual class." "True friends" included the petty bourgeoisie and lower levels of the same intellectual class in which Mao placed secondary school students, schoolteachers, clerks, office functionaries, and small lawyers. In between was the middle bourgeoisie, vacillating and unreliable as allies of the proletariat. In this category also were national capitalists, bankers, businessmen, and "many higher-level intellectual elements." The last included the trained personnel who ran enterprises for capitalists, most returned students, and most college teachers and students.[14]

So unorthodox was Mao's class analysis that later editions of this essay had to be substantially "revised."[15] Yet in Jiangxi, after he had become more of a Marxist and more of a revolutionary, Mao became entangled in the dilemma again, and he seems to have tried to bend the rules of class struggle in order to compromise with rich peasants and intellectuals. The CCP's Jiangxi experience appears retrospectively, then, as a prelude for many conflicts to come. The self-critical currents of the 1920s and 1930s would be pushed to ever higher degrees of intensity as they merged with the perceived necessity of class conflict. And despite the early insights Mao contributed to it, the ensuing contradiction – with revolution as prerequisite for educational development and intellectuals as casualties of revolution – would never be resolved in his lifetime.

Not only did the CCP never find a solution for that most basic contradiction between revolution and systemic education reform, but it also never laid to rest

---

[14] "Zhongguo shehui ge jieji de fenxi" (An Analysis of Classes within Chinese Society), 1 Feb. 1926, in *Mao Zedong ji*, 1:161–174.
[15] See, e.g., *Selected Works of Mao Tse-tung* (Peking: Foreign Languages Press, 1965), 1:13–21; and extracts in Schram, *The Political Thought of Mao Tse-tung*, pp. 143–147.

one of the major issues contributing to the original 1920s backlash. Here, too, the Jiangxi experience served as a prelude, symbolized in the person of Qu Qiubai, who spent only a few months in the region.

Qu had occupied the post of commissar for education and culture in absentia for more than two years while Mao's old teacher from Changsha, Xu Teli, served as acting head of the department. Schooled in the Chinese classical tradition, Qu was a college student in Beijing majoring in Russian literature at the time of the May Fourth demonstrations. His political career began when he led fellow students from his institute into the streets at that time. But he remained essentially a literary man, and his milieu was the Shanghai world of letters. Qu had headed the CCP briefly during the disastrous autumn of 1927. After returning from Moscow in 1930, where he had been called to answer for his errors, Qu was expelled from the ruling bodies of the CCP. When the new base was established in Jiangxi, he was named to head the education department but he remained in Shanghai. There he returned to the cultural world he had abandoned for politics years before. When it became too dangerous for him to stay longer, he finally made the move to Jiangxi, arriving in February 1934.[16]

Meanwhile, Qu had been theorizing eloquently in Shanghai about the need for a truly proletarian culture. During this period he lent his voice to the critical currents of the time, deploring the alienation of Westernized intellectuals from China's mass culture. In their haste to be modern, they had abandoned all that was traditional and conservative. They had come to be regarded as "foreigners" in their own land by ordinary people, among whom old values still held away. Leftist intellectuals, wrote Qu, should work toward a truly "proletarian May Fourth." As members of the educated elite, they should address themselves to the cultural concerns of the masses and ultimately nurture intellectuals among the poor and proletarians. But theorizing about such a culture and actually creating it were two different things. Qu seemed as much at a loss as any other Chinese intellectual might have been upon finding himself suddenly transplanted from Shanghai's cosmopolitan "foreign" environment into one that was not even proletarian but rural and totally "Chinese."

Of his brief Jiangxi experience, Qu wrote that the region was culturally very backward, "like a sheet of blank paper," and had only just started to run a few elementary and teacher training schools. He himself had no expertise in this area. "Concerning the special problems of educating the worker–peasant masses,

[16] For biographies of Qu Qiubai, see Paul G. Pickowicz, *Marxist Literary Thought in China: The Influence of Ch'ü Ch'iu-pai* (Berkeley: University of California Press, 1981); Benjamin I. Schwartz, *Chinese Communism and the Rise of Mao* (Cambridge: Harvard University Press, 1958), chap. 7; Sima Lu, *Qu Qiubai zhuan* (A Biography of Qu Qiubai) (Hong Kong: Zilian chubanshe, 1962); Chen Tiejian, *Qu Qiubai zhuan* (A Biography of Qu Qiubai) (Shanghai: Shanghai renmin chubanshe, 1986). Editions of his works include *Qu Qiubai wenji* (Qu Qiubai Collected Works), 6 vols. (Beijing: Renmin wenxue chubanshe, 1985–1988).

I really had no knowledge, and even my commonsense understanding was insufficient!" He ventured out once or twice to see how peasants' lives had changed after land reform but learned little. "From the first word, there was no 'common language' between us, and I was also very lazy, so nothing was achieved."[17]

Qu was, then, a typical product of China's early-20th-century intellectual establishment. Its members were well educated, internationalist in outlook and training, instinctively attracted to the political arena, and sensitive to the strains between themselves and the majority of their unlettered compatriots. Yet even the theoretical commitment to "proletarian" concerns that came with Communist Party leadership was not enough to alter the elitist urban orientation of university-educated intellectuals. The mundane details of policy and implementation bored them. Hence, if the concerns they expressed so eloquently were ever to be translated into reality, other kinds of people with different inclinations would have to oversee the task.

When it came time to break out of the GMD encirclement and begin the Long March retreat into the Northwest, Qu was deemed unfit for the adventure and left behind with the rear guard. He was a chronic tuberculosis sufferer and in poor health. Mao was just then recuperating from malaria, and, it was said, some wanted to use his health as a pretext for leaving him behind as well. Qu was captured while trying to make his way back to Shanghai and was executed by the GMD in 1935. Many other leftist intellectuals would follow the CCP to its new base, especially after the Japanese began occupying their cities in 1937. But in the Northwest, the contradictions between them and the Party, of which Qu Qiubai's association with the Jiangxi soviet was a symbolic precursor, would provoke the first of many major confrontations.

Yan'an, 1938–1942: mass education as a casualty of united front compromise

Only a few thousand of the 75,000–100,000 people who broke out of the GMD blockade in Jiangxi survived the epic Long March retreat that followed. Leaving Jiangxi in the autumn of 1934, they arrived one year and 6,000 miles later

---

[17] Qu Qiubai, "Duoyu de hua" (Superfluous Words), in *Qu Qiubai shige qianshi* (A Simple Selection of Qu Qiubai's Poems and Songs) (Nanning: Guangxi renmin chubanshe, 1981), pp. 267–268. Secondary and higher level education in the central soviet area was rudimentary. Such institutions were created essentially as cadre training schools concentrating on the most essential military, political, and propaganda work. Military training schools were the most numerous, and most prominent among them was the Red Army University. Institutions for civilian cadres included a number of vocational and teacher training schools plus the Soviet University, Marx Communism University, Higher-Level Teacher Training School, Gorky Drama School, and Central Agricultural School. See, e.g., Chen Yuanhui et al., *Laojiefangqu jiaoyu ziliao*, 1:168–247; Jane L. Price, *Cadres, Commanders, and Commissars: The Training of the Chinese Communist Leadership, 1920–45* (Boulder, Colo.: Westview Press, 1976), pp. 105–134.

in the Northwest. There, the survivors sought refuge in another of the communist base areas that had maintained a precarious existence during the early 1930s. Central Party and military leaders established their headquarters in this region located at the intersection of three provinces. Yan'an became the capital of the Shaanxi–Gansu–Ningxia (Shaan–Gan–Ning) Border Region in early 1937 and remained so throughout the war with Japan (1937–1945).

For the GMD, those years were a disaster. By 1945, its government and armies were so weakened that Japan's defeat came too late to save them. But for Mao and the CCP, the Japanese invasion ended in the opposite result. What the GMD lost, the CCP gained, until the power of the two was just exactly reversed. The Japanese invasion, Mao's theories about guerrilla warfare and his rural peasant focus, plus the ensuing mass-line policies for revolution and civilian administration were all exploited to maximum advantage. By 1945, he had emerged finally as paramount leader. Also by 1945, the CCP had built base areas across northern China from Yan'an to the sea. Their population was estimated at 95.5 million; communist military forces included 900,000 regular troops; and the CCP had 1.2 million members. As it became the nerve center of this expanding communist movement, Yan'an itself grew from a small town of about 3,000 people into a city of 100,000.[18] The communist-led base areas shrank markedly during the early 1940s Japanese offensives against them. But the Shaan–Gan–Ning region lay beyond the reach of the Japanese advance, providing the same sort of refuge for communist leaders that Chongqing in the Southwest did for the GMD.

Many years later, it would become politically fashionable in China to associate leadership differences over education policy and most everything else with an all-encompassing "two-line struggle" allegedly dating back to the CCP's Yan'an decade. In fact, a closer look at the educational history of that period does reveal a relevant dichotomy, although not in any such clear-cut form, with Mao on one side and his enemies on the other, as was later suggested. The historical record suggests instead that the same controversies existing in Chinese education circles generally at the time were reproduced in Yan'an as well after it became the CCP's capital in the mid-1930s.

As refugees in Yan'an, the new arrivals brought with them all their conflicting assumptions and commitments. These then formed the basis of "new" education policies devised for the communist-led border region governments and implemented most systematically in the relative security of the Shaan–Gan–Ning region. Inevitably, a "regular" school system began to develop and a critical backlash soon set in against it. The latter did not include the full force of the CCP's class warfare contradiction, because the Party had temporarily set aside its most revolutionary social aims in deference to the anti-Japanese united

---

[18] "China's Two Possible Destinies," 23 Apr. 1945, in *Selected Works of Mao Tse-tung*, 3:252; Roxane Witke, *Comrade Chiang Ch'ing* (Boston: Little, Brown and Co., 1977), p. 148.

front. But the CCP under Mao's leadership did turn the existing educational critique into a new policy line investing the old issues, briefly, with greater authority than they had ever been able to generate in the 1920s and 1930s.

The relevant dichotomy between the developing regular system and the backlash against it emerged with two sets of education reforms introduced between 1938–1942 and 1943–1947, respectively. Unlike earlier years when he had devoted some time and thought to specific education questions, Mao's name was not attached to any of the associated education decisions. Nevertheless, the second critical set of reforms derived from the CCP's rectification campaign of 1942–1944, which marked a crucial stage in his emergence as paramount leader. Mao dominated that campaign, and it was the vehicle whereby his ideas were finally elevated to the status of official Party orthodoxy. Thus, there is some substance in historical fact to the later claim of an antithetical "Maoist" line emerging at Yan'an, although any direct conflict between Mao and his opponents over education at that time remains to be verified.[19]

Initially in 1935–1936, prior to the declaration of a formal anti-Japanese united front with the GMD, policies continued much the same as in Jiangxi. Once the united front went into effect, land reform and overt class struggle were temporarily set aside for less divisive endeavors. Accordingly, Mao reminded everyone that "there must be no repetition of the incorrect attitude toward intellectuals that existed in many localities within our Party and in many army units during the agrarian revolution. The proletariat cannot produce its own intellectuals without the help of intellectuals already existing in society."[20] Otherwise, education policies continued more or less unchanged.

When Edgar Snow pioneered the journalists' trail to northern Shaanxi in 1936, he remarked on the practical shoestring approach. There were three basic forms of education: general, military, and social. All were organized to produce concrete results: elementary schooling for children, plus basic-level six-month training courses for teachers and cadres; similar two-level training for the military; plus literacy training and social activities for adults. All were infused with political and patriotic content, designed to raise popular consciousness along with the cultural level. Facilities were rudimentary, and the region seemed, to the Long March veterans Snow interviewed, even more backward than Jiangxi.

---

[19] This section is based largely on compilations of Yan'an era documents published or republished in the 1980s. These sources add much interesting new detail, but no startling revelations, to the educational history of the CCP base areas. See, e.g., Peter J. Seybolt, "The Yenan Revolution in Mass Education," *China Quarterly*, no. 48 (Oct.–Dec. 1971), pp. 641–669; Michael Lindsay, *Notes on Educational Problems in Communist China, 1941–47* (New York: Institute of Pacific Relations, 1950); Mark Selden, *The Yenan Way in Revolutionary China* (Cambridge: Harvard University Press, 1971), pp. 267–274.

[20] "Zhongyang guanyu xishou zhishifenzi de jueding" (The Party Center's Decision on Recruiting Intellectuals), 1 Dec. 1939, *Mao Zedong ji*, 7:93.

Xu Teli, who now headed the border region's education office in name as well as in fact, told Snow that in Jiangxi's model county, Xingguo, there were more than 300 elementary schools by the end of the Communists' tenure there, or about the same number as existed in all the northwest border region at the time of their interview.[21] But between 1935 and 1940, the number of schools grew 10-fold (see Table 6.1).[22] By 1940, however, such statistics were being publicized to bolster the argument that elementary schooling had been too precipitous in its growth. Perhaps it was merely coincidental that Xu Teli was transferred to other work in late 1937. According to education department documents, concern began to mount in 1938 over the low quality of education being provided.

Xu was succeeded as head of the department by Zhou Yang, another cultural luminary from Shanghai. What, if anything, Zhou had to do with the mundane details of elementary schooling has yet to be revealed. By the time this new concern for quality peaked in 1942, he too had been transferred to other work. But his arrival in the border region and its education department coincided with the onset of a "regularization" drive that would dominate border region educational development during the next four years.

Low standards became the chief preoccupation. The newly arrived educators now responsible for a burgeoning system diagnosed this defect as the result of setting up too many new schools too quickly in a rural "guerrilla" work style. Virtually all the elementary schools shown on Table 6.1 were only three-year junior-level schools. In 1940, just 1,547 students were studying at the senior elementary level, that is, in the fourth grade or above. Of the schools shown for that year, only 47 were complete schools. Of the 47, 30 were five-year schools, and 17 had a sixth year attached.[23]

[21] Edgar Snow, *Red Star Over China* (New York: Grove Press, 1961), pp. 251–257; Chen Zhiming, *Xu Teli zhuan* (Biography of Xu Teli) (Changsha: Hunan renmin chubanshe, 1984), pp. 117–119, 124; Xu Teli, "Xin de jiaoyu zhidu" (The New Education System), in Tian Jiagu, ed., *Kangzhan jiaoyu zai Shaanbei* (Education in North Shaanxi during the War of Resistance against Japan) (Hankou: Mingri chubanshe, 1938), pp. 13–16.

[22] The reference was to the Shaan–Gan–Ning region only. Between 1935 and 1940, this region grew in size from about 0.5 million people concentrated primarily in northern Shaanxi to between 1 and 2 million. After 1941, the region appears to have stabilized at about 1.5 million people. It was divided into five subregions with a total of 29 counties (*xian*). The latter were divided further into 266 districts (*qu*), containing 1,549 townships (*xiang*), the basic administrative unit in the countryside (Braun, *A Comintern Agent in China, 1932–1939*, p. 148; Warren Kuo, *Analytical History of the Chinese Communist Party*, 3:581–582; Selden, *The Yenan Way in Revolutionary China*, p. 152).

[23] "Zenyang gaijin bianqu de xiaoxue jiaoyu" (How to Improve Elementary Schooling in the Border Region), *Xin Zhonghua bao* (New China News), 22 Sept. 1940, reprinted in Gansusheng shehui kexue yuan lishi yanjiu suo, ed., *Shann–Gan–Ning geming genjudi shiliao xuanji* (Selection of Historical Materials from the Shaan–Gan–Ning Revolutionary Base) (Lanzhou: Gansu renmin chubanshe, 1985) (hereafter, cited as *Shaan–Gan–Ning xuanji*), 4:383; and "Bianqu sinianlai xuexiao jiaoyu menglie zengjia" (The Great Increase of Schooling in the Border Region during the Past Four Years), *Jiefang ribao* (Liberation Daily), 5 June 1941, reprinted in *Shaan–Gan–Ning xuanji*, 4:451.

Table 6.1. *Shaanxi–Gansu–Ningxia Border Region elementary schools and students, 1935–1946*

Date	Schools	Students
1935	120	2,000
Spring 1937	320	5,600
Fall 1937	545	10,396
Spring 1938	705	13,779
Fall 1938	733	15,348
Spring 1939	890	20,401
Fall 1939	883	22,089
Spring 1940	1,341	41,458
1942	1,198	40,366
1943	752	26,816
Oct. 1944	1,090 (574)	33,636
End of 1944	1,181	34,202
Spring semester, 1945	1,377 (1,057)	34,004 (16,797)
Fall semester, 1946	1,249 (940)	34,063 (15,373)

Note: Figures in parentheses are for *minban* schools (schools run by the local people with help from the local authorities; see the section below entitled Yan'an, 1943–1947: The Mass Line and Mass Education) and their students. These figures are included within the overall figures.

Sources: 1935–1940 – "Bianqu sinianlai xuexiao jiaoyu menglie zengjia" (The Great Increase of Schooling in the Border Region during the Past Four Years), *Jiefang ribao* (Liberation Daily), 5 June, 1941, in Gansusheng shehui kexue yuan lishi yanjiu suo, *Shaan–Gan–Ning geming genjudi shiliao xuanji*, 4: 451.

1942–1946 – Jiang Longji, "Guanyu minban gongzhu zhengce de chubu zongjie" (A Preliminary Summary of the People-Managed Public-Help Policy), n.d., mimeo, in Zhongyang jiaoyu kexue yanjiu suo, *Laojiefangqu jiaoyu ziliao*, 2:xia:376.

Initially, in 1938, the education department's concern about quality and standards remained within the context of existing quantitative growth. A directive on work for the second quarter of 1938 continued to promote expansion. But it warned that some schools – with one teacher and only four or five students using the old Confucian primers – were little different from *sishu*. The overall average was something less than 20 students per school. Improvement of quality must therefore be the core task for 1938. Everyone had to stop using "inappropriate" teaching materials and shift to the newly issued textbooks. To help ensure that all the department's instructions were heeded, reporting and inspection "systems" were being established throughout the border region.

The directive nevertheless cautioned that the method of merging schools to achieve larger student bodies should not be used, because in a rural setting it always meant sacrificing quantity for quality. "Past experience proves that, after merging, the number of schools declines and the number of students cannot increase." The sparseness of rural populations, primitive transport, and parents' fear of sending young children to school outside their village all combined to produce that result. Hence, "guarantee that existing elementary schools all remain open," ordered the education department. "Do not let even one close," and "do not let even one trained teacher stand outside education work."[24]

Quality concerns strengthened steadily thereafter. The 1938 midyear summary claimed goals almost completed on some points, but there was still a long way to go. Teachers were generally not adequately qualified either. Many had undergone only short-term training. They had learned a little about the new teaching methods, so they had at least given up the old-fashioned disciplinary style of "hitting and cursing." But many could not teach the new modern subjects such as arithmetic, and sweeping the school yard was the extent of the outside activities they could organize. Persevere in raising quality, admonished the education department. Establish schools "along the regularization [zheng-guihua] road." Overcome the "guerrilla work style." Run schools according to the rules and regulations being laid down.[25]

In 1939, a new set of border region elementary school regulations was issued to strengthen the 1937 curriculum.[26] In 1940, Zhou Yang's August report to a conference of county education cadres sustained the momentum.[27] According to a later account, the 1940 meeting also finally changed course on school mergers, the ultimate step in pursuit of quality and regularization. Each county was authorized to close 10 elementary schools and charged to run well one complete school (i.e., a school with both lower and upper levels). Schools were not to operate with fewer than 20–30 students. All schools were instructed to

---

[24] "Jiaoyuting guanyu gaijin yu fazhan xiaoxue de zhishi: siyuechu zhi liuyuedi gongzuo jihua" (Education Department Directive on Improving and Developing Elementary Schools: Work Plan for April through June), Xin Zhonghua bao, 25 Apr. 1938, reprinted in Shaan–Gan–Ning xuanji, 4:61–65.

[25] "Bianqu gexian bannianlai guofang jiaoyu gongzuo zongjie" (Summary of National Defense Education Work for Various Counties in the Border Region during the Past Half Year), Xin Zhonghua bao, 25 Aug. and 5 Sept. 1938, reprinted in Shaan–Gan–Ning xuanji, 4:89–92.

[26] The courses in the new curriculum at the junior elementary level were Chinese language, arithmetic, common knowledge, art, music, labor, physical education. At the senior elementary level they were Chinese language, arithmetic, politics, natural science, history, geography, art, music, labor, physical education. See Gao Qi, ed., Zhongguo xiandai jiaoyu shi (A History of China's Modern Education) (Beijing: Beijing shifan daxue chubanshe, 1985), p. 207; Wang Bingzhao et al., Jianming Zhongguo jiaoyu shi (A Concise History of Chinese Education) (Beijing: Beijing shifan daxue chubanshe, 1985), p. 417.

[27] "Sankezhang lianxi huiyi zongjie sannianlai de jiaoyu jingyan" (Third Section Chiefs Joint Conference Summarizing Education Experience during the Past Three Years), Xin Zhonghua bao, 12 Sept. 1940, reprinted in Shaan–Gan–Ning xuanji, 4:382. The "third section" within county-level governments at this time was responsible for education.

reorganize grades, classes, vacation times, etc., so as to operate according to uniform plans and schedules.[28]

Directives, instructions, and editorials followed one after another in similar vein throughout the 1940–1941 academic year. One article expanded on the two main problems in elementary schools: student "mobility" and the *sishu* work style of teachers. Precisely those features of traditional schooling idealized by the young Mao for his Self-Study University were now targeted for eradication as border region educators were called to put their house in order. Rules and regulations had to be fixed and followed as to when students might enter school and when they could leave it. This would put an end to students casually dropping in and out of school, sending a younger brother to sit in for an older one who had more work to do at home, and so on.

Concerning the *sishu* work style among teachers, most schools still had no curriculum charts, fixed class schedules, or any established sequence for presenting coursework. The teachers just carried on as they pleased, sometimes spending a whole day on Chinese lessons or reading a book and never organizing activities outside the classroom. Of the estimated 1,700 elementary school teachers in the border region, more than half were "very deficient" in their cultural level and political awareness. Among the prescribed antidotes: unified textbooks and teaching materials, fixed curriculum standards, and uniform teaching plans. Elementary education could not be improved unless all the "necessary systems" were firmly established.[29]

Improved quality also required the "concentration of strength to run complete elementary schools and create their central function of being model schools." In 1940–1941, the Shaan–Gan–Ning Border Region could boast 47 complete elementary schools and perhaps another 50 central (*zhongxin*) three-year junior elementary schools. Altogether these added up to about 100 model schools, although some of the five-year institutions were "very deficient" and

---

[28] Liu Songtao (Xin Ming), "Ban xiaoxue de liangtiao luxian" (The Two Lines for Running Elementary Schools), *Renmin jiaoyu* (People's Education), Beijing, June 1957, pp. 14–18, reprinted in *Laojiefangqu jiaoyu gongzuo jingyan pianduan* (Selections on Education Work Experience in the Old Liberated Areas) (Shanghai: Shanghai jiaoyu chubanshe, 1979), p. 185.

[29] Wen Jize, "Zenyang gaijin bianqu de xiaoxue jiaoyu" (How to Improve Elementary School Education in the Border Region), *Xin Zhonghua bao*, 22 Sept. 1940, reprinted in *Shaan–Gan–Ning xuanji*, 4:383–385. Taiwan historian Wang Jianmin (Wang Chien-min) later provided unsourced statistics which offered more detail about the qualifications of Shaan–Gan–Ning teachers. His 1940 statistics concerned 845 teachers in the 10 counties that made up the Yan'an subregion, or roughly half the total number of elementary school teachers in the border region at that time. Their credentials were as follows:

Teacher training school graduates:	213 (25%)
Senior elementary school graduates:	438 (52%)
Other:	194 (23%)

See Wang Jianmin, *Zhongguo gongchandang shigao* (History of the Chinese Communist Party) (Taibei: Zongyang wenwu gongyingshe, 1965), 3:273–274.

therefore unable to perform their "model functions" as guides and pacesetters in their districts.[30]

The education department therefore instructed county authorities to concentrate their resources on a few good schools. Their guiding principles should be "don't strive for more, but only for running well," and "running one school well will give impetus to 10." Counties were to select a few schools, already well established, allow them larger budgets than others, and assign them the best teachers and cadres. Specifically, counties were to concentrate this model building in the complete elementary schools, ensuring that they mobilized the fixed minimum number of students, that no more than one class or grade of students be assigned to each classroom (it was common in one-room village schools to combine grades), that furnishings be complete (in some schools, students had to bring their own stools), and that enough personnel be assigned to create "model elementary schools in fact as well as in name." A forerunner of the controversial key-point schools of later years, these central schools were following the same pattern formalized in the GMD government directives of the mid-1930s. Nor did the format escape controversy in 1941 apparently. Some people will say this is "just putting on a show," said Deputy Chief Ding Haochuan of the education department, and "so it is" – to show everyone how schools should be run.[31]

Finally, at the start of the 1941–1942 academic year, the education department announced the reorganization of elementary education. The fall conference of county-level education cadres focused that year on concrete methods for closing and merging schools while strengthening those remaining.[32] Coincidentally, both Bo Gu and Luo Fu, two of Mao's antagonists from the Bolshevik returned-students group, spoke at this conference. Also discussed at the meeting were the teaching methods of liberal reformer Tao Xingzhi, who enjoyed great prestige among Yan'an educators.[33] The Party newspaper recapitulated the effort to improve border region schooling. For the past four

---

[30] Ding Haochuan, "Jinnian jiaoyu gongzuo de zhongxin" (Central Tasks of This Year's Education Work), 17 Jan. 1941, originally in *Xin Zhonghua bao*, 2 Feb. 1941, reprinted in *Shaan–Gan–Ning xuanji*, 4:419.

[31] *Shaan–Gan–Ning xuanji*, 4:420.

[32] "Tigao bianqu guomin jiaoyu" (Improve National Education in the Border Region), *Jiefang ribao*, 4 Oct. 1941, reprinted in Zhongyang jiaoyu kexue yanjiu suo, ed., *Laojiefangqu jiaoyu ziliao: kangri zhanzheng shiqi* (Materials on Education in the Old Liberated Areas: The Anti-Japanese War Period) (hereafter cited as *Laojiefangqu ziliao*) (Beijing: Jiaoyu kexue chubanshe, 1986), 2:xia:336.

[33] "Bianqu jiaoyuting zhaoji gexian sankezhang huiyi" (The Border Region Education Department Calls a Meeting of County-Level Third Section Chiefs), *Jiefang ribao*, 2 Oct. 1941, reprinted in *Shaan–Gan–Ning xuanji*, 4:610–611. On Tao Xingzhi's high standing in Yan'an, which evidently survived the 1943–1944 policy shift, see Witke, *Comrade Chiang Ch'ing*, pp. 72–73, 77, 78; *Xu Teli zhuan*, pp. 166–168; Xu Teli, "Tao Xingzhi de xueshuo" (Tao Xingzhi's Theories), *Jiefang ribao*, 12 Aug. 1946, reprinted in *Tao Xingzhi wenji* (Tao Xingzhi's Collected Works) (n.p.: Jiangsu renmin chubanshe, 1981), pp. 1–3.

years, we have been promoting slogans about quality, began the editorial, yet numbers continued to grow while quality had not improved. The first slogan had been "do not have only quantitative development but also improve quality." Next came "pay attention to quality and halt quantitative development." Then in the autumn of 1941 it became "reduce numbers and raise quality." Still nothing had changed.[34]

The lack of qualified teachers remained a major problem. Meanwhile, ordinary folk felt that educating their children was a burden foisted upon them by the authorities. Teachers and school principals were still going personally from door to door arguing with parents in order to mobilize children to attend. Local cadres regarded education work as a thankless task, difficult to do and without much use. In sum, illiterates were too many, intellectuals too few, and material difficulties too great. It would take a century to surmount such obstacles, and the prerequisite of social revolution was not even considered.

Education was therefore to be developed on a restricted basis. Toward that end, the education department had now issued a set of strict standards and authorized investigators to decide who deserved to pass and who did not. Schools and teachers who did would be given material government support to become central, or model, institutions. At the mass level, directives announced that "supplementary troops should be developed for the cultural battlefront." This meant that anyone who wanted to run schools could do so. So long as they obeyed border region laws, the government would not interfere with their aims, systems, curricula, or measures for hiring and enrollment. And that included the old-fashioned "gentlemen" with their *sishu*, since so many rural people were still more inclined to send their children to receive "discipline" from them than to study in modern schools.[35]

By January 1942, then, border region education policy had evolved into a clear "two-track" approach, essentially the same as that prevailing everywhere else. This restricted development, it was argued, was the only way of "guaranteeing quality." Interestingly, economic considerations were mentioned scarcely at all as a justification for the policy, even though the border regions were at this time experiencing serious economic difficulties.[36] The rationale was drawn instead primarily on academic grounds, appealing to the conventional view among professional Chinese educators that, given the obstacles, quality of

---

[34] "Tigao bianqu guomin jiaoyu" (Improve National Education in the Border Region), *Jiefang ribao*, 14 Jan. 1942, reprinted in *Laojiefangqu ziliao*, 2:xia: 337–339.

[35] Ibid.

[36] In 1942, Mao mentioned only in passing that "many official organizations and schools in Yan'an" had been merged during the economy drive for "better troops and simpler administration." All available education documents, however, elaborated only the arguments outlined here. For Mao's statement, see Mao Zedong, "Economic and Financial Problems," Dec. 1942, translated in Andrew Watson, ed., *Mao Zedong and the Political Economy of the Border Region* (Cambridge: Cambridge University Press, 1980), p. 214; *Mao Zedong ji*, 8:324.

Table 6.2. *Reduction of schools and students in selected Shaan–Gan–Ning counties, 1942*

County or town	Schools (%)	Students (%)
Yanchi	44	30.5
Heshui	70	33.8
Yan'an city	50	—
Ganquan	53	—
Huan	56	—
Ansai	—	48

Source: "Shaan–Gan–Ning bianqu jiaoyu ting guanyu yijiusier nian xiaqi tigao guomin jiaoyu de zhishixin" (Shaan–Gan–Ning Border Region Education Department Directive on Improving National Education during the Latter Half of 1942), Sept. 1942, in Zhongyang jiaoyu kexue yanjiu suo, *Laojiefangqu jiaoyu ziliao*, 2:*xia*:342.

necessity meant a concentration of resources and that mass education should be sacrificed to achieve it.

By September, the new line was being enforced at last. In a selected list of counties, the mergers had led to about a 50 percent reduction in the number of schools and a 30 percent or more drop in student enrollments (see Table 6.2). Statistics for the Shaan–Gan–Ning Border Region as a whole later showed that the total number of elementary schools declined from a high of 1,341 in 1940 to 752 in 1943; enrollments fell from 41,458 to 26,816 (see Table 6.1).

Overall, the education department professed satisfaction with the results. Mergers had finally been accomplished; most of the best teachers had been transferred to the complete or central elementary schools; and these were being appropriately strengthened in all other respects as well. Still, quality had not reached the desired level, and so many children had dropped out that the problem of quantity had taken on new meaning. The main tasks for the fall semester 1942 should therefore be to hold the number of schools at the then existing level, mobilize enough students to fill them, and continue to improve quality.[37]

Accordingly, the plan for merging and strengthening would remain unchanged. The stipulated minimum number of students per school had to be met. Separate classrooms had to be maintained for each grade level. Strict examination systems were to be established for admission, semester finals, year-end finals, and graduation. Also strictly adhered to should be the rules

[37] "Shaan–Gan–Ning bianqu jiaoyu ting guanyu yijiusier nian xiaqi tigao guomin jiaoyu de zhishixin" (Shaan–Gan–Ning Border Region Education Department Directive on Improving National Education during the Latter Half of 1942), Sept. 1942, in *Laojiefangqu ziliao*, 2:*xia*:342–346.

and regulations for monitoring class attendance, granting leaves of absence for teachers and students, making reports, holding meetings, and inspecting work.

As for the drastic decline in numbers, however, closing schools seemed to have exacerbated the existing difficulties in mobilizing rural children to attend school. They still had to help their families with farm chores. Their families still lacked enough surplus to allow children to leave home and live at school. Yet the schools were too far away for youngsters to walk back and forth each day. And as an added consideration, some parents who wanted to keep their children at home forever were afraid that if they received too much education, they would want to quit farming to become public officials! The education department therefore worked out guidelines. Families that truly lacked labor power need not send their children to school. Elementary school districts had now been drawn roughly according to a 20 *li* (1 *li* = 0.5 km) radius around each school. But children living more than 5 *li* away had to live at school, that being the conventional walking distance in the region. Children under 10 years of age who lived more than 5 *li* away also need not be required to attend. Local government authorities and not the teachers should be responsible for all mobilization work and compulsion should not be used.[38]

A similar evolution toward regularity occurred at the secondary level as well. There were only two middle schools in the entire region in 1935: the Suide Teacher Training School and Mizhi Middle School, both located in the relatively prosperous Suide subregion. Additional schools were set up between 1937 and 1942, resulting after a number of mergers and name changes in six secondary institutions, four of which were teacher training schools. In 1940, these six schools had a total of 1,062 students.[39] There were also a college-preparatory middle school associated with Yan'an University; a number of complete elementary schools offering a sixth-year of coursework; and a few vocational schools. But the six schools constituted the core of the secondary-level establishment in Shaan–Gan–Ning.

Initially, at least, the newer schools were filled with left-leaning youth who had fled the Japanese-occupied or GMD areas. After short training courses, they were assigned to work as elementary school teachers or local cadres in the border regions. Coursework was gradually lengthened and the curriculum became more complete. By 1940–1941, it included the full range of secondary school subjects. Finally, in 1942, the same year that the regularization drive peaked for the elementary level, the border region issued two sets of "provisional draft regulations," one for the ordinary secondary schools and the other for teacher training schools. The ordinary curriculum was fixed at six years, following the national format, and teacher training at five years. Uniformity

[38] Ibid.
[39] "Bianqu sinianlai xuexiao jiaoyu menglie zengjia," p. 451.

and standardization were the hallmarks of the new regulations. Age limits were fixed along with admissions requirements favoring a formal school background over work experience. All had to pass standardized entrance examinations. Teaching plans and workloads were fixed, and the six schools brought under the direct leadership of the border region education department.[40]

Party rectification and the Sinification of Marxism, 1942–1944

The regularization drive came to an abrupt halt in 1943–1944. Precisely who decided what remains unverifiable, but official accounts of the new direction invariably cited Mao's 1942–1944 rectification campaign (*zhengfeng yundong*) and the associated senior Party conference as the point of origin. He had regained a position within the Party's top leadership during the Long March, 1934–1935, arguing his case in terms of the erroneous political and military decisions made by his rivals that led to the destruction of the Jiangxi base. Mao then spent much of the next decade elaborating the lessons of that "historic punishment" and forcing the Party to memorize them.[41]

Mao officially broached the idea of sending the Party to school in 1938, pursuant to the strategy of joining an anti-Japanese united front with the GMD while simultaneously trying to maintain the independent identity of the CCP. Party membership was expanding rapidly as the Japanese invasion intensified, and the new people knew little of Marxism–Leninism or the CCP's recent history. In establishing his interpretation of events, however, Mao reproduced the classic response of his generation. He accused the CCP of mechanical copying, especially from the Soviet Union in military and political matters via its Comintern loyalists in China. Hence, of all the functions both positive and negative attributed to the ensuing rectification–study campaign Mao orchestrated, those highlighted in Boyd Compton's early study remain the most relevant. Analyzing it as the Sinification of Marxism and the Bolshevization of the CCP, Compton in effect placed the campaign directly within the critical post–May Fourth tradition.[42]

The campaign was not actually launched on an all-Party basis until early 1942. When it ended two years later, all the Party had indeed been to school

---

[40] Seybolt, "The Yenan Revolution in Mass Education," pp. 650–652; "Shaan–Gan–Ning bianqu de zhongdeng jiaoyu gaikuang" (A General Survey of Secondary Education in the Shaan–Gan–Ning Border Region), June 1944, in *Laojiefangqu ziliao*, 2:*shang*:440–449; Gao Qi, *Zhongguo xiandai jiaoyu shi*, pp. 203–205.

[41] The term "historic punishment" is from "Zhongguo geming zhanzheng de zhanlue wenti" (Strategic Problems of China's Revolutionary War), 1936, *Mao Zedong ji*, 5:103.

[42] Boyd Compton, Introduction to *Mao's China: Party Reform Documents, 1942–44*, trans. Boyd Compton (Seattle: University of Washington, 1952).

and the "thought of Mao Zedong" was the main subject matter.[43] Lecturing on Party formalism, Mao traced this evil back to the rebellious iconoclasm of the 1910s, when intellectuals rejected the old Confucian doctrines in favor of Western-style science and democracy. Like other critics of his time, Mao reevaluated that iconoclasm. For its adherents, he recalled, "what was bad was completely bad, bad in every way; what was good was absolutely good, good in every way." Unlike some of his contemporaries who also criticized the earlier intellectual tendency of regarding all that was old and Chinese as bad, and all that was new and foreign as good, Mao now blamed the earlier proforeign formalism on the absence of a genuine and therefore critical Marxist perspective. Thus, some comrades whose mastery of Marxism was evidently lacking had succumbed to the temptation of the times, reproducing the spirit of proforeign formalism within the CCP.

Mao's "Talks at the Yan'an Forum on Literature and Art," a key study document, was the most direct in fusing Marxist–Leninist goals with the early-20th-century critique of China's intellectuals. If writers and artists meant to follow the CCP, said Mao, it was not enough just to move to a base area. They would have to stand on the side of the proletariat as well. To illustrate his meaning, Mao included the de rigueur testimonial about his own "awakening." The complication of Mao's peasant origins was glossed over, whether for literary or political effect is unclear. But Mao claimed he had learned to identify with intellectuals, acquiring their values and mannerisms. Consequently, school life and student status had made him ashamed to be seen doing manual labor.

Like Tao Xingzhi, Mao also focused on the symbolism of clothing. He had come to regard workers, peasants, and soldiers as "dirty" and would not wear their clothes. Only after he joined the revolution and went back to living among them did he rediscover himself. "Then and only then the bourgeois and petty bourgeois feelings taught to me in bourgeois schools began to undergo a fundamental change." He called this a "changing over from one class to another" through "transformation of feelings," a necessary step for all who aspired to work among the masses. In word and theory, everyone did so, but deeds were something else again. There was as yet hardly any difference in this respect between the CCP and the GMD, "since both to some extent had a tendency to despise workers, peasants, and soldiers and to isolate themselves from the masses."[44]

---

[43] Compton translated the earliest versions of many of the study documents in ibid. See also Bonnie S. McDougall, *Mao Zedong's "Talks at the Yan'an Conference on Literature and Art": A Translation of the 1943 Text with Commentary* (Ann Arbor: Center for Chinese Studies, University of Michigan, 1980). Early versions of the main articles by Mao are in *Mao Zedong ji*, vol. 8.

[44] McDougall, *"Talks at the Yan'an Conference,"* pp. 61–67.

Such were the lessons the CCP was required to learn between 1942 and 1944. But since this was a rectification as well as a study movement, each Party branch also had to "apply the documents." Each Party member's work, thought, and life history had to be examined. Those who had erred and were judged incapable of mending their ways or conforming with the new orthodoxy were expelled from the Party. Such people were apparently few in number, but disposition could be harsh. The wartime search for agents and spies was also incorporated under cover of the larger political movement.[45]

For Mao, however, the rectification campaign was perhaps his greatest political triumph. He emerged from the exercise as undisputed leader while his interpretation of Marxism and Party history was elevated to the level of official Party doctrine. Integrated within it were the conclusions he had drawn from the consequences of trying to follow Moscow's directives – lessons that all his contemporaries who had committed themselves to learning from the outside world could not fail to recognize. Those lessons derived from the post–May Fourth credo that foreign ways and means could not be used to modernize China until they had been adapted to Chinese conditions. Also included in that credo was the Chinese intelligentsia's critique of itself as descendants of China's ruling elite, now characterized in Mao's Marxist terminology as a petty bourgeois minority divorced by its learning and lifestyle from the laboring masses.

Finally, Mao's timing and instincts as a revolutionary strategist are only apparent against the backdrop of contemporary events. By 1942, the united front with the GMD existed in name only. Politically, the CCP was now free to resume its revolutionary course. Meanwhile, its membership had been growing rapidly, from about 40,000 in 1937 to 800,000 in 1943. These members were spread all across the far-flung communist-led border regions being carved out of Japanese-occupied China. The Japanese responded to this growing threat in 1941–1942 with a pacification drive which reduced by half the size of the communist base areas' population.

Once the Japanese offensive began to recede after 1943, however, the CCP emerged as the one cohesive political force within these regions. The rectification–study campaign had played an important role in consolidating that strength. It did so by instilling within the new members, many of whom must have been drawn to the Party by its leadership of the anti-Japanese resistance, a larger set of commitments. These produced, among other things, a party that could

---

[45] E.g., Merle Goldman, *Literary Dissent in Communist China* (Cambridge: Harvard University Press, 1967), chap. 2; Raymond F. Wylie, *The Emergence of Maoism: Mao Tse-tung, Ch'en Po-ta, and the Search for Chinese Theory, 1935–1945* (Stanford: Stanford University Press, 1980), pp. 177–190; Peter J. Seybolt, "Terror and Conformity: Counter-espionage Campaigns, Rectification, and Mass Movements, 1942–1943," *Modern China*, vol. 12, no. 1. (Jan. 1986), pp. 39–73; John Byron and Robert Pack, *The Claws of the Dragon: Kang Sheng, the Evil Genius behind Mao, and His Legacy of Terror in People's China* (New York: Simon and Schuster, 1992), pt. 2.

follow Leninist principles of centralism and obedience in the wartime base areas behind the Japanese lines, where strict organizational control was otherwise impossible to enforce.

It was within such an environment, moreover, that the CCP was also marshalling its forces for the shift back from united front to revolutionary politics. The new recruits, who made up the great majority of the CCP's membership, had no memory of the earlier revolutionary days in Jiangxi.[46] Hence the rectification drive also prepared this new party for a reradicalization of its policies, moving from rent reduction back to land reform, class struggle, and the creation of new village power structures, on a scale far grander than the small mountain bases had afforded in the early 1930s. This radicalization began in about the latter half of 1943, as militarily secure areas expanded during the final years of the war against Japan. By the end of rectification in 1944 and Japan's defeat a year later, all the basic ingredients were in place that would guarantee communist victory in 1949.

In this respect, the final key component of rectification was the senior cadres conference convened in Yan'an from October 1942 through mid-January 1943. It marked the connecting link between rectification and its transformation into practice. Mao's nemeses, the Bolshevik returned students, were noticeable by their absence from the roster of those making major speeches. He now dominated the proceedings, which brought rectification to the CCP's topmost ranks. For three months, the participants criticized their past and present work on seven fronts: the Party, government, armed forces, civic or mass organizations, work relations between and among them all, financial matters, and schools.

The resulting financial and economic reforms were introduced on the spot by Mao himself. Across-the-board education reforms were drawn up during the following year. The new policies deriving from the critical reappraisal were based on uniform principles throughout: reliance on the existing economic and educational base, application of existing technology, adaptation of traditional mutual-aid practices as a form of preliminary collective effort, local self-reliance, benefits for the masses and popular mass participation in management, and active Party and government direction. From this conference there then emerged not just a leadership united around Mao's doctrines but new and more radical policies aimed at applying them throughout the north China base areas as the Japanese tide receded but before the GMD could return.[47]

---

[46] At the Central Research Institute, Yan'an's highest political training school, as of 1942, 82 percent of the students were urban intellectuals, 74 percent had joined the CCP after 1937, 79 percent were in their twenties, and 68 percent had never held a regular job before joining the communist-led anti-Japanese resistance movement in Yan'an (*Jiefang ribao*, 31 Oct. 1942; cited in Seybolt, "Terror and Conformity," p. 47).

[47] On the conference, see Selden, *The Yenan Way in Revolutionary China*, pp. 200–207; Andrew Watson, *Mao Zedong and the Political Economy of the Border Region*, passim; *Zhongguo gongchandang lici zhongyao huiyiji* (An Anthology of the Various Important Meetings of the Chinese Communist Party) (Shanghai: Shanghai renmin chubanshe, 1982), pp. 221–228.

Yan'an, 1943–1947: the mass line and mass education

In education, the full rectification cycle took more than a year to complete. The overall reform package for general (as opposed to political and Party) education was not unveiled until the spring of 1944. The proclaimed objective was to halt the trend then under way to reproduce the forms of GMD China's "regular" education system within the communist-led border regions.

The rationale

The precedents invoked were twofold.[48] One was the "new education" introduced at the turn of the century, or rather the ongoing debate it had provoked. The other was Marxist teachings on the role of education in society. Marxists advocated combining production with knowledge and Lenin had put that idea into practice. The border regions did not aim to transplant the proposals of Marx and Lenin but only "to translate them into proper Chinese."[49] The result should be a kind of education joined together with the people, not separated from them. In the border regions, life was dominated by war, revolution, and the struggle for economic survival in an impoverished rural environment, but education was divorced from those realities under the growing influence of a conventional system. Still, even the Yan'an critics could not escape its contradictory appeal.

That system, they explained, was the product of peacetime, of city life, and a high stage of capitalist mechanized production. It was characterized in its European, American, and Japanese variants by a long period of study from first grade through college, with every grade rigidly linked, dozens of compulsory subjects, and hundreds of technical courses. Many Chinese intellectuals were dissatisfied with it. But even though the Chinese version of this foreign system dated only from the turn of the century, because of its international background linked with the whole of human knowledge, "no matter how much it is criticized and attacked, to substitute another system for it is not something that can be done overnight."[50]

Nevertheless, the movement for educational reform in China had failed most basically because the political authorities never backed it. Now, when the

---

[48] The rationale was spelled out in three editorials that were reprinted and circulated with the main education reform documents in 1944: *Shaan–Gan–Ning bianqu jiaoyu fangzhen* (The Education Policy of the Shaanxi–Gansu–Ningxia Border Region) (hereafter cited as *Jiaoyu fangzhen*) (n.p.: Shaan–Gan–Ning bianqu zhengfu bangongting, July 1944), pp. 31–53; translations in Lindsay, *Notes on Educational Problems in Communist China*, pp. 51–63, and in *Chinese Education*, vol. 4, no. 3 (fall 1971), and no. 4 (winter 1971–72).

[49] "Dasui jiu de yitao" (Smash the Old Forms), *Jiefang ribao*, 11 Sept. 1941, reprinted in *Jiaoyu fangzhen*, p. 36.

[50] "Genjudi putong jiaoyu de gaige wenti" (Problems of Reforming Ordinary Education in the Base Areas), *Jiefang ribao*, 7 Apr. 1944, reprinted in *Jiaoyu fangzhen*, p. 39.

border region government had finally committed itself to reform, "dogmatic methods of thought" about education still blocked the way. Naturally, if the conventional system had been found lacking elsewhere, it was even less suited to the border regions. But in recent years, educators there had tried to develop that same system, even though most people were living in sparsely populated villages with backward production techniques and an underdeveloped social division of labor.

Consequently, most young people had only three employment options: return home and work with their families; become cadres, that is, work in some public capacity at the local level; or continue their studies. Yet the border region's education system was preparing students for none of these aims. Upon finishing elementary school, students had no desire to return home. Nor did the system train them adequately to be cadres. As for continuing their studies, the curriculum was designed for that end, but only a small minority even went on to middle school. The border regions had no real universities, and the schools for higher-level cadres were not linked to the middle schools in any way. Meanwhile, the people actually responsible for leading the war and production had nothing to do with the schools, nor vice versa.

The future, of course, would be different. In the industrialized future, every worker would be able to study math, physics, and chemistry. A system wherein students passed on from one grade and level to the next was also one for the future, but not the present. "To forget the future because of the present is incorrect; to forget the present because of the future is especially incorrect."[51]

Henceforth, education in the border regions would be very different from the old system and would have independent objectives directly related to life and work. Such education would be neither preparatory nor attached to the next level above. Many different forms would be used for both the masses and the cadres, including winter schools, half-day schools, night schools, literacy groups, the "little teacher" method, apprentice systems, etc. "In any case, nonuniformity of standards is unavoidable, and so exact linking of the various school grades is almost impossible, but this is absolutely nothing to worry about."[52] Mass elementary schooling should focus on home and village. Cadre schools might still be called middle schools, teacher training schools, universities, or training courses. But all should base their curricula on the armed struggle, border region construction, and production. Courses should be designed to "eliminate the abnormal psychology of students not wanting to do technical work."[53]

[51] Ibid., p. 42.
[52] "Lun putong jiaoyu zhong de xuezhi yu kecheng" (On the System and Curriculum of Ordinary Education), *Jiefang ribao*, 27 May 1944, reprinted in *Jiaoyu fangzhen*, p. 49.
[53] Ibid., passim.

Elementary school reform

The directive for elementary schools was promulgated in April 1944. Applying the reform rationale, it charged that border region schools were divorced from the lives of ordinary people. The solutions, based on experimental trials during 1943, were twofold: change the content and change the forms of schooling. The new form would be called "schools run by the people" (*minban*) with "public assistance" (*gongzhu*). Financially supported and managed by the villages themselves, this new form was not so much an innovation as an adaptation of the continuing *sishu* tradition. The plan was "to give the great majority of or even all elementary schools" to the masses to run in this manner. Local governments would give material help as well as leadership. Specific instructions included the following:

- Uniformity should not be the aim. But in general, all junior elementary schools should eventually be transformed into *minban* schools.
- Fixed standards and restrictions should not be imposed upon such schools for student quotas, teachers, facilities, or whatever. The site of the school, its financing, remuneration of its teachers, and the number of students should all be left to the local people to decide. Local government authorities, if requested, might introduce a teacher. Otherwise, local people could hire whomever they wanted regardless of the person's age.
- Nor should uniformity be imposed on the length and content of courses. This, too, should be decided by local people. The curriculum might be long or short, and classroom schedules should be at the discretion of the community supporting the school. If villagers wanted their school to teach only reading, writing, and the abacus, then they should be allowed to have it their way (although in principle, the government hoped to teach some subjects of practical use for village life that were also relevant to politics or to production).
- Flexibility stopped with textbooks and teaching materials, however. Often rural people did not want to use the new materials prepared by the border region education department but preferred instead the old Confucian primers and glossaries. On this point, the government would not compromise. The old books were things of the past and no longer of any use. Meanwhile, the education department was editing some new materials to meet this local demand, "in the old style, but with new content."
- Finally, *minban* (popularly managed) should not be divorced from *gongzhu* (public assistance). The county, district, and township authorities should not just let the masses go their own way. Leadership should come from the heads of districts and townships (i.e., the general administrative, rather than specifically educational, authorities). Henceforth, inspecting the elementary schools would be part of their administrative duties, whereas the county-level leaders

supervised overall. The past practice of district and township cadres having nothing whatever to do with education had to be changed.[54]

In Shaan–Gan–Ning, quantitative losses suffered during the regularization drive were reversed (see Table 6.1). Other militarily secure areas also claimed impressive gains after adopting the *minban* formula.[55] As experience grew, a number of different models were advertised to demonstrate the versatility of the *minban* approach.[56] It remained official policy and practice in Shaan–Gan–Ning until early 1947, when civil war finally achieved what the Japanese could not in forcing the communists to evacuate Yan'an.

Apparently just prior to the evacuation in March 1947, the deputy director of the education department, Jiang Longji, prepared a report which survived only in undated mimeographed form.[57] It summarized the pros and cons of *minban* schools with unaccustomed candor (the military emergency may have saved the document for posterity from the ministrations of official editors). Published 40 years later, the relatively unvarnished state of the report makes it especially valuable in illustrating the particular nature of the effort that went into implementing this new mass-line policy and the typical development dilemmas its promoters encountered in the north China countryside.

The report provided statistics, albeit "not very accurate," to illustrate growth after the regularization drive was scrapped (shown in Table 6.1). New schools were established, and a "large group" of government-run schools were changed to *minban* status. The report concluded that the new direction adopted in 1944 had greatly benefited border region education. The remaining government-run

---

[54] The above account is taken from the directive itself: "Bianqu zhengfu guanyu tichang yanjiu fanli ji shixing minban xiaoxue de zhishixin" (Border Region Government's Directive on Promoting the Study of Models and Experimentally Running Popularly Managed Elementary Schools), 18 Apr. 1944, in *Jiaoyu fangzhen*, pp. 4–9.

[55] E.g., the claim for the Shanxi–Chahar–Hebei Border Region was over 7,000 *minban* primary schools by 1945; 833 in the Taihang Mountains district; and 3,000 in southern Hebei (Liu Songtao, "Ban xiaoxue de liangtiao luxian," p. 187). Michael Lindsay also reported a rapid growth of schools in these areas after 1944, although the above figures seem exaggerated versions of those he cites (*Notes on Educational Problems in Communist China*, p. 36).

[56] E.g., "Zhixing xin jiaoyu fangzhen de juda shouhuo" (The Great Results of the New Educational Policy), *Jiefang ribao*, 14 Nov. 1944, reprinted in Jiaoyu kexue yanjiusuo choubei chu, ed., *Laojiefangqu jiaoyu ziliao xuanbian* (Selected Materials on Education in the Old Liberated Areas) (Beijing: Renmin jiaoyu chubanshe, 1959, 1983), pp. 268–278 and 260–323 passim; *Xiaoxue jiaoyu de lilun yu shijian* (The Theory and Practice of Elementary School Education) (Hong Kong: Xin minzhu chubanshe, n.d.), passim; Chen Yuanhui, Qu Xingui, and Zou Guangwei, eds., *Laojiefangqu jiaoyu jianshi* (A Short History of Education in the Old Liberated Areas) (Beijing: Jiaoyu kexue chubanshe, 1982), pp. 108–113.

[57] Jiang Longji, "Guanyu minban gongzhu zhengce de chubu zongjie" (A Preliminary Summary of the People-Managed Public-Help Policy), n.d., mimeo, in *Laojiefangqu ziliao*, 2:xia:375–390. "Jiang Longji," in Li Shaoxian, ed., *Zhongguo jiaoyu mingren zhuanlue* (Biographical Sketches of Famous Chinese Educators) (Shenyang: Liaoning daxue chubanshe, 1985), pp. 251–252. The remainder of this section on elementary schooling is based on this summary.

schools had also been influenced and improved by the new, more flexible work style. However, problems remained.

Schools run on the basis of local demands could not but reflect some negative features of the local environment. One such was continued use of the old Confucian primers, for which rural people retained a seemingly unshakable attachment. Another was allowing geomancers, hawkers, ex-soldiers, and even beggars to serve as teachers. Consequently, the teacher's foot rule still controlled many a classroom and corporal punishment was not uncommon. All such defects needed correcting. But these were problems which only educated outsiders found reprehensible. Jiang Longji's report concentrated instead on the "opinions of the masses," which if not addressed would adversely "influence their enthusiasm" for running schools. These opinions revolved around three related concerns, namely, leadership, funding, and teachers.

The report was, of course, not written for the masses either, but for the cadres as mass leaders. It thus offers some interesting insights into the difficulties of trying to sensitize inexperienced local cadres to a new work style which required them to walk the fine line between compulsion, or "commandism," and leaving the masses to their own devices. The *minban* school policy accordingly illustrated the unfamiliar mix of mass-line voluntarism and Party leadership that Mao's rectification campaign was intended to promote.

Basically, local people liked the idea of running schools themselves. They liked to be able to hire the teachers they wanted, to schedule classes around the busy farming seasons, and (for better or worse) to retain control of their children after they finished studying. Such local schools also saved peasant families the expense of sending their children outside the village to school. But the school also increased the economic burden, and many villages decided not to take it up. Others, having tried *minban* schools, soon began demanding that the government take them over. When local authorities refused, some villages refused to continue running their schools. Since government-run and even central schools were never eliminated (see Table 6.1), villagers continued to regard that as an option, viewed it as preferable, and demanded one of their own.

Local cadres, caught in the middle between government policy and the peasants, tended to vacillate between "commandism" and providing no leadership whatsoever. It was, after all, much easier to run a government school and lead by administrative decree. But such administrative methods were now deemed inappropriate. Local cadres, unused to the new way, tended to either keep to the old or do nothing. Some would rush ahead enthusiastically at first and "then just bury their heads in despair" as the problems piled up and they could proceed no further. The report elaborated at length upon the importance of correct leadership, since it meant the difference between success or failure. The second half of the *minban* formula was as important as the first. Schools could not succeed without "public assistance," which meant not just material help but, more important, leadership.

To do their jobs correctly, however, the local cadres themselves had to understand the significance of *minban* schools. Such schools were a means not just of universalizing education but of promoting the mass line, putting down roots in the villages, helping them become self-reliant, and uniting education work with production and society. Such schools were different from their private counterparts, which were controlled by individuals, usually landlords and gentry. A *minban* school was a common collective enterprise of everyone in a village: everyone enjoyed the right to enter the school and also the obligation to support it. *Minban* schools were also different from government-run schools, although the difference was more of degree than of kind. The border region political power was a power belonging to the people themselves, so that a government-run school was actually a school run by all the people. The *minban* school was also a public school, but one belonging to the "small" public of the village.

The report also elaborated at length on concrete obstacles. Cadres who led correctly also had to appreciate the rural environment with its scattered population, insufficient labor power, primitive communications, and inconvenient transport. Traditional ways of thinking constrained people's minds, so that their demands for education were often not great. And herein lay the crux of the problem: the policy itself was decreed from above, yet local cadres were being directed to make *minban* schools a mass-line operation. That meant following the demands of local people, even though local people did not necessarily have any great demand for schooling.

"Many peasants, because their vision is not broad and their thought is narrow, experience only immediate needs that are partial and pressing. They cannot easily grasp the importance of their future, long-term needs." Still, such needs should not be denied. The peasants demanded food and clothing but not better hygiene. Yet "we cannot therefore say the masses do not need good health." Similarly, the peasants understood their needs for labor and production but not necessarily for schooling. They were often willing to sacrifice the latter when it seemed to conflict with the former. But the cadres should not conclude that the peasants did not need culture and education. Hence, the cadres' task must be to enlighten the masses and lead them to understand that some needs, although not clearly apparent, were in fact as important as others that were.

The peasants must be made to understand that literacy was something they really could not do without in real life, and then they would quite naturally be willing to study. "So voluntarism relies on self-awareness; but self-awareness is aroused and induced by the leaders. From this it can be seen that leadership is absolutely not compulsion; and voluntarism absolutely cannot mean noninterference. Management by the people with public assistance is voluntarism plus leadership. These two cannot be separated." Once these points had been grasped, the concrete problems of funding and teachers could be more easily tackled.

Financing came from several sources: a little from the school's own productive endeavors, some from parents in the form of school fees, and some from the entire village or township as a collective contribution. But often the students were too few. Or the parents' burdens were already too heavy. Or the villagers as a whole argued that they had already given their public grain (grain tax in kind). Some families did not even have children in school. Certainly, a *minban* school seemed much greater a burden than one financed by the government. Fair solutions had to be found. Toward that end, the report offered suggestions.

The government should probably give each *minban* school a foundation fee to establish its economic base. If a school had been allocated village land, this must be well managed. The proper method was to see that it was cultivated either by the students' parents or by the teachers' families, in which case the harvest would serve as the teachers' income. Or the land might be cultivated by the school (students, teachers, and staff) and peasants jointly as a production activity with the proceeds used to help meet school expenses. Or a local fund might be established; students' parents might be willing to invest in some enterprise and create a cooperative society to run it, using the profits to support the school.

Finally, good teachers were hard to come by in the villages, and this, too, undermined peasants' enthusiasm. Teachers essentially came from three sources. One was local senior primary school graduates. They were sound politically and enthusiastic in their work; but their cultural level was not very high. They were also young and did not understand enough about human nature. Hence, they were "looked down upon by the masses." Another source of teachers was the small pool of local older people with some education. But they were a mixed lot: some were the old-fashioned teachers with little modern training; others included bankrupt businessmen and ex-military men. Such people only taught school to earn some money and lacked the spirit of serving the masses. The latter only hired them because of personal relations or because they came more cheaply than others. Finally, a third source of teachers were educated people from the GMD areas. Some had come "seeking truth and glory" and were willing to sacrifice for the border region. But some could not care less. They knew little of local conditions, had no interest in politics, and "just worked like hired hands."

When they saw that teachers were wasting the students' time, the masses withdrew support and the schools collapsed. Parents needed to know their children were making progress every day. Often the main problem was not funding at all but how to establish the teachers in the esteem of the villagers. Once this was done, the financial problems often solved themselves. Toward these ends, there were a number of on-the-job methods for helping the existing contingent to improve. A division of labor and leadership should also be maintained: the complete and central primary schools should maintain regular links with ordinary schools; and each remaining government school should be responsible for helping the *minban* schools in its vicinity. Districtwide meetings should be held regularly to discuss teaching methods, content, and the like.

In terms of content and quality, moreover, the *minban* schools should not be seen only as a means of promoting universal literacy. Each school should strive to build itself up to the level of an ordinary junior elementary school, and on to become a complete school as conditions allowed. This quality consideration was especially important for government-run schools – to keep up morale and protect their academic standing – after they were turned over to the people to manage.

Secondary and higher education

At the secondary level, reform also directly contradicted the recent "old-style regularization" trend which had tried to establish a regular college-preparatory curriculum like that existing elsewhere in China. This aim was now rejected as totally inappropriate for a region still trying to create its first vocationalized university. Priorities were reordered to emphasize cadre education and in-service training for those already working rather than for school-age youth. All schooling above the basic elementary level was reconceptualized accordingly. Senior elementary education became a sort of intermediate training course for local cadres. Statistics for 1944 showed 18,161 students in complete elementary schools, of whom only 2,683 were studying at the upper level. In recent years, only about 20 percent of the students at that level returned home to work with their families. Over 70 percent were either assigned work immediately or went on with their studies.[58]

Regular secondary and secondary teacher training schools were given greater responsibility for in-service training. Whereas before rules had stipulated that 70–80 percent of the student body should be elementary school graduates, new regulations directed that when enrolling new students "local cadres should outweigh the graduates of complete elementary schools, and the poor children of workers and peasants should have more opportunity to enter school."[59]

Secondary schools were to develop study plans according to their specific

---

[58] "Zhixing xin jiaoyu fangzhen de juda shouhuo," p. 275.
[59] "Bianqu zhengfu guanyu gezhongdeng xuexiao jinhou zhaosheng biaozhun de zhishixin" (Directive from the Border Region Government on the Standards for Henceforth Enrolling Students in the Various Secondary Schools), 8 May 1944, in *Jiaoyu fangzhen*, p. 15.

training tasks and local conditions. Uniformity was no longer required. In the Suide subregion, where education was most developed, for example, a majority of the senior elementary graduates continued on with their studies. Unlike more typical rural youth, who were often well into their teens when and if they graduated, those in Suide were too young to be assigned work. Hence secondary education there should be planned to accommodate them.

The number of secondary schools in Shaan–Gan–Ning remained essentially unchanged. But major curricular revisions were announced in 1944, cutting formal coursework almost in half, from five or six years to three years. The new course schedule was reduced to only eight subjects and redesigned to teach essential knowledge and practical skills. Music, art, physical education, and military drill were all relegated to the category of extracurricular activities. Specialized vocational training was concentrated in the final semester and developed according to different job requirements. Students were supposed to do 20–30 days of production labor per year.[60]

The reform of higher education was complicated by the "irregular" nature of all such education to begin with. Border region schools had grown around the need for short-term cadre training, both civilian and military. Consequently, when the rectification movement began as a political education drive, it was launched from Yan'an's higher-level cadre training schools, where the future leaders of the communist movement were being produced in short order. Then, once the movement progressed from political rectification to general reform, the latter ironically entailed a kind of regularization. The aim was to change some of the cadre training schools into more conventional institutions, albeit based on the 1944 reform principles.

As of 1941, when rectification was just beginning, Yan'an's higher-level schools were divided into those for CCP members only and "united front" institutions, which accepted non-Party members as well. At the top of the hierarchy, the Central Research Institute trained the highest-level theoretical cadres. The Central Party School trained senior and middle-ranking cadres at both the tertiary and secondary academic levels. The Military Academy similarly trained senior and middle-ranking military cadres. These were Yan'an's main CCP schools as of 1941. The most famous united front school was the Chinese People's Anti-Japanese Resistance Military and Political University (Zhongguo renmin kangri zhunshi zhengzhi daxue), or Kangda for short. Other such institutions included the Lu Xun Academy of Art and Literature, the Natural Science Academy, the Chinese Medical University, the National Minorities Institute, and Yan'an University (or Yanda). During the decade that Yan'an served as nerve center for the expanding communist movement, its

---

[60] "Guanyu zhongdeng xuexiao xin kecheng" (On the New Secondary School Curriculum), *Jiefang ribao* (27 May 1944), reprinted in *Jiaoyu fangzhen*, pp. 18–20; "Shaan–Gan–Ning bianqu de zhongdeng jiaoyu gaikuang," pp. 444–445, 448–449.

schools trained many thousands of "revolutionary cadres." In all the schools, courses were mostly short, and students, sometimes even before they graduated, were moved on quickly to assignments in the field.[61]

After more than a year of rectification and political education among faculty and students, the focus shifted to general reform. Whatever his role in the earlier regularization drive, Zhou Yang now emerged as a staunch supporter of Mao's ideas on rectification. Zhou was appointed head of Yan'an University and concurrently of its reorganization committee. The reform plan was announced in May 1944. Yanda had been created in 1941 as an amalgam of three other schools, and most of the remaining individual united front institutes now merged with it as well. Yanda was being reorganized into a comprehensive university, and its reform plan was a preliminary effort to adapt the new mass-line principles for use in a regular institution of higher learning.

The adaptation remained largely on paper since Yanda enjoyed very few years of "regular" existence after the 1944 reorganization. Nevertheless, the 1944 regulations remained as a record of the ideals that had inspired the CCP's first official effort to reform higher education. The university might also have remained just another of China's many abandoned reform projects had it not been created by CCP leaders who would soon rule all of China as well.

As reflected in the 1944 regulations for Yan'an University, practical application was the overriding aim. Mao set the tone in his address at the opening ceremony of the newly reorganized Yanda in May. It was mainly a university for the study of politics, economics, and culture, he said, and Yanda students must learn how to put those subjects to work in the service of the border region.[62] On-the-job practical training was to be part of each student's study plan, along with productive labor, which was supposed to cultivate in college students the "habits and viewpoints" of the working people. Approximate ratios were fixed for on-campus study, off-campus practice, and productive labor. New teaching methods were to be developed based on three special characteristics. One was the union of study and teaching with practical application. Second, independent study should be primary and instruction supplementary. The third was a democratic spirit.[63]

Reorganized Yanda thus seemed designed as the "regular" equivalent of a

---

[61] E.g., Qu Shipei, *Kangri zhanzheng shiqi jiefangqu gaodeng jiaoyu* (Higher Education in the Liberated Areas in the Period of the Resistance War against Japan) (Beijing: Beijing daxue chubanshe, 1985); *Laojiefangqu ziliao*, 2:*shang*:238–429 passim; Price, *Cadres, Commanders, and Commissars*, pp. 135–188.

[62] From Mao's address at Yan'an University, 31 May 1944, excerpted in *Comrade Mao Tse-tung on Educational Work* (Beijing: People's Education Publishing House, 1958), translated in *Chinese Education*, vol. 2, no. 3 (fall 1969), pp. 38–39.

[63] "Yan'an daxue jiaoyu fangzhen ji zanxing fangan" (Yan'an University's Educational Policy and Provisional Plan), 21 May 1944, in *Jiaoyu fangzhen*, pp. 21–30; "Yan'an daxue gaikuang" (General Survey of Yan'an University), June 1944, in *Laojiefangqu ziliao*, 2:*shang*:391–411.

military–political training school, of which Kangda remained the foremost example.[64] But Yanda was also clearly a descendant, in spirit at least, of Mao's old Self-Study University. Not that Mao's Self-Study University was unique or that the line of inheritance moved directly from Mao's youth in Changsha to his middle age in Yan'an. But the self-study university had grown from the early critique and was part of what had become an ongoing effort to adapt Western-style education to the Chinese environment. That critique – synthesized and recycled through Mao's rectification campaign in the wartime border regions with an admixture of Marxism–Leninism – produced the reformed Yan'an University of 1944.

The Yan'an legacy

The same forces that saved Jiang Longji's report for posterity also brought an end to the 1944 Yan'an reforms. Another survey, written in 1957, recalled how the years 1945–1948 had marked the culmination of China's revolutionary struggle. Full-scale civil war, the GMD armies' invasion of the border regions, the loss of Yan'an, and land reform could not but hinder education work. Then, as the communist-led areas expanded and became more secure, civilian life gradually resumed. North China conferences on secondary and elementary education were held during the 1948–1949 academic year, and with them the course set by the Yan'an reforms was lost as they seemingly went the way of all their republican predecessors.[65] The CCP thus inherited in 1949 the same conventional system that had stood for 30 years impervious to all the reformers' efforts.

The Yan'an experience is important to our story on several counts. First, it provided a sort of controlled experiment that showed how instinctively committed Chinese educators were to the forms and structures of the established system. Given the opportunity, they immediately proceeded between

[64] On the Kangda experience, see Qu Shipei, *Kangri zhanzheng shiqi*, pp. 29–70; *Laojiefangqu ziliao*, 2:*shang*:242–325; Price, *Cadres, Commanders, and Commissars*, pp. 137–150. See also "Gei Lin Biao tongzhi de xin" (A Letter to Comrade Lin Biao), 1936, in *Mao Zedong ji*, 5:171; "Statement on the Third Anniversary of Kang-ta," 30 May 1939, reprinted in *Comrade Mao Tse-tung on Educational Work* and translated in *Chinese Education*, vol. 2, no. 1–2 (spring–summer 1969), pp. 65–67.

[65] Liu Songtao, "Ban xiaoxue de liangtiao luxian," pp. 188–190; Guo Lin, "Guanyu bianqu xiaoxue xuezhi de gaige" (On the Reform of the Elementary School System in the Border Regions), in Bao Xiaying, Tao Duanyu, et al., *Nongcun banxue jingyan* (The Experience of Running Schools in the Countryside) (Beijing: Sanlian, 1949–1950), pp. 79–84. Liu Songtao's characterization of the north China provisional measures was correct. See "Huabeiqu xiaoxue jiaoyu zanxing shishi banfa," Huabei renmin zhengfu, 15 June 1949, reprinted in Huabei renmin zhengfu jiaoyubu, ed., *Shifan xuexiao shiyong: xiaoxue jiaoyu lilun yu shiji cankao ziliao* (Reference Materials on the Theory and Practice of Elementary Education for Use in Teacher Training Schools) (Beijing: Xinhua shudian, 1950), pp. 7–14. But his account of the declining *minban* school ethos is somewhat overdrawn. In fact, it seemed to be taking root but then retreated under the weight of "Sino–Soviet" regularization (see chap. 9, below).

1938 and 1942 to replicate that system regardless of its acknowledged defects and however inappropriate to the time and place.

Ironically, the features of that system stood out more sharply in the reduced-to-scale Yan'an setting than across the larger canvas of republican era development, where they originated. The directives cited above constituted the building blocks of a new structure deliberately fashioned step-by-step to curb the undisciplined growth initially promoted by the Jiangxi veterans. Key features of the "regularization" model reproduced in Yan'an were a preoccupation with quality, to be guaranteed via fixed uniform standards, governed in turn by fixed "systems" of rules and regulations for all aspects of school life; the assumption that in order to guarantee such standards resources must be concentrated in a few centers of strength; a related tolerance for investment priorities that disproportionately and deliberately emphasized those centers of strength; an assumption that quantity must be sacrificed for quality, even to the point of closing down schools and sending children home; and a rationale which cited the lack of demand among illiterates plus ensuing obstacles so great that "a hundred years" would be needed to surmount them.

The pattern also reinforces the conclusion, noted in chapter 4, about the responsibility of professional educators themselves for republican China's poor record in developing mass education. In fact, the assumptions of professional educators about the need for quality and how to structure a quality system must have been at least partly responsible if the decision to reduce enrollments in Yan'an is any indication.

Second, the Yan'an experience played an adaptive function between past and future for the critique of the regular system. This role was developed in the course of carrying out Mao's brief for the Party's rectification campaign as a whole to "Sinicize Marxism" or "translate it into proper Chinese." The then sympathetic observer Michael Lindsay wrote of the 1944 reforms that they "show Chinese communist theory at its best, combining Marxist principles with strong common sense and concern for practical problems."[66] He might more accurately have said that while Marxist principles were being applied to the task of educational reform, at the same time the decades-old critique of China's modern education system was being incorporated within the theory and practice of Chinese communism. This integration, spelled out clearly in the 1944 reform rationale, proved an important step in the growing status of the antiestablishment critique. Previously, it had always remained outside the system, and individual reforms had rarely progressed beyond the experimental stage. Within the 1944 Yan'an experience, by contrast, the reforms acquired a stronger foundation. Their adherents managed to win enough backing to create a policymaking precedent within a new political establishment that was in turn about to win national power.

[66] Lindsay, *Notes on Educational Problems in Communist China*, p. 39.

Third, following from Lindsay's assessment, the 1944 reforms made some positive contributions to China's educational development. One practical insight, enforced by the urgency of the times to be sure, concerned the general need to adapt schooling more closely to the demand for specific manpower needs. Another contribution was the *minban* school concept and the associated understanding about local initiative being a necessary but insufficient ingredient for promoting universal education. Marxist–Leninist principles contributed the other necessary condition, that is, political will or direct government leadership to enforce collective support. And in trying to adapt education to the realities of rural China, the 1944 reforms also applied the post–May Fourth answer to the perceived dysfunctions of dependency, or, in this case, to the negative consequences of depending on transplanted foreign-inspired models.

A fourth point to emphasize, however, is that the official recognition accorded the old critique in rural wartime Yan'an was not enough to establish its preeminence within either the CCP or the wider academic community responsible for running the education system on a nationwide basis. The above-cited *Liberation Daily* editorials suggest that even in 1944 Yan'an, the ambivalence between reform and regularization remained very much alive. Especially, references to the education of the future betrayed the continuing attraction of the regular system.

Consequently, the rectification campaign as a means of enforced intellectual and political conformity introduced an ominous precedent. Unlike the early 1930s in Jiangxi, intellectuals were not compromised by their association with class enemies, because social revolution was held in abeyance during the Yan'an decade. In later years, social revolution would be revived, compounding the negative legacy of rectification, a legacy which would be invoked repeatedly against class enemies and their associates. On the positive side, then, integrating the decades-old critique of modern education within the theory and practice of Chinese communism introduced, at last, the possibility of reforming the system as a whole in conformity with the old reformers' ideals. But conversely, integrating the associated critique of Chinese intellectuals with rectification and class struggle would prove a hazardous undertaking.

In the 1920s and 1930s, the critical ideals were widely popular but the gap between talk and action was never bridged. The 1944 Yan'an solution anticipated the necessary changes but proposed to bridge the gap via induced obedience. In Yan'an itself, education reform was soon overwhelmed by the rush of larger events. But that Yan'an solution, rather than the more benignly ineffective critique preceding it, would later be invoked as precedent. A new reality of two contending "lines" would then be created – pitting regularity against the mass line – with negative consequences for all, including the guardians of the established system, the attempt to reform it, and in dialectical fashion for educational development as well.

Part II

Learning from the Soviet Union

7

Introducing the Soviet Union

By 1949 the basic tasks were fixed and clearly defined. They entailed providing elementary schooling for everyone, higher education for the elite few, and intermediate secondary schooling – all in ways the economy could afford and society would accept. The historical foundations of the controversies surrounding these tasks were well established in China as elsewhere. The new ingredients in the early 1950s came from the Soviet Union as ally, advisor, and inspiration for socioeconomic revolution. One additional important difference between the early 1950s and the Yan'an decade was the nationwide scope of the CCP's power, which now encompassed not just an isolated rural hinterland but the cities, coastal areas, and the South as well.

Nevertheless, the pattern of development that emerged in Yan'an – regularization followed by an antithetical phase deliberately incorporating key elements from the old reformers' critique – continued in sequence for at least 30 years thereafter. Counting the Yan'an decade, the same cycle was repeated three times, with a fourth regularization phase commencing after Mao's death in 1976.

The second cycle began in the early 1950s, when the Soviet Union replaced the West as authoritative reference point, and produced a regularization phase more rigorous than any recorded precedent. The 1958 Great Leap Forward broke out of that phase in search of a more rural-oriented "Chinese way," with deregularization on a similarly unprecedented scale, citing among other things the mass-line lessons learned in Yan'an. The Soviet Union was dropped as an overt model but seemed to provide continuing "internal" reinforcement through a deregularization exercise of its own which occurred at the same time. Between 1960 and 1966, while China recuperated from Great Leap excesses, the cycle resumed and "order" was tentatively restored. The 1966–1976 decade then again attempted to institutionalize the aims of the Great Leap, now phrased more explicitly in terms of 1940s Yan'an precedents. After Mao's death, these were repudiated in favor of the old familiar alternative, while China turned outward once more, looking especially to the U.S. as authoritative reference point. Thus, not only did the cycle itself persist, but its various historical antecedents were deliberately invoked by both sides. Ironically, both sides sought to establish precedents within the modern era itself, reproducing thereby the ancient custom of using past events to gain legitimacy for present innovations.

From 1949 until the mid-1950s, however, the dominant slogan in China was "learn from the Soviet Union" (*xuexi Sulian*). Mao had announced in the summer of 1949 that the CCP must "lean to one side," but before long it seemed more like falling head over heels.[1] The government and the economy, like the CCP itself, were all structured along Soviet lines to a degree that seemed inexplicable given the recent exhortation to Sinicize Marxism.

Education naturally followed the national trend. Russians replaced departing Americans and Europeans. Those most directly responsible for setting up the Soviet model included 10,000 or more Soviet "experts" who served in China during the 1950s, including some 700 who worked in higher education. Moving in the opposite direction, more than 30,000 Chinese scientists, technicians, teachers, students, and workers went to the Soviet Union during the same period for study and training.[2] At the time, people recalled, the Soviet Union loomed overwhelmingly as mentor and guide and was commonly referred to as "elder brother." Those who did not leap on the bandwagon were obliged to follow along in its wake. Those who resisted were criticized, discredited, and silenced.

In the West, these events reinforced all the worst cold war fears about a former protégé and ally fatally clasped in Moscow's embrace. Yet the Chinese reality as always was rather different. The Sino-Soviet alliance actually lasted no more than a decade, and China's infatuation with the Soviet model had an even shorter history. It was as though the game had to be played through again from the beginning in order to reach the same foreordained conclusion. Certain key features that had marked the initial experience of learning from the outside world during the early decades of the century now reappeared: a sudden enthusiastic rush to learn the secrets of the foreigners' success, mechanical copying, transplants that could not but function differently in the Chinese setting, followed by a backlash against the ensuing dislocations and unseemly desire to emulate foreigners in so uncritical a manner.

By the mid-1950s, then, a renewed search was under way for more specifically "Chinese" solutions. Education continued to follow the national trend that began while Soviet-style regularization still held sway. As in Yan'an, however, the search became most evident when it merged with the next deregularization phase in 1958. Once again, the regular education mode was

---

[1] "Lun renmin minzhu zhuanzheng" (On the People's Democratic Dictatorship), 30 June 1949, *Mao Zedong ji*, 10: 296–300.

[2] Chu-yuan Cheng, *Scientific and Engineering Manpower in Communist China, 1949–1963* (Washington, D.C.: National Science Foundation, 1965), pp. 186–217; Theodore Hsi-en Chen, *Chinese Education since 1949* (New York: Pergamon, 1981), pp. 35–40.

explicitly associated with mechanical copying of a foreign model, and once again deregularization was cast as the Chinese antidote.

Two points must nevertheless be noted in this ongoing reaction against dependency while simultaneously trying to learn the secrets of foreign success. One is that no effort was ever made to purge completely Soviet influence from the system. That influence was effectively co-opted and camouflaged but was never expunged, even after it was no longer overtly acknowledged. The second point is that although Soviet influence in its most exuberant form was associated with the regularization phase, Soviet influence was not exclusive to that phase. Hence over time, the net effect for education (and generally) was adaptation of the Soviet example to strengthen both the regularization and the deregularization phases of the development cycle. As a result, and especially after the Sino-Soviet honeymoon ended, it became increasingly difficult to distinguish between changes inspired by the Soviet Union and those that simply reinforced the assumptions of Chinese themselves about how best to reform and revolutionize their system. The borrowing grew ever more selective until post-1949 China absorbed and co-opted the Soviet model, much as pre-1949 China had done with Western influence during the 1920s and 1930s.

Guomindang forces had been defeated and expelled from the Northeast (Manchuria) by the end of 1948, and, not entirely by coincidence, that was also the region where the Soviet presence first made itself apparent. The Soviet Union had led all the other foreign powers in returning to their old spheres of influence in China after World War II. Hence the earliest Chinese references to learning from the Soviet Union, in 1948 and 1949, appear in sources from its old Manchurian redoubt. Autumn semester 1949 brought a flurry of activity there. Chinese educators visited Soviet-run schools in Lushun (Port Arthur) and Dalian (Dairen) established for the children of Soviet personnel. One such visit was recorded in meticulous detail and circulated in numerous reprinted versions.[3] Among the first Soviet experts to arrive in China was a deputy director of the Russian Republic's education department traveling with a Soviet cultural delegation. In late 1949 before returning home, she addressed a gathering in Shenyang (Mukden) at length on Soviet education.[4] Her remarks were also widely reprinted, but her immediate audience could not have known that they were hearing, in effect, a keynote speech for the new era. The details and extent of the movement to learn from the Soviet Union in education had

[3] Zhang Lianfeng, "Xuexi Sulian jiaoyu de jige jiben wenti: canguan Lushun Sulian zhongxue de jianji he ganyan" (A Few Basic Questions on Learning from the Soviet Union: A Short Report and Comments on a Visit to the Lushun Soviet Middle School), *Dongbei jiaoyu* (Northeast Education), no. 9, reprinted in Tianjin shi xiaoxue jiaodao yanjiuhui, ed., *Xiang Sulian xuexi* (Learning from the Soviet Union) (Beijing and Tianjin: Dazhong shudian, 1951), pp. 30–43.

[4] Du-bo-lo-wei-na, "Sulian de jiaoyu gongzuo" (The Soviet Union's Education Work), *Dongbei jiaoyu*, no. 9, reprinted in *Xiang Sulian xuexi*, pp. 1–20, and in *Renmin ribao* (People's Daily), Beijing, 12 Dec. 1949.

yet to be formulated. But aims and principles introduced during the fall of 1949 would dominate Chinese education for most of the coming decade.

First and foremost, the Russians explained, they were recommending the education system then current in the Soviet Union and not any of its previous incarnations. In her Shenyang speech, the comrade deputy director focused on those earlier "errors," to save China from the "winding path" that had earlier confounded Soviet education. In 1917, the Soviet revolution had led the way when there were no models. The Chinese should beware and benefit by coming later. Accordingly, they were enjoined to avoid temptations left and right.

Considerable liberty was taken with the historical context, but the errors mentioned referred mostly to the Soviet Union's experience during the 1920s. Problems on the right referred to those that emerged in the process of negating the old system and building a new one tailored to the specifications of the new revolutionary government. Resistance aimed at preserving the ways and methods of the old system was a kind of "rightist opportunism" which had to be suppressed. In the process, however, "infantile leftist" inclinations emerged. According to the official version as presented to the Chinese, such infantile leftism had been inspired by viewpoints current among American education reformers in the 1920s, when international discourse was still relatively open. Such viewpoints had emphasized education for life and the consequent reform of old-fashioned classroom learning. "This kind of thought was very destructive," warned the deputy director in her Shenyang remarks. "Why? Because to say that life can educate us reduces the function of schools. If the students feel that life can educate us, then teachers are not necessary. Then teachers, schools, and teaching methods cannot develop."[5] Hence the Soviet Communist Party had rectified this deviation as well and gone on to build the system being introduced to the Chinese. Its starting point was the 1931 decision on secondary and elementary education.[6]

That American educators should have been blamed for leftist errors constituted one of the more ingenious sleights of historical hand. Such "errors" had actually culminated, during the late 1920s, in a radical episode evidently promoted by Stalin himself as he moved to consolidate his power against enemies all around. The "education for life" experiments drew inspiration from many sources, including John Dewey, to be sure, but they were only a part of this radical phase, which had many parallels with the cultural revolution episode launched by Mao Zedong in the late 1960s. It also had some parallels with Soviet reform efforts in the mid-1950s, when the earlier, controversial period

---

[5] *Xiang Sulian xuexi*, p. 9.

[6] A Chinese translation of the Soviet document was published in 1951. See "Liangong, bu, zhongyang, guanyu xiaoxue yu zhongxue de jueding" (Decision of the Central Committee, Communist Party of the Soviet Union, Bolshevik, on Elementary and Secondary Schools), 5 Sept. 1931, *Renmin jiaoyu* (People's Education), Beijing, Mar. 1951, pp. 21–24.

of Stalin's past was partially exhumed. It was then portrayed as a kind of inspiration by negative example for the mid-1950s reforms. Such changes were necessary, it was explained to the Chinese in 1956, because the 1931 model had been designed in an overly rigid academic style to correct the unscientific leftist excesses of the 1927–1930 years.[7]

Whatever liberties they had to take with the historical context, however, Soviet advisors initially presented the 1931 system to the Chinese without qualification as the best of all possibilities. In 1931, it was said, students had not been receiving a good foundation in scientific knowledge. Curriculum and teaching methods were thereafter revised accordingly. American-style child psychologists were purged from the system, together with the methods they allegedly advocated of IQ testing and assigning students to different schools on the basis thereof. We feel, explained the Russian deputy director to her Shenyang audience, that differences in level of intelligence are not great and that, with very few exceptions, all children should be taught together. The key variable determining their ability to learn was the classroom environment itself and the methods by which they were taught. Detecting in China an inclination to favor antithetical views, Soviet advisors blamed these on the dangerous remnant influence of American pedagogy and warned their hosts to remain vigilent against them.

The government should issue orders defining clearly the curriculum, teaching and study methods, and disciplinary procedures. There should be strict rules and regulations for all aspects of school life. Nothing should be treated lightly or left to chance. Each student should be tested each semester and methods stipulated for evaluating and recording the individual's study and conduct. Lax discipline should not be tolerated among either teachers or students. As a symbolic feature of the proper school environment, when the teacher entered the classroom each day all students should rise in unison and remain standing until the teacher had taken his or her place at the lectern. The curriculum should be arranged in orderly sequence for each subject, so that each year's coursework was built systematically upon the foundation laid the previous year. This meant a fixed and planned curriculum with teaching outlines for all subjects at all levels.

One of the most difficult challenges for Soviet educators just after the revolution, they said, had been to strike the appropriate balance between past and present. Initially, they had struggled to overthrow the old system in its entirety. But once that was accomplished, they decided that some things might better have been retained. Hence, the Soviet education system as of 1949 was a combination of old and new. Among the latter: change had been built into the

---

[7] See chaps. 10 and 11, below, for further discussion on Soviet education in the 1920s and on the mid-1950s reforms.

system as a mandatory feature. Curriculum and textbooks were constantly revised to incorporate the latest developments in science, learning, and society. Another new feature was the materialist viewpoint used throughout to explain everything. Similarly, the erroneous old notion that study and the curriculum could be divorced from politics had been banished, along with the companion idea that a politics course could be added to the teaching plan while all the other subjects remained unchanged. The content of all courses – whether geography, history, literature, or whatever – had to be revised in accordance with the principle that learning and politics could not be separated. Banished as well were the old teaching methods, which revolved around four points only: teacher, textbook, blackboard, and chalk. The new methods in Soviet schools required all kinds of teaching aids: maps, charts, specimens, equipment, laboratories, and campus gardens. These were regarded as essential for illustration, observation, and hands-on student experimentation.

Finally, errors aside, Soviet education had been marked by three unbroken developments from 1917 onward. The first was mass education for the younger generation inspired by aims that were egalitarian and quantitative. The system was unified in all respects, by conscious contrast with Tsarist times when class differences were manifested in different kinds of schooling and when children of the laboring classes often received none at all. The new Soviet government decreed that all children must attend school free of charge. In 1930, the government announced that compulsory four-year education would be enforced in the countryside and seven years in the cities. In 1949, the seven-year system was decreed for the countryside as well, and the goal of 10 years was announced for the nation as a whole, to be achieved as soon as possible. Also in the early 1930s, the practice of giving preference in college admissions to workers and peasants was dropped. Students were thereafter enrolled according to uniform enrollment criteria regardless of their class origins or family backgrounds.

Second, adult education underwent similar phased development. In 1917, close to 80 percent of the population was said to have been illiterate. The first aim, therefore, was to eradicate illiteracy among the entire population aged between 8 and 50. A movement was launched in which every literate person was required to teach an illiterate. Then additional subjects were added. The effort continued for two decades, and by 1949 it had been successfully concluded. In addition, all kinds of training classes were set up in factories, schools, and enterprises and offered courses of varying duration at all levels in a range of practical subjects. A workers university was also established, specifically to train new intellectuals from among the workers and peasants. Here class background remained an important criterion for admission, and students after four or five years of full-time study could go on to regular universities and specialized institutes. Later, as regular mass education expanded, such preparatory training was deemed unnecessary and phased out, although adult education continued. For example, another form of education was created specifically for urban and rural youth who had been unable to complete their secondary schooling as regular students. This was a national system of night schools for employed young people and offered the same curriculum and advancement prospects as ordinary daytime schools.

The third major development had been to "reform" the "intellectuals," those who staffed the institutions of learning and maintained the nation's intellectual life. This, too, was a task "not completed in a day or two" since many of the old intellectuals were not sympathetic to the revolution, regarded capitalist Western thought as more progressive than Marxism, and felt the proletariat incapable of grasping theory or culture. But by 1949, they were said to have all been brought around to the correct way of thinking.[8]

In this manner, Soviet mentors promoted for China the end product of their own early revolutionary struggles at a stage when those of the newly victorious CCP were just beginning. This was the "classless" (because the original class enemies had been largely defeated) Stalin model education system. It featured a disciplined classroom-oriented academic format designed to produce loyal citizens capable of maintaining the bureaucratic institutions and heavy industries upon which the Soviet Union's centralized planned economy was built.

[8] This account of Soviet educational history is taken from the above-cited 1949 Shenyang speech by the deputy director of the Russian Republic's education department and also from Du-bo-lo-wei-na, "Sulian renmin wenjiao zhongxin Mosike" (Moscow, the Soviet People's Cultural Center), *Renmin jiaoyu*, Jan. 1952, pp. 7–8.

8

The Soviet model for Chinese higher education

For higher education, the main lessons learned from the Soviet Union revolved around thought reform and structural reorganization. According to the official chronology, reorganization was first proposed in mid-1950; the tertiary sector mobilized its forces to resist; thought reform intervened in 1951–1952; and by 1953, the nation's institutions of higher learning had been reconstructed along Soviet lines. As usual, the actual progression of events was rather more complex than the official chronology suggested.

Although political formulas were still phrased in terms of united front class coalitions, Mao's above-cited declaration in mid-1949 about leaning to one side under the aegis of a people's democratic dictatorship anticipated a renewed revolutionary surge. But the speed and intensity of the shift back from united front to revolutionary politics was also closely tied to a hostile international environment, which in turn complicated education reform.

University reorganization was announced at the First National Higher Education Conference in June 1950. Hostilities in Korea began that same month, and in China, domestic tensions escalated with the search for "counterrevolutionaries," or active opponents of the new regime. Chinese troops came to the aid of their North Korean ally in October, and in December, the U.S. government halted the remission of all funds to China. The Chinese responded, freezing American assets in China. Financial supply lines for American-funded institutions (see Table 8.1) on the Chinese mainland were cut. All foreign-subsidized and foreign-operated cultural, educational, relief, and religious institutions were required to register. All those receiving American subsidies were nationalized or transferred to private Chinese control.

Concurrently, a campaign was launched against all foreign missionary endeavors. These were denounced as instruments of cultural imperialism and breeding grounds for disloyal elements bent on undermining the "resist America, aid Korea" war effort. Schools with direct foreign links led the field in declaring their patriotism as a wave of anti-American, anticapitalist, and antimissionary fervor swept the country. Made to serve as model targets for criticism were the two most prestigious American-funded educational institutions in

Table 8.1. *Missionary-affiliated institutions, 1949*

	American subsidized	Total
Education:		
Tertiary	17	20
Secondary	200	300
Primary	1,500	6,000
Medical:		
Hospitals	200	400
Relief:		
Orphanges	200	—
Leper asylums	20	—
Schools for the deaf and mute	10	—
Schools for the blind	30	—

Source: Vice-Premier Guo Moruo, "Report on the Policy for Dealing with U.S.-Subsidized Cultural, Educational, and Relief Organizations and Religious Bodies," 29 Dec. 1950, *Renmin ribao* (People's Daily), Beijing, 30 Dec. 1950. For a list of Protestant and Catholic institutions of higher learning, see Lutz, *China and the Christian Colleges, 1850–1950*, pp. 531-533.

China, Yanjing (Yenching) University and the Beijing (Peking) Union Medical College.[1]

During the spring and summer of 1951, anti-American activities merged into the first nationwide political study movement for educational and literary personnel. This was the campaign to criticize the film *The Story of Wu Xun*. Everywhere college students and faculty were being recruited for off-campus excursions to the countryside. There they learned about social revolution firsthand by observing land reform or the expropriation and redistribution of agricultural land. In September, at the start of the 1951–1952 academic year, a more systematic thought reform campaign was launched; the first general reform plan for the education system as a whole was announced in October; and restructuring at the tertiary level intensified.

[1] Articles denouncing cultural imperialism in American missionary schools proliferated during 1950–1951. The U.S. government press-monitoring units translated a large sample; see, e.g., *Current Background*, U.S. Consulate General, Hong Kong (hereafter cited as *CB*), no. 107 (15 Aug. 1951), and the following issues of *Survey of China Mainland Press*, U.S. Consulate General, Hong Kong (hereafter cited as SCMP): no. 27 (10–11 Dec. 1950), pp. 9–12; no. 46 (11 Jan. 1951), pp. 14–20; no. 52 (19–20 Jan. 1951), pp. 3–5; no. 153 (13–14 Aug. 1951), pp. 27–28; no. 159 (22 Aug. 1951), p. 14; no. 184 (28–29 Sept. 1951), pp. 25–27; no. 236 (14–15 Dec. 1951), pp. 11–12. See also Bullock, *An American Transplant*; Lutz, *China and the Christian Colleges*; and Philip West, *Yenching University and Sino–Western Relations, 1916–1952* (Cambridge: Harvard University Press, 1976).

These activities unfolded simultaneously with two similar campaigns, one for the government bureaucracy, much of which had been inherited from the GMD, and the other for business and industry. Both campaigns embodied the spirit of Mao's "democratic dictatorship" as a preliminary attack against bourgeois behavior. The former, which began in late 1951, was known as the "three-anti" campaign, that is, anticorruption, antiwaste, and antibureaucratism. University administrators were also targeted since most institutions of higher learning were public, and by early 1952 the campaign combined with the thought reform study movement to reach a crescendo of criticism against "bourgeois ideology."

The second campaign, called the "five-anti" campaign, aimed to rectify commercial and industrial activities. The five targets were bribery, tax evasion, theft of state property, cheating on contracts, and stealing economic information for speculative purposes. These campaigns belied the continuing official toleration of united front class alliances. The fines and compensation demanded of wrongdoers during the five-anti exercise were often confiscatory and escalated into outright expropriation. By 1956, capitalists as a class no longer existed, having survived their rural landlord counterparts by only a few years.

Reforming the thought of intellectuals

Thought reform thus unfolded as a companion in the intellectual realm of a fast accelerating socioeconomic revolution at home and open hostilities abroad. Officially, intellectuals did not form a separate social class but most often originated somewhere within the bourgeoisie and had political views to match. They could still be accepted as allies but only on the CCP's terms, that is, by accepting working-class and CCP leadership. Thought reform would ensure that they learned the unfamiliar terms of the new alliance.

The story of this episode has been told many times.[2] The Chinese themselves coined the term "brainwashing" (*xinao*), which was then widely used in the West to suggest the invidious psychological pressures to which victims were subjected. In fact, ideological conversion was probably the least important or effective of the thought reform campaign's aims and consequences. Considering all that has happened since, a more realistic appraisal would probably lie in the political and social, rather than psychological or intellectual, realms. The campaign essentially laid down the parameters within which everyone would henceforth have to live their lives and pursue their careers. Many undoubtedly accepted, either in whole or in part, the logic of the arguments they were obliged to study and learn. Others undoubtedly feigned acceptance, mouthing

[2] E.g., Theodore H. E. Chen, *Thought Reform of the Chinese Intellectuals* (Hong Kong: Hong Kong University Press, 1960), pt. 1; Robert Jay Lifton, *Thought Reform and the Psychology of Totalism: A Study of "Brainwashing" in China* (New York: W. W. Norton, 1963); Allyn Rickett and Adele Rickett, *Prisoners of Liberation* (Garden City, N.Y.: Anchor/Doubleday, 1973); Edward Hunter, *Brain-washing in Red China* (New York: Vanguard, 1953); Merle Goldman, *Literary Dissent in Communist China* (Cambridge: Harvard University Press, 1967), pp. 87–157.

their lessons opportunistically. But everyone most certainly grasped the basic point of the exercise, namely, that a new political authority with a new set of rules would have to be accommodated one way or another.

The CCP marshalled for this initial task many, but not all, the charges that had inspired the radical critique of Chinese education in earlier decades. The issues selected were those that dovetailed with the concurrent drive to learn from the Soviet model. The 1940s rectification movement in Yan'an had begun the process of integrating the old critique with the ideology and practice of Chinese communism during the rural wartime stage of its growth, under the more benign rules of united front politics. By contrast, the main target in the early 1950s at the onset of social revolution was the entire urban intellectual establishment, most of which had opted to remain in China after 1949 rather than flee abroad or move with the GMD to Taiwan. Efforts to merge the two orientations, rural and urban, would only come later.

Specifically, the themes from the recent Chinese past that gave added dimension and credibility to the Soviet-inspired thought reform exercise were the pro-Western and especially the pro-American inclinations of China's intellectuals; the influence of Western and missionary-run education in China itself; the inherited Chinese disdain for practical application, which was responsible for the education system's deficiencies in science and technology training; the intellectual community's self-perception as the modern successor of China's traditional ruling elite; and the individualistic nature of the reform tradition itself.

The prelude, billed as a film critique, was an almost quiet summer break amid the cacophony of political sounds in 1951. Everyone working in education and literacy circles had to attend study meetings and read the propaganda materials criticizing *The Story of Wu Xun*. Wu Xun had been a Chinese-style Horatio Alger in the rags-to-riches tradition. Born in 1839 the son of a poor peasant family in Shandong, he became famous during the last years of the Qing dynasty for his commitment to education. When still a young child, his father died, leaving the family to live as beggars. Their poverty prevented the boy from being accepted in the village school, and this made so deep an impression that he never forgot his vow to promote education for others. As a young man, even after his fortunes began to improve, he continued his old way of life, guided by the motto "begging to build a school." Eventually after becoming a moneylender and landlord, he managed to establish three schools during the last decade of his life. The memory of his commitment continued to be venerated, particularly in his native Shandong, for half a century after his death in 1896. The "spirit of Wu Xun" came to be widely understood in educational circles as meaning a willingness to strive, against overwhelming odds, to promote the cause of education for those in humble circumstances.

Also in time-honored tradition, education reformer Tao Xingzhi was among those who had gone on record in praise of Wu's dedication. Tao's aim had been to draw a parallel between himself and Wu, thereby invoking the latter's traditional-style charity as a precedent to help garner support for Tao's own less conventional methods. It was actually a literary debate over Tao's identification of himself with Wu that was used to launch the campaign. A film based on Wu's life premiered in Shanghai on 31 December 1950 to critical acclaim but was withdrawn in May. The debate that had developed in the interim was then publicized in the national press.[3] Prominent intellectuals came forward one after another with critical commentaries, all clearly following prepared guidelines.[4]

Qinghua University philosopher Feng Youlan probably revealed most about the motivation underlying the campaign when he acknowledged in his contribution that before 1949, the great majority of China's "men of talent" remained in the cities under GMD rule. Meanwhile, the revolution was victorious in Russia, Marxism took root in China, the CCP was founded, and its liberated areas began to grow in the countryside. But most of China's leading academics had participated neither directly nor indirectly in any phase of the revolutionary enterprise. Just as Wu Xun had perpetuated the dominant ideology of his time in both the form and Confucian classical content of his charitable schools, so modern intellectuals continued to stand on the side of reaction, accepting posts from the GMD government and perpetuating its worldview. From that perspective, neither Wu nor his modern successors deserved to be emulated, however worthy their particular contributions.[5]

Tao Xingzhi's praise of Wu Xun obviously presented something of a problem since both Tao, who had died in 1946, and his methods continued to be respected by CCP leaders. The official solution was to separate Tao's own life and work from his attempts to identify himself with Wu. By the end of the campaign, Tao's reputation was rather more tarnished. But once the rhetorical tides had subsided, the basic charge against Wu Xun stood as a Marxist repudiation of the earlier liberal assumptions that education could "save China"

[3] Yang Er, "Tao Xingzhi xiansheng biaoyang 'Wu Xun jingshen' you jiji zuoyong ma?" (Does Mr. Tao Xingzhi's Praise of "The Spirit of Wu Xun" Have Any Positive Function?), *Wenyi bao* (Literary Journal), vol. 4, no. 2 (1951); and Jia Ji, "Bu zu wei xun de Wu Xun" (Wu Xun Is Not Worthy of Emulation), *Wenyi bao*, vol. 4, no. 1 (1951). The former was first reprinted in *Renmin ribao*, 16 May 1951. The editorials calling for criticism appeared on 20 May. All were reprinted together in *Xinhua yuebao* (New China Monthly), Beijing, vol. 4, no. 2 (25 June 1951), pp. 394–405. See also *Jiefang ribao* (Liberation Daily), Shanghai, 20, 21 May 1951; and *CB*, no. 113 (1 Sept. 1951), entire issue.

[4] The critical articles were collected in several sources, e.g., Renmin chubanshe, ed., *Pipan "Wu Xun zhuan"* (Criticizing *The Story of Wu Xun*), 2 vols. (Beijing: Renmin chubanshe, 1951); *Xuexi* (Study), Beijing, vol. 4, no. 5 (16 June 1951); *Xinhua yuebao*, vol. 4, no. 3 (25 July 1951), pp. 682–690; *Renmin jiaoyu*, July 1951, pp. 17–33. Zhou Yang's summary statement marked the campaign's end (*Renmin ribao*, 8 Aug. 1951). At this time, Zhou Yang was a deputy director of the CCP Propaganda Department and a deputy minister of culture.

[5] Feng Youlan, "Guanyu *Wu Xun zhuan* de pipan" (On the Criticism of *The Story of Wu Xun*), *Xuexi*, vol. 4, no. 5 (16 June 1951), pp. 24–25.

or improve the lives of ordinary people. Wu Xun had succeeded only in the small personal sense, whereas his effort was doomed to larger failure since it did not anticipate revolutionary collective action. Yet the Wu Xun tradition served to perpetuate the illusion that fundamental improvements could be achieved through education and by individual reformers.[6]

The main thought reform campaign began in September 1951, with a four-month study program for university personnel in Beijing and Tianjin. It was than extended nationwide for educators at all levels, although activity remained concentrated in higher education. The campaign was directed from the center by the government's Culture and Education Commission and the CCP's Propaganda Department. Hu Qiaomu, as secretary-general of the commission and a deputy director of the Propaganda Department, played a key role, together with Education Minister Ma Xulun. Beneath them, work was coordinated in all major cities by the local government education bureaus, but regional study committees were set up to provide direct guidance and coordination with the center. Ma Xulun was chairman of the University Professors Study Committee for Beijing and Tianjin, with branches in each university. The prominent intellectuals who had by this time been named to head most major universities were directed to lead the branch committees and use themselves as models or typical examples for study and reform. At the "grassroots" level, all faculty members were organized into small "mutual-aid" study groups, which for the individual became the focal point of campaign activity.

In this way, China's ranking academics were introduced to the techniques for achieving ideological discipline that had been pioneered among both non-Party and Party members in Yan'an during the rectification drive there. Similarly, the 1951–1952 effort began with a fixed "core curriculum" of reports and documents which had to be mastered in order to serve as the basis for the small-group exercises. In this way, everyone was supposed to master the art of criticism and self-criticism. Such direct personal confrontation was a new experience for academics, as unfamiliar as it was unpleasant. But it would become a routine feature of teachers' lives in later years as the "struggle–study class" (*xuexi ban*) used in more and less benign forms to enforce discipline throughout the Cultural Revolution decade.

In 1951, the introductory exercise progressed through five stages. The first was dominated by study of Premier Zhou Enlai's five-hour keynote address which launched the campaign on 29 September. He introduced seven topics necessary for the intellectuals' thought reform: their standpoint, attitudes, whom they should serve, problems of thought, problems of knowledge, democracy,

---

[6] E.g., Qian Junrui, "Cong taolun Wu Xun wenti women xuedao xie shenma" (What We Have Learned from the Discussion of Wu Xun's Problems), *Renmin jiaoyu*, Sept. 1951, pp. 11–13; and a later self-criticism by film director Sun Yu in *Guangming ribao*, 10 June 1952. Qian Junrui was a deputy minister of education.

and the practice of personal criticism and self-criticism.[7] The second stage commenced on 18 November with Peng Zhen's report on the three major movements then under way: land reform; resist America, aid Korea; and suppression of political opponents, or counterrevolutionaries. Study materials for the third stage comprised Hu Qiaomu's history of the CCP and an essay by Chen Boda on Mao Zedong's theories combining Marxism–Leninism with the realities of the Chinese revolution.

The fourth stage entailed the study of Li Fuchun's report on economic development and cadre training. The aim was to establish among university and research personnel the idea that their work should serve the needs of economic development and national defense. Specifically, this fourth step aimed to tackle "ideological problems," or resistance to the new plans introduced in mid-1950 for reorganizing faculties and departments, revising curricula, and reforming teaching methods. Finally, the fifth stage entailed summaries of personal ideological problems revealed in the course of the study sessions, an examination of work, and the preparation of concrete measures for implementing the proposed reforms in higher education.

In his keynote address, Zhou Enlai in effect issued a direct, albeit polite, warning to intellectuals that indefinite passive accommodation with the new order would not be enough. There could be no middle ground. Deputy Minister of Education Qian Junrui was more blunt. He admonished the great majority of college teachers for having made so little progress in their thinking since 1949. As a result, they were obstructing reform of higher education. Yet without such reform, those institutions would remain incapable of serving the nation. That service had now been redefined in practical terms, namely, to train 200,000 people capable of implementing the country's ambitious new economic development plans. Such people would be needed especially in industry, agriculture, communications, transport, and medicine. Toward this end, the system, content, and methods of China's tertiary education had to be changed. Qian identified three types of incorrect viewpoints and work styles among college teachers that would have to be overcome.

First was their strong Anglo-American bias. Second, higher-level intellectuals were overwhelmingly motivated in their life and work by self-interest, by their own security, wealth, and prestige. Third, college teachers were dogmatic in their work and divorced from reality, which greatly undermined their effectiveness. Declared Qian: "Reading out from textbooks and the duck-stuffing method are still the most common ways of teaching in our institutions of higher learning. Among them, the most popular and harmful is the mechanical copying of foreign dogmas. Old things studied 10, 20, or 30 years ago in England or America, foreign textbooks, even lecturing in English, making the

---

[7] Zhongyang jiaoyu kexue yanjiusuo, ed., *Zhou Enlai jiaoyu wenxuan* (Selections from Zhou Enlai on Education) (Beijing: Jiaoyu kexue chubanshe, 1984), pp. 38–65.

students take notes and prepare exercises in English – really, what is the point of it?!" Institutions of higher learning were in the process of being reorganized in order to strengthen the specialties needed for economic development. The substance of education would also be revised, including curricula, textbooks, and teaching methods. Thought reform aimed to correct the above erroneous tendencies.[8]

Thereafter, China's best-known academics from its leading universities came forward in succession with statements of criticism and self-criticism.[9] All used similar language, reiterating in different ways the three basic points of criticism outlined by Deputy Minister Qian – which were in turn a reiteration using Marxist terminology of well-established themes from the history of modern Chinese education. The demands being made were thus neither entirely alien nor capricious. They were being phrased in terms familiar enough that few could fail to grasp their logic, which undoubtedly explains the ambivalence within the thought reform movement that few observers also failed to note. It was the same ambivalence that had characterized education reform in China since the 1920s. On the one hand, the academic community did not rush to participate, despite the examples set by their leaders. Accounts from the early stages of the campaign all noted its slow start. Yet China's leading academics also went along with the exercise to a degree that bewildered foreign observers. Nor should the acquiescence be seen as deriving entirely from coercion or the social pressures built into the movement.

Among Americans, accusations that Beijing Union Medical College and Yanjing University had used Chinese children in medical experiments only fanned cold war flames. So too did charges that the gardens of missionary compounds were littered with death pits containing the bodies of Chinese children left to die while foreign missionaries lived in well-fed comfort.[10] American diplomatic observers similarly dismissed the criticism of Hu Shi as an attempt to discredit one of China's most prominent intellectuals for having rejected the new regime. Hu Shi had been singled out as "the most highly representative figure wherein is concentrated all the reactionary aspects of the old scholastic circles."[11] These observers also judged the thought reform campaign to be "in essence a criticism of free scholarship and liberalism."[12]

In China, by contrast, the campaign contained many additional dimensions.

[8] Qian Junrui, "Gaodeng jiaoyu gaige de guanjian" (The Key to Reforming Higher Education), *Xuexi*, vol. 5, no. 1 (1 Nov. 1951), pp. 10–11, reprinted in *Renmin jiaoyu*, Dec. 1951, pp. 6–7.

[9] For a selection of these statements, see *CB*, nos. 169, 182, 213 (all 1952).

[10] *SCMP* contains translations of many articles from the antimissionary propaganda campaign, a selection of which can be found in the following issues: nos. 83, 88, 102, 110, 162 (all 1951), no. 354 (1952).

[11] *Ta Kung Pao*, Hong Kong, 30 Nov. 1951, trans. in *SCMP*, no. 225 (1951).

[12] "The Communists and the Intellectuals: Stage One," editorial comment, *CB*, no. 169 (2 Apr. 1952), p. 4; "The Campaign against Hu Shih," editorial comment, *CB*, no. 167 (25 Mar. 1952), p. 2.

The circulation of atrocity stories was a long-standing tradition each time opinion rose against the foreign missionaries. The most recent serious outburst had occurred in the mid-1920s, as part of the larger nationalistic backlash against the rush to embrace the West during the two decades preceding. The 1951 accusations against missionary hospitals and orphanages were but the latest variation on earlier precedents.[13]

Hu Shi did indeed rank among China's foremost intellectuals, and his refusal to lend his prestige to the new CCP-led government placed him beyond the pale of its united front blandishments. But his well-publicized differences with the modern critics of China's Westernization extended back to 1919, when they were all still friends working together for the common cause of cultural reform and national reconstruction. As the critical consensus hardened during the 1920s and 1930s, Hu Shi refused to join it. He not only had distanced himself from the post-1919 disillusionment with the West at its inception but ultimately became one of its most articulate opponents.

The archtypical cosmopolitan intellectual, Hu Shi maintained that China's salvation lay in its absorption of Western values and attitudes, seen at their best in America. He maintained further that China's universities should be centers for creating the "new gentry" leadership necessary to disseminate that influence. Consistent with this belief, he had remained politically aloof from the post-1919 tides of popular nationalistic protest against foreign incursions in China. He also admired Japan for having succeeded in learning from the West while China failed and was placed increasingly on the defensive as Japan's invasion of China progressed during the 1930s, provoking an ever more militant Chinese nationalism in response. His youthful vow not to succumb to the lure of official position was but a distant memory by the time he was appointed China's ambassador to the U.S. in 1938. As head of Beijing University a decade later, his support for the GMD government in its battle with the communists marked the gulf that finally separated Hu Shi from the contemporary generation of students, for whom active confrontation with the GMD was the norm.[14]

Similarly, the three main points in Qian Junrui's 1951 statement must have been instantly recognized by all who read them as a reiteration of the familiar

[13] E.g., Paul A. Cohen, *China and Christianity: The Missionary Movement and the Growth of Chinese Antiforeignism, 1860–1870* (Cambridge: Harvard University Press, 1963), passim; Mary Clabaugh Wright, *The Last Stand of Chinese Conservatism: the T'ung-Chih Restoration, 1862–1874* (Stanford: Stanford University Press, 1962), p. 276. On the 1920s, see Paul A. Varg, *Missionaries, Chinese, and Diplomats* (Princeton: Princeton University Press, 1958), pp. 180–193; Lutz, *China and the Christian Colleges*, chap. 7.

[14] Grieder, *Hu Shih and the Chinese Renaissance*, pp. 281–282, and passim; Meisner, *Li Ta-chao and the Origins of Chinese Marxism*, pp. 104–112; Keenan, *The Dewey Experiment in China*, pp. 143–154; John Israel, *Student Nationalism in China, 1927–1937* (Stanford: Hoover Institution, 1966), pp. 133–134, 141; Pepper, *Civil War in China*, chap. 3.

arguments against China's educational establishment. When China's academics came forward one after another with their acts of contrition, these could have been paraphrased almost as readily from the old reformers' critique as from the current directives of the CCP's Propaganda Department.

There were, of course, some significant differences between present and past. The differences were most notably the Marxist–Leninist theoretical framework, the centrally controlled format that deprived opponents of their right to speak, the unfamiliar criticism–self-criticism routines, and the Soviet Union as revolutionary role model. A more appropriate comparison, then, was with the Yan'an rectification movement, because the 1951–1952 thought reform campaign was also translating Marxism–Leninism into "proper Chinese" and further integrating the indigenous critique of China's modern Western-oriented intellectuals with the theory and practice of Chinese communism. In this way, the critique was reaffirmed as a link between the pre-1949 past and an uncharted revolutionary future to be governed by the new foreign dogma and strange Soviet model. In this way, too, the Yan'an precedent was in the making as its ominous portents began to be realized. For a second time, the intellectual obedience achieved via rectification was deliberately used as a prerequisite for major education reform.

Nevertheless, this was not just a manipulation of past precedents to gain a measure of legitimacy by integrating well-known Chinese concerns with the unfamiliar Marxist rhetoric. It was also an attempt to use the new order to promote aims that had never been possible under the old. Another important difference, then, between the present and the past was that ranking members of the educational establishment had been maneuvered into articulating views that were previously the hallmark of dedicated reformers and radical youths but were acknowledged at most only in the abstract by everyone else. Now for the first time, a national government was apparently intent on trying to make everyone pay more than lip service to such aims. And as many a reformer had earlier discovered, implementation inevitably marked the painful moment of truth, forcing back all but the most dedicated. Only this time there would be no turning back, at least not in the foreseeable future. All the authority and coercive power of the state stood behind ideological reform and university reorganization.

For the intellectuals who remained in China, as a majority chose to do, the first real test of their commitment to the new order thus began during the 1951–1952 academic year or, more accurately, the year after. Before thought reform, according to another deputy minister of education, Zeng Zhaolun, university personnel had refused to learn from the Soviet Union and had opposed reorganization for almost two years, maintaining that American-style education was superior. Afterward, a new enthusiasm for studying Russian could be detected. But the most important result was to smooth the way for reorganization, allegedly causing faculty to accept transfers "happily and with perfect peace of mind."[15]

Restructuring tertiary education

Reform and reorganization plans had been introduced at the First National Higher Education Conference in June 1950. Higher education must be made to serve economic development. The key lay in technology rather than pure science. Curricula had to be revised accordingly. But higher schools should also open their doors to students of working-class origins. To ensure this new direction, leadership over higher education would have to be unified and centralized under the Education Ministry, which would be given responsibility for determining policy, curricula, teaching materials and methods, as well as appointments and dismissals of university leaders. The institutions themselves and the departments within them were to be reorganized, nationwide, the better to fulfill their new mission. Intellectuals should be sent for training to Soviet bloc countries and Soviet textbooks translated into Chinese. These decisions had already been made at the highest levels, and the academic community, without yet realizing it, was not being asked but told what lay in store.[16]

Following a decision on curricular reform passed at the June 1950 conference, institutions of higher learning had to submit reports of their progress, and investigations of selected departments were conducted by faculty committees. They were checking, among other things, to see whether the stipulated political courses had been introduced; whether theory and practice were being coordinated; whether departments were offering courses in a rational and planned manner; and whether the new teaching research groups (*jiaoxue yanjiu zu*) were being formed.[17] These groups, or *kafedra* in Russian, were advertised as the mainstay of Soviet education. New to Chinese institutions of higher learning, the Chinese version in both name and function was not unfamiliar in principle given its similarity with the education research committees (*jiaoyu yanjiu hui*). These were authorized, as we have seen, by Chinese government directives to improve elementary school teaching in the 1930s.

At the tertiary level, however, the teaching research groups were at first as

---

[15] Zeng Zhaolun, "Sannianlai gaodeng jiaoyu de gaijin" (Improvements in Higher Education during the Past Three Years), *Renmin jiaoyu*, Jan. 1953, pp. 11–12.

[16] The First National Higher Education Conference was widely publicized both before and after the event. Education Minister Ma Xulun's opening and closing speeches were published in *Renmin jiaoyu*, July 1950, pp. 11–16; speech by Deputy Minister of Education Qian Junrui in ibid., Dec. 1950, pp. 8–14; speech by Soviet expert A-er-xin-jie-fu in ibid., July 1950, pp. 25–27. Also on the conference, see ibid., May 1950, pp. 16, 22.

[17] *Renmin ribao*, 31 Jan. 1951; see also *Guangming ribao*, 30 Jan. 1951; Zhongyang jiaoyubu (Education Ministry), "Quanguo gaodeng xuexiao yijiuwuling niandu jiaoxue jihua shencha zongjie" (Summary of the 1950 National Investigation of Teaching Plans for Institutions of Higher Learning), *Xinhua yuebao*, vol. 4, no. 1 (25 May 1951), pp. 176–178.

unwelcome as the new self-criticism routines. Soon all teachers were organized into these groups on the basis of the subjects and courses they taught. The groups served essentially as the basic units for collective course preparation, teacher training, and mutual supervision. The more experienced were supposed to induct the younger members into the practical aspects of the profession. A group's members prepared course outlines and lecture notes together as a team, dividing up the work in different ways. They also attended one another's classes as a basis for group evaluations afterward.[18]

In November 1951, a National Conference on Higher Technological Education finalized plans for the reorganization of all such institutions of learning. Meanwhile, the Education Ministry was reiterating through the columns of its publication *Renmin jiaoyu* (People's Education) and elsewhere the defects of the old Western-influenced system that Soviet-style education would correct. Familiar themes were finally appearing as specific items on a reform agenda, for example: an unbalanced geographic distribution, with institutions of higher learning concentrated in the larger cities, especially of north and east China; inefficient teacher/student rations; insufficient emphasis on technology education, with only a few students in many important specialties such as geology, mining, water conservancy, civil engineering, etc.; a preference for regular courses over specialized post-secondary training programs; high unemployment among graduates due to the isolation of their training from the actual needs of the economy.[19]

The announcement in April 1952 of detailed plans for colleges and departments of technology heralded the restructuring of all institutions during the 1952–1953 academic year. The result, copied from the Soviet system, divided tertiary institutions into three types: comprehensive universities combining science and humanities faculties; polytechnics, with several applied science faculties in a single institution; and specialized colleges, each with a single faculty (see Table 8.2). To illustrate the large-scale uprooting of personnel that occurred at this time, Beijing University's College of Engineering and Yanjing

---

[18] For several descriptions of the unfamiliar "collective teaching" approach promoted by Soviet advisors through the teaching research groups, see, e.g., A-er-xin-jie-fu, "Guanyu Sulian gaodeng xuexiao de jiaoxue yanjiu zhidao zu wenti" (Questions on the Teaching Research Guidance Groups in Soviet Institutions of Higher Learning), *Renmin jiaoyu*, June 1950, pp. 34–36; A-er-xin-jie-fu, "Duiyu jiaoxue yanjiu zu suo ti wenti de jieda" (Answers to Questions Raised on the Teaching Research Groups), in ibid., pp. 49–50; An-de-lie-yang-nuo fu, "Guanyu Sulian gaodeng xuexiao do jiaoxue, xingzheng zuzhi yu zhengzhi sixing jiaoyu deng wenti" (On Teaching, Administrative Organization, Political Thought Education, and Such Questions in Soviet Institutions of Higher Learning), *Renmin jiaoyu*, Sept. 1951, pp. 18–19; Tseng Chao-lun (Zeng Zhaolun), "Higher Education in New China," *People's China*, Beijing, no. 12 (16 June 1953), p. 8; see also Alexander G. Korol, *Soviet Education for Science and Technology* (Cambridge: Massachusetts Institute of Technology; New York: John Wiley and Sons, 1957), pp. 153–154, 221.

[19] E.g., Zhang Zonglin, "Gaige gaodeng gongye jiaoyu de kaiduan" (The Beginning of Reform for Higher Technical Education), *Renmin jiaoyu*, Jan. 1952, pp. 9–12; Zeng Zhaolun, "Sannianlai," pp. 11–15.

Table 8.2. *Distribution of students in reorganized tertiary institutions by school and/or field of study*

Type of institution	No. of institutions (Dec. 1953)	1953–1954		1954–1955	
		Field of study	Planned no. of freshmen (%)	Field of study	Planned no. of freshmen (%)
Comprehensive universities	14	Natural sciences	4,500 (6.43)	Natural sciences	5,740 (6.34)
Polytechnics	39	Humanities	3,000 (4.28)	Humanities	7,110 (7.86)
Teacher training colleges	31	Engineering	30,000 (42.86)	Engineering	33,865 (37.42)
Agricultural colleges	29	—	18,300 (26.14)	Teacher training	24,975 (27.60)
Medical colleges	29	—	3,200 (4.57)	Agriculture and forestry	4,260 (4.70)
Politics and law	4	—	7,200 (10.29)	Medicine	9,200 (10.17)
Finance and economics	6	—	700 (1.0)	Political science and law	2,000 (2.21)
Foreign languages	8	—	2,000 (2.86)	Finance and economics	1,970 (2.17)
Fine arts	15	—	300 (0.42)	Fine arts	385 (0.43)
Physical culture	5	—	800 (1.14)	Physical education	1,000 (1.10)
Minority nationalities institutes	2	—	—	—	—
Total	182		70,000		90,505

Sources: Data on institutions for 1953–1954 are from *Guangming ribao*, 17 Dec. 1953; *Renmin ribao*, 17 Dec. 1953. Tertiary-level figures contained more than the usual unexplained discrepancies at this time, perhaps because of the disruption caused by reorganization and/or a desire to conceal the decline in number of institutions by comparison with pre-1949. For example, in mid-1953, Education Vice-Minister Zeng Zhaolun claimed 185 tertiary institutions before 1949, 210 in 1951, and 218 after reorganization (Tseng Chao-lun, "Higher Education in New China," *People's China*, 16 June, 1953, p. 8).

Data on students for 1953–1954 are from Ma Xulun, "Gaodeng jiaoyu de fangzhen, renwu wenti" (Questions on the Policy and Tasks of Higher Education), *Renmin jiaoyu*, Apr. 1953, pp. 13–14.

Data for 1954–1955 are from *Renmin ribao*, 25 May 1954.

University's engineering departments were all merged within Qinghua University, which became a multifaculty institute of technology. Beijing University became a Soviet-style comprehensive institution absorbing the liberal arts, sciences, and law colleges of both Qinghua and Yanjing. The latter was formally abolished.[20]

The proliferation of specialized colleges was based on the assumption that narrower specialization provided the most efficient training. Academic specialties were also redesigned more narrowly than majors under the old system, the aim being to prepare students more quickly for specific kinds of work as dictated by the economic plan. To create a more rational geographic distribution of academic resources, at least one college each of medicine, agriculture, and teacher training was established in every province. The new-style comprehensive universities were also more or less evenly distributed around the country, with only one each in Beijing and Shanghai. All remaining private institutions were taken over by the state during the 1952–1953 reorganization.

The new system was designed not only to emphasize technical education but to elevate it to a status equal to other fields. Within the old system, the liberal arts and sciences universities enjoyed the highest prestige, in comparison with colleges and technical institutes. Officially, the Soviet-style system placed all on an equal plane, although each category was assigned a different function and offered courses of differing lengths. As a chief selling point of the new system, all tertiary-level graduates, including those of two-year technical training courses and the applied science institutes, were said to enjoy equal status in terms of their academic standing.

This was claimed to be the most effective means of overcoming serious personnel shortages in many key areas while equalizing opportunities for all. In 1952, some 55 percent of all first-year students enrolling in applied science majors were channeled into the two-year post-secondary courses. Contemporary published statistics varied somewhat, but the most detailed breakdown of students by institution and speciality is shown in Table 8.2. Applied science and technology had taken over the commanding heights of the tertiary system. It was officially claimed that students enrolled in these subjects already made up 35 percent of the total number in 1952–1953, whereas in 1946 they had made up less than 20 percent.[21] Simpler breakdowns comparing the late forties and late fifties are shown in Tables 8.3 and 8.4. Comparable data from earlier decades are shown in Table 4.5.

Finally, to ensure that the restructured system performed the functions

---

[20] "Zhongyang renmin zhengfu jiaoyubu, guanyu quanguo gongxueyuan tiaozheng fangan de baogao" (Central People's Government Ministry of Education, Report on the National Restructuring Plan for Technical Institutes), 30 Nov. 1951, *Wenhuibao*, Shanghai, 17 Apr. 1952; see also "Ma Yinchu daibiao de fayan" (Representative Ma Yinchu's Presentation), National People's Congress meeting, 26 Sept. 1954, *Guangming ribao*, 27 Sept. 1954.

[21] Zeng Zhaolun, "Sannianlai," p. 15.

Table 8.3. *Distribution of students in tertiary institutions by field of study*

Field	1947 (%)	1957 (%)
Engineering	17.8	37.1
Agriculture	6.6	9.1
Medicine	7.7	11.4
Teacher training	13.5	24.5
Politics and law	24.4	1.8
Finance and economics	11.5	3.2

Source: Zhang Jian, "Woguo de gaodeng jiaoyu shi yueban yuehao le" (Our Country's Higher Education Is Being Run Better and Better), *Renmin jiaoyu*, Oct. 1957, p. 7.

Table 8.4. *Geographic distribution of tertiary institutions and students*

	1949	1957
Coastal provinces:		
No. of institutions	118	113
% of students	61.5	55.9
Interior provinces:		
No. of institutions	87	114
% of students	38.6	44.1
Total	205	227

Source: Zhang Jian, "Woguo de gaodeng jiaoyu shi yueban yuehao le" (Our Country's Higher Education Is Being Run Better and Better), *Renmin jiaoyu*, Oct. 1957, p. 7.

intended, it was reinforced with unified sets of plans for student enrollment, job assignment, and curriculum content. Available documentary sources do not reveal precisely how this particular mix of centralized structures and functions came into being. Curricula were taken directly from those used in the Soviet Union. The enrollment and job assignment plans were also Soviet imports, their details drawn to meet the predetermined needs of centralized economic planning. The actual procedures whereby students were recruited to fill the slots stipulated by the enrollment plan seem to have been inspired by the Soviet planning ethos but were reinforced by the imperatives of China's own academic traditions. In any event, the end result was a far more rigidly centralized, standardized, and hierarchical enrollment system than had ever been deemed necessary in the Soviet Union. Evidently, the well-known priorities of

Chinese intellectuals inherited from the past constituted the chief imperative. The antidote, however, was also inherited from the past in the form of college entrance examinations that had more in common with the pre-1905 system of bureaucratic selection than the Soviet Union's highly decentralized enrollment procedures.

Centralized enrollment and job placement

Unified state job assignments for college graduates were introduced in 1950, with a proud claim that the pre-1949 students' lament, "graduation means unemployment," was now banished forever.[22] In retrospect, the claim was probably used not just to advertise one of the new benefits of socialist life but to counteract widespread student resentment over the gap between their inherited expectations and the newly enforced "needs of national construction." Tensions were naturally greatest among the transitional generation, who were enrolled under the old system but graduated into the new.

Political consciousness-raising via thought reform was prescribed as an interim solution while plans were laid to channel students into the required slots at the start of their college careers rather than at the end. But instead of leaving it to the redesigned institutions themselves to enroll and train students according to centrally fixed standards and curricula, following Soviet practice, the Chinese pushed centralized personnel planning a step further.[23]

In 1952, they introduced unified national entrance examinations, which all candidates throughout the country took on the same days, at the same time, and in the same sequence. Examination scores were then used to allocate all first-year students in accordance with the unified enrollment plans – coordinated and carefully balanced between the national and regional levels – which stipulated the number of students to be enrolled from each region into each institution and specialty. The aim, once all the plans were fully operational, was to match the number of first-year students enrolled each year in different specialties with the number of employees that would be needed two to four years hence, as decreed by the national economic plan.[24]

---

[22] E.g., Liu Shih, "Two Years of Advance in People's Education," *People's China*, vol. 4, no. 7 (1 Oct. 1951), p. 34.

[23] On Soviet tertiary-level admissions procedures, see Nicholas De Witt, *Education and Professional Employment in the U.S.S.R.* (Washington, D.C.: National Science Foundation, 1961), pp. 242–274; Korol, *Soviet Education for Science and Technology*, pp. 167–190.

[24] The phased introduction of planned enrollment began at the start of the 1950–1951 academic year. The pre-1949 practice whereby most universities gave their own entrance examinations or sometimes cooperated with one another in giving joint exams was replaced where possible by an expanded use of the latter alternative and also by more unified enrollment among groups of universities or within regions. For 1951–1952, enrollment was unified by the major administrative regions into which the new People's Republic was initially divided (North, Northeast, East, Central–South, Southwest, and Northwest). Finally, in 1952, enrollment was centralized with

The students' lot was markedly improved at this time, in comparison with the late 1940s, and the introduction of several other features of socialist life probably had a pacifying effect. Beginning in 1952–1953, free room, board, and health care were added to the benefits of tuition-free education for all tertiary students.[25] But these socialist securities were not sufficient to eliminate frustrations generated by the new enrollment procedures. Candidates were still allowed to list their study preferences and retained the right, which many used, of refusing to accept any other college assignment. Consequently, the 1953 enrollment plan was difficult to enforce. Centrally planned enrollment was "absolutely necessary," it was argued, due to the imbalance between the number of secondary school graduates in the various regions and the regions' tertiary-level freshmen quotas. There was also a great gap between the personal desires of students and the enrollment plans designed to meet national needs. Most candidates were still trying to enroll in a few popular departments, courses, and institutions while for many others, there would have been no way to obtain students without assigned enrollment.[26]

In 1953, the most popular subjects were mechanical and radio engineering, telecommunications, and medicine. The fields that did not receive enough voluntary applications to fill the available vacancies included geology, mining, civil and military engineering, teacher training, mathematics, finance, economics, politics, law, and physical education. Most candidates applied to enter regular four-year courses rather than the two-year post-secondary programs. And the best-known institutions in the largest cities were flooded with applications while newly established schools elsewhere had difficulty filling their enrollment quotas.[27]

Important changes were under way. The new order had at least succeeded in shifting priorities away from politics, law, and liberal arts. But systematic counseling for senior middle school students began at this time and remained a feature of centralized college enrollment ever after. Each year, publicity focused on specialties where supply and opportunities were greatest according to the plan and demand lowest in terms of student preferences. More than

a single set of college entrance examinations taken by all candidates in a procedure that would become increasingly unified and reminiscent of the old imperial civil service examinations. The actual work of administering the examinations and enrollment was coordinated by the greater administrative regions until these were abolished. In 1955, the education authorities of the provincial governments assumed these responsibilities. For relevant enrollment regulations, see *Renmin ribao*, 29 May 1950, 9 May 1951, 26 Sept. 1952, 6 July 1953, 25 May 1954; *Wenhuibao*, 13 June 1952, 20 July 1953; *Guangming ribao*, 25 May 1954, 9 June 1955.

[25] Zhou Enlai, "Zhengwuyuan guanyu tiaozheng quanguo gaodeng xuexiao ji zhongdeng xuexiao xuesheng renmin zhuxuejin de tongzhi" (Government Administration Council Circular on Readjustment of People's Stipends for College and Secondary School Students), 8 July 1952, *Guangming ribao*, 11 July 1952. A less egalitarian form of distribution for college student support was announced in 1955 (*Renmin ribao*, 7 Sept. 1955; *Guangming ribao*, 18 Apr. 1956).

[26] *Renmin ribao*, 25 May 1954.

[27] Ibid., editorial, 25 Sept. 1953.

publicity and counseling, however, the new system depended on central enforcement to obtain the recruits necessary for Soviet-style planned economic development.

The initial goal, once the new system and its priorities were established, had been to adopt the Soviet method, which, like pre-1949 Chinese practice, allowed each institution to examine and enroll its own students. "The present centralized enrollment of students is only a transitional method for a certain period under certain circumstances," explained the *People's Daily* in 1955. "The normal way is for each higher-level institution to organize the enrollment of its own students; henceforth we should improve enrollment methods and gradually have each institution admit its students independently."[28] In fact, the "normal way" was never achieved. Chinese educators would continue their search indefinitely for ways – other than compulsion or the cumbersome ancient method of allocating places "fairly" via the centralized examinations – whereby young intellectuals might be induced to abandon their inherited preferences and accept the assignments necessary to promote national modernization.

Adapting the host environment to fit the plan

The restructuring of higher education had, of course, been designed not just to correct the familiar irrationalities of the old system but more specifically to dovetail with the advent in 1953 of China's First Five Year Plan (FFYP). In late 1952, the Ministry of Education was split, following Soviet practice. Ma Xulun became head of the new Ministry of Higher Education. Zhang Xiruo was appointed the new Minister of Education.[29] Both ministers proclaimed that the new priorities being locked into place by the dual mechanisms of economic and personnel planning were the essence of the Soviet model. The primary task, declared Zhang, was to train personnel for economic development and only secondarily to elevate the educational level of the masses.[30] Ma Xulun was equally blunt. "Educational construction," he said, "should serve economic construction. The key point of economic construction is industry, and the key point of industrial construction is heavy industry."[31]

By the end of the FFYP in 1957, Chinese leaders would acknowledge the poor fit between this Soviet-style industrialization and Chinese realities. Priorities

---

[28] Ibid., editorial, 30 June 1955; see also *Guangming ribao*, 23 June 1955.
[29] Ibid., 27 Dec. 1952.
[30] Zhang Xiruo, signed article in *Ta Kung Pao*, Hong Kong, 1 Oct. 1953, trans. in *CB*, no. 270 (25 Nov. 1953).
[31] Ma Xulun, "Gaodeng jiaoyu de fangzhen, renwu wenti" (Questions on the Policy and Tasks of Higher Education), *Renmin jiaoyu*, Apr. 1953, p. 13; see also Zhang Jian, "Wei shixian guojia gongyehua, jiaoyu gongzuozhe ying dali wei guojia peiyang gongye jianshe rencai" (In Order to Realize National Industrialization, Educational Workers Should Energetically Train Talent for Industrial Construction), *Xinhua yuebao*, no. 8 (1953), pp. 206–208.

were established and pressures created that the newly victorious revolutionary regime could not absorb. As the logic of the unfamiliar planning mode settled over Chinese education in 1953, however, education decision makers seemed to hesitate. Uncertain as to whether the plan should be altered to fit the environment or the environment changed to accommodate the plan, they initially opted for the latter course. Immediate casualties within the Chinese revolutionary environment included quantitative growth, higher education for workers and peasants, and residual Yan'an-style irregularities.

During the first three years of the People's Republic, emphasis had been unremittingly on quantitative growth. Guo Moruo, head of the central government's Culture and Education Affairs Commission, reported in 1951 on the gap between needs and capabilities. Projected personnel requirements for the coming five years, he said, included 150,000 senior technical and administrative cadres, half a million intermediate technical cadres, 10,000 tertiary-level teachers, 100,000 at the secondary level, and 1.5 million for elementary education, plus 200,000 medical personnel. Yet total enrollments in the nation's 195 institutions of higher learning were only 128,000; intermediate-level technical schools had a total enrollment of just over 100,000; and the 600 normal schools for training elementary school teachers had a total of 165,000 students; while China's 4,000 ordinary secondary schools had but 1.3 million students. The only solution would be large numbers of short-term schools, refresher classes, and correspondence courses. Within the coming decade, said Guo, regular schools would continue to be restricted in number and output "while the short-course method must be adopted for the majority of schools, students, and subjects."[32]

Numbers were still a major preoccupation when reorganization began in earnest the following spring. Enrollment plans for the 1952–1953 academic year based on projected national needs called for a first-year class of 50,000. Yet only 36,000 students graduated from senior secondary school in 1952.[33] A year later, however, Ma Xulun had some harsh words to say about "serious defects" in education work. He denounced the lack of planning, inadequate leadership, blind development, equal distribution of strength, and the serious inclination to stress quantity over quality.[34] Thereafter, official statements condemned the obsession with "numbers and speed" as the chief defect in the past three years' work. "Blind adventurism" became the new adversary. Hence, new objectives for 1953 aimed at coordinating education more closely with the FFYP. The new slogan to guide the course correction was "adjust and consolidate, develop key points, raise quality, advance steadily."[35]

[32] Guo Moruo, "Guangyu wenhua jiaoyu gongzuo de baogao" (Report on Culture and Education Work), 25 Oct. 1951, *Xuexi*, vol. 5, no. 2 (16 Nov. 1951), p. 17.
[33] E.g., *Renmin ribao*, 16 Apr. 1952.
[34] Ma Xulun, "Gaodeng jiaoyu de fangzhen, renwu wenti," pp. 12–13.
[35] *Renmin ribao*, 1 Oct. 1953.

A second related issue was education for workers and peasants as the "main body of the nation and creator of society's wealth." After the June 1950 conference on higher education adopted the principle of producing "intellectuals of a new type from among workers and peasants," it was decided that institutions of higher learning should lower their admissions standards for workers and peasants. In 1952, the new system was said to be "daily increasing the opportunity of the nation's youth and especially its worker–peasant youth to enter college."[36]

However, less than a year later Ma Xulun ridiculed the college enrollment work of previous years for granting admission to students who had earned failing grades on their entrance examinations. As a result, he said, "relatively large numbers of students could not keep up with coursework."[37] Zeng Zhaolun was more diplomatic. "Because the worker–peasant laboring people were almost entirely deprived of educational opportunities in the days of reactionary rule," he said, "our present attempt to absorb worker–peasant cadres of a certain tertiary or secondary cultural level directly into institutions of higher learning is bound to be restricted in scope."[38] Thereafter, the annual college enrollment regulations routinely stipulated that only when workers and peasants earned scores on the entrance examinations that met the requirements of departments and majors to which they were applying would such candidates be granted priority in admission.[39]

Another related issue was the question of irregular courses and schools. Initially, "all roads" led to higher education, as in the Soviet system. Entry into institutions of higher learning was not supposed to be limited to students from regular secondary schools. Those from short-term, spare-time, and technical schools could aspire to a college education as well. But among Ma Xulun's complaints in early 1953 was the poor record of the worker–peasant short-course middle schools (*gongnong sucheng zhongxue*). These schools had been inaugurated with much fanfare in 1950 and developed amid much publicity thereafter. Modeled on the Soviet Union's *rabfaks*, or workers' faculties, the aim was to provide a college-preparatory secondary education to adult cadres of worker–peasant origin and/or those who had worked for a certain number of years "in the revolutionary struggle." The schools compressed the regular six-year secondary school course, which students were expected to master in three or at most four years.[40] Planned measures would have to be adopted,

---

[36] E.g., ibid., 26 Sept. 1952.

[37] Ma Xulun, "Gaodeng jiaoyu de fangzhen, renwu wenti," p. 12.

[38] Zeng Zhaolun, "Sannianlai," p. 13.

[39] Compare enrollment regulations for 1951 and 1952 with 1953–1957, in e.g., *Renmin ribao*, 9 May 1951 and 26 Sept. 1952; *Guangming ribao*, 6 July 1953, 25 May 1954, 9 June 1955, 7 Apr. 1956, and 25 Apr. 1957.

[40] *Zhongguo jiaoyu nianjian, 1949–1981* (China Education Yearbook, 1949–1981) (Beijing: Zhongguo dabaike quanshu chubanshe, 1984), pp. 174–177. The schools were formally authorized by the First National Education Conference in Dec. 1949, the First National Conference on Workers'

declared Ma, to turn these schools into proper college-preparatory classes, so as to increase the numbers of qualified worker–peasant students able to continue on to the tertiary level.

In keeping with the new themes of 1953, order and discipline also assumed a prominence not seen since 1949. Suddenly, the political and social concerns that had filled academic life both on and off campus after 1949 belonged to another era. Institutions of higher learning had been "as a rule in a state of confusion."[41] Now, all agreed that teachers must concentrate on teaching and research. A distinction had to be drawn between the bourgeoisie and people influenced by its ideology. In fact, bourgeois culture and learning contained certain progressive components that should be extracted and used. These included the cultural knowledge and scientific technique possessed by the older teachers. The new Communist Party organizations established within the universities tended to overstep the bounds of their authority by confusing political leadership with administration. Such Party organizations could not take the place of professional university administrators, and the two lines of authority had to be respected even when the administrators were not Party members.[42]

Adapting the plan to fit the environment

Having thus moved to curb certain indigenous radical tendencies, the new system of higher education found itself suffused with enthusiasm of another kind as the rush to emulate the Soviet example finally took hold. It must be admitted, editorialized the *People's Daily*, that at first many academics failed to appreciate the value of the Soviet experience. But "apparently, a decided change has occurred in this respect during the past year." Suddenly, learning from the Soviet Union had become "unanimous," to the point of excess, as the "tendency to ask for too much in too short a time" overtook the reform of tertiary education.[43] The mood recalled that of half a century earlier, when intellectuals suddenly began enrolling in the previously despised missionary schools. Once social pressures grew strong enough to breach the wall of resistance, those

and Peasants' Education, in Sept. 1950, and the education reform decree of Oct. 1951. Specific founding directives are cited in ibid., p. 175; see also "Gongnong sucheng zhongxue zanxing shishi banfa" (Provisional Implementation Measures for Worker–Peasant Short-Course Secondary Schools), 10 Feb. 1951, *Renmin ribao*, 17 Feb. 1951; Zhongyang jiaoyubu zhongxue jiaoyu si, "Diyici quanguo gongnong sucheng zhongxue gongzuo huiyi zongjie zhaiyao" (Summary of the First National Conference on Worker–Peasant Short-Course Middle School Work), Dec. 1951, *Renmin jiaoyu*, Feb. 1952, pp. 11–14. For other contemporary references, see *Renmin ribao*, 17, 20 Dec. 1950 and 12 Dec. 1951; and short items in *Renmin jiaoyu*, June 1950, p. 14, and July 1950, pp. 24, 51.

[41] "Ma Xulun daibiao de fayan" (Representative Ma Xulun's Presentation), National People's Congress meeting, 25 Sept. 1954, *Guangming ribao*, 26 Sept. 1954.

[42] E.g., *Guangming ribao*, 31 Jan. 1954.

[43] *Renmin ribao*, 16 Aug. 1953.

same pressures propelled everyone suddenly forward in the very direction they had initially opposed.

The 1953–1954 academic year was therefore devoted to reining in this enthusiasm.[44] The Ministry of Higher Education convened a series of conferences. The first, on technical education, announced that during the previous three years, the chief defect had been a "blind preoccupation" with quantity over quality but that "at the moment" the most serious error was the new tendency among educational leaders to emulate contemporary Soviet standards all at once. As a result, teaching loads were too heavy, teaching materials excessive, and students unable to absorb what they were being taught.[45] Departments were trying to squeeze the regular five-year Soviet college courses into the four-year Chinese system, which initially remained unchanged. The pressure to switch over to Soviet course outlines and syllabi as quickly as possible meant that teachers who had taken crash courses in Russian were just barely able to keep up, translating materials from day to day as they went along. The academic level of China's secondary school graduates was also much lower than that of their Soviet counterparts. Nor was the secondary school curriculum yet comparable, making it doubly difficult for Chinese students to handle the newly imported college materials.

The ministry therefore laid down new guidelines. The aim should be to adapt Soviet ways and means in order to reach Soviet standards. But these could not be reached in a single leap even for a few key points. Curriculum developers must address a single simple question, namely, what kind of technicians would be appropriate for China's actual conditions as well as its scientific and technological levels. Because some questioned whether all of this caution did not contradict the concurrent guidelines for qualitative and key-point development, it was reiterated that the caution actually reaffirmed the quality concerns. Quality could only be achieved by recognizing China's different demands and different rate of advance.[46]

The conference for comprehensive universities revealed a similar excessive shift to the new priorities. Suddenly, everyone wanted either to train engineers or be one, adversely affecting all aspects of work. This conference concluded that the "principal defect" in university reorganization for the comprehensive universities was underestimatation of their importance. Blame was laid upon the "education leaders of the central government" for having failed to clarify

---

[44] *Renmin jiaoyu* reflected the new concerns: e.g., "Jiaoxue jingsai ying quanbu tingzhi" (Teaching and Studying Emulations Must Completely Cease), Aug. 1953, pp. 4–5; "Jiaqiang jilu jiaoyu" (Strengthen Discipline Education), "Tiaozheng jiaoxue gongzuo zhong de guogao guoji yaoqiu" (Correct Excessively High and Pressing Demands on Education Work), and "Fandui pianmian di qiangdiao jitihua" (Oppose One-sided Emphasis on Collective Activities), Sept. 1953, pp. 4–5, 6, and 7–8, respectively.

[45] *Renmin ribao*, 11 Aug. 1953.

[46] Ibid., 16 Aug. 1953.

the status and functions of these institutions. Hence little concern was shown for the historical strengths of different institutions, leaving them weakened and their work impaired. With the absence of firm direction from above, departments generally tended to go their own way, offering courses as they chose. Some science faculties tried to jump on the technology bandwagon by adding so many applied science courses and technical training classes as to interfere with the regular curriculum. Liberal arts and law were largely ignored, reflecting the general impression that these fields had no future in the new China.

As a result, good students were reluctant to enter the comprehensive universities. Some departments had few or no applicants. When first-year enrollment targets were met by persuading candidates to accept unified assignments, many remained resentful. Faculty members transferred to comprehensive universities were similarly depressed and demoralized. Some were unwilling to accept the assignment because they felt these institutions had no important role to play in the new, unanimously accepted "glorious" work of rebuilding the fatherland. Certainly, their faculty members would have no chance of sharing in the exciting inventions and discoveries being made by teachers in technical institutions. Some even now felt the comprehensive universities were a retrogressive throwback to the pedagogical methods of Anglo-American capitalism, since their curricula were so similar to the now discredited liberal arts "general education" of the past.[47]

Work continued throughout the year and into the next to revise and develop curricula in the Soviet manner but tailored more appropriately to China's needs. Up to this point, schools and departments had been using a mix of teaching plans and materials. Some were translated directly from the Russian, others were Soviet inspired, and some were original formulations. From 1953, curriculum development became progressively more systematic and centralized, with the gradual formulation of a single set of teaching plans, syllabi, and materials for each major or specialty and each course within it, to be used nationwide wherever they were taught.

"Standardization and uniformity" were tried and true values idealized as the essence of modern education, compared with traditional teaching methods. But the degree of standardization now enforced was a new departure for Chinese instructors. Teaching plans specified the aims, requirements, and contents of each major, including the courses to be taught within it. The syllabus for each course was so detailed that it included the items to be taught, their sequence, the time to be spent on each item, and the exact material to be covered during each hour of instruction. Textbooks and teaching materials were also similarly compiled.

All institutions had to adopt these uniform teaching plans and syllabi because,

[47] From reports on the comprehensive universities conference: *Guangming ribao*, 26 Sept. and 31 Oct. 1953; *Renmin ribao*, 11 Sept. and 15 Oct. 1953.

it was explained, only through such a totally planned system would it be possible to produce the required numbers of people trained to the specifications of
each grade and level in all the various specialties required for economic development. For this heightened degree of standardization and uniformity in teaching
methods and content, the new teaching research groups served as enforcers. Their
function was to ensure that the faculty actually taught according to the study
plans and syllabi as prescribed for each specialty. "Since all teaching work is
carried out under a unified aim and plan, each subject taught by each teacher is,
both qualitatively and quantitatively, essential for the realization of the general
aim and plan. If the teaching work is not carried out through the guided,
organized, and collective activity of the teaching research office, it will be
difficult to achieve the desired result."[48]

The actual work of developing teaching plans and materials was coordinated
by the Ministry of Higher Education, usually with a few Soviet advisors, plus
leading Chinese academics in each field and representatives of the relevant
government departments, which were now directing activity in all sectors of
the economy. Curricular revision continued in this manner throughout 1954,
working down the list of academic priorities from the applied sciences to
finance and economics, politics, teacher training, medicine, the comprehensive
university specialties, and agriculture. By mid-1954, curriculum revision in the
applied sciences was basically complete. Unified teaching plans for over 170
academic specialties had been revised and authorized for use by year's end.[49]
Older faculty members would later recall the mid-1950s as a time when course
outlines and syllabi, once they were authorized for use, were treated as sacrosanct and enforced "like the law."[50]

Toward a Sino-Soviet regularization model

The 1954–1955 academic year marked the high point of China's attempt to
adapt itself to the received model of Soviet education and vice versa. By 1955,
old modes were clearly reemerging. The immediate excuse was the need for
better-qualified personnel as required by the FFYP. But once quality was
allowed to become the official goal, Chinese educational decision makers moved
as if by instinct back to old familiar ways – exacerbating contradictions between the education system, with its need for talent, and the new revolutionary
regime then in the process of overthrowing the old social structure from which

---

[48] *Renmin ribao*, 24 Apr. 1956; see also *Guangming ribao*, 7 Sept. 1954.
[49] E.g., *Renmin ribao*, 30 July and 23 Aug. 1954, 22 Aug. 1955; *Guangming ribao*, 26, 27 July, 30
Aug., and 11 Sept. 1954.
[50] The centralization of higher education enforced at this time is reflected in "Zhongyang renmin
zhengfu zhengwuyuan, guanyu xiuding gaodeng xuexiao lingdao guanxi de jueding" (Central
People's Government, Government Administration Council, Decision on the Revised Leadership Relations for Institutions of Higher Learning), 6 Oct. 1953, *Renmin ribao*, 11 Oct. 1953.

such talent was drawn. Even as political life grew more radical with the expro-priation of rural land and urban capital, adjustments continued within the education system until Chinese-style "regularization" could be seen co-opting the Soviet transplant at many points.

The subtle shift was encapsulated in the phrase "spirit and essence" to explain how the Soviet experience should be used, rather than "mechanically" copying every detail. Because the Soviet educational experience had not been properly learned, its spirit and essence had not been grasped. The relationship between Soviet conditions and Chinese application was therefore poorly under-stood, and the Soviet model was poorly adapted to its new environment.[51] The old arguments against copying Western education models were now being recycled for use against the most recent effort at international emulation.

How to "guarantee quality" within the Chinese environment thus became the key concern. This was because "cultural and education work at present has a widespread basic defect, namely, quality too low to meet the demands of national construction." Blame was laid upon "some comrades" who thought that in so poor a country, quantitative demands were more urgent. But, "as everyone knows, the 156 projects which the Soviet Union is helping us build as the core of our industrial construction use the most advanced techniques and equipment." Without technical talent to match, continued the official rationale, such enter-prises could not go into production. And "a one-sided pursuit of quantity without giving attention to the conditions within institutions of higher learning or the number and quality of the teachers or the source and quality of students or teaching materials, etc., cannot achieve the aim of training qualified talent."[52]

Without adjustment, the system could not meet the demands being made upon it. Annual first-year enrollment had leapt from 35,000 in 1950 to 94,000 in 1954. The college intake each year was greater by several thousands than the number of students graduating from the senior secondary level. To fill the gap, employed and unemployed young people were recruited. Academic, political, and physical standards were, of necessity, lowered in order to meet enrollment quotas. As a result, dropout rates due to poor academic performance were high. Those who just managed to hang on created differences of ability so great that teaching plans could not be followed, lowering the quality of education for everyone else.

To teach all the new students, 20,000 new faculty members were hired to make a total tertiary-level teaching force of 38,000 in 1955. Over half that number, however, were only teaching assistants, and especially in the engineering faculties a large proportion of the new teachers were recent graduates of the

[51] E.g., Zhang Jian, "Luetan gaodeng xuexiao xuexi Sulian xianjin jingyan de chengjiu he wenti" (A Brief Discussion of the Accomplishments and Problems of Tertiary Institutions Learning from the Advanced Experience of the Soviet Union), *Renmin jiaoyu*, Feb. 1955, pp. 12–15.
[52] *Renmin ribao*, editorial, 23 June 1955.

post-secondary courses or students allowed to graduate early from regular college programs.

In sum, the cycle of quantitative growth had to be broken and curricula further adjusted. Toward these ends, several important decisions were announced in mid-1955. They included stricter college enrollment standards, the suspension of most post-secondary courses, the extension of regular college programs from four to five years, and the abolition of the worker–peasant short-course middle schools.[53]

Entrance requirements were strengthened. Academically, standards were "not to be lowered under any circumstances." But politically, "because our country is still in the transition period, class relations are extremely complicated, and struggle between the working class and the classes that have been or are about to be eliminated is growing sharper daily." Political quality therefore had to be considered closely when enrolling new students.[54]

The post-secondary courses, which had been a major target for enrollment particularly in the applied sciences, were curtailed. Training intermediate-level technicians was transferred to the specialized secondary schools. Beginning with polytechnic and comprehensive universities, coursework was extended to five years as needed to accommodate Soviet curricular requirements.[55]

Most striking of the 1955 adjustments, both for its political implications and historical antecedents, was the demise of worker–peasant short-course middle schools. A total of 87 had been established in cities throughout the country by the time the experiment ended. They were credited with having enrolled some 64,700 students overall.[56] The 1955 enrollment plan for 33,000 new students was announced in March and would have brought total enrollment in these schools to 84,000.[57] The schools were nevertheless ordered to suspend enrollment

---

[53] The new system was widely criticized in mid-1955 to justify these decisions, and the above summary is taken from those critical commentaries, e.g.: *Renmin ribao*, 12, 23, 30 June 1955; *Guangming ribao*, 19, 23 June 1955.

[54] *Guangming ribao*, editorial, 23 June 1955.

[55] *Renmin ribao*, 22 Aug. 1955.

[56] *Zhongguo jiaoyu nianjian, 1949–1981* (China Education Yearbook, 1949–1981) (Beijing: Zhongguo dabaike quanshu chubanshe, 1984), p. 175; Fang Junfu, "Zhongxue jiaoyu youmeiyou chengji, chengji zai nali" (Have There Been Achievements in Secondary Education and If So What Are They?), *Renmin jiaoyu*, Oct. 1957, p. 14. A 1954 compilation (in *Guangming ribao*, 23 Apr. 1954) showed the following occupational backgrounds of students in 58 schools:

Government and CCP cadres:	56.51%
Industrial workers:	25.47%
Military:	8.76%
Other:	8.88%
Peasants:	0.38%

Data on class or family origin are not available; such information would have produced a different profile, revealing perhaps more worker–peasant "good" class origins than suggested here, but also "bad" bourgeois backgrounds as well.

[57] *Guangming ribao*, 9 Mar. 1955; see also ibid., 28, 29 Mar. 1955.

work in July, effective immediately, and the entire project was abandoned as impractical. These schools, it was now said, were impossible to popularize, were unable to "guarantee the necessary quality," and could not compete with the regular method of "gradual progress in the proper sequence." Many students were held back in the same grade from year to year and ultimately dropped out because they could not keep up. Some were promoted to the tertiary level, in keeping with the original aim, but "the great majority" did not produce good academic results.[58]

The case of the short-course schools demonstrated yet again the clash between regular and irregular education modes. Despite much publicity about the "splendid job" these schools were doing, the Ministry of Higher Education had issued a directive reminding college educators of their obligations to these students shortly after the first batch of about 1,500 graduates entered college in 1953. The source of the problem was twofold. The students were "unfamiliar with the regular way of study" and often had a poor foundation in math, geometry, physics, and chemistry and none at all in Russian. Also, some educators were "still unable to appreciate sufficiently the political significance of educating intellectuals of the working class." Some still regarded such students as "stupid" and demonstrated great impatience in teaching them.[59]

The 1955 directives canceling the short-course schools prescribed that in the future, all workers and peasants, whether cadres or not, should take the same entrance exams and study in the same schools as regular students. Otherwise, the new preferred alternative was spare-time education, which was promoted as a more effective method of gradually raising the cultural level of all those who for whatever reason could not compete within the regular school system.[60] The short-course middle schools thus met the same fate as all the other "irregular" education experiments that had gone before. The regular system rejected them now as previously, albeit this time in the name of Soviet-style modernization, which had ironically been built on just such irregular expedients in its own early stages.

The worker–peasant short-course secondary schools therefore symbolized some important differences between the Soviet and Chinese efforts to transform their education systems in accordance with similar revolutionary ideals. The Soviet *rabfaks* were introduced in 1919 and were, unlike their Chinese counterparts, attached to universities from the start. Although openly despised by regular faculty and students, they nevertheless managed to fulfill their

[58] *Renmin ribao*, editorial, 23 June 1955; *Guangming ribao*, 14 July 1955.

[59] *Guangming ribao*, 21 Mar. 1954. Achievements were nevertheless still regarded as primary and defects secondary at this time. E.g., ibid., 23 Apr. 1954; Zhongyang jiaoyubu gongnong sucheng zhongxue jiaoyuchu, "Wunianlai de gongnong sucheng zhongxue" (Worker–Peasant Short-Course Secondary Schools during the Past Five Years), *Renmin jiaoyu*, Nov. 1954, pp. 34–35.

[60] *Guangming ribao*, 28 Aug. 1955.

mission of preparing workers for college. A decade later, *rabfaks* were providing about 30 percent of all first-year students to tertiary institutions.[61] By contrast, the Chinese equivalent was deemed unable to perform its intended function, quickly succumbing under the combined weight of Chinese academic tradition and Soviet-style industrialization.

By the mid-1950s, then, the "mechanical copying" phase had already peaked, and a Sino-Soviet compromise was emerging as Chinese educators found common cause with the foreign import. In later years, even those whose memories extended back to the 1950s would be hard put to distinguish which of the tertiary system's features were "Chinese" and which Soviet inspired. The two had come together most effectively in the college entrance examinations, which merged Soviet-style economic and personnel planning with the old Chinese selection procedure to create a new unified enrollment and job assignment mechanism far more rigid than the Soviet counterpart. But this mechanism helped ensure that the restructured tertiary system with its newly designated prestige categories in the applied sciences would overcome inherited intellectual priorities to produce the talent needed for economic development. The mechanism would also go on to become an established feature of Chinese higher education, restored with alacrity after each of the two massive irregular interruptions to follow.

Companion features of the system that Chinese educators would also accept as their own were the nationally unified teaching plans and the teaching research groups. Of the latter, teachers and administrators alike would later wonder how universities could ever have been run without them. And at lower academic levels as well, teachers would find the "teaching research" function indispensable to the practice of their craft (see chap. 16). At the same time, moreover, the rigors of Soviet-style management provided Chinese educators with a ready excuse to begin eliminating certain irregular residual features transplanted along with the Soviet model, the better to adapt it to "Chinese conditions." Inevitably, the CCP's demand for worker–peasant college enrollments was compromised as well by this emerging mix of Sino–Soviet regularity.

[61] Sheila Fitzpatrick, *The Commissariat of Enlightenment: Soviet Organization of Education and the Arts under Lunacharsky, October 1917–1921* (Cambridge: Cambridge University Press, 1970), pp. 79–81, 220–221, 225–226; Gail Warshofsky Lapidus, "Educational Strategies and Cultural Revolution: The Politics of Soviet Development," in Sheila Fitzpatrick, ed., *Cultural Revolution in Russia, 1928–1931* (Bloomington: Indiana University Press, 1978), p. 83.

9

Sino-Soviet regularization and school system reform

Elementary and secondary education reform followed the same course as that at the tertiary level. Initially, features from the mid-1940s Yan'an past seemed to be carrying over into the new era. Education would "take workers and peasants as the main force and train large numbers of new-style worker–peasant intellectuals."[1] The First National Conference on Workers' and Peasants' Education, in September 1950, promoted the same line. "Different forms and methods may be employed and no forced uniformity or regularity is necessary." The "people teaching people" concept would be applied until enough regular staff could be trained.[2] But different regions were already issuing provisional regulations which owed far more to their GMD government antecedents than to the post-1942 Yan'an reforms. These regulations, carefully collected and reprinted for general reference, stipulated all the old rules for "raising quality," complete with provisions for central elementary schools and a few "well-run" middle schools in each locality to serve as leaders and models.[3]

The conflicting aims were written into the first "Decision on School System Reform." Promulgated on 1 October 1951, the decision marked a kind of

---

[1] From a report on the First National Education Work Conference in *Renmin ribao*, 24 Dec. 1949. See also ibid., 6 Jan. 1950; Lu Dingyi, "Xin Zhongguo de jiaoyu he wenhua" (New China's Education and Culture), and Qian Junrui, "Dangqian jiaoyu jianshe de fangzhen" (The Present Policy of Educational Construction), both in *Dangqian jiaoyu jianshe de fangzhen* (The Present Policy of Educational Construction) (Guangzhou: Xinhua shudian, 1950), pp. 3–13, 21–49, respectively.

[2] See Education Minister Ma Xulun's report on the conference (*Renmin ribao*, 20 Dec. 1950). See also on the conference, ibid., 21, 24, 30 Sept. 1950; "Quanguo gongnong jiaoyu huiyi yingyu de sixiang zhunbei" (Necessary Thought Preparation for the National Conference on Worker–Peasant Education), editorial, *Renmin jiaoyu*, Sept. 1950, pp. 7–9; Huang Fujin, "Ji diyici quanguo gongnong jiaoyu huiyi" (A Record of the First National Conference on Worker–Peasant Education), *Renmin jiaoyu*, Nov. 1950, pp. 49–51; Qian Junrui, "Wei tigao gongnong de wenhua shuiping, manzu gongnong ganbu de wenhua yaoqiu er fendou" (Struggle to Raise the Cultural Level of Workers and Peasants and Satisfy the Cultural Demands of Worker–Peasant Cadres), report to the conference, 30 Sept. 1950, *Renmin jiaoyu*, May 1951, pp. 12–16.

[3] E.g., "Dongbei renmin zhengfu guanyu tigao zhongdeng jiaoyu gongzuo de jueding" (Decision of the Northeast People's Government on Raising Up Secondary Education Work), reprinted in *Dangqian jiaoyu jianshe de fangzhen*, pp. 54–58. The North China Provisional Elementary School Measures are cited in chap. 6, n. 65.

transitional attempt to regularize irregularity.[4] It listed the system's defects inherited from the past: lack of formal standing for worker–peasant cadre schools, training classes, etc.; no system of technical education; the division of six-year elementary schooling into separate junior and senior levels. As a result, technical schools were not recognized as part of the regular system, nor were they provided with any regular status; different kinds of training had no rightful place anywhere; and the great majority of rural children who entered elementary school dropped out after the junior level.

In order to "guarantee an equal opportunity for the children of all urban and rural laboring people to receive a complete elementary education," the 1951 decision therefore reduced it from six to five years and abolished the junior–senior distinction. Applying the principles upon which Soviet education had been built, the different kinds of short courses and training classes would be designed to provide equivalency training for overaged students at all levels. Graduates would be eligible to advance into regular classes upon passing the requisite examinations, following the same pattern as the college-preparatory short-course middle schools for worker–peasant cadres.[5] The aim was "not only to equalize the position of worker–peasant cadres and the worker–peasant masses in receiving education" but also to bring their schools, "according to their various disparate levels, completely within the regular school system, causing them to be basically linked with it so as to guarantee the possibility of offering the various levels of education."[6] Irregular forms were to be integrated throughout the regular system.

The official announcement accompanying the decision declared that it represented the first attempt to merge the regular system of the GMD era with the new-type education of the pre-1949 CCP base areas. Still, the old ambivalence remained, evidently compounded by the mixed signals coming from the Soviet model: between its earlier effort to incorporate education for workers and peasants and its Stalin-era regularity. In any event, as the economy grew more sophisticated, continued the official Chinese commentator, the school system would surely evolve accordingly, "to become more strict, uniform, and standardized." Finally, as if reiterating the admonitions of Soviet advisors: "all who advocate ways of thinking and action which would abolish the school system and the examination system, and one-sidedly emphasize the importance of living experience while neglecting systematic knowledge and theoretical studies, are mistaken and will end in failure. We firmly oppose this erroneous inclination. In carrying out the new school system, we must develop this kind

---

[4] "Guanyu gaige xuezhi de jueding" (Decision on School System Reform), *Renmin ribao*, 3 Oct. 1951, reprinted in *Zhongguo jiaoyu nianjian, 1949–1981*, p. 686.
[5] "Guangyu gaige xuezhi de jueding."
[6] Qian Junrui, "Yong geming jingshen shishi xin xuezhi" (Use a Revolutionary Spirit to Implement the New School System), *Renmin jiaoyu*, Nov. 1951, p. 6.

of two-line struggle, in order to guarantee the complete realization of the
. . . Decision on School System Reform."[7]

The "two-line struggle" at the elementary level, 1951–1955

The 1951 solution for the two-line struggle lasted only about a year – suggesting that the old reform axiom of change as the only constant would hold even truer in the new China than in the old. The revised five-year curriculum was launched on schedule for first graders in the fall of 1952. The plan was to proceed year by year until the changeover was complete for all grades in 1957. Implementation was begun among continuing claims that it would "close the gap between urban and rural elementary education." China had an estimated 400,000 elementary schools but only about 10 percent had senior-level sections, and these were concentrated in urban locations. The goal was to achieve universal complete five-year elementary schooling within a decade.[8]

Yet, by mid-1952, a shift in emphasis was already discernible. Among the first indicators was a new reservation about *minban*, or local community-run schools. The *minban* formula had initially been promoted to fill the gap between public and private as regular private schools were taken over by the state and *sishu* were (finally, after half a century of unrecognized existence) closed or reorganized. But a national education administration conference was told in August that "henceforth elementary schooling should be mainly public." *Minban* schools were to be run only under the following conditions: "the masses are completely willing in the absence of compulsion; the masses have legitimate and reliable sources of funding and manpower which can be maintained for a definite number of years; and the matter has first been passed by the *xiang* people's representative committee and then approved by the county people's government."[9]

By 1953, the concerns underlying regularization at the tertiary level were beginning to dominate the system along its lower reaches as well. Among the defects recognized as part of the "lack of planning and foresight" syndrome were "blind and rash advance and the deviation of emphasizing quantity over quality in anti-illiteracy work and elementary school education."[10] Virtues had suddenly become vices.

---

[7] *Renmin ribao*, editorial, 3 Oct. 1951.

[8] E.g., Qian Junrui, "Yong geming jingshen shishi xin xuezhi," pp. 6–9; Wu Yanyin, "Beijingshi xiaoxue shiyan shiyan wunian yiguanzhi liangnianlai de chubu jingyan" (The Preliminary Experience of Experimenting with the Five-Year Integrated Elementary School during the Past Two Years in Beijing), *Renmin jiaoyu*, Dec. 1952, pp. 4–16; *Renmin ribao*, 31 May, 19, 20, 21 Aug., and 24 Sept. 1952.

[9] *Renmin ribao*, 19 Aug. 1952.

[10] From the State Statistical Bureau communiqué for 1952 work (ibid., 30 Sept. 1953). The present study focuses on the development of the regular school system (and its irregular equivalents) but not the related subjects of literacy programs, adult education, cadre training, etc. See, e.g., works by Glen Peterson and Vilma Seeberg (cited in the Bibliography) incorporating these added dimensions.

Without knowing exactly who was making which decisions at this time, it is only possible to look at changing policy patterns and speculate on their origins. But it was as if the need to regularize the tertiary sector to meet FFYP demands had provided an excuse for conventional assumptions to resume paramount influence over the system as a whole. That a decisive turning point had occurred in this respect was apparent by early 1953, when regional conferences were held to explain the implications for elementary education of the "new" line, that is, "adjust and consolidate, develop key points, raise quality, advance steadily."[11]

The north China conference discovered after "exhaustive discussion" that an "acute ideological struggle is indispensable in order to turn cultural and education work from the path of blind development to regular planning." Local cadres failed to appreciate the benefits of national planning and opposed the new policy for restricting development. Nevertheless, plans were announced to "readjust" elementary schools as well as to "curtail junior secondary teacher training schools and close down short-course teacher training classes." Also, "the past revolutionary practice of setting up temporary affiliated classes should now be integrated into the established regular schools."[12]

East China authorities similarly announced that in their region's elementary schools, "blind attempts were made to enroll large numbers of students and train large numbers of teaching personnel, as well as to set up large numbers of junior teacher training schools and short-course training classes." Henceforth, the east China conference was told, "it is necessary to improve understanding of the plan, that the plan is the law . . . and that one must be held responsible under the law for failing to fulfill the plan." The region was also trimming its targets for the anti–illiteracy drive, from 10 to 1.2 million people, to conform to the spirit of central directives.[13]

A central government directive on elementary education in December 1953 formally overturned both the letter and spirit of the 1951 goals for that level. All talk of closing the urban–rural gap ceased as the forces of regularization took hold. The five-year unified elementary school was abandoned. Enforcement of the new system was suspended and the junior/senior division exonerated. Funding would come mainly from the state, but public school development should be promoted most vigorously in the cities and less so in the countryside, where the above-cited conditions for running *minban* schools were reiterated.

Primary school enrollments stood at 55 million, an increase of 135 percent in comparison with 1946, the peak year under the old regime. But the quality of

---

[11] *Renmin ribao*, 3 Feb. 1953; *Guangming ribao*, 17, Nov. 1953.

[12] *Renmin ribao*, 26 Mar. 1953; see also ibid., 6 Mar. 1953. Affiliated or attached classes referred to the expedient of allowing an existing school to "wear a cap" (*daimao*), used most commonly to expand junior secondary enrollments. After graduation, students simply remained at their elementary school for a year or two of secondary-level instruction.

[13] *Jiefang ribao*, Shanghai, 22 Feb. 1953.

teachers was poor and facilities were inadequate. Hence the need for reorganization. "Hereafter, emphasis should be given to the successful operation of elementary schools in the cities and in industrial and mining districts, as well as to the complete and central elementary schools in the countryside." Since 1949, teachers and students had also been distracted by too many social and political activities. The directive therefore placed strict time limits on such nonacademic endeavors.[14]

The government's dilemma, explained the official commentary, was that the mass demand for education had greatly increased, so it would be wrong to neglect or belittle elementary school work. But universal elementary schooling was premature because "all other endeavors should only be carried out in coordination with industrial production." Since 1949, elementary schooling had actually developed faster in the countryside than in the cities, a fact inconsistent with industrialization. Hence, "this directive stipulates that in the future, the country should place the center of elementary school development in the industrial and mining districts and the cities, especially in the big cities, so as to accommodate the daily expanding needs of industrial construction."[15] The new policy would seek to "overcome egalitarianism" and emphasize "key-point development" in terms of regions, tasks, schools, and resources. The idea was, among other things, to "concentrate expenditure" and "make key-point schools . . . a practical success so as to set examples for general mobilization."[16]

The reason cited was planning for industrialization, and the Soviet Union provided the model for curriculum development as well. Unified elementary and secondary school teaching plans for science subjects, patterned on those of the Soviet Union in both content and form were also issued by the Ministry of Education in 1953.[17] But all the imperatives and external reference points seemed to provide educators with the excuse they needed to fall back on their old ways of guaranteeing a quality product. Just as they had done in Yan'an between 1938 and 1942, education decision makers now used the quality-versus-quantity rationale to curtail growth, concentrate resources in key centers of strength, and try to reimpose regularization patterns within a system that had just experienced four years of "adventuristic progress and confusion." In a replay of those Yan'an years, enrollments declined during the first half of the FFYP while old familiar rules and regulations were invoked in the name of quality.

Later, the decline was blamed on vacillating leadership from the center over *minban* schools. The state could not afford the investment necessary to run

[14] "Zhengwuyuan guanyu zhengdun he gaijin xiaoxue jiaoyu de zhishi" (Directive on Reorganizing and Improving Elementary Education), 26 Nov. 1953, *Renmin ribao*, 14 Dec. 1953, reprinted in *Zhongguo jiaoyu nianjian, 1949–1981*, pp. 732–733.
[15] *Renmin ribao*, editorial, 14 Dec. 1953.
[16] Ibid., 16 Dec. 1953.
[17] *Guangming ribao*, 4 Mar. 1953.

enough public schools for all children, but neither could decision makers agree on the irregular *minban* alternative – hence the restrictions introduced in 1952. Overaged youngsters could not attend. Each class had to have a certain minimum number of students. Schools with fewer than a certain number of classes could not continue in operation. Facilities had to be comparable to those of regular state-supported schools, and so on. Applying these restrictions, local authorities closed down some schools, took over others, refused permission for some to open, and did little or nothing to encourage the development of those remaining. After a year or so, this course was officially reinterpreted as a mistake, and *minban* schools began to revive. But without clear guidelines from above and concrete encouragement from local officials, the rate of development was slow. In 1955, there were only about 28,000 such schools nationwide, with an enrollment of 1.76 million.[18]

Reflecting the "vacillations" of decision makers, elementary school statistics also fluctuated, sometimes even retroactively. The most conservative compilation, issued by the education ministries in 1954, attributed the discrepancy between it and other sources to "revisions necessitated by changes in the scope of the data."[19] The more commonly cited figure for 1952 was the State Statistical Bureau's 55 million. According to the bureau's figures, elementary enrollments declined from 55 million to 51.2 million in 1954.[20] As shown in Table 9.1, however, the bureau subsequently issued a revised set of figures.

Regularization at the secondary level

Secondary, or middle, schools (*zhongdeng xuexiao*) continued to fall between two stools, treated alternately as an extension of one or preparation for the other. At the junior level (grades 7–9), numbers began to increase in the early 1950s as an unintended consequence of expanding elementary school enrollments. Policymakers then sought, albeit not very successfully, to curb these unplanned pressures for more schooling when the regularization mode was revived at the onset of the FFYP. Thereafter, the main emphasis for secondary education

---

[18] The retrospective on *minban* school policy is from editorials in *Guangming ribao*, 21 July 1955, and *Renmin ribao*, 27 Feb. 1956.

[19] "Quanguo geji xuexiao xuesheng renshu de fazhan jiyu jiefangqian de bijiao" (The Development of National Student Enrollments at the Various Levels of Schooling and a Comparison with before Liberation), figures compiled jointly by the Ministries of Education and Higher Education, dated Sept. 1954, in *Renmin jiaoyu*, Oct. 1954, pp. 34–36. These figures are reproduced in Table 9.1.

[20] State Statistical Bureau, "Guanyu yijiuwuernian guomin jingji he wenhua jiaoyu huifu yu fazhan qingkuang de gongbao" (Report on the Restoration and Development of the National Economy, Culture, and Education for 1952), *Renmin ribao*, 30 Sept. 1953; "Zhengwuyuan guanyu zhengdun he gaijin xiaoxue jiaoyu de zhishi," 26 Nov. 1953; and State Statistical Bureau, "Guanyu yijiuwusi niandu guomin jingji fazhan he guojia jihua zhixing jieguo de gongbao" (Report on National Economic Development and the Results of Implementing the National Plan for the Year 1954), *Renmin ribao*, 23 Sept. 1955.

Table 9.1. *National student enrollments, 1946–1958*

Institution	Peak pre-1949	1949/50	1950/51	1951/52	1952/53	1953/54	1954/55	1955/56	1956/57	1957/58
Tertiary (graduate and undergraduate)	(1947/48) 155,036	117,133	138,731	155,570	194,378	216,765	258,000	292,000	403,000	441,000
Secondary (ordinary and specialized):	(1946/47) 1,878,523	1,267,809	1,566,540	1,964,071	3,145,866	3,628,264	4,246,000	4,473,000	—	7,059,000
Ordinary senior middle	317,853	207,156	237,950	184,393	260,433	359,532	478,000	580,000	780,000	—
Ordinary junior middle	1,178,021	831,808	1,066,957	1,383,691	2,230,477	2,571,636	3,109,000	3,320,000	4,340,000	—
Elementary (millions)	(1946/47) 23.68	24.39 (24.39)	28.92	43.15	49.76 (55.00) (51.10)	51.50 (51.66)	51.22	53.13	63.00	64.28

Sources: The figures for pre-1949 through 1953/54 are from "Quanguo geji xuexiao xuesheng renshu de fazhan jiyu jiefangqian de bijiao" (The Development of National Student Enrollments at the Various Levels of Schooling and a Comparison with before Liberation), figures compiled jointly by the Ministries of Education and Higher Education, dated Sept. 1954, in *Renmin jiaoyu* (People's Education), Beijing, Oct. 1954, pp. 34–36. Pre-1949 figures are from GMD Ministry of Education statistics, as cited in this source. The figures for 1954/55 and 1955/56 are from Zhonghua renmin gongheguo guojia tongjiju (State Statistical Bureau), *Guanyu 1955 niandu guomin jingji jihua zhixing jieguo de gongbao* (Report on the Results of the National Economic Plan for 1955) (Beijing: Tongji chubanshe, 1956), p. 47.

The secondary and elementary enrollment figures for 1956/57 are from *Jiaoshibao* (Teachers News), Beijing, 1 Jan. 1957. Tertiary and secondary enrollment figures from the above sources agree for 1949/50, 1952/53, and 1953/54. Only the elementary-level figures diverge. Those shown in parentheses are from the 1956 SSB compilation except for the 55 million figure, which is from the SSB's "Guanyu yijiuwuernian guomin jingji he wenhua jiaoyu huifu yu fazhan qingkuang de gongbao" (Report on the Restoration and Development of the National Economy, Culture, and Education for 1952), *Renmin ribao*, 30 Sept. 1953.

The figures for 1956/57 (tertiary only) and 1957/58 are from SSB, *Ten Great Years* (Peking: Foreign Languages Press, 1960), p. 192. This source actually shows figures for all levels from each year, 1949 through 1958, but these figures differ sometimes quite substantially from other sets of official statistics published earlier, which are those shown here. The discrepancies remain unexplained.

Table 9.2. *Proportion of private to public schools and students, 1949*

	Private schools (% of total)	Private school students (% of total)
Tertiary	41	27
Specialized secondary	54	39
Ordinary secondary	56	39
Elementary	10	11

Source: "Jinianlai woguo jiaoyu shiye de fazhan gaikuang" (A Survey of Our Country's Educational Development in Recent Years), *Tongji gongzuo tongxun* (Statistical Work Bulletin), no. 20 (1956), reprinted in *Xinhua banyue kan* (New China Semimonthly), Beijing, no. 24 (1956), p. 93. According to this source, all private tertiary institutions had been converted to public management by 1953, and the same was "basically" true at the lower levels by 1955.

was to develop its college-preparatory function, with attention focused on the senior-level (grades 10–12) and the regular, full-course middle schools.

The "blind adventurism" of the immediate postliberation years (1949–1951) had also exhibited the same uncertainty, albeit to reverse effect. Initially, when elementary enrollments were doubling and those in junior middle schools also rising, numbers at the senior secondary and the tertiary levels dropped sharply. But the Education Ministry could only plead for an end to the "chaotic conditions" that obtained at the secondary level and above, where students and teachers were routinely pressed into service for a multitude of postliberation activities.[21]

Also disruptive, at the secondary level especially, was the collapse of all private financing. According to figures issued later, the proportion of private to public schools was, by the late 1940s, greatest at the secondary level (see Table 9.2). But land rent constituted a major source of private school income, which disappeared once agrarian reform was completed in the early 1950s. As a combined result of all the disruptions, senior secondary enrollments were most seriously affected and did not return to their pre-1949 level until the 1953–1954 academic year (see Tables 9.1, 9.3).

Unlike the tertiary and elementary sectors, however, early reform decisions left the structure of secondary education essentially unchanged. The basic division of secondary schooling into two separate streams, one ordinary (*putong*, i.e., general academic or college preparatory) and the other specialized (including both technical and teacher training schools), was retained. The October

[21] E.g., *Renmin ribao*, 6 Aug. 1951; "Jianjue kefu xuexiao jiaoyu gongzuo zhong de hunluan xianxiang" (Resolutely Overcome Chaotic Phenomena in School Education Work), *Renmin jiaoyu*, Aug. 1951, p. 8.

Table 9.3. *Number of students in secondary schools, 1946–1957 (unit: 1,000 persons)*

Type of schooling	1946/1947	1949/1950	1950/1951	1951/1952	1952/1953	1953/1954	1954/1955	1955/1956	1956/1957	1957/1958
Specialized (zhongzhuan):	137	77	98	163	290	300	300	318	—	778
Schools	74	77	23	39	77	56	—	—	—	—
Classes	63	—	75	124	213	244	—	—	—	—
Teacher training (shifan):	246	152	159	220	344	369	308	219	320	—
Schools	169	91	98	151	252	252	—	—	—	—
Classes	77	61	61	69	92	117	—	—	—	—
Ordinary (putong):	1,496	1,039	1,305	1,568	2,491	2,931	3,587	3,900	5,120	6,281
Senior middle schools	318	207	238	184	260	360	478	580	780	—
Junior middle schools	1,178	832	1,067	1,384	2,230	2,572	3,109	3,320	4,340	—
Worker–peasant short-course middle schools	—	—	4	13	20	28	51	—	—	—

Sources: The figures for 1946/1947 through 1953/1954 are from "Quanguo geji xuexiao xuesheng renshu de fazhan jiyu jiefangqian de bijiao" ("The Development of National Student Enrollments at the Various Levels of Schooling and a Comparison with before Liberation), figures compiled jointly by the Ministries of Education and Higher Education, dated Sept. 1954, in *Renmin jiaoyu*, Oct. 1954, pp. 34–36. Pre-1949 figures are from GMD Ministry of Education statistics, as cited in this source.

The figures for 1954/1955 are from State Statistical Bureau (SSB), "Communiqué on the Development of the National Economy and the Results of Implementing the State Plan for 1954," issued 21 Sept. 1955. The data presented here are from the statistical tables appended to a subsequent publication of the communiqué by the Statistical Publishing House, as translated in *Current Background*, no. 382 (29 Mar. 1956), p. 22.

The figures for 1955/1956 are from "Jinianlai woguo jiaoyu shiye de fazhan gaikuang" (A Survey of Our Country's Educational Development in Recent Years), *Tongji gongzuo tongxun*, no. 20 (1956), reprinted in *Xinhua banyue kan*, no. 24 (1956), p. 93.

The figures for 1956/1957 are from *Jiaoshibao*, 1 Jan. 1957, p. 3.

The figures for 1957/1958 are from SSB, *Ten Great Years*, p. 192.

Table 9.4. *Specialized secondary school enrollments, 1949–1956*

	1949/1950	1952/1953	1953/1954	1954/1955	1955/1956
Engineering	21,400	111,400	129,700	151,700	177,600
Agriculture	21,700	66,600	68,700	58,700	53,300
Public health	15,400	59,400	57,700	58,600	57,300
Finance and economic	14,800	52,300	42,300	28,800	26,000
Teacher training	151,700	345,200	369,000	308,000	219,000
Fine arts and others	3,800	700	1,000	2,200	3,900
Total	228,800	635,600	668,400	608,000	537,100

Source: Zhonghua renmin gongheguo guojia tongjiju, *Guanyu 1955 niandu guomin jingji jihua zhixing jieguo de gongbao* (Report on the Results of the National Economic Plan for 1955) (Beijing: Tongji chubanshe, 1956), p. 51.

1951 decision on school system reform left the regular full-course middle school at six years or, alternatively, divided into two separate junior and senior middle schools of three years each.

The specialized schools (*zhongdeng zhuanye xuexiao*, or *zhongzhuan* for short) were to be maintained and developed at both junior and senior levels. Their fields of specialization ranged from industry and agriculture to pharmacology and banking, but most numerous in the specialized category were the normal, or teacher training, schools (see Table 9.4). These offered courses qualifying their graduates to teach at the elementary and kindergarten levels. Specialized secondary courses were usually two to four years in length. The two main innovations have already been mentioned, namely, the worker–peasant short-course middle schools and formal recognition for technical and spare-time education by granting it status equivalent to the regular academic stream.[22]

The attempt to integrate technical and irregular modes within the regular system was seemingly doomed from the start. Despite the October 1951 declaration that the principal reform tasks were to be "education for worker-peasant cadres, technical education, and elementary education," the first two concerns had scarcely emerged from the shadow of the academic stream before its primacy of place was officially reasserted. Chief indicators of that restoration were (1) the regularization of specialized technical education and the narrow, functionally specific role to which it had been relegated by the mid-1950s; (2) the shift in official enrollment priorities from technical to ordinary education; (3) the designation of senior secondary college preparation as the new primary task; (4) the selection of "key-point" schools within the academic stream to serve as seedbeds for quality instruction; (5) an apparent deemphasis

[22] "Guanyu gaige xuezhi de jueding."

on class background as a criterion for student admissions in deference to academic achievement; (6) the systematic revival of quality-control measures within the academic stream; and (7) the already mentioned demise of the worker–peasant short-course schools.

Specialized secondary education

Existing ratios between technical and general education were initially held to be "incompatible with the needs of national construction." At the time, in 1951, there were approximately 5,000 secondary schools nationwide, of which only about 500 fell into the specialized category (not including those in teacher training). The "energetic development" of specialized education was officially proclaimed as an objective of prime importance, even to the extent of transforming ordinary schools into the specialized variety in order to begin redressing the balance.[23] No uniform age limits were to be enforced for these schools, "in order to ensure that elementary school graduates, young workers and peasants unable to continue their studies, and adults all have the opportunity for admission."[24]

Table 9.3 shows pre- and post-1949 enrollments in the specialized and ordinary academic streams but indicates that in fact the ratios between them did not change much. According to the mid-1950s version of what happened, there had been great "recklessness" in specialized-school development during the early postliberation years. "At that time, the secondary specialized school establishment lacked planning, training objectives were not well defined, the school system was chaotic, subjects were numerous and overlapping, equipment was poor, leadership relations were not clear, and teaching quality was very low," all of which was incompatible with the needs of national construction.[25]

Regularization proceeded accordingly. The schools were reduced in number from about 800 to 650 overall by 1953–1954 and stabilized at 557 (not including

---

[23] *Renmin ribao*, editorial, 5 Apr. 1951. See also *Xinhua yuebao*, vol. 4, no. 1 (25 May 1951), pp. 173–174; "Diyici quanguo zhongdeng jiaoyu huiyi jingguo" (The Convention of the First National Secondary Education Conference), *Xinhua yuebao*, vol. 4, no. 1 (25 May 1951), pp. 174–175; *Renmin ribao*, 8 Apr. 1951; Ma Xulun, "Diyici quanguo zhongdeng jishu jiaoyu huiyi kaimuci" (Opening Statement at the First National Secondary Technical Education Conference), *Renmin jiaoyu*, Aug. 1951, p. 23.

[24] "Zhongdeng jishu xuexiao zanxing shishi banfa" (Provisional Measures for Secondary Technical Schools), *Renmin ribao*, 28 Oct. 1952. See also *Guangming ribao*, 8 Apr. 1952. These schools were often referred to interchangeably as secondary technical schools (*zhongdeng jishu xuexiao*) and secondary specialized schools (*zhongdeng zhuanye xuexiao*), although the former was usually not used with reference to the secondary-level teacher training schools while the latter often, although not always, did include them. Students of all such schools graduated to become middle-ranking technical or professional cadres. The training they received was typically of a more advanced level than that provided by vocational schools (*zhiye xuexiao*), which produced skilled workers.

[25] *Guangming ribao*, 5 Oct. 1955.

teacher training schools), or close to the original number.[26] In 1953, recruitment of students at the junior middle level was curtailed, the aim being to standardize all specialized education as senior secondary equivalent.[27] In 1954, overall leadership authority was transferred from the Ministry of Education to the Ministry of Higher Education, and the dual command structure under which the specialized schools were to operate was more clearly defined. All were placed under the "unified leadership" of the latter ministry, but other central government departments were also granted direct administrative control over those schools which trained in specialties related to their work. Such dual leadership was the same as that used for specialized tertiary institutions. Since it accompanied the already mentioned downward transfer of all post-secondary programs within institutions of higher learning to the specialized secondary schools, this upgrading of their leadership was presumably intended to standardize and preserve the intermediate status of technical training. The 1954 decisions also stipulated the principles to be followed in drawing up and revising curricula and teaching plans.[28]

By 1955–1956, the results could be more or less precisely stated. Specialized education had been "drawn into the sphere of the state plan," and students were being trained to meet the specific needs of the planned national economy. Schools had been placed under the jurisdiction of 29 ministries and departments of the central government and offered some 200 specialties. Approximately 2,000 subjects were included in their curricula, and teaching outlines for most had been completed under the leadership of the various central ministries. The "backward" practice of not teaching in accordance with these unified plans had been "thoroughly eradicated."[29] Institutions of higher learning were thus relieved of yet another "irregular" burden. All intermediate technical training was now streamlined and standardized at the senior secondary level. Admissions requirements were also being upgraded.

In form, the new enrollment regulations adopted in 1955 were similar to those being prepared for the tertiary level but never actually introduced there. Following Soviet practice, each school was allowed to enroll new students on its own. To ensure student "quality," the Higher Education Ministry drew up

[26] *Renmin ribao*, 8 June 1954. The 557 figure is from *Zhongguo jiaoyu nianjian, 1949–1981*, p. 206.
[27] "Zhongyang renmin zhengfu jiaoyubu, guanyu shifan xuexiao jinhou shezhi fazhan yu tiaozheng gongzuo de zhishi" (Central People's Government Ministry of Education, Directive on the Future Work of Developing and Adjusting the Teacher Training School Establishment), discussed in *Renmin ribao*, 20 June 1954.
[28] For these 1954 decisions and regulations, see *Guangming ribao*, 27 June 1954, on the National Specialized Secondary Education Administration Conference; "Zhongdeng zhuanye xuexiao zhangcheng" (Secondary Specialized School Regulations), 9 July 1954, *Guangming ribao*, 16 Oct. 1954; "Gaijin zhongdeng zhuanye jiaoyu de jueding" (Decision on Improving Secondary Specialized Education), 26 Sept. 1954, discussed in *Renmin ribao*, 17 Oct. 1954, and published in *Renmin jiaoyu*, Nov. 1954, pp. 65–66.
[29] *Guangming ribao*, 5 Oct. 1955.

a set of entrance examination guidelines. The subjects were, for most schools, limited to only three: Chinese language, math, and politics. Each school was also instructed to tailor its questions "both in degree of difficulty and in scope to suit the actual level of junior middle school graduates in its locality." But standards otherwise were not to be lowered for anyone, although priority was supposed to be granted to the usual categories of candidates when their scores were the same as others. The categories were workers, peasants, and the children of both; revolutionary cadres; dependents of those killed in service to the revolution and of military personnel; demobilized and disabled military personnel; national minorities; and returned overseas Chinese.[30]

In its formal explanation of these 1955 regulations, however, the ministry found itself trying to convince professional Chinese educators on two main counts, namely, the number of examination subjects and preferential admissions. The ministry argued that three subjects were ample. It was unnecessary to test for all the junior middle school courses, since students had to earn a passing grade in every one to graduate, and a graduation standard was now the prerequisite for admission to the specialized secondary schools.

Educators were also reminded that the "basic spirit" of the enrollment regulations was to increase the proportion of students from worker–peasant backgrounds and also to implement government intentions toward the national minorities and Chinese returning home from overseas. But in order to "raise quality" and ensure that they could "smoothly complete their study task" after being admitted, all had to sit for the entrance exams, and only when their scores were the same as others' could such students be granted priority in admission. The ministry nevertheless compromised in allowing schools to use the percentage grading system (rather than the more general five-point Soviet method then being promoted, comparable to the A through F American system). And in using percentage points, schools could further classify examination results within a limited point range in order to determine "comparable" performance for admissions purposes.[31]

By the mid-1950s, then, China's specialized secondary schools had been led through the same phases of regularization as the system as a whole. With recklessness and revolutionary idealism in ill-repute by 1953, these schools were soon tailored, trimmed, and upgraded to fill a particular niche within the

---

[30] Ibid., 23 May 1955.

[31] Ibid., 21 June 1955. As practice developed in later years, the classification range was typically fixed at 10 percentage points. If this same range was used in the mid-1950s, a student from the preferred categories would have been granted priority only over other students falling within that same 10-point range, e.g., 90–99 percent, 80–89 percent. Under this procedure, if the student scored 89 percent but there were enough candidates scoring 90 percent or above to fill the enrollment quota in the specialty and school to which the student had applied, then he or she would not be admitted regardless of family background. Such a student would have to accept an alternative choice, agree to whatever else was still available, or try again the next year.

regular system that bore little resemblance to the early aims of 1951. As of 1955, the regular system at the secondary level was again dominated by the college-preparatory stream. The specialized schools themselves, under Ministry of Higher Education leadership, had begun to demonstrate the same convergence of interests then occurring throughout the system between the "regular" modes of Soviet and of Chinese educators. Such convergence was nowhere better illustrated than in the arguments over the 1955 enrollment regulations. The main concern was to find an acceptable common ground between Soviet and Chinese examination procedures that would satisfy both the official requirement to learn from the Soviet Union and the demands of Chinese educators to "guarantee quality" via their favorite method of ever more numerous, unified, and meticulously graded examination subjects. As it happened, the 1955 enrollment procedures for specialized secondary schools marked, in their own small way, the zenith of the attempt to transplant Soviet methods into Chinese education. That endeavor, as pursued in the early 1950s, was abandoned before the more difficult task of introducing these same enrollment procedures at the tertiary level could be attempted.

The academic stream

The academic stream's preeminence was actually foreordained by decisions made in 1951, even as declarations for technical and worker–peasant education were at their height. Most relevant in this respect was the decision made at the 1951 National Secondary Education Conference to "select 250 middle schools with relatively good conditions to be conscientiously run in order to gain and gradually extend experience."[32] With the forces of regularization by then gathering strength, in 1953 *People's Education* advertised the importance of such selective "key-point" school development:

> The various provinces and cities should select some middle schools with better conditions to serve as key-point [*zhongdian*] schools. Their human and material conditions should be strengthened in a planned manner (by assigning them better teachers and improving their facilities), and so should their teaching–research organizations for the various subjects be strengthened, to lead in the collective study of teaching materials and methods and the study of the Soviet Union's advanced experience.[33]

The key-point concept would develop later, in the early 1960s and again during the late 1970s, into a systematic and controversial mechanism for resource concentration including not only the best teachers, leadership personnel, and

[32] Ibid., 22 July 1951.
[33] Shi Weisan, "Sannianlai de zhongxue jiaoyu" (Middle School Education during the Past Three Years), *Renmin jiaoyu*, Jan. 1953, p. 28.

facilities but unified enrollment procedures that concentrated the "best" students as well. This last was specifically prohibited by Soviet pedagogy which, must be why key-point middle schools received so little overt recognition during the 1950s. In any event, the initial application of the key-point concept within the education sector replicated old patterns combining the central school format most commonly used at the elementary level throughout China before 1949 and the "model," or key-point, approach to policy implementation much favored by the CCP. New policies were typically introduced on an experimental or selective basis where conditions were most conducive to success prior to general implementation.[34]

According to interviewees (see Appendix), the schools so designated in the early 1950s, and referred to as key points thereafter, typically included the best of those inherited from the per-1949 era. By using such schools in this way, however, the new aim of strengthening regular academic secondary schooling played an important role in perpetuating the elitist traditions against which the old reformers' critique had been so assiduously honed in the past.

To reiterate briefly, before 1949, admission to all schools, from kindergarten on, had been governed by examinations designed to select the mentally and physically most advantaged. Given the small size of the system overall, such an enrollment process inevitably favored children from better-off families. Schools generally gave their own entrance examinations and enrolled individually. But since the number of applicants was always much greater than the places available at the most "famous" elementary and middle schools, the competition tended naturally to produce higher-scoring student bodies at these institutions. Admission to schools with the best reputations, both public and private, was also based on *guanxi*, or connections, however. It helped, in other words, if one's father knew the headmaster. And it was from among these best-appointed and most-prestigious schools that the first group of key points was selected in the early 1950s.

According to data published much later, 196 middle schools had been selected to serve as key points by 1953. These schools were located throughout the country, but the largest numbers, of 10 or more per locality, were concentrated in the three cities of Beijing (20), Tianjin (10), and Shanghai (10) and in the provinces of Liaoning (15), Jiangsu (14), Anhui (10), Fujian (10), and Sichuan (15). All other provinces had fewer than 10 such schools.[35]

---

[34] The central (*zhongxin*) school pattern was specifically reaffirmed in the Provisional Elementary School Regulations of 1952, but the companion Provisional Secondary School Regulations mentioned neither the central nor the key-point formula. Both sets of regulations are reprinted in *Zhongguo jiaoyu nianjian, 1949–1981*, pp. 727–731. As we have seen, the central school pattern, authorized by GMD government directives in the 1930s, was adopted in the CCP liberated areas as well. Transitional 1949–1950 directives such as the provisional elementary school measures for north China and the secondary school regulations in the Northeast, both cited above, also perpetuated this conventional pattern.

[35] "Zhongxue jiaoyu" (Middle School Education), *Zhongguo jiaoyu nianjian, 1949–1981*, p. 168. See Table 13.3 below.

A second step reaffirming the status of the academic stream was recorded in Education Minister Ma Xulun's report to an August 1952 conference of education administrators: "The large-scale development of middle schools, especially ordinary [*putong*] middle schools, will be of crucial importance in educational construction for several years to come."[36] And so the die was cast. The need to meet the planned college enrollment quotas took precedence over all other considerations at the secondary level throughout the FFYP, and the inherited academic stream naturally served as the foundation upon with the developing college-preparatory stream was built.

At the secondary level, then, the course corrections that accompanied the "readjustment and consolidation" phase formally inaugurated in 1953 were essentially a confirmation of an already existing emphasis on the regular college-preparatory stream. Decisions and directives needed only to be rephrased in a more forthright admission of that aim, now placed within the context of FFYP demands on the education system. "To cope with the demands of the nation's socialist industrialization," noted a 1954 report confirming the trend, "greater importance should in principle be attached to senior than to junior middle schools, and to big cities and industrial districts rather than to ordinary districts."[37] "In the development of secondary education," noted the subsequent formal directive, "the emphasis is on senior middle schooling while junior middle schools are also developed appropriately in accordance with existing conditions."[38]

For content, curriculum development, teaching plans, and textbooks, the system's builders still retained the Soviet Union as their primary reference point. For enforcement of quality, however, Chinese educators resorted increasingly to their own inherited ways and means. Deriving from the conclusion that the "principal defect" of education work was "low quality," the model prescription circulated nationally "for reference" was the "Decision on Raising the Quality of Secondary and Elementary School Education in the City of Beijing," issued by the Beijing municipal CCP Committee in mid-1954. This decision was subsequently recommended by the Ministry of Education as containing the concrete measures most suitable for translating into

---

[36] *Renmin ribao*, 19 Aug. 1952.

[37] Ibid., 2 Feb. 1954. The report concerned another secondary education conference convened to redefine programs and tasks more clearly in terms of planning and key-point development. The conference also confirmed the leadership principle necessary to guarantee the application of the key-point concept to secondary school development. Provincial government education bureaus, under the leadership of the provincial CCP committees, were authorized to administer directly a few selected middle schools while leaving the lower-ranking city or county bureaus and CCP committees in charge of the rest.

[38] "Zhongyang renmin zhengfu zhengwuyuan guanyu gaijin he fazhan zhongxue jiaoyu de zhishi" (Central People's Government Administration Council Directive on Improving and Developing Secondary Education), 8 Apr. 1954, *Renmin ribao*, 12 June 1954, reprinted in *Zhongguo jiaoyu nianjian, 1949–1981*, pp. 733–734.

reality the aims of recent directives on improving elementary and secondary education.[39]

Using scores on the 1953 college entrance examinations as a standard, the Beijing decision began with the revelation that 70 percent of the city's candidates failed to achieve a "passing" score (in absolute terms, meaning a score of 60 points out of 100 points). Of Beijing's 44 middle schools, students at only 7 achieved an average of above 60 points. The reasons were many but chief among them was deemed to be a failure of leadership. The responsible CCP and government authorities had not introduced the measures necessary to raise quality simultaneously with the increase in quantity. Hence, there were no effective plans for training and promoting teachers, no "stringent selection" procedures for new personnel, no "rigorous inspection" of work, and no system of rewards and punishments. For students, there were no "strict standards and systems to govern admission, promotion, and graduation."

Under the circumstances, quality must take precedence over quantity. Students must be trained to pass their examinations, and the key-point schools must be run well. Toward those immediate aims, the Beijing decision outlined a series of measures, all standard features of the "regular" education repertoire from days gone by, now prescribed as the remedy of choice to cure the ills diagnosed within the school system.[40] Among the first of these measures to be introduced in Beijing and promoted by the Education Ministry was the controversial *tongkao*, or unified examinations of 1930s fame, which now became the pivot around which quality control revolved. While the Beijing decision was being drafted, unified examinations in mathematics and Chinese were administered to 8th and 11th graders throughout the city. The results then served as the chief standard for judging the "quality" of teachers' work and their success in adhering to the prescribed teaching plans and syllabi.[41]

---

[39] "Xuexi Beijingshi tigao zhong xiao xue jiaoyu zhiliang de cuoshi" (Study Beijing's Measures for Raising the Quality of Middle and Elementary School Education), *Renmin jiaoyu*, Aug. 1954, pp. 5–6; "Zhongguo gongchandang Beijingshi weiyuanhui, guanyu tigao Beijingshi zhong xiao xue jiaoyu zhiliang de jueding" (Decision by the Beijing City Communist Party Committee on Raising the Quality of Elementary and Secondary Education in Beijing), 23 June 1954, ibid., pp. 17–19; *Guangming ribao*, 8 Sept. 1954.

[40] "Guanyu tigao Beijingshi zhong xiao xue jiaoyu zhiliang de jueding."

[41] "Xuexi Beijingshi tigao zhong xiao xue jiaoyu zhiliang de cuoshi." Both the practice and the controversy continued. Three years later, educators criticized the practice, noting that the Beijing Education Bureau ranked schools each year on the basis of their exam scores but never considered the schools' differing conditions or cared how the scores were achieved (*Wenhuibao*, Shanghai, 6 May 1957). A Beijing school administrator complained that the rank order of various schools, based on their students' average college entrance examination scores, was publicly announced instead of being used for internal reference only, as ostensibly intended. The negative consequences for learning were great, because schools concentrated only on pushing up exam scores in a manner "not much different from the nature of the pre-1949 unified examinations" (*Guangming ribao*, 16 May 1957, comment by Zhao Dexian, p. 3). See also "Jiaoshi tan jiaoyu gongzuo neibu maodun" (Teachers Discuss Contradictions within Education Work), *Renmin jiaoyu*, June 1957, pp. 6–13, for selected comments from another meeting of Beijing middle school teachers (9 May 1957), including complaints about the practice of ranking schools (pp. 8, 9–10).

As in tertiary institutions and specialized middle schools, strengthening the regular college-preparatory stream also led to a quiet revision of enrollment priorities. Revisions concerned both the kind of student recruited and the kind of schools granted first pick of the student crop. Pursuant to the initial "policy of opening the doors for workers and peasants," the March 1951 secondary education conference had resolved with respect to middle school enrollment that "localities should variously fix relative quotas for the children of workers and peasants."[42] Whether such quotas were ever actually established is uncertain, but localities did make great claims about recruiting working-class youth at the secondary level.[43] The Education Ministry's 1952 national enrollment guidelines for senior secondary and technical schools also stipulated specifically that preference should be granted, including lower admissions scores, to the children of revolutionary martyrs, workers, and peasants, as well as to army dependents, workers, young peasants, national minorities, and returned overseas Chinese.[44]

By 1953, however, the regulations stipulated that only when their examination scores were equal to those of other students should these categories of candidates be granted preference.[45] It was claimed that, as of 1953, 57 percent of all middle school students were of worker–peasant origin and that some 70 percent overall were the "children of workers, peasants, and other laboring people."[46] But such claims soon disappeared. The 1954 regulations stipulated only that the children of revolutionary martyrs be given priority in admission, leaving it to the various localities to give preference to others as local conditions warranted.[47] In 1955, the regulations cautioned localities to "emphasize and grasp the principle of guaranteeing quality" when enrolling the previously preferred categories.[48]

A related question nevertheless remains unclear, that is, the extent to which newly designated key-point schools were allowed to enroll the "best of the best" students during the first round of selection. This practice became the linchpin of the increasingly regimented school hierarchy during the early 1960s by ensuring that the best schools had first choice from among all students scoring highest within a city, district, or county on unified local secondary school entrance examinations. It seems unlikely that such schools enrolled on a par

---

[42] From Ma Xulun's report, in *Guangming ribao*, 22 July 1951. This stipulation was also written into the 1952 Provisional Secondary School Regulations (article 7).

[43] *Renmin ribao*, 21 June 1950. For a sample of the publicity, which was strong on claims but weak on detail (as to how many of what kind of students were admitted to what kind of schools with scores how many points lower than others), see *Tianjin ribao*, 13 July 1952; *Jiefang ribao*, Shanghai, 15 July and 15 Aug. 1952; *Changjiang ribao*, Wuhan, 1 Dec. 1951; *Fujian ribao*, Fuzhou, 8 Aug. 1952; *Nanfang ribao*, Guangzhou, 23 Aug. 1952.

[44] *Guangming ribao*, 11 July 1952; *Wenhuibao*, Shanghai, 12 July 1952.

[45] *Guangming ribao*, 22 July 1953; *Wenhuibao*, Shanghai, 1 Aug. 1953.

[46] E.g., *Guangming ribao*, 16 Jan. and 12 June 1954.

[47] Ibid., 6 June 1954.

[48] Ibid., 17 June 1955.

with others in the 1950s, as the central elementary schools were in theory supposed to do. But Soviet pedagogy specifically prohibited streaming or concentrating students by ability in separate classes or schools, and published enrollment regulations were silent on the status of key-point schools in the admissions process.

Interviewees, although hazy on this question, nevertheless agreed that initially, just after 1949, secondary schools continued to enroll individually. Each school prepared and administered entrance examinations to candidates who applied directly to it for admission. Hence the same sort of "natural" selection, whereby the most prestigious schools attracted the most-advantaged students, continued to operate after 1949 as it had before. General regulations and guidelines were, of course, issued by the central authorities. Besides stipulating the preferential categories of students, general procedures, and the like, national guidelines fixed enrollment targets for the different kinds of middle schools and for each of the greater administrative regions into which the early People's Republic was divided. Actual enrollment work was conducted under the authority of provincial and city government education bureaus, which were responsible for applying the regulations locally.

In 1952, however, central regulations stipulated "unified enrollment" for specialized and senior middle schools.[49] Although this seems initially to have been a provisional measure, which was not even extended to include all schools, it nevertheless marked the onset of a unification trend that would soon become an institutionalized feature of the school system. As such, unified secondary school entrance examinations would perform the same function for the country's middle schools within their local enrollment districts that the national college entrance examinations played at the tertiary level: ranking schools and channeling students throughout the school hierarchy on the basis of their exam scores.

In 1952, however, unified enrollment for public senior middle schools seemed only a somewhat more efficient version of the old method. In Beijing, for example, a single set of examination papers was given to all candidates; correcting and grading were also unified; and admissions were coordinated citywide. Students listed several preferences but sat for the examinations at their first-preference schools, each of which then selected first from among its own self-selected group of candidates.[50] The net result for elite schools was thus much the same as before, depending, that is, on how seriously they were expected to take the new worker–peasant preference schemes. The main point that remains

[49] *Renmin ribao*, 11 July 1952.
[50] *Guangming ribao*, 12 July 1952. Several cities announced similar unified enrollment procedures at this time: e.g., *Tianjin ribao*, 13, 15 July 1952; *Jinbu ribao*, Tianjin, 29 July 1952; *Xinhua ribao*, Chongqing, 25 Aug. 1952; *Nanfang ribao*, Guangzhou, 8 Sept. 1952; *Jiefang ribao*, Shanghai, 5 July 1952; *Fujian ribao*, Fuzhou, 29 June and 5 Aug. 1952.

unclear is precisely when the "best" students within a given catchment area began to be channelled systematically on the basis of unified examinations into the key schools.

For Shanghai, one interviewee recalled unequivocally that this point was reached in 1956, just after all remaining private schools were taken over to become part of the public system. A middle school student herself at the time, she described a procedure similar to that of later years, with minimum passing-score requirements fixed by key junior and senior middle schools in a ranked hierarchy moving upward from district key junior middle schools to all-city key senior middle schools. Students who listed such schools on their application preference forms were only admitted if they achieved the requisite minimum passing scores on their entrance examinations. Candidates were encouraged to apply at their nearest district key school, but crossing boundaries was possible depending on availability of places and number of applicants.[51]

According to a former Shanghai school administrator responsible for enrollment work in the late 1950s, all examination papers were at that time collected together, graded, ranked, and grouped by the candidates' first-preference schools. Enrollment inspectors from the key schools then converged on the collection center to make their choices, each school starting with its own first-preference applicants. Other schools were allowed to enroll only after the key points had completed their selection.

Other cities, however, did not arrive at so systematic and hierarchical a procedure at so early a date, according to interviewees (see also chap. 13). Published regulations also suggest that the systematic concentration of student talent probably occurred only gradually with the unification of school district and all-city examinations and enrollment procedures during the 1950s. National regulations thus continued to stipulate that schools could enroll either individually or jointly within a given district depending on local conditions, and in 1957 the regulations even advised "in general" against the "unified enrollment method."[52]

Development dilemmas and the Soviet model

That Stalin-era socialist planning would not safeguard China against the most basic "dysfunctions" of development had thus become evident within less than

---

[51] Shanghai's published enrollment regulations distinguished between academic and specialized secondary schools but made no mention of a key-point hierarchy within the academic stream (*Wenhuibao*, Shanghai 13, 15, 21 July 1952, 9, 26 July, and 1, 7, 16 Aug. 1953, 9, 20 July and 10 Aug. 1954, 4 July 1955; *Jiefang ribao*, Shanghai: 10 July 1955, 6 July 1956, 12, 29 July 1957). The complete takeover of Shanghai's private elementary and secondary schools was announced in early 1956 (*Wenhuibao*, Shanghai, 25 Jan. 1956).

[52] *Guangming ribao*, 6 June 1954, 17 June 1955, 23 May 1956, 21 Apr. 1957; *Renmin ribao*, 30 Apr. 1956.

a decade's effort spent emulating the Soviet model. Far from sparing China the consequences of the Soviet Union's earlier mistakes, that model's urban-based, heavy-industry focus actually seemed to compound the contradictions. As of mid-1956, and despite unprecedented quantitative growth, only 52 percent of the age-group had entered elementary school, and 78 percent of the total population was still classified as illiterate.[53] Yet under the imperatives of the plan, China had retreated from its original goal of closing the urban–rural elementary school gap within a decade. Also abandoned for the same reason were the various supplementary and irregular means of adding more secondary school places to the limited regular supply.

The number of students at the senior elementary level had nevertheless increased on an average of 20 percent per year since 1952, in contrast with an average annual increase of only 14 percent at the junior middle level. As a result of this imbalanced growth, only about one-third of all elementary school graduates were able to go on to the junior middle level after 1953, whereas some 70–80 percent were doing so before. And at this level, too, the urban–rural gap seemed unbridgeable. As of 1955, close to 80 percent of all urban elementary school graduates were entering junior middle school, while only 30 percent were doing so in rural counties.[54]

Even the political goal of quickly creating a new generation of worker-peasant intellectuals had been compromised to meet the plan's demands for quality-controlled college students and development personnel. Soviet-style goals for industrialization and the Chinese resources available for meeting its requirements, including certain inherited assumptions about how to guarantee educational quality, then conspired to return the regular college-preparatory stream to its old dominant place within the school system. Tables 9.5 and 9.6 help illustrate the extent of the dilemmas in the making.

Yet the only counsel promoters could offer was patience, and the only excuse, poverty. In China as elsewhere, however, one of the first distress signals of a developing system could not be ignored and was impossible to cover up. At the start of the fall semester 1953, Education Minister Zhang Xiruo went on the radio in an attempt to pacify students and parents. Addressing specifically the problem of elementary school graduates, he pointed out that the national secondary school enrollment of 3 million was already 80 percent higher than before 1949. But elementary enrollments stood at 55 million and were growing at a faster rate. Moreover, most junior elementary graduates wanted to advance to the next level, and most senior elementary graduates

[53] Zhang Xiruo, "Muqian guomin jiaoyu fangmian de qingkuang he wenti" (Present Situation and Problems of National Education), National People's Congress report, 20 June 1956, *Renmin jiaoyu*, July 1956, p. 9; also in *Renmin ribao*, 21 June 1956.

[54] "Jinianlai woguo jiaoyu shiye de fazhan gaikuang" (A Survey of Our Country's Educational Development in Recent Years), *Tongji gongzuo tongxun* (Statistical Work Bulletin), no. 20 (1956), reprinted in *Xinhua banyue kan* (New China Semimonthly), no. 24 (1956), p. 94.

Table 9.5. *Opportunities to continue schooling within the regular system, 1953–1957*

	(1) Elem. school graduates	(2) Jr. middle entrants	(3) Elem. graduate promotion rate (%)	(4) Jr. middle school graduates	(5) Sr. middle entrants	(6) Jr. middle graduate promotion rate (%)	(7) Sr. middle school graduates	(8) Tertiary freshmen	(9) Sr. middle graduate promotion rate (%)
1953	2,935,000	818,000	27.87	398,000	161,000	40.45	56,000	81,544	145.61
1954	3,325,000	1,236,000	37.17	576,000	195,000	33.85	68,000	92,280	135.71
1955	3,229,000	1,282,000	39.70	870,000	221,000	25.40	99,000	97,797	98.78
1956	4,051,000	1,969,000	48.61	785,000	374,000	47.64	154,000	184,632	119.89
1957	4,980,000	2,170,000	43.57	1,112,000	323,000	29.05	187,000	105,581	56.46

Note: This table is a revised version, using Chinese statistics published in the 1980s, of Table 9: Opportunities to Continue Schooling, 1953–1957, in Thomas P. Bernstein, *Up to the Mountains and Down to the Villages*, p. 48. Bernstein's Table 9 was based on earlier compilations. The data are "basically" the same, that is, comparable but not identical, with the exception of the elementary school graduate figures. The original source for this column on Bernstein's table was the State Statistical Bureau's *Ten Great Years*, p. 194, which differs substantially from the later compilation shown here. The latter, moreover, yields promotion rates much closer to other contemporary sources.
Source: *Zhongguo jiaoyu nianjian, 1949–1981*, p. 1021 (col. 1), p. 1001 (cols. 2, 4, 5, 7), p. 969 (col. 8).

Table 9.6. *Students of worker–peasant origin* (percentage of all students)

Academic level	1951/1952	1952/1953	1955/1956	1956/1957	1957/1958	1958/1959	1959/1960
Tertiary	19.08[a]	20.46[b]	29.20[b]	34.29[b]	36.42[b]	48.00[c]	51.00[d]
Tertiary freshmen[a]	—	—	—	36.69	44.00	62.00[c]	—
Famous big-city universities[e]	—	—	—	10–20	—	—	—
Graduate students, universities[f]	—	—	—	17.46	—	—	—
Graduate students, Academy of Sciences[f]	—	—	—	5.92	—	—	—
Preparatory classes for study in USSR[f]	—	—	—	30.10	—	—	—
Secondary, ordinary[g]	51.27	56.10	62.20	66.02	69.10	75.20	—
Secondary, technical[h]	56.60	57.10	62.00	64.10	66.60	77.00	—
Elementary	—	—	—	80.00+[i]	—	90.00+[c]	—

[a] *Renmin ribao*, 27 Dec. 1957, p. 7.

[b] "Education: Training Worker and Peasant Intellectuals," *Peking Review*, vol. 1, no. 12 (20 May 1958), p. 16.

[c] Yang Xiufeng, "Woguo jiaoyu shiye de da geming he da fazhan" (The Great Revolution in and Great Development of Our Country's Educational Enterprise), in *Jiaoyu shinian* (Ten Years of Education), p. 2.

[d] Hu Qili's National Students Association report, in *Renmin ribao*, 5 Feb. 1960.

[e] Zhang Jian, "Woguo de gaodeng jiaoyu shi yueban yuehao le" (Our Country's Higher Education Is Being Run Better and Better), *Renmin jiaoyu*, Oct. 1957, pp. 6, 10.

[f] Guo Moruo, in *Renmin ribao*, 6 July 1957. The 1956/1957 percentage cited for preparatory classes for study in the USSR in fact refers to the proportion of worker–peasant students among all those in such classes between 1952 and 1956.

[g] Fang Junfu, "Zhongxue jiaoyu youmeiyou chengji, chengji zai nali" (Have There Been Accomplishments in Secondary Education and If So What Are They?), *Renmin jiaoyu*, Oct. 1957, p. 14; and State Statistical Bureau, *Ten Great Years*, p. 200.

[h] State Statistical Bureau, *Ten Great Years*, p. 200.

[i] Guo Lin, "Bu xu dongyao jiaoyu xiang gongnong kaimen de fangzhen" (The Policy of Opening the Doors of Education for Workers and Peasants Should Not Waver), *Renmin jiaoyu*, Sept. 1957, p. 12.

were demanding access to junior middle school. These upward pressures amounted to an immediate demand for universal schooling through the junior secondary level, a demand that was objectively impossible for the state to meet. To the many critics who were asking why China did not open enough schools to accommodate all those wanting to enroll, Minister Zhang provided the standard explanation, namely, that people's cultural needs would be met gradually upon a foundation of "great economic strength and heavy industry."[55]

Students and parents were reminded repeatedly that China was now embarked upon the same planned and phased course of development as that pioneered by the Soviet Union, where resources were concentrated in heavy industry and in urban, rather than rural, development.[56] But listeners were hard to convince. Minister Zhang repeated the message in 1954 and again in 1955, noting that tensions had been high for three summers running over this issue. "Some people are in the habit of voicing support for socialist industrialization," he admonished. "But once they find that their own children cannot gain admission to a higher school, they turn to blame the government for not establishing more schools."[57]

Chinese leaders found themselves trapped in the classic dilemma. Bearing as it did the banner of socialist superiority, the new CCP government was officially committed to ridding China of the stigma of illiteracy. Yet immediately that commitment was set in motion, popular expectations were aroused that could not be met. The authorities then had to choose whether to backtrack on their original commitment or allow the dynamic of development to carry them where it would: in terms of increasing numbers of "displaced" young people demanding jobs and study opportunities that did not yet exist.

After a preliminary bout of blind adventurism, Chinese leaders opted for Soviet-style concentrated development in combination with centralized planning and job assignment as the control mechanism for misplaced aspirations. Even so, the inherent coercion and social pressure were not enough. Consequently, a steady stream of publicity was churned out each year and timed to coincide with the graduation and enrollment cycles in hopes of counteracting the "emotional upset" produced by negative entrance examination results.

---

[55] Zhang Xiruo's radio speech was printed in *Guangming ribao*, 24 Sept. 1953.

[56] E.g., see also Zhang Xiruo's speech at the First National People's Congress, 26 Sept. 1954, *Renmin ribao*, 27 Sept. 1954; "Zhonggong zhongyang xuanquanbu, guanyu gaoxiao he chuzhong biyesheng congshi laodong shengchan xuanquan tigang" (Chinese Communist Party Central Propaganda Department, Propaganda Outline on Senior Elementary and Junior Middle Graduates Engaging in Labor Production), 22 May 1954, *Renmin jiaoyu*, June 1954, pp. 7–10; Zhongguo gongchandang zhongyang Huanan fenju xuanquanbu, ed., *Gaoxiao he chuzhong biyesheng congshi laodong shengchan xuanquan jianghua* (Propaganda Talk on Senior Elementary and Junior Middle Graduates Engaging in Labor Production) (Guangzhou: Huanan renmin chubanshe, 1954), p. 35.

[57] From Zhang Xiruo's report to a National People's Congress meeting, 22 July 1955, *Guangming ribao*, 23 July 1955.

Acknowledging that most of the 4 million senior elementary and 600,000 junior middle graduates that year wanted to continue their studies but could not, a 1954 national Youth League directive acknowledged also that preparing these graduates to participate in labor "is still an unfamiliar problem for us." The task was to "develop a correct public opinion" from the prevailing view that for a student to join the ranks of labor was an "injustice and a disgrace."[58] Old ideas about the distinction between mental and manual labor were being reproduced in successive generations, along with the most basic rudiments of education, in even the most nonacademic of settings.

Despite the proclaimed intention to adjust the balance between junior and senior secondary development, however, neither level was able to meet the demands made upon it throughout most of the FFYP period (see Table 9.5). Elementary education continued to expand at a faster pace than that at the junior secondary level, and the latter, despite slower growth rates, was soon producing more students than the senior level was allowed to absorb. Meanwhile, the senior level could not keep pace with the planned enrollment quotas for the tertiary sector. This remained true generally despite the slowdown in growth at the elementary level between 1953 and 1955 and the sudden increased demand, explained below, for junior middle graduates precipitated by Mao's first unplanned "leap forward" in 1956.

[58] *Renmin ribao*, 24 Apr. 1954.

10

Blooming, contending, and criticizing the Soviet model

With higher education restructured to produce the talent needed for industrialization, the gradual 20th-century separation of Chinese intellectuals from their inherited association with bureaucratic and political power seemed virtually complete. Professionally, however, Chinese educators were far from being disempowered. They had already registered marked success in adjusting their realm to suit old assumptions about how schools should be run, under the guise of adapting the Soviet import to Chinese conditions. At every point where such adjustments occurred, they merged right rather than left, that is, in a line of convergence with China's own regularization mode rather than its critical countercurrent. Just how far professional educators would have liked to go in that direction became evident during 1956 and 1957 – as did the full extent of the forces arrayed against them.[1]

The revelations were part of a much larger exercise initiated by CCP leaders themselves in an effort to regain their balance after leaning so heavily "to one side." No sooner had they made that decision in 1949 than Josef Stalin died, in 1953, preparing the way for important changes within the Soviet bloc. These changes were heralded by new Soviet leader Nikita Khrushchev's report criticizing Stalin at the Soviet Union's 20th Communist Party Congress in February 1956. The consequences for the CCP were at best politically embarrassing and nowhere more so than in its relationship with the academic community, where initial reluctance to jump on the Soviet bandwagon was well known.

The Chinese were supposed to benefit by coming later, avoiding the youthful errors of Soviet big brother and moving at once into a state-owned centrally planned model of socialist heavy industry that had taken most of two decades to establish in the Soviet Union. But whatever the benefits, they were more than matched by errors of judgment and timing, that is, by the costs of having launched China once more into the orbit of a passing foreign star, and one that was about to fall at that. Disengagement and damage control began in the mid-1950s,

---

[1] For a different approach to the convergence question, see Ronald F. Price, "Convergence or Copying: China and the Soviet Union," in Hayhoe and Bastid, *China's Education and the Industrialized World*, pp. 158–183.

217

reflecting early post-Stalin trends in the Soviet Union itself. Inevitably, old Chinese concerns reemerged, with dependency and mechanical imitation in the forefront. These were unavoidable but awkward admissions for a party that had earned its nationalist credentials in long years of battle against the Japanese and other foreign intruders.

Even prior to Khrushchev's report, the rigidities of Soviet intellectual life began to ease, and China followed suit accordingly. The new emphasis in 1954 on "spirit and essence," rather than mechanical reproduction, of the Soviet experience probably derived from that shift. But the first acknowledged step taken by the CCP to distance itself from the Soviet mentor was announced at a special January 1956 conference on the question of intellectuals. In his keynote address, Premier Zhou Enlai said that China lacked sufficient numbers of trained personnel to meet the needs of national development. Science and technology were still backward. "We are still unable to acquire and use many of the world's latest scientific achievements. We are also still unable to solve independently of the Soviet experts many of the complex technical questions now arising in our construction work."

Yet China had failed even to exploit fully the talent it had due to "certain sectarian attitudes" or prejudices against non-Party intellectuals. But these prejudices derived from the Party's assessment of them, which Zhou did not deny. On the contrary, it was estimated that perhaps 40 percent of higher intellectuals were progressive or active supporters of the CCP and socialism, he said, although even many of these still entertained "individualistic" attitudes and work styles reflecting their bourgeois origins. Another 40 percent were middling elements who accepted the new order but were "not sufficiently progressive." Something over 10 percent were probably "backward" and opposed to socialism, including a few actual counterrevolutionaries. China's intellectuals were, in other words, a mixed lot with "complex historical records," bourgeois family ties, and ideological commitments to match.[2]

The same contradiction Mao had identified in the early 1930s between the CCP's need for and suspicions of intellectuals was now magnified many times over. The Party was in effect being ordered by its leaders to do the impossible, namely, seize the initiative in promoting the nation's intellectual life, produce more qualified personnel, ensure their political loyalty even though most were deemed to some degree unreliable, and reduce China's intellectual dependence on the Soviet Union. Nevertheless, Zhou's 1956 report contained recommendations for coping on all these points.

[2] Zhou Enlai, "Guanyu zhishi fenzi wenti de baogao" (Report on the Question of Intellectuals), speech delivered 14 Jan. 1956, *Renmin ribao*, 30 Jan. 1956, trans. in Robert R. Bowie and John K. Fairbank, eds. *Communist China, 1955–1959: Policy Documents with Analysis* (Cambridge: Harvard University Press, 1962), pp. 128–144.

On the correct orientation toward the Soviet Union, he said: "We must first discard all servile thinking, which shows a lack of national self-confidence." Soviet aid was still needed to overcome China's scientific backwardness. But there was a right and a wrong way to accept that aid. The latter was "to seek a solution from the Soviet Union to every question, great and small, that arises and to send mostly secondary school graduates, rather then scientists, to study in the Soviet Union. The result would be to remain forever in a state of dependence and imitation." The right way was "to make an overall plan that distinguishes between what is essential and urgent and what is not, and to systematically use the latest achievements of Soviet science so as to bring ourselves abreast of Soviet levels as rapidly as possible."

Following Khrushchev's report, the CCP issued its own statement in April 1956, similarly criticizing Stalin's errors.[3] The Party then took the initiative in May, when Mao himself launched a new slogan – "Let a hundred flowers bloom, let a hundred schools of thought contend" (*baihua qifang, baijia zhengming*) – and with it a new movement. The "hundred schools" slogan was intended to evoke as precedent China's ancient age of philosophers (770–221 B.C.). According to tradition, it was a time when many schools of thought flourished, but none dominated. The difference between then and now, explained the CCP, was that society then was in a chaotic state, and contention was "spontaneous." Now, the "unified leadership" of the Party would establish the guidelines and explain the rationale. The motives were typical 20th-century Chinese modern: if the nation was to become rich and powerful, the arts and sciences must prosper. But the prerequisite was freedom of thought, debate, and creativity. The question was how much freedom and for whom.

The formal guidelines for literature, art, philosophy, and the social sciences raised more questions than they answered. But the prescription for the natural sciences was clear and the change important. The natural sciences, it was now said, had no "class character" but instead followed their own laws of development. Hence attaching labels like "feudal" and "bourgeois" to them was wrong. The prescription, adapted from changes under way in the Soviet Union itself, also reopened some doors to the West. Whereas before, there was no need, because the Soviet Union had already absorbed all that was of value from the capitalist world, now all its intellectual merits should be "studied critically."[4]

The story of the subsequent blooming-and-contending experiment and its

---

[3] *Renmin ribao*, 5 Apr. 1956.
[4] Mao's speech launching the slogan remained unpublished, but its import was elaborated in countless official forums while Lu Dingyi, head of the CCP Propaganda Department, provided the official public elaboration. The above quotes are all taken from his statement: Lu Dingyi, "Baihua qifang, baijia zhengming" (Let a Hundred Flowers Bloom, Let a Hundred Schools of Thought Contend), speech delivered 26 May 1956, *Renmin ribao*, 13 June 1956, trans. in Bowie and Fairbank, *Communist China*, pp. 151–162.

political dénouement in the Party's antirightist campaign against its intellectual critics is well known.[5] Less so are the debates over specific questions of education reform that took place at the same time. But while China's intellectual community was engaged in elaborating the officially anointed critique of dogmatism and dependency, Party leaders embarked on an enterprise of their own, not criticizing the early 1950s Soviet model in so many words but disrupting it massively in action. Professional economic planners were evidently no less appalled than professional educators at the consequences. These added fuel to fires already burning and, in the more relaxed climate of 1956, inspired further the arguments in defense of academic regularity.

Socialist upsurge and the case for Chinese-style "irregularity"

The new approach began in 1955, midway through the FFYP, and derived from the Party's changing economic policies, with those for agriculture in the lead. The accelerated collectivization of agriculture during the latter half of 1955 was followed by the ambitious 12-year development plan adopted in January 1956. Between July and December 1955, the number of Chinese rural households farming collectively increased from 17 million to 70 million, or to about 60 percent of the 110 million total. The increase was many times faster than originally planned. A year later, close to 90 percent had pooled land, labor, animals, and implements under the collective management of the new basic-level work unit in the countryside known as the agricultural producers cooperatives (APCs).

In response to the socialist upsurge, Mao wrote: "This event tells us that the scope and speed of China's industrialization as well as the development of science, culture, education, public health, and so on, can no longer be entirely the same as originally thought. All must be appropriately expanded and accelerated."[6] The Draft Program for Agricultural Development, 1956–1967, aimed therefore to hasten rural development along every dimension from grain yields to social welfare. For education, the objective was universal elementary schooling

---

[5] E.g., Roderick MacFarquhar, ed., *The Hundred Flowers Campaign and the Chinese Intellectuals* (New York: Praeger, 1960); Roderick MacFarquhar, *The Origins of the Cultural Revolution: Contradictions among the People, 1956–1957* (New York: Columbia University Press, 1974); Roderick MacFarquhar, Timothy Cheek, and Eugene Wu, eds., *The Secret Speeches of Chairman Mao: From the Hundred Flowers to the Great Leap Forward* (Cambridge: Council on East Asian Studies/Harvard University, 1989), pp. 113–372; Chen, *Thought Reform of the Chinese Intellectuals*, pt. 2; Goldman, *Literary Dissent in Communist China*, chaps. 8–9; Mu Fu-sheng, *The Wilting of the Hundred Flowers: The Chinese Intelligentsia under Mao* (New York: Praeger, 1963).
[6] Mao Zedong, "Zhongguo nongcun de shehuizhuyi gaochao xuyan" (Preface to *Socialist Upsurge in China's Countryside*), 27 Dec. 1955, first published in *Renmin ribao*, 12 Jan. 1956.

in the rural areas within 12 years and the elimination of illiteracy within 7. The village *minban* schools were designated as the medium that would make this possible. Only the "people" responsible for running them now were the new collectives.[7]

Reviving rural goals

The official revival of the old formula capped a critical reassessment of the 1952–1955 years for having abandoned the "school in every village" ideal. Yet commentaries demonstrated the ambiguities that Chinese society had created for itself – with some new arguments now added to old – over the deceptively simple task of universalizing elementary schooling. Blame was placed upon "some people" responsible for education work at levels high and low who did not appreciate the importance of *minban* schools. Some argued that education should be entirely state funded, and some also argued that the state was doing well enough without *minban* schools. Some argued that the rural masses were neither willing nor able to assume such a burden themselves. People committed to regularity said that schools run by the people would be "irregular in quality" and thus unable to guarantee genuine universalization in any case. Official commentators tried their best to refute such arguments.

According to the principles of socialism, wrote Education Ministry official Li Pingjie, the economy had to grow proportionally, with appropriate ratios of state investment in each sector. Heavy industry remained the key to national construction and therefore had to take precedence in state financing over education. Yet the 51 million children in elementary school constituted only about half the nation's school-age population. If we follow the old way of thinking, namely, that universal education must be free and state financed, he continued, then schooling for the other half must be postponed indefinitely because the state cannot afford such an investment.[8]

As for willingness, rural people had a "glorious tradition" of running their own schools, which had been tapped during the Yan'an decade. More recently, many thousands of villages had continued to run schools despite the lack of official encouragement. Concerning their uncertain quality, better a school that could at least teach children a few characters than none at all, which would only add to the generations of rural illiterates. There was, moreover, no need to judge the future by the past. Henceforth, the new collectives would be

---

[7] Article 29, Draft Program for Agricultural Development, 1956–1967, promulgated 23 Jan. 1956, *Renmin ribao*, 26 Jan. 1956, trans. in Bowie and Fairbank, *Communist China*, pp. 119–126. The draft program was also known as the "12-year agricultural program" and the "40 articles."

[8] *Guangming ribao*, 22 Feb. 1956. Li Pingjie was deputy director of the Elementary Education Office, Ministry of Education.

responsible for providing the leadership necessary, giving new life to the 1940s "run by the people with public assistance" formula.[9]

The Education Ministry also chided itself for having suppressed the development of specialized teacher training schools, the main supplier of teachers for the elementary level.[10] An estimated 1 million extra teachers would have to be added to the profession in order to meet the new goals put forward. The only solution was to revive the one-year teacher training classes and recruit graduates from ordinary junior middle schools to fill them.[11]

Racing to meet expectations

The upsurge in elementary schooling soon spread to the next level as well. Elementary schools were again allowed to "wear caps" (*daimao*) as the quickest, most economical way of meeting the demand. Primarily a rural expedient, about 3,000 such *daimao* junior middle schools were created in 1956, half the total number of 6,000 regular secondary schools nationwide.[12] At the senior secondary level, enrollment quotas were expanded in 1956 sufficiently to accommodate all junior middle graduates. Suddenly, there were not too many junior middle graduates but too few. Education Minister Zhang could therefore report that the "false impression" of surplus at this level created by graduates unable to continue their studies and unwilling to join the work force had given way to scarcity.[13]

The potential of 1955–1956 was highly tentative, however. Agricultural collectivization continued, along with the final expropriation of all private enterprise. But Mao's subsequent effort to "liberate the forces of production" collapsed within a year. Apparently against the better judgment of professional economists and Party planners, Mao had pushed through his preliminary "leap forward" in early 1956, as a kind of trial run for the 1958 Great Leap Forward policy, to vindicate socialist transformation. The result was a program calling for across-the-board production increases in all sectors including industry as

---

[9] This case for reviving and updating the *minban* school formula was presented in many sources, e.g., Li Pingjie in *Guangming ribao*, 22 Feb. 1956; Education Minister Zhang Xiruo in his report to the National People's Congress, 22 July 1955, *Renmin ribao*, 23 July 1955; editorials in *Renmin ribao*, 23 June 1955 and 27 Feb. 1956, and *Guangming ribao*, 21 July 1955 and 12 Aug. 1955.

[10] Education Minister Zhang Xiruo's report to the National People's Congress, 20 June 1956, *Renmin ribao*, 21 June 1956. According to another source, only 57,000 new students were enrolled in such schools nationwide during the 1953–1955 consolidation phase for elementary schools ("Jinianlai woguo jiaoyu shiye de fazhan gaikuang," p. 93). See Table 9.4, above, which shows the declining enrollments in these schools in the mid-1950s.

[11] Yang Wei, "Let Us Help the State Enforce Compulsory Primary Education," *Shih Shih Shou Ts'e* (Current Events), no. 4 (25 Feb. 1956), trans. in *Extracts from China Mainland Magazines*, U.S. Consulate General, Hong Kong (hereafter cited as *ECMM*), no. 33 (30 Apr. 1956), p. 46.

[12] Su Ren, "Zhong, xiaoxue jiaoyu fazhan wenti de wojian" (My Views on the Developmental Problems of Secondary and Elementary Education), *Renmin jiaoyu*, May 1957, p. 11.

[13] Education Minister Zhang Xiruo's report of 20 June 1956.

well as agriculture and education. The 12-year agricultural plan targets, already ambitious by measured FFYP standards, were further accelerated – hence the sudden upsurge in demand for educated personnel at all levels. Within months, however, the economic upsurge was overtaken by a new backlash against "blind adventurism."[14]

The high-speed experiment in economic development was officially repudiated at the Eighth National CCP Congress in September 1956, but a critical appraisal of the education component was ready for public consumption in June. Contained within Zhang Xiruo's above-cited report to the National People's Congress on 20 June, it noted that the correction of blind adventurism in 1953 had produced an attitude of "passive withdrawal," and anti-illiteracy work had virtually ceased between 1953 and 1955. The growth rate in elementary school enrollments had also declined. But then in early 1956, another round of adventurism had commenced. Zhang took responsibility, blaming the "excessive zeal of the Education Ministry's leadership" for the response of the local authorities. A year later, he was even more contrite. "There was," he reported, "a high tide of socialist construction last year and because all enterprises were expanding by leaps and bounds, it was possible for our schools at all levels to enroll more students. But this brought many difficulties to our work . . . it is unthinkable that our schools can continue to develop as they did last year."[15]

The arguments that appeared in the interim – roughly coinciding with the year of blooming and contending from May 1956 to May 1957 – suggested further how an alliance of interests had emerged between professional educators and the CCP's bureaucratic planners as architects of the heavy-industry model. Mao's early-1956 "leap" received a drubbing from officials and academics alike as voices rose to champion the virtues of measured development against the follies of "blind and rash advance."

People's Education writer Dai Shuren contributed an orthodox defense of the official line restoring regularity. He quoted from Liu Shaoqi's political report to the Eighth National CCP Congress on the need to "accumulate every *yuan* of construction funds and use it in the most effective way." Dai elaborated the "chaotic conditions" produced by the 1956 leap, together with its underlying assumption that there was "no need to fear imbalance." The 1957 cutbacks were "unlikely to satisfy the needs of the masses in the immediate future," but they would have to learn that moderation was in their own best long-term interests.[16]

---

[14] MacFarquhar, *Origins of the Cultural Revolution*, pp. 26–32, 57–74, 86–91.
[15] Education Minister Zhang Xiruo's report to a Chinese People's Political Consultative Conference (hereafter cited as CPPCC) meeting, 16 Mar. 1957, *Renmin ribao*, 19 Mar. 1957.
[16] Dai Shuren, "Cong jige sheng, shi kan jinnian jiaoyu shiye de fazhan" (The Development of This Year's Education Enterprise as Seen from Various Provinces and Cities), *Renmin jiaoyu*, Jan. 1957, pp. 13–15. For the text of Liu Shaoqi's report, see *Renmin ribao*, 17 Sept. 1956, trans. in Bowie and Fairbank, *Communist China*, pp. 164–203.

Ironically, the only relief from three years of tension over student demands for more education and jobs came with the 1956 leap. But the professionals seemed unimpressed. According to an Education Ministry spokesman: "it was mainly due to the rather excessive expansion of enrollment plans for tertiary and secondary schools that comparatively many graduates from the secondary and elementary levels were able to continue their studies in 1956. At the same time, under last year's high tide of socialism, with all kinds of enterprises developing in a big way, schools had to enroll more students to meet the need for more personnel. But this was a special one-time phenomenon. Starting this year our construction enterprise is returning to normal, and what happened last year should not happen again." As for elementary education, that "a rather long time" would have to pass before all children could attend was deemed "very natural."[17]

The unkindest cut, however, came from the Education Ministry's new publication, *Teachers News* (*Jiaoshibao*).[18] A discreetly anonymous back-page article traced the origins of the CCP's 1956 "great stride" to the controversial years in the Soviet Union before the heavy-industry model was established. Soviet agriculture was collectivized in 1929, and in 1930, Stalin published his essay "Dizzy with Success," criticizing the delusion, born of early victories, that all problems could be solved at once. "This explains that such a situation also occurred at that time in the Soviet Union, where it was even more serious than in China. Looking at the experience of the Soviet Union and China, it seems very likely that this is something difficult for a country to avoid during the early stages of socialist construction." But for the sake of true educational development, the error of detaching subjective hopes from objective economic realities should not be repeated.[19] The efforts of early Soviet advisors had evidently been in vain. China would not, after all, be able to avoid the winding path.

Improvising a substitute for the Soviet model

This time around, however, the attack on adventurism did not herald a typical regularization reversal. Had professional educators and the mass media not been so preoccupied with blooming and contending, the mixed signals coming from the center on education reform might have attracted more attention as leaders began improvising a substitute for the Soviet model. But in retrospect, they were obviously moving toward solutions antithetical to the mainstream

---

[17] *Renmin ribao*, 16 Mar. 1957.
[18] The newspaper was launched in May 1956 to promote the multiple objectives anticipated in Zhou Enlai's January report on intellectuals (see the inaugural statement, *Jiaoshibao*, Beijing, 1 May 1956).
[19] Ibid., 12 Apr. 1957.

views being elaborated by the academic community in 1956 and 1957. These emerging solutions – *minban* schools, labor education, and rural work assignments – were all grouped at the "irregular" end of the education reform spectrum and were being deliberately revived from the Yan'an precedent.

Growth rates would be more realistic, according to Education Ministry pronouncements. But universal elementary schooling remained the goal, and it could not be realized without the supporting effort of collectively run *minban* schools in the villages and enterprise-run schools in town.[20] The solution for secondary schooling emerged more slowly. Junior middle caps had returned to the unwanted list, and as of January 1957, they were still being doffed. By March, however, they were seen as a "good method," not to be disbanded unless especially "lacking" and the masses agreed. But "uniformity with city schools should not be required" as a prerequisite. Moreover, the past policy of concentrating secondary education in urban areas was deemed incorrect. City schools were now packed to overflowing, and rural students were adding to the strain. They also encountered the typical problems: costs half again as much as if they could be educated closer to home, few job opportunities in town, no desire to return to their villages after graduation, etc. Junior middle caps had greatly expanded in 1956, but "some people ... used the old-fashioned concept of regularity to view the problem," judging them too inferior and irregular rather than a turning point for rural education. They "should not be casually merged and closed." The basic curriculum should be the same as in city schools, to allow some students to continue their studies. Otherwise, differences should be encouraged to accommodate local needs and cultural levels.[21]

Official emphasis again shifted back from quality to quantity, contradicting regularity's logic to argue that more was better. "In general, it is better to run more schools than few, and better to be literate than illiterate."[22] By extension, since everyone was to be educated, most everyone would be joining the work force afterward and should be prepared for that end.[23] The Education Ministry acknowledged furthermore that despite all the propaganda about the glories of labor over the years, little else had been done to prepare young people for the world of work. Even the propaganda had been conducted sporadically because labor education had few genuine supporters. The continuing ignorance of production and work habits naturally did nothing to dilute the inherited "contempt

[20] Ibid., 1 Jan. and 29 Mar. 1957.
[21] Rural secondary school proposals are from ibid., 27 Nov. 1956; 1 Jan., 29 Mar., and 2 Apr. 1957. After a long silence on the subject of education reform, Mao appears to have again turned his attention to the issue. He gave his blessing to junior middle caps at this time ("Talk with the Heads of Departments and Bureaus of Education," 7 Mar. 1957, in MacFarquhar, Cheek, and Wu, *Secret Speeches of Chairman Mao*, p. 214).
[22] *Renmin ribao*, 29 Mar. 1957.
[23] "Shelun: jinian jiaoyu gongzuozhong zhide zhuyi de jige wenti" (Editorial: A Few Problems That Merit Attention in This Year's Education Work), *Renmin jiaoyu*, Jan. 1957, pp. 4–6.

for labor." Henceforth, the regular curriculum would include instruction in labor education to be conducted both at school and organized as an outside and extracurricular activity.[24]

In fact, the sporadic treatment of "production technique" represented another area where the concerns of professional Chinese educators meshed with the Soviet transplant. They tended to regard "handicrafts" (*shougongyi*) as well as practical application and fieldwork as vocational training, out of place in the regular academic stream. The Soviets had also eschewed such training as an example of pedagogical pragmatism. Hence "technical" education was introduced to China much as it was taught in the Soviet Union, primarily via regular classroom instruction along with conventional academic subjects such as physics, chemistry, and biology. Apparently, a handicraft course was initially introduced but then allowed to lapse. It was formally reinstated at the elementary level in 1955 and in secondary schools the next year.[25]

These mid-1950s adjustments followed a new concern in the Soviet Union itself about the predominantly academic orientation of polytechnic or comprehensive technical education (*zonghe jishu jiaoyu*). This had actually begun in the early 1950s and was promoted further during the Khrushchev era. The Chinese equivalent, "education in basic production technique" (*jiben shengchan jishu jiaoyu*), was advertised with some fanfare in 1955 and 1956. Yet however inconclusive the public commentary, decisions were obviously being made. The reinterpretation of technical education to include production skills as well as production knowledge and the official promotion of such vocational-type training – including both labor practice and classroom instruction for *all* students – date from this period. So too did the shift in rationale: from Soviet precedents to Chinese needs.[26]

The most pressing need, however, was what to do with all the young school leavers. Thus, rounding out the emerging solutions was the first large-scale "down to the countryside and up into the mountains" (*xiaxiang shangshan*) movement, designed to integrate the assignment of urban youth to rural work with the downward transfer of urban personnel generally. The movement did not move into high gear until the autumn of 1957. And given the accompanying polemics, it seemed more a function of the political antirightist campaign (see below) than of the need to redistribute the work force. But personnel retrench-

---

[24] Education Minister Zhang Xiruo's report to the CPPCC, 16 Mar. 1957; see also "Shelun: jinian jiaoyu," p. 4; and *Renmin ribao*, 8 Apr. 1957.
[25] *Guangming ribao*, 6 Sept. 1955 and 16 Aug. 1956; *Renmin ribao*, 1 Sept. 1956.
[26] For the 1955–1956 Chinese promotion of education in production technique following the Soviet example, see the following issues of *Renmin jiaoyu*, for 1955: Jan., pp. 19–22, 27–30; May, pp. 36–42; June, pp. 5–8, 29–36, Nov., pp. 20–26; and for 1956: Feb., pp. 27–56, 63–64; Apr., pp. 57–61; June, pp. 7–30. For the 1956–1957 Chinese criticism, see the following section on "blooming and contending."

ment had actually begun early in the year, following the excessive growth of 1956. Students due to graduate in 1957 were also being prepared for their likely assignment to rural work given the lack of sufficient urban opportunities. Initially, then, plans for urban–rural transfer seem to have been laid prior to the retribution campaign against intellectual critics, which only developed later.[27]

Blooming, contending, and the case for Chinese-style regularity

Mao's 1955–1956 leap may have united Party planners and professional educators in opposition to socialist irregularity, but the old ambivalence could be seen lurking not too far beneath the surface. Everyone was being forced to reevaluate inherited assumptions about the aims of schooling. And the same bureaucratic planners who derided quick steps forward were ready enough to champion the virtues of labor once illiterate masses began passing through the system in ever increasing numbers to emerge as educated youth.

The blooming-and-contending debates over education and political reform then compounded the contradictions. For a time, conventional views prevailed as intellectuals and educators indicated just how far they might have gone in restoring the old ways. Ambiguities were nevertheless built into the exercise from the start. Blooming and contending had initially been introduced as a means of cutting the umbilical cord of dependency with the Soviet Union, even though the initial inspiration to launch the exercise came from Moscow. Khrushchev's ideas about education were also cited as a starting point, yet his starting point in turn was the disturbingly familiar issue of relating education to work.

At first, educators showed little independence of any kind. Official commentaries acknowledged widespread "doubts and misgivings" about blooming and contending.[28] People allegedly had yet to grasp the importance of free academic debate and were afraid of making mistakes. Such people were reassured that since the Soviet Union itself was now criticizing its past practice of disregarding scientific and technological progress in capitalist countries, China must do likewise.[29] But official commentaries also acknowledged the contradiction between the need for intellectual independence and citing Moscow as the authority for change. *People's Education* appended an advisory to the report of a Soviet delegation sent to explain the significance of the 20th Party Congress

---

[27] Two key indicators in this regard were a *Renmin ribao* editorial (8 Apr. 1957) and a message from Vice-Premier Deng Zihui. See Deng Zihui, "Xiang nongcun qingnian he zhongxiao xuesheng jinyiyan" (A Word to Rural Youth and Secondary and Elementary School Students), *Zhongguo qingnian*, no. 10 (16 May 1957), p. 8.

[28] E.g., *Guangming ribao*, 21, 25 May 1956; *Renmin ribao*, 2, 21 July 1956.

[29] Unsigned editorial, "Thoroughly Implement the Policy of 'Let All Schools Contend,' Actively Develop Free Discussions in the Academic Field," *Kexue tongbao* (Science Journal), no. 6 (June 1956), trans. in *ECMM*, no. 47 (13 Aug. 1956), pp. 3–7.

for education reform. The advice: this time around avoid superficiality and mechanical copying.[30]

The editors nevertheless spelled out what was expected, quoting from Khrushchev's criticism of Soviet education at the congress. He had pointed to "serious weaknesses" in Soviet education on grounds that teaching was divorced from life and students were not receiving enough practical training. Hence Soviet educators were currently discussing how to reform their teaching plans and outlines, how to develop comprehensive technical education, whether to allow senior secondary education to be divided into separate science, technology, and liberal arts streams, and whether to allow electives at the junior middle level. This proved after all that "educational science is not really unchanging and immutable." Soviet education had actually undergone many experiments and much discussion before 1931. Afterward, the unified labor schools, vocational training for all, and teaching materials linking education with life were deemed inappropriate. Now the Soviets themselves had decided to revive some of the old concerns. Since the USSR was engaged in such debates, China should do likewise, and the center had decreed that "these academic debates must be developed forcefully." As to the specific topics for debate, national construction and the needs of social development should be the central focus. Relevant concerns included China's past and present educational theories, including the work of Tao Xingzhi; different opinions on Soviet pedagogy; how to combine teaching for "all-around development" in the Soviet manner with Chinese-style teaching for individual aptitude; how to reform methods and materials; how to combine teaching with life; and how to link theory with practice.[31]

Opinions at the tertiary level

At least so far as the published record shows, Chinese educators kept to the letter of their working brief. But as for its spirit, Khrushchev's concerns evidently were not theirs. In particular, the quantitative excesses of socialist upsurge seemed to provide the perfect cover under which to revive the modern Chinese educators' favorite quantity–quality contradiction. Especially for higher education, it became the centerpiece of the floral arrangement, with the rigidity of Soviet-style curriculum plans running a close second.

Summing up the sense of several discussion meetings convened by the Ministry of Higher Education in June and July 1956, *Guangming ribao* (Enlightenment Daily), reported that the big increase in schools, faculty, and students had been

---

[30] "Duanlun: yinggai renzhen yanjiu Sulian jiaoyu daibiaotuan de baogao" (Short Comment: The Report of the Soviet Education Delegation Should be Conscientiously Studied), *Renmin jiaoyu*, July 1956, p. 14; Mo-luo-zi-ang, "Sugong diershici daibiao dahui de jueyi he Sulian xuexiao de renwu" (The Decisions of the Soviet Union's 20th Communist Party Congress and the Tasks of the Soviet Union's Schools), ibid., pp. 15–19.

[31] "Pinglun: luelun jiaoyu kexuezhong de baijia zhengming" (Commentary: Brief Discussion on Blooming and Contending in Educational Science), *Renmin jiaoyu*, July 1956, pp. 4–5.

cited by educators as a major problem. Foundations in China were weak, and conditions lagged far behind those in the Soviet Union. Hence the tendency, or so critics argued, was to overemphasize standardization and conformity while overloading the system in an effort to catch up. With too heavy a study load and too many students, learning and teaching inevitably suffered.[32]

Additionally, within engineering faculties, disagreement continued over the relative merits of specialized versus theoretical and foundation courses. Teachers criticized the narrowly specialized applied science approach which characterized the Soviet-style curricula. Some argued that with a better foundation, students would actually be able to grasp at a faster rate the specialized technical knowledge needed for practical application in the workplace. It was in any case agreed that course loads were too heavy, that the total number of study hours should be reduced, and that the subjects which were not essential to any given major should be dropped from the teaching plans.

Educators were also critical of different imported methods, including the five-point grading system and especially oral examinations. Teachers complained that while these might promote comprehension as the Soviets argued, most classes in China had more students than did their Soviet counterparts. If all students were tested orally in all subjects following Soviet practice, the work would be "too strenuous and tiresome both for teachers and students." Nor did Chinese teachers much like the Soviet method of teaching for "all-around development" (*quanmian fazhan*) rather than "teaching according to individual aptitude" (*yincai shijiao*). Teachers argued that if the aim was to teach students to think, work, and solve problems independently, then why not go back to the pre-1949 curricula with their mix of optional and compulsory courses? This allowed the brighter students to augment their study programs and others to learn according to their own ability. Chinese educators objected to the Soviet emphasis on uniform collective advancement in everything, whereby "all activities were required to proceed at the same rate, and the social life of the students, their time, and the content of their self-study were all uniformly fixed."[33]

At a meeting of historians and others, also convened by the Ministry of Higher Education in July, some argued that the teaching outlines and plans should be scrapped since they prevented the free expression of ideas in the classroom. Others thought they could be retained but used for reference only. The sense of the meeting, as announced, was that the teaching plans were essential for systematic learning, but ways should be found to prevent the dogmatic adherence to only one school of thought as presented in the plans.[34]

In August, a two-week meeting of university leaders prepared for the fall

---

[32] *Guangming ribao*, 31 July 1956.
[33] Ibid. On these questions at this time, see also *Guangming ribao*, 29, 30 July and 1 Aug. 1956.
[34] *Renmin ribao*, 24 July 1956. For discussions of similar issues in Tianjin higher education, see *Tianjin ribao*, 4 Sept. 1956; and in arts and science teaching at teacher training institutes, see *Guangming ribao*, 15, 21, 28 Aug. 1956.

semester. The Beijing gathering again focused on the quantity–quality dichotomy. "Many" participants held that the "fundamental" problem at the tertiary level was too many students. More college graduates had been produced since 1949 than during the entire period between the 1911 revolution and 1949. As a result, tertiary institutions were enrolling students of "uneven attainment," unlike preliberation days, when they could pick and choose 1 from among every 20 candidates. Participants requested the authorities to "study thoroughly" whether such a large number of college-trained people were really needed for national construction.[35]

A lengthy commentary in the *People's Daily* elaborated the same point, questioning whether the quantitative growth was really necessary and worth the qualitative costs. Because the numbers enrolled in college each year were greater than those graduating at the secondary level, in-service cadres had to be mobilized to take the college entrance examinations. The supply of teachers was also overstretched. Faculty/student ratios as usual showed the numbers to be more than adequate. But young assistant teachers, themselves recently graduated, made up a majority of all faculty members, and many of these inexperienced young assistants were being allowed to teach college courses.[36]

Despite the controversy obviously raging in official and professional circles over quantity, however, the arguments were dismissed without even the courtesy of a rebuttal. The 1956 first-year class was the largest ever, reflecting the "special requests from various quarters" for trained personnel deriving from socialist upsurge.[37] Otherwise, the rules governing school life changed abruptly in line with the emerging critique of the system.

According to provisional regulations authorized by the Ministry of Higher Education for the fall semester, the number of subjects in teaching plans and the number of hours allocated for them were too great. Students needed more time for independent study. The number of classroom hours per week might be reduced by two or three hours. Schools themselves might also introduce changes as they deemed necessary in the sequence of each subject, the number of classroom hours devoted to some activities, and the number of subjects to be examined each semester. The teaching plans issued by the ministry should remain the guiding documents for instruction, but teachers should be allowed to modify them somewhat, to prepare different course outlines, and to present their own personal views and theories.[38]

Whereas teaching plans had been enforced like "the law," suddenly in September 1956, students could do what they liked after class; the time allocated

---

[35] *Renmin ribao*, 17 Aug. 1956.
[36] Ibid., 4 Sept. 1956.
[37] *Renmin ribao*, 17 Mar. 1956; *Jiaoshibao*, 19 June 1956; Chang Chien (Zhang Jian), "Why Fewer Students Are to Be Enrolled in Universities and Middle Schools This Year," *Shih Shih Shou Ts'e* (Current Events), no. 7 (6 Apr. 1957), trans. in *ECMM*, no. 88 (24 June 1957), p. 8.
[38] *Renmin ribao*, 5, 17, 18 Aug. 1956; *Guangming ribao*, 17 Aug. 1956.

for political study was reduced; written exams replaced Soviet-style orals; and many other modifications began to appear as well. Beijing University, for example, added several new optional courses in the departments of philosophy, economics, and law. A course on "idealist philosophy," including lectures on Bertrand Russell and Hegel, was introduced for purposes of criticism and comparison with dialectical materialism. Other new courses included the "bourgeois" economic theories of Keynes and Anglo-American law.[39]

Following further upon the aims Zhou Enlai had outlined in January for an end to scientific dependency, a new graduate student program was also announced to begin training China's first Soviet-style associate doctoral (*fu boshi*) candidates. Just over one thousand graduate students were enrolled nationwide in what would have been the first post-1949 graduate degree program.[40] Major scientific initiatives included the drafting of a 12-year plan for science in 1956, with carefully delineated scientific priorities and concrete provisions for projects in the most urgently needed fields as anticipated by Zhou in his January address. Science budgets, facilities, and staff all registered marked increases in 1956, combining Zhou's priorities with Mao's up-beat variation on Soviet socialist planning.[41]

Debates and developments continued in this manner for most of 1956 without official summation or authoritative conclusion. A speech by Jiang Nanxiang was printed twice in October as an authoritative reminder that parameters were nevertheless being drawn. Jiang was then president of Qinghua University but had long been associated with the central leadership of the Communist Youth League. After the Party introduced its new policy of promoting free discussion, said Jiang, some began to question the correctness of learning from the Soviet Union. He acknowledged that the exercise had initially been doctrinaire and the ensuing mistakes even "laughable" at times. But he asserted that "we must definitely not deny the need for learning from the Soviet Union" because of such deviations or "abandon the new socialist education policy – the policy of thoroughly realizing overall development." "Overall development" had become a catchphrase referring to all aspects of Soviet-style pedagogical planning, while "teaching according to individual ability" was identified with independent thinking in the 1956 debates. Intellectual critics saw their opening in the new official concern for "learning to solve problems independently" and

[39] *Zhongguo qingnian bao* (China Youth News), Beijing, 25 Aug. 1956; *Jiaoshibao*, 7 Dec. 1956; Rene Goldman, "Peking University Today," *China Quarterly*, no. 7 (July–Sept. 1961), pp. 101–111.

[40] *Jiaoshibao*, 20 July 1956; *Wenhuibao*, Shanghai, 14 Dec. 1956.

[41] Cheng, *Scientific and Engineering Manpower*, pp. 10–28; John M. H. Lindbeck, "Organization and Development of Science," in Sidney H. Gould, ed., *Sciences in Communist China* (Washington, D.C.: American Association for the Advancement of Science, 1961), pp. 4, 12–13, 16–17; Richard P. Suttmeier and Genevieve Dean, "The Institutionalisation of Science," in *Science and Technology in the People's Republic of China* (Paris: Organisation for Economic Co-operation and Development, 1977), pp. 71–76.

rushed to elaborate a range of meanings which in effect challenged the entire restructured system.

"Certain comrades today have grossly misinterpreted the policy for overall development," continued Jiang, noting the argument that overall development might be acceptable for middle school students but that it would "obliterate individuality and special talent" at the tertiary level. Overall development was the "basic goal" of education, while teaching according to the individual student's abilities was only an "educational method." The two aims should not be confused as antithetical. The policy of overall development was embodied in the teaching plan, with its requirements for politics, physical education, basic knowledge, specialization courses coordinated with fieldwork, extracurricular activities, and so on. Individual capacities could only be developed on the basis of such a rational foundation. Yet, "some people consider that the pedagogical plan in the schools today obstructs the development of individuality and special talent. They maintain that the schools in old China allowed completely free development and some scientists were trained, but the pedagogical plans today have provided too concrete, too rigid rules for the students, and talent cannot be fostered." Jiang's verdict: the old system was costly and wasteful, unsuitable for producing the large numbers of people necessary for national development. We cannot allow students to study what they want, he declared, because if we do the state's personnel needs will not be met. "Objective needs come first, individual wishes and special capabilities are born and developed on this objective foundation, and individual wishes are not immutable."[42]

Opinions on elementary and secondary education

At the elementary level, schooling remained under the disruptive and quantitative impact of socialist upsurge – to the unabashed dismay of *Teachers News*. The atmosphere was likened to the early 1950s, before order was restored and local authorities were forbidden to disrupt school routines. And the "main reason for the revival of chaos is the high tide of socialist reform (especially agricultural cooperativization)."[43] "This is the most chaotic year for elementary

---

[42] Jiang Nanxiang, "Luelun gaodeng xuexiao de quanmian fazhan de jiaoyu fangzhen" (A Brief Discussion of the Educational Policy of Overall Development for Institutions of Higher Learning), *Zhongguo qingnian*, no. 20 (16 Oct. 1956), pp. 9–12; *Zhongguo qingnian bao*, 18 Oct. 1956; see also Zhang Yeming, "He Jiang Nanxiang tongzhi shangque jiaoyu fangzhen wenti" (Discussing Questions of Education Policy with Comrade Jiang Nanxiang), *Renmin jiaoyu*, Dec. 1956, pp. 5–8. The 1956 debate over all-around development was never officially concluded, however. Contributors were especially prolific in the pages of *Renmin jiaoyu* and *Jiaoshibao* between September and December. For a summary of the arguments in those two publications, see *Wenhuibao*, Shanghai, 17 Nov. 1956. For earlier discussions, see the following issues of *Renmin jiaoyu*: June 1951, pp. 19–23; and for 1955: Feb., pp. 44–49; May, p. 59; June, pp. 56–59; Aug., pp. 43–49; Sept., pp. 54–57.
[43] *Jiaoshibao*, 12 Oct. 1956; see also 2, 30 Nov. 1956.

schooling since liberation," lamented a report from Changsha. The city had just universalized schooling but without adequate preparation. The local education bureau had relied on public security statistics, only to find over 2,000 more seven-year-olds than anticipated on the enrollment lists. Several weeks into the semester, many schools still lacked enough teachers and administrators, and some could not hold regular classes.[44]

Yet strangely, given the pressures building up beneath them at the elementary level, secondary school educators did not focus specifically on the quantity–quality issue. Perhaps the phenomenon was not so extreme for them and they had accepted existing growth rates. In any case, the written record suggests they chose to fight the battle on different ground, namely, quality education for the few and something less for everyone else – hence their preoccupation with all-round development versus aptitude teaching. The record yields no clues as to whether students anywhere were already being systematically divided by ability into separate streams. But arguments indicated clearly whence pressures to do so originated. They were traced to the traditional assumption, evident in the teaching methods of old-fashioned literacy classes and *sishu*, that individual students learned at different speeds and should be taught accordingly.[45]

In earlier years, this traditional assumption had not been directly challenged by the critics of modern schooling. On the contrary, they (recall Mao and the mid-1940s Yan'an reforms) accepted the old *sishu* logic that children should be taught at their own pace and criticized modern schools wherein everyone had to progress together through all the grades and levels. Modern educators, for their part, had accommodated the tradition by maintaining a quantitatively limited system which in effect segregated students according to social background if not intellectual prowess. Even before socialist upsurge, then, the "modernized traditional" assumptions of professional educators had been sorely tried by the decrees of Soviet pedagogy for quantitative growth combined with all-round development. The crisis precipitated by de-Stalinization, and the perceived need for intellectual quality plus independence, gave new life to old "Chinese" assumptions. Only now they would have to be adapted for use within a newly socialized system growing at truly unprecedented speed.

Like most everyone else, secondary school educators in the city of Tianjin discussed all the related questions without reaching many conclusions. One of the few items on which "almost everyone" agreed was the need to call a halt to the "outstanding class [*youxiuban*] system" – a kind of academic hybrid that combined Soviet egalitarianism with Chinese intellectual elitism. Students were typically organized into individual classes and received all instruction as a group, remaining together in the same class from year to year. At their summer

[44] Ibid., 16 Oct. 1956.
[45] *Wenhuibao*, Shanghai, 17 Nov. 1956.

1956 discussion meetings, Tianjin educators decided that trying to elicit an all-around outstanding (*youxiu*) performance, or five points in all subjects, from all students in a class had too many negative side effects. These included excessive competition, average development (*pingjun fazhan*), and lack of independent thinking. The better students were unable to do their best because they had to help the underachievers, whereas the latter became dependent on the former and great pressure was placed on the poorest students.[46]

On the question of curricular content, the teachers noted that before 1949, students during their first year of senior middle school had to take only one math course and either physics, chemistry, or biology. Now they had to take all three science courses plus three math classes. Yet despite the heavier course loads, students could only memorize exam questions and lacked the ability to think independently or grasp scientific concepts.[47] No one seemed quite sure how to remedy the situation, however. The key evidently lay somewhere within the developing debate over all-around education and aptitude teaching, but where?

Even at the elementary level, educators disagreed over the relative merits of the two approaches. The Ministry of Education sent out four investigation teams during the fall semester of 1956, and all reported back great "confusion" among schoolteachers everywhere over the all-around development debate.[48] The team sent to Jiangxi Province had visited many schools and sponsored many discussion meetings but could report no conclusions. The then "prevalent deviation of average development [*pingjun fazhan*] and insisting on uniformity [*qiangqiu yilu*]" was associated with the overall development approach. But aptitude teaching led to the "new deviation of training talent [*tiancai jiaoyu*]." Teachers would concentrate on a few bright pupils in the class and ignore the rest. Some Jiangxi educators held that both secondary and elementary education were fundamental and since students' individuality was not yet fixed at that age, accommodating individual differences was not justified at either level. Others advocated dividing students into science and liberal arts streams in senior middle school. Still others suggested the use of electives to accommodate students' differing interests and abilities, and so on.[49]

In Hebei Province, three secondary schools were selected to experiment with aptitude teaching. Among the measures they reported were organizing the curriculum into compulsory and elective courses, posing more difficult questions for the better students, lecturing less and summarizing concepts more, encouraging greater student participation in the classroom, organizing fewer

---

[46] *Tianjin ribao*, 13 Aug. 1956; *Guangming ribao*, 6 Aug. 1956; see also Yang Zhihong, "Yaoqiu xuesheng 'men men wu fen' dui ma" (Is It Correct to Demand "Five Points in Every Subject" of Students?), *Renmin jiaoyu*, Feb. 1957, p. 26.

[47] *Tianjin ribao*, 3 Aug. 1956.

[48] *Wenhuibao*, Shanghai, 3 Dec. 1956.

[49] *Jiaoshibao*, 9 Oct. 1956.

extracurricular group activities, and leaving students more free time. But despite the upbeat front-page report of the experiment, page 2 of the same issue on the same day carried a sober critique of the measures adopted by the three schools in their experiment.[50]

A major reason for the confusion over Soviet and Chinese approaches, however, seemed to be that Chinese educators themselves could no longer distinguish easily between them. If forcing everyone into the straitjacket of a uniformly presented teaching plan was the Soviet way and loosening the jacket for individualized instruction was posited as the Chinese alternative, then why did everyone suddenly throw up their hands in horror at the consequences of relaxation in the autumn of 1956? "Students' thought has been activated as never before," intoned the *People's Daily* in October. "The air is filled with the smell of independent thought and study" and with several other "unhealthy phenomena" as well.[51]

From Shanghai, it was reported, "many leadership cadres feel that although the past practice of controlling too rigidly and interfering excessively was of course not correct, the present attitude of not daring to lead and just letting things go is also clearly wrong." In Jiangxi, the investigation team had discovered another "new deviation": schools unable to distinguish between correct and incorrect restrictions on student life. They "eliminated some systems that should not have been eliminated, and a form of anarchy ensued." Some schools abandoned the noon rest period, mealtime regulations, and many others governing campus life, including self-study and extracurricular activities. Some schools went so far as to give students complete freedom in the use of their after-class time, and "chaos" resulted.[52] Everywhere, it seemed, students were refusing to take their afternoon naps and spent their free time dancing, singing, playing cards, reading novels, cruising the streets, and refusing to join organized after-class activities.

Obviously, there were limits to freedom and independent thinking beyond which Chinese educators did not wish to venture. The convergence and confusion between Soviet-style order and Chinese regularity, most apparent at the secondary level, were also reflected in the search for new guidelines. "Everyone knows," declared a defensive *Teachers News*, "that we oppose interfering with students too much and too rigidly. But no one has ever said a school can relax leadership and do without discipline, systems, or Youth League and Young Pioneer activities. We advocate paying attention to the spirit of 'aptitude teaching,' and students interests and abilities must be accommodated. But no one has ever said the students can scatter freely to develop individualistic

---

[50] Ibid., 28 Dec. 1956. The three schools were Baoding Girls Middle School, Zhuo County Number One Middle School, and Shijiazhuang Teacher Training School.
[51] *Renmin ribao*, 28 Oct. 1956.
[52] Comments from Shanghai and Jiangxi are in, respectively, *Guangming ribao*, 29 Oct. 1956, and *Jiaoshibao*, 9 Oct. 1956.

thinking."[53] At year's end, the public debate over all-around development wound down after the Education Ministry concluded that "too much" had already been said. Henceforth, emphasis should be placed on research into actual "measures and methods" of aptitude teaching.[54]

Rectification: in pursuit of a Chinese communist way

Mao then raised the stakes by adding Party rectification to blooming and contending. Critics both inside the Party and out were now invited not just to debate problems but to seek their cause in the leadership's mistakes. Elaborating the old distinction between the people and their enemies, Mao declared that contradictions could exist among the people in a communist state and that "the people" referred to all classes willing to work for socialist construction. All kinds of contradictions, even those between the proletariat and the bourgeoisie could be treated as nonantagonistic and resolved peacefully. Only those between the people and their enemies need be regarded as antagonistic and treated accordingly.

These ideas elaborated in Mao's February 1957 speech on contradictions among the people were hailed briefly as a new addition to the Marxist lexicon, reducing China's dependence on Moscow thereby and pointing toward a more liberal kind of communism. Mao's speech set the stage for the rectification campaign that followed as an exercise in resolving nonantagonistic contradictions among the people. The main participants were drawn from the same educated elite stratum as before but now included not just academics, writers, and journalists but people from the full range of professional occupations, entrepreneurs, civil servants, and members of the small political associations that the CCP had allowed to continue in existence as part of its united front policy. Everyone was encouraged to help the Party improve itself by publicly criticizing its shortcomings in all sectors.

After a few weeks of such "open-door" rectification, however, the Party launched a sudden counterattack against its critics in the form of an "antirightist" campaign. Six criteria, apparently added to Mao's February speech when it was finally published in June, defined the limits of criticism. The application of these six criteria during the months that followed, to assess retroactively the nature of the criticisms raised in May, had a lasting impact on the intellectual community's political relationship with the CCP.[55]

---

[53] *Jiaoshibao*, editorial, 9 Oct. 1956.

[54] Ibid., 1 Jan. 1957.

[55] Mao Zedong, "Guanyu zhengque chuli renmin neibu maodun de wenti" (On the Correct Handling of Contradictions among the People), 27 Feb. 1957, first published in *Renmin ribao*, 19 June 1957, trans. in Bowie and Fairbank, *Communist China*, pp. 273–294. According to the six criteria, words and deeds could be rejected as erroneous to the extent that they harmed national unity, socialist transformation and construction, the people's democratic dictatorship,

The immediate aim of rectification was evidently to preempt the kind of authority crisis, such as the Hungarian uprising, being precipitated by de-Stalinization elsewhere in the Soviet bloc. The sudden antirightist backlash in June 1957 therefore caused much speculation as to whether Mao had deliberately laid a trap for his critics or was taken off guard by their vehemence. The latter seems especially unlikely, because CCP leaders were under no illusions as to intellectual loyalties. Zhou Enlai's January 1956 assessment was reiterated even more coldly by Mao a year later. And so reluctant were other Party leaders to open up rectification to non-Party participants that Mao had to agree ahead of time to limit the exercise to only a few weeks. The idea of a trap seems more accurate (especially for those who felt they had fallen into it). But as Deng Xiaoping's final summation suggested, the explanation should probably be phrased otherwise: as an inevitable consequence of the CCP's social revolution and the mass movement method used to activate it.[56]

Thus, Party leaders were well aware of the Chinese revolution's late-stage development. But they were also committed to pursuing it in all sectors, including agriculture, industry, commerce, and the superstructure (political and intellectual life), before their late-blooming revolution was nipped in the bud by the post-Stalin drift of international communism. This probably helps explain why the Chinese rushed through in only six years a socialization process that took at least twice as long in the Soviet Union. Seeking a formula that might do the job, that is, save the revolution and the CCP's face at the same time, Party rectification was added to blooming and contending, with active non-Party participation as a key ingredient. But once the decision was made to launch the whole effort as a movement, that is, to mobilize popular participation for a specific purpose, leaders by definition had to shift to the ad hoc campaign mode of management.

In accordance with the "law" of all the CCP's mass movements, top leaders in effect improvised as they went along, using different guidelines at different times to mobilize, channel, and control the popular response. Such an exercise always had a beginning and an end. Guidelines announced at the start were rarely the same as those that ended it and never what they were in between when mass mobilization was at its height. In such a game, excesses were expected as inevitable, useful, and nothing to be feared. But their precise nature could not

democratic centralism, the leadership of the CCP, and international socialist solidarity. For an elaboration of the six criteria, see Tung Fang-ming, "What Fragrant Flowers and What Poisonous Weeds?" *Shih Shih Shou Ts'e* (Current Events), no. 16 (21 Aug. 1957), trans. in *ECMM*, no. 107 (12 Nov. 1957), pp. 15–19. An original version of the speech is translated in MacFarquhar, Cheek, and Wu, *Secret Speeches of Chairman Mao*, pp. 131–189.

56 In launching Party rectification, Mao overrode close to half the top leaders to open up that exercise, typically an intra-Party affair, to non-Party participation. In return, unchecked criticism was to be limited to only a few weeks (MacFarquhar, *Origins of the Cultural Revolution*, pp. 104–105, 111–121, 140–144, 219, 241–249). Mao's March 1957 comments on intellectuals and Deng's September summation of intervening events are both cited below.

be predicted in advance. It was the leader's right, in accordance with the "law of the mass movement," to decide when and where to draw the line in relation to costs and benefits. Depending on the movement, risks and dangers could be great: both for leaders if their timing was off and for participants who refused to take their cues as the winds shifted. Many could not or would not obey, and confusion emerged as a common side effect. Since the movement was orchestrated in such a way as to provoke a spontaneous response, some participants inevitably did not grasp until too late that their response was spontaneous only within the confines of a movement manipulated from above over which they ultimately had no control. Individual participants might well perceive entrapment even though the "fault" was really theirs for having acted without grasping or heeding the laws governing the movement – an understandable lapse since these were never announced in advance in order to maintain the appearance of spontaneity!

Such movements always presupposed leaders who did understand the laws, however, because it was the leaders' job to stand above the fray and orchestrate the movement by manipulating them. Mao, of course, emerged as the grand master in using the movement to build revolutionary power. The cavalier approach he brought to this enterprise is best exemplified in the directive he issued at the start of land reform in the mid-1940s, when he advised against worrying too much about excesses, which were unavoidable in any case: "as long as it is really a conscious struggle of the broad masses, any excesses that have occurred can be corrected afterward."[57]

The events of 1956 and 1957 – mobilization through blooming and contending, the accelerated rectification phase in May 1957, and the antirightist backlash in June – seem best explained in this way. Mao's barnstorming speeches in March 1957 were clearly part of escalating mobilization as he repeatedly championed the cause of blooming and contending for intellectuals, characterized 80 percent of them as bourgeois in outlook, and prepared the Party for rectification of its own work style.[58] The two sides – intellectuals and Party members – were being deliberately set up and primed for struggle against each other.

Rectification was announced on 1 May 1957. The Party provided the general guidelines for its rectification, designating the familiar sins of bureaucratism,

[57] "Rent Reduction and Production Are Two Important Matters for the Defense of the Liberated Areas," inner-Party directive dated 7 Nov. 1945, in Selected Works of Mao Tse-tung (Peking: Foreign Languages Press, 1961), 4:72. This conception of the mass movement style of leadership derives from an earlier study of the land reform campaigns in the late 1940s. Contemporary internal CCP documents described the process in terms of the "law of the mass movement" as a way of explaining shifts in central policy to confused local cadres. With the benefit of hindsight, this concept seems useful as a guide to understanding erratic policy shifts – albeit only those that occurred during the CCP's mass movements – when leaders deliberately mobilized popular participation toward some specific end. On the 1940s land reform campaigns, see Pepper, Civil War in China, chap. 7.

[58] MacFarquhar, Cheek, and Wu, Secret Speeches of Chairman Mao, texts 4–13.

sectarianism, and subjectivism as the targets. For the education sector specifically, the Education Ministry's CCP small group announced conditions for rectification a few days later. Serious manifestations of the three sins had caused three main contradictions to flourish in education work. The contradictions were between the people's need for education and the limited resources available for providing it; between demands for quality and the inability to meet them; and between the aspirations of school graduates to continue their studies and the possibility of their doing so, exacerbated by their low opinion of manual and especially agricultural labor. Such contradictions were not caused by leadership failures, but these hindered solutions.

Concerning the three deviations, "bureaucratism" meant ignoring real problems in deference to administrative routines. "Sectarianism" led to insufficient cooperation with non-CCP people. "Subjectivism" encouraged dogmatism, which included "overlooking our country's actual situation and mechanically using international experience." The Education Ministry further identified several specific issue areas to serve as focal points for discussion: teacher training, political education, policies for general education during the Second Five-Year Plan, *minban* schools, work assignments for school graduates, and reducing burdens by revising yet again the structure of the school system (*xuezhi*), curriculum, and teaching materials.[59]

The minister of higher education announced that discussions begun in April on contradictions lacked the necessary critical spirit. "Open-door rectification" must therefore begin. Off-limits were the "long-term contradictions" which could not be solved at once, such as those between quantity and quality and between Marxist–Leninist thought and the hundred-flowers spirit. Since the aim was to improve the CCP's leadership of higher education, discussion should focus on concrete problems such as mechanically copying (*shengban yingtao*) the Soviet experience, ignoring China's own heritage, excessive unification, and relations between Party and non-Party people.[60]

In addition to Party rectification as the main difference between May 1956 and May 1957, the subjects authorized for discussion within the education sector had evolved in some important ways. Most significant was learning from the Soviet Union, which had now been officially promoted to the list of China's 20th-century international indiscretions as yet another exercise in mechanical copying. The center had also devised a tactic for managing the quantity–quality issue that intruded so sharply in 1956. Now it was discouraged at the tertiary level but deliberately authorized for discussion otherwise, along with the related question of graduate employment and the officially sponsored solutions (i.e., *minban* schools, political education, and blue-collar job assignments for school graduates). In this way, the authorized topics could be seen to reflect the academic community's concerns but also the parameters being pinned down around them.

The critics again speak out

Again, participants kept to the letter of their assignment, albeit now within the spirit of the final mobilization-phase upsurge. All the authorized issues were addressed, while the unauthorized overriding theme this time was the seemingly rudderless nature of Beijing's leadership. Educators rose en masse to ridicule the "chaos" (*luan*) in a system now seemingly bereft of all authoritative external models and internal reference points.

"I have participated in this sort of meeting many times," complained a Nanjing University professor at the preliminary April discussions. "Everything is well arranged, you can approve or disapprove, but when it comes to actual implementation, in fact, the discussion is just a waste of time. So now I have no interest in such meetings."[61] "For some work they seek out people and hold meetings," said the president of Nanjing Teacher Training College. "In promoting 'five-year integrated' elementary schooling, for example, the Ministry of Education wanted me to attend, but not to discuss problems or listen to opinions. It was only to talk us around and convince us. As a result, after one year the experiment was stopped."[62]

The 1956 all-around development debate was a favorite target: "As for discussing the policy of all-around development, that was a big thing for education circles, but it clearly suffered from a serious bout of dogmatism. The discussion was conceptually superficial and did not analyze concrete realities, so it had no explanatory power."[63] Nor did anyone know what, if any, conclusions had been drawn from it.[64]

This line of argument developed easily into a general attack on the Education Ministry for its vacillating leadership. At the lower (elementary and secondary) levels, it shared the limelight along with mechanical copying. One of the late-April meetings concentrated on both, with teachers likened to weathervanes "turning in the wind" and China's effort to learn from the Soviet Union "like a blind man feeling an elephant."[65] Perhaps anxious to deflect blame, local government education bureaus set the pace in targeting central leaders for "issuing orders in the morning and changing them by nightfall" (*zhaoling xigai*).

The Hunan provincial education bureau derided the Education Ministry's

[61] Ibid., 25 Apr. 1957.
[62] Ibid., 30 Apr. 1957.
[63] Ibid. (article by Chen Yousong).
[64] E.g., ibid., 6, 18 May 1957; *Jiaoshibao*, 14, 17, 24, 28 May 1957 and 4 June 1957.
[65] *Wenhuibao*, Shanghai, 6 May 1957.

habit of "seeking many opinions at the lower levels" and then ignoring them. Even worse, decisions issued one year changed the next. Socialist upsurge had disrupted the five-year plan's targets for secondary schooling, but the junior middle school "caps" were the most erratic of all. As of mid-1957, they were again part of the secondary education repertoire, but directives had yet to be issued on what they should teach or how or to whom.[66]

The Hubei education bureau criticized the ministry's vacillations between quantity and quality from year to year: quantitave development in 1952, reorganization in 1953, key-point development in 1955, and the "great stride" in 1956. "The masses blamed us," complained the bureau of the shifting line on *minban* schools. "Because of this problem, the lack of concrete analysis, and vacillations left and right, great losses have been registered in the development of elementary education."[67]

On the ubiquitous theme of mechanical copying, everyone could list a grievance. Most common was the five-point grading system, which deliberately equalized distinctions by limiting the gradations to only five.[68] Educators also used the mechanical copying argument against technical education. The Russians were now much concerned about relating education to life. The 20th Soviet Communist Party Congress had therefore resolved to emphasize "comprehensive technical education" in regular academic schools and guarantee close coordination between classroom teaching and students' social labor obligations.[69] Chinese teachers complained that in rushing to develop a curriculum for the Chinese equivalent, "basic-production technical education," much money was wasted buying equipment and materials, which usually remained as inadequate as the teachers' ability to give instruction and the students' learning result.[70]

As with socialist upsurge, however, the sharpest wit came from an anonymous *Teachers News* writer. Picking up on the conclusion Zhou Enlai had articulated in his January 1956 report on intellectuals, the sarcastic rebuttal mocked Party leaders for themselves emulating the Soviet Union in all things while singling out the education sector to serve as scapegoat for the pervasive national habit:

---

[66] *Jiaoshibao*, 4 June 1957.

[67] Ibid., 28 May 1957.

[68] E.g., ibid., 17 May 1957 (article by Kai Feng), and 31 May 1957; "Jiaoshi tan jiaoyu gongzuo neibu maodun" (Teachers Discuss Contradictions within Education Work), *Renmin jiaoyu*, June 1957, p. 8.

[69] E.g., Xie Na-wu-mo-fu (general advisor to the Chinese Ministry of Education), "Genju Sulian gongchandang diershici daibiao dahui jueyi de jingshen: tan Sulian guomin jiaoyu de jixiang renwu" (In Accordance with the Spirit of the Resolutions of the Soviet Union's 20th Communist Party Representative Congress: A Discussion of the Various Tasks of the Soviet Union's National Education), *Renmin jiaoyu*, Jan. 1957, p. 7.

[70] E.g., *Wenhuibao*, Shanghai, 6 May 1957; *Jiaoshibao*, 24 May 1957; "Jiaoshi tan jiaoyu gongzuo neibu maodun," p. 8. On the Chinese difficulty in defining "basic-production technical education," see *Jiaoshibao*, 8 May and 20 July 1956.

> I often think that the Party center leads China's revolution very well. No matter what the policy, all issue from China's own actual conditions. For example, the Soviet Union calls its army the Red Army, while ours is named the People's Liberation Army. The Soviet Union has established soviets, whereas we have created representative people's congresses. The Soviet Union has no democratic parties, whereas we not only allow them to exist but also permit "long-term coexistence and mutual supervision." We have no tractors, yet we also have cooperativized agriculture. . . . But in our education work, we only know mechanical copying. After the 1911 revolution, we copied Japan. During the GMD era, we copied the U.S. And after liberation, we copied the Soviet Union. . . . In the past, no matter who we learned from, we never could abandon mechanical copying, and because of this we have been unable to build our own educational science.[71]

At the tertiary level, by contrast, these mundane issues of education and history were overshadowed by more immediate political concerns.[72] For a few weeks, Party rectification allowed Chinese intellectuals to be Chinese intellectuals again, and they seized the moment with all their old vigor. Epitomizing this revival was Chu Anping, who had won fame as a political commentator in the late 1940s. Now, as editor of the briefly independent *Guangming ribao*, he demonstrated the same rhetorical skills he had perfected a decade earlier against the GMD, indicating also that his views had changed little in the interim. Of the CCP in 1957, he wrote: "Is it not too much that within the scope of the nation, there must be a Party member as leader in every unit, large or small, whether section or subsection; or that nothing, big or small, can be done without a nod from a Party member? . . . I think this idea that 'all under heaven belongs to the Party' is at the bottom of all sectarianism and the root of all contradictions between the Party and non-Party people."[73]

Applying this theme to institutions of higher learning, faculty and students challenged the Party's monopoly of power within them at virtually every point. Some advocated the withdrawal of Party committees altogether or at least an end to CCP leadership. Some argued that institutions of higher learning should be run by academic professionals alone.[74] On the ever contentious issue of job assignments for graduates, faculty and student opinion was reportedly united

---

[71] *Jiaoshibao*, 17 May 1957 (article by Yi Si, p. 3).

[72] For an eyewitness account summarizing both education and political themes, see Rene Goldman, "The Rectification Campaign at Peking University: May–June 1957," *China Quarterly*, no. 12 (Oct./Dec. 1962), pp. 138–153.

[73] Chu's commentary appeared in both *Renmin ribao* and *Guangming ribao* on 2 June 1957. The CCP's United Front Work Department had just decided to withdraw the CCP committee from *Guangming ribao*, a paper specializing in news of interest to intellectuals. The paper was to be run independently by the democratic parties to encourage blooming and contending. But this arrangement soon lapsed, and Chu was removed as editor during the subsequent antirightist backlash (see *Guangming ribao*, 15 July 1957).

[74] E.g., ibid., 7, 8, 13 May and 1, 2 June 1957; *Renmin ribao*, 8, 11, 14, 16, 17, 25 May 1957.

in calling for an end to the "absolute authority" of university personnel offices, which were all controlled by the university Party organization.[75] Faculty members complained that assistant teachers were assigned without prior consultation. Academic departments had to accept them however unqualified or unsuitable. Professors accustomed to tapping favorite students to remain at school as assistant teachers after graduation now had to seek permission from the personnel office, which often overruled faculty nominees on political grounds.[76]

Another major complaint, also associated with the Party-dominated personnel office, was the use of class background and political criteria in the allocation of all benefits. Most important of these benefits were admission to college, job assignments for graduates, overseas study, research assignments, faculty appointments, and promotions. The most-favored class or social backgrounds were naturally workers, peasants, and revolutionary cadres. Political criteria included CCP and Youth League membership and political activism. Faculty and students complained that these considerations, rather than academic qualifications, determined who could become assistant teachers, who received the most-coveted high-status big-city jobs, and who could study in the Soviet Union. From those who could not meet the new political criteria for whatever reason, there flowed a long litany of grievances arising from their status reversal. For them, "sectarianism" took the form of relationships and attitudes marked at every turn by the new lines of discrimination being drawn ever more sharply against the old-style "bourgeois intellectuals" and in favor of the new "red experts."[77]

The Party strikes back

Open-door rectification ended on 8 June, when the Party signaled that it had heard enough. The *People's Daily* lashed out at "rightist elements" who had revealed their continuing preference for capitalism and Anglo-American democracy. In the antirightist campaign that followed, the Party's most prominent critics were forced to recant and be criticized in turn.

Having drawn the general guidelines at the outset, the Party now announced the limits beyond which its critics would be rebuffed and their opinions redefined as wrong or antagonistic. The rules were documented in the above-mentioned six criteria published in June, and all that had been said previously was now reassessed in accordance with them. Deng Xiaoping, as general secretary of the CCP Central Committee, gave the summation. He called rectification a "socialist revolution on the political and ideological fronts" that was

---

[75] E.g., *Renmin ribao*, 20 May and 2 June 1957; *Wenhuibao*, Shanghai, 19 May 1957.
[76] E.g., *Renmin ribao*, 22, 25 May and 2 June 1957.
[77] E.g., ibid., 7, 14, 17, 20, 22, 25 May 1957; *Guangming ribao*, 8, 19 May and 1 June 1957; *Wenhuibao*, Shanghai, 20, 22 May 1957.

necessary because changing the ownership of the economic means of production in agriculture, industry, and commerce was not sufficient to consolidate the revolution. The aim of the exercise just past had been to uncover and solve contradictions. Those perpetrated by the "reactionary bourgeois rightists" were most serious and were not just among the people after all but between the people and their enemies: "antagonistic, irreconcilable, life-and-death contradictions."

Such contradictions, explained Deng, originated primarily among the bourgeoisie and the intellectuals, most of whom were still from bourgeois and petty bourgeois families. This antagonistic force could be found in business and industry, within the democratic parties, among government bureaucrats and college students, and in all the professions, including education, journalism, publishing, literature, the arts, science, technology, and medicine. Politically, the rightists still possessed status, capital, and influence while professionally they monopolized China's intellectual resources. Hence, "the bourgeoisie and especially the intellectuals now constitute the main force that can challenge the proletariat." Deng also summarized the essence of the views now deemed antagonistic that had been put forward by these rightists: opposing the socialist economic and political system; opposing the CCP's basic policies; denying the achievements of the revolution; denying the ability of the CCP to lead national construction; opposing the CCP's leadership in all sectors; and demanding that CCP leadership be removed, especially from institutions of higher learning, the press, and publishing houses.[78]

Specific verdicts for the education sector emerged piecemeal during the latter half of 1957 in a series of authoritative pronouncements beginning with Zhou Enlai's government work report in June. Those who wanted the education system to return to its pre-1949 state were wrong, he said, but the education departments had made mistakes. Chief among these were "rejecting certain factors that were rational in the old education system, failing systematically to sum up and carry forward the experience of revolutionary education in the liberated areas, and failing to adapt the Soviet experience sufficiently to China's actual conditions."[79]

Official thinking had obviously been moving toward this conclusion for some time. In early May, another anonymous contributor had already elaborated the rationale that underlay this new summation and that would be used to exorcise "mechanical copying." The rationale looked back to the pre-1949 modern system that was "unified in form and diverse in content" and was supplemented by *sishu*, which remained outside the system and not recognized by it. Elementary and middle schools within the system were governed by

---

[78] Deng Xiaoping, "Guanyu zhengfeng yundong de baogao" (Report on the Rectification Campaign), 23 Sept. 1957, *Renmin ribao*, 19 Oct. 1957, trans. in Bowie and Fairbank, *Communist China*, pp. 341–363.

[79] From Premier Zhou's report to the Fourth Session of the First National People's Congress, 26 June 1957, *Renmin ribao*, 27 June 1957, trans. in Bowie and Fairbank, *Communist China*, pp. 299–329.

unified rules and regulations determining the curriculum, hours per course, vacation times, the form of internal organization by class (*ban*) and grade (*ji*), standards for buildings and equipment, etc. But the content of textbooks and teaching materials was not unified except for politics, and the GMD authorities made little effort to enforce the use of their officially sponsored texts. At the college level, content was even less regulated, with teachers essentially making their own decisions about what to teach.

During the Yan'an decade, education in the liberated areas was just the opposite: disparate in form but "basically unified" in content. Schooling was adapted to the time and place: towns, villages, mountains, plains, guerrilla areas, behind enemy lines, and so on. By contrast, after 1949, all aspects of education work were planned and unified. Accommodating particular needs should be the new guiding principle for both form and content. The latter should be flexible enough to accommodate local production needs and changing current events – like the Hungarian uprising, which raised many questions in students' minds that the existing curriculum did not address. Course content should be easy to adapt for students of different backgrounds and abilities, and the form should be flexible enough to accommodate rural children especially, following the example set in the old liberated areas.[80]

On the question of learning from capitalist countries, science and technology were acceptable but other lessons were not, including the rightist calls for a two-party political system, bicameral legislature, the bourgeois class stand in education and ideology, and liberal lifestyles. CCP committees would therefore not be withdrawn from schools. Leadership over teaching and curricular planning would not be abandoned, and individual freedom in scientific research would not be tolerated. Western or non-Marxist social sciences would not be restored and political courses would not be made optional. The personnel system would continue to rely on political and social criteria.[81]

An Ziwen of the CCP Central Committes's Organization Department defended the proposition that the CCP most certainly could lead education, science, and culture. Large numbers of Party members had been transferred to work in these fields, he said, acknowledging that perhaps a few had not been qualified. But rather than withdraw, the CCP had decided to *strengthen* its presence by transferring in more of its best cadres and training others. This would henceforth enable it to exercise direct leadership not just in terms of policy and personnel but over academic and technological matters as well.[82] A

[80] Shu Ming, "Lun jiaoyu gongzuo de tongyixing he difangxing" (On the Unified and Local Natures of Education Work), *Renmin jiaoyu*, May 1957, pp. 6–9.
[81] E.g., Zhang Jian, "Xuexi Sulian jingyan de chengji bushi zhuyao de ma" (Have Not the Achievements Been the Main Thing in Learning from the Soviet Experience?), *Renmin jiaoyu*, Aug. 1957, pp. 16–18, 12.
[82] An Ziwen, "Gongchandang nenggou lingdao kexue, wenhua he jiaoyu gongzuo" (The CCP Can Lead Science, Culture, and Education Work), *Zhongguo qingnian*, no. 13 (1 July 1957), pp. 5–6.

few months later, recalling that since 1949 close to one thousand Party cadres had been transferred into higher education to lead administrative and political work, the CCP Central Committee sent in an additional one thousand high- and middle-ranking cadres. Their assignment was to shore up leadership work as the heads and deputies of universities, research institutes, and newspaper offices.[83]

Nor were many points conceded on the contentious personnel question. Zhou Enlai acknowledged in his June report that academic standards had sometimes been too loosely applied in selecting students for study abroad. Also, henceforth, only older students would be sent overseas for specialized courses not yet available at home. But political criteria for selection would not be abandoned. Nor would he accept the accusation that too many children of high-ranking officials were among those selected in the past. Between 1952 and 1956, he claimed, 6,435 individuals were sent abroad for study, of whom only 3.5 percent were sons and daughters of "revolutionary cadres."

Guo Moruo, president of the Chinese Academy of Sciences, addressed the challenge about "special privilege" and "unequal treatment" in personnel matters generally by declaring that political qualifications must remain an "absolutely unshakable" criterion. CCP and Youth League members whose academic standing was up to par would continue to receive preference. He also defended the practice of giving workers, peasants, and others preference in college admissions when their entrance exam results were the same as others.[84]

The question of political and social criteria had an added dimension, however, that neither critics nor defenders seemed willing to expound fully in public debate. The critics, not wanting to appear overtly antagonistic to working-class students, focused instead on the preferences and privileges enjoyed by cadres' children. Similarly, when the Party answered back, it too took the high ground, focusing on the new opportunities for the previously underprivileged masses. In fact, the two categories often overlapped, since many "revolutionary cadres," or those who joined the CCP and the revolution before 1949, had been born into peasant or worker families. Thus their children could still claim to be of worker–peasant class background, regardless of their parents' current cadre status. They represented one of the ironies of class-based communist revolutions in that, once victorious, the revolutionaries became the new rulers, exchanging places with the old, albeit in the name of the working class.

That same irony was reproduced in China immediately and enlivened the arguments over who should gain access to higher education and other benefits, with the old intellectual elite leveling charges of unfair advantage against the privileges of the new. Zhou Enlai at least had tried to answer the charge

---

[83] *Renmin ribao*, 23 Oct. 1957; Zhang Jian, "Woguo de gaodeng jiaoyu shi yueban yuebao le" (Our Country's Higher Education Is Being Run Better and Better), *Renmin jiaoyu*, Oct. 1957, p. 9.
[84] Guo Moruo, in *Renmin ribao*, 6 July 1957.

directly about high-level cadres' children studying abroad. Guo Moruo and most others simply ignored it. Statistical approximations on student class background are shown in Table 9.6. Since a majority of students at the tertiary level still came from bourgeois and landlord families, declared Guo, the Party should actually be doing more, not less, to redress the balance.

One of the few presentations to address directly the irony of new elite privileges hiding behind preferential treatment for the underprivileged allowed the significance of the contradiction to be all but lost in the clumsy attempt to deny it. The specific charge being addressed was not access to higher education but to elite education at lower levels in the form of schools established for cadres' children. These were different in principle if not always in fact from quality-oriented key-point schools. The writer, Guo Lin, was a former headmaster of Yan'an Elementary School. Such special schools for cadres' children had their origin during the pre-1949 war years, he explained, when cadres, troops, and liberated-area government offices were constantly on the move. No one questioned then the need to provide some semblance of regular schooling for dependents, war orphans, and refugee children. The students, like everyone else in those days, lived on austerity rations: two sets of clothes per year and three ounces of millet a day.

After 1949, however, the schools moved into town and everything changed. No longer the waifs of war, some youngsters arrived at school each day in chauffeur-driven cars. Yan'an Elementary moved to Beijing and became the famous Yucai Elementary School, which sent many of its graduates on to the equally famous Middle School Number 101. But the students were allegedly trained not to behave like a "privileged class," and Premier Zhou Enlai himself was said to have ordered parents to stop sending their children to school in official cars immediately he learned of this practice. Moreover, all such special institutions were brought into the regular public school system in the mid-1950s, claimed Guo, although the aura of special privilege still clung to them by reason of who the parents were. He nevertheless maintained the theoretical pretense even in this case of equating the CCP with the proletariat, declaring that the rightists had slanderously "compared the children of workers, peasants, and revolutionary cadres with the scions of royal families in feudal society and children of the aristocracy in capitalist countries."[85]

On the procedures for applying these political and social criteria, the Party strongly reaffirmed the role played by the personnel offices. One spirited rebuttal called the personnel file an "indispensable tool" in assessing individual character and ability as a basis for employment and promotion. Among other things, the personnel file allowed the state "to identify the political features of

---

[85] Guo Lin, "Bu xu dongyao jiaoyu xiang gongnong kaimen de fangzhen" (The Policy of Opening the Doors of Education for Workers and Peasants Should Not Waiver), *Renmin jiaoyu* (Sept. 1957), pp. 11–12.

every worker, forestalling the infiltration of counterrevolutionaries and sabo-
tage elements and ensuring the purity of the revolutionary ranks." Since the
dossiers also similarly recorded "the reactionary words and deeds and odious
histories of those rightists," it was little wonder they demanded that the files be
burned and the personnel assessment system abolished.[86]

Only on the issue of job placement for college graduates did the official
response appear conciliatory. Some students had wrongfully demanded an end
to state job assignments. Still, there had been many problems with the scheme
that went beyond the desires of the graduates themselves. These problems
were well known. Factories were unpopular and the countryside even more so.
But the crux of the problem was acknowledged to be China's overall lack of
experience in coordinating personnel planning with economic development
needs. Sometimes, in making job assignments, "we have to grope our way in
the dark to a certain extent and have no clear understanding as to what are the
actual personnel needs of the different work units." Such problems could only
be solved with experience, but in the meantime the "impractical and bombastic
propaganda" that had created unrealistic aspirations among students must be
stopped. Too much publicity had been given to the bright future of socialist
construction and not enough to the practical difficulties young graduates were
likely to encounter.[87]

On learning from the Soviet Union, errors of mechanical imitation were also
conceded, including too many courses in the curriculum, specialties and majors
too narrowly divided, the Soviet five-point grading system, and oral examinations. Nevertheless, achievements were greater than defects. Quantitatively,
between 1928 and 1948, China had produced only 150,000 college graduates,
in comparison with 360,000 between 1949 and 1957. The number of college
teachers nationwide had risen from about 16,000 in 1949 to 68,000. True, the
quantitative development had raced ahead of the system's capacities. But that
did not validate the charge that quality was higher before 1949 than after. As
for university reorganization, the largest proportion of pre-1949 students had
always been graduates in politics and law. Since 1949, engineering graduates
numbered 96,000 of the total, or more than three times the number produced
during the entire first half of the century. Of the 331 majors in China's
institutions of higher learning as of 1957, 191 were in engineering fields all
designed to serve the needs of industrialization. Only the planned and proportionate development possible under socialism could have solved this most basic
of Chinese education's inherited weaknesses.

Finally, smarting under the charge that learning from the Soviet Union was

[86] Wang Liang, "Refute the Rightists' Malicious Charges against Cadre Policy and Personnel
Work," *Shih Shih Shou Ts'e*, no. 16 (21 Aug. 1957), trans. in *ECMM*, no. 107 (12 Nov. 1957),
pp. 20–24.
[87] *Renmin ribao*, 15 July 1957.

but another form of dependency, or educational "colonialism," the official rebuttal took refuge in the old critique claiming the CCP to be its sole legitimate heir. As everyone knew, many in the past had "worshipped foreign countries," perpetuated the old saying that "even the moon is rounder in America," and supported the collaborator government in the Japanese-occupied areas during World War II. The nation was not liberated from this colonial mentality until the CCP came to power, fought the U.S. in Korea, took over all foreign-run cultural institutions on Chinese soil, and mobilized people everywhere to cast off their cultural dependence on American imperialism. The relationship with the Soviet Union was, by contrast, based on "independence, sovereignty, patriotism, and internationalism."[88]

Having thus defined right and wrong views, the next step was to determine who held them. Unfortunately for many, the decisions were made by the very same work-unit personnel authorities who had borne the brunt of everyone's wrath in May. Approximations vary. A year later, Mao declared there to be 300,000 rightists in all, of whom fully one-third were elementary school teachers.[89] After his death, a 500,000 figure circulated. It included many Party members but was primarily a designation for non-CCP professionals of all kinds who had responded too enthusiastically to the CCP's call for criticism. About 26,000 had their rightist labels removed in 1959 as part of an amnesty declared to mark the 10th anniversary of the People's Republic.[90] But most carried the labels, duly recorded in their dossiers, through the Cultural Revolution decade, when it became one of the five bad categories after landlords, rich peasants, counterrevolutionaries, and bad elements (*di, fu, fan, huai, you*). All of these designations brought varying degrees of discrimination for the holders and their immediate families, which intensified progressively from 1957 onward until all such labels were removed after Mao's death for the great majority of those who bore them.

When the instructions for job placement work were issued in mid-1957, for example, they contained two changes from previous years. One concerned technical procedures designed to promote a more rational distribution of talent

---

[88] E.g., Zhang Jian, "Xuexi Sulian jingyan de chengji bushi zhuyao de ma"; and the following, all also from *Renmin jiaoyu*: "Jiaoyu zhiliang shibushi 'jin bu ru xi'? Beijing shida jiaoshou chi youpai fenzi dui jiaoyu zhiliang de wumie" (Is It True That Educational Quality Today Cannot Compare with the Past? Beijing Teacher Training University Professors Denounce the Rightists' Slander of Educational Quality), Sept. 1957, pp. 30–36; Zhang Jian, "Woguo de gaodeng jiaoyu shi yueban yuehao le"; Chen Xuanshan, "Banianlai gaodeng shifan jiaoyu de juda chengjiu bu rong mosha" (The Great Achievements in Higher Teacher Training during the Past Eight Years Must Not Be Written Off), Oct. 1957, pp. 11–14.

[89] Mao Zedong, "Zai bada erci huiyishang de jianghua: disanci jianghua" (Talks at the Second Session of the Eighth Party Congress: Third Talk), 20 May 1958, in *Mao Zedong sixiang wansui* (Long Live the Thought of Mao Zedong) (1969), p. 215.

[90] MacFarquhar, *Origins of the Cultural Revolution*, p. 314; MacFarquhar, Cheek, and Wu, *Secret Speeches of Chairman Mao*, p. 13.

given available job openings. But the second was to enforce more stringent political criteria. A political examination was required for all graduating seniors that consisted mainly of self- and group assessment as to each person's behavior during the rectification campaign. Those found to be guilty of errors so serious as to be deemed counterrevolutionary were given prison terms, either "reform through labor" or the less severe "reeducation through labor." Others deemed antisocialist were placed under public surveillance, which is to say, on good behavior for specified periods. They were assigned to low-status jobs that carried no titles, ranking, or remuneration except living expenses.[91]

According to interviewees, those with rightist views not serious enough to warrant a label were dealt with in various ways. Most common for graduating seniors that year was an "inferior" job assignment. One such person had been tapped as an outstanding graduate student in the associate doctoral program to remain as a teacher at his university, but permission was denied on political grounds. As a result, he spent his entire career from 1958 onward in a less prestigious teacher training college. In another case, an agronomy student at a Wuhan college had articulated views deemed rightist in 1957. In return, he was assigned to a state farm, unable to win a transfer for more than 20 years, during which he worked not in his specialty but as a middle school teacher. The associate doctoral degree program was abandoned – whether because of the prevailing bourgeois orientation of the candidates or simply as a matter of principle is unknown. For everyone else, the "rightist" demand that political study be made optional was answered by increasing the number of hours required for compulsory "socialist ideological education" and related social activities, including stints of manual labor.

By the end of 1957, however, everyone's fate was being painted onto a much larger canvas which included not just the antirightist and rectification campaigns but a reordering of developmental priorities as well. The final year of the FFYP marked the formal end of the 1950s model that China had tried to copy from the Soviet Union. The model was not abandoned but it was substantially altered. "We believe that learning from the Soviet Union has been absolutely necessary," declared a defensive Zhou Enlai in his June report. "The question lies in how we ourselves do the learning." Deng Xiaoping's September summation with its dual emphasis on rectification and economic priorities contained, in effect, the Party's answer. According to the key passage in Deng's report, much cited thereafter to justify the new emphasis on agriculture and rural work assignments: "Simultaneously while giving priority to heavy industry, we must exert great effort for the development of agriculture. In the past few years, we have been conducting somewhat more propaganda for

[91] *Renmin ribao*, 20, 31 July 1957; Goldman, "The Rectification Campaign at Peking University," p. 153.

industry and assigned a large group of cadres to industrial work. . . . Now we should emphasize the importance of agriculture in our propaganda to change the bad atmosphere which has appeared in the past two years of looking down on agricultural production, of peasants wanting to enter the cities, of city people unwilling to go to the countryside, and of people in the plains unwilling to move into the mountains."

Henceforth, the lessons of Party rectification, the antirightist campaign, and changing economic priorities would be joined. According to the official diagnosis, the main cause of the Party's failings was that a majority of its 12.7 million members had joined after 1949 and so had no direct revolutionary experience. The 1.8 million intellectuals among them also had no training in productive labor. Every Party member and especially those in leadership or cadre positions must therefore be tested, and all cadres, whether Party members or not, would have to be "steeled in production work." College graduates, warned Deng, should first be assigned to manual or menial work as the prerequisite for subsequent job placement. For everyone else, the prescription was "vigorous retrenchment," or an escalation of the movement under way since early 1957 whereby urban functionaries were being transferred to basic-level production posts.[92]

Lessons learned from the Soviet Union

In many ways, then, the CCP paid an immediate and heavy price for its initial decision to emulate the Soviet Union in all things great and small. Surprisingly, given their recent Yan'an experience, Party leaders seem not to have anticipated the dangers of such a course. Hence it was only after the intervening embarrassment of de-Stalinization compromised its new foreign model that the CCP shifted gears in the mid-1950s to pick up where it had left off a decade earlier when civil war interrupted rural-oriented mass-line reform. And again in the 1950s, as in earlier years, the old issues incorporated within that line found ready, if not uniformly willing, adherents at points high and low throughout the system.

"Mechanical copying" attracted the most varied cross section of critics. Cooptation had actually set in almost at once between the Soviet transplant and its host environment, as Chinese educators demanded "adaptation to Chinese conditions." Many such adjustments occurred at the expense of the Soviet model in deference to its regular Chinese counterpart. By 1956, the points of adjustment already included the demise of five-year integrated elementary schooling, the demise of worker–peasant short–course middle schools, the creation of key-point schools, the pattern of quantitative decline associated with qualitative reorganization at the elementary level, the use of unified examinations

---

[92] Deng Xiaoping, "Guanyu zhengfeng yundong de baogao."

to rank schools, and the introduction of a unified national college entrance examination. After mechanical copying was officially authorized as a subject for criticism in 1956, the ensuing debate suggested just how much further the regular education system might have gone, if allowed, in rejecting the Soviet model.

At the same time, *minban* schools, junior middle caps, ad hoc teacher training courses, and anti-illiteracy work were all residual features from the CCP's own "irregular" rural past that suffered setbacks as regularization proceeded in the form of a genuine Sino-Soviet compromise. In all the "necessary systems" relied upon by Chinese educators to maintain order, discipline, and daily routines, as well as in their ambivalent approach to manual labor and practical training, it was often difficult to see where regular Chinese modes stopped and those of Soviet educators began.

A conventional urban-oriented college-preparatory system had obviously been deemed essential to meet demands for trained personnel once planned Soviet-style heavy industry was accepted as the basis of Chinese modernization. The Soviet model thus provided a ready opportunity for Chinese educators to reassert inherited assumptions about how to produce a quality product. And on that basis, they were by the mid-1950s already well on their way to taking over the Soviet import.

Yet for Chinese intellectuals, communist victory had marked the nadir of their 20th-century slide from the top of the social and political hierarchy. Early 1950s thought reform coupled with university reorganization constituted the first round in what would become a protracted struggle under CCP rule to expropriate the remaining power, prestige, and social influence of China's educated elite. Its members found themselves not only reclassified as potentially suspect associates of the bourgeoisie but effectively confined in a more modern way to the specialized world of their own professional pursuits.

That a newly victorious CCP would not be able to live with the contradictions inherent in such a system, whatever its mix of regular Soviet and Chinese features, should also have been anticipated but evidently was not. In effect, the CCP's most basic challenge at this juncture was its inability to reconcile or ignore the conflicting demands created by Soviet-style industrialization, Chinese socioeconomic realities, and the CCP's own revolutionary commitments.

The regular education system continued to rest upon a base of mass illiteracy which such a system could offer little hope of eliminating in the foreseeable future. The demand to improve quality as needed for Soviet-style modernization and as implemented by Chinese educators could only be achieved at the cost of reducing the number of students and the rate at which teachers were trained to teach them. The goal of universal elementary schooling would recede even further into the future under a rigorous application of the Sino-Soviet convergence model. The only way there could be a school in every village was by reverting to the Yan'an philosophy of not worrying too much about quality and uniform standards since these could only be achieved in a regular state-supported system staffed by conventionally trained teachers.

Tensions were also mounting at other points. The unprecedented growth of elementary and secondary schooling that had occurred meant increasing numbers of graduates for whom there were no places available at the next higher level. Far from safeguarding the Chinese against these development dilemmas, the Soviet model actually seemed to compound them. In any event, the Chinese found themselves reproducing some classic "dysfunctions." Providing new places at the elementary level was easier than expanding secondary schooling. Similarly, it was easier to increase secondary school enrollments than to provide appropriate opportunities on the job market once the new students graduated. Another potentially disruptive symptom of development was therefore looming in the form of young people whose aspirations for more schooling and/or employment commensurate with their new education could not immediately be met. Ironically, the only relief from these tensions came in 1956 as a result of Mao's new high-speed development program with its adventuristic plans for growth in all sectors.

Zhou Enlai, in his June 1957 report, had acknowledged these development pressures underlying the political upheaval of rectification. His report emphasized the need to devise forms of secondary schooling that would be college preparatory for some but terminal and work-oriented for the majority, at the same time that recent rapid growth had created a corresponding rise in expectations. Because of the great need for development personnel, Zhou noted, most secondary school graduates since 1949 had been able to continue on to college. But expansion at the tertiary level could not continue to match that at the secondary. Henceforth, an increasing number of elementary- and secondary-level graduates would have to reconcile themselves to "productive labor" in agriculture and industry.

The events of 1955–1957 should therefore be seen as deriving from the search for an alternative to the Stalinist model that would better accommodate the CCP's conflicting commitments. In reviving the old Yan'an formula, however, Party leaders had to consider two important differences between Yan'an in the 1940s and China a decade later. First, the CCP was now legislating not just for an isolated rural hinterland but for the entire country. In education, this meant that demands for quality, trained personnel, and, more recently, intellectual independence from the Soviet Union had to be accommodated. The Yan'an reforms postponed such concerns for a future that had now arrived.

Second, the entire country was also in the throes of socioeconomic revolution as the CCP insisted on fulfilling its revolutionary mandate to eliminate private ownership of the means of production and overthrow the existing class structure. Yet the need for trained personnel meant that the existing educated

elite would perpetuate itself into the indefinite future, especially after the
Party's early hopes for high worker–peasant college enrollments disappeared
under the weight of Sino-Soviet regularization. And the educated elite was not
only bourgeois by reason of its birth but evidently remained unchanged in
many of its concerns and commitments, which were being passed on to the
younger generation as well.

Hence one additional contradiction – not authorized for discussion in May
1957 but clearly uppermost in Mao's calculations as he embarked upon his
preparatory barnstorming speeches to Party leaders that spring – concerned
the conflicting prerequisites for development and revolution. Long before,
after the CCP began its class-based revolution in a few Jiangxi counties, Mao
declared that discriminating against bourgeois teachers had been detrimental
to its complementary goal of educating peasants. During the united front of
cooperation against Japan, Party rectification in Yan'an had incorporated the
old reform critique within the theory and practice of Chinese communism,
albeit minus the active class-war component. In 1957, however, Party rectification and the antirightist campaign finally joined the old critique with the full
force of the Chinese revolution.

Mao calculated the nation's intellectuals at 5 million, of whom about 2
million ran the education system and another 3 million were scattered throughout the Party, government, army, business, and industry, as well as in literary
and artistic circles. Without them, said Mao, China would have no teachers,
scientists, or engineers. "We can't move without them. If we leave them, we
won't be able to move a single step. This is why we must take pains to unite
with them." But he entertained no illusions about the difficulty of that task,
since at most only 500,000 accepted Marxism. Perhaps another 10 percent
consciously opposed it, while 80 percent were only "half-hearted," going along
with the new communist order but wavering at every provocation. Basically,
the intellectuals as a whole remained bourgeois in their views and values,
declared Mao, and the CCP's long-term aim was to eliminate the bourgeoisie
as a class.[93]

The self-serving intellectual of earlier pre-Marxist polemics had been redefined
as the unreliable appendage of a class marked for extinction. At the same time,
ideals previously honored only in the breach were becoming the daily life reality of an obligatory job assignment and a category of punishment for political/
intellectual indiscretions. The old tension between regularity and its critics was
being incorporated within a "two-line" class-based struggle between the proletariat and the bourgeoisie that was designated, in turn, as the prerequisite for
success in all things. In this way, the possibility of suppressing the intellectuals'

[93] See text 11, "Talk at the Conference of Party Member Cadres of Shandong Provincial Organs,"
18 Mar. 1957, in MacFarquhar, Cheek, and Wu, Secret Speeches of Chairman Mao, esp. pp. 311–
317, and texts 5–13.

independent political influence was realized, and so too was the possibility of suppressing the professional educators' influence and transforming the entire system in accordance with the old critical ideals, although that final step would not be taken until the 1966–1976 period.

From 1957, however, the reform mentality of earlier decades shifted into revolutionary high gear, a state maintained for most of the next 20 years until Mao's death. Far from coming to rest in the new communist order, China's 20th-century quest for the ideal model of national reconstruction accelerated as newly empowered CCP leaders discovered that solutions did not appear automatically with revolutionary success. Directives followed one upon the other, reversing themselves from year to year as the two-line struggle, having been set in motion, proceeded on to its logical conclusion.

Part III

Cultural revolution and radical education reform

11

On Stalin, Khrushchev, and the origins of cultural revolution

Much as the regular modes of Chinese education co-opted the initial Stalin model, so Khrushchev's attempt to reform that model in the Soviet Union was soon taken over in China by a new strain of Chinese radicalism. China's 1958 Great Leap Forward marked that takeover. But the syncretism contained within it was obscured by the developing Sino-Soviet rift and the CCP's need to neutralize its embarrassing new image as a mechanical copier. Unfortunately, much of the evidence for this line of reasoning is only circumstantial. But once mustered, this evidence suggests that the Chinese debt to Khrushchev, and Mao's debt to Stalin before him, were substantial enough to warrant some adjustments in the conventional interpretation.

In China, the radicalism began with Mao's "great stride" of 1956 and continued two years later as the even more ambitious Great Leap Forward. This adventure in high-speed socialist development included extensive education reforms introduced in 1958 as part of a "cultural revolution." The radical education reforms introduced that year were then reincarnated in the Great Proletarian Cultural Revolution of 1966–1976, which sought to combine and institutionalize the earlier radical adventures as essential features of an evolving Chinese communism.

According to conventional periodization, moreover, the 1958 leap marked the end not just of mechanical copying but also of direct Soviet influence. Thereafter, China set out self-consciously in search of its own distinct route to socialism, which culminated in the 1966–1976 Cultural Revolution. The chronology was reinforced by Chinese claims to originality as the lessons of dependency just relearned escalated into an open breach with the Soviet Union, signified most dramatically by the withdrawal of Soviet advisors from China in 1960. Much was made thereafter of the ideological differences between the two fraternal systems. The older continued along its so-called revisionist path while the younger claimed to be maintaining a purer, albeit more rough-hewn, revolutionary line tracing its Marxist–Leninist roots in a direct line of descent back through the Yan'an reforms of the mid-1940s (when Moscow's influence over the CCP was at a minimum).

Mao began articulating the differences between the two systems in the late

1950s. He argued that seizing state power and the means of production were necessary but not sufficient means for achieving socialism and ultimately communism. Nor, having seized political and economic power, was Soviet-style economic development a sufficient condition. Nor was Soviet-style development even capable of maximizing material and technological growth. In Mao's view, the Soviets had simply wedded heavy industry to a centrally planned, publicly owned economy under Communist Party rule and called it socialism. But in reality, the Soviets had put their revolution on hold since they were ignoring the superstructural concerns necessary for creating genuine socialism and were thereby inhibiting economic development as well.

Mao seemed to be making two points, namely, that the Stalinist Soviet model was bad socialism per se and that it was especially inappropriate for China at that time. Khrushchev's efforts to the contrary notwithstanding, Mao argued that the Soviets were disregarding the role of production relations, ideology, culture, politics, and people in the ongoing development of the revolutionary enterprise. Instead, the Soviets were preoccupied with technology, expertise, central planning, hierarchical management, bureaucratic organizations, and material incentives.

So far as can be ascertained from the documents available, Mao did not give Khrushchev any credit for trying to reform any of these features of the system he had inherited. And with Khrushchev's political demise in 1964, the question became academic in any case since his reform efforts were overthrown with him. By way of defense for having promoted so inappropriate a system in the early 1950s, Mao said only that the CCP did not know what else to do: "In the early stages just after liberation, we had no experience with managing the economy of the entire nation, so during the period of the FFYP we could only copy the Soviet Union's methods, but were generally dissatisfied with them."[1]

The Chinese may have relearned the lessons of overt mechanical copying at this time as the pattern of attraction and reaction played itself out once more. But the 20th-century habit of dependency, as manifested in the penchant to follow the dominant world trend of the day, was evidently hard to break. In any event, no effort was made to expunge all Soviet influences. On the contrary, the new protestations of independence seemed to mask an ongoing debt to the Soviet experience, and that debt almost certainly included the strain of mass movement radicalism in Soviet revolutionary history that ran, also in a direct line of descent, from the Soviet Union's own FFYP (1929–1933) through

---

[1] Mao Zedong, "Sulian *Zhengzhi jingji xue* dushu biji" (Reading Notes on the Soviet Union's *Political Economy*), 1961–1962, in *Mao Zedong sixiang wanxue* (1969), p. 395. For the conventional Chinese argument as formulated between 1958 and 1962, see Mao Tsetung, *A Critique of Soviet Economics*, trans. Moss Roberts and Richard Levy (New York: Monthly Review Press, 1977). For a preliminary unedited presentation dating from 1958, see MacFarquhar, Cheek, and Wu, *Secret Speeches of Chairman Mao*, texts 17–19.

Khrushchev's reforms during the 1950s. Although Mao himself did not acknowledge it, the Chinese debt to that strain was well documented for education between 1956 and 1958, opening thereby a small window on the radical skeletons locked firmly away in everyone's closets.

The main clue pointing to such antecedents appeared in the revised version of Soviet educational history presented to the Chinese by way of explanation for Khrushchev's reform proposals. Their historical pedigree was clearly drawn, being traced back to the controversial years between 1925 and 1931, and "especially between 1927 and 1930," when many serious errors had been committed. As noted above, these errors were introduced to the Chinese in 1949 as something to be avoided. Not fully rehabilitated in 1956, they were nevertheless reinterpreted as the point of origin for current Soviet concerns.

The dubious influence of Dewey's pragmatism was still blamed, together with such utopian leftist ideas as the "withering away of the school." These ideas were now not only acknowledged but explained in some detail. According to the withering-away concept, for instance, schools need not exist as separate institutions in a socialist society and could disappear, like the state itself. Learning could occur in farms and factories, returning to its original form in the school of life. Soviet teaching in the late 1920s, it was explained, had been highly eclectic, concentrating on practical subjects rather than conventional courses. Production techniques were emphasized but not the knowledge from which those techniques derived, in the style of Western vocational training, which left a partially educated work force at the mercy of its capitalist exploiters.

All of this had ended with the 1931 decision on education which decreed that modern production required the systematic presentation of basic scientific knowledge. The centralized teaching plans, syllabi, texts, and materials were then developed, and classroom teaching became the mainstay, as a reaction against the excesses of earlier years. Hence, "throughout the 1930s, teaching and production were separated." This "weakness" was soon recognized, but between 1938 and 1952, little was done to correct it. The matter was revived in 1952, and Khrushchev was now carrying it forward. Since the Chinese had adopted the Soviet Union's post-1931 system, they too should discuss how best to reintroduce technical and labor training within the regular school curriculum.[2]

[2] This summary of Soviet educational history is based on the report of Chen Zenggu, a deputy education minister, who led a teachers delegation on a two-month trip (Oct.–Dec. 1955) to the Soviet Union. See Chen Zenggu, "Guanyu fu Su fangwen kaocha de zong baogao" (General Report on an Investigation Visit to the Soviet Union), Renmin jiaoyu, Apr. 1956, p. 13 (full report, pp. 9–22). See also Chen Zenggu, "Fu Su fangwen kaocha de jingguo he shouhuo: 2 yue 8 ri zai jiaoyubu di 40 ci buwu huiyi shang de baogao" (The Course and Results of an Inspection Visit to the Soviet Union: Report to the 40th Ministry Affairs Meeting on 8 Feb.), ibid., Mar. 1956, pp. 7–10; "Duanlun: Yinggai renzhen yanjiu Sulian jiaoyu daibiaotuan de baogao" (Short Comment: The Report of the Soviet Education Delegation Should be Conscientiously Studied), ibid., July 1956, p. 14. For a summary of changing Soviet views toward labor and polytechnic

The internal documents that must have been circulating in China to explain further the extraordinary changes of the Khrushchev era remain unavailable, so it is not clear how much more those in the need to know were told about the years 1927–1930 in Soviet history beyond the above style of allusions. But the contemporary sources available suggest further that Chinese leaders must have been aware of what occurred in the Soviet Union during that period even if they would not authorize the full story for public consumption.

The evidence includes especially (1) the rationale for continuing revolution, beginning with the 1957 argument for rectification as a "socialist revolution on the political and ideological fronts," intended to break the remaining influence of intellectuals as an essential corollary in the superstructure to socializing the economy (see Deng Xiaoping's report cited in chap. 10); and (2) the introduction of the 1958 Great Leap education reforms as a "cultural revolution" in a formulation synchronized almost to the day with Khrushchev's developing proposals for Soviet education. These latter were, in turn, evoking ideas and aims reminiscent of the late 1920s "cultural revolution" period of Soviet educational history.

The Russian cultural revolution

Despite passing references to cultural revolution in the late 1920s, historians have generally glossed over the period to concentrate on events just before (especially the demise of the New Economic Policy) and after (the emergence of Stalin's centralized, repressive bureaucratic system). The years in between were usually portrayed as a transitional period when the foundations of Stalinism were laid.[3] We are therefore indebted to Sheila Fitzpatrick and a small group of American historians for the light they have shed on those mysterious years, 1927–1930, so often mentioned by Chinese and Russians in China during the 1950s but never fully explained.[4]

The years cited by these historians are actually 1928–1931, defined as a four-year interlude when Stalin and the Communist Party of the Soviet Union (CPSU) leadership adopted as official policy a leftist interpretation of cultural revolution which included militant, mass-activated class struggle. Fearful of a

---

education specifically from the 1920s through the 1960s as the background for Chinese practice, see Ronald F. Price, *Marx and Education in Russia and China* (London: Croom Helm, 1977), chap. 5.

[3] On passing references to cultural revolution, see, e.g., Charles Bettelheim, *Class Struggles in the USSR, Second Period: 1923–1930* (New York: Monthly Review Press, 1978), pp. 222–236; John E. Rue, *Mao Tse-tung in Opposition, 1927–1935* (Stanford: Hoover Institution, 1966), pp. 119–125.

[4] The following discussion is taken from Sheila Fitzpatrick, *Education and Social Mobility in the Soviet Union, 1921–1934* (Cambridge: Cambridge University Press, 1979); and Sheila Fitzpatrick, ed., *Cultural Revolution in Russia, 1928–1931* (Bloomington: Indiana University Press, 1978).

bourgeois restoration or the revival of unreconstructed forces on the cultural front, this interpretation denounced peaceful cultural development as "the most dangerous distortion of the Party line in cultural work."[5]

The more conventional, nonmilitant Soviet interpretation of cultural revolution or cultural development (followed both during the 1920s and later) included the gradual reeducation and reorientation of bourgeois intellectuals inherited from the old regime; the growth of literacy, mass education, etc.; and the elevation of those who received it (workers, peasants, women, and national minorities) into the ranks of the intelligentsia through higher education and job assignments.[6]

The change in 1928 seemed to derive from Stalin's disagreement with his "rightist" opposition over the speed of industrialization and agricultural collectivization. The rightists were also held to be conciliators of bourgeois intellectuals, among whom support for the revolution was noticeable by its absence. A campaign to discredit the rightist opposition was therefore linked with efforts to create a new proletarian intelligentsia while breaking the authority of the old. Public vigilance was aroused against intellectual saboteurs and wreckers in industry. The proletariat was called upon to resist the influence, traditions, and customs of the old society. Simultaneously, large numbers of adult workers were recruited into higher education and then promoted into the new jobs created by rapid industrialization.

The process was also characterized by local initiative and popular mass mobilization. In this manner, dismissals and expulsions of faculty and students occurred at all levels. The targets in government offices were corrupt and incompetent bureaucrats. These were purged "spontaneously" by militant workers, peasants, youth groups, and local Party organizations. Workers were even invited to participate in the tenure confirmation of university professors. Youth League (Komsomol) participants appeared the most enthusiastic in attempting to simulate the spirit of the October Revolution and subsequent civil war with their cultural "armies" and "ambushes" (used for assaulting illiteracy and defending against bourgeois counterattacks). Suspicious of the government education bureaucracy, militants initially developed their movement outside of it in an attempt to reorganize the basis of the education system.

Since it was a time for attacking conservative ideas as well as bureaucratic methods, radical alternatives flourished. One such pedagogical concept was indeed the withering away of the school. Another proposal aimed to give the "bourgeois" secondary school over entirely to vocational training. Gradual expansion gave way to enlarged enrollments and accelerated courses to meet

---

[5] Quoted in Gail Warshofsky Lapidus, "Educational Strategies and Cultural Revolution: The Politics of Social Development," in Fitzpatrick, *Cultural Revolution in Russia*, p. 90.

[6] E.g., Gilbert Rozman, *A Mirror for Socialism: Soviet Criticisms of China* (Princeton: Princeton University Press, 1985), pp. 137–138.

the immediate demands of an economy developing via forced marches and crash programs. Besides linking education more closely with production, the new education principles demanded that students engage in socially productive labor as part of their schooling. This work included participation in the adult world of political campaigns and manual labor. Schools were often emptied of students, who were sent out on work assignments to help fulfill the state economic plans. All schools had to attach themselves to production enterprises, as society itself became the school, breaking down the "authoritarianism" of the teacher and the formal classroom environment. There was even a proposal to make the entire education system self-supporting by relying on student labor.

It was also at this time that Soviet universities were reorganized into specialized technical institutes, designed to meet the needs of high-speed industrialization and scientific economic planning. Large numbers of students could then be trained more quickly to fill the specific slots decreed by the centralized economic plan. Expanded enrollments at the tertiary level included a deliberate effort to recruit large numbers of adult workers and CPSU members with several years' on-the-job experience. These new students, often enrolled in groups of a thousand at a time, usually had not completed secondary school and were of lower-class origins. So great were their numbers and so urgent was the demand for their services that even the shortened route for such students could not meet the demand. The two- to three-year *rabfak* (workers collegepreparatory secondary school) courses took too long to complete and so were supplemented by quicker expedients of a year or less.

As a result, the working-class composition of all college students rose from about 25 percent in 1927–1928 to more than 50 percent in 1932–1933 (up from 15 percent in 1923–1924). Fitzpatrick calculates that two out of every three students in Soviet higher education as of 1932–1933 would not have gained entry into the pre-1928 system. And of those two "new" students, one was promoted from the adult worker and CPSU category while the other was from a more mixed background which included peasants, teachers, and lower-level office workers.[7]

When the policy changed in the early 1930s and class or social background ceased to be a criterion for enrollment, the new students were not purged from the system but went on to become the foundation of the Soviet Union's new educated and political elites. It was on this basis that the new proletarian and

---

[7] Fitzpatrick, *Education and Social Mobility*, pp. 188–189; Lapidus, "Educational Strategies and Cultural Revolution," p. 83. According to official figures, workers constituted 51.4 percent of all tertiary students in early 1934, and laboring peasants accounted for another 16.5 percent. See J. V. Stalin, "Report to the Seventeenth Party Congress on the Work of the Central Committee of the C.P.S.U. (B)," 26 Jan. 1934, in *Works*, 13 vols. (Moscow: Foreign Languages Publishing House, 1952–1955), 13:345.

old bourgeois intellectuals ultimately merged. But the adventure in radicalism to which the former owed their rise was soon officially repudiated and then "lost" by historians both Western and Soviet, each for their own reasons. The militants who implemented the adventure became a forgotten generation of political activists. This left the regimented industrial model with its "classless" new elite to stand alone as the sole legacy of the Stalin era.[8]

By the early 1950s, however, the CPSU's Central Committee of 125 full members included at least 37 who gained admission to institutions of higher learning under the late 1920s adult promotion programs. One of the 37 was Nikita Khrushchev, who had entered the Moscow Industrial Academy from a working-class background at age 35. At this institution then "teeming with rightists," Khrushchev studied and led the struggle against them between 1929 and 1931, when he was a staunch defender of Stalin and the Party's "general line." Underlying that struggle was Stalin's observation, which Khrushchev endorsed even 40 years later, that Stalin's Trotskyite and rightist opponents had taken refuge in scientific and technological institutions after being removed from Party posts, whereas those responsible for Party work who "stood firmly for the General Line" had no opportunity to further their education. Not surprising then that in the mid-1950s, Khrushchev would revive some of the ideas and aims of the earlier period and even recall some of its aging activists in the service of his more famous struggle against the Stalinist legacy created in the interim.[9]

It was also appropriate that Mao should honor his host with the highest form of flattery when the leaders of the international communist movement gathered in Moscow for the 40th anniversary of the Bolshevik Revolution in November 1957. Khrushchev's fond remembrance of things past evidently extended also to Stalin's adventurous production targets during the Soviet Union's FFYP. Khrushchev announced in a November 1957 speech that the Soviet Union would overtake the United States in the production of both heavy industry and consumer goods within 15 years. Mao had already convinced CCP leaders to have another go with his great leap approach. In Moscow, he could therefore match Khrushchev's boast by vowing to overtake the United Kingdom economically within 15 years.[10]

---

[8] For a more conventional account, see Fainsod on higher education in Smolensk between 1929 and 1931. The events he describes are much the same as the above but Fainsod interprets them as part of the overall effort to communize Soviet society and bring education under CPSU control rather than as a distinct cultural revolution interlude (Merle Fainsod, *Smolensk under Soviet Rule* [London: Macmillan, 1958], chap. 18).

[9] *Khrushchev Remembers*, trans. Strobe Talbott (London: Andre Deutsch, 1971), pp. 38–39, and also pp. 36–44. See also Fitzpatrick, *Education and Social Mobility*, pp. 246, 328 n. 5; Fitzpatrick, "Cultural Revolution as Class War," in Fitzpatrick, *Cultural Revolution in Russia*, p. 40.

[10] Roderick MacFarquhar, *The Origins of the Cultural Revolution: The Great Leap Forward, 1958–1960* (New York: Columbia University Press, 1983), pp. 16–17.

Early Stalin and late Mao: mechanical copying backward
in time?

Another set of clues can thus be found in Khrushchev's memories of Stalin's general line and the CCP's 1958 response in kind. As indicated, cultural revolution–type activity was not the only noteworthy feature of the Soviet Union's FFYP. The period has, in fact, always been best known for its high-speed approach to industrial production and agricultural collectivization. It was the sum total of these events which combined to form the "general line" of Khrushchev's remembrance. A few quotations from Stalin himself should suffice to set the scene for comparative purposes.

In his report to the 16th CPSU Congress in June 1930, Stalin characterized the time as "a period of intensified socialist construction both in industry and in agriculture." The 16th Congress was "the congress of the *sweeping offensive* of socialism *along the whole front*, of the elimination of the kulaks as a class, and of the realisation of complete collectivisation. There you have in a few words the essence of our Party's general line."[11] Implementing the new line meant "amending and giving precision to the five-year plan by accelerating tempo and shortening time schedules." Production targets doubled and tripled.[12]

As to how such rates of growth were possible, Stalin in 1930 sounded like Mao many decades later: "The Central Committee is of the opinion that the reconstruction of the technical basis of industry and agriculture *under the socialist organisation of production* creates such possibilities of accelerating tempo as no capitalist country can dream of."[13]

> It may be said that in altering the estimates of the five-year plan so radically the Central Committee is violating the principle of planning and discrediting the planning organisations. But only hopeless bureaucrats can talk like that. For us Bolsheviks, the five-year plan is not something fixed once and for all. For us the five-year plan, like every other, is merely a plan adopted as first approximation. . . . Only bureaucrats can think that the work of planning *ends* with the drafting of a plan. The drafting of a plan is only the *beginning of planning*.[14]

Socialist construction was also complicated by a reflection of the class struggle within the CPSU itself. Since it was the very moment when the "roots of capitalism" were being torn out, rightists posed a greater threat than leftists because the former were inclined to compromise with the class enemy. Rightists were distinguished by their belief that socialism could be "built on the

[11] J. V. Stalin, "Political Report of the Central Committee to the Sixteenth Congress of the C.P.S.U. (B)," 27 June 1930, in *Works*, 12:352, emphasis in the original.
[12] Ibid., pp. 355–356, 359. See also Isaac Deutscher, *Stalin: A Political Biography* (New York: Vintage Books, 1960), pp. 317–332.
[13] "Political Report to the Sixteenth Congress," pp. 358–359.
[14] Ibid., p. 357.

quiet, automatically, without class struggle."[15] Stalin had earlier elaborated the rightist danger as a tendency "to depart from the general line of our Party in the direction of bourgeois ideology" by denying the need for an offensive against capitalist elements in the countryside, demanding a slowdown in industry, or rejecting the need to fight against bureaucratism by methods of self-criticism, all of which strengthened the possibility of capitalist restoration.[16]

On other relevant points, Stalin emerged during this period as an eloquent Maoist-like champion of mass action: for developing production, as an active component of class struggle, and in the cultural revolutionary sense of combining educational development for the masses with the exercise of public power. On mass action in production: "Certain 'comrades' of the bureaucratic type think that emulation is just the latest Bolshevik fashion. . . . In point of fact, emulation is *the communist method of building socialism*, on the basis of the maximum *activity* of the vast masses of the working people."[17]

On mass action in class and cultural struggle:

> Why has the slogan of self-criticism acquired special importance just now, at this particular moment of history, in 1928? . . .
>
> Because the subversive activities of the class enemies of the Soviet Government, who are utilising our weaknesses, our errors, . . . are more glaringly evident now than they were a year or two ago. . . .
>
> It is not just *any kind* of self-criticism that we need. We need such self-criticism as will raise the cultural level of the working class, enhance its fighting spirit, fortify its faith in victory, augment its strength and help it to become the real master of the country.[18]

Further on mass action in cultural revolution:

> The question of the cultural powers of the working class is a decisive one. Why? Because, of all the ruling classes that have hitherto existed, the working class, as a ruling class, occupies a somewhat special and not altogether favourable position in history. . . . The working class differs . . . among other things, in that it is not a wealthy class, that it was not able formerly to train in its sons the knowledge and faculty of government, and has become able to do so only now, after coming to power.
>
> That, incidentally, is the reason why the question of a cultural revolution is so acute with us. . . . therefore, every means capable of promoting the development of the cultural powers of the working class, every means capable of facilitating the development in the working class of the faculty

---

[15] Ibid., p. 369.

[16] J. V. Stalin, "The Right Danger in the C.P.S.U. (B)," 19 Oct. 1928, in *Works*, 11:234–235.

[17] J. V. Stalin, "Emulation and Labour Enthusiasm of the Masses," 11 May 1929, in 12:114–115, emphasis in the original.

[18] J. V. Stalin, "Against Vulgarising the Slogan of Self-Criticism," 26 June 1928, in *Works*, 11:136, 138, emphasis in the original.

and ability to administer the country and industry – every such means must be utilised by us to the full.[19]

On the corollary questions of education and management, the "broad mass of the workers" had to participate in the management of industry. The working class had to "master technical knowledge." And technical colleges had to do a better job of training "Red experts." "The method of training them must be changed, and changed in such a way that already in their first years of training in the technical colleges they have continuous contact with production, with factory, mine and so forth." Otherwise, they "will never get the upper hand over the old experts, who have been steeled by practical experience but are hostile to our cause."[20]

Stalin also displayed a Maoist-like ability to manipulate the mass campaign, pushing it from right to left and then back to center or through the necessary phases from inaction, to excess, achievement, and consolidation. "Our campaign for intensifying self-criticism began only a few months ago," he wrote in mid-1928, but the returns were already beginning to come in. On the positive side, workers production conferences and temporary control commissions were being restored, production managers were "beginning to smarten up" after criticism, the press was growing livelier, and worker and village journalists were becoming "a weighty political force." But balanced against these positive results were the excesses: "vulgarizing the slogan of self-criticism" by distorting it with witch-hunts and kangaroo courts.[21] The 1930 "Dizzy with Success" article was written in the same vein. Having launched the drive to collectivize agriculture at full speed and destroy the kulaks, Stalin then cautioned against the use of excessive force and the assumption that the process could be achieved at one stroke.[22]

By the 17th CPSU Congress, in January 1934, however, the high tides had passed. At the 15th Congress (1927), said Stalin, we still had to prove the Party line was correct, and at the 16th Congress we had to deal final blows against the opposition. "At this congress, however, there is nothing to prove and, it seems, no one to fight. Everyone sees that the line of the Party has triumphed."[23] Stalin also chose this forum to end the Soviet experiment with agricultural communes in favor of the artel, or collective farm. The latter socialized only the means of production, whereas the former "until recently" had socialized all aspects of everyday life. In order to save themselves from extinction, claimed

[19] J. V. Stalin, "The Work of the April Joint Plenum of the Central Committee and Central Control Commission," 13 April 1928, in *Works*, 11:41.

[20] Ibid., p. 64.

[21] "Against Vulgarising the Slogan of Self-Criticism," in *Works*, 11:133–144.

[22] J. V. Stalin, "Dizzy with Success: Concerning Questions of the Collective-Farm Movement," 2 Mar. 1930, in *Works*, 12:197–205.

[23] J. V. Stalin, "Report to the Seventeenth Party Congress," in *Works*, 13:354.

Stalin, the communes "have been compelled to abandon the system of social-ising everyday life; they are beginning to work on the basis of the workday unit, and have begun to distribute grain among their members, to permit their members to own poultry, small livestock, a cow, etc." The commune could still be honored in theory as the higher form of the collective farm movement, but in practice, it should be left to the future when it could be re-created on the basis of more "developed technique" and an "abundance of produce."[24]

The basic similarities between the course followed by Stalin during the Soviet Union's FFYP and that adopted by Mao during China's second are striking. The key features in common were high-speed socialization of agricul-ture, rapid industrial growth, and cultural revolution, all formulated as a "general line for socialist construction." Otherwise known as the Great Leap Forward, the Chinese version of the general line was formally launched in May 1958. The CCP declared itself to be "entering a new period of socialist con-struction centered on the technical and cultural revolutions."[25]

Concrete measures were announced throughout the summer. For steel pro-duction, Mao himself doubled the 1958 output target (by comparison with 1957) and then trebled it for 1959. Chinese agriculture had already been collec-tivized in 1955–1956. Now the small agricultural producers cooperatives, aver-aging 164 households each, were merged and expanded within a matter of months to include several thousand households organized into communes. These socialized all aspects of rural life and were proclaimed as the vehicle for launching China into a state of pure communism. Claims to originality were clearly implied if not declared outright. "In 1958, a new social organization appeared like the sun rising above the broad horizon of East Asia," began the formal Party resolution on the communes.[26]

The cultural revolution was declared under way in June 1958. It was defined as including both conventional education development and a class-based mass-line movement led by the CCP rather than by professional educators. "The cultural revolution is a movement for the cultural emancipation [*fanshen*] of all the laboring people."[27] If in overall conception the Great Leap seemed to reflect a more distant past, specific reforms for education also had a more immediate reference point. Indeed, so closely did the official Chinese directive parallel contemporary Soviet efforts that the former was published on 20 September, just one day ahead of Khrushchev's proposals for Soviet education, which appeared in penultimate formulation on 21 September.

[24] Ibid., pp. 358–361.
[25] *Renmin ribao*, 29 May 1958; see also Liu Shaoqi's work report delivered on 5 May 1958, in *Renmin ribao*, 27 May 1958, trans. in Bowie and Fairbank, *Communist China*, pp. 416–438.
[26] "Guanyu renmin gongshe ruogan wenti de jueji" (Decision on Some Problems concerning the People's Communes), 10 Dec. 1958, *Renmin ribao*, 19 Dec. 1958, trans. in Bowie and Fairbank, *Communist China*, pp. 488–503.
[27] *Renmin ribao*, 9 June 1958; see also *Jiaoshibao*, 10 June 1958.

The 1958 education reforms: mechanical copying by another name?

By September 1958, of course, the Chinese had become more circumspect in acknowledging their debts of inspiration to the Soviet Union. During 1956 and 1957, however, exchanges between the two communist partners continued as before, leaving the Chinese well informed about the reforms being discussed in the Soviet Union. We have already seen how delegations moving between the two countries publicized the Soviet reform proposals and how these proposals entered into the Chinese blooming-and-contending debates of those years. In early 1957, the Soviet reform proposals were being explained as a search for solutions in four specific areas: (1) how best to implement the resolutions of the 20th CPSU Congress and universalize secondary schooling during the Sixth Five-Year Plan, (2) how to teach effectively comprehensive technical and labor subjects, (3) how to create new-style boarding schools for the especially talented, and (4) how to improve the quality of ordinary schools.[28]

After Party rectification had devolved into the antirightist campaign, authoritative commentator Zhang Jian elaborated the Soviets' reform proposals as measures to correct their previous one-sided emphasis on theory and academic learning. He singled out the proposal – clearly a successor of earlier adult promotion schemes – whereby young people would have to work for a few years after secondary school before going on to college. Having acquired the habit of labor, they could then enter college as true "worker–peasant intellectuals."

University graduates would also have to complete two to three years of practical work before receiving their diplomas and job titles. Soviet schools, reported Zhang, were also trying to simplify courses and strengthen ties with production. Not all these new measures would be applicable to China, but "their direction and basic demands must be of great use to our country's educational enterprise in terms of inspiration and the lessons drawn from them." Especially as an antidote for mechanical copying, Soviet lessons should be combined with those learned about popular education in the old liberated

---

[28] Yi. An. Kai-luo-fu, "Guanyu gaijin he tigao Sulian putong xuexiao de jiaoyu zhiliang wenti" (On the Problems of Improving and Raising Educational Quality in the Soviet Union's Ordinary Schools), *Renmin jiaoyu*, Mar. 1957, pp. 4–9. Visiting-delegation reports have been cited above (Chen Zenggu, "General Report on an Investigation Visit to the Soviet Union," and Mo-luo-zi-ang, "The Decisions of the Soviet Union's 20th Communist Party Congress and the Tasks of the Soviet Union's Schools"). Also on Soviet reforms at this time, see Ma-er-gu-she-wei-qi, "Guanyu Sulian putong xuexiao shishi zonghe jishu jiaoyu de jige wenti" (On Some Problems of Carrying out Comprehensive Technical Education in the Soviet Union's Ordinary Schools), *Renmin jiaoyu*, June 1956, pp. 7–15; Xie. Na-wu-mo-fu, "Tan Sulian guomin jiaoyu de jixiang renwu" (Discussing Some Tasks of National Education in the Soviet Union), ibid., Jan. 1957, pp. 7–12.

areas before 1949.[29] This statement indicating the Chinese intention to combine a reformed Soviet model with their Yan'an heritage was nevertheless among the last to advocate learning from the Soviet Union directly in any form.[30]

Changes along these lines had actually begun for Soviet education in 1954–1955 with the introduction of manual skills training and a more practical orientation in science teaching. Despite Khrushchev's much-quoted comments about the weaknesses of Soviet education at the 20th CPSU Congress, however, Soviet educators resisted the reform proposals in practice. Only about one-fourth of all general secondary schools were following the new experimental curriculum by mid-1958: hence Khrushchev's more drastic formulation published in *Pravda* under the Dewey-like title "Strengthening the Ties of School with Life" on 21 September 1958. This version formed the basis of an education reform law promulgated in December.[31]

The impetus underlying the Soviet reforms appeared to be both practical and ideological. Khrushchev expressed concern about the developing white-collar mentality, which disdained practical work and manual labor. He also complained that only a few students in Moscow's tertiary institutions were of worker–peasant origin. But the Soviet system was also moving toward full and universal secondary schooling, heightening typical developmental concerns about how to create a system that would be college preparatory for some and terminal for most. The proposals therefore anticipated more practical content at the elementary and lower-secondary grades, with expanded availability to make eight years of schooling universal. Grades 9 and 10 were to become work oriented. Several work–study options were promoted for these grades. Most

[29] Zhang Jian, "Xuexi Sulian jingyan de chengji bushi zhuyao de ma" (Have Not the Achievements Been the Main Thing in Learning from the Soviet Experience?), *Renmin jiaoyu*, Aug. 1957, p. 18.

[30] The Soviet reforms themselves, however, continued to be well covered by the Chinese press, including Khrushchev's 21 Sept. formulation and the final version promulgated in Dec. 1958 (e.g., *Renmin ribao*, 22 Sept. and 22 Dec. 1958). The Soviet education reforms were described as running parallel to their contemporary Chinese counterparts and were described in similar terms by the Chinese press through mid-1959 (e.g., *Renmin ribao*, 1958: 23 Jan., 1, 29 Apr., 6 June, 18 Sept., 5, 17 Nov., 16, 25 Dec.; and 1959: 27 Feb., 13 Apr., 6, 20, 29 June, 30 July, 21 Aug.). Soviet experts and advisors were recalled in Aug. 1960 (Mikhail A. Klochko, *Soviet Scientist in Red China*, trans. Andrew MacAndrew [New York: Praeger, 1964], chap. 13).

[31] Western sources on the Khrushchev era reforms for Soviet education include Nigel Grant, *Soviet Education*, 4th ed. (New York: Penguin, 1979), pp. 102–104, 109–117; Mervyn Matthews, *Education in the Soviet Union: Policies and Institutions since Stalin* (London: George Allen and Unwin, 1982), pp. 15–39; Mervyn Matthews, *Privilege in the Soviet Union: A Study of Elite Life-styles under Communism* (London: George Allen and Unwin, 1978), pp. 114–117, 126–130; George Z. F. Bereday, William W. Brickman, and Gerald H. Read, eds., *The Changing Soviet School* (Boston: Houghton Mifflin, 1960), pp. 86–100, 290–291; Jaan Pennar, Ivan I. Bakalo, and George Z. F. Bereday, *Modernization and Diversity in Soviet Education* (New York: Praeger, 1971), pp. 102–117.

students would also have to work for at least two years prior to entering college.

Strangely, given their otherwise egalitarian and working-class ethos, the reform proposals up through their 21 September formulation also called for the creation of special boarding schools as highlighted in the early 1957 Chinese report. These were to be the destination of the nation's brightest youth – not only in the fine arts as was already customary but in the sciences as well – where students would receive instruction appropriate to their talents. Apparently, this idea derived from a concern about preserving quality in a mass system. But the proposal proved too controversial due to its elitist implications and was dropped from the reforms as officially promulgated in December 1958. The school system remained officially, at least, unstreamed, uniform, and coeducational, with the old academic orientation replaced by a combination of academic and practical training in some variation for everyone.

Among other reforms, the rigid rules for classroom behavior were relaxed. Emphasis on homework was reduced. Students were made responsible for school cleaning and maintenance. Year-end final exams at the secondary level were replaced by grade assessments. In keeping with the tenor of the reforms, some effort was also made at this time to reduce income differentials generally. In 1959, a new law authorized the work unit to recommend candidates for college from among employees, with the understanding that they would return to the enterprise upon graduation.

The Chinese equivalent was the Directive on Education Work issued on 19 September 1958.[32] It called for a cultural revolution and criticized education work for the errors of neglecting politics, Party leadership, and productive labor. The new aim was to "train tens of millions of red and expert working-class intellectuals." Quantitative goals were as extravagant for education as for the economy. Within three to five years from 1958, illiteracy was to be basically eradicated and elementary schooling universalized. Within the same time, every agricultural producers cooperative would have a secondary school, and nurseries and kindergartens would be established for all pre-school-age children. Within 15 years, college education would be available for everyone with the necessary qualifications who wanted it; improving the quality of higher education could then be pursued during the 15 years thereafter. To achieve these aims, many different forms of schooling would be used: schools run by the state and by the people; general education and vocational training; education

---

[32] Published in *Renmin ribao*, 20 Sept. 1958. The directive was much reprinted, together with the official elaboration of the new line it represented, by Lu Dingyi. Lu's statement, which actually predated the decision, was first published in the CCP's new theoretical journal, *Hongqi* (Red Flag): Lu Dingyi, "Jiaoyu bixu yu shengchan laodong xiangjiehe" (Education Must Be Combined with Productive Labor), dated 16 Aug. 1958, in *Hongqi*, Beijing, no. 7 (1958), pp. 1–12.

for children and for adults; full-day schools, work–study schools, and spare-time schools; and schools that charged tuition as well as those that did not.

The September 1958 directive also contained a measure comparable to Khrushchev's boarding-schools proposal, however. In the Chinese version, some existing schools should be given responsibility for raising the quality of education. Such schools were to maintain a complete curriculum and pay attention to raising the quality of their own teaching and research. Thus, even this most radical of directives had a place in its heart for key-point schools, although the term was not actually used to identify the institutions that would be entrusted with maintaining system quality. And unlike the Khrushchev proposals on this point, the quality schools soon emerged to dominate the Chinese system of the early 1960s.

Nevertheless, productive labor was to be introduced into the curriculum in all schools at all levels, and every student would be required to participate. Politics was the extra feature in the Chinese directive, and it stipulated measures for more, rather than less, CCP leadership over education, reaffirming the Party's response to the "rightist" challenge of 1957. Additionally, in order to consolidate the break with bourgeois academic authority in all schools at the secondary and tertiary levels, six measures were advanced. These were designed to institutionalize the participation (under the leadership of each school's Party committee) of teachers, students, and staff in management, teaching, and research.

The first of these six "mass-line work methods" was the free airing of views (*daming dafang*) and big-character posters (*dazibao*), a reference to the conventional ways and means of Chinese student protest which were now advocated for common use: to raise political consciousness, improve teaching quality, and promote unity. Teachers and students should participate together in preparing school education plans and course outlines. The professional teaching staff should be augmented by people with practical experience. Students were to participate in assessing the performance of their classmates. Leadership personnel, including Party and Youth League cadres, were instructed to fraternize as much as possible with students in life and labor. Teachers were to maintain close contacts with students, establishing mutual relationships based on "democratic equality." School finances and building plans should be made public to allow teachers, students, and staff to participate in management.

No wonder Khrushchev was so angry with the Chinese. He must have felt as though he was seeing himself twice removed in a kind of double-vision mirror. One image reflected his current attempts to reform the Soviet system, the other reflected more dimly his own radical youth, and the Chinese were claiming original credit for both without giving him so much as a footnote of recognition. Adding insult to injury, they were also flouting his criticism of

Stalin's personality cult by fulsomely citing Mao Zedong as the font of all their revolutionary "innovations."

CCP theoretician Chen Boda did the honors during a mid-1958 speech at Beijing University in what should have been billed as the introductory formulation of the Party's renewed search for an independent identity. "Marx and Lenin are our great teachers," said Chen, "but revolution must rely on the people of each country. . . . Everyone knows that the reason Comrade Mao Zedong became the great standard-bearer of the Chinese revolution was just because he worked ceaselessly to accomplish this mission. . . . Comrade Mao Zedong is able to examine and explore China's various characteristics without being bound in the least by formalism." Chen listed Mao's many contributions. He had rejected the old view that socialist ownership was sufficient without continuous struggle on the political and ideological fronts. As far back as Jiangxi, he had combined revolution with construction. After 1949, he emphasized "the great and latent power of the Chinese working people in the development of the productive forces." After socialist transformation, he emphasized the question of scale. Cultural education was also moving in the direction advocated by Mao, that is, transforming workers and peasants into intellectuals and the latter into workers and peasants. The conception of the commune as the basic unit of society was "a conclusion drawn by Comrade Mao Zedong from real life." Under the direction of Mao's thought, it was possible to envisage the "gradual transition of our country from socialism to communism."[33]

The great irony underlying the 1958 Chinese adventure and the 1966–1976 Cultural Revolution, then, was their promotion as a distinct Chinese path without crediting Soviet precedents. Yet the 1966–1976 episode would ultimately reproduce in essence, style, and aims the earlier 1928–1931 Soviet period. And the key connecting link between them was the experience of 1956–1958, when Khrushchev's attempts – containing elements revived from his own youth as a cultural revolutionary – to reorient the Stalinist model were initially acknowledged by the Chinese as an inspiration for their own similar efforts.

Certainly, one cannot but question how much longer it might have taken Chinese education decision makers to hit upon the particular solutions they did for the tensions building up around their imported Stalin model without Khrushchev's conveniently timed proposals. And concerning the concept of cultural revolution as a necessity to prevent capitalist restoration by breaking bourgeois influence over the superstructure, one must also question whether the Chinese endeavor, first in 1958 and then again more ambitiously between 1966 and 1976, would have taken the peculiar form it did without the prior Soviet example.

---

[33] Chen Boda, "Zai Mao Zedong tongzhi de qizhi xia" (Under the Banner of Comrade Mao Zedong), *Hongqi*, no. 4 (1958), pp. 1–12; from Chen's speech at Beijing University commemorating the 37th anniversary of the founding of the CCP.

Since no smoking guns have as yet emerged from CCP archives, it must be left to others to document Mao's conscious reliance on Stalin and Khrushchev for inspiration after 1958. But at least it cannot be argued that the Chinese were ignorant of the similarities between their own "winding path" and that followed by the Soviet Union before them. And just as they were well briefed on Khrushchev's reform proposals, so they also must have known what else happened in the Soviet Union between 1927 and 1931 besides high-speed industrialization and collectivization. Even if the Soviets did not provide the necessary internal documents detailing Soviet educational history more candidly than the revised outline presented in 1956, Chinese Party theoreticians could still have deduced all they needed to know from the above-cited version of Stalin's works, published in Chinese translation as they were in English during the 1950s.[34] Erudite contributors to *Teachers News* were not alone in referring to Stalin's earlier writings. Similar scattered references ran throughout the political discourse of the period.

One of the few direct, albeit unelaborated allusions to his presumed debt of inspiration appeared in Mao's early-1960s critique of Soviet economics when he indicated both that he was familiar with the earlier Soviet experience and that his quarrel was with the Soviet present rather than its past:

> In 1928, the Central Committee of the CPSU passed a resolution saying: "Only with the Party and the great masses of workers and peasants mobilized to the greatest extent will it be possible to solve the task of technologically and economically catching up with and overtaking the capitalist countries." This is very well put. It is exactly what we are now doing. At that time, Stalin had nothing else to rely on but the masses, so he demanded the Party and the worker–peasant masses to mobilize to the greatest degree. Later, when they had a bit more, they did not rely on the masses in that way.[35]

The assumption here, in any case, is that similarities between the Soviet and Chinese experiences were too great to be purely coincidental. Nor should they be written off as spontaneously generated phenomena of early-stage Marxist–Leninist revolutions – as the *Teachers News* writer had so diplomatically suggested upon reading Stalin's 1930 "Dizzy with Success" article. Similar functional necessities existed, to be sure. In 1958, the CCP found itself at a stage comparable to that of the Soviet Union, not in the mid-1950s, but circa 1928, a decade into its revolution with little yet to show for its claims of socialist superiority. And as the hundred-flowers episode had just confirmed, Chinese intellectuals were still unreconstructed, recalcitrant, and reproducing themselves in the younger generation. In both cases – that is, Russia in 1928 and

[34] *Sidalin quanji* (Stalin's Collected Works), 13 vols. (Beijing: Renmin chubanshe, 1953–1958). My thanks to Nina Halpern for this citation.
[35] Mao Zedong, "Sulian *Zhengzhi jingji xue* dushu biji," p. 392.

China in 1958 – committed Communists could rightly assume that without extraction, the "roots of capitalism" might well produce a restoration.

That the Chinese were self-consciously continuing their effort to translate Marxism–Leninism into proper Chinese also seems clear, however. Less so is whether the line they drew from 1958 through the 1966–1976 Cultural Revolution met the criteria for creative adaptation or was only another instance of mechanical copying. The reinterpretation here suggests that Maoist claims to originality were exaggerated, to say the least. Not only did Chinese leaders have to relearn the lesson of mechanical copying the hard way at a stage when they should have known better, but even after Stalin's death they seemed not to have outgrown the habit of intellectual/political dependency. Mao and the political strategists around him were evidently looking backward for inspiration and authoritative foreign precedents to an earlier time when the Russian revolution was at a stage of development closer to their own in the late 1950s. The resulting adaptation therefore did not deserve its self-proclaimed status as a Chinese original inspired by superstructural concerns of cultural revolution and rural-oriented mass activism.

A seemingly more appropriate interpretation would portray China's post-1949 experience with its communist import as similar to that of earlier decades: characterized by a pattern of attraction, followed by a reaction against the overt dependency and dislocations fostered in the process. A fact of ongoing importance, however, was the ambivalence also inherent in the process, ensuring that the bonds were never entirely broken. American influence in Chinese education, which peaked during the early 1920s, retreated before the subsequent critical backlash but never disappeared entirely. Similarly, the CCP led the rush to embrace Soviet big brother in a dependency relationship fostered, as Mao said, by inexperience. But he lacked experience in conceptualizing cultural revolution as well and probably did not venture into that unknown territory without the prop of authoritative foreign references. Hence, what was presented to the world in the 1960s as China's distinctive socialist path should be seen more accurately as a Sino-Soviet synthesis of mass movement radicalism.

The foregoing reinterpretation of Maoist claims to originality does not, however, negate the Chinese experience after 1960 in defining their own way independent of the Soviet Union *at that time* and going it alone in practical terms without Soviet experts, advice, aid, etc. Returning to a basic question posed at the outset of this study, namely, whether and to what extent the Chinese model of the 1970s was actually what it purported to be, the claim that it had surmounted the dependency syndrome afflicting other Third World countries was not unfounded. However qualified by their debts of inspiration to the prior Soviet example, the Chinese version of cultural revolution was also different in degree and played a central role for Mao that was soon rejected by

Stalin. The latter's assertion of unity in the early 1930s signified the end of his brief mass-line adventure and his shift to other "bureaucratic" means of dispatching his enemies. By contrast, the Chinese soon sharpened the relatively benign 1958 definition of cultural revolution into an overall strategy for perpetuating mass-activated class struggle that would characterize their way until Mao's death in 1976.

Even as the Chinese economy reeled under the dislocations created by the Great Leap Forward in 1958 and 1959 – or perhaps because those dislocations signified the fantasy of leaping into pure communism – cultural revolution emerged as the centerpiece of Mao's new line. The Soviet Union had stopped midway. The Chinese would use cultural revolution to keep their quest alive. By 1960, the concept was being publicized as a key feature of continuous revolution, which was, in turn, the prerequisite for achieving communism. Such aims were elaborated in June at a highly publicized national conference of cultural revolutionaries (advanced education and culture workers of proclaimed worker–peasant origins). The struggle, said keynote speaker Lin Feng, would be conducted both by universalizing education and by "thorough eradication" of the bourgeoisie's still pervasive "class ideology."[36]

Accordingly, education for workers and peasants was a necessary condition but not, as some "bourgeois intellectuals" thought, the only one. In addition, the Party's "militant program" (*zhandou gangling*) for educational development stipulated that manual labor must be accepted by all as the "first necessity of human life," essential for realizing communism.[37] In this manner, the old pre-1949 critique of education was moving forward with Chinese communism into its most radical cultural revolution stage.

[36] From Lin's speech in *Renmin ribao*, 2 June 1960. Lin Feng was a leader from Yan'an days. See also Lu Dingyi's speech in ibid. Lu still headed the CCP Central Committee's Propaganda Department at this time and was also a vice-premier of the national government. Also on the conference, see chap. 13, n. 51, below.

[37] Chi Liaozhou, "Wenhua jiaoyu gongzuo de zhandou gangling" (A Militant Program for Cultural and Educational Work), *Zhongguo qingnian*, no. 12 (June 1960), pp. 2–3.

12

The great leap in education

The claims for 1958 were extravagant, befitting the high tide of a national mass movement on all fronts. Production targets for industry and agriculture began leaping and bounding. "As I see now, there has never been such an upsurge of enthusiasm and initiative among the masses of the people on the production front," declared Mao in his February 1958 guidelines for the Great Leap Forward.[1]

In the countryside, agricultural producers cooperatives merged to form much larger communes. Instead of hundreds of people working together and jointly sharing the income earned, now thousands did so. Cooking pots went into local smelters, bolstering the great leap in iron and steel production. Commune mess halls were promoted as successors to the family kitchen while nurseries and "happiness homes" cared for young and old. Freed from household chores, women were mobilized to join the work force outside the home in numbers greater than ever before, and they were needed as never before. China's enormous population was transformed overnight from a liability into an asset, much as the mini-leap of 1956 had turned too many school graduates into too few. Now all hands were needed for massive public works, farmland capital construction, dam building, canal digging, coal mining, smelting, and all the projects necessary to create communist economies of scale upon a base of only just collectivized and not yet mechanized peasant producers.

In north China, preparations commenced to restore Pingyuan Province, created originally from the communist border regions in the 1940s, at the juncture of Henan, Hebei, and Shandong. Now it was to become the first province to achieve communism, based upon the system of wartime remuneration in the old liberated areas, where people had worked for austerity rations of food and clothing and little else. Similarly, in communist Pingyuan, wages were to be abolished and material goods distributed according to need.

---

[1] Mao Zedong, "60 Work Methods (Draft)," issued by the CCP Central Committee, 19 Feb. 1958, trans. in *CB*, no. 892 (21 Oct. 1969). For background discussion of this document, see MacFarquhar, Cheek, and Wu, *Secret Speeches of Chairman Mao*, text 15, pp. 377–391.

Mobilization

Along with Mao's guidelines, the February 1958 National People's Congress meeting marked the onset of full-scale mobilization in all sectors. Major speeches launched the movement for education. In an act more symbolic than substantive, the congress formally abolished the Soviet-style ministerial division and recombined the two education ministries into one.[2] Most widely publicized among educators, however, were the special meetings convened by Premier Zhou Enlai and addressed by Kang Sheng. The latter seemed an unlikely choice but quickly emerged as chief public promoter for the Great Leap's educational component, known as the "education revolution of 1958." Kang Sheng appeared repeatedly in 1958, both alone and with others, to champion the causes ultimately formalized in the 19 September directive (discussed in chap. 11).[3]

In February, Zhou and Kang challenged educator representatives at the

[2] *Jiaoshibao*, 4, 11, 14 Feb. 1958. Minister of Higher Education Yang Xiufeng was named to head the newly reconstituted Ministry of Education.

[3] Kang Sheng's main areas of expertise were Party organization, political intelligence, and ideology, from the 1920s until his death in 1975. He spent the mid-1930s in the Soviet Union, returning to Yan'an with Sinicized Russian and a similarly Sinicized view of his experience. He allegedly used his friendship with fellow Shandong provincial Jiang Qing, who was about to become Mao's wife, to gain access to Mao's ear, which he filled with a distorted interpretation of all things Soviet (according to hostile Soviet witness Peter Vladimirov: *The Vladimirov Diaries: Yenan, China, 1942–1945* [Garden City, N.Y.: Doubleday, 1975]). Hence it is tempting to speculate that he played the role of idea man – perhaps along with Chen Boda – helping Mao translate into proper Chinese Stalin's ways and especially his cultural revolutionary means, although none of Kang's biographers drew this particular link. But he emerged as a prominent champion of Maoist proletarian cultural goals during each of their three main "high tides." In Yan'an, he was not only chief of security and intelligence but head of the five-man standing committee in charge of the Party rectification campaign (Seybolt, "Terror and Conformity," p. 46; John Byron and Robert Pack, *The Claws of the Dragon: Kang Sheng – The Evil Genius behind Mao* [New York: Simon and Schuster, 1992], chaps. 7–8. The pinnacle of his career in these respects came much later, however, when he assumed a high-profile leading role during the mobilization phase of the 1966–1976 Cultural Revolution. Unfortunately, Kang's activities in between – when the concepts and goals of cultural revolution were being formulated for application in Chinese practice – remain obscure.

Apparently in self-imposed retirement during the early 1950s, Kang was demoted from full to alternate member status within the ruling CCP Political Bureau in 1956. Then, resuming his career, he became deputy head of the Party's Central Group on Culture and Education in early 1957, the highest body with responsibility for propaganda, education, and culture. His brief was further refined when he became head of a "theoretical small group" within the larger body. Chen Boda headed the Political Research Office set up by the Political Bureau in 1956. Both men sustained their careers at this time by exploiting their close relationship with Mao and their expertise as Marxist theoreticians (Byron and Pack, *Claws of the Dragon*, chap. 11). Kang threw himself into "superstructural" work between 1957 and 1959, serving as chief Party promoter for the mobilization phase of the education revolution. This role during the Great Leap clearly presaged his emergence as a leading cultural revolutionary 10 years later. His public promotional activities during the Great Leap are recorded in the following issues of *Guangming ribao*: 23, 25, June, 11 July, 6 Aug., 9, 26 Oct., 27 Nov., and 23 Dec. 1958; 4 May 1959; 10 Feb. 1960. See also *Renmin ribao*, 15 Feb. and 23 Sept. 1958.

congress meeting to carry forward the struggle on two fronts: one, against remnant bourgeois intellectual behavior; and the other, for socialist construction following the "more, faster, better, cheaper" formula. Specifically, two methods with time-honored reformist credentials were promoted to ensure the "great forward advance" in education: "diligent work and frugal study," or work–study, for students; and *minban*, or mass-run, management for schools. Kang Sheng said that whether one looked at Marxist theory or at practice in the anti-Japanese base areas and in the Soviet Union, experience everywhere proved that unifying education with production was correct.[4]

Mao's February guidelines had listed all the ways that work–study might be arranged, and all were written into the promotional materials.[5] These dismissed concern that work–study would harm quality.[6] Fears about declining quality were as unfounded as the rightists' contention that education since 1949 was "not as good as previously," declared Kang Sheng. Teaching plans and textbooks had to be rewritten to incorporate the new requirements for students' labor and a more practical orientation in the subject matter. These revisions were supposed to be done "democratically" by students and technicians working along with professional educators.[7]

In September, Kang was off to Taiyuan with the CCP Propaganda Department director, Lu Dingyi, where they both expounded on the theme of workers studying and students working.[8] In October, Kang issued "important

---

[4] "Zhou zongli zhaokai jiaoyu wenti zuotanhui; Kang Sheng tongzhi baogao jiaoyu he shengchan jiehe wenti" (Premier Zhou Convenes Discussion Meetings on Education; Comrade Kang Sheng Reports on the Problems of Combining Education with Productive Labor), in *Qingong jianxue xuexi ziliao* (Study Materials on Diligent Work and Frugal Study) (Hangzhou: Zhejiang renmin chubanshe, 1958), pp. 29–33 (originally in *Renmin ribao* and *Guangming ribao*, both 15 Feb. 1958).

The term "diligent work and frugal study" dated from the early decades of the century and seemed to mark the onset of Chinese intellectuals' self-consciousness over their traditional exemption from manual labor. As the cultural revolutionary ethos intensified, the term was dropped, apparently due to its past bourgeois associations. Its best-known application had been in self-support schemes for study abroad, in contrast with the purer unremunerated labor of later years. In 1958, the term was explicitly defined to exclude these connotations (see below, the summary of the Apr. 1958 Fourth National Education Administration Conference, point 3). On the earlier experience, see, e.g.: Zhou Tiandu, *Cai Yuanpei zhuan* (A Biography of Cai Yuanpei) (Beijing: Renmin chubanshe, 1984), pp. 71–83; Huadong shifan daxue jiaoyu si, jiaokesuo, ed., *Zhongguo xiandai jiaoyu shi* (A History of Modern Education in China) (Shanghai: Huadong shifan daxue chubanshe, 1983), pp. 9–24; Paul Bailey, "The Chinese Work–Study Movement in France," *China Quarterly*, no. 115 (Sept. 1988), pp. 441–461; Marilyn A. Levine, *The Found Generation: Chinese Communists in Europe during the Twenties* (Seattle: University of Washington Press, 1993).

[5] Mao Zedong, "60 Work Methods," articles 48–50.

[6] E.g., the Communist Youth League's January 1958 "Decision on Diligent Work and Frugal Study for Students." The decision and the Education Ministry's endorsement circular were printed in *Jiaoshibao*, 31 Jan. and 4 Feb. 1958, respectively.

[7] E.g., *Guangming ribao*, 9, 11 July 1958; *Jiangxi ribao*, Nanchang, 12 July 1958.

[8] *Renmin ribao*, 23 Sept. 1958; *Jiangxi ribao*, 24 Sept. 1958.

instructions" after inspecting schools in Anhui. He emphasized the need for all kinds of educational institutions as the essence of the "mass line in education," which was based on two key principles: (1) proletarianization of intellectuals and intellectualization of workers and peasants; (2) "wearing caps and boots," that is, "taking secondary schools as the base while building higher-level institutions above, with elementary schools and kindergartens below," allowing the masses to move unobstructed up the educational ladder. He also visited five institutions of higher learning, bestowing an appropriate revolutionary homily at every stop: for engineering, medicine, teacher training, etc. Overall, he said, the tertiary level should rely on the experience of Party cadres and the enthusiasm of young teachers to counteract the influence of bourgeois thought in the old universities.[9]

Meanwhile, new elementary schools had been springing up everywhere "like bamboo shoots after a spring rain."[10] Additionally, some 60 million people were said to have joined the "high tide" of battle against illiteracy, and "tens of millions" attended new spare-time schools for adult peasants.[11] Making it all possible, as in Yan'an days, was the *minban* formula. It was applied increasingly during the drive to set up communes in the countryside, and in the urban areas as well. The agricultural middle school, combining the *minban* concept with work–study, represented the first attempt to promote mass secondary schooling in the countryside. As a result, secondary school enrollments were said to have doubled between 1957 and 1958.[12] The *minban* method was even applied at the tertiary level, pursuant to the goal of popularizing higher education.

Epitomizing these developments was the new Communist Labor University inaugurated in Jiangxi Province on Army Day (1 August) 1958 as a secondary and post-secondary agricultural extension program with a difference. Its network of 30 branches and 30 farms soon grew to include every county in the province. Evoking the tradition of the Jiangxi soviet, some of the first branches were established in the old base areas at Jingganshan and Ruijin, like communist versions of 1930s rural reconstruction schemes. Provincial leaders backed the project and provided it with a "ready-made" infrastructure in the form of land reclamation sites located throughout a province scarred by decades of rebellion, civil war, disease, and neglect. The aim was to break through all the

---

[9] *Guangming ribao*, 27 Nov. 1958; *Anhui ribao*, Hefei, 24 Nov. 1958.
[10] *Renmin ribao*, 10 Feb. 1958; "Never So Many at School," *Peking Review*, 23 Sept. 1958, p. 4; "Third Quarter Results: Still Faster Growth," *Peking Review*, 14 Oct. 1958, p. 14.
[11] "Zhonggong zhongyang, guowuyuan guanyu zai nongcunzhong jixu saochu wenmang he gonggu fazhan yeyu jiaoyu de tongzhi" (CCP Central Committee and State Council Circular on Continuing to Eradicate Illiteracy and Consolidating the Development of Spare-Time Education in the Countryside), 24 May 1959, reprinted in *Zhongguo jiaoyu nianjian, 1949–1981*, p. 898, trans. in Joint Publications Research Service (hereafter cited as JPRS), trans., *Compendium of Laws and Regulations of the People's Republic of China* (hereafter cited as *Compendium of Laws*), General Series: 14,346 (2 July 1962), p. 321.
[12] "Third Quarter Results."

old taboos: intellectuals would attend school and remain in the countryside as rural cadres upon graduation; while studying they would labor like ordinary peasants doing the hardest of all agricultural work by opening up wasteland on field and forest reclamation sites.[13]

A new form of college admissions was also adopted. The national unified entrance examinations were not held that year. Instead, institutions of higher learning gave their own examinations either individually or jointly, as they had prior to 1952.[14] This change actually brought China closer to Soviet practice, except that the use of political criteria also intensified. They now began to be applied not just positively but also negatively. Young people with certain kinds of family backgrounds found themselves subjected to varying degrees of discrimination. Most problematic at this stage were those whose immediate relatives had been singled out as targets in recent campaigns. If the problem was serious enough – such as having in the immediate family an active-duty GMD military officer who had fled to Taiwan – students could be prevented from entering college altogether.

Candidates of worker–peasant origin and cadres who had participated in revolutionary work were given priority. In 1958, they could be admitted on the basis of recommendation only, without taking any written entrance examinations, in contrast with recent years past when they could only be granted priority within a 10-point score range on the unified national examinations. Others similarly exempted included "young intellectuals" who had worked in industry or agriculture for two years after leaving middle school.[15] As a result of the renewed emphasis on politics and class, those from "good" worker–peasant backgrounds in China's tertiary institutions increased from 36 percent of all students in 1957, to 48 percent in 1958, and on up to 51 percent in 1959 (see Table 9.6).

Consolidation

After such excess, consolidation had to follow. The extent to which the claims of 1958 were fabricated or simply unsustainable was never revealed. Without actually acknowledging that they had been overassessed, Zhou Enlai in his government work report for 1958 presented enrollment figures somewhat lower than those issued a few months previously. His figures and those issued simultaneously by the State Statistical Bureau were 660,000 at the college level; 12

---

[13] E.g., *Jiangxi ribao*, 2 Aug. and 6 Sept. 1958.

[14] From the 1958 admissions regulations issued by the Education Ministry on 1 July 1958, published in *Guangming ribao*, 3 July 1958.

[15] From the 1958 enrollment regulations; see also explanations in *Renmin ribao* and *Guangming ribao*, both 3 July 1958; Sun Si, "Tantan jinnian gaodeng xuexiao zhaosheng gongzuo zhong de jige wenti" (Discussing a Few Questions about This Year's College Enrollment Work), *Zhongguo gingnian*, no. 13 (July 1958), pp. 19–21.

million at the secondary; and 86 million elementary school students, representing 85 percent of the age-group. One of the highest assessments for 1958 had claimed enrollments at those three levels to be 700,000, 14 million, and 92.6 million respectively (see Tables 12.1–12.3). "Last year," said Zhou, "schools at all levels experienced great development." Next must come "adjusting, consolidating, and upgrading."[16]

The episode overall, of course, was not so benign. The "law of the mass movement" decreed consolidation as a time for righting wrongs and correcting excesses. The usual retrenchments and recriminations began while the players found themselves rearranged to the right or left depending on their interests and inclinations as events developed. Defense Minister Peng Dehuai took his famous stand in opposition at the Lushan plenum of the CCP Central Committee in July–August 1959 and ended his days in political oblivion as a result. Mao Zedong stood his ground but not without accepting a measure of responsibility for some of the excesses, and targets were revised downward. Nevertheless, this was probably the first time that his instincts for manipulating the movement were seriously off cue, because the correctives did not come in time to avert disaster. Compounded by bad weather and the Soviet withdrawal, economic disruption and dislocations propelled the country into three years of severe postleap recession.

Two decades later, Mao would have to accept greater responsibility, albeit posthumously, for the debacle. Relevant statistical indicators were kept carefully hidden after 1960. But in the critical reassessment of all things associated with his rule that followed Mao's death in 1976, newly published data and calculations based thereon for the Second Five-Year Plan (1958–1962) revealed an average annual *decline* in agricultural production as well as in national income. Industrial production rose by only 3.8 percent, as compared with 18 percent during the FFYP. The per capita grain ration fell from 203 kilograms in 1957 to 163.5 kilograms in 1960, and the national mortality rate doubled during that time.[17]

Quantitative retrenchment and growth

The statistics published retroactively for education, shown in Tables 12.1–12.3, paint a somewhat different picture, however. Given the dramatic

[16] Zhou Enlai, "Zhengfu gongzuo baogao" (Government Work Report), 18 Apr. 1959, *Renmin ribao*, 19 Apr. 1959; and State Statistical Bureau, "Guanyu 1958 nian guomin jingji fazhan qingkuang de gongbao" (Report on the National Economic Development Situation for 1958), *Guangming ribao*, 15 Apr. 1959.

[17] The post-1976 Chinese data are cited in MacFarquhar, *Origins of the Cultural Revolution*, pp. 329–330. For a recently published compilation of provincial mortality rates, see Jin Zhong, "Dayuejin e si ren de xin ziliao: Zhonggong guanfang renkou tongji yanjiu" (New Data on Starvation Deaths during the Great Leap Forward: Research on Official CCP Population Statistics), *Kaifang zazhi* (Open Magazine), Hong Kong, Jan. 1994, pp. 49–53.

Table 12.1. *Number of schools and students at the elementary level during the
Great Leap Forward and its aftermath, 1956–1965*

Year	Schools	Students In millions	Students Est. % of age-group entering school
1956	—	63.46[a]	52[b]
1957	—	64.28[a]	—
1957	547,300[c]	64.28[c]	—
1958	936,000[d]	92.61[d]	—
1958	—	86.00[e]	—
1958	—	86.40[f]	85[f]
1958	776,800[c]	86.40[c]	—
1959	—	90.00[g]	—
1959	737,400[c]	91.18[c]	—
1960	726,500[c]	93.79[c]	—
1961	645,200[c]	75.79[c]	—
1962	668,300[c]	69.24[c]	56[h]
1963	708,000[c]	71.58[c]	—
1964	1,066,000[c]	92.95[c]	—
1965	1,681,900[c]	116.21[c]	84.7[i]

[a] State Statistical Bureau (SSB), *Ten Great Years*, p. 192; see above, Table 9.1.
[b] Zhang Xiruo, "Muqian guomin jiaoyu fangmian de qingkuang he wenti" (Present
Situation and Problems of the Nation's Education), 20 June 1956, *Xinhua banyuekan*,
no. 14 (1956), p. 76.
[c] *Zhongguo jiaoyu nianjian, 1949–1981*, p. 1021.
[d] "Third Quarter Results: Still Faster Growth," *Peking Review*, 14 Oct. 1958, p. 14.
[e] Zhou Enlai, "Zhengfu gongzuo baogao" (Government Work Report), *Renmin ribao*,
19 Apr. 1959; State Statistical Bureau, "Guanyu 1958 nian guomin jingji fazhan
qingkuang de gongbao" (Report on the National Economic Development Situation
for 1958), *Guangming ribao*, 15 Apr. 1959.
[f] SSB, *Ten Great Years*, pp. 188, 192; Yang Xiufeng, "Woguo jiaoyu shiye de da
geming he da fazhan" (The Great Revolution in and Great Development of Our
Country's Educational Enterprise), in *Jiaoyu shinian* (Ten Years of Education), p. 1.
[g] Zhang Jichun, "Gengkuai genghao di fazhan wo guo de jiaoyu shiye" (Develop Our
Country's Educational Enterprise Faster and Better), *Hongqi*, no. 3 (1960), p. 11;
Guangming ribao, 1 Feb. 1960.
[h] John Gardner, "Educated Youth and Urban–Rural Inequalities, 1958–66," in
Lewis, *The City in Communist China*, p. 246.
[i] *Peking Review*, no. 5 (3 Feb. 1978), pp. 16–17.

Table 12.2. *Number of schools and students at the secondary level during the Great Leap Forward and its aftermath, 1957–1965*

Year	Specialized/technical		Agricultural/vocational		Ordinary	
	Schools	Students	Schools	Students	Schools	Students
1957	—	778,000[a]	—	—	—	6,281,000[a]
1957	1,320[b]	777,939[b]	—	—	11,096[b]	6,281,300[b]
1958	—	—	—	—	150,000[c] (all-inclusive)	14,000,000[c] (all-inclusive)
1958	—	—	—	—	—	12,000,000[d] (all-inclusive)
1958	—	1,470,000[a]	—	2,000,000[a]	—	8,520,000[a]
1958	3,113[c]	1,469,812[c]	20,023[c]	1,999,900[c]	28,931[c]	8,520,200[e]
1959	—	—	—	—	—	12,900,000[f] (all-inclusive)
1959	—	—	—	—	—	7,000,000[g] (jr. middle only)
1959	3,706[c]	1,469,613[c]	22,302[c]	2,189,900[c]	20,835[c]	9,178,700[c]
1960	—	—	30,000[h]	2,960,000[h]	—	—
1960	6,225[c]	2,215,869[c]	22,597[c]	2,302,000[c]	21,805[c]	10,260,100[c]
1961	2,843[c]	1,203,017[c]	7,260[c]	611,700[c]	18,983[c]	8,517,600[c]
1962	1,514[c]	534,911[c]	3,715[c]	266,600[c]	19,521[c]	7,528,000[c]
1963	1,355[c]	451,360[c]	4,303[c]	307,800[c]	19,599[c]	7,616,100[c]
1964	1,611[c]	531,557[c]	15,108[c]	1,123,400[c]	19,214[c]	8,540,300[c]
1965	1,265[c]	547,447[c]	61,626[c]	4,433,400[c]	18,102[c]	9,337,900[c]

[a] State Statistical Bureau (SSB), *Ten Great Years*, p. 192.　　[b] *Zhongguo jiaoyu nianjian, 1949–1981*, pp. 981, 982, 1000, 1001.

[c] "Third Quarter Results: Still Faster Growth," *Peking Review*, 14 Oct. 1958, p. 14.

[d] Zhou Enlai, "Zhengfu gongzuo baogao," *Renmin ribao*, 19 Apr. 1959; SSB, "Guangu 1958 nian guomin jingji fazhan qingkuang de gongbao," *Guangming ribao*, 15 Apr. 1959.

[e] *Zhongguo jiaoyu nianjian, 1949–1981*, pp. 981, 982, 1000, 1001, 1017.

[f] Zhang Jichun, "Gengkuai genghao de fazhan wo guo de jiaoyu shiye" (Develop Our Country's Educational Enterprise Faster and Better), *Hongqi*, no. 3 (1960), p. 11; *Guangming ribao*, 1 Feb. 1960.

[g] Lu Dingyi, in *Guangming ribao*, 23 Mar. 1959.　　[h] *Renmin ribao*, 16 Mar. 1960.

Table 12.3. *Number of schools and students at the tertiary level during the*
Great Leap Forward and its aftermath, 1956–1965

Year	Schools	Students
1956	—	403,000[a]
1957	227[b]	441,000[b]
1957	229[c]	441,181[c]
1958	1,065[d]	700,000[d]
1958	—	660,000[e]
1958	—	660,000[f]
1958	791[c]	659,627[c]
1959	841[g]	810,000 (full time)[g]
		300,000 (spare time)[g]
1959	841[c]	811,947[c]
1960	1,289[c]	961,623[c]
1961	845[c]	947,166[c]
1962	610[c]	829,699[c]
1963	407[c]	750,118[c]
1964	419[c]	685,314[c]
1965	434[c]	674,436[c]

[a] State Statistical Bureau (SSB), *Ten Great Years*, p. 192; see above, Table 9.1.
[b] "Never So Many at School," *Peking Review*, 23 Sept. 1958, p. 4; SSB, *Ten Great Years*, p. 192.
[c] *Zhongguo jiaoyu nianjian, 1949–1981*, pp. 965, 966.
[d] "Never So Many at School"; "Third Quarter Results: Still Faster Growth," *Peking Review*, 14 Oct. 1958, p. 14.
[e] Zhou Enlai, "Zhengfu gongzuo baogao," *Renmin ribao*, 19 Apr. 1959; SSB, "Guanyu 1958 nian guomin jingji fazhan qingkuang de gongbao," *Guangming ribao*, 15 Apr. 1959.
[f] SSB, *Ten Great Years*, p. 192; Yang Xiufeng, "Woguo jiaoyu shiye de da geming he da fazhan," in *Jiaoyu shinian*, p. 2.
[g] Hu Qili's National Students Association report, in *Renmin ribao*, 5 Feb. 1960; "Educational Big Leap," *Peking Review*, 16 Feb. 1960, p. 5.

reassessments in most sectors, including the qualitative aspects of education, that followed Mao's death, a much greater downward revision might have been expected in the quantitative indications of educational growth for the Great Leap and its aftermath. But figures published in the early 1980s retain the State Statistical Bureau revisions as cited by Zhou Enlai in 1959. These were also reproduced in the standard State Statistical Bureau compilation for the period, *The Ten Great Years*.[18]

---

[18] The continuity in nationally aggregated enrollment figures for all academic levels was marred only by the major, unexplained discrepancy in the elementary school graduate statistics for the

The post-1976 figures show growth continuing through 1960 at all three academic levels. Even at the lowest point, in 1962, enrollments did not fall to their 1957 levels, which were already substantially elevated by the first, 1956 leap. After the 1962 low point, elementary and secondary enrollments rebounded, quickly reaching or surpassing their Great Leap peaks by 1964–1965. The continuing gradual decline in tertiary enrollments between 1961 and 1965 is presumably related to causes other than Great Leap disruptions. Nor, despite the decline, did tertiary enrollments ever return to the 400,000 level achieved by the mini-leap of 1956. The statistics published after 1976 suggest that in quantitative terms, at least, the cause of extending and popularizing education benefited substantially from the two mass mobilization leaps in 1956 and 1958. Interview data also support the general impression of educational growth in the 1970s being built upon an extensive already-existing mass base.

Qualitative consolidation and selective development

Especially in terms of student enrollments, Table 12.2 suggests further how the regular academic stream surged ahead to dominate the system. Recollections of people who worked and studied within it, summarized in chapter 13, will tell the rest of the story. We will also turn briefly to the question of who might have been responsible for such consequences since that question became the most contentious political issue within the education sector as it moved forward from the cultural revolution introduced in 1958 to its more grandiose successor a decade later. But our immediate concern here is to illustrate the nature of the consequences themselves as the regular–irregular dichotomy reemerged once more.

We have seen how in earlier decades regular education typically resisted populist reform efforts, forcing them into a marginal existence outside the system. That pattern had reappeared most recently during the mid-1950s, as Chinese-style regularity adapted with relative ease to the demands of Soviet-style planning and an industrializing economy. Even so, and despite the process of mutual co-optation obviously under way, Chinese educators could not let the hundred-flowers opportunity pass without reiterating their views on the qualitative consequences of quantitative growth. Thereafter, the antirightist campaign and the Great Leap episode, in effect, served notice on a still reluctant education system and its guardians that there would be no turning back. Among other things, the events of 1957 and 1958 forced quantitative modernization and mass-line reform upon a system that had more or less successfully resisted them throughout all the controversial decades of its history. And in this respect, the precedent set in Yan'an between enforced intellectual obedience

1950s (cf. State Statistical Bureau, *Ten Great Years*, p. 194, and *Zhongguo jiaoyu nianjian, 1949–1981*, p. 1021).

and radical education reform, repeated in the early 1950s via thought reform and tertiary-level reorganization, was repeated again. With rectification and the antirightist campaign still fresh in everyone's memories, the "education revolution of 1958" rolled unobstructed over the regular system.

To say that radical change was imposed to an unprecedented degree is not to say it was imposed uniformly, however, at least not yet. Since "irregular" alternatives could no longer be pushed outside the system, a functional equivalent was devised in the form of separate compartments to accommodate them – a solution spelled out clearly in the "revolutionary" 19 September directive on education reform. The relevant passage in that directive, introduced above, stipulated more fully that there would be three main types of schools: full time, work–study, and spare time. But the three types were collapsed into two main functional distinctions: with quality maintenance listed first and popularization second. According to the directive:

> Of the three types of school, some will be responsible for the task of upgrading. These schools must have a complete curriculum and pay attention to raising the quality of their own schoolwork and the work of scientific research, and raising the level of their various subjects. These schools, under the condition of not harming their original level, should energetically assist in the work of building new schools. But if the level of these schools is lowered, it will be detrimental to the entire educational enterprise.

Work–study and spare-time schools could promote popularization because they were financially self-supporting and did not need a professional staff but could rely on the principle of "whoever is capable can teach." Such schools would over time become more complete in terms of their curricula, teachers, and facilities. The distinctions between spare-time and work–study schools would gradually disappear. But the directive said nothing about eliminating the differences between regular, quality schools and the mass-based work–study alternatives. On the contrary, the guiding principle was to "walk on two legs" and specifically "not just on one."[19]

Educators, whether bourgeois or otherwise, need have looked no further than the 19 September directive itself for authorization to continue running the regular stream much as they had before. And this they did, albeit with added vigor. The new impetus derived from the Great Leap's consolidation phase, which was officially promoted for education essentially as an exercise in *qualitative adjustment* designed to accompany *continuing quantitative growth*. Key-point schools were liberated from the closet to which they had been consigned by Soviet egalitarian tradition to become the chief focus of qualitative adjustment.

[19] *Renmin ribao*, 20 Sept. 1958.

The consolidation phase thus began seemingly on schedule, and if Mao or anyone else *at that time* had any reservations about the course being adopted, those reservations remain a closely guarded secret. Just as the string of directives issued between 1938 and 1942 showed how a regular school system could be carved out of the north Shaanxi wilderness, so a steady stream of circulars and decisions from 1958 to 1963 illustrated how to preserve the regular system as a qualitatively secure zone within the national mass education drive.

The guidelines. No secret was made of the solution. The February mobilization phase instructions of Zhou Enlai and Kang Sheng were still being reprinted in the provinces, and popular activism everywhere was being fanned to new heights, with quality a secondary concern at best. But planning was already under way for the postmobilization phase. Proposals were discussed both in public and internally throughout 1958, giving Mao plenty of time to intervene on the education front had he so desired before his power allegedly waned following his partial withdrawal from active leadership in 1959.

Specific guidelines for the entire movement from mobilization through consolidation were extensively publicized during the Fourth National Education Administration Conference convened by the Education Ministry in March and April 1958.[20] *People's Education* treated its readers to an uncharacteristically concise summary of the conference proceedings:

(1) The cultural revolution was to be promoted through five great tasks: a literacy campaign, popularizing elementary education, establishing agricultural middle schools, improving teacher training, and "reforming the education system, content, and methods, in accordance with Chairman Mao's education policy to meet the needs of socialist construction."

(2) Popularization would necessitate upgrading or "walking on two legs," that is, one leg for popularization and the other for quality maintenance. *Minban* elementary schools, agricultural middle schools, and spare-time schools were mainly for popularization. After popularization would come consolidation and upgrading. But "there must be no turning back" the quantitative gains during consolidation. Hence upgrading on that basis would require many years of struggle. Meanwhile, to satisfy the needs of the tertiary level, regular schools must be run "even better."

(3) Both "diligent work and frugal study" (i.e., part-work, part-study) and "half-work, half-study" were basic measures necessary for fulfilling educational objectives. But they were not to be confused. Half-work, half-study was meant to promote economic self-sufficiency for *minban* and agricultural middle schools. Part-work, part-study was meant to round out the political and academic training of regular students. "Therefore, in state-run

---

[20] Ibid., 10 Apr. 1958.

secondary, elementary, and teacher training schools, physical labor is necessary but it must be appropriate and properly arranged; in general, do not do half-work, half-study, and do not seek economic self-sufficiency."

(4) Henceforth, a basic school task was to demolish capitalism and establish socialism.

(5) The great leap in education must rely on the Party's leadership and follow the mass line.[21]

Liu Shaoqi articulated this two-legged approach in his famous "two-systems" formulation a few weeks later. His statement was not published at the time but circulated in Party circles after he presented it at an expanded CCP Political Bureau meeting in May 1958. The existing regular full-time system should continue, he said, but be paralleled by work–study schools which could also be built into "one kind of regular school system." The latter would help young people in both town and countryside who for financial reasons, including both the state's and their own, could not continue their studies in the full-time system whether at the secondary or tertiary level.[22]

The 19 September directive then sanctioned the concern to maintain an island of quality within the burgeoning mass system and incorporated the "two-systems" solution in principle if not in so many words as a means of institutionalizing the Great Leap's goals for education. With the basic policy decisions thus made, specific directives for the early consolidation phase were all formulated accordingly. Education Minister Yang Xiufeng set the tone on the last day of 1958, when he repeated some of the highest Great Leap claims on the one hand while calling for consolidation and key-point development on the other.[23]

Liu Shaoqi's two-systems formulation, reiterated during his own inspection tour of Anhui in October 1958, just a few days before that of Kang Sheng, now emerged into fuller public view. Although the comments of both men had originally been treated with a mobilization-phase gloss in national and provincial accounts, by January 1959 the same remarks had been polished to fit the cause of consolidation more explicitly. In his widely circulated summary of their visits to Hefei Industrial University, its Party secretary quoted both Liu

---

[21] "Disici quanguo jiaoyu xingzheng huiyi de chengguo" (The Results of the Fourth National Education Administration Conference), *Renmin jiaoyu*, no. 5 (1958), p. 20. See also "Jiyao puji, yeyao tigao" (If There Is Popularization, There Must Also Be Upgrading), ibid., p. 21. All of these points were elaborated in the press while the conference was in session (e.g., *Jiaoshibao*, 25, 28 Mar. and 1, 4, 8, 11 Apr. 1958).

[22] "Wo guo yingyou liangzhong jiaoyu zhidu, liangzhong laodong zhidu" (Our Country Should Have Two Kinds of Education System and Two Kinds of Labor System), 30 May 1958, in *Liu Shaoqi xuanji* (Selected Works of Liu Shaoqi), 2 vols. (Beijing: Renmin chubanshe, 1981–1985), *xia*: 323–327.

[23] From Yang Xiufeng's report to a conference of representatives from advanced agricultural units on 31 Dec. 1958, as reported in *Guangming ribao*, 3 Jan. 1959.

and Kang repeatedly on the need to find a middle ground somewhere between bourgeois academic thought and erroneous views like stressing labor equally with study in regular schools and practice over theory. Liu's two-systems formulation featured much more prominently than it had two months before. He was quoted as having said that:

> At present, your schools should still take study as the main thing. Only use a little time for labor because university education is still not common and there are still not many institutions of higher learning. Universities should now take study as the main thing, while schools run by factories and farms should take production as the main thing. . . . Only in this way will our construction and educational enterprise be benefited, causing in the future the two forms gradually to become closer until they finally become the same.[24]

Adjust, consolidate, upgrade. Virtually every kind of educational endeavor at every level now began checking in with its progress report for the next phase of the movement.[25] In March 1959, the State Council approved six directives stipulating how to consolidate and upgrade within the context of quantitative growth.[26] Zhou Enlai's above-cited government work report to the National People's Congress in April summarized their import:

> The regular schools of the full-time system should make raising the quality of teaching a constant fundamental task. They should, moreover, first concentrate relatively great strength to run well a group of key-point schools, in order to facilitate the training of even higher special talents for our country, to raise rapidly the level of our country's science and culture.[27]

Due to inexperience in 1958, Yang Xiufeng told the congress, schools had cut out too many classes for the sake of productive labor and practical learning. The balance must be redressed. Academic courses should not be weakened at the tertiary level. Elementary and secondary schools should improve quality. Productive labor should be listed as part of the regular curriculum, but the amount of time allocated for it should be arranged differently by the different kinds of schools. For those in the full-day system, classroom education should

---

[24] Sun Zongrong, "Dangqian jiaoyu gemingzhong de jige wenti: zuexi Shaoqi, Kang Sheng tongzhi lai benxiao shicha shi suo zuo tanhua de jidian tihui" (Some Problems in the Current Education Revolution: Study a Few Points of Experience from What Was Said by Comrades Shaoqi and Kang Sheng When They Came to Our School on an Inspection Visit), *Zhongguo qiangnian*, no. 2 (1959), pp. 7–9; reprinted in *Guangming ribao*, 16 Jan. 1959, and *Xinhua banyuekan*, no. 3 (1959), pp. 104–106. For the official Nov. version of Liu's remarks, see *Guangming ribao*, 14 Nov. 1958; *Anhui ribao*, 6 Nov. 1958. Kang Sheng's remarks were reported in *Guangming ribao*, 27 Nov. 1958; *Anhui ribao*, 24 Nov. 1958.

[25] E.g., see *Guangming ribao*, 13, 16, 18, 21, 26, 31 Jan., 4, 6, 14, 18, 24 Feb., 2, 3, 6, 13, 23, 28 Mar. 1959.

[26] Ibid., 23 Mar. 1959.

[27] *Renmin ribao*, 19 Apr. 1959.

be their main concern. Wherever elementary schooling had been universalized, continued Yang, work should shift to consolidation and upgrading. Elsewhere, achieving universal elementary education should remain the first priority. Schools set up in 1958 should concentrate on consolidation. To ensure quality, authorities at all levels from the center to the county should designate a few full-day schools to serve as key points for selective development. These schools should not be too large in size, strict qualitative demands should be imposed upon them, they should be run well, and they should produce results. Reiterating the point from the 19 September directive on the need for a division of labor between mass and quality schooling, he said: "Only if we adopt large-scale popularization and selective upgrading, that is, the policy of 'walking on two legs,' will we be able to solve the contradiction between quantity and quality."[28]

The six new directives spelled out the details. At the tertiary level over 700 new schools had been set up in 1958. "Some of the schools correspond to the standard of higher-level institutions and can be continued," noted the relevant directive. It went on to list the specific criteria to be used in determining whether or not a school should be allowed to continue in operation and, if so, the precise name that should be given to it, for example, college, technical school, or cadre training class.[29] The national unified college entrance examinations were restored in 1959 and held every year thereafter until 1966.[30]

On the experimental revision of the school system, another directive noted that many schools had carried out such experiments with official encouragement during the 1958–1959 academic year. Now strict limits must be placed on such efforts, which involved curricular changes, teaching methods, and a reduction of combined elementary and secondary schooling from 12 to 10 years. Henceforth, only a few authorized schools were to continue the experiment, which was to be brought under Education Ministry control. All other full-time schools were ordered to continue operating under the old system.[31]

Here, too, Soviet influence could be seen hovering. After the abortive 5-year

[28] From Yang Xiufeng's report as printed in *Guangming ribao*, 29 Apr. 1959.

[29] "Zhongguo gongchandang zhongyang weiyuanhui, Guowuyuan, guanyu zhengdun 1958 nian xin jian de quanrizhi he banrizhi gaodeng xuexiao de tongzhi" (Circular of the CCP Central Committee and the State Council on Reorganizing the Full-Time and Half-Time Institutions of Higher Learning Newly Established in 1958), 24 May 1959, printed in *Zhonghua renmin gongheguo fagui huibian, 1959 1 yue–6 yue* (Compilation of Laws and Regulations of the People's Republic of China, Jan.–June 1959) (n.p.: Falu chubanshe, 1959, 1982), pp. 258–259, trans. in JPRS, *Compendium of Laws*, pp. 318–320.

[30] *Guangming ribao*, 11 June 1959. In 1959, however, the enrollment regulations stipulated that workers, peasants, and cadres could still be admitted on the basis of recommendation and individual examination by the institutions they wished to enter, without having to take the national examinations.

[31] "Zhongguo gongchandang zhongyang weiyuanhui, Guowuyuan, guanyu shiyen gaige xuezhi de guiding" (CCP Central Committee and State Council Decision on the Experimental Reform of the School System), 24 May 1959, printed in *Zhonghua renmin gongheguo fagui huibian, 1959 1 yue–6 yue*, pp. 262–263, trans. in JPRS, *Compendium of Laws*, pp. 324–325.

elementary school experiment in the early 1950s, China had retained the 12-year system. But in 1958–1959, even as the mechanical copying themes of 1956–1957 still reverberated, experiments with a 10-year format, standard in Soviet education, were officially encouraged.[32] The aim, however, was to achieve greater efficiency and economy for the regular full-day system while sacrificing nothing in terms of quality, and the experiment remained quality-oriented from 1959 onward. Some localities experimented again with the 5-year elementary school; some with 5-year secondary schooling; and still others with an integrated 10-year curriculum.[33]

On labor and study schedules for regular full-day schools, no more than two to three months per calendar year were to be devoted to productive labor activities at the college level, and the Education Ministry retrieved some of its recently relinquished powers, including the right to decide teaching-time requirements for academic courses. Labor time was fixed at 8–10 hours per week for senior middle school students; 6–8 hours per week at the junior secondary level; and 4–6 hours per week for elementary school students from age nine.[34]

The shift from mobilization to consolidation was accomplished with greater ease in some quarters than others. Party leaders in Fujian seemingly adapted like ducks to water, turning their province, not otherwise known for its academic achievements, into a national pacesetter for the consolidation phase. According to an official account, Fujian's leadership had taken firm control of secondary schooling in particular. As a result, 63 percent of those taking the 1959 college entrance examinations passed, in contrast with only 5.6 percent in 1954. Thus, "the experience of Fujian and other places proves that educational quality of middle schools can be raised rapidly."[35] Provincial Party leader Lin Xiude outlined Fujian's winning formula. The goals were traditional: examination success. Leadership and slogans were contemporary: great leap modern, including direct local Party attention to every detail. The methods were a mix of mass movement activism, competitive grade-point emulation, and Soviet-style curriculum management.[36]

[32] The 5-year elementary school and 10-year integrated-school experiments of the early 1950s were still being criticized as an example of mechanical copying at the Fourth National Education Administration Conference in early 1958 (*Jiaoshibao*, 28 Mar. 1958).

[33] See reports by Yang Xiufeng and Lu Dingyi in *Guangming ribao*, 9 Apr. 1960, and *Renmin ribao*, 10 Apr. 1960, respectively; see also Robert D. Barendsen, "The 1960 Educational Reform," *China Quarterly*, no. 4 (Oct./Dec. 1960), pp. 55–65. The standard-bearer of the comprehensive 10-year curriculum into the 1990s was Beijing's Jingshan School (Jingshan xuexiao). Established in 1960, its graduates quickly achieved one of the highest possible promotion rates into college (*Guangming ribao*, 8 June 1960).

[34] "Guowuyuan guanyu quanrizhi xuexiao de jiaoxue, laodong he shenghuo anpai de guiding" (State Council Decision on Teaching, Labor, and Living Arrangements for Full-Day Schools), 24 May 1959, printed in *Zhonghua renmin gongheguo fagui huibian, 1959 1 yue–6 yue*, pp. 263–268, trans. in JPRS, *Compendium of Laws*, pp. 326–331.

[35] *Renmin ribao*, editorial, 21 Dec. 1959.

[36] Ibid., 21 Dec. 1959; see also *Fujian ribao*, Fuzhou, 22, 26 Dec. 1959.

The 1959 consolidation phase directives evolved through several formulations into a comprehensive set of regulations and curriculum plans issued between 1961 and 1963. Together, these represented yet another major overhaul of education at all levels, formally replacing the 1950s Soviet model with a Chinese version which tried to graft "irregular" Great Leap solutions onto the existing regular system. Quantitative growth was affirmed along with all the formulas necessary to deliver it. So too was Party leadership. Labor was written into the curriculum, albeit further reduced by contrast with the 1959 guidelines.

Yet the regular system emerged from the radical interlude not much different from before. The shortened curriculum was never confirmed, although the "experiment" continued, with a few of the best schools in each city adopting 5- or 10-year programs. Most schools, however, retained the 12-year format. Experimentation and flexibility were strictly contained, with the return of fixed rules, regulations, and systems for everything. Full-time secondary and elementary schools were expected to regard teaching as their main work and classroom teaching as its main form. They were ordered to use the nationally unified teaching plans, outlines, and textbooks stipulated by the Education Ministry. Schools and localities were expressly forbidden to make arbitrary revisions.[37]

Indeed, the most ironic consequence of the period was the new status accorded key-point schools. They now came into their own as a specifically Chinese solution to the problem of quality control within a high-growth system. Perhaps Khrushchev's interest in a similar solution for the Soviet Union emboldened CCP policymakers to compromise with Chinese educators, whose familiar quantity–quality conundrum had created a major point of friction during the 1950s. But it was Mao's radical Great Leap Forward that finally exonerated their preference for training talent and legitimized the systematic national development of elite schools.

[37] The open publication of such regulations ceased in the early 1960s, so contemporary sources are unavailable. The regulations for secondary and elementary schools were published in the late 1960s for criticism (see Susan Shirk, "The 1963 Temporary Work Regulations for Full-Time Middle and Primary Schools: Commentary and Translation," *China Quarterly*, no. 55 [July/Sept. 1973], pp. 511–546). See *Zhongguo jiaoyu nianjian, 1949–1981*, for the following documents: Zhonggong zhongyang, "Zhonghua renmin gongheguo jiaoyubu zhishu gaodeng xuexiao zanxing gongzuo tiaoli (caoan)" (Provisional Work Regulations for Institutions of Higher Learning Directly Subordinate to the Ministry of Education of the People's Republic of China [Draft]), Sept. 1961, popularly known as the "60 Articles," pp. 693–699; Zhonggong zhongyang, "Quanrizhi xiaoxue zanxing gongzuo tiaoli (caoan)" (Provisional Work Regulations for Elementary Schools in the Full-Day System [Draft]), Mar. 1963, pp. 699–701; Zhonggong zhongyang, "Quanrizhi zhongxue zanxing gongzuo tiaoli (caoan)" (Provisional Work Regulations for Secondary Schools in the Full-Day System [Draft]), Mar. 1963, pp. 702–705; "Jiaoyubu guanyu shixing quanrizhi zhong xiaoxue xin jiaoxue jihua (caoan) de tongzhi" (Ministry of Education Circular on the New Teaching Plan [Draft] for Secondary and Elementary Schools in the Full-Day System), 31 July 1963, pp. 737–740. The Ministry of Higher Education was reestablished in early 1964.

A 1962 Education Ministry circular reaffirmed the solution. Key schools were still not being taken seriously enough. Many localities were still using their strength in too egalitarian a manner, spreading resources too thinly. Accordingly, all provinces and cities were instructed to select and run well a small group of middle schools within the full-day system, and city districts and counties were to do the same for elementary schools. In these schools should be concentrated the strongest leadership personnel, the most qualified teachers, the best students, and the most complete facilities. To concentrate the "best" students, the catchment area from which they were enrolled could be expanded beyond each individual school district, to the entire county, city, etc., as appropriate. The number of students per class was not to exceed 40–45, and the size of such schools had to remain limited. The full 12-year curriculum was to be rigorously and completely followed and stability guaranteed.[38]

In the hyperactive political climate of the 1960s, everyone was called upon to hold high the "three red banners," that is, to support the aims of the general line for socialist construction, the Great Leap Forward, and the people's communes. Key schools had a national mission to promote quality, and it was measured in the currency of the day, by examination success. In the spirit of the national publicity given Fujian, these schools were driven to demonstrate their qualitative prowess by pushing up scores and promotion rates with an intensity unprecedented in all China's long history of competitive examinations.

Whose mistake?

Briefly, on the contentious political question of who was responsible for what, Lu Dingyi in his 1958 introduction to the Great Leap education reforms had identified their opponents as "bourgeois educators" and "some of our comrades" who agreed with them in wanting to restrict the extent and speed of educational development. They advocated one type of school system, state run and state funded, with regular full-time schools only. But such a course would have postponed indefinitely the goal of universal education because the state could not afford the financial investment necessary to achieve it. Hence, the new course was adopted in 1958 because "we communists are not the same as bourgeois educators."[39]

A decade later, when the 1966 Cultural Revolution heralded an even more radical set of reforms, Lu Dingyi himself would be blamed for all that had occurred during the intervening 1959–1965 years, along with Mao's erstwhile

[38] "Jiaoyubu guanyu you zhongdian de banhao yipi quanrizhi zhong, xiao xuexiao de tongzhi" (Ministry of Education Circular on Running Well in a Key-Point Manner a Group of Secondary and Elementary Schools within the Full-Day System), 21 Dec. 1962, in *Zhongguo jiaoyu nianjian, 1949–1981*, pp. 736–737.

[39] Lu Dingyi, "Jiaoyu bixu yu shengchan laodong xiangjiehe," p. 4 (originally cited in chap. 11, n. 32, above).

heir apparent, Liu Shaoqi, and vestiges of an education system "millenniums old." They were charged with responsibility for having distorted Mao's revolutionary line on education by perversely turning his "walking on two legs" principle into "two kinds of education": one regular and the other work–study.

Liu, Lu, and their alleged confederates within the government education bureaucracy and academia were also declared responsible, retroactively, for a host of sins associated with the predominance of "regular" education extending all the way back to 1949. Reinterpreted as a deliberate betrayal of Mao's omniscient revolutionary line were actions as diverse as denigrating the Yan'an experience with education reform; transplanting the Soviet model; upholding the cause of bourgeois academics; abandoning the 5-year elementary school experiment in the early 1950s; promoting the quality-oriented experimental 10-year curriculum; altering the content of work–study; stressing the development of regular full-time and elite key-point schools; and promoting the national emulation of Fujian Province after it achieved success on the college entrance examinations. Yet the 19 September directive itself, which had sanctioned quality concerns, remained curiously unscathed by the polemics of the late 1960s.[40]

Such accusations raise obvious questions. If Mao was so offended by Liu Shaoqi's line on education (and other matters), why did Mao wait so long to move against him? Especially, why did Mao formally accept Liu as his heir apparent, a role confirmed by Liu's succession to the post of state chairman in 1959? Why did Mao not at least nip Liu's two-systems solution in the bud, since he had articulated it many months before it was finally written, in principle, into the 19 September directive? Indeed, why was the 19 September directive never criticized as the source of Liu's pernicious two systems for education, when the directive clearly authorized just such a course? And why did Mao not try to stop or alter that course, which unfolded quite openly and methodically from April 1958 onward? To accept the late 1960s charges, in other words, we would also have to accept the standard Maoist defense as well,

---

[40] E.g., see the basic Maoist document of accusation for education issued in the late 1960s: "Shiqi nianlai jiaoyu zhanxian shang liangtiao luxian douzheng dashiji" (Chronology of the Two-Line Struggle on the Educational Front during the Past 17 Years), *Jiaoyu geming* (Education revolution), 6 May 1967, reprinted in *Hongweibing ziliao* (Red Guard Publications) (Washington, D.C.: Center for Chinese Research Materials, Association of Research Libraries, 1975), vol. 2, trans. in Peter J. Seybolt, ed., *Revolutionary Education in China: Documents and Commentary* (White Plains, N.Y.: International Arts and Sciences Press, 1973), pp. 5–60. The actual authorship of the 19 Sept. 1958 directive remains uncertain. For example, one of the many Red Guard compilations from the late 1960s presents extracts from the directive along with other quotes from Mao on education (*Mao zhuxi jiaoyu yulu* [Quotations from Chairman Mao on Education], ed. Hongdaihui, Zuozhanbu doupigai bangongshi [Beijing: Beijing dianji xuexiao, dongfanghong gongshe, 1967]). But in such a source, the sentences might have been selected to represent Mao's spirit rather than his actual words. None of the main compilations of his works, official or unofficial, include this directive, nor do contemporary sources cite Mao as its author.

that he had been rendered powerless by the coalition of scheming bourgeois revisionists around him. This defense was assisted by Mao's voluntary partial "retirement" in 1959 to make way for younger successors. He had relinquished his post as head of state at that time but retained his Party chairmanship.

Isolating fact from fabrication in the Cultural Revolution's articles of accusation would, of course, require a separate volume in itself. That task should not detain us here except to reiterate the general assumptions concerning those charges upon which the following account rests. The assumptions are not only that Mao's revolutionary line owed more debts than acknowledged to the Soviet experience but also that Mao accepted the two-systems approach for education in 1958, personally approved its general inclusion within the September directive, probably without troubling himself to any great extent over the likely consequences, and only changed his mind about five years later, after the full social consequences became evident. These assumptions derive in turn from another, namely, that the shifting and often contradictory events from 1958 through the early 1960s, like those of 1956–1957 before and 1966–1976 after, are best explained in terms of the mass movement's "laws" of progression.

Evidently, the art that Stalin toyed with briefly during the early years of his dictatorship was developed by Mao and the CCP into a standard method of political action and policy implementation. The CCP relied on mass movements for a diversity of aims both revolutionary and mundane, including socialist transformation and construction as well as more basic work like combating corruption and infectious diseases. There were many mass movements of varying size, duration, and purpose. But all followed a similar course from mobilization through consolidation and beyond, when the goals for which a movement was launched could be deemed accomplished or at least sustainable thereafter through more routine means. Introduced above with specific reference to the rectification and antirightist campaigns, the operational principles inherent in this mechanism perhaps deserve further elaboration since it was so central to CCP rule under Mao's leadership and by inference to the political question posed here.

Essential to this mechanism was a paramount leader powerful enough to stand above the fray: setting the movement in motion, defining the issues around which to mobilize public opinion, and, most crucial of all, deciding when mass activism had peaked and the shift to consolidation should commence. Timing was essential in the calculation of costs and benefits. The opposition had to be sufficiently intimidated so as no longer to present a significant threat, and local leaders had to be ready to implement the aims for which the movement was launched in the first place. This was the point before which the costs had to be estimated and after which they had to be paid, while errors and excesses were corrected in the balance. Naturally, not all the mistakes could be so easily compensated, especially when violence was involved, which was not uncommon.

Naturally, too, some participants refused to heed the signals sent out by the leader as the movement progressed from one phase to the next. This was an easy enough mistake to make since the rules of the game, by its definition, were never announced in advance or even clearly articulated – as Wuhan University Party Secretary Liu Yangqiao so artfully suggested while discussing the changing emphasis from productive labor in 1958 back to book learning in 1959. He revealed the dilemmas experienced by local Party leaders caught up in the shifting currents of a mass movement, unable to anticipate the shifts or escape responsibility for their actions as it developed:

> After conducting our investigations, we were keenly aware of the need to analyze and study more fully not just the many problems raised in the past but also the new problems thrown up by the new situation. Especially there is the need for enough political sensitivity to be able to ascertain quickly the direction of the wind and to find the laws governing it, since only then can the movement's development be correctly guided.[41]

Those without the ability to grasp the movement's governing laws or whose sense of timing failed them or who simply refused to accept the leader's cues for whatever reason had to be calculated among the costs of this method. Especially vulnerable were the younger, less experienced participants and local leaders who emerged during the early stages of the movement. They were essential in whipping up popular opinion but prone to take too literally the excessive goals of the mobilization phase and their own "spontaneous" association with them. Like the Russian cultural revolutionaries in the late 1920s, Chinese land reform cadres in the 1940s, and rightist intellectuals in the 1950s, such participants were regularly swept aside by the shifting currents of consolidation and paid a heavy price. So too did the movement's formal targets, against which excessive behavior could be temporarily condoned.

Assuming he was still in power when it ended, the initiator also had the right to interpret the movement's twists and turns afterward to portray himself to best advantage. But he would not actually have been able to control all the twists and turns. If it was a true mass movement, based on the mobilized and spontaneous participation of many people outside the regular channels of CCP leadership, it would for a time have been allowed to develop in an ad hoc fashion and take on a life of its own. This was necessary given the functions of excess and the leader's political need to distance himself therefrom, ends best served by allowing a movement to escalate temporarily out of control.

According to Mao, excesses were essential to overcome resistance and to

---

[41] Article by Liu Yangqiao, CCP committee secretary, Wuhan University, in *Wenhuibao*, Shanghai, 3 Sept. 1959.

right wrongs. "In correcting wrongs," he had written in his 1927 report on the Hunan peasant movement, "it is necessary to go to extremes or else the wrongs cannot be righted." Much quoted during the next five decades, this passage became the leitmotif of the Chinese communist revolution. Mao had added "must" to the four-character phrase "*jiaowang guozheng*" (to exceed the proper limits in righting a wrong) and built the concept into a deliberate strategy of mass movement action. The above-cited corollary followed logically: "as long as it is really a conscious struggle of the broad masses, any excesses that have occurred can be corrected afterwards."[42]

Such a strategy of course made it difficult for anyone else to determine who had actually been responsible for what at any given time. But this was also what made the mass movement such a useful political instrument. It gave the initiator an overwhelming advantage of mass strength against the forces of opposition, whoever or whatever they might be. And it was usually possible for him – so long as he remained in control of the Party center and its propaganda apparatus – to camouflage responsibility for errors and excesses by deflecting it onto the actual perpetrators of wrongdoings committed as the movement progressed.

As initiator, he therefore retained the right of defining what was and was not a wrongdoing and also of changing the definitions as events developed. Violence might be inevitable and even beneficial to promote excesses at one stage, but harmful at another. In this manner, political allies became enemies and what was advocated as correct for one period was cast aside and condemned during the next. Especially complex was the consolidation phase, when whatever forces of opposition remained might regroup in various ways to recoup some of their losses.

Following this line of argument, when Mao activated the next major movement in 1966, events of the intervening years since 1958 were simply reinterpreted as a progressive perversion by Liu Shaoqi and his confederates of Mao's "correct" line as advanced in 1958. A more plausible explanation, however, is that developments in education progressed very much *in accordance* with the provisions of the 19 September directive, sanctioned by Mao, and the mass movement method whereby it was launched, also sanctioned by Mao. But having progressed in that manner, the contradictions inherent in such a course also developed accordingly.

Thus, the decision to develop key schools and the regular full-time system, together with work–study alternatives, may have initially been thought to give

[42] The original source on the necessity of going to extremes is "Hunan nongmin yundong kaocha baogao" (Report on an Investigation of the Peasant Movement in Hunan), 28 Mar. 1927, in *Mao Zedong ji*, 1:214 (from the section "The Question of 'Excess'"). The corollary on correction is from the 1940s land reform period: "Rent Reduction and Production Are Two Important Matters for the Defence of the Liberated Areas," 7 Nov. 1945, in *Selected Works*, 4:72.

equal emphasis to quality and quantity as everyone declared. But in implementing that line, the inevitable distinctions between the two kinds of schooling became clear. To declare a policy of walking on two legs while assigning the regular stream to one leg and irregular work–study to the other ensured that one leg would grow much stronger than the other.

Probably, it was only within this developing context that Mao himself belatedly realized the flaw in his two-legged principle – whereupon he decided to redefine the issue as part of a more systematic second attempt at cultural revolution. Further in this respect, Liu Shaoqi and Kang Sheng were not alone on the school inspection circuit at the start of the 1958 fall semester. And unlike both of them, Mao was reported to have said nothing at all about quality, concentrating instead on the work–study projects under way at Tianjin and Wuhan Universities and an Anhui middle school.[43]

The record also suggests, however, that Mao, like everyone else, including both Liu and Kang, accepted "full-day schools, work–study schools, and spare-time schools" in 1958 as the answer to the quantity–quality dilemma. At the Anhui middle school, Mao asked its headmaster whether any students were doing half-work, half-study. When told there was only one class in such a program (i.e., students in one classroom, probably between 30 and 50 individuals), Mao asked how much labor time was arranged for all the other regular students. He was told one and a half days per week and, according to the account, raised no objection. Instead, he "nodded his head smiling" and moved on.[44]

Similarly, at Tianjin University when told that 98 percent of the student body was participating in "diligent work and frugal study" activities, and that preparations were under way to admit a few classes (ji ge ban) of students for half-work, half-study during the coming semester, Mao did not protest this introduction of the two-systems approach. On the contrary, "the chairman said, 'this is very good,'" and went on to praise both programs for producing students who would be at once cultured and laborers.[45]

As for Kang Sheng, who remained at Mao's side throughout, it would be tempting to read into his and Liu Shaoqi's 1958 Anhui comments the origins of the divide that would separate them a decade later. But the differences between their respective statements as published in November 1958 were minimal, like variations on the single mobilization theme, by comparison with the differences in tone between their November 1958 comments and the "updated"

---

[43] *Mao zhuxi shicha xuexiao* (Chairman Mao Inspects Schools) (Beijing: Zhongguo shaonian ertong chubanshe, 1959), pp. 3–24. Despite its title, only 3 of the 11 chapters in this booklet actually record school inspection visits. See also "Instruction Given on an Inspection Tour of Tientsin University," 1958, and "Instruction Given on an Inspection Tour of Wuhan University," 1958, both in *Mao Zedong sixiang wansui*, trans. in *CB*, no. 891 (8 Oct. 1969), pp. 30–31.

[44] *Mao zhuxi shicha xuexiao*, p. 6.

[45] Ibid., p. 9.

composite version of both men's remarks once consolidation became the chief concern in January 1959. Kang Sheng's mobilization-phase statements in Anhui and elsewhere during 1958 also contained many qualifications in deference to regularity and an implicit acceptance of the two-systems formula.

In any event, there is no evidence that Mao tried to stop or substantively alter the directives designed between 1959 and 1963 to develop the education system in accordance with the two-systems approach. It was only in the early 1960s, after the consequences of implementing that approach had become evident, that Mao began talking again more pointedly about labor and practical learning for everyone, elites and masses alike.[46]

It follows, therefore, that Liu Shaoqi's greatest "error" was also probably committed only later, after 1963–1964, when he miscalculated and missed his cues while Mao was deciding on a course correction. Perhaps Liu failed to anticipate the extent of the second cultural revolution upsurge. Or being an old mass movement veteran himself, perhaps he decided that as heir apparent he could now play the game against its aging grand master and survive. Liu, in any case, continued to champion the course he had articulated in 1958 for two separate kinds of education: one regular and the other irregular work–study. But whoever was responsible and however styled, trying to build an education system based on a division of labor between regular and irregular separate forms of schooling was bound to fail – for reasons that both Mao and Liu might have anticipated even at the start.

---

[46] Mao's most famous statement in praise of half-work, half-study, the 30 July 1961 "Letter to Jiangxi Communist Labor University," is ambiguous. During the 1966–1976 years, it was used to promote some version of work–study for everyone. But read within the context of his Great Leap era two-legged approach, Mao could just as well have been referring to one leg only since his comments were addressed specifically to Party and government offices and mass organizations, which he advised to establish work–study schools for their employees. The labor university itself was administered by and within the state land reclamation farm system of Jiangxi Province and was not part of the regular school system. Since Mao did not say that all schools should do half-work, half-study, he was presumably still thinking in terms of two legs as two systems at this point (the labor university and Mao's letter are discussed below).

13

A system divided: walking on two legs into the 1960s

The verdict of history might excuse both Mao and Liu for failing to anticipate the consequences of their two-legs/two-systems strategies, because China's educational development was heading into the uncharted territory of mass elementary and secondary schooling with no real precedents for guidance. And even had anyone been inclined to heed the arcane advice of colonial development experts, Philip Foster's formulation of the parity principle at work in Africa had yet to be published, much less assessed against any Asian experience.

Tables 12.1 and 12.2 summarize the essence of the story. What failed was not the Great Leap education strategy but only its irregular work–study component. By contrast, regularity thrived. It emerged triumphant yet again, but with some important differences which finally transformed China's modern school system into one with a permanent mass base. Those differences began in turn to redefine the nature of both regular education and its irregular alternatives.

We will return to elementary schooling in chapter 16, which indicates a continuity of growth from 1958 through the 1966–1976 decade. By the early 1960s, universal elementary education had been basically achieved in urban areas, albeit with an assist from the *minban* formula at that time. But how to do the same for the rural majority was the ultimate challenge, pursued most systematically during the 1966–1976 years.

Higher education had been the centerpiece of educational development throughout the 1950s and remained in a holding pattern thereafter. The Sino-Soviet compromise model that evolved during the FFYP remained essentially unchanged while Great Leap quantitative increases were absorbed. But for the intensifying use of political and class background criteria in the governance of school life, higher education essentially reverted to its mid-1950s state, as affirmed in the "60 Articles" directive of 1961.[1]

At the secondary level, however, the Great Leap had a major formative

[1] The 1961 directive is cited in chap. 12 n. 37, above. The period of reversion was limited, however. Excessive labor, experimentation with shortened curricula, and so on, continued in varying degrees from 1958 to 1960. The socialist education campaign as a prelude to reviving cultural revolution concerns then began disrupting regular academic routines on college campuses during the 1964–65 academic year.

impact, deriving both from its successes and from its failures. Secondary education had until then been left to grow largely as it would, responding variously to upward pressures from new elementary-level graduates for more schooling and to the demands of tertiary institutions for more recruits. Lip service to the contrary notwithstanding, the need to define secondary education as an end in itself was several years overdue, despite the relatively slow growth rates at that level during the 1950s. The Great Leap thus initiated the first concerted effort to focus on secondary schooling, and it was also the first time that the goal of universalizing junior secondary education was seriously raised.

To summarize the moral of this story at its beginning, the Great Leap strategy addressed the challenge of trying to devise secondary schooling that would be terminal for the majority and college preparatory for the few by promoting all kinds of schools, both regular and irregular, but assigning them functionally specific tasks. It was the attempt to achieve such a specific divide that proved the scheme's undoing rather than the irregular alternatives per se.

Quantitative growth of the regular system, together with its newly legitimized key-point stream, produced a competitive race to join the college-preparatory elite unknown in earlier years, when the demand for tertiary-level students usually outstripped the supply.[2] Passing the college entrance examinations, unified nationally in the 1950s, had already become the chief aim of secondary schooling. The key-point schools then locked quickly into place as the chief source of college candidates. The net result was to guarantee that regularity would successfully adapt once more – this time to the first onslaught of a communist-led cultural revolution – leaving all irregular alternatives to languish on the sidelines.

In fact, the 1958 cultural revolution combined with China's modernization goals and its inherited traditions to reproduce more intensely than at any time since 1905 the ancient Chinese view of education as the means and examination success the chief end. Hence, it was in the midst of this anachronistic revival they seem to have unwittingly promoted that Mao and his cultural revolution allies had to begin thinking in concrete terms about the problem of educational parity, or "equality," arising from their strategy of allocating different kinds of education to different kinds of students. The issue was forced upon them in this instance not just as an ideological imperative of their Marxist revolution but also from below as a natural by-product of the developmental forces they had set in motion. Probably it was only at this point, sometime in the early 1960s – with the aims of his cultural revolution still unfulfilled and the consequences of the 1958 formula becoming apparent – that Mao decided to distance himself from the latter, however styled.

---

[2] Cf. Tables 9.5 and 13.1 on opportunities to continue schooling at all levels in the 1950s and 1960s.

Table 13.1. *Opportunities to continue schooling within the regular system, 1957–1965*

Year	(1) Elem. school graduates	(2) Jr. middle entrants	(3) Elem. graduate promotion rate (%)	(4) Jr. middle graduates	(5) Sr. middle entrants	(6) Jr. middle graduate promotion rate (%)	(7) Sr. middle graduates	(8) Tertiary freshmen	(9) Sr. middle graduate promotion rate (%)
1957	4,980,000	2,170,000	43.57	1,112,000	323,000	29.05	187,000	105,581	56.46
1958	6,063,000	3,783,000	62.39	1,116,000	562,000	50.36	197,000	265,553	134.80
1959	5,473,000	3,183,000	58.16	1,491,000	656,000	44.00	299,000	274,143	91.69
1960	7,340,000	3,648,000	49.70	1,422,000	678,000	47.68	288,000	323,161	112.21
1961	5,808,000	2,218,000	38.19	1,892,000	447,000	23.63	379,000	169,047	44.60
1962	5,590,000	2,383,000	42.63	1,584,000	417,000	26.33	441,000	106,777	24.21
1963	4,768,000	2,635,000	55.26	1,523,000	434,000	28.50	433,000	132,820	30.67
1964	5,674,000	2,866,000	50.51	1,386,000	438,000	31.60	367,000	147,037	40.06
1965	6,676,000	2,998,000	44.91	1,738,000	459,000	26.41	360,000	164,212	45.61

Source: Zhongguo jiaoyu nianjian, 1949–1981, p. 1021 (col. 1), p. 1001 (cols. 2, 4–6), p. 969 (col. 8).

The "failure" of half-work, half-study

Agricultural work–study middle schools were initially touted as the innovation of the period and the means of achieving universal junior secondary education for the rural population. The agricultural middle school appeared at first glance to be a development planner's dream come true – designed to discourage rural–urban migration while harnessing the revolution of rising expectations to productive ends. The schools were to be largely self-supporting, leaving the regular education budget essentially intact. No longer would aspirant rural students have to "run away" to the cities for lack of secondary schools at home, a problem already registered in the mid-1950s. The agricultural middle school would prepare young people to remain in the countryside as educated peasants rather than provide them with a way out of agriculture.

The logic was faultless and agricultural middle schools seemed set to vindicate the claims. Some 20,000 such schools with 2 million students appeared from nowhere in 1958. The highest claim, made in 1960, was 30,000 schools with almost 3 million students.[3] The experiment was launched in Jiangsu Province, with Party propaganda chief Lu Dingyi as its leading promoter.[4] On the first anniversary of their inauguration , Lu acknowledged that China had at least 37 million 13- to 16-year-olds (the junior secondary age cohort), while regular schools at that level could accommodate only about 7 million. Most of the other 30 million were rural youth, and if they were to receive any formal schooling at all, work–study was the only way since the state could not yet afford the expense of giving them all a regular education.[5]

On the second anniversary of their birth, he was even more emphatic in advertising the economic benefits of work–study. He used one set of widely quoted figures from Jiangsu which showed costs to the state per student annually as being 187 renminbi (rmb) in regular junior middle schools but only 13 rmb in the agricultural equivalent. Additionally, the cost to the individual family in each case was estimated at over 100 rmb and over 30 rmb respectively.[6] But the third anniversary went unheralded. Having sprouted like bamboo shoots in spring rain, the schools withered just as quickly in the economic drought that followed. By 1962, they had all but disappeared (see Table 12.2).[7]

---

[3] See Robert D. Barendsen, "The Agricultural Middle School in Communist China," *China Quarterly*, no. 8 (Oct./Dec. 1961), pp. 106–134; and an update by the same author: *Half-Work Half-Study Schools in Communist China: Recent Experiments with Self-Supporting Educational Institutions* (Washington, D.C.: U.S. Dept. of Health, Education, and Welfare, 1964).

[4] *Guangming ribao*, 19 Mar. 1958.

[5] Ibid., 23 Mar. 1959.

[6] Lu Dingyi, "Nongye zhongxue chuangban erzhounian" (Two Full Years of Agricultural Middle Schools), *Renmin jiaoyu*, no. 2 (1960), reprinted in *Xinhua banyuekan*, no. 5 (1960), p. 83.

[7] Only Jiangsu seemed to keep the faith: Wu Tianshi, "Ban hao nongye zhongxue" (Run Agricultural Middle Schools Well), *Jiangsu jiaoyu* (Jiangsu Education), no. 2 (1962), reprinted in *Xinhua yuebao*, no. 4 (1962), pp. 118–120.

The effort to try again as the economy revived was noted, internally, by a "preliminary draft opinion" from the CCP Propaganda Department in March 1963 on reorganizing junior middle schools and strengthening technical education for agriculture and industry.[8] A commemoration of Jiangsu's fifth agricultural middle schools anniversary launched the revival, which continued until 1966.[9] Junior middle schools reappeared, with the addition of work–study schools at the elementary and senior middle levels, and urban equivalents as well.[10]

Liu Shaoqi now became their leading promoter, advertising them as part of his two–systems solution, and barnstormed the country, reputedly carrying his message personally to eight provinces. So literally was it taken that a parallel bureaucracy even began to form, with provinces and cities creating separate "second" education departments and bureaus (dier jiaoyu ting, ju) to manage work–study while existing offices continued to run the regular system.[11] It was this revival, highlighted by the Education Ministry's two national conferences on rural and urban work–study education in April and November 1965, respectively, that precipitated the post-1966 criticism of two separate systems as a perversion of Mao's "walking on two legs" concept. Thereafter, the separate half-work, half-study option as an economic expedient was abandoned in favor of varying combinations of part-work, part-study for everyone.

Given the chronology of their dual rise and fall, it would seem logical to blame Great Leap economics for the agricultural middle schools' first demise and Cultural Revolution politics for their second. When the work–study idea was revived after 1963, however, official promoters revealed reasons for its initial failure that seemed to reach beyond both economics and politics. Reflecting those reasons, the target group such schools were intended to serve allegedly regarded them as a second-rate alternative to "real" education, or that offered by the regular, full-time system.[12]

Up to this point, we have followed our sources and portrayed the failure of

---

[8] *Zhongguo jiaoyu nianjian, 1949–1981*, p. 180.

[9] Ouyang Huilin, "Xinxing de xuexiao yuanda de qiancheng: wei jinian Jiangsusheng nongye zhongxue chuangban wuzhounian er zuo" (Great Prospects for a New Form of School: Written in Commemoration of the Fifth Anniversary of Jiangsu's Agricultural Middle Schools), *Renmin ribao*, 2 Apr. 1963, reprinted in *Xinhua yuebao*, no. 5 (1963), pp. 57–60.

[10] E.g., *Renmin ribao*, 19 Oct. 1964; 6 Jan, 30 May, 13 July, 28 Sept., and 6, 11 Dec. 1965.

[11] Zhang Yanjing, "Liang zhong jiaoyu zhidu" (Two Kinds of Educational System), *Zhongguo dabaike quanshu: jiaoyu* (Chinese Encyclopedia: Education) (Beijing and Shanghai: Zhongguo dabaike quanshu chubanshe, 1985), p. 224; *Yangcheng wanbao* (Guangzhou Evening News), 14 Feb. 1965; interviews 78/GD/8, 79/GD/1.

[12] E.g., *Renmin ribao*, 19 Oct. 1964; Chen Guang, "Jiangsusheng nongye zhongxue chuangban qizhounian" (Seven Full Years of Agricultural Middle Schools in Jiangsu Province), *Hongqi*, no. 4 (1965), pp. 36–47; John Gardner, "Educated Youth and Urban–Rural Inequalities, 1958–66," in John Wilson Lewis, ed., *The City in Communist China* (Stanford: Stanford University Press, 1971), pp. 242–250; Glen Peterson, "State Literacy Ideologies and the Transformation of Rural China," *Australian Journal of Chinese Affairs*, no. 32 (July 1994), pp. 119–120.

all earlier irregular alternatives largely as the fault of an inhospitable political environment and/or the professional educator's commitment to regular education. Reformers, politicians, and educators were the key players. But with quantitative growth came an active new dimension, in the expectations of "nonintellectual" parents and students. This added dimension began to appear almost immediately, in the demands of urban elementary and junior middle school graduates for more education and jobs commensurate with their newly acquired status. On the surface, it seemed like misplaced elite aspirations – the typical Third World phenomenon of disdain for manual labor acquired along with even the most basic rudiments of education – and Chinese leaders responded in kind. But eventually, popular demands began creating constraints that could no longer be eased, as in the early 1950s, by a radio broadcast from the Education Minister chastising parents and students for expecting too much too soon.

In 1958, as policymakers shifted to high-speed growth and took their first leap into the unknown realm of rural mass secondary schooling, they ran sharply up against a wall of rural indifference for the proposed work–study scheme. Some city-bred intellectuals could still profess surprise at the uniform rural rejection of the agricultural middle school idea after it was recycled yet again in the late 1970s. Since rural people could not realistically aspire to higher education, it was reasoned, they should be content with some such appropriate alternative. Rural teachers and others closer to the scene, however, saw the rejection as entirely rational. It seemed to derive from and certainly reinforced the professional educator's quality-oriented view: "better no school than an irregular one." But this rural version also reflected the practical calculations of family decision makers about present costs and future benefits.

Times had clearly changed since the 1920s and 1930s, when everyone's social surveys revealed that peasants preferred old-fashioned irregular *sishu* to modern "foreign" schools. Now, rising elementary enrollments testified to the increasing acceptance of "regular" mass education at that level even in the countryside. So did the presence of rural youth crowding into town schools, a pressure point reflected in the mid-1950s vacillations over junior middle "caps" and how to meet the growing demand for more secondary schooling in the countryside. The measure of modernization could thus be seen in the expectations of these new rural students – a substantive change from their own formative rural experience that neither Mao nor Liu Shaoqi seem to have grasped in the late 1950s.

Still, the new demand from below was not just for regular education but more specifically for education that justified the cost in time and trouble of supporting young people in middle school rather than putting them directly to work. Agricultural middle schools were simply not accepted in that equation by their intended audience, and people therefore refused to support or attend them. The issue seems never to have been formulated explicitly in terms of "equality." But by the late 1950s, the growing rural clientele was demanding in effect a kind of parity and Beijing policymakers ultimately had to accept that challenge as a condition for further development. Interviews conducted in Hong Kong with former rural residents help illustrate those calculations.

Although the interviews focused on the post-1966 period, many of the older teachers with longer professional memories were able to reminisce about earlier years, as did younger teachers about their own student days. Of the 82 people interviewed for this study, 30 could claim direct firsthand or plausible second-hand knowledge of 109 half-work, half-study agricultural middle schools and four labor universities in their immediate localities, that is, in the counties, communes, or suburban districts where they worked or studied.[13] Only one person had actually studied in such a school; another had begun his teaching career therein; and a third had worked briefly "on loan" at a county-run labor university, the higher-level equivalent of an agricultural middle school. Several had relatives, classmates, and colleagues who were associated as either students or teachers with the schools. And almost everyone recalled them in the same negative terms – as poorly managed and unpopular – including those set up in 1958–1959 and later in 1964–1965. Most had closed down or ceased operating on a half-work, half-study basis after only a few years, in a pattern similar to that indicated by official statistics as shown on Table 12.2 for the country as a whole. Official statistics record no such schools for the 1966–1976 decade, but a few people reported that work–study middle schools had either been set up in their localities or continued to operate during those years, accounting for 7 of the 113 schools and the only success story among them.

Typically, the middle schools began with one or two *ban* (classes) totaling fewer than 100 students, and two or three teachers drawn from miscellaneous sources. Some schools enrolled new students for two or three years and so grew in size. The main subjects taught were Chinese language, math, politics, and agricultural knowledge. Localities varied widely in the material support they provided. Hence, the burdens of building construction or opening up waste-land allocated to the school for cultivation could fall heavily upon students and teachers. Accordingly, the work schedules also varied widely, sometimes with more work and less study rather than half and half. Yet regardless of the labor

---

[13] See Appendix on the interview data and the distinction between firsthand and secondhand information used in summarizing it. The following tabulation classifies the 30 interviewees responding to this question (and the 113 schools, in parentheses) by province:

Guangdong:	10	(19)	Shanghai suburbs:	2	(21)
Fujian:	6	(45)	North China:	1	(1)
Jiangsu:	2	(2)	Yunnan:	2	(5)
Anhui:	2	(3)	Guizhou:	2	(2)
Zhejiang:	1	(13)	Sichuan	1	(1)
			Xinjiang	1	(1)

schedule, such schools were treated as a course of last resort by all concerned, and achievements were modest at best. The relatively well managed schools in a suburban commune near Shanghai, described by Teacher Wu, provide a case in point.

Teacher Wu had himself graduated from a regular senior middle school in the county but found his route blocked thereafter by family political problems. He was thus available when his commune's agricultural middle school "system" began to expand in 1964–1965. The main school located in the commune headquarters town had started up with only one class of students in 1958 and after a checkered history could boast by the mid-1960s about 150 students and 10 teachers. They followed a three-year junior middle curriculum which tried to duplicate that of the regular schools with the addition of a course in agricultural basic knowledge.

In 1963, two production brigades had set up night schools to accommodate elementary school graduates unable to continue their studies, and in 1964, the night schools were superseded by two new agricultural middle schools, one of which Teacher Wu was recruited to staff. As its one and only teacher, he taught all subjects to the first class of 30 students. The school doubled in size the next year and closed down in 1966, after which all three agricultural schools merged with the regular commune middle school. The entire operation, in Teacher Wu's view, had been promoted solely to universalize junior middle schooling. Once that had been achieved in the early 1970s, there was no more need for agricultural middle schools.[14]

Speaking of another suburban Shanghai county, Teacher Wang recalled: "There were two things people did not like because both were inferior and they tried to get rid of them as soon as possible: one was agricultural middle schools; the second was *minban* schools. Peasants did not want to send their children to such schools because the education provided was inadequate. Neither teachers nor peasants liked these schools . . . despite their convenience." Just about every newly created commune in the country set up its own agricultural middle school in 1958, but Teacher Wang could remember only two that survived until 1966, whereas "most closed down right away." The two that survived soon expanded to include both junior and senior middle sections and, like the schools in Teacher Wu's commune, did their best to duplicate the regular curriculum. Tuition and all expenses were "free," paid for with the students' labor. But only if students could not get into a regular institution, recalled Teacher Wang, would they consent to attend an agricultural school. Especially in the rural areas, he explained, 16-year-olds could join the agricultural

---

[14] Interview 82/S/6, pp. 26–30. Teacher Wu recalled that his commune had a population of about 25,000 in the late 1970s, divided into 14 production brigades (village-based collective work units), each with about 2,000 people.

work force so they calculated that an agricultural school was a losing proposition whereby they earned nothing and learned little.[15]

Teacher Liao told a similar story. All the new communes in his relatively prosperous south Fujian county had set up agricultural middle schools in 1958 and allocated land to support them. But all had varied histories of no more than a few years, enrolling students who could not gain admission elsewhere. He dismissed half-work, half-study as a failure and said that the national model in that regard, Jiangxi Communist Labor University, was not admired in his county. The agricultural middle schools were not well run, he said, because no one took them seriously. "Students were not taught well during the half-day in class, so there was no real result. Neither parents nor students wanted such schools; even when the authorities ran them, no one wanted to attend."[16]

From northern Jiangsu and coastal Fujian respectively, Headmaster Chu and Teacher Lin assessed the problem in even more prosaic terms. Rural students were always looking for a way out of rural life. Since village youth "use study to get out of the village," they did not like the agricultural middle schools, which led to no such job assignment.[17] Teacher Zhu's verdict from his central China commune was the same. Agricultural middle schools neither taught much agricultural technology nor offered a way out of the village, he said, so they could not be popularized. "There were not many people who wanted to study in such schools and because there were no students, there could be no schools. They were all soon abandoned."[18]

The one success story was atypical in almost all respects. It was told by Commune Cadre Wen, a man of varied experience not prone to exaggerate the positive about life in China. The setting was a small commune in west Xinjiang. About 80 percent of its 8,000–9,000 inhabitants were recent Han Chinese settlers – people from all over China who like Wen himself were trying to put their troubles behind them. Politically, the region remained after 1949 what it had been before: a place to assign people with problematic pasts. Economically, the official effort to settle the border regions had provided an unofficial escape route for many thousands of economic migrants during the early 1960s depression years. The region, although isolated and pervaded by a certain "Wild West" atmosphere, had rewarded them with living standards that compared favorably with their home provinces even in good times, according to Wen and two other teachers with personal knowledge of the region. Relations in Wen's commune between the Han settlers and the non-Han minority population (a mix of several ethnic groups) were not particularly good but neither were they

[15] Interview 80/S/4, pp. 7, 10–11.
[16] Interview 83/FJ/26, p. 33.
[17] Interview 83/JS/6, p. 5; 80/FJ/8, p. 61.
[18] Interview 82/NC/15, p. 12.

very bad. The latter lived mostly by raising animals in the hills, and a separate elementary school was maintained in the commune seat for the more sedentary among them.

The agricultural middle school was actually a tribute to the initiative of one man, the commune's leader and Communist Party secretary. He, too, was an outsider, having been demoted to that far-off post for "errors" of a personal nature, although he was otherwise energetic and capable. Open-minded politically, he did not hesitate to tap the commune's miscellaneous assortment of talents. These he mobilized to produce an economic surplus and to staff the school, endeavors both calculated to redeem himself within the Party bureaucracy. After trying unsuccessfully to obtain help from the provincial government, he built and staffed the school entirely with commune resources in the early 1970s.

Cadre Wen agreed that such schools were unpopular everywhere else that he had ever heard of, but he insisted the reverse was true in his Xinjiang commune. He attributed the school's success to good leadership and the commune's working conditions since it already had the necessary material and technical resources in the form of a functioning farm machines station, two irrigation engineers, a clinic, and a well-managed commune-run farm staffed by over 10 men. Since the Party secretary was personally leading the project, commune staff could not refuse to cooperate, which they might otherwise have done. They therefore served as teachers for the three main "subjects": farm machines and irrigation for boys and public health for girls. The school did not try to teach conventional subjects, concentrating instead on apprentice-like practical instruction for one year only. With an enrollment of no more than 100, numbers were not so great as to disrupt commune work routines. There were also "results" lacking elsewhere in that students acquired basic skills which prepared them to move into on-the-job training slots in three essential areas of commune life.

Yet, the tale ended as an exception that did not disprove the rule. Students were mostly all ordinary commune members from "poor and lower-middle" peasant families. Cadres' children preferred to attend the regular county town middle school, and most did so unless they were exceptionally poor students. Following from this observation, Wen reasoned that despite its popularity the work–study enterprise had "no hope for the future." Subjects were too limited, and the need for people so trained would soon be filled. "Another reason," he said, "is that society progresses. It wants to go forward in ways appropriate to the environment. Students will want to go on to a higher and more regular kind of education."

This conclusion pointed to one additional reason underlying the successful work–study operation, namely, the absence of an alternative. For reasons unexplained, the Party secretary had applied his energies to work–study rather than to mobilizing support from the state through the county education bureau to follow the then typical practice of building a regular middle school within the commune's boundaries. Perhaps mitigating factors were the commune's small population, the non-Han pastoral minority, and the unusually slow growth of elementary schooling, to which the Party secretary might have devoted more attention had he not been trying to make a fast impression with something more spectacular. But for whatever reason, the county did not authorize a regular junior middle school for this commune until the mid-1970s and it did not begin enrolling students until 1978. Hence Wen concluded that the new school would probably have an adverse influence on its work–study predecessor, although he left the locality before any such impact was apparent.[19]

Evidently by an accident of circumstance, the Xinjiang school succeeded where most others failed in putting together the prerequisites for a work–study enterprise. In so doing, that one isolated case also helps reconcile the great gap between work–study's overall failure and its premier success in Jiangxi's famous Communist Labor University (Jiangxi gongchanzhuyi laodong daxue, or Jiangxi Gongda, for short). That institution, a provincewide network of branches administered from the main Nanchang campus, not only survived the early 1960s depression but went on to become the work–study standard-bearer for schools at all academic levels and the national demonstration model for agricultural education in particular. In the end, after Mao's death, Jiangxi Gongda finally met the same fate as its counterparts everywhere. This work–study model was forced to bow by government decree to the triumph of regularity, however, and did not collapse of its own accord. Also unlike others, its faculty remained defiantly committed to their enterprise. Nor could its success be explained wholly in "Hawthorne effect" terms: wherein models succeed precisely because of the attention they generate as models, a result by definition impossible to achieve under ordinary circumstances.[20]

That principle could be seen at work in Chinese models such as Gongda. For them, the attention generated typically included tangible material assistance as well, but only *after* the endeavor had already demonstrated some potential for success. The potential remained as the point of origin and featured in interviews of a different sort, conducted not in Hong Kong but on the Gongda campus itself in 1980.[21] With all its branches recently severed, the

---

[19] Interview 82/XJ/13, pp. 64–73.

[20] The reference is to the Western Electric Company's Hawthorne Works in Cicero, Ill., and the pioneering behavioral studies done there in the late 1920s. Experiments tried to determine the variables responsible for increasing productivity. Yet no matter what innovations were tried, barring physical obstruction of the work itself, production always increased. Researchers ultimately concluded that it was the human/social factor or being part of the experimental situation itself, rather than any technical input, which was the key variable inspiring workers to greater productivity; see F. J. Roethlisberger and W. J. Dickson, *Management and the Worker* (Cambridge: Harvard University Press, 1939).

[21] Gongda was one of the dozen universities visited by the author in 1980, under the national U.S.–China scholar exchange program administered by the Committee on Scholarly Communication

university was awaiting reorganization. Inevitably at such a time, faculty and staff were conducting their own postmortem, dissecting the anatomy of their successes and failures. In the process, they revealed more clearly than could the isolated Xinjiang case why their winning formula was so difficult to reproduce nationwide. At Gongda, they said, that formula was applied with greatest success during the first decade of its life, or from 1958 until 1966.

The university's history was reflected in the rise and fall of its branches (see Table 13.2). Half were lost in the early 1960s, but its status was affirmed by Mao's 30 July 1961 letter praising Gongda's work–study orientation.[22] This was subsequently tapped by Liu Shaoqi during his two-systems revival in the mid-1960s, when the school emerged as a national model. Local leaders and educators came by the thousands from all over China to learn how a half-work, half-study enterprise should be run and returned home to set up hundreds of schools in its image.[23]

Accordingly, Gongda found itself in the middle of the epic struggle between Mao, for the forces of cultural revolution, and Liu Shaoqi, recast as the revolution's archenemy in all sectors. But with Mao, Zhou Enlai, and veteran army chief Zhu De also on record as its supporters, Gongda survived the 1966–1968 struggles. It emerged scarred but unbowed to become a model for the 1970s, when the revolutionary logic of work–study for everyone replaced the two-systems formula. Expansion peaked at this time, in the early 1970s, after which Gongda became tangled in controversy once more, during the last upsurge of the cultural revolutionaries between 1974 and 1976. Apparently, they were in the process of supplanting Gongda with their own, "purer" work–study model, the Chaoyang Agricultural College in Liaoning Province, when Mao's death ended all such designs.[24]

---

with the PRC. Except where otherwise noted, this brief account of Jiangxi Gongda's work is based on interviews conducted at the main Nanchang campus and the former Nancheng County branch during a weeklong stay in late October 1980.

[22] The letter was not officially published until much later (in *Renmin ribao*, 30 July 1977), but it was circulated in unofficial compilations after a copy was exhibited at Gongda in 1965 (e.g., *Mao Zedong sixiang wansui* [1967], pp. 267–268).

[23] E.g., see Jonathan Unger's compilation for Guangdong Province, which shows only four agricultural labor universities in 1961–1962 but 115 in early 1966. With a total enrollment of 20,000, these schools averaged 174 students each, smaller even than Jiangxi Gongda's individual branches (Unger, *Education under Mao*, table 3–2, p. 54). In Guangdong, the Xinhui County school was the most famous. Built upon the county's system of work–study middle schools and boasting among its visitors Zhou Enlai himself, the Xinhui County Agricultural Labor University survived into the late 1970s. Jiangxi appears to have been unique, however, in establishing a provincewide system with top provincial leaders assuming personal responsibility for its unified administration, as indicated below (Christine Wong, Xinhui County Labor University, trip notes, 11 June 1977; Ou Meng-chueh, "Farm–Study Schools Prove Their Worth," *China Reconstructs*, vol. 14, no. 9 [Sept. 1965], pp. 7–9).

[24] See press accounts at the time Mao's letter of 30 July 1961 was finally published, especially a full-page history that accompanied its publication (in *Renmin ribao*, 30 July 1977), and *Hongri zhao zhengcheng: ji Jiangxi gongchanzhuyi laodong daxue* (Arduous Journey under a Brilliant Red Sun: Commemorating Jiangxi Communist Labor University) (Shanghai: Shanghai jiaoyu chubanshe, 1977). Events in the mid-1970s are summarized in chap. 17, below.

Table 13.2. *Jiangxi Communist Labor University: number of branches and students*

	Branches and schools	Students (approx.)
1958	30	11,000 (main campus and branches)
1959	77 branches 38 vocational schools	40,615
1960	88 branches 14 vocational schools	50,000 (main campus, branches, and schools)
Early 1960s	46	17,000
1964	46	13,000 (main campus and branches)
1965	23 branches: provincial and prefectural specialized senior middle schools 23 branches: county-run vocational junior middle schools	14,000
1966	112	31,000
Late 1960s	126	52,000
1972	130	50,000 (main campus and branches)
Mid-1970s	108	37,000
1976–1979	104–105	—
Fall semester, 1979	—	37,000 (branches only)
Dec. 1979	All branches severed	
Oct. 1980	—	1,886 (main campus only)

Sources: 1958 – *Jiangxi ribao*, 2 Aug. 1958. 1959 – *Jiangxi ribao*, 14 May 1959. 1960 and 1965 – *Renmin ribao*, 17 Apr. 1965. Early 1960s, late sixties, and mid-1970s through Oct. 1980 – Interview notes, Jiangxi Gongda, Oct. 1980. 1964 – *Jiangxi ribao*, 26 Aug. 1964. 1966 – *Jiangxi ribao*, 17 June 1966. 1972 – "University Combined Education with Labor," *China Reconstructs*, Beijing, vol. 21, no. 9 (Sept. 1972), p. 7.

Yet its personnel, looking back over the years, spoke far less of struggle and glory than of economics and administration as the prerequisites for success. Gongda's chief competitor had always been recognized as the regular system. In the mid-1960s, University Party Secretary Zhang Yuqing wrote of the difficulties. Many people believed, he said, that because work–study was not "regular" such a school could not be built and that if built could not survive.

All doubts were concentrated in three questions: "Should such schools be built? Can they be operated well? Do they have a future?"[25]

Personnel 15 years later described a school system that had been designed with precisely those questions in mind, by emphasizing the same three key features identified in the Xinjiang case: active local government and CCP leadership, adequate material and technical support, and tangible benefits for the student clientele. Gongda owed its strength to that formula, which was orchestrated with a precision rarely seen in most civilian educational endeavors, perhaps reflecting also the interest of so many old veterans in the project. It had been launched by Jiangxi's top provincial leaders in coordination with the central Ministry of State Land Reclamation Farms (Nong ken bu). About 50,000 cadres and demobilized soldiers had been sent down in late 1957 as part of the province's ambitious land and forest reclamation program. The original 30 farms were actually comprehensive land reclamation state farms, and a branch school was attached to each, with the main campus serving as academic guide and coordinator.[26]

The main initial work–study activities of students and staff were reclaiming barren wastelands for cultivation and restoring forests by planting trees under contracts allocated by the provincial land reclamation department. School buildings were also constructed with student and staff labor. But strictly speaking, the enterprise operated on a half-work, half-study schedule only during its first academic year, 1958–1959. Thereafter, students labored progressively fewer months each year. After 1962, when basic construction was completed and everyone was becoming more quality conscious, only about one-third of the students' time was devoted to labor. From 1962 also, students at the main campus were enrolled via the national unified college entrance examinations.

The Gongda complex was also never entirely self-sufficient or able to survive without state subsidies in some form. But the complex throughout its history did rely for a considerable portion of its income on student labor and school-run productive enterprises. Over time, these grew to include, besides land reclamation and afforestation, factories, forestry centers, orchards, and livestock farms. All of this required in turn an extensive network of county- and prefectural-level support for the allocation of unreclaimed lands, assignment

---

[25] Chang Yü-ch'ing (Zhang Yuqing), "The Great Victory of the Half-Work (Farming) and Half-Study Educational System: Introducing Kiangsi Communist Labor University," *Chung-kuo nung-ken* (China's Agricultural Land Reclamation), no. 1 (5 Jan. 1965), trans. in *Selections from China Mainland Magazines* (*SCMM*), no. 466 (1965), p. 12. For a similar full-page account of Gongda's work by its president Liu Junxiu, see *Renmin ribao*, 17 Apr. 1965. Zhang Yuqing was at this time concurrently a deputy secretary-general of the Jiangxi Provincial CCP Committee; he was Gongda CCP secretary between 1961 and 1968.

[26] *Jiangxi ribao*, 2 Aug. 1958 and 14, 15 Feb. 1959; *Guangming ribao*, 9 June 1960. The farms were known as *nonglin xumu zonghe kenzhi chang* (comprehensive agricultural, forestry, and animal husbandry reclamation farms).

of afforestation and irrigation contracts, and the guaranteed allocation of supplies, transport, and marketing facilities. But the main reason local authorities cooperated, given competing local demands for the scarce resources needed to maintain any given school, was the unified provincewide system held together by its "command and control" network.

At the top, the university's founder was the then provincial CCP secretary and governor, Shao Shiping, whose revolutionary credentials extended back to the Jiangxi soviet period and beyond. Another secretary of the provincial CCP committee, Liu Junxiu, was concurrently the first president of Gongda's main campus, and its CCP secretary was none other than the deputy governor of Jiangxi Province, Wang Dongxing, Mao's personal bodyguard from Yan 'an days.[27] Crucial to the whole operation, however, was not so much who these men were as what they were. The pattern of interlocking positions was replicated throughout the system, making the heads or Party secretaries of prefectures and counties concurrently the leaders of prefectural- and county-level branch schools. Hence, when anyone complained about the added burdens – a common reaction among local officials – the governor could argue that as he was responsible for the system as a whole, so individual county leaders should be able to look after a single school. If the man still refused to cooperate, he would be transferred to other work.

The interlocking directorate became a prerequisite in order to guarantee access to the resources necessary to sustain the operation. A county chief could order that contracts be allocated to the school rather than to other production units. He could also order that scarce materials and spare parts be allocated to the school on time as needed, guaranteeing that the output of its orchards and farms need not be bartered for favors but could bring the income needed to feed students and keep the school running. A simple country schoolmaster or even the county education bureau lacked such powers. In this respect, the system functioned most smoothly during its early years. The 1966–1968 factional struggles shattered the concurrent leadership custom, which was never fully restored after 1970, although the complex remained strong enough to continue operating most of its branches.

Students were mainly in the secondary and tertiary age brackets. The first 1958 class contained many cadres who had been sent down to the land reclamation sites, but adults were never the main source of students. These were

---

[27] On these men and their positions in 1958–1959, see *Jiangxi ribao*, 2 Aug. 1958 and 14, 15, 23 Feb. 1959; biographic sketches are in *Who's Who in Communist China* (Hong Kong: Union Research Institute, 1969–1970), 1:438–439, 2:558–559, 699. Liu Junxiu was university president for 10 years, from 1958–1968. Shao Shiping died in 1965. Wang Dongxing served as university Party secretary between 1958 and 1961. Wang was also a vice-minister at the national Ministry of Public Security in the mid-1950s and remained in the role of central elite guard until Mao's death. Kang Sheng had been Wang's superior within the Yan'an security apparatus (Byron and Pack, *Claws of the Dragon*, p. 289).

recruited in a variety of ways and, initially at least, came from widely varying educational backgrounds ranging from semiliteracy through senior secondary. Together, county and prefectural branches plus the main campus offered a variety of programs at all academic levels from junior middle through college. The branches were led in academic and policy matters by the main campus, and the entire complex was devoted throughout its life primarily to agriculture and forestry.

The university's objective from the start was to train rural cadres, and of the 200,000 students who had graduated from the Gongda complex by 1980, most did eventually become "basic-level cadres in agriculture" although they were not necessarily assigned as such upon graduation. Two different principles governed job allocation for Gongda graduates. Students of the county-level branches usually returned to their own communes and were subsequently assigned work therein as needed. Many of these graduates later became production brigade and team leaders within their communes. Graduates from the prefectural-level branches and the main campus, which had many out-of-province students before 1966, also sometimes returned to their own localities. Or such students were assigned jobs under the unified state plans, becoming cadres in the county and provincial bureaus responsible for agriculture, forestry, reclamation, and other areas for which Gongda at times offered courses of instruction. Many of these graduates later became commune Party secretaries.

University personnel did not draw any parallels between themselves and a much earlier generation of education reformers. But the incongruous sight of an old church, built in Gothic cathedral style, rising along the road south from the main campus to the Nancheng County branch reminded the traveler that this was once missionary country. Just beyond Nancheng on the Fujian border lies Lichuan County, site of George Shepherd's vain effort in the 1930s to recruit educated young people willing to "serve as the communists do – for living expenses only" in such isolated rural backwaters. He would undoubtedly have been even more impressed by Gongda, with its work–study philosophy and branches in every Jiangxi county. But unlike Shepherd, Gongda personnel were under no illusions regarding the full range of resources necessary to maintain their idealistic tradition in a materialistic world.

Yet the more things changed, the more they stayed the same. Gongda personnel remained unrepentant in their commitment to labor as an antidote for intellectual and bureaucratic elitism, however great the acknowledged difficulties of realizing work–study's other aims. As individuals, at least, they would undoubtedly carry that commitment with them wherever their subsequent assignments took them, ensuring that the controversy between them and conventional educators would carry on as well. The latter, too, had remained unmoved by all the forces of revolution ranged against them. "We hated that place" was a typical view. It was inspired by the practice in later years – as work–study was being transformed from a pragmatic second system into a uniform requirement for all – of sending teachers and students out on their labor assignments in emulation of Jiangxi Gongda.

In the post-1976 end, of course, regularity would again prevail. But its protagonists then, as they tried to confine labor to its "rightful" place in a revived work–study agricultural middle school alternative, seemed oblivious still as to how a newly educated mass base had changed the nature of the debate. Work–study had been promoted from 1958, not just as a form of penance for the ancient intellectual exemption from manual labor, but also as a practical means of universalizing secondary schooling. On paper, it had seemed the perfect solution: affordable education appropriate to ordinary rural lives. In reality, the experiment failed because the student bodies and communities it was intended to serve rejected it as an inferior version of the real (i.e., regular) thing. Evidently, the only way work–study could succeed in competition with the regular system was by offering a kind of parity or comparable tangible results. And the only way that could be done was by reproducing the winning formula as demonstrated by prototype Jiangxi Gongda and its miniature Xinjiang replica.

Ultimately, then, whether it was foisted upon the masses as a practical alternative or upon intellectuals as a political imperative, everyone would resist work–study, leaving it back where it began as an ideal honored by all in theory and only the dedicated few in practice. But just as it had been used to promote different ends, one political and the other economic, so it was rejected for different reasons, one old and the other new, reflecting the complex popular interests developing along with a fast-growing system of mass education.

The "success" of the regular system

By contrast, the regular system emerged from the Great Leap Forward more vigorously competitive than ever before in modern times. Whether the intrusion was Western learning, the Soviet model, or a radical socialist orientation, Chinese educators seemed infinitely able to adapt. Only this time, they had the weight of Mao's two-legged solution behind them as they set about rebuilding the regular system and especially the key schools within it. These latter could be seen as the CCP's compromise with its disaffected educational establishment by allowing it a qualitatively secure zone designed to keep the quantitative excesses of a modernizing socialist revolution at bay. The Party's motive undoubtedly was to guarantee talent for modernization rather than to placate bourgeois educators. But the net result was the same, allowing inherited assumptions about turning out a quality product to survive yet another historic assault.

If the promoters – whether Mao, Liu, or the Education Ministry – thought at all about the social contradictions such quality education might generate, they must have calculated that tensions could be contained by discreetly unpublicized regulations, carefully contrived external appearances, intensified use of political criteria in school management, and massive doses of political study. In fact, to have promoted such a solution, whether as two legs or two systems, during the radical cultural revolution phase of the CCP's history was like trying to erect a lightning rod in the middle of a thunderstorm. The designer's dream would soon turn into a nightmare for all concerned.

Quality-oriented key schools were institutionalized within the regular system at every level from kindergarten through university. But quality orientation was defined specifically to mean college preparatory. And since the ultimate tangible proof of success was admission to college, the lives of everyone within the key-point stream revolved from 1959 onward around the single aim of passing the national college entrance examinations. Given that aim, the secondary level quickly emerged as the crucial link since it performed the final tasks of sorting and prepping.

Statistics published only later leave many questions still unanswered but suggest the differentiation that occurred after 1958. From a pre–Great Leap high of 11,000 in 1957, regular middle schools probably at least doubled and then leveled off at about 19,000 in the early 1960s. Student enrollments also doubled from 6 to at least 12 million and leveled off at between 7 and 8 million (see Table 12.2). Since the only available set of national key-point middle school totals is from 1963 (see Table 13.3), we can use that year to profile the secondary school system during this period (see Table 13.4).

About 19,600 regular middle schools were recorded for 1963, of which only 4,303 were senior level or complete junior/senior middle schools. This number included the 487 key-point schools shown in Table 13.3. Junior secondary enrollments predominated, accounting for 6.4 million of the total 7.6 million students enrolled.

Of the 4,303 senior middle schools, 1,414 were located in urban areas, 2,408 in county towns, and 481 were designated rural. Beyond this point, however, the national statistics reveal none of the educational hierarchies created at every level as localities struggled to fulfill the terms of central decisions and directives on key-point management. The 487 key schools listed were only the tip of the iceberg; that is, they were the key schools run directly by provincial education bureaus (and all-city bureaus in the case of independently administered Beijing, Shanghai, and Tianjin).

Beneath them was a much larger configuration of prefectural, city, and county key-point schools designed to serve as backup and feeder schools. The configuration was intended to absorb as much quality talent as possible while providing all regions with some opportunity to compete in the annual college enrollment sweepstakes. At the base of the key-point pyramid, as the system developed after 1958, each county typically tried to maintain one middle school

Table 13.3. *Number of key-point schools, full-time regular secondary,*
1953 and 1963

	1953		1963	
	No. of schools	% of total	No. of schools	% of total
Beijing	20	27.7	12	2.7
Tianjin	10	—	—	—
Hebei	8	3.1	37	2.8
Shanxi	4	4.4	41	11.3
Inner Mongolia	2	6.4	11	4.3
Liaoning	15	4.9	52	6.0
Jilin	4	3.3	23	5.3
Heilongjiang	7	5.8	11	1.6
Shanghai	10	5.4	13	3.3[a]
Jiangsu	14	3.3	18	1.2
Zhejiang	9	4.6	7	1.2
Anhui	10	6.8	12	2.0
Fujian	10	5.7	14	4.6
Jiangxi	4	1.8	24	4.0
Shandong	8	4.2	36	3.9
Henan	5	2.5	19	2.1
Hubei	7	5.3	18	2.3
Hunan	6	2.5	20	2.1
Guangdong	7	1.6	10	.9
Guangxi	4	2.5	9	2.4
Sichuan	15	3.5	30	3.5
Guizhou	3	3.6	10	4.6
Yunnan	3	2.1	9	3.9
Tibet	—	—	—	—
Shaanxi	6	4.2	10	1.9
Gansu	2	—	17	7.1
Qinghai	1	—	4	12.5
Ningxia	1	12.5	4	1.2
Xinjiang	1	2.1	16	5.6
Total	196	4.4	487	3.1[a]

[a] The 3% calculations are reproduced as shown in the source cited. But the total number of middle schools given elsewhere in the same source (p. 1009), both for Shanghai and for the entire country, yields a lower proportion of key schools than that shown here. The total number of regular middle schools in Shanghai in 1963 was given as 521 (and the total number for the country as a whole, 19,599). With only 13 recognized key schools in Shanghai, and 487 nationwide, the percentages should both be 2.5.

Source: *Zhongguo jiaoyu nianjian, 1949–1981*, p. 168.

Table 13.4. *National statistical profile, regular secondary schools, 1963*

	Jr. middle	Sr. middle	Jr. middle grads.	Sr. middle freshmen	Sr. middle and complete jr./sr. middle	Sr. middle grads.	College freshmen
No. of schools (total: 19,599):	15,290				4,303[a]		
Urban	2,594				1,414		
County town	2,899				2,408		
Rural	9,797				481		
No. of classes (ban) (total: 168,574):	140,490				28,084		
Urban	50,409				11,973		
County town	39,640				14,111		
Rural	50,331				2,000		
No. of students (total: 7,616,100):	6,380,800	1,235,300	1,523,000	434,000		433,000	132,820
Urban	2,491,000	543,000	469,000	191,000		180,000	—
County town	1,750,000	605,000	431,000	213,000		218,000	—
Rural	2,139,000	87,000	623,000	30,000		35,000	—

[a] Including 487 key-point schools.

Source: *Zhongguo jiaoyu nianjian, 1949–1981*, pp. 168 (key points), 969 (college freshmen), 1000, 1001, 1005, 1006.

"in the key-point manner," concentrating therein the county's best teachers and students. Most of the 2,408 complete or senior middle schools shown on Table 13.4 as located in county towns (averaging slightly more than one per county, with a national total of approximately 2,000 counties) should therefore be regarded as county-level key points. Usually, the key-point school offered the only senior secondary instruction in the county. The above-cited statistics show a total of 2,889 senior secondary schools at the county level or below, averaging about 1.4 such schools per county nationwide. National statistics for the entire hierarchy have not been published, but Guangdong revealed, for example, that in 1963, besides its 10 provincially run key schools, an additional 25 middle schools were designated as prefectural key points and 130 as city or county key points.[28]

These schools were administered in a mix of overlapping jurisdictions and enrollment areas rendered more complicated by almost annual changes and adjustments during the early 1960s. The changes followed in turn from the regular system's need to digest the enormous quantitative increases of the Great Leap while simultaneously undertaking the first nationwide attempt to superimpose on a modern Chinese system what were in effect educational hierarchies adapted from the imperial past.

Historical prototypes were everywhere. One of the best known was Guangya Middle School in Guangzhou. Opened in 1888 as Guangya Academy (*shuyuan*), its founder was modernizing Qing dynasty official Zhang Zhidong, when he was governor-general of Guangdong and Guangxi. The school was designed to accommodate only 200 students, enrolled in equal numbers from those two provinces, living on campus in separate provincial halls. Students were all *juren*, or provincial-level degree holders, and were recruited to Guangya on a quota basis of one per county, to spend three years preparing for the metro-politan examinations in Beijing. The academy was in fact a transitional institu-tion with a reform-minded curriculum. Guangya converted to a modern curriculum and became a secondary school after the imperial examinations were abolished.[29]

In the early 1950s, when Guangya was tapped as one of the original Guangdong key points, the school continued to hold its own entrance exams and enrolled

[28] "Guangdongsheng jiaoyu" (Guangdong's education), *Zhongguo jiaoyu nianjian, 1949–1984: difang jiaoyu* (China Education Yearbook, 1949–1984: Local Education) (Changsha: Hunan jiaoyu chubanshe, 1986), p. 909. China's contemporary prefectures (*zhuanqu* or *diqu*; the former terminology was changed to the latter in the early 1970s) are subprovincial administrative units. In 1963, Guangdong's 93 counties were divided among 6 prefectures, the greater Guangzhou area, and the Hainan Island Administrative District. See Zhonghua renmin gongheguo minzhengbu, *Zhonghua renmin gongheguo xianji yishang xingzhengqu huayange* (The Evolution of the Administrative Divisions at the County Level and above within the People's Republic of China) (n.p.: Cehui chubanshe, 1987), 2:634–648.
[29] Interview 80/GD/1, pp. 13, 138; Ayers, *Chang Chih-tung and Educational Reform in China*, pp. 58–59.

from throughout Guangdong Province as it had before 1949. After 1958, however, key-point enrollment was systematized as the old imperial formulas were adapted for use nationwide. But principles designed to mediate competition among a relatively small exclusive elite produced mammoth complications between 1958 and 1966, when the educational hierarchies had to be superimposed on a truly mass base. Nor were socialism and modernization the only imperatives decreeing that the distribution of elite benefits had to be orchestrated, if not equally and fairly, then at least with the appearance of same.

Guangya Academy had been designed in accordance with Qing dynasty standards for creating candidate pools and allocating degrees on the basis of regional quotas. The formula was deliberately drawn to mediate two contradictory aims represented by (1) the intellectual goal of identifying individual talent through competitive examinations and (2) a regional parity principle whereby educationally less developed regions were guaranteed an opportunity to compete. Thus, the original Guangya had not aimed to enroll the best 200 students from Guangdong and Guangxi, but only the best from each county therein. This formula had evolved through centuries of intra-elite controversy, going back at least to Song times, inspired by a system that awarded bureaucratic power and status both official and unofficial, as necessary for empirewide governance, on the basis of intellectual achievement.

The precedent-setting debate in this respect between officials Sima Guang and Ouyang Xiu had actually occurred in the year 1064. Their debate followed the southward shift of the population in Song times and the consequent rising preeminence of degree-holders from the Southeast within the Song bureaucracy. Not surprisingly, Sima, who was from the old northern heartland, argued for regional parity, while Ouyang, from the new South, argued for individual merit. Sima's argument was not accepted at the time, but the concept of regional parity had already been introduced in the year 1009, when quotas were created to limit the number of successful candidates in lower qualifying examinations. Periodically adjusted, the quotas were fixed on the basis of the average number of candidates in recent past examinations from each prefecture rather than from the empire as a whole.[30]

Over the centuries thereafter, successive dynasties mediated conflicts created by regional disparities plus increasing numbers of candidates and competition by adding ever more degrees, preliminary qualifying examinations, and regional quota refinements.[31] However elitist China's traditional intellectual hierarchy may have been, concerns about fair access and opportunity to compete had been integral to that tradition for at least a thousand years. Accordingly, those same concerns and compromises were reproduced in some form

[30] Chaffee, *The Thorny Gates of Learning in Sung China*, pp. 35, 120–122, and passim.
[31] On the complicated quota arrangements worked out during the Ming and Qing dynasties, see Ping-ti Ho, *The Ladder of Success in Imperial China*.

everywhere – within provinces, prefectures, cities, and their districts – as the key-point formula was systematically imposed after 1958.

Also following old principles, however, the main additional criterion in designating key points, balanced against concern for fair regional distribution, was a school's actual performance. Promotion rates were the chief measure of success. These were calculated each year as the percentage of successful candidates among the total number of graduates or, alternatively, successful candidates among the total number taking the entrance exams for the next level above. If the candidates were elementary school graduates in a district where all went on to junior middle schools, the "pass rate" would be calculated in qualitative terms as the percentage gaining admission to district or all-city key points. At the most important senior middle to college level, two principles applied, that is, both quantitative and qualitative.

Essentially, the only constants during the early 1960s were these general principles governing the developing hierarchies. The hierarchies themselves were in constant flux. At each administrative level, the government education bureaucracy and Party authorities were directly responsible for running schools in the key-point manner, which meant guaranteeing them the best of everything available within their administrative jurisdictions. Each locality worked out its own ways of designating the schools and of sharing (or competing for) the resources in question. The usual, although not inevitable, result was that the key provincial schools run by provincial education bureaus were guaranteed first choice, and others lined up in rank order beneath them. But even the provincial key points were designated according to the regional parity principle and were therefore located throughout the province rather than concentrated within a single urban/cultural center, where the largest pools of talent would typically concentrate. As a result, only two of Guangdong's 10 provincial key middle schools were located in its largest city, Guangzhou, while the remainder were designated roughly on a prefectural basis.[32]

Further following the parity principle, the provincial key points in the 1960s were not allowed to enroll throughout the province. The two in Guangzhou, Guangya and Huafu, thus recruited primarily within Guangzhou itself, and those applying for admission took the Guangzhou city entrance examinations. The other provincial key points enrolled from only a few designated neighboring counties or at most the prefectures within which they were located. These schools were not intended to enroll the highest-scoring students in the province as a whole but only the highest-scoring students in each region of the

[32] "Guangdong sheng jiaoyu," p. 909; and interviews 79/GD/7, p. 31, 80/GD/1, p. 118; 80/GD/2, p. 41. The Guangzhou schools were Guangya Middle School and South China Teacher Training College Attached Middle School (Huafu). Others included Jinshan Middle School (Shantou Prefecture), Dongshan Middle School (Mei County), Beijiang Middle School (Shaoguan Prefecture), Jinian Middle School (Zhongshan County), Taishan Middle School Number One (Taishan County), Jiangmen Middle School Number One. (The Zhongshan, Taishan, and Jiangmen schools were all located in Foshan Prefecture.)

province. Guangzhou's Middle School Number One, a city key point, could therefore usually boast higher pass rates than outlying provincial key points but typically followed Guangya and Huafa in the Guangzhou city rank order. This last result was produced by the general rule which allowed the highest (jurisdictional) level school to enroll first or take the pick of the crop in any enrollment area where more than one school was competing for the same pool of candidates.

Within such a system, the assumption was well founded that if one gained admission to a top key senior middle school, one's ticket on to college was all but written. At its pinnacle, the key-point stream created a kind of artificial island simulating conditions enjoyed in the 1950s by the system as a whole, when virtually all of its graduates could continue their studies. But having structured secondary schooling in this manner, competition was naturally pushed outward and downward – which was indeed the official intention. In this spirit, Fujian's experience was publicized as an academically undistinguished province that pulled itself up from nowhere to win top honors in the race for examination scores and admission rates to college.

Passage at every level was governed by exit and entry examinations, while rank-order lists recorded scores and compared promotion rates. These lists were compiled for "internal" use only and were jealously guarded as the system's trade secrets. But they inevitably spread by word of mouth from teachers to pupils and parents. Stakes were further raised as the possibility of a rural work assignment increased during the 1960s for those who failed to achieve high scores.

Pressures for parity, or the chance to compete from below, thus combined with the system's design and official prodding from above. The results were traditionally "Chinese" in form but unprecedented in degree, leaving irregular alternatives to wither outside the growing vortex of the competitive circle. And so it came to pass that ways and means from an earlier age were adapted, with the blessing of all the CCP's top leaders, to form the core of communist China's rapidly growing mass-based school system. Little wonder that a Jiangxi Gongda–type operation was required to mount a credible "irregular" counteroffensive.

The regular system of the 1960s has been the subject of much research based on interviews conducted in Hong Kong primarily with former students from Guangdong Province. We are indebted to that work for our understanding of how the system functioned during those years.[33] Interviews conducted for this study reinforced the earlier findings for the 1960s by adding the teacher's

---

[33] The main studies resulting from this interview research done in Hong Kong during the 1970s are those by Anita Chan, Stanley Rosen, Susan Shirk, Jonathan Unger, and Gordon White. See the Select Bibliography for books and articles by these scholars (as well as for those of others who did not rely primarily on the interview method, e.g., Thomas Bernstein, Julia Kwong, and Ronald F. Price).

perspective, since most of the individuals interviewed were former teachers (see Appendix). But that perspective was presented with a difference that also reflected the shifting political norms of the post-Mao era. Although the "key-point manner" of running schools was officially sanctioned in 1958, much concerning their modus vivendi remained hidden, in mute testimony to the contemporary educational principles and socialist ideals they contradicted. Hence, the 1962 circular promoting key-point management was not actually published until the early 1980s. The hidden contradictions left a fertile field for Red Guard investigators ransacking school files when Mao finally rebelled and turned the full force of his second cultural revolution against the educational establishment as an exercise in class warfare. It was the system's hidden secrets, uncovered in this way, plus their own recollections filtered through the radical Maoist critique of key-school elitism, that contributed so many insights to the earlier research interviews with dissident members of the Red Guard generation who fled to Hong Kong in the early 1970s.

By 1980, however, class warfare had been repudiated, and the critical norms of that generation had been turned on their heads. Teachers interviewed in the post-1976 era, rather than reflecting one orthodoxy or the other, appeared to have internalized the contradictions between them: proud of the system's "glorious" past while scorning its easily manipulated pretensions. Here, too, they seemed to be reproducing the old ambivalence whereby everyone paid lip service to certain popular ideals even while ignoring them in practice. Two sets of recollections are especially useful. One is from Shanghai in the 1950s and 1960s, which offered a well-organized urban environment for early experimentation with key-point management in a modern system. The other is from Fujian, where educators won national recognition between 1959 and 1966 for their application of such skills in a very different setting.

Shanghai: building a mass-based key-point stream

Although key-point school origins in the 1950s remain obscure, the recollections of Shanghai teachers indicate that development was already well advanced there by 1958.[34] But as noted in chapter 9, they sketched a far more symmetrical pattern than was reported for other cities at the same time, suggesting that Shanghai probably played an unheralded pioneering role in developing mass-based key-point education during the 1950s. Aiding that role were Shanghai's unique "natural" resources, including its status as a self-contained

---

[34] Fifteen of the teachers interviewed had themselves been educated in Shanghai's inner-city schools, including those at the elementary, secondary, and tertiary levels, during the 1950s and 1960s. Four of those 15 had also spent all or the greater part of their own professional teaching careers in Shanghai's inner-city elementary and secondary schools (see Appendix). Relevant data were also gleaned from a visit to East China Teacher Training University Attached Middle School Number Two, Shanghai (interview notes, 28 Nov. 1980).

city-state, its concentrated urban population, and, especially, by Chinese reckoning, the inherited concentration of higher-level intellectual institutions, high-level intellectuals, and their better-educated offspring. According to interviewees, the Shanghai system by 1958 already contained superior state-financed kindergartens, a network of central (*zhongxin*) elementary schools, and ranked middle schools administered as key points (*zhongdian*) on both all-city and district bases at both the junior and senior secondary levels.

Most difficult to build was the key-point structure at the secondary level, and this work had actually begun about 1951 or 1952, the same years that mention of key middle schools began appearing in the documentary sources cited earlier. Perhaps as many as 20 schools were tapped for the experiment. Then, as conditions allowed, the least-qualified personnel were transferred out, and the best from other schools were transferred in. Concentrating students was more troublesome given the disparate admissions practices of those days. Since the experiment was conducted on a district basis, some districts also had more resources to concentrate than others.[35] Hence, not every school initially tapped succeeded in producing the desired results. It had been decided at the start to focus on the senior secondary level and give the experiment a three-year gestation period. Success was determined by comparing students' college entrance exam scores.

The 13 key schools shown on Table 13.3 for 1963 were those that passed the test and were designated all-city key points administered directly by Shanghai's education bureau. Additionally, former teachers identified a larger network of key schools administered by the districts, estimated to total at least twice that number. Financially, by the mid-1960s, the annual budgets of Shanghai's city key points were reputed to be about double those of their ordinary counterparts. The extra costs were necessary to maintain the prestige schools in the manner accustomed, with their well-equipped buildings, spacious dormitories, multiple playing fields, parklike grounds, etc.

Probably, Shanghai's solution to the problem of guaranteeing "student quality" appeared around 1956, after all remaining private schools were taken over by the state. The city then began to enforce a unified key-point enrollment

---

[35] This section on Shanghai's regular and key-point school development concerns the inner-city districts only and not the suburban counties. During the early 1950s, Shanghai was divided into several districts (18 in 1956–1957). Reorganization in 1958 produced a Greater Shanghai composed of inner-city districts (*qu*) and suburban counties (*xian*), the latter incorporated from surrounding Jiangsu Province. In 1964, the familiar 10 districts and 10 counties emerged and remained in that configuration until 1980, when the number of districts again began to increase. See Zhonghua renmin gongheguo minzhengbu, *Zhonghua renmin gongheguo xianji yishang xingzhengqu huayange*, 2:2–9. Shanghai's population in 1963 was 10.7 million, with 6,390,000 in the inner-city districts and 4,346,000 in suburban counties (*Shanghai tongji nianjian, 1989* [Shanghai Statistical Yearbook, 1989] [Shanghai: Zhongguo tongji chubanshe, 1989], p. 92). Individual inner-city districts in the 1960s varied in population size from 100,000 to over 0.5 million, according to former residents.

formula whereby each district gave its own junior middle entrance examination, in Chinese language and math. The exams differed from district to district, but standards were more or less uniform throughout the city. Following tradition, essay composition was still regarded as an important test of ability and counted for at least half the grade on the language exam. The highest-scoring students were then assigned, primarily on the basis of these exam results, to the district's key junior middle school(s). Other students with passing scores were assigned usually to the nearest ordinary school in their neighborhood. Similarly, all graduates at the junior middle level who wanted to continue their studies took a unified examination in three subjects (politics, language, and math) to determine who could study at which of the key and ordinary senior secondary schools, since all soon came to be ranked informally on the basis of their past promotion rates.[36]

The unified exams were disrupted in 1958.[37] But by the early 1960s, Shanghai was enrolling students on a comprehensive basis, channeling the highest-scoring candidates on district entrance exams into the city key points, which maintained higher minimum passing scores than the district key schools. These latter, in turn, received higher-scoring students than ordinary schools, and the *minban* variety were ranked last (in cities, *minban* schools were run by streets and neighborhoods). As a rule, especially the city key schools at the senior middle level were allowed to expand their catchment areas in accordance with annual regulations specifying approximate numbers to be enrolled by each school from each district.[38]

At the elementary level, however, the discreetly unpublicized task of developing an elite stream proved especially awkward. Shanghai followed the old pre-1949 "central school" tradition, maintaining a few better-equipped schools in each district. They fulfilled their guiding (*fudao*) responsibilities for neighboring schools by holding a series of open classes each semester to demonstrate teaching methods. But Shanghai's central elementary schools, from at least 1956, did not practice key-point enrollment. Central and ordinary schools

---

[36] Students were actually assigned on the basis of both their entrance exam scores and their own list of written preferences. But the best students were coached by teachers and parents to list the top key schools as their first or second preference. This usually produced the desired result of channeling the highest scorers into the best schools, because the schools were given first choice but could only exercise it among those candidates who had in turn listed such schools as their own first preference.

[37] *Wenhuibao*, Shanghai, 11 July 1958.

[38] With uncharacteristic candor for the 1960s, Shanghai published the names of schools that enrolled on a multidistrict basis in 1964. The list included a mix of urban and suburban schools. But those heading the list for the senior middle level included topmost Shanghai Middle School and the East China Teacher Training College Attached Middle School Number Two. Both at that time were all-city key points. Others heading the list were the middle schools attached to Fudan, Jiaotong, and Tongji Universities and Shanghai Teacher Training College; Songjiang Middle School Number Two; and Yangpu Middle School (*Wenhuibao*, Shanghai, 3 July 1964).

were alike in having to admit all children, regardless of ability or background, who resided within each school's predetermined (but constantly readjusted) enrollment area.[39]

Responsibility for elementary school enrollment work fell upon Shanghai's famous all-knowing residents committees (*jumin weiyuanhui*), which informed each school as to the number of school-age children to expect each year. Since Shanghai was striving for universal elementary schooling by the late 1950s, all children had to be accommodated. Class (*ban*) size was maintained at 48–50 students, with one head teacher or class master (*banzhuren*) for each class plus two or three other teachers responsible for individual subjects. If a school did not have enough rooms and teachers to accommodate all the children in its designated catchment area, residents committee enrollment personnel had to look for space elsewhere. If this was found in a school deemed inferior to the original and if parents complained, committee personnel were responsible for "persuasion." Once the schools and authorities made a decision, parents had to accept it.

Another of Shanghai's compromises – given the concerted quality building otherwise under way – was the city's aversion to streaming or grouping students by ability *within* individual schools. Teachers reported the practice as being forbidden at both the elementary and the junior middle levels, although it is unclear whether the prohibition was enforced uniformly throughout the city or only on a district basis. Students were usually organized into classes by their home addresses. When all the youngsters from one lane had been accommodated, those from the next would be added until the full complement of 50 students was reached. In this manner, however, a kind of "natural" social streaming occurred which might or might not be deliberately broken up.

The big dividing line in the teachers' view was that between children from white- and blue-collar families. Since these tended to live in different lanes, their children tended to be grouped in different classrooms. If a school in a working-class district had three classes of first graders, it could easily happen that all the youngsters from white-collar families (managers, technicians, clerks, etc.) were taught together. And although the head teacher typically changed along the way, students usually remained in the same class from the time they entered a school until they left it. Hence the term "classmate" took on a special meaning in the Chinese context, where students studied, worked, played, and

[39] Estimates of the numbers of central elementary schools vary. Older teachers remembered a formula of one per district, but that seems to have been the 1950s norm when Shanghai's districts were more numerous than the 10 which became standard from 1964. For the mid-1960s, teachers spoke of "two or three" central schools per district. One later source claimed cryptically: "In 1959, the city districts established 60 key-point elementary schools, but the central schools continued to exist" ("Shanghaishi jiaoyu" [Education in Shanghai], *Zhongguo jiaoyu nianjian: difang jiaoyu*, p. 407). No one interviewed acknowledged such a distinction in practice, however, nor did anyone estimate so large a number of schools in the elite category.

competed together in the same group for several years and had little contact with youngsters in other classes.

Teacher Gan, who had been the head teacher for many central school classes over the years, still recalled it as a "glorious" achievement that 15 students from one class of sixth graders in 1957 were admitted to the district's key junior middle schools. But although "it was never admitted publicly," she knew why more students succeeded from this than any other graduating class that year: the others all had greater numbers of working-class children, whereas youngsters from white-collar families "always did better . . . and more of them were admitted to key middle schools." Such students were "better behaved and more studious" because they were "influenced by their parents to study and to appreciate books."[40] By contrast, working-class parents (especially ordinary laborers rather than factory production workers) were "too busy" and their family lives too chaotic, making their children the most difficult to teach. Another year, not one of Teacher Gan's students proved to be key-point material. Of course, there had to be an investigation, and "they found the reason although they could not announce it openly: the students in that class were all from very poor families."

Later, in the 1960s, when schools and classes were all competing more openly to raise promotion rates, Gan and some like-minded colleagues proposed to divide the sixth graders more systematically on the basis of their academic performance. They argued that the brightest needed as much coaching as they could take while the others needed extra help of a different kind, but she admitted that their real aim was to place as many of the better students

[40] Teacher Gan was using the term *zhiyuan*, or "office worker," best translated as "white collar." In this case, she meant simply to distinguish students whose parents engaged in physical labor from those who did not, and to express the conventional educator's view of that difference. In fact, *zhiyuan* was also a formal occupational designation applied to all "white-collar" jobs, including technical managers in factories, administrative personnel, professionals, and teachers. It was the formal equivalent, used in personnel files, of the general term "intellectual." The usual definition of the latter was anyone with a secondary education or above, including both students and graduates (e.g., *Selected Works of Mao Tse-tung*, 2:303 n). In popular usage, "higher-level intellectual" (*gaoji zhishi fenzi*) distinguishes college professors, famous writers, etc., from the rank and file. These styles evolved in turn from the equivalents drawn during the turn-of-the-century transition years between the imperial examination system and modern schools. The equivalents varied, but, roughly, a *jinshi* degree holder corresponded to a university graduate, and the provincial *juren* degree to post-secondary higher schooling, while all the lesser ranks and titles corresponded to different levels of elementary and secondary education (e.g., Franke, *The Reform and Abolition of the Traditional Chinese Examination System*, p. 66). Thus, "intellectual" became a general term applied to all who had passed the requisite exams and formally progressed beyond the elementary level, just as the *xiucai*, or scholar-in-waiting, status of old marked the dividing line at its most basic level between commoner and educated elite. Lest equivalents be further drawn in the reader's mind between secondary school students in modern Western societies and those in China, the small number of Chinese relative to the whole population who acquired even this level of education, whether traditional or modern, through the 1950s must be borne in mind.

as possible in key middle schools. Other colleagues criticized the proposal, using the standard argument from the 1950s Soviet period, namely, that the slower students would fall even further behind when separated from the stimulation provided by the others. Also, no one wanted to teach the slower students. Ultimately, however, the problem was solved for them by city authorities, who ruled against such deliberate tracking. Another Shanghai school at this time went so far as to enforce mutual-help schemes by seating fast and slow learners side by side, paired together in the double-seat desks common in Chinese classrooms. The debate nevertheless continued over whether or not to stream students by ability within individual schools at the senior elementary and junior middle levels.

Yet the pristine order of Shanghai's organization grid was marred throughout by exceptions and "special interests" (*tequan*), both intellectual and political. The former is best exemplified by the key-point kindergarten. Never actually called "key points," they were nonetheless regarded as such because they were fully financed by the state, well equipped, and professionally staffed and enrolled only the "best." The most experienced Shanghai teacher interviewed, who had been for many years a secondary school class master, described the "entrance examination" conducted by these kindergartens to decide which children to admit. Parents filled out application forms designed to reveal their own social status and educational backgrounds, while the children had to answer simple questions such as their parents' names and work units. Some children could not respond quickly, "like the children of workers," because "they do not bother to teach their children anything when they are young, not even the names of their own parents." Such children would be "sent to the *minban* kindergartens" in their neighborhoods.

Teachers estimated that probably no more than half the age-group could be accommodated in Shanghai's regular pubic kindergartens overall in the early 1960s. After the three years of "regular" training they provided, a youngster could enter first grade knowing a great deal more than others. Such kindergartens were therefore "linked" informally with nearby central schools for enrollment purposes. In this way, a child who had fulfilled expectations in kindergarten was essentially guaranteed admission to a central elementary school, regardless of whether the youngster actually lived within its catchment area. The conventional educator thus assumed that children from educated families represented the greatest potential for academic success, and the regular system, over which these educators presided, encouraged decisions based upon that assumption from babyhood onward. Such also were the "centers of strength" upon which the quality-oriented key-point stream was built, an ironic but inevitable consequence of the CCP's revolutionary 1958 decision on education reform.

Countervailing political interests are more difficult to assess because the official criteria defining them were imprecise, constantly changing, and always open to varying interpretation in practice. Tertiary admissions were governed by the formal regulations, already noted, and were followed essentially as announced. To reiterate, except during the early 1950s and 1958–1959, only "a few points of preference" on entrance exam scores were given to candidates from favored family backgrounds: workers, peasants, revolutionary cadres, martyrs, national minorities, and returned overseas Chinese. These same rules tended to apply at the senior middle level as well. But those *against* the dependents of class and political enemies were never formally announced, and the political enemies list in particular varied from one political movement to the next.

Even more uncertain was the application of all such criteria to children at the lower levels of schooling. The Shanghai teachers agreed that through the junior middle level, family political problems were of no significance in determining whether a child could enter school and would also (generally) not prevent a student from entering a (district-level) key school. At the senior middle and college levels, however, a family's unmitigated bad class or political standing would likely prevent an otherwise qualified candidate from entering an all-city key school and the most prestigious college courses. In this way, many students from problematic family backgrounds were sidelined into unpopular teacher training colleges and teaching careers, including several individuals interviewed for this study.

Former teachers and students also remembered a marked intensification everywhere after 1962 of both positive and negative discrimination: in favor of those from "red" family backgrounds (workers, poor and lower-middle peasants, revolutionary cadres, soldiers, martyrs) and against "blacks" or "whites" (terms used interchangeably to denote class and political enemies, most commonly landlords, rich peasants, counterrevolutionaries, bad elements, and rightists). This intensification was seen in retrospect as following upon Mao's celebrated 1962 declaration, "never forget class struggle," marking the revival of cultural revolution concerns from their quiescent early-1960s phase.[41] Prior to this time, class consciousness was not very well developed among students, at least, and most reportedly had little clear impression of their classmates' family backgrounds. Afterward, the issue was so intensely articulated that young people of that generation could recall even a decade later the family circumstances of virtually every classmate.

Consequences of the emphasis on class varied from place to place. Nothing

---

[41] Many interviewees referred to Mao's 1962 statement in this way, although the quotation itself did not become commonplace until a few years later. The declaration was made at the 10th Plenum of the 8th Central Committee in September 1962. E.g., see *Mao Zhuxi jiaoyu yulu*, p. 7; "Long Live the Invincible Thought of Mao Tse-tung! Outline of the Struggle between the Two Lines from the Eve of the Founding of the People's Republic through the 11th Plenum of the 8th CCP Central Committee," undated Shanghai pamphlet, trans. in *CB*, no. 884 (18 July 1969), p. 20; Richard Baum, *Prelude to Revolution: Mao, the Party, and the Peasant Question, 1962–1966* (New York: Columbia University Press, 1975), chap. 1.

was absolute. Individual exceptions did not disprove the rule, but there were also many mitigating circumstances. One was the student's own political behavior. Another was willingness to disavow or draw a clear line (*huaqing jiexian*) between one's self and one's problematic relations. Old family friends and more distant relatives who might be on the other side of the class divide could also be helpful. Yet another important consideration was the student's own ability. Much could be overlooked for the truly gifted and the exceptionally talented. But the net result of the post-1962 trend was to make life more difficult for young people from bad class and political backgrounds, especially in terms of continuing their education beyond junior middle school and job placement. Young people from such families who had expected to continue their studies found their applications increasingly blocked and their options restricted to "volunteering" for unpopular job assignments.[42] At the same time,

---

[42] The good and bad categories represented the CCP's basic constituencies, or the socioeconomic classes and political backgrounds which the regime was committed to reward and punish. "Revolutionary cadre" referred to those, both civilian and military, who had "joined the revolution" and the CCP before 1949, regardless of their actual economic status. The latter was determined by the main source of income of a family's leading male member (chief breadwinner) three years prior to 1949 or prior to land reform in those districts ruled by the CCP before 1949. This yielded the basic classes: workers, peasants, landlords, and capitalists.

Intellectuals, as noted, did not constitute a separate class but were usually of bourgeois family backgrounds (and, by Mao's 1950s reckoning, of bourgeois political inclinations as well). The *zhiyuan*, or white-collar, category used to designate most "intellectual" occupations nevertheless indicated their intermediate or middling status, suspended somewhere between propertyless proletarians and property-owning exploiters.

Over time, the basic social divisions were further refined according to political need as the revolution continued. For example, the "rightist" category of political enemies was composed largely of white-collar or intellectual critics who went too far in 1957. Most serious on the negative side, however, were counterrevolutionaries and bad elements. The former concerned political crimes, and the latter ordinary crimes. As a general rule, young people with such individuals in their immediate families, or individuals being formally investigated for such offenses, would not be permitted to attend college or key senior middle schools. This rule extended back at least as far as 1958 and continued to be applied after 1976 as well, even though by then the definition of what constituted counterrevolutionary behavior had been turned upside down.

Under the intensifying class line after 1962, and especially after 1966, two additional categories came to be treated as bad or borderline bad without being formally defined as class enemies. These were capitalists and people with overseas Chinese relations (*haiwai guanxi*). Capitalists were not categorically labeled as class enemies in the same manner as landlords, evidently following the CCP's initial recognition of the former's historically "progressive" economic role – hence, the early designation "national capitalist" to denote those among them worthy of becoming united front allies. Overseas Chinese were also initially granted preferential treatment in recognition of their patriotic material contributions to the nation, despite their typically bourgeois economic status. As class conflict intensified, however, both categories shifted in practice from potential united front allies to potential class enemies and were (with the inevitable exceptions) treated as such especially during the 1966–1976 decade. On the complexities of the class background question generally, see Richard Kraus, *Class Conflict in Chinese Socialism* (New York: Columbia University Press, 1981). On the application of class and political criteria in school life, see Unger, *Education under Mao*, pp. 12–15 and passim; Rosen, *Red Guard Factionalism*, pt. 1 and passim; Gordon White, *The Politics of Class and Class Origin*; Shirk, *Competitive Comrades*.

students whose parents were "neither red nor white" (i.e., primarily white collar: intellectuals, office workers, clerks, etc.) found themselves under increasing pressure to compensate for a middling inheritance by demonstrating their own personal ability and activism.

The combination of revolutionary purity and key-point quality also produced aberrations such as the *gaoganban*, or special classes for higher-level cadres' children, at top-ranking Shanghai Middle School. One teacher recalled his youthful dream of attending that school, where students could study foreign languages and instructors lived like college faculty members in spacious campus accommodations. But alas, he failed to qualify because one "had to have the right background to get in: your parents had to be either high-level cadres or famous high-level intellectuals."

Another teacher claimed to know more of Shanghai Middle School's secrets. It followed the practice not just of giving a few points of preference to the usual categories but of giving special preference at both junior and senior levels to the children of Shanghai's ranking district and city Party and government officials. The points of preference, in their case, could be "expanded" to mean entrance examination scores a full 10 or even 20 points below those required of other successful candidates. Those who really could not keep up were expected to withdraw along the way, but for the others special coaching was given. In this manner, the politically privileged sons and daughters of the revolution were inducted into the regular world of the educated elite without doing serious damage to the school's college promotion rates. Between 1964 and 1966, separate classes were even formed to accommodate these lower-scoring students when there were 40 or more of them at any grade level. These were the *gaoganban*, organized by the school to show its special concern (*zhaogu*) for the red class offspring of revolutionary cadres. At the time, no one protested. But later, during the next mass movement mobilization phase in 1966 and 1967, the details were well publicized.[43]

In the memories of these former teachers and students, then, Shanghai's regular system and especially the elite schools within it stood as the ultimate stabilizer, drawing everything into its orbit. At the lower reaches, *minban* and work–study alternatives could not survive in its shadow, and the experimental 10-year curriculum was effectively absorbed as well. Collectively run *minban* schools were set up in great numbers and were responsible for universalizing education in Shanghai at both the elementary and junior middle levels by the mid-1960s. But these schools received little public assistance. They were pieced together instead by the residents committees: housed in spare rooms and old

---

[43] Shanghai Middle School's efforts were not uncommon in the mid-1960s. Rosen reported similar practices in Guangzhou (*Red Guard Factionalism*, pp. 76–77, 259–260 n. 18; on the intensifying class line which benefited primarily cadres' children in the best schools between 1964 and 1966, see ibid., chaps. 1–2).

buildings, equipped with neighborhood supplies, and staffed by local house-wives. Financing came from students' tuition, occasional neighborhood contri-butions, and profits from factory workshops run by the residents committees.

Despite aggressive publicity in the local press, however, pressures for regu-larization began almost at once. "People criticized such schools as inferior and did not like to send children to them, so they were very quickly phased out." "No one wanted to send their children to *minban* schools but there was no other way." Hence, the process of regularizing began immediately and went on continuously. Teachers recalled the early 1960s as a time of constant motion in this respect. Whenever a *minban* school appeared, it would soon begin to transfer out students as space was made available in nearby regular schools. By the late 1960s, according to everyone's recollections, most *minban* schools had been similarly absorbed into the Shanghai city school system.

At the opposite end of the school spectrum, only the strongest were allowed to continue experimenting with a shortened curriculum in the 1960s. Teacher Gan had participated in the experiment and explained how it was effectively scuttled. The aim had been to revise the fixed and unvarying formulas adopted during the 1950s. Teacher Gan and many others recalled the formulas clearly. For example, the first day of a new history lesson was divided into five parts: 5–10 minutes for reviewing the previous lesson; another few minutes for linking that lesson with the new one; most of the class period would then be devoted to reading aloud the new lesson; then consolidation; and, finally, questions for the students. On the second and third days, the lesson would be further analyzed, discussed, and summarized; students' comprehension tested; a homework assignment given; and so on, all following prescribed plans and methods. Instead of using them to create a shorter system as in the Soviet Union, Chinese educators had quickly given up that aim in the early 1950s and retained their old 12-year format. Then, in 1958, the rigorous emulation of these Soviet methods was criticized. But paradoxically, the criticism was cou-pled with the demand for a shorter, more efficient regular system. The system reacted with utmost caution, as suggested by the above-cited consolidation-phase guidelines. Schools so authorized typically created an "experimental class" of the best students to serve as guinea pigs. Experiments were then conducted to see whether the same curricular content could be taught and learned while reducing the stages of Soviet-style course presentation, with unified examinations used to compare and verify results at every step. Natur-ally, "only the best students and teachers could succeed" in such an exercise.

The experiment seems to have been most successful at the elementary level, and Shanghai maintained a number of five-year schools in the 1960s, all re-garded as superior to their ordinary six-year counterparts, as judged by com-parative promotion rates into key junior middle schools. But overall, the effort was never formally concluded one way or the other in the early 1960s and so "did not pass beyond the experimental stage," recalled Teacher Gan. For their part, teachers more or less agreed that the 1950s methods were "after all the best way of presenting a lesson."

Fujian: pushing up pass rates

Not for Shanghai were clumsy procedures such as Guangzhou devised with its three categories of middle schools, three separate entrance examinations, key-point classes for elementary school students, and so on.[44] Also not for Shanghai was the unseemly race to push up pass rates which won for Fujian a place among the top-scoring eight provinces every year from 1959 to 1965. Indeed, so confident were Shanghai educators in the natural superiority of their resource base and the methods used to exploit it that they seemed unaware of how the system worked elsewhere. Hence their chagrin in 1977, when unified college entrance examinations were restored after the 1966–1976 hiatus and Fujian came in first nationwide. Shanghai (and other localities) rushed investigation teams to the spot while Fujian educators relished the irony, vowing never to tell anyone the innermost secrets of their success. But by 1980, everyone knew its essential ingredients.

The Education Ministry had asked the major universities receiving Fujian students to monitor their progress, and it was found that, although good, the general performance of these students did not match their high entrance exam scores. They were not among the most brilliant, and on the average were "not as good as Shanghai students." The lesson, which everyone but Fujian educators seemed to have forgotten, was the difference that a concerted effort to

---

[44] Guangzhou's struggle to work out a viable key-point enrollment formula peaked in 1962 (see ibid., pp. 18–21). For the next three years, there were only two groups and two examinations (*Yangcheng wanbao*, Guangzhou, 18 July 1961, 10 July and 15 Aug. 1962, 12 July 1963, 22 Aug. 1964, 11 July and 20 Aug. 1965). The information about streaming in the upper grades of elementary school is from former Guangzhou students.

Guangzhou's key-point system was also fairly haphazard compared with Shanghai's stream-lined network. To recapitulate: the two top-scoring schools in Guangzhou were provincial key points, Huafu and Guangya. Next in line were Guangzhou city key points, the top-scoring of which was Guangzhou Middle School Number One. Additionally, there were only "four or five" other schools actually designated as city key points (the list seems never to have been published; interviewees usually named Middle Schools Numbers One, Two, Five, and Seven and Zhixin Girls). Unlike Shanghai, Guangzhou appears not to have maintained the distinct second-tier level of district key points in the 1960s. The term "key point" quickly caught on, however, and was often used popularly with reference to all the top-scoring schools, whether or not they were officially designated as such. Thus, not all the top 12 schools in the Rosen and Unger survey data actually bore the formal designation, even though people regarded them as (and boasted of attending) "key points" (Unger, *Education under Mao*, pp. 26–27; Rosen, *Red Guard Factionalism*, pp. 22–31).

One similarity between Shanghai and Guangzhou: Guangzhou also used the *minban* neighborhood school expedient to boost enrollments after 1958, and most of these schools were soon absorbed into the regular city system, according to interviewees.

push up exam scores could make.[45] The winning formula had reemerged in Fujian as if by magic immediately the all-clear sounded following Mao's death in 1976.

The formula, noted above, had already been publicized in general terms as early as 1959. Former Fujian school people revealed a few more of the secret details remembered from the 1960s, albeit nothing that had not already been held up for public scrutiny by radicalized students and teachers in 1966–1967.[46] Fujian teachers who recounted the story as participant observers were as bemused by the twisting hand of fate as they were ambivalent over the outcome. They regarded many of the stratagems used before 1966 and again after 1976 to push up exam scores as being of dubious educational value at best, even while taking pride in the record-high pass rates achieved.

Fujian's resource base, or at least the one exploited for this purpose, was confined to the coastal region between Fuzhou and Xiamen (Amoy). The area around the ancient port city of Quanzhou and its modern successor, Xiamen, is referred to locally as the overseas Chinese district (Qiaoqu), due to the large numbers of inhabitants who have migrated overseas to Taiwan, the Philippines, and Southeast Asia. This fact is related to the educational development of the Fujian coast for reasons not fully understood but popularly attributed to population density and the infertility of the soil.

Teacher Fang, from northern Fujian, offered the conventional explanation. "In the North, land is plentiful and people few, so children do not study. They just go out to work and earn money. In the South, it is different. There are many people and not enough land, so people want their children to learn more and even go to college. That is why the educational level is not the same in the North and South ... and why so many people left the South to become overseas Chinese in the first place."[47] Nor should this tradition be mistaken as a modern phenomenon. An account from 1184, during the Song dynasty, explained in almost identical terms why people were quitting agriculture: "The land of Fu-chien is cramped, and inadequate to feed and clothe them, so they scatter to all the four quarters. For this reason wherever studying goes on, there Fukienese literati will be found."[48]

Teachers further characterized the south coast in the mid-20th century as being "neither urban nor rural" but a region of villages separated by small plots

[45] Interview notes: Fudan University, Shanghai, 17–21 Nov. 1980, p. 52; East China Teacher Training University, Shanghai, 22–28 Nov. 1980, p. 35; Shandong University, Jinan, 29 Nov.–5 Dec. 1980, p. 17; Nanjing University, 10–14 Nov. 1980, p. 78.
[46] Unless otherwise noted, the following account is based on the recollections of seven former Fujian teachers interviewed in Hong Kong. Only one was an out-of-province person; the others were native sons, although one of these was a returned overseas Chinese from Indonesia. All but the outsider had spent the entire 1960s decade in Fujian schools as either students or teachers.
[47] Interview 83/FJ/25, p. 4.
[48] Quoted in Chaffee, The Thorny Gates of Learning in Sung China, p. 153.

of land where people "cultivated stones" rather than crops, ate the lowly sweet potato (*digua*) rather than rice, and lived on remittances from relatives overseas. Following from the emphasis on study and migration as the traditional escape routes out of poverty, the custom had developed – much stronger than in neighboring Guangdong, from which many millions had also migrated overseas – of remitting money back to hometowns and extended families for school construction and maintenance. So strong was the custom, which continued until 1966 and resumed after 1976, that up to half the village elementary schools in some Jinjiang prefecture communes were financed directly by overseas remittances, with more than enough schools to achieve universal junior elementary education by the mid-1960s. Many middle schools were also built in the same manner.

It was upon this foundation that Fujian's 1960s achievement was built. The more conventionally rural and mountain counties in northern and western Fujian remained outside the competitive circle. The Fujian coast tradition had first won fame for its scholars during the Song dynasty when the region became one of the leading producers of degree holders. Success in that regard continued through Ming times (1368–1644), when Fujian produced the highest number of *jinshi* degree holders per million population, sharing overall primacy of place with Zhejiang, Jiangsu, and Jiangxi Provinces.[49] But Fujian was eclipsed during the Qing dynasty (1644–1911), leaving it to Shanghai and the surrounding Jiangsu–Zhejiang hinterland to perpetuate the southeastern intellectual tradition in modern times. Hence it was a bizarre accident of historical circumstance which allowed Wang Yugeng to tap Fujian's unique underlying foundation of that same tradition – kept alive by centuries of emigration, family ties, and overseas remittances – to re-create Fujian's ancient glory in modern guise.

Wang Yugeng headed the provincial education bureau from 1955 until 1966 and was seen by all as the driving force behind Fujian's success. Her unusually high profile derived about equally from her status as wife of provincial CCP leader Ye Fei and the energy she devoted to her apparently self-appointed role as chief promoter of Fujian's high-scoring college candidates.[50] During her 10-year career, Wang traveled the coast road repeatedly as she personally took up the task of boosting pass rates (*shengxuelu*) in Fujian's main secondary schools which lay along that route.

Xiamen Middle School Number Eight was one such school which figured

---

[49] Ibid., chap. 6; Ping-ti Ho, *The Ladder of Success in Imperial China*, chap. 6.
[50] The 1955 date is from my interview notes, Xiamen Middle School Number Eight, 21 Oct. 1980. Husband Ye Fei, whose revolutionary cadre status extended back to Fujian's earliest guerrilla days in the late 1920s, was named first CCP secretary and governor of Fujian, as well as general in the People's Liberation Army (navy), all in 1955. Ye remained first party secretary until 1966, but his concurrent posting as governor ended in 1959 (*Who's Who in Communist China*, 2:769).

prominently in her campaign. The school was founded in the 1920s and run by overseas Chinese until 1949. Wang first paid a visit in 1957, when its performance was still unremarkable. The school was designated a key point three years later in recognition of its progress. Having "grasped the red flag" of pass rates, to use the terminology of that time, Number Eight was honored at the marathon national conference of outstanding cultural revolutionaries in 1960.[51] Thus, Fujian's efforts to raise examinations scores had adapted easily to the logic of the Great Leap Forward. But while the 1960 conference marked the onset of a temporary national respite from revolutionary activism, Wang Yugeng's emulation campaign style remained the dominant fact of educational life in Fujian from 1959 to 1966.

Ironically, Fujian did not do all that well at building a key-point college-preparatory stream and concentrating talent within it. All the requisite hierarchies of county, prefectural, and provincial key points were quickly created, but they could not be run efficiently because too many strong schools were vying for the coveted designation. Following standard practice, the provincial key schools could only enroll within a single city or prefecture at most. But in Fujian, they had to compete with many lower-level schools. These "selfishly" lured the highest-scoring local students with promises of extra coaching and expert tutors who could promise results equal to those of the provincial key points. Reflecting this competition, the list of Fujian's key-point schools was in a state of perpetual adjustment and expansion between 1957 and 1963.[52] Hence, what set Fujian apart was not so much its key-point concentration of talent as heightened competition based upon the relatively large number of quality schools.

Even more distinctive, however, was the way all schools in the coastal region, whether key point or not, were drawn into the race. Virtually every examination seemed the occasion for drawing up a rank-order list, and frequent unified exams (*tongkao*) were given for no other purpose than comparative ranking and evaluation. The competition was pervasive and relentless,

---

[51] Interview notes, Xiamen Middle School Number Eight (formerly Shuangshi, or Double Ten, Middle School), 21 Oct. 1980. The 1960 conference marked an interim "last hurrah" for the cultural revolutionary ethos of the Great Leap Forward. Thereafter, the country settled into the politically quiescent "three bad years." Cultural revolution rhetoric revived along with the economy after 1963, culminating in the Great Proletarian Cultural Revolution launched in 1966. The 1960 "conference of heroes" met from 1 to 12 June and was attended by more than 6,000 "advanced workers" in education, culture, health, gymnastics, and journalism. They were selected for having grasped the three red flags of the "general line, the Great Leap, and the people's communes" by making outstanding progress in their professional work during the mass movements of cultural and education revolution (see *Guangming ribao*, 10 Feb. and 1–14 June 1960). The provinces held preliminary conferences in May. Double Ten Middle was one of nine middle schools (and one of 1,000 advanced work units and individuals) named at Fujian's conference of heroes (*Fujian ribao*, 30 May 1960).

[52] "Fujian sheng jiaoyu" (Fujian's education), in *Zhongguo jiaoyu nianjian, 1949–1984: difang jiaoyu*, p. 637.

coloring even ordinary classroom routines with the banners of success (red) and failure (white).

Tension was naturally greatest where the stakes were highest, that is, on the examinations governing passage on to the next level: junior middle, senior middle, and college. For these exams, rank orders were drawn not by score but by the rates of successful admission. Fujian middle schools were further ranked on their college pass rates at three levels: within counties, within prefectures, and within the province as a whole. The drive to excel was fanned by public praise for winners and humiliation for losers. Like other provinces, Fujian did not publish or otherwise announce its rank-order lists. "This was because, officially, the scores were not supposed to be used to judge whether schools and education were good or not."[53] The rank ordering was euphemistically intended for "internal reference" purposes only. But unlike other provinces, Fujian did publicize the names of top-ranking "red-flag" schools each year following the college entrance examinations. Individuals responsible for successful exam coaching were also honored by name as advanced (*xianjin*) teachers.[54]

Internally, however, the names of "white-flag" schools scoring lowest were also circulated in written reports and announced at meetings. Wang Yugeng personally led this practice with her regular reports praising winners and those registering marked improvement, while prodding losers to try harder. Her reports were delivered in a style recalled by one teacher as "really something: nonstop smoking and nonstop talking both at the same time." But the game was especially cruel for ordinary small-town schools in the region, which had to compete but could not possibly win. One well-known story in Jinjiang Prefecture from the early 1960s concerned a headmaster who committed suicide because he could no longer bear the gibes of townspeople after his school failed one year to send a single graduate to college. The remark most remembered later came from the barbershop. When Headmaster Lian went for his regular haircut, the barber tried to make light of the latest town gossip and asked in jest if he wanted his head shaved instead – referring to the old custom of preparing for the ultimate self-mortification.

Beyond key points and red flags, however, lay the final step of sharpening

---

[53] Interview 80/FJ/3, p. 26.
[54] Besides Fuzhou Middle School Number One, which reputedly always achieved the highest number of college admissions to the highest-ranking tertiary institutions, others most consistently named each year as red-flag schools for achieving the highest average scores on the college entrance examinations provincewide were Xiamen Middle Schools Numbers One and Eight, Jimei Middle School near Xiamen, and Putian Middle School Number One. A list of second-tier high-scoring schools would usually include Quanzhou Middle Schools Numbers One and Five and Yangzheng Middle School, all in Jinjiang Prefecture; and Zhanzhou Middle School Number One and Longhai Middle School Number One, in Longxu Prefecture. Former teachers indicated no letup in the pre-1966 drive to push pass rates. But from 1962 on, the main provincial newspaper, the *Fujian ribao*, registered a clear reduction in publicity for individual high-achieving schools and teachers.

the points (*jianzi*, literally, "sharpies" or "the best of the best"). This practice preceded entrance examinations at every level but was most concerted for the all-important college sweepstakes. Fujian educators seem to have elevated the art of cramming to its highest possible stage of development, in a process similar in kind but more intense in degree than that reported anywhere else. And herein lay the essence of the secrets which teachers in 1980 vowed never to share with outsiders. Indeed, they would not even tell their own "fraternal" neighboring schools, so seriously was the competition taken.

The key lay in exam preparation, which for graduating middle school seniors took precedence over all other work during the final semester. Prepping was led by the *banzhuren* (head teachers) for each class and by a few others especially skilled in this work. Schools compiled their own review materials for each subject based on previous examinations and edited from year to year, focusing on questions of continuing importance while discarding others. But it seemed as if the procedures as well as the structures of the imperial past were all being revived at once as the centralized plans, quotas, and examinations of a modernizing communist state settled over the land. Without actually acknowledging the ancient tradition they were carrying forward or how it had been kept alive through half a century of alternative enrollment procedures, teachers nevertheless described cramming formulas inherited from days long gone.[55]

Teacher Lu described the process generally. For each subject, "there was usually one overall review and after that several key-point reviews. Just before the examination, there would be concentrated guidance in all subjects, and teachers would lead students through the exercise of 'anticipating the questions.'" Some teachers specialized in this last, applying their mastery of previous examinations and the unified middle school curriculum to guess what the questions would be. These were the teachers especially honored by name when their guesses proved accurate, and these were also the teachers whose reputations schools exploited to lure students in the first place. For the Chinese language exam, all the different kinds of essays would be printed up and circulated as part of the final preparation. "The majority of candidates then memorized these model essays so as to remember them. And in this way, one entire school's candidates might write exactly the same essay on the examinations, the length, structure, and sentences all completely the same."[56]

Additionally, however, the effort included a host of stratagems designed to boost scores and competitive advantages. One common practice was to "persuade" the worst students not to take the entrance examinations. This helped when pass rates were calculated as the percentage of successful candidates

---

[55] On the past, see, e.g., Miyazaki, *China's Examination Hell*, p. 17.
[56] Interview 80/FJ/3, pp. 10–11.

among those taking the exams. To discourage that practice, the calculation might be changed to the proportion of successes among those graduating. Schools responded by preventing the worst students from doing so, either by making them repeat a year, with the aim of encouraging them to drop out, or by declaring them to be school leavers rather than graduates.

Even worse, a school might, through its various "intelligence" channels, go so far as to calculate its own students' chances against those of its nearest competitors and decide the numbers to force out on that basis rather than on the students' actual performance. But to be done well enough to influence a school's pass rate was not easy. If too many seniors were forced out, everyone would have known immediately what was afoot, shattering the formal facade of disapproval for all such maneuvers. Hence the weeding out had to begin much earlier and work its way back through all the grades as students were passed or failed on the basis of their estimated college pass rate potential.

Teacher Liao witnessed these practices firsthand in a small-town school otherwise at a comparative disadvantage with the number one county-town key point nearby. No one said anything at the time and parents did not realize what was going on, but it all came out later. Teacher Liao blamed county officials for demanding high pass rates rather than the headmaster or his colleagues, who only tried to produce them. He also blamed the Great Leap mentality which forced educators "like peanut farmers" to search for ever more ingenious ways of pushing up their production figures.

Just across the border in northern Guangdong, another small-town school had actually won great glory for itself by manipulating precisely the same strategy. Everyone was emulating Fujian in those days. Because they were so close, educators from the county often visited Fujian schools to audit their classes, to see how they prepped students, and especially to try to learn how they anticipated the exam questions. But inevitably, other points were mastered as well. Teacher Ye's school had kicked off its campaign in 1959, soon after Headmaster Kuang returned from a meeting in Guangzhou bearing the consolidation-phase message that quality must be grasped at all costs. The next year, the school declared a mix-up in registration procedures, leaving many second-year senior middle students unregistered and therefore ineligible to continue. Parents complained to no avail. Many students just dropped out; some tried their luck in neighboring counties. By their senior year, only about 30 students remained, and so "teachers were able to grasp quality." With this group, the numbers going on to college began to increase.

Thereafter, weeding out was done more systematically. The students with the lowest grades, usually from rural families, never made it into senior middle school. Typically, in the 1960s, the senior middle section enrolled four classes of first-year students, or about 200 total, and then failed or held back approximately 25 percent each year. By senior middle three, only three classes remained, each with 20–30 students. These had already been tapped as successful college material. To ensure that result, they were divided into the three classes by ability, where they spent their senior year prepping for one of the three sections on the national college entrance exams. In the early 1960s, these were divided into (1) science and technology; (2) medicine, agronomy, and forestry; and (3) liberal arts. The top-scoring students were placed in the science and technology class, while the others were divided between the other two.[57] In this manner, the school's college pass rate allegedly increased from virtually nil in 1959 to 60 percent by the mid-1960s.[58]

Inevitably, however, a few county-level CCP committee members' children remained in Teacher Ye's school despite poor grades. But the most concise statement on this point came from a Shanghai-based teacher who had worked briefly in several small east China towns during his 20-year career. Describing the typical balancing act performed by county-town key-point middle schools in the 1960s, he said the practice they aimed to perfect was "appropriate preference" (*shidang zhaogu*) for the children of county government and CCP leaders. It meant, roughly within a 10-point range on the entrance examinations, giving preference in admission to such students whose general deportment was also good. "The point of special but appropriate preference is that it should not be obvious. Otherwise, people would notice and complain. Therefore, it had to be done in such a way as not to influence the school's promotion rates."[59]

Teacher Liao's points were never so concisely made, but his story also illustrated how difficult the balancing act could be for a small-town school trying to push up pass rates and adjust to its social milieu at the same time. Due to an accident of local administration, many cadres (including both government office staff and local Party leaders) lived nearby, so their children

---

[57] The examination subjects for the three groups respectively were (1) Chinese language, politics, math, physics, chemistry, a foreign language; (2) Chinese language, politics, physics, chemistry, biology, a foreign language; and (3) Chinese language, politics, history, a foreign language. Group two was abolished in 1964, but the group one examination subjects remained the same, with all science and technology candidates taking the group one examination in 1964 and 1965. Liberal arts subjects also remained unchanged. The enrollment regulations were published each year in the main national and provincial newspapers (e.g., *Renmin ribao*, 4 June 1960; *Guangming ribao*, 13 May 1961; *Renmin ribao*, 18 June 1962, 31 May 1963, 4 June 1964, 11 June 1965). For two years after the unified national college entrance examinations were instituted in 1952, all candidates took the same set of exams (subjects: politics, Chinese language, Russian or English, Chinese and foreign history and geography, math, physics, chemistry, biology) (*Wenhuibao*, Shanghai, 13 July 1952, 20 July 1953). But from 1954, the examinations were divided into science/technology and liberal arts, with candidates selecting one or the other (*Guangming ribao*, 25 May 1954). In 1955, the science/technology category was further divided to form the above three examination groups, which remained standard until 1964 except for the 1958 hiatus (*Guangming ribao*, 9 June 1955, 7 Apr. 1956, 25 Apr. 1957, 11 June 1959).
[58] Interview 82/GD/7, pp. 61–68, 91–94.
[59] Interview 82/SD/14, p. 30.

attended Teacher Liao's school instead of the number one county-town key point, which was the usual residential pattern. He estimated that these children accounted for perhaps 20 percent of the school's student body, or about 10 in every class of 50 students. The parents were not very well educated themselves but "had great expectations for their children," a few of whom were unfortunately not very bright. Teacher Liao estimated further that of the 10 cadre children in every class, one or two could not have been admitted on the basis of their grades alone. But Headmaster Chen was himself a member of the county CCP committee and "since he had such close working relations with the parents, of course he would take care [zhaogu] of the children." He obliged by organizing extra tutorials especially for the cadres' children on weekends, a humble county-town equivalent of Shanghai Middle School's special classes. Here, however, other students could participate but usually did not since most lived at school (where two hours per day of extra tutorials for all was already the rule) and spent weekends at home.

Still, this school never tried to contravene the local rule against internal streaming. All students were taught together regardless of ability and there were no special key-point, or sharpies, classes. In evaluating students' abilities, however, teachers here as elsewhere judged academic performance as a function of socioeconomic status. Students from rural households (nongye hukou, or families deriving their livelihood from agriculture) were the equivalent of laborers' children for Shanghai educators. The worst grades were usually earned by rural students – because of their "economic situation at home" and the time they had to spend doing farm chores. Indeed, one of the reasons for this school's natural disadvantage vis-à-vis its main competitor was the latter's entirely urban catchment area. Accordingly, the various stratagems designed to push up pass rates by holding back and pushing out those with the poorest grades were most likely to affect rural students, whereas their parents were the least likely to understand how the rules were being manipulated against them.[60]

Some lessons from history and the 1960s

If co-opting the Soviet model was the dominant feature of China's educational history between 1949 and 1958, then 1959–1966 should be remembered for the unsuccessful effort to build a national secondary school system based on the old regular–irregular dichotomy. The strategy was based on a simple idea, namely, that the most rational way of using scarce educational resources was to create functionally specific compartments into which students would be channeled on the basis of ability and background. The regular system would continue to expand quantitatively, but a separate key-point stream within it would "guarantee

[60] Interview 83/FJ/26, pp. 246, 254.

quality" for the tertiary sector. At the pyramid's base, irregular alternatives could provide some form of schooling for the masses and especially for rural youth.

Irregular work–study and *minban* alternatives nevertheless failed in the early 1960s, just as they had in all earlier incarnations, except that the causes of failure had acquired an important new dimension. Professional educators were no more or less receptive than before. But the communist government had used its political strength to override their indifference only to discover that the target population also rejected irregular alternatives as an inferior form of education.

Promoters undoubtedly did not anticipate the extent of the rejection they would encounter among the intended clientele. But the early 1960s was not like the 1920s and 1930s, when peasants in everyone's rural surveys preferred old-fashioned irregular forms of literacy training to regular "foreign" schools. Nor was it even like the early 1950s, when the first school leavers from an expanding system began making demands not easily met. Now, the CCP's national mass mobilization and development drives were bearing fruit in ways its leaders did not yet fully grasp, as the revolution of rising expectations began to take hold throughout.

The best parallel in the international development literature seems to be Foster's work on Ghana, where he found that a century of colonial effort to develop "appropriate" agricultural and vocational education had failed. Africans preferred regular academic secondary schooling and continued to seek it even when they pragmatically anticipated no more than skilled or semiskilled worker jobs upon graduation from the junior secondary level. To reiterate, Foster found the reasons to be threefold: (1) the near impossibility of devising effective vocational education directly relevant to the jobs available; (2) the realistic assumption that academic education could enable many individuals to move from the subsistence economy into modern-sector jobs where such education was an asset; and (3) noneconomic "pressures for parity" or demands for access to the best academic stream, generated first by the competition between African and European colonial elites and continuing after independence as the competition widened to ever-expanding circles of the population.

The interview data summarized here suggest much the same reaction occurring in China between 1958 and 1966, when the rural population was presented with work–study agricultural middle schooling and rejected it forthwith as an inferior version of the real thing. Similarly, the *minban*, or locally financed, school might have become the vehicle for achieving universal urban junior middle education. But the schools themselves were unpopular, transitional, and achieved their purpose by being quickly incorporated within regular city school systems.

It followed, therefore, that irregularity's greatest failure was a function of regularity's success and the pressures for parity it generated. Epitomizing that success was a new nationwide system of key-point college-preparatory schools. These schools represented the CCP's compromise with professional educators, who had fretted throughout the 1950s over the Soviet Union's egalitarian teaching methods. Freed at last from that particular burden of dependency, CCP leaders allowed educators to address their quantity–quality concerns by creating an exclusive quality stream within the expanding system.

Key-point schools in the 1950s had remained isolated islands of quality run much as they had been before 1949, when all schools enrolled independently. Contravening as it did all of the social and pedagogical principles of the new China, key-point school development also remained discreetly unpublicized. With documentary references still scarce to nonexistent, we must rely on interviewees, who date, for both Shanghai and Guangzhou, the onset of unified enrollment from about 1956. That year marked the final transformation of all private schools into public institutions, which facilitated unified student re-cruiting within a given geographic area. This development made it possible, in turn, to round out key-point schools' potential by systematically channeling the "best" students into them from larger pools of candidates. Nevertheless, such key-point enrollment seems not to have become explicit national policy until 1958 and was still not being uniformly pursued everywhere in 1962, according to the directive promoting key schools issued that year.

Precisely how or why educational designers hit upon the particular method of key-point hierarchies has yet to be revealed. But the method was unique in its attempt to adapt for nationwide use in a modern system principles of regional representation and educational achievement inherited from the impe-rial past, when carefully controlled pools of candidates were maintained at each level and in every region. Topping out this modern reincarnation of the ancient institution and serving as its functional imperative were, of course, the college entrance examinations themselves, unified nationally in the early 1950s.

The formula would have seemed anachronistic in any 20th-century setting but was especially incongruous for China between 1958 and 1966. One reason was the pervasive regional representation, extending like the old examination system itself down to the basic county level as required for the sake of fairness, appearances, and the training of local elites. But the modern version also served to strengthen the hold of the regular system as ever more schools were drawn into the race. The imposition of key-point hierarchies, and the height-ened competition for scarce local educational resources they generated, thus helped ensure the rejection of irregular alternatives being promoted at the same time.

Even worse, considering the costs that later came due in human terms, was to have deliberately encouraged Chinese educators to reestablish their elitist traditions in the midst of the CCP's developing cultural revolution. There could scarcely have been a more bizarre mix than that represented by the 1958–1966 educational strategy which used the strength of a centralizing communist state to re-create educational forms and functions modeled directly on those of the imperial bureaucratic past, even as the CCP was intensifying its use of class-based criteria for continuing social revolution.

Suggesting the hazards for which educators were being set up – although no one seemed to anticipate it at the time – was the increasing emphasis on politics and class background as admissions criteria after 1962. At least two Guangzhou key schools did interpret that positively to mean enrolling a few genuine peasants (rather than just negatively against class enemies). Zhixin Girls Middle School enrolled about 200 new students each year, and beginning in 1963, a quota of 15 or so "poor and lower-middle peasant" students were admitted. Huafu did likewise. Former students recall that these two schools recruited from Guangzhou's suburban Hua and Conghua Counties and from neighboring Taishan as well. But the rural students had a lower educational level than others and could not compete successfully with their big-city classmates. A more common response was for key-school headmasters to do the politically correct thing by relaxing admission standards especially for revolutionary red cadres' children and then organizing special tutorials to help them on their way.

The class composition of student bodies naturally reflected these biases and enrollment criteria. Rosen and Unger provided a good indication of whose children were being accommodated where in the hierarchies of prestige and achievement, based on their questionnaire circulated among 74 former Guangzhou students living in Hong Kong in the mid-1970s. According to the results of this survey, which referred to the 1962–1966 years, working-class youth predominated only in the poorer regular junior middle schools with the lowest pass rates. These tended to be the newer and *minban* schools only recently established in working-class neighborhoods which previously had no middle schools. About 42 percent of the students surveyed in such neighborhood schools were of worker–peasant background, and 8 percent were from cadre families. By contrast, at the best key junior middle schools, only 11 percent of the students were of worker–peasant background, whereas 48 percent were revolutionary cadre children and 32 percent were from intellectual families. At the senior secondary level, where places were fewer, competition was more intense, and academic standards were higher, the proportion of cadre children declined. At the best key schools, they occupied 27 percent of the student body, and worker–peasant youth, 12 percent. The children of intellectuals represented 34 percent, and those of other middling groups, 16 percent.[61]

---

[61] The survey results are presented in Rosen, *Red Guard Factionalism*, p. 26; and Unger, *Education under Mao*, pp. 26–27.

These findings and all the anecdotal evidence, which agrees with them, suggest that the official late-1950s claims (shown in Table 9.6) of 50+ percent worker–peasant class composition among college students were probably a distortion. To the extent that these claims had substance in fact, they may have represented a deliberate merger of all the revolutionary reds into a composite "worker–peasant" category. And if so, that category was also serving to disguise another merger of historic proportions: revolutionary cadre parents had learned the value of coaching and cramming and began imitating intellectual elite lifestyles with similar "high expectations for their children."

Among educated Chinese, the cycle of upward social mobility is well known. One need not therefore have studied Ho Ping-ti's (He Bingdi) lists of *jinshi* degree holders from the Ming and Qing dynasties to be able to recite the conventional wisdom that upward mobility or new blood is always greatest among officials at the start of a new dynasty and then declines steadily thereafter as succeeding generations inherit the status of their fathers.[62] But given the thousand-year history of the examination system, the essential mechanism for this inheritance was intellectual as children of educated fathers benefited not just from the status and wealth the latter enjoyed as officials but from the household environment they provided their offspring.

That same tradition was vividly reproduced in the post-1949 revolutionary era. Two features of the 1958–1966 years in particular – the strengthening emphasis on class background and on the college-preparatory key-point stream – combined to hasten just such intergenerational succession. Genuine worker–peasant youth growing up in largely illiterate or semiliterate households could count themselves lucky to graduate from a newly established *minban* junior middle school. That left the "revolutionary red" field open to the children of the new CCP elite, who responded by encouraging their offspring to compete academically, in a trend which extended nationwide from county-town key points to the most prestigious middle schools in Shanghai and Beijing.

In this manner, educational development during those years also contrived to fulfill another related prophecy of the Chinese bureaucratic tradition, arising from its seductive ability to co-opt outsiders and alien dynasties. With the Soviet model already thus dispatched, the next target was the CCP itself. The Party's peasant roots had placed it beyond the traditional pale, beyond which, indeed, the great majority of all 20th-century contenders for Chinese political power had originated. Now, however, the CCP was promoting via key schools and family background criteria for enrollment a course foreordained to assimilate its revolutionary sons and daughters into the rarefied world of China's intellectual elite.

As for the intellectuals, key-point hierarchies and all that went with them

[62] Ping-ti Ho, *The Ladder of Success in Imperial China*, chap. 3.

addressed the contradiction Mao had long perceived between the prerequisites for revolution and those for development. With one hand, then, the CCP had done its best to discredit the "old" intellectuals for their bourgeois orientations and, in 1957, to expropriate any of their remaining independent political influence. But with the other hand, the Party had reaffirmed their authority over the education sector, even allowing them for the sake of Chinese national independence and modernization to use that authority in the most traditional of ways.

During the early 1930s, when the emerging "Stalin model" declared an end to class-based criteria for college enrollment in the Soviet Union, the new and old Russian intellectuals were merged within the new system. That merger had nevertheless occurred on the Communist Party's terms both politically and socially as the Khrushchev generation of working-class college graduates moved into positions of power and responsibility. Thereafter, they may have all gone their combined revisionist ways. But the Chinese formula as designed in 1958 brought together a far greater clash of political and social subcultures by actually reviving educational traditions that had lain dormant for half a century and then proceeding to incorporate the CCP's new goals and new elites within them. At the same time, the ongoing rhetoric of continuous revolution served as a constant reminder that at least some CCP leaders would not be able to live for long with the terms of that formula whatever its success in guaranteeing quality for modernization.

Meanwhile, as the system expanded quantitatively, increasing numbers of graduates had to be accommodated. In order to contain the potentially destabilizing consequences of disappointment, large doses of "political thought education" were administered each year to prepare students "with one red heart for the two possibilities," that is, pass or fail. But the clearly divided system clarified the consequences as well. Success meant key schools and college. Failure meant a life of labor. And for the failures, prospects seemed to worsen during the 1960s, as the government placed ever tighter restrictions on rural–urban migration. Rural youth were mobilized as part of the annual "preparation" to return home (*huixiang*) to work with their families in the countryside. Additionally, with the urban economy not even growing fast enough to provide employment for its own, urban youth were also assigned in increasing numbers to work in the countryside. According to official statistics, some 1.2 million urban school leavers were assigned to work in the countryside between 1956 and 1966, in a trend that increased from the early 1960s.[63]

A rural work assignment nevertheless remained the least desirable of all options. Like earlier generations of intellectuals who had paid mostly lip

---

[63] Cited and analyzed in Thomas P. Bernstein, *Up to the Mountains and Down to the Villages: The Transfer of Youth from Urban to Rural China* (New Haven: Yale University Press, 1977), chap. 1.

service to the idea of rural reform, most everyone viewed working in the countryside as a fate to be avoided by whatever means. Yet official policy and practice actually reinforced the negative associations by treating the country-side as a dumping ground for urban rejects. The Urban Work–Study Confer-ence in 1965 had affirmed, for example, that young people who were able to continue their studies or obtain jobs could stay in the cities (as bad-class youth increasingly could not in both instances). The remainder would have to be resettled in the countryside. A rural work assignment had become a form of class retribution and carried the stigma of failure within the urban hierarchy of status and achievement as well.[64]

Essentially, all that is known about Mao's views on these matters was ex-trapolated after the fact and after he launched the next mass movement mobil-ization phase in 1966. We must still therefore proceed like archeologists, piecing together fragments of information from cryptic commentaries and polemical arguments. Hence, we may never know more of Mao's role in creating the tracks and streams of the 1958–1966 education system. We may also never know if Mao was aware of the general rural rejection of work–study agricul-tural middle schools, or what he thought of the class composition within China's developing key-point school hierarchy, or indeed what he thought of that hierarchy itself.

Nevertheless, after it was all blamed on Liu Shaoqi and vestiges of a tradi-tion millennia old – a charge which our analysis suggests had more substance in fact than heretofore thought – Mao's comments at the 1964 Spring Festival forum were cited retroactively as signaling his renewed interest in education. The forum had also signaled yet another round of education reform by an-nouncing yet another recently authorized small-group investigation of needed improvements. Mao had used the occasion to criticize the pedantic and im-practical nature of the regular elementary and secondary schools. Their 12-year curriculum was too long; the subjects covered were too many and too complicated; examinations were too rigid. "It won't do," he said as if recalling his self-study university manifesto from 40 years previously, "for students just to read books all day, and not to go in for cultural pursuits, physical education, and swimming, not to be able to run around, or to read things outside their courses." His solutions: chop the syllabus in half; take a nap if lectures are too boring; crib on exams; and send all urban intellectuals periodically down to work in villages and factories.[65] Mao's number one priority at this time was

[64] Stanley Rosen, *The Role of Sent-down Youth in the Chinese Cultural Revolution: The Case of Guangzhou*, China Research Monograph, no. 19 (Berkeley: University of California, 1981); D. Gordon White, "The Politics of Hsia-Hsiang Youth," *China Quarterly*, no. 59 (July/Sept. 1974), pp. 491–517.

[65] "Remarks at the Spring Festival," 13 Feb. 1964, trans. in Stuart Schram, ed., *Mao Tse-tung Unrehearsed, Talks and Letters: 1956–71* (Harmondsworth: Penguin, 1974), pp. 201–211.

obviously with cultural revolution and class struggle as prerequisites for consolidating achievements already won by the overthrow of the old economic and political power structures. But Mao had begun his public life as an education reformer, and his sporadic commentaries on the subject throughout his career as a professional revolutionary remained consistent with his earliest inclinations. We can therefore speculate without fear of distorting too greatly the still unverified facts that Mao simply changed his mind sometime in the mid-1960s concerning the solutions he had authorized in 1958. With the consequences of those 1958 decisions fully apparent by the mid-1960s, Mao must have then decided to exercise his prerogative as mass movement leader, redefine his own position in favor of a more radical approach, and launch it as part of his second, more grandiose attempt at overall cultural revolution.

14

Education reform as the catalyst for cultural revolution and class struggle: the 1966–1968 mobilization phase

An event as contentious as the Great Proletarian Cultural Revolution naturally lends itself to dramatically differing interpretations. Since our interests are limited primarily to the impact on educational development, we need not tarry over these controversies except to reiterate the interpretation and chronology followed here. The line of argument has been introduced in chapter 11, namely, that Mao drew upon the concept of cultural or superstructural revolution to consolidate what had already been achieved in the economic base. Evidently, neither the idea nor the specific forms it took were original with him. But the Chinese version was at least unprecedented in degree and scope by comparison with the Soviet Union's earlier experience.

Mao and his allies had first raised the idea of cultural revolution in 1958, as part of the great leap into communism with emulation campaign economics as the centerpiece of that movement. The mistake of campaign-style economics was not repeated, but Mao's commitment to cultural revolution emerged from the early-1960s famine years as if strengthened by the experience. Thereafter, cultural revolution was recast in the leading role of his quest for a Chinese route to socialism, with class struggle defined as the motive force. Targets were all-inclusive and the class enemy was everywhere.

To launch such an undertaking, which entailed not just changing wrong ideas but seizing power from those who espoused them, Mao turned to the mass movement, and the interpretation used here was also introduced in chapter 11. He manipulated the movement to unleash its mass energy against the targets, much as he had used it to seize power in the villages of China during the land revolution of the 1940s. Just as land reform could not have succeeded while the old power structure dominated the countryside, so Mao's line and policies for socialist construction could not succeed until the power and authority of those opposed to them were broken.

Using the masses in this way also had a number of important related functions besides attacking targets. It permitted the masses to participate directly in the power struggle, thus giving them a personal stake in the process; and the natural leaders that emerged among them during the movement provided a source of new recruits to succeed the overthrown power holders. Especially, it would provide the successor generation to continue Mao's revolution after his demise. Naturally, there would be "excesses." But Mao had discovered long before that excesses were important to his cause, a lesson reiterated and reprinted countless times during the early mobilization stage of this movement.

These were the rules by which Mao had activated previous mass movements, and the same pattern was evident during the Cultural Revolution, launched in 1966. Accordingly, he radicalized the movement, allowing it on the one hand to take on a life of its own while on the other manipulating it to attack all the points of resistance he had targeted, including leaders at the very top of the Party hierarchy. With the destructive phase having achieved its purpose, the excesses could be corrected and a new superstructure built by a new or at least a chastened set of leaders. The changes introduced into the education system between 1968 and 1976 are thus treated as integral to the reconstruction phase of the movement since they could not have been instituted under the pre-1966 leadership.

Alternative interpretations by scholars and participants have referred to the 1966–1968 mobilization phase only as the Cultural Revolution and everything else as "after the Cultural Revolution." This was a common style while events were unfolding. Another cutoff date was the CCP's Ninth Congress in 1969, which signaled the rebuilding of the Party and the return of its conventional leading role, albeit under Maoist leadership, plus the accession of army chief Lin Biao as Mao's successor, replacing the disgraced Liu Shaoqi. Still other interpretations dated the end of the Cultural Revolution from Lin Biao's fall in 1971, and even from the 10th Party Congress in 1973.

All of these chronologies focus on the struggle for political power, whether in the narrow sense of Mao's attack against his opponents at the top of the Party hierarchy or in the broader sense of the mass movement he ignited against the Party and state structure. The assumption here, however, is that Mao used the power struggle and mass activism as means more than ends, reserving to himself the right to make the rules and define the limits of mass participation. He then did so not in accordance with any predetermined master plan but in an ad hoc fashion as the movement developed and in relation to his general vision for socialist construction. The chief rationale was to prevent the kind of creeping capitalism under way elsewhere in the communist world, and mass spontaneity was always manipulated toward that end. But the aim itself was open-ended, to be pursued through consolidation and not declared won or lost with the end of the mobilization phase.

Also contributing to the uncertain chronologies was the absence of a declaration formally ending the Cultural Revolution at any of the above-cited dates. Mao had even said, at the end of the first year of mass mobilization, that consolidation would last for at least a decade.[1] Hence the interpretation here also accepts as most appropriate the official termination of the Cultural Revolution by the 11th Party Congress in 1977, which heralded a comprehensive return to pre-1966 ways and means in all sectors, thereby marking the final posthumous defeat of Mao's grand design.

Educational issues figured prominently in both the initial mobilization and later consolidation phases. During the former, they served as easy catalysts to activate young intellectuals or college and middle school students. But reborn as Red Guards and rebels, they soon left such "small" concerns behind, forgotten in the excitement of seizing power and making revolution. Then, their destructive job done, students were (with some difficulty) reined in, returned to school, graduated, and sent out again, this time into the real world of work. Meanwhile, the consolidation phase commenced, known like its Great Leap predecessor as an "education revolution." New school leaders and a new generation of students were assigned to translate the revolutionary critique of the pre-1966 system into guidelines for a new era.

Our interest lies mainly in the later, consolidation period, bringing us back full circle to China's revolutionary development model which generated so much international attention in the early 1970s. But since the initial, destructive phase loomed so large as a pretext in China itself for discrediting the entire episode after 1976, we should first note the ties between the destructive and the reconstructive phases, which contemporary outsiders invariably factored out of their equations.

Mass mobilization

A definitive history of this episode may be impossible to write, but multiple segments of the story have been told and retold. The outline here seeks to highlight only certain key features of particular relevance for the subsequent, reconstructive phase. These include especially the intimidation and radicalization of school communities, as well as the class-based factionalism which divided them. All had an impact extending beyond the destructive, mobilization phase itself.

The prelude is well known as a sequence of events, fixed clearly in the minds of people who lived through them: Mao's 1962 declaration never to forget class struggle; increasingly class-based measures introduced into the school system and elsewhere thereafter; a political rectification movement (known as the

---

[1] "Dui Aerbania junshi daibiaotuan de jianghua" (Talk to the Albanian Army Representatives' Group), 1 May 1967, in *Mao Zedong sixiang wansui* (1969), p. 677.

socialist education or four-cleans campaign against "unclean" manifestations of capitalism) in the countryside with work teams of Party and university personnel sent down from the cities to participate in 1964–1965; the introduction of this same campaign into some universities and middle schools, accompanied by renewed criticism of education following Mao's 1964 spring festival commentaries; and the revival of cultural revolution concerns in literature, art, and ideology.[2]

The latter concerns – education and culture – were then used as catalysts for the big event, with Kang Sheng now appearing openly in the role of Mao's spokesman. Kang's role as advisor to the new Cultural Revolution Small Group, with which Mao led the movement, suited perfectly the manipulative skills necessary to grasp its laws and survive. Most of the other actors, less experienced than Kang, were not so lucky, including his first accomplice on the education front, Nie Yuanzi, a philosophy instructor and departmental CCP secretary at Beijing University (Beida). Kang stood in as her *houtai* (behind-the-scenes backer) and encouraged her to write a "big-character" poster denouncing Lu Ping, the university president and Party secretary, for trying to suppress radical criticism by students and teachers. The poster, put up on 25 May 1966, was broadcast nationwide on 1 June, activating the Cultural Revolution's mass mobilization phase.[3]

Events followed thereafter in rapid succession as the movement, orchestrated from Beijing, spread rapidly, if somewhat unevenly, to universities and middle schools throughout the country. In early June, Lu Ping was only the first to lose his job. Spearheading the action were newly organized groups of militant "good-class" youths calling themselves Red Guards. Credit for the first such group, set up in late May, goes to the middle school attached to Qinghua University in Beijing.[4]

---

[2] Increasing class-based concerns in education and Mao's 1964 commentaries were introduced in the preceding chapter. On the four-cleans socialist education campaign ("cleaning up politics, ideology, organization, and the economy"), see Baum, *Prelude to Revolution*; Richard Baum and Frederick C. Teiwes, *Ssu-ch'ing: The Socialist Education Movement of 1962–1966*, China Research Monographs, no. 2 (Berkeley: University of California, 1968); Anita Chan, Richard Madsen, and Jonathan Unger, *Chen Village: The Recent History of a Peasant Community in Mao's China* (Berkeley: University of California Press, 1984), chap. 2. On the developing cultural controversies, see, e.g., Merle Goldman, *China's Intellectuals: Advise and Dissent* (Cambridge: Harvard University Press, 1981), chaps. 2–4.

[3] E.g., Byron and Pack, *The Claws of the Dragon*, chaps. 15–16; Victor Nee, *The Cultural Revolution at Peking University* (New York: Monthly Review Press, 1969), pp. 42–60; Julia Kwong, *Cultural Revolution in China's Schools, May 1966–April 1969* (Stanford: Hoover Institution Press, 1988), pp. 3–8; "Flagrant Facts Demonstrating That Big Party Lord Peng Zhen Really Struck Blows at the Revolutionary Left and Undermined the Socialist Education Movement in Peking University," *Zhan Bao* (Battle News), 18 Jan. 1967, trans. in *Survey of China Mainland Press – Supplement* (hereafter *SCMP-S*), no. 165 (10 Mar. 1967), pp. 8–9; interview 82/BJ/17, p. 25.

[4] Nee, *The Cultural Revolution at Peking University*, p. 72.

In mid-June, examinations were suspended to allow students to devote themselves full-time to the movement. A 13 June proclamation postponed college enrollment for a semester pending one more thorough reform for an education system that had long since lost count of its incarnations. Criticism in these early days focused on education and school affairs, or more specifically on how authorities had perpetuated the old bourgeois system and corrupted the younger generation while discriminating against proletarians. Yet even at Beijing University, ominous features of the criticism movement appeared immediately: the practice of *chaojia*, or ransacking a suspect's home to search for hidden incriminating evidence, and physical abuse at public criticism meetings. Following an early house search, Lu Ping was criticized for his bourgeois lifestyle as well as for suppressing criticism of education. Lu and some 60 others were targeted as Beida's "black elements" at a dramatic criticism–struggle (*pidou*) meeting on 18 June.[5]

The struggle had only just begun, however, and central Party leaders were not united behind it. Work teams were sent into leading universities and middle schools throughout the country to provide guidance for the movement in early June. Liu Shaoqi and Deng Xiaoping were still in charge of day-to-day Party leadership, and the work teams operating under their authority evidently tried to put a lid on the movement.

Mao ordered the teams withdrawn in July, and Kang Sheng came out again in person, as he had done in 1958. He visited Beijing University along with Mao's wife, Jiang Qing, and Chen Boda to point the way forward. Kang told the dissidents that it was they, not the work teams or anyone else, "who are the masters of the Cultural Revolution. This is what Chairman Mao has first asked us to accomplish." The masses would be masters, but Kang was spelling out their mission in advance: "struggle" school leaders first, academic authorities next, and then revolutionize education. Beida had struggled its Party secretary president, Lu Ping, and then philosopher Feng Youlan, representing the new communist and old intellectual authorities, respectively. The next step was to resolve questions of teaching, research, work–study, etc.[6] The specific targets were thus to be the intellectual establishment as a whole, including its Party leadership, and the education system over which it presided.

Thereafter, Mao made a major mistake, given his standard modus operandi.

[5] Ibid., pp. 59, 62; Yan Jiaqi and Gao Gao, *"Wen ge" shi nian shi* (A History of Ten Years of "Cultural Revolution") (Hong Kong: Wannianqing chubanshe, 1989), *shang*: 29.
[6] "Record of Speeches by Comrades Jiang Qing, Chen Boda, and Kang Sheng at Beijing University (July 22, 1966)," trans. in *Selections from China Mainland Magazines–Supplement* (hereafter *SCMM-S*), no. 16 (5 June 1967), p. 7; "Comrade Kang Sheng's Speech in His July 28 Interview with Part of the Students of Institutions of Higher Learning," trans. in *CB*, no. 819 (10 Mar. 1967), pp. 1–3; Roxane Witke, *Comrade Chiang Ch'ing* (Boston: Little, Brown, and Co., 1977), pp. 320–324.

For the first time ever, he emerged into full public view – no longer a behind-the-scenes manipulator – to take personal command of the mobilization phase. Hence any excesses committed in the process could be blamed directly on him, an opening his enemies would exploit to the full, albeit only many years later, after his death. He wrote a poster himself, dated 5 August, praising Nie, criticizing the work teams, and blaming "certain leading comrades at the center and in the localities" for repressing dissident views.[7]

The CCP's 8 August "16-Point Decision" authorized all that followed – in terms reminiscent of Stalin's exuberant struggle against capitalist restoration in 1928–1929.[8] The comprehensive targets spelled out in August were those in authority going the capitalist road, reactionary academic authorities, and bourgeois ideology, including old ideas, culture, customs, and habits (article 1). Cultural revolution was revolution, and the targets would resist, but resistance would crumble once the masses were aroused (article 2). Boldly activate the masses (article 3). Let them educate themselves in the struggle. Cast out fear. Don't flinch from disorder. Use big-character posters and great debates, criticize wrong views, and expose all "ghosts and monsters" in order to raise the political consciousness of the masses and identify enemies (article 4). Do not penalize students for problems created in the movement (article 7). An important task of cultural revolution was to transform the education system and the old ways of teaching. Bourgeois intellectuals must no longer dominate (article 10).[9]

Radical teachers and rebellious students were formally vindicated, along with any "problems" they might create. House searches, accusation meetings, and physical abuse became standard features of the mobilization phase, all justified in the hunt for ghosts and monsters. "Cow-ghosts and snake-spirits" (*niugui sheshen*) of traditional lore were evil spirits capable of taking human form. Their spell and their power could only be broken by penetrating the human disguise and confronting the demons within. Class enemies were first and foremost those in authority taking the capitalist road, that is, the Party's own leadership cadres. With their aims of capitalist restoration heretofore hidden by reason of their overt revolutionary credentials, these were the main "ghosts and monsters" that now had to be exposed by the masses in every school.

---

[7] Mao Zedong, "Bombard the Headquarters," 5 Aug. 1966, *Xin Beida* (New Beijing University), Beijing, 18 Apr. 1967, trans. in *SCMP-S*, no. 182 (11 May 1967), p. 1.

[8] For the similarities between the Soviet experience in the late 1920s and the Chinese cultural revolution launched in 1966, see chap. 11, above.

[9] "Decision of the Central Committee of the CCP Concerning the Great Proletarian Cultural Revolution," 8 Aug. 1966, reprinted in *CCP Documents of the Great Proletarian Cultural Revolution, 1966–1967* (Hong Kong: Union Research Institute, 1968), pp. 42–54 (first published in *Renmin ribao*, 9 Aug. 1966).

School authorities as first targets

Had Mao been more of a bureaucrat and less committed to the mass movement method of revolutionary politics, he would simply have ordered everyone from middle school headmasters and CCP secretaries upward to tender their resignations pending reorganization of the leadership in all schools, work units, and government bodies. Then, individuals more committed to his priorities could have been recruited, thereby fulfilling the basic aim of the mobilization phase. But staffing the power structure with Maoists from top to bottom was only half the task; the other half was to activate the masses to do the job themselves, in accordance with the "laws" of a revolutionary movement – hence the progression through a sequence of stages that the participants often found as confusing as did outside observers.

The movement was activated around two concrete objectives: deciding precisely who should take the blame for the bourgeois education system and who should lead the attack against it, or defining targets and participants. Oddly, given the uncertainties surrounding the movement at the start, no one challenged directly the new verdict, proclaimed from all official sources, which suddenly recast the education system as bourgeois in all of its manifestations. Nevertheless, the work teams had a mixed record in designating both targets and participants.

In Beijing, where leaders carried the message in person from Mao's side, the consciousness-raising search for enemies fixed immediately upon school headmasters and Party secretaries.[10] There, accusations against them began either before or soon after the work teams arrived in early June. But conventional channels of command and control were suddenly in abeyance since the movement was being directed by only a few top CCP leaders against the Party-led bureaucracy as a whole, with the masses being mobilized to act on their own.

---

[10] In the mid-1960s, some university presidents and middle school headmasters, or principals, concurrently headed the organization of CCP members within the school, and some did not. Hence sometimes, as at Beijing University, the president concurrently held the post of university Party secretary as well. Additionally, deputy leaders also might or might not wear two (administrative and Party) hats.

Such leaders in universities and middle schools were of diverse origins. Some were genuine "revolutionary cadre" intellectuals who had joined the Party before 1949, and others had joined after. In the major tertiary institutions, at least, top leaders combined appropriate academic qualifications with their political credentials. But arrangements varied; for example, in some middle schools the leading positions were not occupied concurrently by the same person. In such cases, a professionally qualified headmaster might serve together with a less well educated CCP secretary.

Statistics for later years are not available, but as of 1956, when the CCP's total membership stood at 10.7 million, only 11.7 percent were classified as intellectuals; 69 percent were of peasant origin and 14 percent were workers. In terms of current occupation, only 3.8 percent of the Party's membership were then employed in "culture and education," whereas 57.8 percent were working in agriculture (*Shih Shih Shou Ts'e*, no. 18 [25 Sept. 1956], trans. in *CB*, no. 428 [19 Nov. 1956], pp. 1–2).

Recalled former student Han from Beijing: "The school CCP committee should have led this movement but could not because . . . it was actually a movement against the people who were usually relied upon to carry out the center's movements. . . . So at the start, there really was no one leading."[11]

Outside Beijing, the targets were not immediately understood or were deliberately misunderstood by local authorities, who mounted their own defensive actions.[12] But the order of battle as Kang Sheng had initially defined it was soon clarified and confirmed, if not by the work teams themselves in June or July, then by traveling Red Guards from Beijing in August, whose mission was to "scatter revolutionary sparks" nationwide, and by activists from bigger provincial cities fanning out to smaller towns as the autumn semester began.[13]

At the tertiary and secondary levels, school leaders, whether administrative or political, were rare indeed who managed to escape censure as the primary targets responsible for running a bourgeois education system antithetical to Mao's line.[14] Even the leaders of work–study model Jiangxi Communist Labor University and all its branches came under fire. In fact, it was this experience which undermined the efficiency of the whole complex, since so many county political authorities were reluctant to return to the pre-1966 system of concurrent university postings, being afraid to seat themselves on potential powder kegs once more. Overall, the leaders' fate was often, but not always, shared with leading "old" targets among the teachers, especially rightists and those with "historical" problems, whom these same leaders had often treated similarly in previous campaigns. Sometimes the leaders' protégés and political

[11] Interview 83/BJ/2, p. 165.
[12] Neale Hunter, *Shanghai Journal: An Eyewitness Account of the Cultural Revolution* (Boston: Beacon, 1969), passim; interviews: 78/S/5, p. 14; 82/SC/12, p. 64; 82/BJ/17, pp. 22–27.
[13] The official verdict of repression on the work teams, reinforced by the long argument over what to do with the "black materials" they had gathered on school activists, evidently had more to do with their attempt to control who would participate in the movement than with their choice of school personalities to take the blame. In any event, the movement developed unevenly, and the work teams were sometimes the first to direct attention in any given school to the first intended targets, namely, its own leaders. On the work teams' role in redirecting attention from bourgeois intellectuals to the school authorities in Guangzhou, see Ruth Earnshaw Lo and Katharine S. Kinderman, *In the Eye of the Typhoon* (New York: Harcourt Brace Jovanovich, 1980), pp. 11–24; Gordon A. Bennett and Ronald N. Montaperto, *Red Guard: The Political Biography of Dai Hsiao-ai* (Garden City, N.Y.: Doubleday, 1971), chaps. 1–2. But Rosen notes the variable instructions given by the city CCP authorities to Guangzhou work teams to protect some middle school leaders more than others (*Red Guard Factionalism*, pp. 105, 180). See also Hong Yung Lee, *The Politics of the Chinese Cultural Revolution* (Berkeley: University of California Press, 1978), pp. 26–63, 112–113; Hinton, *Hundred Day War*, chaps. 4–6; and on the argument over black materials associated with the work-team period whether or not a school actually had a team, see Neale Hunter, *Shanghai Journal*, pp. 62–63 and chap. 6.
[14] Of those interviewees contributing substantive recollections of the 1966–1968 years (see n. 27, below), only one reported a middle school (in rural suburban Beijing) where the school leaders were not subjected to some degree of criticism and struggle. The only other such case reported was a national minority district on the Burma border, where traveling Red Guards were not permitted to enter and the movement was not activated apparently for security reasons.

favorites among the younger teachers were also tapped as accomplices. Thus, 1950s rightists and mid-1960s activists were swept up together in the fervor of the mobilization stage.

All school leaders, bourgeois academics, and sympathizers of whatever stripe were not necessarily subjected to public struggle sessions, however, and not all leaders were criticized with equal severity. The degree of accusation varied greatly depending on many factors, including the individual's own political credentials, personality, defensive tactics by local protectors, timing, and academic level. During this early mobilization phase, reports indicate that physical violence against the targets was most extreme in middle schools. At the elementary level, where students were too young to understand or participate fully, the whole exercise followed a more subdued course, leaving the adults mostly to criticize one another, with younger teachers taking the lead against older or against the principal. In elementary schools, the greatest disruption seemed to be caused by former students returning to settle old scores with teachers against whom they harbored childhood grievances.

In June and July, the treatment of struggle objects – whether they were rightist teachers in Guangzhou, middle school headmasters and Party secretaries in Beijing, or the Beida president himself – followed the same pattern: accusations on wall posters; debates among students; investigation; interrogation of the "accused"; confession statements; evaluation; countercharges; revised statements; reevaluation; and one or more public criticism–struggle meetings for those determined to be true ghost/monsters. At such meetings they had to stand in shame, sometimes alone and sometimes with an escort of accomplices, to be charged before the assembled masses. At some point, the accused would also be paraded around campus wearing dunce caps and signs proclaiming their alleged crimes and misdemeanors, ex post facto in relation to Maoist educational standards now ascendant. The struggle objects would also be punched and prodded and splattered with ink or black paint, and sometimes held incommunicado while the investigations and interrogations continued. After the worst was over, a process that might drag on for weeks, designated ghost/monsters remained under surveillance by student guards and were assigned to do manual or menial labor.[15]

The dunce caps, accusation meetings, and house searches also re-created scenes from the pre-1949 land revolution. Mao's 1927 report on the peasant movement in Hunan was widely reprinted to serve as precedent. The report had celebrated the movement, when peasants swarmed into the houses of rural gentry, arrested them at will, paraded them through the streets in dunce caps,

---

[15] See Lo and Kinderman for a typical account. They describe the ghost/monster status of the Foreign Language Department leaders at Zhongshan University, contrasting it with the secondary critique of bourgeois academics and the greater physical violence in middle schools (*Eye of the Typhoon*, pp. 45–53).

and created "terror" in the countryside. The report concluded with Mao's famous declaration against those who feared that the peasants were going "too far." "Frankly speaking, a short period of terror must be created in every village or it will be impossible to suppress the activities of counterrevolutionaries and overthrow the gentry's power in the countryside. Proper limits must be exceeded in righting wrongs or else the wrongs cannot be corrected."[16]

Accordingly, the violence escalated in August and September, after the work teams withdrew. Mao's 5 August poster had derided the work-team period in June and July as the 50 days of "white terror," because student radicals had been dubbed counterrevolutionary. Now followed what the radicals themselves proudly proclaimed as a "red terror" in August and September. Restraining hands were lifted, and within middle schools especially, the interrogation process was further brutalized as physical coercion became a common means of extracting confessions.

The targets were also expanded somewhat to include "bad-class" students and others not initially tapped. These might be teachers never actually labeled "rightist" but known to harbor such sympathies, those with families and contacts abroad, or those who had studied abroad before 1949 and continued to enjoy a foreign, bourgeois lifestyle, although they had otherwise committed no political errors. Hidden Guomindang "agents" and other bad elements were ferreted out as well, along with hidden "collaborators" from World War II and people who had studied in Japan during the 1930s. Previously, there had been explicit rules defining "historical counterrevolutionary" in terms of past associations with the GMD. Now "investigators" ignored these rules, because it was a time for mass action free of bureaucratic control.

Typically, interviewees estimated that in addition to the top administrative and political leaders, who were routinely targeted and deposed or at least "set aside," about 10 percent of the teaching staff were designated as ghost/monsters in middle schools and colleges.[17] This estimate was made of the total number of targets, including some adjustments up and down that occurred in later months (but not including the retribution among and punishments for participants following factional demobilization in 1968).

For everyone else, practice varied. But the usual course of action included

---

[16] "Hunan nongmin yundong kaocha baogao," in *Mao Zedong ji*, 1:212–214.

[17] In middle schools, the top leaders deposed or set aside but not necessarily all tagged as ghost/ monsters were the headmaster or principal, the Party secretary, and the supervisor (*jiaodao zhuren*). The supervisor was often, although not always, a CCP member, and the job description varied, sometimes including both day-to-day academic management and overall discipline and sometimes only one or the other function. Larger schools usually also had deputies for each of the three top posts. Sometimes the deputies were targeted along with the top leaders and sometimes not, depending on what investigators could turn up on any given individual. In universities, the targets included, besides the top administrative and CCP leaders, those of academic departments as well. Sometimes heads of university administrative departments were also struggled.

evaluation of teachers' backgrounds and performance by student investigators, criticism of teachers by students, mutual criticism among teachers, and self-criticism. The aim was to assess how the ways and means of bourgeois education had manifested themselves in everyone's personal behavior. Wall posters and discussion meetings were the normal venue. Criticism ranged from trivial (e.g., wearing leather shoes), to personal (promiscuous sexual behavior), to professional (pushing up pass rates), to the illegal (examination scams, cheating, corruption) and political (criticizing the CCP).

Asked how students knew what to write or what standards to use, Student Han elaborated his theme that they had worked it out for themselves. After the work teams left, "there was no leadership of the movement beneath the central Cultural Revolution Small Group," and it "led only in spirit." There were no detailed instructions. He recalled the official statement that education during the past 17 years since 1949 had basically followed the capitalist road. He recalled too that the central group promoted Mao's talks with his nephew, Mao Yuanxin, as a "theoretical basis" and reference source. But otherwise, "they left the Red Guards to criticize the details and content of the bourgeois line in each school."[18]

In any event, few teachers escaped criticism, but for most the matter ended with the posters, discussion meetings, and self-assessments. Most also rode out the storm as more or less active participants rather than victims. The less active would undoubtedly have preferred observer status, but that option was difficult to exercise, especially during the early months of the mobilization phase. Revolutionary fervor was such that everyone had to participate or risk being criticized in turn. Later in the autumn after the main body of students left school to exchange revolutionary experiences, younger teachers went out as well, leaving others to "rest" at home. Teachers returned to school in the spring and were then drawn into subsequent phases of the movement with the students as noted below. The rehabilitation and return to work of ghost/monsters could take years to accomplish, during which time these main targets, if physically able, were assigned to manual or menial labor either at school or outside. But lesser cases were sometimes resolved quickly, with the first such adjustment coming during the factional realignment of early 1967.

The early criticism activity, of course, yielded many important secrets, including most of those introduced in chapter 13. Sensitized as they had recently been to the class-status question, students investigated every nuance and slight,

[18] "Talks with Mao Yuanxin" was a collection of commentaries for the younger generation, made between 1964 and 1966, which circulated widely in 1966. In them, Mao lectured his nephew on the criteria for successors, on politics, on class struggle, on the superiority complex of cadres' children, and on education reform. Mao cited his own early credentials as a schoolteacher and advocated learning directly from workers and peasants, an end to the obsession with exams and grades, a shortened curriculum, and more political training (translated in Schram, *Mao Tse-tung Unrehearsed*, pp. 242–252).

from every angle: preferences for cadres' children, preferences for intellectuals' children, bias against white-collar children, disdain for workers and peasants, etc. Living quarters were not the only venues for raiding parties, and many different stratagems were used for gaining access to the previously sacrosanct personnel offices, where everyone's files were kept. Sooner or later, everyone's secrets were revealed in this way. Students and teachers alike savored the unprecedented opportunity of seeing the contents of their own files, with the confidential life-determining evaluations of class masters and Party personnel cadres contained therein. Such were the investigative exercises that enabled students and teachers to recall even a decade later the family backgrounds of virtually every classmate and colleague. By delving into files, investigators were able to compile the socioeconomic data on students, teachers, and leaders that filled wall posters and sustained polemics in the Red Guard press for over a year.[19]

In Fujian, Wang Yugeng's high-profile leadership of the competitive "red-flag" system – with all its tactics for pushing up pass rates and pushing out low-scoring students – provided prime material at all the schools that had thrown themselves into the competition. Most memorable was the march north along the coast road led by Luo Sulan and her vanguard of student rebels from Xiamen Middle School Number Eight in late August 1966. Students were mobilized at schools all along the route by criticizing Wang Yugeng's "capitalist" methods for bringing glory to Fujian on the college entrance examinations. They arrived in Fuzhou demanding to "pull out" Wang Yugeng, and their challenge at a mass meeting on 29 August was commemorated in the name of one of Fujian's two main Red Guard factions, "Eight–Two–Nine."

For whatever reason, however, school leaders in Fujian paid an especially heavy price for their former glory. The region that had achieved some of the highest college entrance exam scores in the country now produced some of the most sensational struggles, leading themselves in turn to the most sensationalized of accounts.[20] As a ranking provincial official, Wang at least enjoyed some measure of physical protection, although she was not spared the ordeal of mass struggle meetings in the autumn. But once Wang fell, the headmasters who had followed the pace she set were left swinging in the wind as the movement's prime targets.

Poor Headmaster Chen, who had driven his teachers in a vain effort to provide tutorials for all, please everyone, and outscore the competition, ended up literally in such a state. So vicious did his struggle sessions become that

[19] A selection of these materials is reprinted in *Hongweibing ziliao* (Red Guard Publications), 20 vols. (Washington, D.C.: Center for Chinese Research Materials, Association of Research Libraries, 1975), and *Supplement*, 8 vols. (1980).

[20] Ken Ling, *The Revenge of Heaven* (New York: Putnam, 1972). Although obviously based on an eyewitness account, this book should be read as a dramatized memoir rather than a factual record. Luo Sulan is portrayed as the character Piggy.

students finally stuffed him into a gunnysack and slung him up over the rafters like a giant piñata. No one at school dared intervene, and he would surely have been beaten to death but for the timely intervention of a large peasant rescue party organized by desperate relatives. From another of Fujian's coastal counties came one of only three interviewees who admitted in so many words to having personally participated in such brutality. He was then a student and the victim was his county-town middle school headmaster, who might also have been beaten to death had he not committed suicide instead.

Participants

The early consciousness-raising activities mobilized participants, not just to depose school leaders and uncover their secrets, but also to serve as the spearhead against much higher targets, namely, all those in authority going the capitalist road. Thus, more important than anything the work teams did or did not do in June and July to repress student activism was the overall obstacle they posed to further mobilization. Given his still hidden agenda against all capitalist-roaders even in the topmost echelons of CCP leadership, Mao had to order the teams withdrawn as a logical next step. But although we can identify most of the escalation buttons Mao pushed from above, the ensuing divisions and subdivisions of school communities nationwide into a shifting kaleidoscope of groups, factions, and alliances marked the multiple points whereby the movement took on a life of its own.

In June and July 1966, the work teams' brief had included organizing students to lead the movement in each school. This new echelon of student leadership was composed predominantly, although not exclusively, of good-class (five-reds) youth. Such students and those who supported the work teams were made leaders of the Cultural Revolution preparatory committees set up in each school. When the work teams withdrew, the committees were left in charge of the movement, although they were soon overshadowed by new activist groups, of which good-class Red Guards were the first. But other groups also began to form almost immediately. School communities responded naturally to the divisive impetus provided by two key factors, namely, the class line and the unclear signals coming from Beijing against "those in authority." As a result, two distinct inclinations, conservative and radical, appeared to form spontaneously.

Student Han recalled the earliest division in July and his own small role therein. He had been a student leader by reason of his own talent and activism rather than family background, which was only middling. The strongest criticism at his school came initially from a small number of students whose fathers were all ranking cadres in one particular central government ministry "since based on internal information, they knew where the orders were coming from."

But he and his friends thought those students had gone too far and so wrote a poster of their own saying so.

Initially, "loyalists," or "conservatives," were those inclined as Han had been to support, if not their own school authorities, then the work teams, and by inference Liu Shaoqi and the Party organization. School preparatory committees served as the leadership for this inclination while radicals – such as college teacher Nie Yuanzi and Student Han's well-connected classmates – began to define themselves in opposition. Students whose class background was not unblemished red (i.e., who were not the children of cadre and working-class parents), and who therefore did not qualify to join the first Red Guard groups set up independently in each school, also began organizing their own rebel formations.

Nevertheless, good-class youth led the movement into the extremist "red terror" phase after the work teams withdrew. The Red Guards now gained international attention as they marched out of their schools to attack the "four olds" – old ideas, culture, customs, and habits – wherever they might be found.[21] In some schools, revolutionary discipline was so strict that good-class Red Guards posted sentries at the school gate permitting no one but their own kind out on the search-and-destroy missions. At other schools everyone went out, albeit divided into different formations with good-class Red Guards in overall command.

Also in August, everyone began traveling around the country free of charge to "exchange revolutionary experiences." Beijing youth moved out into the provinces while provincial youth converged on the capital. There they participated in a series of huge rallies used by Mao to further mobilize and guide the movement. The first such rally was held on 18 August and reviewed by Mao himself. Some 13 million young people journeyed to the capital that autumn, before the offer of free travel was withdrawn. And if more proof was needed as to Mao's intentions, a directive was issued in September on his personal instruction forbidding workers, peasants, and city residents from organizing in defense against the students.[22] Strictly speaking, Headmaster Chen's rescue party was an illegal assembly.

[21] For a participant's account of this episode, see Bennett and Montaperto, *Red Guard*, pp. 74–79. Victims not surprisingly had a different perspective, e.g., Lo and Kinderman, *Eye of the Typhoon*; Anne F. Thurston, *Enemies of the People: The Ordeal of the Intellectuals in China's Great Cultural Revolution* (Cambridge: Harvard University Press, 1988); Nien Cheng, *Life and Death in Shanghai* (London: Grafton Books, 1986). Interviewees distinguished more meticulously between "legal" and "illegal" searches. The former was approved by some higher authority pursuant to an investigation or in search of the four olds; the latter referred to bands of young people who treated the exercise as a kind of entertainment, returning time and again to "borrow" items from bourgeois households (interviews: 83/BJ/2, p. 168; 83/AH/7, p. 63; 83/AH/8, p. 5).

[22] "Four-point Decision Transmitted by the CCP Central Committee on September 11," in *CCP Documents of the Great Proletarian Cultural Revolution, 1966–1967*, pp. 73–76.

Given the heights to which he aspired, however, Mao could not rely primarily on good-class Red Guards, who still dominated the movement in August and September, because these were, if not led by children of the very ranking cadres he aimed to overthrow, then inclined to protect them. Good-class Red Guards could be mobilized easily to attack school headmasters and Party secretaries. But when the targets pointed clearly upward and much closer to home, the usefulness of this section of the revolutionary vanguard became more problematic.

Whether intended or not, then, Mao had little choice but to recognize the force building up within the movement or risk losing command over its direction before the main targets had been toppled. Toward that end, he threw his support behind the rebels, who had been on the defensive since June. They dominated the rally in Tiananmen Square on 6 October for specially invited non-red groups from all over the country. Everyone, not just those of good-class background, would henceforth be encouraged to participate in the struggle to bring down those in authority going the capitalist road.

In late July, cadres' offspring at the Beijing Aeronautical Institute's attached middle school had begun to promote their right to lead under the slogan "father a hero, son a great fellow; father a reactionary, son a rotten egg."[23] The ensuing controversy raged for a time, but good-class Red Guards were already in command and Mao's support for their movement seemed to vindicate their theory of inherited "natural redness." Yet simultaneously, their monopoly of power was provoking an antithetical reaction among the student "masses," who had all been activated alike under Mao's banner but had been excluded from full participation. Stanley Rosen found that the single most important issue underlying the formation of Guangzhou middle schools' rebel factions was opposition to the "bloodline" theory of Red Guard leadership.[24]

The theory of natural redness was officially criticized by central Cultural Revolution leaders. Loyalist strength began to wane while that of the rebels grew. Some ranking cadres' children who had led the movement at the start moved over to the rebel side; a few moved on to become antiestablishment ultraleftists; some became conservative; others simply dropped out as the targets suddenly appeared too close for comfort. The most notorious ultraleft response was the United Action Committee, formed by cadres' children from several elite Beijing middle schools and banned as a counterrevolutionary organization in January 1967.[25] With the monopoly of the original "good-class"

---

[23] Yan Jiaqi and Gao Gao, *"Wen ge" shi nian shi*, pp. 106–116.

[24] Rosen, *Red Guard Factionalism*, p. 126.

[25] Hong Yung Lee, *Politics of the Chinese Cultural Revolution*, pp. 110–118; Yan Jiaqi and Gao Gao, *"Wen ge" shi nian shi*, pp. 116–122; David Milton and Nancy Dall Milton, *The Wind Will Not Subside: Years in Revolutionary China, 1964–1969* (New York: Pantheon, 1976), pp. 159–162.

movement broken, its vanguard came to be known as the "old Red Guards" to distinguish them from their rising rebel successors.

Interviewees described, not unsympathetically, the harsh lessons of mass movement politics their privileged classmates had to learn as targets shifted upward against parents, turning children almost overnight "from red to black." A new term was coined – black cadre children (*hei gan zidi*) – to describe those whose ranking cadre parents became targets. One student had been a "model" Red Guard – until middle-class rebels made her ranking cadre father the early target of a poster campaign. The daughter thereupon became "protective" of authority and organized a support team to tear down the critical posters. Another interviewee knew some of the United Action (Liandong) students who had similar protective impulses, such as wanting to curb the indiscriminate house searches (as targets began moving closer to home). Ultimately frustrated, they turned against Jiang Qing and the Small Group itself, thus bringing an inglorious end to their efforts and placing them among the first activist casualties – a common fate among young participants unfamiliar with the inevitably shifting laws of the mass movement. They became the first to raise the lament about "being used," in this case to launch the movement only to be cast aside when they refused to obey the signals coming from Mao's command headquarters.

In the meantime, students had been allowed to extend their range by entering factories and government offices to struggle with authorities there. Suddenly, the "small" concerns of education and schools receded before the heady world of "real" revolutionary power. The original struggle objects seemed trivial by comparison and had in any case been forgotten, left to recuperate as best they could once the main body of students moved out to exchange revolutionary experiences.

In the new phase, extorting confessions by force was officially forbidden, as it had not been earlier. But with the Party's authority in a state of suspension and normal government operations virtually paralyzed by year's end, this was one of many rules often honored only in the breach. Now, mixed-class rebel Red Guards demonstrated themselves as adept at perpetuating revolutionary violence in other people's offices and work units as their red classmates had been in leading the struggle against school leaders, bourgeois intellectuals, and the "four olds."

Nor should it be assumed that the students were alone in these activities. Most teachers and lower-ranking cadres did not qualify as targets, being neither "bourgeois academics" nor "those in authority taking the capitalist road." Especially the younger teachers became active participants not just during the consciousness-raising criticism stage when participation was de rigueur but later during the revolutionary tourism phase, and still later as rebel strength grew. Sometimes, as at Beijing University, students and teachers participated together in the same groups from the start. Elsewhere, teachers set up their own groups, divided along conservative/rebel lines, and established links with like-minded student allies. Younger teachers, it was said, tended to side with the rebels, and older with the conservatives, but lines were not strictly drawn by age. As a whole, teachers continued to participate more or less actively either by joining such groups or by identifying with the inclinations of those who did, by contributing to the multitude of "Red Guard" publications that sprang up at this time, doing propaganda work, helping with loudspeaker broadcasts, and so on.

Seizing political power

By the end of 1966, the ultimate target was revealed: Liu Shaoqi was the chief capitalist-roader to be toppled. It had taken just half a year to escalate the movement from schools and universities to the Party center. In January 1967, the Cultural Revolution leadership called upon workers and peasants to join radicalized intellectuals in seizing Party and state power. The January power seizure in Shanghai was endorsed as official policy and then swept the country, engulfing Party and government organs at all levels. Chaos ensued as competing Red Guard groups and the power holders themselves embarked upon a struggle that was soon duplicated in every province, city, and county throughout the country. The Party organization, carefully constructed to penetrate every work unit and administrative level, ceased to function. The popular movement spread until virtually the entire top echelon of the Party with the exception of Mao and his new heir apparent, Lin Biao, was subject to mass criticism.

Where protection was lacking, even national leaders found themselves subjected to the same kind of treatment that their own offspring had just a few months earlier orchestrated for lower-ranking targets. The treatment was especially galling since it re-created by design the struggles of long ago against rural elites. Now a kind of harsh revolutionary justice took hold, recasting capitalist-roaders within the Party as the successors of their own original class enemies. Liu Shaoqi had himself led the land reform movement through one of its most violent episodes in the late 1940s. Now his wife, Wang Guangmei, was humiliated at a mass meeting orchestrated by student rebel leader Kuai Dafu at Qinghua University in April 1967. Liu himself suffered the same fate at a more private session a few months later.[26]

The first back-to-school call was issued on schedule after one semester but fell largely on deaf ears. Everyone began returning but not to teach or study. Indeed, trying to force interviewees even 15 years later to focus on mundane questions of educational development was often a strain once recollections of

---

[26] Hinton, *Hundred Day War*, chap. 8; Thurston, *Enemies of the People*, pp. 122–124.

the 1966–1968 years had been aroused. Nor was there much difference in this respect between those who had been students and those who had been teachers, or even between participants and targets.[27]

Eyes still lit up at the memory of having seen Chairman Mao in Tiananmen Square during the 1966 rallies. Indignation revived at the memory of having traveled all the way from Guangzhou only to be told that those with overseas Chinese connections could not be reviewed by Mao. Zhou Enlai himself came to the rescue, sending word that they could. Anger also still flared over the refrigerator lost to Red Guard carpetbaggers, and the humiliation of being criticized by fellow teachers. Yet most memorable seemed to be the political life of the mobilization phase thereafter as students, teachers, sent-down youth, contract workers, etc., savored and then as quickly lost unprecedented freedom:

[27] Given the distractions they posed, discussion of 1966–1968 events was encouraged only when time permitted. Nevertheless, 50 (of 82 total) interviewees contributed firsthand accounts of those years, 45 of them school related. Of the 45 interviewees, only 1 was from a pure-red background, without any overseas Chinese connections, as of mid-1966. Nine were of apparently unmitigated bad backgrounds at that time. The rest were either undeclared or in between (neither red nor white), usually by reason of class reinforced by the overseas Chinese connection, which most already had in 1966. A few acquired it by marriage thereafter, as did the one pure red. Three would otherwise have been from red families (two poor peasant and one worker) but for their overseas Chinese connections (see Appendix for class backgrounds of all interviewees).

All but six of the accounts concerned urban, suburban, or small-town schools. Conventional wisdom held that rural schools, like elementary schools generally, suffered much less disruption than urban schools, and the six accounts seemed to conform to that pattern. Of the 45 interviewees, in 1966 23 were teachers, 1 was a headmaster, and 21 were students. Only 1, an elementary school teacher, admitted to having been targeted as a full-fledged ghost/monster and, being from a landlord family, was one of the 9 bad-class individuals. Additionally, 2 college teachers, 1 student, and 1 middle school teacher were singled out for more than ordinary criticism but were not formally labeled. Several students' parents were criticized to varying degree after the movement began, sometimes influencing a participant to drop out and sometimes not. The one headmaster, from a rural commune school in northern Jiangsu, claimed he was "set aside" but not severely criticized and returned about 1969 to join the school's new revolutionary committee. Half the teachers and 18 of the 21 students identified themselves as having been active participants, either in 1966 or 1967 or during both phases of the movement.

The 44 teachers and students, by academic level:

	Teachers (participants)	Students (participants)
Elementary	8 (4)	3 (1)
Secondary	11 (7)	13 (13)
Tertiary	4 (1)	5 (4)
Total	23 (12)	21 (18)

The 45 accounts, by locality:

Beijing: 7	Zhejiang: 3
Shanghai: 7	Anhui: 1
Guangdong: 12	Yunnan: 3
Fujian: 6	Heilongjiang: 1
Jiangsu: 3	Henan: 1
	North China: 1

to organize their own action groups, start their own political publications, liaise with counterparts in other towns, lobby in Beijing or the provincial capital, make and break alliances, participate in dramatic battle scenes with factional enemies, and generally play their own power games as miniature versions of and even as participants in those going on at the provincial and central levels.[28]

Rebuilding the power structure

Mao's initial use of the masses not just to attack the power holders but actually to overthrow them was interpreted by many, observers and participants alike, as the most significant feature of the Cultural Revolution. Certainly, it was unprecedented for a communist leader to have allowed the non-Party masses to participate in a power struggle to this degree. Thus, disillusionment set in as the promise of mass participation in the subsequent exercise of political power gradually eroded after January 1967. Central policy shifted quickly to curb the unworkable excesses created by January's unlimited power seizures. Mao himself endorsed the revolutionary committee (rather than the mass-dominated Paris Commune style of government initially promoted) as the most appropriate form for rebuilding the leadership structure in government and in work units. The new revolutionary committees were to be based on "three-in-one combinations," initially comprising former leaders (who had produced acceptable self-criticisms), members of the army, and mass leaders.

Mao also gave the army a major role in the reconstruction process, sending it into schools, like Liu Shaoqi's work teams of outsiders, to control the movement. The first call for elementary and secondary school students to make revolution by returning to class (*fuke nao geming*) came in March 1967.[29] Army representatives or military training teams were then sent into middle schools and universities throughout the country. Even at the basic level, the small garrison units stationed in every county did the honors in its middle schools. The center issued a warning that mass leaders must not be relegated to a supporting role on the new revolutionary committees. But from this point, the center would never again allow the mass organizations to play an autonomous leading role. Thereafter, the history of the movement was one of balancing and compromising with all forces in the power equation: the Party–state bureaucracy, led by Zhou Enlai; the military, led by Lin Biao; the Cultural Revolution

---

[28] Several accounts of these events are available, e.g., Jean Daubier, *A History of the Chinese Cultural Revolution*, trans. Richard Seaver (New York: Vintage, 1974); Keith Forster, *Rebellion and Factionalism in a Chinese Province, Zhejiang, 1966–1976* (Armonk, N.Y.: M. E. Sharpe, 1990); Julia Kwong, *Cultural Revolution in China's Schools*; Hong Yung Lee, *Politics of the Chinese Cultural Revolution*; Milton and Milton, *The Wind Will Not Subside*.
[29] *Renmin ribao*, 7 Mar. 1967.

Small Group, which was itself not always united; and the feuding mass organizations at the local level.

The immediate task was daunting even for individual work units and schools. The case of every person who had been in a position of authority now had to be evaluated to determine the nature of his or her errors and standpoint in relation to Mao's thought both before 1966 and during the struggles thereafter. Those whose errors were deemed not significant and who produced appropriate self-criticisms could be rehabilitated and even allowed to join the new leading revolutionary committees. But consensus was nearly impossible to achieve because the mass organizations were split into a plethora of groups in every school and work unit. With the strife of recent months still fresh in everyone's memory, it was difficult to make people sit together in the same classroom much less agree on who the new leaders of the school should be.

By default if not design, the newly arrived army representatives in each school became the deciding force as they set about reorganizing the feuding mass groups into a single united all-school Red Guard unit. Those of good-class background were supposed to be the "mainstay" of the new united units. Students who "were not born of the families of the laboring people" could also join if they loved Chairman Mao, had a proletarian spirit, and had behaved "comparatively well" both politically and ideologically.[30]

For their part, "non-red" teachers and students resented this reemergence of the class line which had initially excluded them from full participation in the movement. Now the new power structure was being rebuilt, and they were being relegated to second-class status once more. Some of them even refused to join the new Red Guards, and it was in this manner, over the formation of the new leadership bodies, that the conservative–rebel split readjusted and stabilized in the spring of 1967. The line between the two sides was drawn, as before, primarily over power relationships and, as before, was reinforced by the issue of class.

Some participants stayed where they had always been, on one or the other side of the dividing line; others, like Student Han, shifted from loyalist to rebel; some shifted back and forth more than once before coming to rest or dropping out. At Beijing University, radical activist Nie Yuanzi became a "conservative," more lenient in orientation toward the Party authorities, by contrast with academic authority Zhou Peiyuan, who emerged as a leading "rebel."[31] With the final targets now identified and awaiting judgment, teachers were drawn more easily into this phase of the movement since it entailed rebuilding the power structure within individual work units, where everyone had a personal stake in the outcome.

Although many different independent groups of students and teachers might now exist in any given school, these positioned themselves on either side of the conservative–rebel divide, which was soon reinforced by citywide and provincewide factional alliances. In Beijing, conservative groups associated themselves with the Heaven Faction, so named because of the dominant role played by a group at the Aeronautics Institute, where middle school students had sparked the "bloodline" debate in July 1966. The opposing, rebel Earth Faction was led by a group from the Geology Institute. Similarly, conservative middle school groups affiliated themselves with the Four–Four (April Fourth) Faction, which in turn allied when necessary with college-level Heaven. Middle school rebel Four–Threes associated with Earth. The home bases were appropriately symbolic. Aeronautics specialties were politically and academically chic, admitting primarily red-class youth. Geology was an unpopular field and hence the more likely fate of middling-class students.

In Guangdong, conservative groups rallied with the East Wind Faction, whereas rebels followed the Red Flags. In Fujian, loyalists rallied under the banner of the Revolutionary Rebellion Committee (Geming zaofan weiyuanhui), also known as the August Eighteenth Faction after the date Mao first honored the old Red Guards. This faction grew from the loyalist group initially formed to protect Wang Yugeng, whereas the August Twenty-ninth (Ba-er-jiu) Faction remained the rebel standard-bearer.

Even after the factional alignments stabilized in early 1967, the division between the two sides was never absolute; groups continued to split off and merge and did not always conform to the dominant pattern of class affiliation. Nevertheless, such a pattern did seem to develop, qualifications listed below to the contrary notwithstanding. Thus, civilian and military cadres and their children tended to dominate the "conservative" groups (baohuang pai), and they were reputedly more inclined to protect the Party organization but seemed more radical in acting against other targets. People from middle-class and white-collar backgrounds led the opposing, "rebel" side (zaofan pai), which tended to be more radical in opposing the Party power structure but less so toward other targets with whom its members had many ties. Those from bad-class backgrounds were also more likely to be found on the rebel side if they participated at all. People of working-class origin, who were counted among the reds but not usually among the leaders of either side, divided between the two and participated in both.[32]

---

[32] The best illustration of class-based factional divisions derives from the questionnaire data compiled by Chan, Rosen, and Unger from former Guangzhou middle school students living in Hong Kong in the mid-1970s. These data were first published in their joint "Students and Class Warfare: The Social Roots of the Red Guard Conflict in Guangzhou," *China Quarterly*, no. 83 (Sept. 1980), pp. 397–446. These same questionnaire data used by Rosen and Unger,

Central direction was nevertheless compromising and ambiguous as it officially tried to maintain the revolutionary momentum of January while searching for a viable balance to govern over the longer term. This allowed ample scope for individual leaders to manipulate the mass forces on all sides, until armed conflict erupted among them as the participants ultimately turned their destructive impulses directly against each other. When army representatives entered schools and began military training, the purpose was to promote alliance and instill discipline, which in some instances it did. But the military also added a new dimension as factional strife escalated into actual armed clashes in many provinces during the spring and summer of 1967, with both sides raiding local army units for weapons.

This period also inspired a renewed rebel upsurge as the full force of its opposition matured. Some groups began attacking the entire power structure and all cadres within it whether or not they were "good" Maoists. Some called for a complete and continuing redistribution of social and political power. They were now attacking simultaneously government leaders, conservative mass organizations, and the army. Again Mao intervened on the side of moderation. The radical May Sixteenth (Wu-yao-liu) group, led by some members of the central Cultural Revolution leadership, was "exposed" in August; a planned radical campaign against power holders in the army was called off; and Jiang Qing retracted her famous rallying cry of a few months earlier: "defend with weapons, attack with words."

Measures were also announced that signaled the unmistakable onset of consolidation. The tasks of rebuilding the Party and purifying class ranks were announced in the autumn. Workers, rather than students, were officially cited as the main force of the Cultural Revolution, and the students were criticized for having committed errors. They were told again, as they had been in the spring, that it was time to return to school. Mao issued a series of instructions in late 1967, all in the same vein, aimed at narrowing the targets, reaffirming a lenient rehabilitation policy toward the cadres, upholding the integrity of the army, and unifying the feuding mass factions. Ultimately, the new provincial governing revolutionary committees were formed. Leaders representing the provincial contenders for power, including the cadres, the army, and the mass organizations, were called to Beijing, where they negotiated settlements to create the new provincial governments.

Demobilization and qualification

The central leadership issued orders banning armed conflict in July 1968 and finally enforced them. When some groups still refused to desist, Mao ordered

respectively, are also cited in the final section of the preceding chapter. See also Anita Chan, "Images of China's Social Structure: The Changing Perspectives of Canton Students," *World Politics*, Apr. 1982, pp. 295–323.

another kind of work team, composed of production workers, into the schools to stop the fighting and collect weapons. His famous gift of Pakistani mangoes to the Workers' Mao Thought Propaganda Team stationed at Qinghua University, where Kuai Dafu was holding out to the bitter end, was advertised nationwide to indicate Mao's support for the workers. Together with the army, they then ended campus-based armed conflict and the mass-based political groups which fueled it.

Simultaneously, the campaign to purify class ranks (qingli jieji duiwu) aimed to finalize verdicts once and for all. The shrinking body of original targets was now those deemed beyond redemption and unfit for positions of authority, namely, unregenerate capitalist-roaders (however defined) and individuals who themselves (not including their children) carried bad category labels. Everyone else who had been targeted before was supposed to be rehabilitated and returned to work, albeit after a spell of purifying manual labor preferably in some rural locale. All teachers had to undergo one last round of mutual criticism and self-criticism to assess their behavior during the movement and before. Some new recruits were also added to the list of targets as the movement progressed to its inevitable conclusion. These were the mass leaders who had gone to excess, especially during the armed-struggle phase.

In Guangdong, the lines were clearly drawn; factional retribution was swift and often violent. Recalled Teacher Song, an active participant on the rebel side: "The dividing line at the start was over the army, which side supported it and which did not. The issue was the same all over Haikou and all over Guangdong. So those in power went on to clear out class ranks and control the other faction in this way. . . . For this some were killed and injured. Can anyone forget that? No. The key was their calling us cow-ghosts and snake-spirits."

Teacher Ye recalled events in his northern Guangdong county the same way: "At first, the Red Flags were in power. But in 1968, the East Winds supported the county revolutionary committee and overthrew the Red Flags." All teachers in the county were summoned to a struggle–study meeting that continued throughout the month of August. Such meetings, euphemistically called "study classes" (xuexi ban), were common throughout the Cultural Revolution decade. Content varied widely, ranging from political study and periodic work assessment to personnel discipline and even criminal investigations. If a session entailed struggle or discipline and investigation, as well as study, all participants might be held incommunicado from the outside world for days or weeks at a time. Examples were usually made of a few individuals, who were hauled up before full sessions for public denunciation and self-criticism. Some resisted and refused to admit wrongdoing. A suicide or accidental death was not uncommon during full-fledged countywide struggle sessions, which became intensified versions of the earlier rectification and thought reform exercises.

In this case, rank-and-file rebel teachers were forced to watch while the "stronger rebellious spirit" they had so recently shown against the local leading cadres was turned against their own, including Teacher Ye himself, who had led a small group which rallied under the Red Flag banner. But some county-town rebel leaders in Guangdong survived 1968, he said, only to be overthrown after Lin Biao's downfall in 1971, under the pretext of purging the fallen successor's followers.[33]

Especially in light of the post-1976 inclinations to apportion and deflect blame, however, some qualifications to the pattern drawn above must be appended. Thus, commenting sardonically on the newfound amity within the post-Mao coalition of his victims – with "intellectuals" as an undifferentiated category heralding Deng Xiaoping as their "liberator" – one interviewee noted how intellectuals had actually suffered most at the hands of the early Red Guards, when these were led by the children of the same Party leaders returned to power after 1976. Another interviewee recounted, in turn, the story about Deng Xiaoping's unyielding bitterness toward some of the rebels, so much so that he was still reputedly blocking the appointments and promotions of minor faction leaders more than a decade after their deeds were done.

Such conclusions would also seem to follow logically from the general pattern sketched here: between good-class loyalist Red Guards led by cadres' children and inclined to protect the CCP establishment while attacking other targets more fiercely, and mixed-class rebels doing just the opposite. Without qualification, however, these generalities can be misleading and appear gravely out of focus if applied to any particular time, place, event, or individual. In terms of individuals, for instance, within the small group of 45 interviewees who contributed school-related recollections of the mobilization years, 30 declared themselves to have been active participants (12 as teachers and 18 as students) in the events of 1966 or 1967. Of the 30, 21 also declared their factional affiliations: 17 rebels and 4 conservatives.[34] Except for 1 white, the rebels all fit the pattern of neither red nor white. But the 4 conservatives did

---

[33] Four former Guangdong participants active in groups affiliated with the Red Flag Faction (two middle school teachers, one college student, and one middle school student) described their 1968 reversal of fortunes in the same way. A fifth (a middle school teacher and rebel leader in western Guangdong) was removed from his school's revolutionary committee in a countywide purge of rebel school leaders, enforced via an all-county struggle–study meeting in late 1971. Between 1969 and 1971, his school had achieved a genuine alliance by including on its revolutionary committee two faction leaders, one rebel teacher and one loyalist teacher, who divided political and academic work between them and were responsible for day-to-day school management while the military representative headed the committee.

[34] Rebels, by province: Guangdong, 10; Beijing, 3; Fujian, 2; Zhejiang, 1; Henan, 1. Conservatives: Fujian, 3; Anhui, 1. These factional affiliations are as declared at the time of demobilization and job assignment (described in the following chapter). Thus, Student Han began as a conservative in 1966 but then shifted to the rebel side at some point thereafter and so is counted as a rebel. Given their views and job assignments, Teachers Yang (Jiangsu) and Lu (Fujian) were probably conservative loyalists by 1967–1968. But since they did not declare their factional affiliation in so many words or acknowledge participating in any faction-based activity, they are not counted among the conservatives here.

not fit, since they, too, were all mixed-class (middling and bad) individuals who, for reasons of personal commitment or family circumstances, identified with school and Party authorities. So strongly, in fact, did one teacher retain this commitment that he was angered by questions about the preferential treatment shown to local cadres' children in his school. Overall, however, the most relevant qualifications to the generalized pattern of factional affiliations drawn above are the following.

The general pattern is especially confusing if applied at the start, during the summer months of 1966, when good-class youth actually began by positioning themselves on both sides of the early conservative–rebel divide. At the tertiary level in particular, students, teachers, and early good-class Red Guards alike immediately began taking sides for and against the work teams – despite the exemplary loyalist role assumed by Liu Shaoqi's wife and daughters.[35] The vanguard of the movement against school authorities as well as the four olds was thus drawn from among the early good-class Red Guards, who, at that brief point in time, emerged not as protectors of authority but leading the rebellion against it.

Nor should it be assumed that the Beijing Red Guards succeeded in imposing their strict class-based regimen on all Red Guard formations everywhere, since many reports suggest otherwise. And when everyone went out to smash the four olds, mixed-class rebels were not necessarily more protective of old customs than their red classmates, who still led the movement at this stage (and whose higher-level cadre homes by that time contained many fine old objects as well). On the contrary, it was a time when middle-class youth could prove their credentials by "drawing a clear line" (huaqing jiexian) between themselves and their families' bourgeois habits by conforming as required to the revolutionary mores of the time. When the tide turned in their favor, rebel Red Guards organized "open houses" at higher-level cadre homes and compounds so everyone could come and see the bourgeois lifestyles enjoyed by their leaders, complete with thick carpets, overstuffed furniture, and "American Standard" toilet fixtures.

The general distinctions also seemed to have little practical significance for school leaders, at least once it became clear in any given locality that they were officially intended as the first persons in authority to be targeted. Whether or not like Lu Ping at Beida they concurrently held the position of CCP secretary, middle school headmasters were particularly vulnerable as the highest-profile authorities responsible for trying to combine the academic-quality-oriented

---

[35] For a full account of these complexities in Guangzhou, see Rosen, *Red Guard Factionalism*, chap. 5 and pt. 2, passim. The Liu daughters who figured in Red Guard sagas were Liu Tao at Qinghua University and Liu Pingping at Beijing Teacher Training University's attached middle school. Liu's wife, Wang Guangmei, had been active at Qinghua during the work-team period.

and politically motivated class-line policies of the mid-1960s. Accordingly, these leaders were targeted from all sides, especially during the red days of August and September 1966.

Finally, the pattern of emerging conservative power is based primarily on Beijing and Guangdong, for which information is most complete. The pattern is also drawn from hindsight – with a certain assumption of historical inevitability – assessed against the steady erosion of autonomous mass-based power from early 1967 onward, as the "policy was implemented" (*luoshi zhengce*) of narrowing and rehabilitating targets. The pattern strengthened after the 1971 downfall of Mao's successor, Lin Biao, in an apparent contest of strength with Zhou Enlai. This paved the way for Deng Xiaoping's rehabilitation as the main surviving target and Deng's coup against remaining Maoist leaders after Mao's death.

Still, the pattern of emerging conservative power did not necessarily apply everywhere to the same degree, at least not as early as 1968. In Fujian, for example, the rebels were not suppressed in the same definitive manner as in Guangdong, nor was the convergence between class and faction as consciously drawn. Guangdong interviewees were actually unique among all those responding to these questions in the degree of factional/class convergence and antagonism they articulated. Instead, something approximating the original aim of a factional alliance was achieved in Fujian, and interviewees indicated that a similar compromise occurred in Jiangxi, Anhui, and Henan as well. The nature of the alliance, they said, was determined by the armed struggle and the inclinations of provincial military leaders, who were usually divided like everyone else between rebels and loyalists. In Guangdong, Huang Yongsheng consistently favored the loyalist side, whereas in Fujian, Han Xianchu protected rebel August Twenty-ninth leaders from 1966 until he was transferred out of the province in the mid-1970s.[36]

Factionalism (*paixing*), or autonomous political activity by the mass groups, was officially banned in 1968. The groups themselves were dissolved and their publications terminated. But their influence continued and was measured by the representation granted leaders on work-unit and government revolutionary committees as well as by the job assignments subsequently allocated to rank-and-file members. Rebel Red Flags were clearly the losers in Guangdong from

[36] Huang Yongsheng was commander of the Guangzhou military region in 1966 and concurrently chairman of the Guangdong Revolutionary Committee from 1968. Han Xianchu headed the Fuzhou military region and the Fujian Revolutionary Committee (*Who's Who in Communist China*, 1:221, 313). On Huang Yongsheng as the rebel's nemesis, see Rosen, *Red Guard Factionalism*, pp. 219–220. The link between August Twenty-ninth leaders and Han Xianchu in the late 1960s is also indicated in the Ken Ling account (*Revenge of Heaven*). The Fujian careers of both Ye Fei and Wang Yugeng ended in 1966. Also on continuing rebel power, see Forster, *Rebellion and Factionalism in a Chinese Province*. My thanks to Richard Kraus for helping to clarify certain points in the Fujian story.

1968, whereas August Twenty-ninth leaders in Fujian were assigned to official positions throughout the province.

Hence, unlike Beijing rebel Kuai Dafu, who spent most of the years after 1968 in semidisgrace as an ordinary laborer before being imprisoned in the late 1970s, Luo Sulan remained a prominent figure in Fujian provincial politics until just after Mao's death. She and six other August Twenty-ninth leaders were then arrested as counterrevolutionaries, ostensibly for having joined Jiang Qing's 1975 drive against Zhou Enlai. Simultaneously, a major purge of their local colleagues commenced, complete with the fearsome "study classes" and, in the Xiamen area at least, several executions of affiliated commune cadres as well as arrests of local leaders, including educators.

One rebel teacher-participant described his fear during the 1977 study class in terms identical to those used by Teacher Ye concerning his August 1968 experience. Another rebel Fujian teacher told how his relative, a commune education cadre, feared for his life in 1977 and was lucky to get off with a five-year prison sentence. Hence this late 1970s rebel purge, said to have been ordered by Deng Xiaoping himself, did reproduce the fate suffered by Red Flag Faction members in Guangdong, but only in a kind of delayed-action sequence one full decade later.[37]

Toward consolidation and education reform

The Ninth Party Congress, in April 1969, claimed victory. But the revolution was not yet over, since the threat of capitalist restoration would presumably never die. It remained to continue "struggle–criticism–transformation" (*dou-pi-gai*) and to "carry the socialist revolution in the realm of the superstructure through to the end." Toward that end, Mao's proletarian policies were to be carried out.[38] But the Cultural Revolution was proceeding more or less along the course he had initially charted as Mao the mobilizer became Mao the consolidator. The theme of *dou-pi-gai*, reiterating the logic of the mass movement, persisted from the August 1966 16-Point Decision, to Mao's March 1967 instruction sending the army into the schools, to the Ninth Party Congress, and on into the 1970s. The policy line for the revolution in education as part of this process was also similarly outlined from the start both in the June 1966 decision on changing the system of enrollment and in the August 16-Point Decision (article 10).

According to these two decisions, the education system would be thoroughly

---

[37] Interviews: 80/FJ/8, pp. 75–92; 82/FJ/4, pp. 43–44, 46–47, 89–90; 82/FJ/11, pp. 3–6, 20; 82/FJ/26, pp. 53 ff.; 82/BJ/17, p. 30; 83/AH/7, pp. 55 ff.
[38] The Ninth Party Congress documents are translated in *CB*, no. 880 (9 May 1969); see also *CB*, no. 904 (20 Apr. 1970).

transformed.[39] A new way of enrolling students in college and senior middle school would be devised because the existing method had failed to free itself from the set patterns of the bourgeois examination system. A new method of selection, based on recommendation and proletarian politics, would aim to give greater access to working-class youth. In addition, all the arrangements for schooling, testing, and promotion would have to be changed, together with the content of education.

The formula for educational transformation – combining the old critique of the regular school system that Mao began reviving in 1964, along with the developing class-struggle theme that he began reviving in 1962 – served as the framework upon which his Cultural Revolution was built. Educational issues became the catalyst used to mobilize the nation's academic community, but the actual transformation of schooling was then thrust into the background as mobilized youth moved off campus to complete the rest of their mission.

When the first call came to continue the revolution by returning to class in March 1967, the participants were still locked in struggle. At Qinghua University, factional leaders on both sides rejected the call, arguing that power was the crucial issue and that discussing specific reforms was meaningless until the question of which side would control the university was settled. In Guangdong, it was the conservatives who more readily accepted the center's shift to consolidation-stage education reform. The rebels initially resisted it as a conservative ploy to suppress the larger revolution and remained preoccupied with the power struggle, which they were then in the process of losing.

By autumn it was clear that returning to school could not be delayed much longer. The official press began laying the groundwork, calling upon schools and localities to begin making their reform plans. But having helped bring down all relevant targets, the factions created in the process essentially returned to the question that had galvanized them at the start, namely, who was more responsible – bourgeois academics or Party authorities – for the bourgeois education system. Yet if Mao was reading the coverage on education reform in Guangdong Red Guard newspapers during 1967 and 1968, he must have been pleased to see how well everyone had learned their lessons and internalized his aims.

The conservative side blamed teachers and bourgeois academics for the education system, which rewarded academic achievement and college admission above all else. If Party leaders were to blame, it was for having left leadership over education in the hands of bourgeois intellectuals. The rebel side, by contrast, blamed the power structure, from the school Party authorities to

---

[39] The two decisions were first published in *Renmin ribao*, 18 June 1966 and 9 Aug. 1966, respectively.

national policymakers and Liu Shaoqi himself. Cadres' children were able to exploit their good-class backgrounds and parental connections to claim preference in admission to the best schools, usurping the preferential seats that should have been reserved for workers and peasants.[40] But no one ever challenged Mao's verdict on the bourgeois nature of the education system itself. Of the 45 interviewees who discussed the 1966–1968 years for this study, no one reported, nor could anyone recall, even a single instance when factional arguments developed around anything like such a challenge.

Mao might well have congratulated himself, then, on the Machiavellian brilliance of his strategy. Once again he seemed to have successfully set up intellectuals against the Party and vice versa. Not only had his verdict on education been established as the new orthodoxy, but he had manipulated the movement so that the successors of the two main protagonists he targeted – that is, the children of cadres and intellectuals – had ended with each side blaming the other side's parents for the faults all now accepted. All that remained was to devise positive prescriptions for change, induce the participants to live by them, and prevent the targets from seeking redress! But for the first time since Mao entered public life as an education reformer 50 years earlier, the entire education establishment and all its political allies had been humbled and disempowered. For the first time, radical education reform did not need to be set up outside the regular system or in separate compartments within it. Instead, the entire system could now be re-created in the image of radical reform.

[40] These arguments from the Guangdong Red Guard newspapers are summarized by Rosen (*Red Guard Factionalism*, pp. 227–233) and Hong Yung Lee (*Politics of the Chinese Cultural Revolution*, pp. 306–309).

15

Education reform as the culmination of class struggle: the professional educator's perspective

Returning to the basic question posed at the start as to how the Chinese could have declared in 1980 that not one good thing had come from the Cultural Revolution, we can now anticipate the answer. It was not accidental that Mao reminded everyone in 1966 about his early days as a teacher and elementary school headmaster.[1] The lessons learned in those days from the then developing critique of modern schooling had obviously grown into a lifelong commitment. Having adapted the concept of cultural revolution as class struggle to overthrow the education establishment between 1966 and 1968, Mao then spent his remaining years trying to impose what was in essence the old reform ideals upon the entire system. Even one or the other of those two aims – either class struggle or radical across-the-board education reform – would undoubtedly have been enough to provoke a mighty backlash. But to have combined the two ensured that all the enemies Mao created along the way would unite to demolish his grand design.

Nevertheless, for eight years, from 1968 until his death, Mao presided over the most radical set of reforms to be imposed upon China's modern school system since its founding at the turn of the century. And it was this set of reforms that caught the eye and imagination of the international development community. In fact, polemical distortions to the contrary notwithstanding, neither the negative nor the positive claims were overdrawn! We will therefore present the argument from a dual perspective as the worst of times (from the professional educator's viewpoint) and the best of times (for the radical reform ideals).

At this point, we must also rely more heavily than in earlier chapters on the Hong Kong interview data since the rhetorical content of official publications reached saturation point during the 1968–1976 years, and all unofficial publications disappeared. Also, central documents and directives comparable to

---

[1] "Talks with Mao Yuan-hsin: Third Talk," 1966, trans. in Schram, *Mao Tse-tung Unrehearsed*, pp. 251–252 (see chap. 14, n. 18, above).

those cited for earlier decades remain unpublished at the time of writing (early 1990s), leaving oral histories as the only alternative.

The professional educator's perspective is easiest to present because all the interviewees to some degree shared it regardless of age, political inclination, or factional affiliation. This is not surprising, because most were either trained as regular teachers or at least educated within the regular pre-1966 system, and were speaking after 1976, when the intervening events were already in official disrepute (see Appendix for relevant data on the Hong Kong interviewees). Yet their ability to reproduce the professional educator's perspective did seem at odds with the roles that many had played as active participants in the events of 1966–1968.

All acknowledged that when the radical reform principles were used to launch the assault against headmasters and teachers, the principles themselves were never challenged. The closest that factional antagonists ever came to a "policy" debate was the question of who was more or less responsible for betraying Mao's revolutionary trust. But revolutionary arguments seemed to be one thing, and teaching a classroom of students something else again. It was a contradiction interviewees could only acknowledge, not explain.

For all of its consciousness-raising and power-building, then, the net result of Mao's Cultural Revolution seemed to be a climate of academic opinion not unlike that of the pre-1949 years. In the old days, radical reform ideals evoked an ambivalent response: so popular that almost everyone felt obliged at least to pay them lip service even while ignoring them in practice. During the 1966–1976 decade, they could not be ignored in practice, but the response among educators was still ambivalent. Of the ideals themselves, interviewees would often, although not always, express genuine approval. Of radical reform as implemented, interviewees were generally, although not uniformly, negative.

The radical reform ideals in socialist guise

Although central directives ordering specific changes remain unavailable, the changes themselves were soon evident, reproduced more or less uniformly in nationwide practice and well advertised in the official press.[2] They mirrored the 1966–1968 Red Guard polemics, which, on the content of education reform,

---

[2] The "official" press in those days referred to the "two newspapers and one journal" (*liang bao yi kan: People's Daily, Liberation Army Daily, Red Flag*) authorized as most "reliable" in transmitting the Maoist orders of the day from central command headquarters. This accounted for the "sameness in diversity" as a multitude of groups busily turned out their own newsletters, combat bulletins, investigation reports, etc. Inevitably, Beijing groups formed within government ministries and leading schools had access to more authoritative information from the center, and their publications were most frequently reprinted and rewritten by fraternal groups in other cities.

always elaborated a line similar to official press accounts – while all in turn claimed authority from Mao's cryptic commentaries and instructions.[3]

With the entire body of rules, regulations, precedents, and traditions supporting the old system now overthrown, designers returned to the drawing boards. They began by hanging a series of tentative proposals and draft programs on a string of relevant Maoist quotations. Most frequently cited were his commentaries dating from 1964, including those at the Spring Festival forum and his talks with nephew Mao Yuanxin.[4]

Under the circumstances, there is no way to identify the boundaries of the evolving Maoist system or which experiments were operating within its limits and which extended into the realm of resistance beyond. Nevertheless, a composite summary drawn from the proposals of 1968–1969 can serve as an introduction to the substance of the radical reforms since the principles upon which they were based remained constant until 1976, even though the details in practice seemed suspended in constant animation.

The key quote as classes resumed was a passage from Mao's 7 May 1966 letter to Lin Biao, saying that education should be revolutionized, the school term should be shortened, and students "should, in addition to their studies, learn other things like industrial work, farming, and military affairs."[5] The second most quoted phrase authorized the working class to exercise leadership in everything. To prevent bourgeois intellectual domination, the working class had been sent into the schools via army training groups and worker propaganda

---

[3] E.g., *Renmin ribao*, 18 July 1967 (article by Shi Yanhong) and 19 July 1967 (article by the Ministry of Education's Yan'an Commune). The reader will recall that the basic argument against the pre-1966 education system, which underlay all discourse on the 1966–1976 education reforms, has been assessed and found wanting in earlier chapters. For other elaborations of the two-line struggle in education, see, e.g., "Shiqi nianlai jiaoyu zhanxian shang liangtiao luxian douzheng dashiji" (Chronology of the Two-Line Struggle on the Educational Front during the Past 17 Years), *Jiaoyu geming* (Education Revolution), 6 May 1967, reprinted in *Hongweibing ziliao*, vol. 2 (1975), and trans. in Seybolt, *Revolutionary Education in China*, pp. 5–60; "Chronology of Important Events in the Struggle between the Two Lines in the Field of Higher Education" (jointly authored by Red Rock Fighting Detachment of the Beijing Commune and July First Fighting Detachment, both of the Ministry of Higher Education, and the Torch Fighting Detachment of the New Beijing University Commune), in *Jiaoxue pipan* (Pedagogical Criticism and Repudiation), no. 2 (1967), trans. in SCMM-S, no. 18 (26 Feb. 1968); "Chedi pipan Liu Shaoqi xiuzhengzhuyi jiaoyu luxian" (Thoroughly Criticize and Repudiate Liu Shaoqi's Revisionist Education Line) (jointly authored by three groups from three academic departments at the Tianjin Work–Study Industrial Teacher Training College), 8 Apr. 1967, reprinted in *Hongweibing ziliao*, vol. 16 (1975), pp. 5211–5212.

[4] Mao's relevant quotations are widely available in Chinese and English, e.g., Schram, *Mao Tse-tung Unrehearsed*; John N. Hawkins, *Mao Tse-tung and Education: His Thoughts and Teachings* (Hamden, Conn.: Linnet Books, 1974); *Mao Zedong sixiang wansui* (1969); *Chairman Mao on Revolution in Education* (Beijing and Guangdong: People's Publishing House, 1967–1969), trans. in *CB*, no. 888 (22 Aug. 1969); *Mao Zhuxi jiaoyu yulu* (Quotations from Chairman Mao on Education), ed. Hongdaihui, zuozhanbu doupigai bangongshi (Beijing: Beijing dianji xuexiao, dongfanghong gongshe, 1967).

[5] "Wu qi zhishi" (May Seventh Directive), in *Mao Zedong sixiang wansui* (1969), p. 643.

teams. The latter were to remain indefinitely to guarantee proletarian control while schools in the countryside would be led by poor and lower-middle peasants, rural allies of the urban proletariat. Since a coherent system based on radical principles was easier to conceptualize for the countryside, city schools were initially asked to learn from the idealized rural designs.[6]

Mao also said that intellectuals must be reeducated by workers, peasants, and soldiers, and that all cadres must engage in manual labor.[7] Two Mao quotes foreordained the future for tertiary education. "After graduation from a senior middle school," Mao had said in a December 1965 speech, "one should first perform some practical work. . . . After performing a few years of work in this way, two more years of study will be sufficient."[8] Later he said: "Students should be selected from among workers and peasants with practical experience, and they should return to production after a few years' study."[9]

Accordingly, one or two years' work replaced graduation from senior middle school as the new prerequisite for college. The unified national college entrance examinations were abolished. Instead, colleges selected students from among pools of candidates recommended by their own work units. National unified curricula were abolished, leaving each institution to rebuild its own based on the radical principles of shorter courses, less classroom learning, and more practice plus labor and politics. The declared aim was to equalize the chances for workers' and peasants' children to join the ranks of cadre and intellectual offspring at the tertiary level, or, in Mao's words, "to make intellectuals of the laboring people and laborers of intellectuals."[10]

Mao's famous diatribe against the "Ministry of Urban Health" addressed the problems of medical education in particular: "Tell the Health Ministry that it only serves 15 percent of the population and mainly old men of rank at that. The extensive rural population cannot get medical treatment." Since medical school graduates did not want to go down (to the countryside), others would have to be trained differently, following Mao's maxim that "the more books people read, the dumber they seem to become." Health workers with an elementary education and three years of basic training would "at least render better service than quacks and witch doctors."[11]

---

[6] E.g., "Yisuo lilun he shiji yizhi de xinxing xuexiao" (A New School That Integrates Theory with Practice) and "Gongren jieji yiding yao yongyuan lingdao xuexiao" (The Working Class Must Always Lead Schools), both in *Hongqi* (Red Flag), no. 4 (1968), pp. 24–31, 39–40.

[7] E.g., *Renmin ribao*, 5, 6, 8 Oct. 1968.

[8] *Chairman Mao on Revolution in Education*, p. 16.

[9] *Renmin ribao*, 5 Sept. 1968; *Hongqi*, no. 3 (Sept. 1968), (joint article on the Shanghai Institute of Mechanical Engineering).

[10] E.g., *Renmin ribao*, 25 July 1968 (article by Chen Yonggui); see also *Renmin ribao*, 9 Aug. 1968 (article by Tongji University, May Seventh Commune).

[11] "Dui weisheng gongzuo de zhishi" (Directive on Health Work), 26 June 1965, in *Mao Zedong sixiang wansui* (1969), pp. 615–616, reprinted in the Red Guard press and trans. in *SCMP-S*, no. 198 (16 Aug. 1967), p. 30; see also *Hongqi*, no. 3 (Sept. 1968) (article on the revolution in medical education for "barefoot doctors").

Proposals for the overhaul of elementary and secondary schooling proliferated in 1968–1969. Everything was introduced as tentative and experimental in
the form of model experiences and investigation reports published for discussion and reference. Rural experiments in education reform were introduced
first and the formulas then applied in urban settings, deliberately reversing the
usual order of priorities. Many of the formulas and features so advertised
would become part of the new order; others proved unworkable from the start;
still others were implemented only in modified form. Taken as a whole, they
represented the new formula for revolutionizing Chinese education.[12]

The aims were self-consciously anti-elitist, egalitarian, and designed to
reduce the "three great distinctions" – between town and country, industry
and agriculture, mental and manual labor. They were promoted everywhere by
expanding the quantitative base of the educational pyramid and leveling its
qualitative top. In this respect, the proposals as a whole also demonstrated far
greater consistency than was evident either in Mao's own pronouncements
(in their original contexts) or in the first, 1958 education revolution.

An adaptation of the old *minban gongzhu* (popularly run with public assistance) formula from Yan'an days was proposed for all rural schools. To reduce
the inevitable distinctions between *gongban* and *minban* (regular state-run versus inferior, locally financed schools), all would be managed and financed
under the same arrangement, not to be called *minban* but *jitiban*, or collective
run. Middle schools would be administered by communes and elementary
schools by village-level collectives (production brigades).

Existing state-run schools in the countryside would be transferred to this
new arrangement. All elementary school teachers should be paid in work points,
valued like the peasants' earnings according to each collective's annual income.
The purpose was to eliminate the guaranteed higher state wages, which set
teachers apart from peasants. State subsidies would assist as necessary. Elementary school teachers should also be hired locally, drawn from the local
pools of educated peasants, demobilized soldiers, and resettled city youth. The
Party organization and revolutionary committees at commune and brigade
levels would be responsible for school management, together with school leaders. Poor and lower-middle peasant representatives should supervise and review work as a spare-time responsibility.

For students, the rationale was to achieve universal schooling. As a corollary,
they would have to overcome the idea that "education is useless" if it did not

[12] The summary presented here is a composite drawn from an extended series of articles in the
People's Daily that began in September 1968 and continued throughout the 1968–1969 school
year, advertising experiences in educational reform from localities throughout the country.
Many of the articles were translated in *CB*, no. 868 (31 Dec. 1968), no. 869 (15 Jan. 1969), and
no. 870 (27 Jan. 1969). The first two numbers were devoted to rural reports and the third to
urban. Most formal of the model experiences was the "Draft Program for Elementary and
Secondary Schools in the Chinese Countryside," from Lishu County, Jilin, albeit published
only for "discussion" (*Renmin ribao*, 12 May 1969).

lead outward and upward. Schools should be located as close to home as possible. Every production brigade should run its own complete elementary school, with branches in isolated villages as well if necessary. Complete elementary schools should also "wear junior middle hats," and each commune should, in addition, have its own middle school, where enrollment would be based not on unified entrance examinations but on recommendation plus ability, with priority given to worker–peasant youth. The 1960s stratagems for pushing up pass rates by holding back and forcing out low-scoring students would be forbidden, along with regulations that restricted attendance for whatever reason. Old norms from *sishu* days should be tolerated, such as overaged students and erratic attendance. Fees must be waived or abolished. If family chores threatened, younger siblings could be brought to class and animals left to graze at the school gate.

The nationally unified curricula and teaching materials would be shortened and decentralized to the province and below. Among the decisions thus "sent down" would be the length of elementary and secondary schooling, that is, whether to cut 2 years or 3 from the old 12-year system and how to arrange the new curriculum to combine practical skills with book learning. But labor for labor's sake need not be a feature of rural schooling since students routinely labored with their parents throughout the year. Agricultural middle schools disappeared as a separate work–study alternative. Homework, tests, and exams should all be given, but not in the old formalistic ways.

When applied in cities, however, formulas designed for the countryside encountered immediate problems. The urban equivalent of peasant management could only be schools run by factories and street organizations, neither of which had much potential for universal urban development. This particular effort to reduce urban–rural distinctions proved too literal, and urban school reform inevitably had to adapt more specifically to the different conditions of city life. In any event, key-point schools were abolished along with the competitive entrance examinations which had channeled students into them. Also abolished were all other kinds of special schools, including those for cadres' children, those for army children, and those attached to universities, where intellectuals' children received priority. All alike became ordinary state-run schools. At the unpopular inferior end of the spectrum, urban *minban* schools were not so much abandoned as incorporated within the leveled state-financed system wherein everyone attended their nearest neighborhood schools. All followed shortened curricula combining similar proportions of labor, practice, and classroom learning for all students regardless of their social or academic standing.

Interviewees contributed a wealth of insight and opinion about the education system that resulted as these proposals were implemented between 1968 and 1976. If we distill the opinions as we have the proposals themselves, however,

Table 15.1. *Resumption of classes by year and academic level*

	Number of schools		
	Elementary	Secondary	Tertiary
No interruption	4	1	—
1967	7	3	—
1968	2	18	2
1969	1	8	1
1970	—	1	2
1971	—	—	—
1972	—	—	1

Note: Data from interviewees' firsthand knowledge of their own schools.

the result comes up primarily negative. And the most common point in the negative assessment concerned neither political conformity nor the many manifestations of class struggle but the damage done to quality by quantitative dilution, shortened curricula, and the disruption of regular academic routines. Rural resettlement and rural job assignments for urban teachers – the latter in turn a result of quantitative expansion in the countryside – emerged as a second major source of complaint.

Back to school and down to the countryside

The tertiary level suffered the greatest losses by whatever standard, including quantity, quality, and the length of time that elapsed before classes resumed. Table 15.1 illustrates the number of years lost by academic level, to the best of the interviewees' recollections for their own schools only. Elementary schools were least disrupted, and a few (one urban, one suburban, two rural) continued to hold classes without serious interruption, while a few others (two urban, two suburban) lost only one semester. One rural middle school was set up in 1966 and held classes without interruption thereafter in a Guangdong mountain district. But most middle schools resumed classes only after peace was enforced in 1968. Later sporadic outbreaks of factional violence and consequent disruption in the early 1970s were reported from two provinces (Sichuan and Guizhou). By contrast, tertiary institutions according to all accounts did not begin enrolling new students on a regular basis until 1970, roughly synchronized with the new requirement of one or two years' labor between middle school and college. Some ran makeup and experimental classes for demobilized Red Guard students and others from 1968, however, accounting for the early activity shown on Table 15.1 at the tertiary level.

Meanwhile, academic communities everywhere were struggling with the terms of their new revolutionary contract. The leading revolutionary committees could take many months to form at all government levels and in all schools, leaving everything under military and/or worker propaganda team authority during the interregnum. The two years of strife had taken their toll, with greatest damage to discipline and facilities reported from urban middle schools. Desks had been smashed and equipment looted. Windows were broken; chemistry labs and compounds had been used to make explosives; the remains of countless layers of posters covered walls both inside and out.

These were tense times all around as soldiers and workers disarmed factional fighters, disbanded political action groups, closed down their publications, decided who deserved what degree of punishment, cleared class ranks among faculty and staff, and organized a hasty departure for three years of graduating seniors (the classes of 1966, 1967, 1968) to make room for three years of entering first-year students. Mao's ultimatum of October 1968 that all cadres must engage in manual labor simplified matters, making labor the only option for everyone lacking an immediate task.

The most common venue for all government cadres and college teachers was a "May Seventh Cadre School," usually a school-run farm or hastily converted labor reform correctional facility where the new arrivals did farm labor, swept their own floors, washed their own clothes, and devoted long hours to political study. Some with problematic pasts (unrehabilitated ghost/monsters) stayed on for years. Others were rotated back to offices and institutes as work resumed after only a few months or even less. Except for the few who did not pass the final clearing-class-ranks test, elementary and secondary school teachers as a whole did not participate in such long-term mandatory farm labor. The reason, they said, was the sudden surge in demand for their services with the resumption of classes, backlog of students, and immediate quantitative expansion.

For students, the Red Guard generation at the senior middle level (the *lao san jie*, or "three old classes," i.e., students in their first, second, or third year in 1966) were declared graduated and sent on their way. Rustication, or resettlement in the countryside, was now the main destination. Whereas before 1966, increasing numbers of young middle school leavers with no urban job prospects were mobilized to volunteer for a rural assignment, now they were required to "volunteer" – following Mao's instructions that educated youth should go down to the countryside. Mao's instructions were actually interpreted to mean that all educated youth (secondary school leavers and graduates) must engage in manual labor, a requirement that could be fulfilled in town or countryside. But the countryside had to absorb most of the 1966–1968 Red Guard generation since their numbers were far greater than the city jobs available.

After 1970, "rustication" of city youth continued, and each city worked out its own arrangements, but with the 1966–1968 backlog cleared, the chances of drawing an urban slot increased. A year or more of such labor service also became a new prerequisite for admission to college. All Red Guard generation college students were also declared graduated but had to do a year of mandatory farm labor, usually under military supervision, before qualifying for their first job assignments.

The rural refrain that began in China as a romantic ideal when Mao himself was a student had now matured along with the concern about manual labor into a national movement of unprecedented proportions. And simultaneously, the rural focus as officially presented in ideal-type form began to attract international attention because it coincided so perfectly with the new emphasis on rural poverty or the growing imbalance between urban and rural development. But what the outside world did not know, or had long since forgotten, was the history of ambivalence in China itself over the rural–urban gap. Nor did official accounts ever do more than allude to the related prejudice that governed the implementation of Mao's idealistic solutions. Sentiments against those solutions were still such that in reality they could only be surmounted by a massive show of force such as that generated through his Cultural Revolution. Ultimately, even that would not succeed, leaving the question forever open as to whether less power and prejudice would have achieved a more lasting effect.

Because of the political handicap they all shared deriving from their overseas connections, the experience of Hong Kong interviewees in this adventure must be considered with care. It is conceivable that a similar group without such handicaps would contain many more genuine volunteers who relished the experience. Such people did exist. They were among those, for example, who had volunteered to participate in the Jiangxi Communist Labor University experiment in the late 1950s and remained committed to the social value of rural labor even as their enterprise was being dismantled in the post-Mao backlash 20 years later. But because of their backgrounds, the Hong Kong interviewees were at least well qualified to explain the negative connotations also associated with the downward movement and the biases built into it all along the way. And given the extent of the late-1970s backlash, it is probably safe to assume that on this issue the Jiangxi people represented the minority radical reform tradition only, while interviewees were more typical of cadre and intellectual inclinations overall.

Interviewees participated in all dimensions of the down-to-the-countryside movement. As explained in the Appendix, 82 individuals were interviewed in Hong Kong: 62 teachers, 13 students, and 7 others. The teachers came from all academic levels (see Table 15.2). Each of the six college teachers spent two–three years at May Seventh Cadre Schools or their equivalent. All who had been college students in 1966 did one or two years of manual labor before receiving their first job assignments. And 30 interviewees were resettled in the

Table 15.2. *The 62 teachers interviewed, by academic and geographic levels (for the main work experience described)*

Level	Number of teachers
Tertiary	6
Secondary	
Urban (prefectural seats and above)	7
Rural suburbs	6
County town	5
Rural (commune seats and below)	23
Total	41
Elementary	
Urban (prefectural seats and above)	3
Rural suburbs	2
Rural (commune seats and below)	10
Total	15

countryside (*xiaxiang*) after attending urban middle schools. Most of the 30 had been students in 1966, but a few were resettled in the years just prior, and a few were early-1970s graduates who drew rural assignments.

The usual practice was to resettle as close to home as possible, that is, county-town residents within their own counties, those from prefectural cities within their home prefectures, and provincial-capital youth within the province. Among interviewees, only those from the individually administered cities of Beijing and Shanghai were scattered further afield. Shanghai youth were resettled in Anhui, Yunnan, and the Northeast. Those from Beijing were transplanted to Shanxi, Shaanxi, Gansu, and the Northeast. Many made regular visits home, often spending one or more months per year during the slack farming seasons in this way. Additionally, three others were born and raised in rural areas, attended middle schools in towns nearby, and then returned to the countryside (*huixiang*) after graduation.

Of the 33 total resettled and returnee youth among the interviewees, three were assigned to army-run state farms where they earned fixed wages as farm laborers. Everyone else took up residence in village production brigades where they labored together with the locals and were in all but a few cases paid in the same way. The basic collective unit for most was the production team (typically several tens of households). All working adults received a share of the collectively earned income as measured in work points for the amount of labor performed each day. Actual work-point value varied annually with the team's income. Usually, after a year or more of such labor, young people were eligible

Table 15.3. *Interviewees' elementary and secondary school teaching experience, by location and status*

Status	Urban (prefectural cities inclusive)	County town	Commune and village production brigades	Total
Gongban (state salaried)	9	4	23	36
Minban (locally hired)	1	1	18	20
Total	10	5	41	56

Note: Many interviewees described more than one school-related work or study experience. For example, five interviewees served as *minban* teachers in temporary or substitute capacities, but since these positions were secondary to the main experience described by the five, who had worked mainly as accountants, stenographers, etc., their extra work is not included in the *minban* teacher totals.

for other work, which was assigned at the discretion of village-level production brigade leaders and commune authorities above them.

In this way, 20 of the 33 were subsequently tapped to teach in village schools, continuing to be paid in work points calculated either at the annual value of those in their adoptive teams or at some average value for the whole brigade, a common means of remunerating brigade cadres. Such teachers received an additional small cash subsidy paid monthly by the state to supplement the annual share-out of work-point income, but otherwise they lived like the peasants, with pension and welfare benefits minimal to nonexistent. Those hired in this way were called "popularly hired teachers" (*minban laoshi*), a term living on from the old *minban* school concept even though the name fell out of fashion for the village schools themselves.[13] Resettled and returned youth were also tapped to serve as accountants, stenographers, and health workers (barefoot doctors) in the same way and under the same conditions, accounting for three additional interviewees. Two of the *minban* teachers were soon recruited to work in nearby towns, where they nevertheless retained their irregular status and are the two nonrural *minban* teachers shown on Table 15.3.

Obviously, the best way of avoiding an extended stint of rural labor was to have been a state-salaried elementary or secondary school teacher as of 1966,

[13] The distinction between *minban* and *gongban* was in fact formally eliminated (see chap. 16). As part of that decision, *minban* teachers were guaranteed a state subsidy at the national average rate of 170 *rmb* and 210 *rmb* per year, for elementary and secondary level teachers respectively. Interviewees all reported receiving monthly cash payments approximating these national averages, which are cited in *Zhongguo jiaoyu dashidian, 1949–1990* (Dictionary of Major Educational Events in China, 1949–1990) (n.p.: Zhejiang jiaoyu chubanshe, 1993), *shang*, p. 136.

Table 15.4. *The 56 elementary and secondary school teachers, by their own level of formal education and employment status*

Status	College graduates (4–5 yr. courses)	Post-secondary (2–3 yr. courses)	Specialized sr. secondary	Regular sr. secondary	Regular jr. secondary
Secondary school teachers (41):					
Gongban	19	11	3	—	—
Minban	—	—	—	7	1
Elementary school teachers (15):					
Gongban	—	—	3	—	—
Minban	—	—	—	5	7

and 36 interviewees fell into this category. Only two of their number did time at May Seventh Cadre Schools. Everyone else attended at most on a short-term rotational basis or participated in other manual labor exercises limited to a few weeks per year.

Nor were the uniform status distinctions based on educational qualifications ever challenged. Everyone with a specialized secondary school education or above always qualified for and received state job assignments which carried with them guaranteed salaries and associated benefits, the most important being retirement pensions and health insurance. The relationship between educational qualifications and employment status shows up clearly on Table 15.4. Only one interviewee reported one case where a state-salaried rural elementary school teacher (his mother) was transferred to a work-point pay system following the early proposals outlined above. But a state subsidy was paid to make up the difference between her previous salary and the work-point value of her teaching time, and the arrangement lapsed within a year or two.

Regular teachers were called upon to serve in other ways, however, by assignment and reassignment downward following the renewed emphasis on rural school development. They took all their salaries and benefits with them, but down they went nonetheless. Of the 36 *gongban* teachers, 13 were directly affected by this downward transfer of personnel in the late 1960s. Five were transferred: one from Beijing to a small prefectural seat and the others from county towns to communes. All eight Red Guard generation college graduates were similarly assigned – beneath their level of expectations – to backwater county towns or rural communes. All but one of these "downward" assignments were made to expand and strengthen rural professional services; the one exception resulted purely from factional conflict. Additionally, seven regular teachers had also been assigned, beneath their level of expectations, to commune schools earlier in the 1960s.

Interviewees had clearly been participants in an urban-to-rural movement of historic dimensions. Without the movement, at least 40, including both the resettled *minban* and assigned *gongban* teachers, would probably never have contributed their talents in any rural capacity. Nor was the outside world's attention misplaced, since the movement was unique in reversing the rural-to-urban drift from impoverished countryside to overcrowded cities typical of modernization generally. Some interviewees could appreciate this line of reasoning, but most did not. How could this Chinese experience have ever been adopted for use in other countries, they wondered, when it could not even be made to work in China without the coercion generated from a Maoist-style mass campaign, itself of unprecedented scope?

In this manner, interviewees articulated the inherited nonrural aversion to rural life that the personnel movement aimed to surmount. But they also revealed how the movement itself was implemented everywhere in virtually all its dimensions with a bias that both derived from the inherited aversion and generated even greater antipathy in the process. Thus, despite the uniformly idealistic and evenhanded official publicity, rural assignments were treated not just as a form of penance but also as punishment. They became, in effect, the fate of losers in factional power struggles and the course of last resort for people with no other options.

The nonrural aversion to rural life

Instructor Yin, a college teacher and the first person interviewed for this study, articulated the basic aversion as well as anyone that followed her. She was a medical professional whose practical research, political savvy, and good luck had combined to keep her as safe as anyone in Chinese tertiary education could be, throughout her 25 years' association with it. Nor had she suffered any adverse consequences for her rebel affiliations in 1967–1968. At that time she had just transferred to a north China medical college. Her labor service obligations were fulfilled during what she regarded as wasteful years of enforced idleness after 1968, when all faculty members were sent down to live at county-town hospitals and do periodic farmwork in nearby villages as the equivalent of a May Seventh Cadre School assignment.

After returning to campus in the early 1970s, faculty members were supposed to do one month of alternating farm and factory labor each year. The factory work she performed willingly; the rural labor she always found an excuse to avoid. She agreed that Chinese factories of that time could be fearsome places, with their noxious fumes, bubbling cauldrons of corrosive liquids, and other horrors. She even cited some statistics indicating that rurals had a better chance than urbans of surviving beyond the age of 80. But she disagreed emphatically with the common foreigners' conclusion that a patch of good

Chinese earth would be preferable to city life any day. She also did not hesitate to claim she spoke for "everyone" when she said that teachers and students alike preferred to labor in factories rather than in the countryside because life there was too dull and boring. "The food is dull and so are the people and so is the work. Peasants are interested in nothing but their own work and in no one but themselves." The work was physically exhausting and many villages had no electricity so there was nothing to do but "work, sleep, and play poker."[14]

Shanghai middle school teacher Yan could afford to be more detached. Except for her own school days during the Great Leap, she had spent no extended time in the countryside, but she retained a sympathetic attachment both to her family village and to the students whom she had to prepare for resettlement. She listed the reasons why most urban youth dreaded the prospect: "Work is bitter and wages low. . . . the sun turns complexions dark and old. . . . dirt everywhere. . . . the peasants wear the same clothes covered with mud for 10 days at a time. . . . bathing is difficult. . . . bugs and mosquitoes devour city youth. . . . there is no culture, no music, no movies, no entertainment. . . . not enough light to read by even when houses have electricity. . . . the peasants say you have to be born to this way of life to be able to endure it. . . . not only do they work in the fields all day, but when they return at night they work at their sidelines. . . . city youth don't know how to do these things and at the end of a day in the fields, they are too tired even to try to learn. . . . the peasants' world is selfish and small. . . . it is a matter of economics and the facts of their lives. . . . they have always been tied to their tiny plots of land."[15]

Others were impatient of such intellectual detachment, dismissing the reasons as self-evident: "bitter . . . filthy . . . unbearable stench. . . . people living like animals. . . . Americans could never stand it. . . . a truly rural person would never be able to understand and answer your questions. . . . even if they let me be a commune cadre, I still would not have stayed."

Medical professionals bore witness to the same aversion and to the roots of Mao's diatribe against urbanized health care. In Zhejiang, regular hospital staff, including both doctors and nurses, were transferred down like teachers from county towns to communes. Nurse Weng was transferred down along with another nurse and a doctor to become the first practitioners of modern medicine ever to grace a relatively prosperous but isolated commune that had previously shared a single doctor with several communes in the district. Nurse Weng and her colleagues also oversaw the newly introduced contingent of village barefoot doctors, who were well received locally. Indeed, everyone was happy with the new arrangements except the clinic staff themselves, who petitioned repeatedly along with their neighbors, the middle school teachers, for transfers back to town. To the familiar list of complaints, however, Nurse

[14] Interview 77/NC/1, p. 16.
[15] Interview 78/S/2, pp. 10-11, 26.

Weng added another. At least, she said, the teachers had fixed hours and could remain in the commune seat while their students came to them. But the new commune clinic routines mandated village sick calls when the barefoot doctors could not cope – the one condition she most resented.[16]

In the same vein, Doctor Niu was part of a teaching-hospital complex re-located from Beijing to Gansu in 1970. He was not overly put out by the move, which he assessed as "good for his health but bad for his career." Initially, they ran training courses for barefoot doctors and then in 1974 added a two-year specialized secondary school (zhongzhuan) course to train doctors for com-mune clinics. Doctor Niu estimated that about half the graduates of the regular course "went through the backdoor" to secure positions in town. Some even accepted lower-paying lower-status nursing jobs to escape the commune clinic assignment. He said it was probably just as well, given the low level of training, that some accepted these nursing jobs. But the acceptance illustrated the determination to avoid rural health work even after only two years of regular schooling.[17]

In the early 1980s, a Yunnan provincial education bureau official stunned a visiting British educator with the new post-1976 line that rural youth living in the hills did not need to attend middle school since they could learn all they needed to know about agriculture from their fathers. Among interviewees, such hard-line conventional attitudes were rare among those who had them-selves grown up in rural or small-town circumstances. To find such views, one had to look instead to individuals who had traveled the furthest social distance, from better educated big-city backgrounds to village assignments (see Table 15.5, for interviewees' social transfer characteristics).

Minban teachers Liu and Mei were two such people who had nevertheless remained for many years in their respective Anhui and Jiangsu communes. Both were resettled big-city youth but both had been assigned to relatively prosperous counties and neither complained of physical hardship. On the contrary, Liu's health had improved markedly. He was also one of the minority who had married locally and insisted he would have remained in the country-side had his wife not been able to emigrate with him. Yet both teachers had deserted their posts, where they had been key people responsible for establish-ing regular elementary schooling in their adoptive villages, without any con-cern about who their replacements might be.

Having described her quite considerable efforts which kept the small one-room school in her isolated village a going concern for seven years and won her local commendation as a model worker, Teacher Mei then dismissed the whole experience with contempt: "Sent-down youth cannot have good relations with the peasants because the peasants have no knowledge, no culture, no thought. . . .

[16] Interview 83/ZJ/12, pp. 17–18.
[17] Interview 83/GS/17, pp. 37–38.

Table 15.5. *Rural, suburban rural, and county-town teachers (46 total), by origins and employment status*

Status	Urban born and raised	Rural born and raised
Gongban (state salaried; sr. secondary education and above)	17	10
Minban (locally hired; jr. or sr. secondary education)	16[a]	3[b]

[a] *Xiaxiang* (resettled youth).
[b] *Huixiang* (rural educated youth).
Note: Strictly speaking, none of the interviewees were born into rural households or those where the source of income derived wholly from agriculture. However, 14 were born and raised in rural areas in China. In such families, typically, one parent or guardian (usually the mother) engaged in agricultural pursuits while relatives contributed to the family's upkeep by sending remittances from overseas. The 10 rural-born teachers and the 3 rural educated youth shown here were raised in such households. Among the 14, 2 were classified as "poor peasant" with overseas Chinese relations; 1 was "middle peasant" with a serious historical political problem; and 4 were of former landlord families in varying states of post–land reform decline.

They are illiterate. They can read neither books nor newspapers. All the peasants know how to do is eat and sleep. . . . They have no spirit [*jingshen*]."[18]

Teacher Liu had been better integrated into the life of his commune and knew considerably more about its overall educational growth, although he had been a teacher for only about half the decade he spent there. But having participated in the annual expansion of the commune education system, which succeeded in enrolling virtually every child in the first grade, in doubling junior middle enrollments between 1968 and 1978, and in opening a senior middle section as well, he nevertheless derided the effort as an unnecessary intrusion of the communist state into the peasants' natural condition of illiteracy. "They only ran these schools because it was the policy of the CCP . . . . They only ran them because there is no democracy in China and they were forced to run schools. . . . A junior middle student who returns home to till the land will soon forget all but the most basic characters. . . . Since there is no opportunity to arrange better work for the peasants, they have no need of education."[19] Just like the hypothetical people in the official polemics, Teacher Liu felt education was "useless" if it led neither to college nor to a better job outside agriculture.

[18] Interview 83/JS/10, p. 74.
[19] Interview 83/AH/22, pp. 70–71.

This view of schooling and peasants as contradictions in terms nevertheless seemed to go beyond a simple aversion to the rigors of rural life or the standard pragmatic approach to education. Groping for a way to explain the assumptions underlying such an attitude, reflected to some extent in the comments of several interviewees, Student Tan finally fixed upon race relations in the United States as the appropriate parallel. Tan was somewhat atypical among interviewees in that she had experienced the Cultural Revolution decade first as a middle school rebel, then for five years as a rusticated youth, and finally as a recommended worker–peasant–soldier college student. Not having lived in the U.S. and too objective to express such views herself, she nevertheless concluded that the prejudice against blacks, such as she had read about, must be similar to the nonpeasant bias against peasants she had observed in China.

Virtually all the teachers interviewed spent some time in a rural area, however defined. And virtually all interviewees participated in farm labor of varying duration. Yet only five retained enough of their original idealism to recall the experience in largely positive terms. Many had been volunteers or had made the necessary adjustments and learned to work effectively in rural locales. But for most, initial enthusiasm was recalled as youthful innocence long since tempered by Teacher Yan's sober realities – and by the prejudiced hand of fate.

Punishment and prejudice

Leading cadres and college faculty all had to attend May Seventh Cadre Schools. But no similar uniform enforcement mechanism governed rural teaching assignments and resettlement, leaving more "natural" laws to dominate and reinforce prevailing sentiments. One important means of expanding educational opportunity was to "deconcentrate" the resources centered in key points. New schools were opened and good teachers from the key points were transferred out to strengthen staff at new and ordinary schools. This occurred both in cities and in the countryside, where the best teachers had been concentrated in the county-town key points. Now the new norms decreed a middle school in every commune, and county-town teachers were often transferred down while new college graduates were assigned to join them as "backbone" staff, usually augmented by locally hired and lower-paid *minban* teachers.

The enterprise seemed entirely fair and egalitarian, but from the teachers' perspective it was neither. Since few wanted to go down, assignments were made by school and county authorities. Always announced officially in terms of reducing the three great distinctions or using strength to supplement weakness, in reality decisions were usually made on the basis of class, politics, and factional loyalties. Four teachers were transferred in this way, as were all eight of the new college graduates who received rural assignments.

"As soon as the teachers heard of Mao's statement that all but the old and infirm must go down to the countryside," recalled Teacher Yang, "everyone was afraid." Not everyone, of course, went down. The factional divide in her county-town main middle school had pitted less-qualified hometown rebels against better educated nonnative conservatives. When the time came in 1969, about 20 teachers, or half the total number, were transferred to less well appointed schools throughout this rural Jiangsu county, with one or two sent into each commune middle school. In this case, all the better-educated teachers were sent out, conveniently leaving only the victorious rebels back in town. Teacher Yang drew the poorest school in the most distant commune and left no stone unturned until she had won her transfer back to town four years later.[20]

Teacher Liao had a similar experience in his southern Fujian county, where rebels also emerged victorious after 1968. As a loyalist sympathizer, he was the first at his small-town school to be tapped when a nearby commune requested help in staffing its new middle school. Teacher Liao had retreated to the safety of his own village when factional strife was at its height and had not been an active participant in the events of 1967 and 1968. But he could never forgive the rebels who led the struggle against Headmaster Chen and therefore sympathized with the loyalists. Still, Liao felt secure enough to dig in his heels at first and refused to answer the summons. He only gave in after months of persuasion by the army representative who then headed the school's new revolutionary committee and promised the transfer would be temporary, which it was not.

Unlike many others, however, Liao was both a dedicated teacher and of rural origins himself. Before long he had become so attached to his new commune school that he almost forgot he ever opposed the move. But he was under no illusions about how and why he was transferred. Altogether, about 30 teachers, or half the total number at his original school, were reassigned in the same way, with August Twenty-ninth–affiliated rebels responsible for clearing class ranks and making assignments. "Openly, they explained it in ways that sounded nice, that the school was too large, so some teachers could be released to work with the poor and lower-middle peasants," but in fact, "all the teachers left in school were either rebels or rebel sympathizers."[21]

Teacher Huang found an identical situation awaiting him when he returned from Fuzhou to his home county in Jinjiang Prefecture as a new college graduate in 1970. Half the teachers in his old middle school had been reassigned and less-qualified substitutes hired on to replace them. County education authorities and the leaders of all the county's schools were August

[20] Interview 83/JS/9, pp. 30–33.
[21] Interview 83/FJ/26, pp. 63–64.

Twenty-ninth rebel sympathizers, which Teacher Huang was not, and they assigned him accordingly, to the junior middle section of a small village elementary school. He demanded redress but to no avail. "On the surface, they said that the teachers were being sent down to raise quality in the localities since such teachers were well qualified. But in reality, they were being sent because of factionalism."[22]

One additional reason why Teacher Liao had settled so smoothly into his new surroundings, however, was another phenomenon of the times: a kind of political inversion that could develop at the end of the line when like-minded people disembarked together. Thus Liao's immediate superiors, the commune leaders, included reassigned loyalists with inclinations similar to his own. The same phenomenon was even more evident in Teacher Fang's north Fujian county, where the new head of the propaganda and education group (successor to the pre-1966 county education bureau) under the county government revolutionary committee was a ranking provincial educator demoted for loyalty to Wang Yugeng. Down but not out, Comrade Min used his remaining power as head of education in an academically underdeveloped county to mobilize all the similarly demoted talents accumulating therein.

Teacher Fang had been assigned as a new college graduate from out of province, and he might well have been sent on to work at the commune level but for Comrade Min's decision to rebuild the staff of the county-town main middle school. There the factional fault line had divided less-qualified locals against college graduate outsiders, most of whom (20 of 80 teachers total) had already been transferred down to new commune schools. After arriving in the county about 1970, Min halted the downward transfer of college graduates and then proceeded to merge as best he could the quantitative goals of the early 1970s with the qualitative norms of the decade preceding.[23]

In Fujian, where the loyalists lost, they went down. In Guangdong, it was the rebels who bore the brunt of the downward movement in 1968–1970. Teacher Tang had grown up in a small town and adjusted well enough to his first assignment: a newly established commune middle school in northern Guangdong. But his sympathies lay with the Red Flag rebels. Articulating the strong factional and class antagonism which set the Guangdong interviewees apart, he declared himself the "sacrificial victim of factionalism." The East Winds, he said, were good class and the Red Flags were middling to bad. The East Winds also won and had job assignments to prove it. "They remained in Guangzhou or were assigned to prefectural seats and they were also assigned to administrative work." A classmate with worse grades than his own had been assigned to the Shaoguan Prefecture Education Bureau. Meanwhile, "Red

[22] Interview 82/FJ/4, pp. 89–90.
[23] Interview 83/FJ/25, pp. 31–34.

Flags were all sent down to be commune school teachers and to really bad places at that." When he and his mates were together discussing their fate, "we never thought it was beneficial for the peasants to have people like us with good grades from a provincial teacher training college to teach them; we just looked upon it as a bad job assignment." The county-town key-point school teachers were the same. Officially, "it was said they were being sent down to help the commune middle schools improve their quality, but that was just said because it sounded good. Actually, East Winds were in power when the teachers were sent down, and the assignments were all made on the basis of faction and class."[24]

The same biases were also evident in the resettlement program for secondary school students. Interviewees agreed without exception that whenever there was room for maneuver, the losers, whether by faction or by class, were more likely to go down or were the first down and the last back. According to official figures issued in the late 1970s, when the program was abandoned, 17 million young people had been resettled in the countryside since 1968, of whom 7 million had already transferred to urban work. Just under 1 million had married and established permanent households locally.[25] The 17 million represented about 10 percent of the total urban population and about half the relevant age-group.[26] Conventional wisdom among interviewees in the early 1980s held that virtually all but those who had married locally (and many of them as well) had joined the exodus back to the cities that was permitted after Mao's death – illustrating better than anything else how rusticated youth regarded their adventure.[27] While it was under way, however, the other half of the age-group who never went down and the 7 million who had already transferred out by 1978 represented the room for maneuver.

Each city and town made its own arrangements each year in relation to the number of school leavers and urban jobs available within its jurisdiction. Some graduating classes were "lucky" and some were not. Teacher Yan recalled how students, teachers, class masters, and school leaders, after lengthy discussions and "democratic assessment," decided who should go. But recalled Teacher Yan further, when choices had to be made, informal rules decreed that students with bad records and bad-class backgrounds would be tapped.

Initially, the Cultural Revolution generation was told their resettlement

---

[24] Interview 82/GD/9, pp. 6–7.
[25] Cited in Pepper, "Chinese Education after Mao," *China Quarterly*, no. 81 (Mar. 1980), p. 48.
[26] Estimates in Martin Whyte and William Parish, *Urban Life in Contemporary China* (Chicago: University of Chicago Press, 1984), pp. 39–40.
[27] The claim of virtually complete return to the cities after 1979 is also made in *Zhongguo qingnian yundong liushi nian, 1919–1979* (Sixty Years of the Chinese Youth Movement, 1919–1979) (Beijing: Zhongguo qingnian chubanshe, 1990), p. 610. For an account of resettlement in the Northeast, see *Beidahuang fengyun lu* (Recollections from a Time in the Great Northern Wilderness) (Beijing: Zhongguo qingnian chubanshe, 1990).

would be permanent. But different cities interpreted this rule differently. Beijing and Guangzhou youth began leaving the countryside for work or study as early as 1969–1970 – indicating another opportunity for favored sons and daughters. Such allegations cannot be proved, given the lack of pure-red interviewees. But the one such individual in the group of 82 (see Appendix Table A.10) fit the alleged pattern perfectly. She had spent only one year in a suburban commune just one hour's bus ride from her provincial capital city home, moving on to "cultural work" in the army (a favorite escape hatch for good-class youth), and from there into a factory job, where one of the factory's allocated quota seats for college was reserved just for her (all in only three years' time).

Quality, content, and conventions: the worst of times

Always in the past, irregular alternatives had failed essentially because they could not compete with the regular system. In the 1960s, demands were such among both purveyors and consumers that neither the agricultural middle schools nor the *minban* expedient could survive for long. The basic contradiction seemed insurmountable. Inferior expedients were essential at least in the short run if education was to be made universal. Yet inferior expedients could not survive in the shadow of the regular system. The extent to which these particular development concerns contributed to the designs of 1968–1969 is unclear since they were presented entirely within the context of cultural revolution, class struggle, and the three great distinctions. But the net result was, in effect, to try and solve the contradiction by deregularizing the regular system. The latter would then not be able to serve as the standard for parity because it would no longer exist.

The best functional precedent, although not acknowledged, could be seen, ironically, in the birth of the regular system itself. Modern foreign-inspired schooling was introduced into China as an irregular unorthodox alternative, and modernizing officials found their new schools could not survive in the shadow of traditional learning capped by the examinations system. If the new alternative was to take root, it needed students, teachers, and funds, none of which would appear so long as the old system remained dominant. This calculation led to the abolition of the old system, whereupon the new one quickly supplanted it.[28]

Mao's education revolution was thus neither designed nor intended to promote equality per se, a common assumption outside China based on non-Marxist interpretations of the proclaimed Chinese aim to reduce the great distinctions. The distinctions would be reduced not by pursuing equality but by establishing irregularity as the new norm. In such a system, nonuniformity

---

[28] E.g., Franke, *The Reform and Abolition of the Traditional Chinese Examination System*, pp. 59–60; Ayers, *Chang Chih-tung and Educational Reform in China*, p. 240.

for all helped level the playing field but, by definition, tolerated a host of lesser inequalities at every level and within every sector. In this manner, the old reformer's dream turned into a professional educator's nightmare come true.

Concentration of talent within the key-point stream was now reversed, with a great transfer of personnel especially at the secondary level. The resented downward transfers were part of this rearrangement. Including the 12 who were themselves either reassigned downward or assigned beneath their level of expectation, interviewees volunteered accounts of 29 separate instances where regular state-salaried teachers were transferred out of key points and/or assigned to strengthen ordinary schools. They moved within urban districts, from county town to rural commune, and from commune to village schools. Additionally, four accounts concerned movement in the opposite direction: from rural suburb to city or from village to commune.[29]

Between 1968 and 1970, student numbers were especially great due to the three-year backlog. But enrollment pressures were maintained thereafter, following the official demand to maximize quantity and universalize elementary and secondary schooling as quickly as possible. It was perhaps an exaggeration to claim that the secondary school entrance examinations were abolished. What was abolished was the rigorous unified exams that had channeled youngsters into the hierarchy of key and ordinary schools in any given locality. Suddenly, as of 1968, the neighborhood school became the new norm.

Wherever all children of a given age-group could not yet be accommodated, however, the school itself gave an entrance exam for its own catchment area. Students were then admitted or not on the basis of their grades, behavior, and family class and political history. Such weeding out occurred at both the junior and senior middle levels. But it was more common at the latter both in town (where junior secondary schooling was often already universal) and in the countryside (where the supply of seats provided in junior middle classes attached to elementary schools tended to dovetail with demand, whereas senior secondary schooling was a much rarer privilege).

Teacher Shu recalled this period well, along with the consternation she had felt as a student – having been reared by parents and coached by teachers to anticipate the college-preparatory stream – upon entering her neighborhood junior middle school for the first time in 1968. Elementary schooling had continued uninterrupted in her northern city, so the 1967 graduating class stayed on for an additional year while middle schools were "doing the cultural

---

[29] These calculations do not include lateral "musical chairs" reassignments made for purely factional or personal reasons. This was common in the early 1970s, when individuals, such as Teacher Ye, did their penance and were cleared to return to their original schools but found antagonisms there still too intense. This was especially true of the main leadership targets – headmasters and CCP secretaries – who often exchanged places with counterparts in neighboring schools upon returning to work.

revolution." Then one day in the fall of 1968, the head teacher for her class marched all its 60 students over to the nearby middle school.

"Suddenly, there were no entrance examinations and no key schools . . . and no feeling of having progressed to the next stage of life." And what a sorry place the new school was, not at all like the nearest key point she had planned to attend. "The walls were covered with grime and glue from wall posters. The furniture was all broken, and everything was very dirty." It was also a newly built school in a neighborhood, with "all kinds of people," and the teachers were young and inexperienced. Recalling what she had learned between 1967 and 1971 (during which time this city replaced the old six-year secondary curriculum with one four years in length), and comparing it with what her elder sister had learned just before her, Teacher Shu estimated that content had been reduced by about 50 percent. Calculating what had been cut out and allowing for the extra labor and practical study activities, the new four-year complete middle school curriculum was about equal to the pre-1966 three-year junior secondary course.[30]

The syllabus chopped in half

Everyone who was in a position to compare curricular content before and after 1966, whether for secondary or tertiary education, produced essentially the same balance sheet as Teacher Shu. Curiously, on many other points of the radical reform package, interviewees would refer back to some Mao statement as the chief source of inspiration. But on the matter of content and quality, they did their calculations without ever once citing Mao's relevant quotation from the 1964 Spring Festival forum: "The syllabus should be chopped in half."

Such calculations, of course, broke the very first rule of the new order, which was to render such comparisons and equivalents impossible to make. The aim was to "disunify" and decentralize, leaving each locality to work out its own arrangements, allowing for maximum variability in content, quality, and results. The nationally unified curricula for elementary and secondary schooling were abolished. They had standardized six years at each level, with the five-year experimental schools based on the six-year standard and claiming the same results. By contrast, the new formula deliberately sought to reduce both study time and content while maximizing student numbers, with decisions about how to balance resources made by each locality. Communes, counties, and city districts worked out their own combinations.

A sample of the results for reduced course length is shown in Table 15.6. Usually, elementary schooling was cut by one year and secondary by two. In

---

[30] Interview 82/NC/20, pp. 12–29.

Table 15.6. *Number of schools by length of school courses, 1968–1976*

	Course length			
School level	6 years	5 years	3 years	2 years
Elementary	8	43	—	—
Junior middle	—	—	26	31
Senior middle	—	—	2	52
Specialized secondary	—	—	—	1
Tertiary	—	—	7	2

Note: Data from interviewees' firsthand knowledge.

Junior and senior middle schools are listed and counted separately here even when combined in a single school. Junior middle schools attached to elementary schools are also counted separately.

the early 1970s, as two-year junior middle education was universalized, a third year was often added. This development was more common in cities. The two-year junior middle "cap" attached to five-year village elementary schools remained the most common pattern in the countryside, with a two-year senior middle section added to the main commune seat school as and when conditions allowed and when sufficient students were educated to that level.

Teachers recalled 1968–1970 as the years of greatest uncertainty. Draft curriculum outlines would appear. No one seemed to know exactly where they originated – perhaps from the new city district or county revolutionary authorities. Without textbooks, relying on the mimeograph machine and blackboard, schools and teachers then improvised. Mao's writings were used for Chinese-language teaching ("at least he was a good poet," said someone); politics was taught from newspaper editorials; previous years' materials were used for math. So much "freedom" posed few political dangers since the political environment was now completely "safe," at least for the time being. Few would have dared introduce materials contradictory to Mao's line, the *People's Daily*, and *Reg Flag*. If they had, instant correction would have been ready to hand.

Once they graduated, Red Guard student activists quickly disappeared from school revolutionary committees everywhere and were not replaced by a successor generation of student representatives. But politically correct cadres and teachers remained at the helm. More important, the military representatives (not withdrawn until the early 1970s) and worker propaganda teams (usually composed of factory CCP-member cadres as well as workers, not withdrawn until after 1976) remained to enforce not only student discipline but political rectitude as well. In the countryside, these functions were performed by village production brigade leaders and commune authorities.

By about 1970, unification of sorts resumed with the publication by each province's education bureau (or its revolutionary equivalent) of textbooks and teaching materials based on recommended curricula, all edited and published following the "spirit" of central guidelines. The published materials provided something to hang on to but were intended as standards to be approximated only and were used as such. Localities and schools continued to fix their own curricula based on local demands, the initiative of individual local leaders, and availability of teachers. Prefectures and counties published their own supplementary books and materials. And teachers continued to improvise within the limited range of options open to them.

Nor were the provincial standards themselves either static or uniform. Guangdong initially adopted a four-year middle school system but then added a third year at the junior middle level intended for use primarily in city schools. Thereafter, two sets of materials were issued: one edited by Guangzhou for a five-year system and the other edited by the province for four-year schooling. Usually, but not invariably, rural schools used the latter and urban the former.[31]

Shanghai followed a similarly mixed system, but the purpose was allegedly to maintain quality in the former central and key schools (now all officially abolished). The city continued to regard itself and to be regarded by others as an intellectual cut above the rest. Localities not satisfied with their own provincial editions would send off for Shanghai's materials to use instead. And besides two national minorities areas (in Yunnan and Jilin Provinces) which kept the six-year elementary school, Shanghai was the only other locality reporting six years at that level (see Table 15.6).

In the mid-1970s, foreign visitors also were told that Shanghai had a unified six-year elementary system (with four-year middle schools to keep within the spirit of central guidelines). But one interviewee, in a position to know, insisted that elementary schools remained mixed as they had been before 1966, when many followed the quality five-year curriculum. In the 1970s, however, the balance was reversed. Most elementary schools offered a five-year course, except for a few of the best in each district which were allowed to follow a "six-year experimental system," ostensibly to compare results in order to "maintain the quality of basic-level schooling" for the masses. The four-year middle school was also administered in such a way that the better schools (former key points) maintained four full years of classroom work, allowing in effect a fifth year for labor and practical learning.[32]

The new provincial curricular standards were, however, "*datong xiaoyi*," or basically similar with minor differences. Revisions in course content were sometimes issued annually but tended all to follow the spirit of the same

---

[31] On the education revolution in Guangzhou city schools, see Jonathan Unger, *Education under Mao*, chap. 9.
[32] Interview 82/SD/14, pp. 45–46; also 83/AH/8, p. 12.

shifting winds from Beijing. Before 1966, the main secondary school courses were Chinese language, politics, math (including algebra, geometry, and trigonometry), physics, chemistry, biology, history, geography, foreign language, music, and physical education. Under the new order, Chinese, politics, and math, although revised, remained separate courses and the irreducible minimum without which a school could not be run. Chinese and math were usually allocated five or six class periods per week each, and politics three or four. But most everything else was rearranged into an assortment of combinations all geared to practical learning.

Physics was usually redesigned to become industrial knowledge while biology became part of an agricultural knowledge course and chemistry might or might not be mixed with both. Since reducing the three distinctions remained a constant, urban and rural students alike were usually required to study both, although content and emphasis could vary between town and countryside given the varying conditions available for practical application. Or conditions might not vary at all if big-city schools had access to a hinterland large enough to set up branch schools or farms (like Guangzhou and Beijing but unlike Shanghai). The rural branch then became the venue not just for manual labor but for practical learning as well. Foreign language remained a common addition, with Russian taught in northeastern schools and English the language of choice elsewhere. Especially in Guangdong and Fujian, even commune middle schools tried to teach students their ABC's at least. History, geography, and art might be combined into a "revolutionary culture" course. Or foreign language, history, and geography might disappear altogether, depending on the availability of teachers, which was always most problematic in rural schools.

The manual labor requirement was now doubly resented both for itself and for the time it consumed in the shrinking curriculum. The most common recommended standard was about one month of manual labor per 22–24 week semester, for middle school students. Schools generally arranged this at the rate of one or two afternoons a week plus a few days during spring and fall when urban students went out to suburban communes or school farms to help with spring planting and autumn harvest. Rural youth worked with their own families during the busy farm seasons. But as shown in Table 15.7, many schools approximated the standard while just as many did not. Nor do the annual averages estimated for the table necessarily reflect the reality of the requirement, since it varied from school to school and year to year. Most irregular of all were two schools (shown in the Nonquantifiable column of Table 15.7), which earned much local acclaim for abandoning the new recommended curriculum altogether and developing their own integrated labor and practical-learning schedules.

Under the circumstances, sometimes students learned more and sometimes less. Young Teacher Dai, whose own college education between 1965 and 1969

Table 15.7. *Student labor and practical learning outside the classroom, secondary schools, 1968–1976 (no. of schools, interviewees' own only)*

	Approximate number of weeks each 10-month school year[a]					
	4 weeks or less	5–8 weeks	9–12 weeks	13–16 weeks	17–20 weeks	Nonquantifiable
18 urban (including county-town) schools	1	9	4	2	1	1
25 rural schools	6	9	6	1	2	1

[a] The lengths of summer and winter vacations varied but were usually about 40 days and 21 days, respectively, for students. Interviewees usually calculated between 22 and 24 weeks in a semester as the block of time available for all activities, including classroom teaching, practical learning outside the classroom, labor, and examinations, which continued to be given everywhere as midterms and finals each semester.

had been completely disrupted, nevertheless remained as conventional as teachers trained in more conventional years. He could therefore estimate quite precisely how much of the middle school Chinese language coursework prepared for each semester's use had been completed: between 1970 and 1972, about one-third of the material; between 1972 and 1974, about three-fifths; finally in 1974, disruptions were sufficiently reduced to allow him to complete the entire year's lessons.[33]

Teacher Lei, from a rural Xunde county school, would not even try to make such an estimate. "There was no chemistry or physics in those days," he said. "Instead it was industrial knowledge: motors, pumps, tractors, how to fix small farm tools, so that students could do these things later in their villages. . . . But it was very chaotic [*luan*]. . . . They didn't hold class for one period or one hour at a time. No. They would just study industry for three weeks and then agriculture. The teachers had to go out and find a tractor, to make contact with the production teams. . . . it was a real headache for the teachers. Students were happy though. They didn't learn anything."[34]

Given such variations, the estimated 50 percent reduction in content should obviously be treated as a very rough rule of thumb and especially should not be applied across the urban–rural divide. Teacher Shu was comparing content between two urban schools, one a pre-1966 key point and the other a post-1966 ordinary school. Had she been able to compare pre- and post-1966 content in either of those two schools themselves, the gap would probably have been less. Interviewees agreed that despite the dilution of staff and student bodies, and

[33] Interview 80/GD/2, p. 26.
[34] Interview 80/GD/5, pp. 19–20.

even without a concerted Shanghai-style effort, key schools were still regarded as better than others since they usually retained at least half their original teachers, had better facilities, were located in advantaged neighborhoods, etc.

On the other hand, if Teacher Shu had been comparing a pre-1966 key point with a post-1966 rural school, the gap would likely have been greater. Teacher Dai made such a comparison between the highest pre-1966 standard for Chinese language and the realities of his post-1966 commune school. According to the old 12-year standard, an elementary school graduate should have learned to read and write 2,000 Chinese characters; a junior middle graduate, 3,000; and a senior middle graduate, 4,500. But Teacher Dai estimated that his 9-year commune school system produced elementary graduates who knew only 1,000 characters and middle school graduates with a functional grasp of only about 2,000.[35]

The logic of the new arrangements nevertheless remained consistent. Given that logic, inequality and dilution of standards were "nothing to worry about" because the inequality was enforced everywhere at every level of education. Two accounts stood out in specifying the consequences from the professional educator's perspective. College instructor Yin provided the single best illustration of the damage done at the tertiary level, while Teacher Liao presented a classic lament over the shattered conventions that were the professional Chinese educator's stock in trade.

Instructor Yin's account is significant because of the pivotal role her college played as the largest of only two such tertiary-level medical faculties serving a province of some 60 million people. Her account illustrates in detail one of the worst-case scenarios from the typical 50 percent reduction in curricular content estimated by interviewees for the regular secondary and tertiary system. Instructor Yin, professionally experienced and politically correct if not enthusiastic, had participated in both developing and teaching the new 1970s curriculum. She insisted that the college itself was entirely responsible for this work, which was led by faculty members. They cut the various courses and requirements standardized nationwide in the pre-1966 five-year medical college curriculum on instruction from the provincial education authorities, whose only recommended guidelines were Mao's general thoughts on education plus relevant articles in the "two newspapers and one journal." Additionally, the provincial authorities circulated materials for reference detailing the experience of model medical schools elsewhere in shortening course content.

The medical course was divided into preclinical, clinical, and internship. Before 1966, the first and second years were devoted to preclinical coursework, and the fifth to internship. After 1966, all the material that had been covered in four years was combined into two; the last year of internship remained the

[35] Interview 80/GD/2, pp. 26–27.

same. The school year was 44 weeks in length plus 1 week each semester devoted to final examinations. These were the only exams given during the semester, and students were promoted regardless of performance. Political study and labor did not pose major intrusions. The amount of political study was increased from only four hours per week to six hours, although individual political campaigns sometimes meant extra hours. A directive from the provincial education bureau suggested one month of physical labor per year. But students themselves requested this be broken up since they were hard-pressed for study time as it was. They therefore spent Saturday afternoons doing odd jobs on campus and a week or so at the school's farm during the summer.

Besides the abbreviated curriculum, a second major change concerned the students. The first formal post-1966 class was not enrolled here until 1972. Not only had all worked for at least two years prior to admission, but they were of widely diverse backgrounds, a majority being only junior middle graduates. Instructor Yin estimated that about 30 percent had great difficulty keeping up with coursework. Perhaps 10 percent found the work too simple. The majority could just keep up with the curriculum, and Instructor Yin estimated their professional competence upon graduation at about the level of what well-trained barefoot doctors should be.

This college more than doubled the size of its student body, however. Before 1966, it enrolled new students at the rate of only 200 per year. During the years 1972–1976, it admitted close to 500 students annually. Of these, 60–70 percent were admitted from the rural areas, and upon graduation most were returned there following the new emphasis on expanding rural health care. But most were actually assigned to county-town hospitals rather than commune clinics.[36]

Instructor Yin's account thus illustrates most clearly the consequences of applying uniformly the radical reform principles at all levels. Intermediate medical training in the province was also provided by 10 specialized secondary schools, with one in every prefecture. Hence the reformed medical college was not filling demands for lower-level commune clinic staff that could not be met by other institutions.[37] Meanwhile, the college continued its original mission of training doctors for county-town hospitals.

The net result of the revisions in this case, then, was to expand the supply of intermediate personnel while eliminating tertiary-level medical training in the province altogether. In so doing, the revisions transformed the then

---

[36] Interview 77/NC/1, pp. 10–25. This account was initially written up in Pepper, "Education and Revolution," *Asian Survey*, Sept. 1978, pp. 865–867.

[37] Dr. Niu's above-cited prefectural secondary school in Gansu was of this type, intended to train commune clinic doctors (*yishi*, by comparison with tertiary-trained *yisheng*), although many of its graduates found ways of staying in town. Dr. Niu similarly calculated that the mid-1970s two-year course reduced content by about half that of its three-year predecessor. Graduates of the latter were allowed to perform simple operations unassisted, whereas the two-year students were not (interview 83/GS/17, pp. 13, 30).

popular question about the extent to which scarce resources in Third World countries should be concentrated in advanced medical training. So radical were the Chinese reforms that the question became instead whether such a country could afford to do without that training altogether. Over time, the reforms would even have undermined the new rural-oriented health care system itself since it was based on expanded availability of village and commune services while relying on upward referral for patients needing more sophisticated treatment from commune to county and provincial hospitals.

Systems and conventions destroyed

For Teacher Liao, however, the drama lay elsewhere. Whatever the circumstances of his transfer, he and another experienced teacher reassigned from town soon became the "backbone elements" of a newly established commune school. They helped build it into a local model famous for its application of Maoist curricular demands. Liao himself was something of a rarity as a college graduate born and raised in humble rural circumstances. Such a background was not easy to find in the 1960s, and it perhaps explained his eclectic approach to the new revolutionary mandate. The dilution of curricular content made some sense to them there in his adoptive commune, and they made sense of it in the name of developing practical content that would encourage students to remain in the countryside and contribute to its modernization.

Yet Teacher Liao was a man whose soul seemed truly torn between his role as a Maoist model teacher and his original incarnation as a conscientious young drill master back in the days when he and Headmaster Chen had chased pass rates along with the best of them. On the one hand, Liao proudly related his new school's practical-learning achievements and those of its most successful students, who went on to become the locality's first-ever college graduates. But on the other hand, he mourned the destruction of the old ways as only a Chinese teacher could.

He conceptualized all school management in terms of systems (zhidu). At least 10 such systems, he declared, were necessary to run a school properly and all were "wrecked" by the Cultural Revolution: the enrollment system, the promotion system, examinations, rewards and punishments, teachers' course preparation, organization (Youth League and teachers unions), finances, work and rest, the keeping of records and files, etc.[38] All had been governed by fixed rules and regulations, as indeed the curriculum itself had been with its systematic progression through each semester's lessons. Everything had been neatly laid out with a place for everything and everything in its place, predictable, controllable, and above all regular (zhenggui). If even half a day's unplanned

[38] Interview 83/FJ/26, pp. 157 ff.

activity intruded, the whole fine-tuned mechanism would be thrown off balance.

Teacher Liao had a tendency to ramble, however, and his loyalties were in any case mixed. Dour and angry, Teacher Lu felt no need to temporize and stated his position far more succinctly. "Before the Cultural Revolution, teaching activity in middle schools was on the right track," he said, because policies were clear, leading cadres capable, and "teaching systems" strictly followed. Especially the last he valued above all else. Nothing was as important, not the physical plant or even the qualifications of the teachers themselves. "If you do not have a set of systems for promoting students and for teaching, quality will be difficult to raise."[39] Hence, even had there been no political intrusions, no struggles, and no downward rural transfers, professional educators would still have been profoundly unsettled by the basic reform package, just as professional educators had always been.

Like both Liao and Lu, not everyone found cause to complain about the shortened course length and experiments in practical learning. Like them, too, most rural teachers at least also did not complain about disrespect and disorderly conduct as the norm for student behavior after the mobilization phase ended.[40] But no teacher interviewed, of whatever age, level, generation, or faction, failed to complain about the destruction of at least one of Liao's systems and conventions. Most frequently mentioned were enrollment, examinations, promotion, and punishment.

At first it seemed odd that otherwise conscientious interviewees would complain about the abolition of the unified secondary school entrance examinations in their locality and then report that a certain school continued to give examinations as a basis for enrolling students each year. Interviewees were also much prone to complain that all examinations had been abolished – and then go on to describe the full repertoire of quizzes, tests, midterms, finals, homework, and report cards, which elementary and middle school teachers uniformly admitted to having maintained either in whole or in part throughout the 1968–1976 years. Some schools and localities even sometimes administered the long-controversial *tongkao*, or unified exam, to evaluate and compare student performance, ostensibly "for reference only." But what interviewees meant was that the "systems" had been destroyed, leaving form with no substance.

In the case of tests and examinations, most teachers recalled that at some time during the period, their schools had experimented with new methods, whether open-book, open-door, collective assistance, or whatever. But unlike the 50 percent reduction in course content, Mao's 1964 Spring Festival comments were invariably blamed. He had likened testing methods in China's schools to the style of the old imperial examinations, saying students should be graded instead for creativity and allowed to copy one another's test papers. Clearly, examinations administered in such a manner were not really examinations; hence it could be said that for all intents and purposes they had indeed been abolished.

The spectrum of student punishments had run from a warning, to a small demerit, a large demerit, suspension, and expulsion. The conditions under which students could be made to repeat a grade were also carefully prescribed. But because 1960s schools in pursuit of glory had abused this rule by failing too many students and then holding them back or encouraging them to drop out, the relevant rules underwent, as Teacher Lu said, "a very great relaxation." Interviewees therefore claimed that requiring students to repeat a grade was forbidden – even though exceptions to the new rule were also widely reported (e.g., two or three students per classroom, rather than 10–15 percent).

In this same vein, teachers had difficulty accepting the basic concept of universal junior middle schooling since it meant that "no matter what their records in elementary school," everyone was promoted – which explained the general consternation over the demise of the "enrollment system." Education was not a right but a privilege to be earned, in accordance with fixed standards, or withheld. Schools that failed to enforce such standards "were not really schools."

Without the rules and regulations, of course, teachers would not have been able to cope, especially in big-city non-key schools, where classrooms usually contained 50 or more students. A careful "system" of classroom organization divided students into small groups, each with a leader. These and other student monitors or class cadres helped maintain order, and this system, too, was maintained throughout. But given the persistence of so many systems, which originated in an earlier era when students were far fewer, the question was not whether the rules and regulations existed to maintain order in large classrooms but whether it was not the rules and regulations that had enabled classes to expand to such a size. In any event, from the teacher's perspective, discipline and order were necessary, but not sufficient, conditions for the practice of their craft. The systematic nature of that endeavor was so intimately bound up with the process of educating that it became impossible to distinguish which was prior in the teachers' view: the rules and regulations or the knowledge imparted thereby.

Teacher Hu was another with commitments on both sides, and he could rationalize better than most the dilemmas involved. He was the one college graduate who had requested a rural assignment in the early 1960s and regretted nothing except perhaps his transfer back to town in the mid-1970s. It was a time when both quantitative growth and "open-door" learning were at their height. He approved the growth which allowed Beijing, like several other major cities, finally to claim universal (two-year) senior middle schooling. Hu's transfer resulted from that expansion, and as an experienced teacher, he was assigned to curriculum management work in his new school. He could still remember how the semester had been divided – leaving only about 13 weeks for classroom teaching and exams in each 22–24 week semester. The rationale he accepted; the realities he could not. Students were too young, and the experiments never adequately coordinated classroom and out-of-class teaching, "so there was little concrete result." Still, he blamed his colleagues, albeit only in the abstract.

The central government wanted a new education system, he said, so the old one was overthrown. Then, in 1968, they started editing new materials. "Content was changed and new methods were raised. This was the education revolution. But the teachers really did not know how to do it." Trained in their "old-fashioned" ways of teaching and lecturing in the classroom, and secure in their familiar network of support systems, "they were not clear about what was expected of them" in terms of the new content and methods. There was a certain kind of teacher, including both men and women, he explained, who had strong organizing ability and personal prestige (weiwang) – the latter deriving in part from their "ability to manage everything in minute detail." Such teachers could command the respect of students and cope with the educational experiments at the same time. There were such strong teachers. But they were few and far between.[41]

[41] Interview 82/BJ/18, pp. 16–20.

16

Education reform as the culmination of class struggle: the critical ideals triumphant at last

Ultimately, the "professional educator" and the "radical reformer" emerged as ideal types more than real people. Such individuals undoubtedly existed somewhere. But the reality as described by interviewees suggests that the best way of illustrating the endemic ambivalence they had inherited was to let everyone assume their place along a hypothetical spectrum where most would have fallen between the two extremes while combining varying elements of both. Had the reform package appeared in some less radical version, then, it probably could have mustered a much larger constituency of support.

Many approved the shortened 10-year curriculum at the elementary and secondary levels, for example. Resentment was expressed over labor, politics, and practical learning in unplanned excess but never per se. Sentiment against the pretensions of key-point schools was widespread. Their elitist hierarchical form may have had ancient roots, but its deliberate extension nationwide within a fast-growing modern school system dated only from 1958.

The associated practices of cramming and pushing up pass rates could also boast ancient pedigrees – as could the body of critical literature deploring them. Teachers generally still accepted the 1950s arguments from Soviet pedagogy on the drawbacks of streaming students by ability, an obvious contradiction with the principle of key-point development that many acknowledged and pondered.

Yet, had the reform package been advanced in less radical terms, its most widely acknowledged success – quantitative growth – could not have been achieved to the same degree. Given the inherited formalistic definitions of quality and the pressures for parity they were generating within the "regular" system, educators seemingly could not have it both ways: one had to come at the expense of the other. And their familiar quandary was being reproduced on the grandest of scales: trading a 50 percent decrease in quality overall for massive quantitative gains at the elementary and especially the secondary levels. Unfortunately, only a very few localities conducted their experiments in such a way as to sidestep the dilemma – too few to have any real success in undermining the contention that quality and quantity could not be pursued together without seriously compromising one or the other.

Teacher Wang thus recalled that his small town had built two new elementary schools, adding a total of 33 classrooms of students (at 50 students per class). The surrounding rural communes had also opened many new schools in his suburban Shanghai county. "By comparison with before the Cultural Revolution, numbers and percentages certainly increased," but quality was not the same. "It was a question of quality versus quantity. All the teachers said so."[1] Headmaster Chu's recollections of northern Jiangsu were the same. "During the Cultural Revolution . . . agricultural production increased a lot, so education could develop too. The peasants did not make revolution. They stayed home and cultivated their fields, so village middle schools developed as well. . . . Yes, there is a contradiction: on the one hand, there was the wrecking of teachers' knowledge and cultural levels. But on the other, schools developed at that time."[2]

Even Teacher Zhang, among the most embittered of all interviewees, readily volunteered the point. He credited the dual education revolutions of 1958 and the late 1960s for the growth of schooling in his suburban Beijing commune of some 20,000 people: from only 1 elementary school in the 1950s for the entire commune area to 12, or 1 in every production brigade, with 95 percent of all school-age children in attendance by the early 1970s. "The Cultural Revolution was a disaster especially in the cities," he recalled. "They said we could close universities for many years. Since we didn't have them in Yan'an, we could do without them now as well. And so the universities were ruined. But in the countryside, it was different. There, they actually set up more schools."[3]

Quantitative gains

Without any of the internal working directives from the 1968–1976 years, we can only deduce what they must have been from what was actually done insofar as it can be ascertained. Toward that end, only two sources of data are available: officially published Chinese statistics and the recollections of interviewees. Contemporary aggregate statistics for the country as a whole were publicized only sporadically during the 1970s and were generally assumed to be unreliable. After the education revolution was discredited, however, official statistical compilations did not follow the lead of other official sources in declaring all revolutionary claims null and void. Instead, the high mass enrollment figures for the 1968–1976 years were retained. Tables 16.1 and 16.2 illustrate these later compilations and show the extent of growth at the elementary and secondary

[1] Interview 80/S/4, p. 4.
[2] Interview 83/JS/6, p. 6.
[3] Interview 80/BJ/9, pp. 1–6.

Table 16.1. *National student enrollments, 1965–1977*
(number of students in school)

| Year | Elementary (millions) | Secondary | | Tertiary |
		Ordinary (millions)	Specialized	
1965	116.21	9.34	547,400	674,400
			(4,433,400 agric.)[a]	
1966	103.42	12.50	470,300	533,800
1967	102.44	12.24	307,800	408,900
1968	100.36	13.92	128,100	258,700
1969	100.67	20.21	38,500	108,600
1970	105.28	26.42	64,000	47,800
1971	112.11	31.28	217,600	83,400
1972	125.49	35.82	342,500	193,700
1973	135.70	34.46	482,500	313,600
1974	144.81	36.50	634,300	430,000
1975	150.94	44.66	707,300	501,000
1976	150.05	58.37	689,900	564,700
1977	146.18	67.80	689,200	625,300

[a] Agricultural middle schools were not counted separately during the Cultural Revolution years.
Sources: *Zhongguo jiaoyu nianjian, 1949–1981*: elementary, p. 1021; secondary, ordinary, p. 1001; secondary, specialized, p. 982; agricultural middle schools, p. 1017; tertiary, p. 966. For official figures issued during the 1970s, see Suzanne Pepper, "Chinese Education after Mao," *China Quarterly*, no. 81 (Mar. 1980), p. 6.

levels and the concurrent decline in tertiary enrollments. Yet without elaboration, such statistical tables are of little use in explaining the anomaly of major quantitative gains during a period dismissed by all other official sources as a "decade of disaster" for Chinese education. The interview accounts are therefore especially helpful in corroborating the gains and demonstrating how they were achieved.

As explained in the Appendix, interviewees with rural experience were especially sought out because the rural rationale loomed so large in the overall aim of reducing the three great distinctions, and because building a first-ever mass education system for a rural population was generally acknowledged to be among the most difficult of development tasks. China was no different in this respect, however great the changes since the 1920s and 1930s, when rural reconstruction first became the reformers' cause célèbre. Some 80 percent of the total Chinese population still lived in tens of thousands of dispersed rural villages, without adequate financing or motorized transport, encumbered further by a

Table 16.2. *National promotion rates, 1965–1977*

I. School-Age Children Enrolled at the Elementary Level			
Year	National elem. school-age cohorts (millions)	No. of school-age children who have entered elem. school (millions)	School-age children entering elem. school (%)
1965	116.03	98.29	84.7
1976	121.94	118.39	96.0

II. Pass Rates through the System			
Year	(1) Elem. graduates entering jr. middle school (%)	(2) Jr. middle graduates entering sr. middle school (%)	(3) Sr. middle graduates entering college (%)
1965	44.9	26.4	45.6
1967	22.0	7.5	—
1969	68.7	28.8	—
1971	89.8	38.4	4.2
1973	84.4	40.0	4.3
1975	90.6	60.4	4.3
1976	94.1	71.4	4.2
1977	92.0	63.7	4.7

Sources: I. *Zhongguo tongji nianjian, 1988* (China Statistical Yearbook, 1988), p. 889. Apparent anomalies in this set of figures, especially in relation to the number of students in elementary school shown on Table 16.1, are discussed in Pepper, *China's Education Reform in the 1980s*, p. 82 n.

II. *Zhongguo jiaoyu nianjian, 1949–1981*, calculated from pp. 1001, 1021 (col. 1), p. 1001 (col. 2), pp. 969, 1001 (col. 3).

living tradition of rural mass illiteracy which continued to project agricultural life as the antithesis of civilized literate existence. If the education revolution's claims had any validity in fact, they would therefore have to be measured in the development of rural education or not at all, and it is to the interview accounts that we must turn for an assessment of the claims.

Quantifying responses presented some difficulty since interviewees could at best provide only impressions and estimates, for example, recalling the number of households in a village where home visits were needed to mobilize reluctant parents, or the size of first- and fifth-grade classes in an elementary school to approximate dropout rates. Ultimately, the most reliable means of quantifying recollections was the official standard first advertised in the 1968–1969 "back-to-school" publicity, namely, that there should be an elementary school in every production brigade and a middle school in every commune. Virtually all interviewees with rural experience knew the formula and recalled it as the general standard honored locally.

The demands "from above" which had governed education work were actually more ambitious than the initial publicity suggested, however. At the elementary level, the working rule was that facilities should be provided for all school-age children within reasonable walking distance from home given their age and the local terrain. This typically necessitated at least one complete five-year elementary school per production brigade, which was the standard most localities followed. But since the size and concentration of rural populations varied widely, that standard was sometimes insufficient to achieve the goal and sometimes it could be met with less. Complete elementary schools were supposed to add junior middle sections to supplement the main junior middle school in the commune seat. This latter was in turn supposed to add its own senior middle section once one or two classes of junior middle graduates were willing and able to continue their studies. Nevertheless, since the standard of one complete elementary school per brigade and one complete middle school per commune did provide an indication of growth, and since interviewees could usually recall quite clearly this basic structure of commune and brigade schools, their presence or absence was used as the rough rule-of-thumb criterion of quantitative development.

The results are presented in Tables 16.3 and 16.4, which are based on interviewees' firsthand experience or plausible secondhand information. The latter derives most reliably from teachers' required attendance at frequent commune and county meetings, where, among other things, the work of constituent schools was reported and assessed. Of the 720 production brigades for which interviewees were able to contribute such recollections, only 27 did not have at least one complete elementary school. Of these, four represented localities where the standard was not necessary to achieve universal elementary schooling, as in some suburban Beijing and Shanghai communes where populations were concentrated and transportation adequate. Of the remaining 23 brigades, 13 were inhabited by "minority nationalities" (ethnic groups distinct in language, culture, traditions, etc., from the majority Hans), where the standard educational development demands were not enforced. The secondary-level standard was less uniformly achieved, with 80 of 466 communes able to boast no more than junior middle schooling. Of the seven communes with no secondary education at all, five were again located in the same national minority districts of Sichuan, Yunnan, and Guizhou, which were lacking at the elementary level as well.[4]

---

[4] This study does not deal with the complicated question of minority education. China's 1982 census revealed a minority population of 66.36 million divided into 50–60 separate ethnic groups scattered throughout the country (e.g., *Statistical Yearbook of China, 1983*, pp. 29–34). The minorities are of widely varying cultural levels, ranging from the Koreans in Jilin Province, who

Table 16.3. *Rural elementary schooling, extent of maximum growth, 1968–1978*

	No. of communes (and production brigades) *with* at least one complete elem. school per production brigade	No. of communes (and production brigades) *without* at least one complete elem. school per production brigade
Rural communes:		
Guangdong	9 (92)	—
Guangxi	1 (8)	—
Fujian	21 (305)	1 (3 of 14)
Zhejiang	1 (10)	1 (2 of 7)
Jiangsu	2 (21)	—
Anhui	3 (26)	—
Shandong	—	1 (4 of 11)
Shaanxi	—	1 (3 of 18)
Xinjiang	1 (8)	1 (4 of 6)
Northeast	1 (9)	—
Sichuan	—	2 (6 of 11)
Yunnan	2 (11)	1 (1 of 2)
Guizhou	—	1 (2 of 3)
Suburban communes:		
Beijing, Shanghai, Hangzhou, Hefei, Guangzhou, Kunming	7 (90)	1 (2 of 12)
State farms[a]	5 (56)	—
Total (no. of production brigades reported = 720):		
No. of production brigades with complete five-year schools	(693)	
No. of production brigades with no schools or with junior elementaries only		(27)

Note: Data from interviewees' firsthand experience and plausible secondhand information (as explained in the Appendix).

[a] Regular state farms (and their border region military equivalents, the production construction corps, *bingtuan*) during the 1960s and early 1970s were organized according to the standard of 20,000 people per farm or corps, subdivided usually into companies (*liandui*) that were roughly the equivalent of the commune's production brigade subdivision.

Table 16.4. *Rural secondary schooling, extent of maximum growth, 1968–1978 (number of communes)*

	At least one complete four-yr. jr.-sr. middle school or one sr. middle per commune	At least one detached jr. middle school per commune	No detached middle school per commune
Rural communes:			
Guangdong (101)	89	12	—
Guangxi (1)	1	—	—
Fujian (73)	73	—	—
Zhejiang (82)	62	20	—
Jiangsu (36)	23	11	2
Anhui (7)	5	2	—
Hubei (23)	23	—	—
Shandong (11)	4	7	—
Shanxi (28)	28	—	—
Shaanxi (11)	—	11	—
Gansu (15)	11	4	—
Xinjiang (2)	—	2	—
Northeast (9)	9	—	—
Sichuan (2)	1	—	1
Yunnan (11)	—	8	3
Guizhou (2)	1	—	1
Suburban communes:			
Beijing, Shanghai, Hangzhou, Hefei, Guangzhou (36)	34	2	—
State farms:			
Regular farms, corps (15)	15	—	—
Dependents farm (1)	—	1	—
Total:			
Communes, farms, all kinds (466)	379	80	7

Note: Data from interviewees' firsthand experience and plausible secondhand information (as explained in the Appendix). The compilation does not include vocational, specialized secondary (*zhongzhuan*), or agricultural middle schools.

In reality, of course, the "commune" and "brigade" were highly artificial standards for comparison and should be defined more carefully since rural educational development was so closely integrated with this form of collective organization. Briefly, in 1958 existing small collectives were merged into huge 5,000-household communes heralding the advent of agrarian communism. Afterward, both the economic and political significance of the communes were reduced to more modest proportions. The small production team (*shengchan xiaodui*) of 20–50 households became the basic unit of rural collective ownership, labor cooperation, and income sharing. The team also became the base of a three-tiered administrative structure, with seven or eight teams making up a production brigade (*shengchan dadui*), composed of one or more natural villages. Ten or more such brigades in turn formed a commune. As of 1980, China's rural population numbered 807 million, or about 80 percent of the national total, divided into some 5 million production teams, 699,000 brigades, and 53,000 communes. The last averaged 25 per county, with about 15,000 people per commune.[5]

Among interviewees, 46 had lived and worked in these communes and recalled that all units actually varied widely, ranging from communes with 40,000 or more people in Guangdong and Fujian to their minuscule counterparts in Sichuan and Guizhou with large land areas and dispersed populations of 5,000 or fewer "scattered over several mountaintops." The number of communes was also greater than average, and population size per commune smaller, in provinces such as Zhejiang and Anhui, which maintained a district (*qu*) level of government between county and commune. A small proportion of China's rural population (11 million) also lived and worked on (2,000) state farms or land reclamation farms usually operated in sparsely inhabited areas by migrants and resettled personnel.[6] Five interviewees had worked on such farms in Heilongjiang, Xinjiang, and Guangdong, and all were organized according to a standard population size of 20,000.

For our purposes here, we need only note further that the communes had in effect become the basic unit of local government, implementing central policies, overseeing rural economic production, managing local resources, and coordinating rural administrative services. Commune leaders and staff received

---

outperform everyone in terms of education development, to others which lack even a written language. The 13 underdeveloped brigades listed here represented four ethnic groups: Uighur, Dai, Yi and Miao. In the interviewees' experience the national standard was enforced among three other groups: the Yao and Zhuang of northern Guangdong and the Koreans. Interviewees nevertheless reported "special consideration" for all schools, however few, that were maintained in minority areas (Koreans excepted) primarily in terms of extra funds for teachers' salaries, operating expenses, and capital construction.

[5] *China: Socialist Economic Development* (Washington, D.C.: World Bank, 1983), 2:32–38; see also *Statistical Yearbook of China, 1983*, pp. 147–148.

[6] *China: Socialist Economic Development*, 2:38–40; *Statistical Yearbook of China, 1983*, p. 202.

regular fixed state salaries and were the only individuals in the commune area besides regular teachers and doctors to do so. Everyone else, including the production brigade leader and its CCP secretary, brigade accountants, the village policeman, production team leaders, etc., were all paid in work points. These were earned through their daily performance of agricultural labor and/or services but valued according to the variable annual total income from all labor and services by the work unit as a whole. In most cases, this unit was the production team, the income of which derived from land cultivation and collectively managed agricultural sidelines. Additionally, production brigades maintained small-scale enterprises, repair shops, brick kilns, etc., income from which was shared among the member teams or used for collective purposes. Communes might also run similar kinds of enterprises, with income distributed or invested locally.

It was this kind of rural existence, tied to the daily accumulation of work points and the necessity for extra labor in individual family sidelines and on private plots, that resettled urban youth found so demoralizing. For this reason, a state farm was almost always the preferred assignment. The kind of physical labor required was equally "bitter," but pressures around the margins of survival were less intense. This was because all farm earnings accrued to the state and were in turn redistributed by the state in the form of fixed monthly cash wages for all staff and workers or at least a guaranteed work-point value, regardless of actual farm income during any given season. Everyone was assigned enough work, and conditions for performing it were provided within the security of the farm organization to maintain a basic living standard. By contrast, commune members in bad years could "borrow" from the collective against future income. But often there would be no cash share-out at all once the value of grain and other goods distributed in kind throughout the year was deducted from work-point earnings. Such families, like the resettled youth among them, were left to their own devices and had to rely on their private sidelines (or outside remittances) to make ends meet.[7]

Such was the milieu within which schools had to operate. At the elementary level, when the main school in the largest production brigade village was too far for young children to attend on a daily basis, the old junior elementary classes remained the most common fallback solution. Usually, older children could walk to the main village school, which meant they could also continue on for a year or two of junior secondary instruction as well when such classes were attached at the village level. But the main middle school in the commune seat had to arrange some form of dormitory accommodation since distances were usually too great for a daily commute.

Since most interviewees had spent many years in their localities and sat through many report meetings on their history, recalling when schools had

---

[7] Many studies of rural life in China during the 1960s and 1970s are available, e.g., those listed in the Select Bibliography by Chan, Madsen, and Unger; Friedman, Pickowicz, and Selden; Hinton; Madsen; Mosher; Oi; Parish and Whyte; Potter and Potter; and Zweig.

Table 16.5. *Pattern of school development, rural areas and rural communes*
(number of schools)

	When established and/or closed[a]				
School level	Before 1949	1949–1957	1958–1965	1966–1978	1979–1983
Complete 5- or 6-year elementary, or 2-, 3-, or 4-year jr. elementary	+5	+16	+154	+51, −17	—
Attached 1- or 2-year jr. secondary	—	—	+12, ±14	+387, ±14, −4	−63
Detached 2- or 3-year jr. secondary	+5	+7	+74	+9	−1
Complete 4-, 5-, or 6-year secondary, or 2- or 3-year sr. secondary	+6	+9	+12	+258, −7	−110, +1

[a] Denoted as follows: + = established; ± = established and closed within the same time period; − = closed.
Note: Data from interviewees' firsthand experience and plausible secondhand information (as explained in Appendix). The compilation does not include vocational, specialized secondary (*zhongzhuan*), or agricultural middle schools.

been established was relatively easy. Tables 16.5 and 16.6 record these recollections. Many interviewees – depending on their own origins and the relative size of a county seat – insisted that its schools should also be regarded as "rural." In fact, although county-town schools served primarily the urban town population, such schools did often educate youngsters from the countryside and from families who lived in town but worked in the surrounding brigades. Nevertheless, all the obstacles to operating rural schools were substantially reduced in county towns, as well as in the suburbs of big cities, which seemed reason enough to present separate calculations as shown in the two tables.

As one final measure of quantitative rural growth, previous chapters have noted the marginal development of rural secondary schooling. The highest standard cited for pre-1966 was between one and two senior middle schools per county, and such schools were usually located in county towns. This pattern corroborated conventional wisdom and anecdotal evidence, which always suggested that genuinely rural youth raised in families who lived by agricultural labor rarely attended college. Again, statistics published in the early 1980s, shown in Table 16.7, illustrate the extent of growth in this sector in a pattern consistent with the recollections of interviewees. They were able to contribute relevant accounts for 51 counties through 1976 (47 rural and 4

Table 16.6. *Pattern of school development, county towns and suburban communes (number of schools)*

	When established and/or closed[a]				
School level	Before 1949	1949–1957	1958–1965	1966–1978	1979–1983
Complete 5- or 6-year elementary, or 2-, 3-, or 4-year jr. elementary	+ 7	+6	+8	+11, ±7	−6
Attached 1- or 2-year jr. secondary	—	—	±1	+20,±1	−9
Detached 2- or 3-year jr. secondary	+ 8	+2	+8	+22	—
Complete 4-, 5-, or 6-year secondary, or 2- or 3-year sr. secondary	+14	+6	+10	+32, −1	−9

[a] Denoted as follows: + = established; ± = established and closed within the same time period; − = closed.

Note: Data from interviewees' firsthand experience and plausible secondhand information (as explained in Appendix). The compilation does not include vocational, specialized secondary (*zhongzhuan*), or agricultural middle schools.

suburban). Only four counties had essentially not progressed beyond the pre-1966 standard of between one and two senior middle schools per county located in town (one county each in Sichuan, Yunnan, Guangdong, and Shaanxi, of which only the Sichuan county was in a minority area).[8]

Reducing distinctions, increasing responsibilities

The obstacles inhibiting mass education in rural communes, by contrast with county towns and suburbs, were of course the same obstacles perpetuating the

[8] The Guangdong county had only two senior middles located in the county seat; the Shaanxi county added a second senior middle in another town; and the Yunnan county only relocated its one school out of town and failed to add any others. Additionally, five or six counties in Yunnan and Xinjiang had not gone beyond the old standard for the indigenous population whether Han or minority. But these counties all had state farms or large state-run enterprises (mines and a factory) which administered schools from separate state budgets for the families of staff and workers. In such enterprises, like the state farms, most personnel were usually transferred or resettled from elsewhere, although at least a few locals always benefited in various ways. For example, a few local children – especially cadres' children – from adjacent communes could usually make their way into the neighboring work-unit's schools.

Table 16.7. *Complete secondary and senior secondary schools, 1963–1977*
(number of schools nationwide)

Year	Urban	County town	Rural
1963	1,414	2,408	481
1965	1,315	2,193	604
1971	863	1,479	11,819
1973	5,139	4,301	19,925
1975	6,170	5,015	27,935
1977	7,610	6,377	50,916

Source: *Zhongguo jiaoyu nianjian, 1949–1981*, p. 1005. Total number of counties as of 1982: 2,133 (*Statistical Yearbook of China 1983*, p. 1).

urban–rural intellectual divide generally. Interviewees usually explained the root cause of these obstacles in economic terms: the economics of school finance inhibiting growth on the one hand and the economics of rural family finances inhibiting enrollments on the other. At their most basic, these economic differences meant guaranteed state allocations for all the items on the budgets of all city schools. In the countryside, only a single school – the commune seat's middle school and perhaps its elementary school as well – could count on such largess. Then, like the proverbial loaves and fishes, rural communes had to transform this basic state allocation into enough schools to educate populations of 20,000 or more, scattered over a wide landscape where bicycles were usually of little use and the school bus nonexistent.

Meanwhile, most people living in urban households (*jumin hukou*) had long since become salaried. They ate commercial grain (*shangpinliang*) and could count that and other low-priced rationed necessities as one of several benefits, along with pensions and health care, enjoyed by urbanites in a state-run economy. In the countryside, agricultural households (*nongye hukou*) enjoyed no such benefits, neither pensions nor anything but the most rudimentary health care. They had to produce their own grain and other foodstuffs. Invariably, all family members were drawn into the daily struggle for economic survival, even though children under age 16 were not supposed to be assigned work-point earning tasks by the collective. But children often performed the lightest work assigned their parents and helped out with many household chores as well.

Thus, despite the much proclaimed aim of reducing the great distinctions, Mao's China never escaped the harsh laws of unequal development. These were marked most clearly in the differences between state and collective forms of economic ownership, and their respective domination in city and countryside. Urban areas remained always at an advantage, and the countryside always struggled under multiple handicaps: fewer educated people, fewer economically secure people, fewer schools, and fewer resources with which to create more. Considering the implications of these handicaps, state farms and rural communes should also have been calculated separately. State farm schools were managed like their city counterparts. If the policy was fixed at so many schools for so many children, money would be allocated and personnel assigned to meet the prescribed standard – as in all the state farms with which interviewees were familiar.

Nevertheless, Mao's education revolution was unique not just in its destructive leveling at the top of the pyramid but also in expanding its mass base and especially in trying to reduce the rural handicaps. Nor were the teachers themselves the most important part either of the problem or of its solution. Most significant, instead, were the decisions made in Beijing about how the state's budgetary allocations for education were to be spent, together with the related demands enforced through the Party–state bureaucracy to distribute those funds down to the commune level and beyond. The key decisions were to authorize state funds to finance the new standard of one middle school per commune and to provide assistance (however limited) in financing virtually all brigade-run schools as well.

The initial 1968–1969 publicity was thus somewhat misleading in its enthusiasm for communes and peasants running their own schools, or perhaps the arrangements were only worked out by trial and error later. In any case, interviewees reported uniformly that the new rural middle schools were indeed located at the commune level and served the commune population, but these schools were all state run and financed in the same manner, if not to the same degree, as urban schools. This made the county education bureau responsible for recruiting teachers, meeting all recurrent expenditures, and authorizing capital construction funds for new buildings. Teachers were recruited via the state job assignment plan and paid in accordance with unified state salary scales. Such teachers also had to meet customary academic requirements whereby tertiary and specialized secondary training was necessary to qualify as state-salaried secondary and elementary teachers respectively. The county education bureau also had final say in deciding whether to establish a school, when to add senior middle sections, the size of enrollments, and the number of classrooms. Commune authorities might or might not fuss over a school, contribute to its amenities, interfere with its routines, and plead its case before the powers that be. But the county education bureau had final power over the basic decisions governing middle school development.

By contrast, elementary schools and their attached junior middle caps were the responsibility of the teams and brigades in which they were located. Management was, however, always coordinated by the commune as the lowest extension of state authority responsible for putting together the mix of state-salaried and locally hired teachers, plus state and local funds and resources, that sustained every commune's school "system." The locally hired teachers were either natives of the commune itself or resettled youth. All were paid, like other commune members, according to the value of their team or brigade work points. As noted in chapter 15, these teachers also received a small state subsidy, which was standard practice nationwide by the early 1970s, although the actual amount varied slightly from place to place.

Similarly, just as remuneration for *minban* teachers varied within a common pattern, so the specific local resource mix used to support brigade schools was also subject to infinite variation, albeit within a standard administrative format. It was usually called collectively run (*jitiban*) or brigade run (*daduiban*) for elementary schools and their attachments, and state run (*gongban*) for the commune middle schools. The old term, "*minban*," remained in use everywhere but only with reference to the locally hired teachers themselves. Such were the institutional origins of the distinction between interviewees with college educations who had been assigned to work as state-salaried teachers in commune middle schools and others with only secondary-level training who were tapped to work as *minban* teachers after being resettled in the countryside. Otherwise, for school management, the *gongban/minban* distinction formally disappeared.

Related to its success in "deconcentrating" resources and distributing them, however thinly, throughout the country was the way this pattern of school management also effectively subdued the ever-present pressures for parity. We have noted how these pressures shaped Chinese educational institutions throughout their history, and the most recent experience with the unpopular *minban* and agricultural middle schools was still fresh in people's minds. After 1968, both alternatives were simply absorbed into the reformed system. The story of Shanghai's *minban* schools was repeated everywhere as the ad hoc arrangements of the early 1960s were incorporated within regular city school systems. Rural areas, reflecting their different financial arrangements, handled the problem differently. But so thoroughly unfashionable had the *minban* alternative become that only five localities of all those for which interviewees contributed any kind of information were actually still using the term "*minban*" with reference to their village elementary schools by the mid-1970s.

In reality, all brigade schools were run in accordance with the old "popularly run with public assistance" formula, which was redefined as collectively run with state assistance. The collective, having become the lowermost public authority at the village level, was seen as granting "regular" public status to the brigade-run schools. It was a subtle kind of deception but effective nonetheless given the communes' function as the basic units of local government and the role of their constituent brigade and team parts within the bureaucratic chain of command.

The arrangement could thus eliminate the public's perception of two separate kinds of school, *minban* and regular, and the consequent rejection of one as inferior. Indeed, so effective was the deception that it allowed some localities to gild the lily further and declare all their brigade-run elementaries to be "state run," or *gongban*, even when they were managed just like everyone else's, with the typical mix of local collective management and minimal state contributions, including the *minban* teachers' monthly cash subsidy. In such cases, village junior elementary classes would still be distinguished as collectively run by brigades and teams but were always linked in some way with the main brigade elementary school into a mini-system which further blurred the status distinctions between and among them.

This new "Cultural Revolution regular" system also assumed certain attributes of its predecessor in another way: by ignoring less regular alternatives that had also been promoted in 1968–1969. Hence, no one had more than hearsay knowledge of such expedients – sometimes called *fangniuban* (classes for cowherd children) or *gengduban* (classes held during work breaks in the fields). Such measures had often been discussed or tried briefly and then abandoned, but they were reported nowhere as a routine feature of rural schooling.

The search for "*minban* schools" by any other name actually became one of the most tedious mysteries of the entire interview exercise, providing many clues about the strategy and tactics adopted to surmount obstacles and reduce handicaps. The logic of the old Yan'an principles did still dominate. The only way there could be schools in every village and commune was by forcing every locality to assume responsibility for its own. But these principles had come a long way in practice since the 1940s. First and foremost, they had proven themselves incapable of surviving in competition with the regular system – hence the decision to enforce a merger of the two by diluting standards, by redistributing resources, and especially by camouflaging the invidious regular–irregular distinction within a single mass-based system.

The common pattern of funding and management could, however, only reduce handicaps and blur distinctions, not eliminate them. Interviewees identified two kinds of variables, one potentially quantifiable and the other not, governing school growth in rural areas. The former included economic wealth, the technical level of development, location, transport, and population density. The subjective variables included popular traditions, leadership initiative, and managerial skills. Following the laws of unequal development, wealth produced more wealth, and people living in denser concentrations with adequate transport represented economies of scale. Such localities always had more schools and better schools, which was why urban areas represented one end of the education development spectrum and border region national minority districts the other.

State education budgets for rural counties were governed by the same principles, with relatively larger budgets for richer, more populous areas. This
explained why the suburban communes nearest big cities, like the cities themselves, could always seem to boast fully state-funded elementary schools while
those further away could not.[9] It also explained why most Guangdong and
coastal Fujian counties had relatively more to spend on their schools and why
even some of their rural communes could claim one or more (almost) completely state-financed elementary schools per brigade, while communes elsewhere had to make do with little more than the small standard allocations to
help pay their teachers' salaries.[10]

These principles also explained why some communes and brigades in richer,
more populous areas of Jiangsu and Zhejiang could probably have done without state funding altogether, so profitable were their various collective endeavors.
But such were the laws of unequal development advantage that the budgetary
process sought only to modify, not eliminate. Hence in the allocation of county-
controlled funds, interviewees reported two variations on the set pattern of
state funding for commune middle schools.

At the more prosperous populous end of the scale, communes in Guangdong
and Jiangsu were actually encouraged to set up their own senior middle sections to help meet growing demand and save state funds. Then once the
commune had borne the burden of start-up costs, the county would step in and
take over the school. In such cases, personnel and prestige, rather than recurrent expenditures, were the main concerns. Usually, even a prosperous commune could not staff a middle school from its own population. Nor could
communes alone easily recruit such individuals, given the intellectual aversion
to rural life, without the "coercive" power of the state assignment mechanism.
Additionally, in such a county, for a commune not to have its own state-
authorized complete middle school became "a great loss of face," as the parity
principle left its inevitable mark.[11]

By contrast, counties in more sparsely populated, poorer regions sometimes
drew the line at the junior middle level and would not allow further growth
even when commune authorities requested it. The basic policy decision on
whether or not to promote rural senior middle schools was, however, made by
the province while counties only implemented the overall mandate. Thus one
province, albeit only one among those represented, opted to retain the old
pre-1966 pattern and specifically did not allow the development of commune-
level senior secondary education. In this case, the prohibition included even

---

[9] Interviews 80/BJ/9, pp. 2–3; 82/S/6, p. 17; 82/FJ/11, pp. 15–18; 82/BJ/18, p. 4; 83/BJ/3,
p. 55; 83/AH/7, p. 29.
[10] Interviews 82/GD/2, p. 14; 82/GD/9, pp. 61–62; 80/FJ/8, p. 41; 82/FJ/4, pp. 31–32; 82/
FJ/11, pp. 15, 18; 83/FJ/25, pp. 10–13.
[11] Interviews 80/S/4, p. 13; 80/GD/5, pp. 6–8; 83/JS/6, pp. 12–18.

predominantly Han communes, in suburban areas, with well-attended systems through the junior middle level.[12]

In the interviewees' experience, however, the most common pattern was the progressive growth of schooling through the senior secondary level, with commune authorities seeking and receiving authorization on a case-by-case basis from the county education bureau for the addition of a senior middle section to the existing state-run junior middle school in the commune seat. Building materials would then be allocated, and teachers with some kind of post-secondary education would be assigned. The new staff was usually a combination of recent graduates from the nearest teacher training college, allocated through the provincial job assignment plan, plus experienced "backbone elements" transferred from established schools in the vicinity. But besides buildings and staff, which the county could guarantee, the main prerequisite was the commune's own "system" of schools, which at a basic minimum had to be developed sufficiently to produce a steady supply of about 100 students annually.

Once the focus shifted further downward from the county and state-funded commune seat schools to their village-level foundations, the second cluster of variables – local tradition and especially leadership – grew in importance. Without the right combination, schools even in prosperous regions floundered, and with it, the consequences of poverty could be minimized.

Within a commune and county, the most isolated, distant, and sparsely populated brigades and communes would usually be the last to meet the new standards. Such brigades and communes predominated among those noted above that failed to meet Cultural Revolution quantitative standards. But such brigades and communes could be found everywhere, as pockets of resistance, even in the most prosperous regions, including Guangdong, southern Fujian, and suburban Shanghai. In such cases, interviewees were likely to blame a "leadership problem" and conversely to credit leadership initiative or careful management where schools flourished. This was because rural schools did not spring up "automatically" by administrative fiat as they seemed to do in town. Such leadership was related to many other conditions, including local custom and tradition. But all other things being equal, as they were in Teacher Shao's Zhejiang county, the active interest of brigade and commune leaders was crucial because of the effort (mafan) required.

With at least three generations of county-town politicking behind him, young Teacher Shao seemed to know whereof he spoke. The active interest of these leaders was essential because only they had the clout to beg, borrow, barter, and otherwise procure all the resources necessary – including both people and materiel – to maintain a school. More distant communes and isolated brigades inevitably could not activate their interest to the same degree as those close to

[12] Interviews 82/SC/12, pp. 21 ff.; 82/SC/19, pp. 41 ff.; 82/NC/15, p. 9; 83/SX/20, pp. 18, 73.

the county and commune seats, where power over resource allocation lay, because the necessary connections and exchange relationships were more difficult to sustain from a distance. The law of unequal development advantage was still at work, but individual initiative was the intervening variable mediating its impact.[13]

Stories from many regions served to illustrate the mediating impact of local traditions, leadership, and managerial skills on revolutionary goals. Three accounts stand out, each for different reasons. The Fujian coast tradition interacted negatively with the antibourgeois ethos of the time to produce the only reports of rural school closures. A second account is from the Yangzi River valley region of Hubei, Anhui, and Jiangsu, where remnants of the old *sishu* tradition were still strong enough to influence modern development. A third story concerns the Koreans of Jilin Province, who outperformed everyone else and put to shame some conventional Chinese assumptions about education, including those of both elites and masses.

Coastal Fujian

The Fujian coast tradition was important in developmental terms because it seemed to refute the most commonly expressed conventional wisdom that poverty and schooling were antithetical. According to this wisdom, the worst-educated localities and families were always the least economically secure. Teacher Fang, introduced in chapter 13, had used the Fujian inversion of this maxim in his explanation for the great gap in academic achievement between north and south Fujian. Because his northern county was relatively prosperous, he said, children quit school early to begin earning money for their families. In the South, too little land and too many people made study "the only way out."

This variation of the usual theme, peculiar to the Fujian coast and neighboring Shantou Prefecture in Guangdong, extended back many centuries to the time when family strategies had to focus on the imperial examinations since there were so few other sources of wealth and security in the region. But the question Fujian people could never answer was why they had taken to study as the way out when other poor people did not. Likewise, the question others could not answer was why their impoverished regions and families had not caught on to the Fujian way. In fact, there were no answers, because the Fujian case did not really disprove the conventional wisdom nor did it present a solution that could necessarily be duplicated elsewhere.

The key intervening variable in this case was the companion centuries-old custom of overseas migration and the continuing loyalty to home villages over many generations, giving rise to the custom of remitting money specifically for

[13] Interview 83/ZJ/16, pp. 24ff.

school construction and maintenance. As the wealth of overseas communities grew and the principle of universal mass education gained acceptance, the Fujian coast tradition adapted to the modern demand for a school in every village. Responding to that demand, overseas communities joined the campaigns to modernize their homeland by mail and remittance check. As a result, some Jinjiang County communes in the heart of overseas Chinese country could indeed boast at least one junior elementary school in every village by 1966, with up to half built and maintained through overseas contributions. This flow of funds was disrupted by the Cultural Revolution and the rise in hostility against bourgeois overseas Chinese ways. Some of the village schools closed, accounting for the only decline in elementary school numbers during the period reported by interviewees (see Table 16.5).

Teachers Lin and Huang, from two different Jinjiang County communes, reported the same pattern of rural elementary school financing with little locally generated support whether from the brigades themselves or student work–study projects. Instead, village schools all relied primarily on the state, student fees, and overseas endowment funds. When the endowment funds were depleted and not replenished during the early 1970s, some schools closed while others were maintained by state allocations at the rate still of at least one school per production brigade. Both teachers, who remained at their commune posts throughout the 1970s, maintained that the number of students in school probably declined little if at all because only the village junior elementaries were disrupted and these had been overbuilt, based not always on need but on family considerations, feuding clan loyalties, and the like.[14]

Overseas money had been widely invested all along the coast at the secondary, as well as elementary, level. But nowhere was the custom as pervasive as in Jinjiang County, and nowhere else did it contribute so greatly as in the counties of Jinjiang Prefecture to rural mass education. Hence the Fujian coast communities may still have been poor enough to keep their ancient tradition alive and their remittance checks flowing. But along the way they had created a unique kind of security net for themselves and especially for their schools that existed nowhere else to the same degree. Even neighboring prefectures in Fujian itself, with less dense concentrations of overseas Chinese families, could not rely on the remittance method alone to promote mass education without substantial local input.

Yet however unique their circumstances, these communities did demonstrate that the elite tradition could be transposed for general use into a modern system wherein almost every child, rural or otherwise, if provided with a school, would attend it. Four interviewees with at least 10 years' teaching experience each in four Jinjiang Prefecture communes all estimated attendance

---

[14] Interviews 80/FJ/8, pp. 26–41, 65–70; 82/FJ/4, pp. 31–36.

rates in the mid-1970s that were more comparable to urban than rural stand-ards: with virtually all children entering elementary school, few dropouts, and most continuing on to the junior middle level. A fifth, Teacher Liao, was also a Jinjiang native, having been born, raised, and educated in local schools there. Not coincidentally, he was the only pre-1966 college graduate among the interviewees who could claim to be of humble rural origins.[15]

The heartland

Nevertheless, the Fujian coast – best characterized as neither urban nor rural, dependent on overseas remittances, and outward looking to a degree unimagined in most inland locales – was far removed from the rural norm. More typical was the Yangzi River region of Hubei, Anhui, and Jiangsu. There, people with even "a little bit of overseas connection" by reason of a distant relative living in Hong Kong or Taiwan could be few to nonexistent. In such areas, the overseas Chinese lifestyle, sustained by consumer habits and parcels of extra food and foreign-style clothing, was little known. When the locals did know of such things, they tended to disapprove of them, as modern vices in commun-ities where socialist values only reinforced traditional rural virtues of frugality and thrift. Rural overseas Chinese families in Zhejiang's Jinhua Prefecture found themselves subject to such disapproval from their neighbors. In rural Jiangsu and Anhui, there were often no such families to disapprove of. Within entire communes, resettled youth and reassigned teachers might be alone in such connections. Consequently, the communities also had no sources of "foreign capital" or overseas relatives to exploit.

Seven interviewees told the story of education in this rural heartland, in-cluding two locals and five urbanites transferred from nearby cities. All seven counties and communes were estimated as being average to moderately pros-perous, reflecting the practice of not resettling city people in the most desti-tute, disaster-prone localities of the region. These accounts were important because they illustrated the best and worst possible outcomes from a more typical combination of rural resources. The region was also of historical inter-est as the only one where interviewees reported the old *sishu* tradition still at work, for better and for worse, influencing modern development.[16]

Many small mysteries became clearer in the presence of these partially preserved holdovers from an earlier time. For example, the regular–irregular controversy that had now assumed systemic proportions and dangerous polit-ical overtones could be seen in something like its original state. Here it was still essentially the same conflict mentioned in pre-1949 accounts, between

---

[15] Interviews 80/FJ/3; 80/FJ/8; 82/FJ/4; 82/FJ/11; 83/FJ/26.
[16] The only eyewitness account of a living *sishu* remnant came not from this area, however, but from Xunde County, Guangdong (see chap. 18, section Reaffirming the Urban–Rural Divide).

proponents of the new modern schools and "backward" basic-level remnants of the old learning.

Yet the origin of the political overtones also became clearer in this region since it included the Jiangsu hinterland around Nanjing, where, in the 1920s, emerging ironies were already apparent. The same geographic and intellectual heartland was still producing them half a century later. Before 1966, Jiangsu was always among the highest-scoring provinces on the national college entrance examinations. Yet it was still unable to meet contemporary mass education standards, leaving its "illiterate peasants" to the tender mercies of conscripted urbanites like Teachers Mei and Liu.

Mysteries remain, of course, as to why the region had clung so tenaciously to its *sishu* tradition and whether it may actually have inhibited the development of modern mass education. In Chu Prefecture, Anhui, just across the Yangzi River from Nanjing, *sishu* continued to thrive until the early 1950s. In his 1947–1948 study of Chu County within the prefecture, Morton Fried remarked on the two different kinds of elementary education available there, one offered by the new public schools and the other traditional, taught by a single teacher in a one-room schoolhouse. Typically, "the traditional curriculum was little altered, consisting in largest part of learning the classics by rote." As for the sons of poor peasants and rural tenants, any kind of formal schooling was still "patently beyond the realm of possibility."[17]

Teacher Bao, from the same prefecture, was the only interviewee actually educated in a *sishu*. He attended from age 7 to 18, when he transferred to public school. The year was 1951. Land reform was under way, the landowning families in the district were being expropriated, and all the *sishu* thereabout finally stopped operating at that time. He recalled the school well since it was held in a spare room of his family's house, the largest in the village. Boys of all ages had gathered there every morning. They began with an hour's warm-up of cacophonous recitation when everyone shouted out their lessons in full voice. Then each student, beginning with the youngest, would recite his lessons individually from memory with his back to the teacher (*beishu*) while everyone else listened. All they did all day was recite from memory, grind ink, do writing exercises, and learn to use the abacus, interrupted by breakfast and lunch breaks. If the teacher had to be absent, students were happy to take a day off. For beginners, individual characters were taught first, including both recognition and writing, followed by simple children's stories and then moving on through the Confucian classics – the only curriculum this *sishu* ever offered.

Teacher Bao estimated that most boys, rich or poor, in his village attended a *sishu*, but the poorest dropped out after only a year or two and most girls received no schooling whatsoever. His family provided the room rent free, and

---

[17] Morton H. Fried, *Fabric of Chinese Society: A Study of the Social Life of a Chinese County Seat* (New York: Octagon Books, 1974), pp. 133, 184.

students paid tuition to the teacher in measures of rice, more from the rich and less from the poor, who also worked out other arrangements such as personal services to the teacher in return for their children's instruction. Modern schools were nonexistent in this locality, and rural youth attended *sishu* or nothing at all until the early 1950s.[18]

On the plus side, the old *sishu* obviously provided models and precedents for an irregular style of education suited to village life. They also provided a supply of local literates and teachers to staff new schools, an important consideration given the urban concentration of regular schooling and unwillingness of city people to relocate in the countryside. From further upriver, Teacher Zhu recalled the development of rural schools in his county as being almost totally dependent upon the old *sishu* teachers, who were sent back to school in the early 1950s for retraining in politics, the new curriculum, and more modern teaching methods. At that time, he had attended the first modern elementary school in his district, serving an area that would later become two communes.

The school had five classes of students, all taught by retrained *sishu* teachers, most of whom were his relatives. These same teachers were then transferred to the agricultural middle schools set up in 1958, and to the regular junior middles which replaced them in the early 1960s. Returning to his commune's middle school in the early 1970s, Teacher Zhu was one of only two college graduates among its 18 teachers, 12 of whom still dated from the old *sishu* days. Physics, chemistry, and math were usually left to younger colleagues while the old teachers concentrated on their traditional strong points: Chinese language and history.

In this case, a key input was the unrelenting effort to retrain which began in the 1950s and continued throughout the Cultural Revolution decade, according to Teacher Zhu. This region, too, experienced the full range of political movements, downward transfers, and regular struggle–study sessions as a political control mechanism. But through it all, modern rural schools grew as elsewhere from virtually nothing in the early 1950s to the standard complement of brigade and commune schools. Accompanying school growth at each step of the way were teacher training programs and refresher courses orchestrated by the prefectural and county education bureaus together with local normal schools. Even during the early 1970s, teachers for the new commune senior middle schools were produced through the same kinds of short courses and training arrangements devised initially to modernize the *sishu* generation.

On the minus side, left to themselves in a rural setting, these decaying remnants of the old tradition could surely inspire the regular teacher's hallmark credo: "better no school..." Such was commune clerk Tao's reaction, back in Chu Prefecture, to the village elementary schools that made it possible for his adoptive commune to claim universal attendance. A resettled youth

---

[18] Interview 83/AH/7, pp. 5–8.

from Shanghai, Tao seemed happy never to have been tapped for service in the local school system, but he knew something of its workings from his clerical job at the commune headquarters. Land area was relatively great, requiring on the average a one-hour walk from brigade seats to surrounding villages. The commune's solution was to run first- and second-grade classes in the villages, with a three-year senior elementary school in each brigade center.

Most of this development took place in the early 1970s. But from Tao's perspective, it hardly mattered that every child probably did study for at least one or two years, because the new village arrangements were "schools in name only." They were all one-room affairs with earthern walls, thatched roofs, no glass in the windows, and no electricity. Even the desks were made of pounded earth and students brought their own stools. Worst of all, these village schools were run in corrupted *sishu* style with little apparent concern from any quarter about what went on within them. Everything was casual, careless, and "not at all regular" like a school should be. Leadership from the teams, brigades, and commune seemed virtually nonexistent, leaving the teachers to do as they pleased. Often they would read or chat with friends and ignore the students, or just disappear for a day and cancel classes. Each school also had only one such teacher; Chinese language and arithmetic were the only subjects taught; and students would also come and go as family responsibilities demanded.[19]

In neigboring rural Jiangsu, the same conditions were duplicated at the secondary level. This occurred in the commune to which Teacher Yang had been banished in 1969, and her exasperation was understandable. It was the most backward of any middle school introduced and a classic case of deprivation: everything that could possibly be wrong was. The commune was the most distant, poorest, sparsely populated, and least accessible in the county. In Teacher Yang's view, however, the real problems lay elsewhere. "Life was bitter, yet the teachers were enthusiastic and the masses actually demanded schooling. But the leaders above did not grasp education. There were many problems in this place and they all concerned leadership." And at the heart of the leadership problems was an old *sishu*.

Commune leaders did not move themselves to promote elementary schooling, nor did the county goad them to it. County education bureau leaders did, however, establish the requisite "state-funded" middle school in every commune. But in this case they only rechristened an ancient *sishu* famous locally for its long history and little else. A headmaster was formally appointed along with three state-salaried teachers, two of whom were college graduates. All expenses were met by the state, the headmaster traveled frequently to the county seat for meetings, and so on. But the negative consequences of the county's inertia were manifold in terms of the school's location, its personnel, curriculum, enrollments, and teaching plan.

[19] Interview 83/AH/21, pp. 7–17.

What must have been an auspicious site for generations past was no more. Located in a secluded spot, the school was more than one hour's walking time from the commune headquarters, and student dorms were nonexistent. The headmaster was a native of the brigade and had been educated in this school when it was still a *sishu* before 1949. He was personally responsible for having kept its tradition alive, standing out as a man of culture in a locality where illiteracy remained common. His calligraphy was elegant, he could play musical instruments, and he had taken up carpentry to support himself in lean times. He also taught politics but was not a Communist Party member, and in any case, political intrusions were minimal here. Alas, also minimal was his knowledge of how to run a modern school.

The school could accommodate at most 40 students in the old *sishu* building, which was solid but small and totally lacking in amenities. Electricity was finally installed about 1973. The supply of textbooks and teaching materials here as elsewhere was never a problem, one of the courtesies of a communist state. Initially, the books were edited and printed by the county. Then, in the early 1970s, the provincially unified materials became available. But this was the Cultural Revolution decade, when new rules decreed that each school could fix its own curriculum and teach what it chose. Since the headmaster in good *sishu* tradition remained uninterested in science, these subjects were not taught. Nor did he bother with history. He also enrolled new students only once every other year, to avoid the nuisance of teaching two grades at the same time. All 40 students were taken together through the school's two-year junior middle curriculum and only then, when they graduated, would a new batch be enrolled. Anyone wanting to complete the third year had to seek it elsewhere. There was no other secondary-level schooling available in this commune of about 10,000 people.

Such were the consequences, in a modern teacher's view, of the old *sishu* tradition left to itself. Although she had many political grievances, Teacher Yang's assessment of this school was made on other grounds. She especially looked to the commune and county to provide the kind of leadership, such as Zhu reported, that would have brought the headmaster up to standard or else. Instead, the only professional (*yewu*) activities they had was a monthly trek to the commune seat for all teachers to summarize work and an all-county meeting for one week each summer. Even the more common "teaching-research" work was absent, including the demonstration teaching exercises arranged in many communes whereby teachers audited and evaluated one another's classes. Teachers relied upon such activities for course preparation, keeping up with trends political and otherwise, shoptalk, and especially in helping to train the many inexperienced people being drafted for work at this time.[20]

Teachers Liu and Wan, by contrast, found themselves in two rural Anhui

[20] Interview 83/JS/9, pp. 33–54.

counties where leaders were able to exploit a similar combination of resources
to far better advantage – demonstrating also the effort required. Liu and Wan
were both resettled youth from Shanghai, but their accounts were different in
many respects, not the least being the temperaments of the two men telling
them. We have already noted Liu's views on the academic potential of rural
people. In the early 1970s, he had moved from agricultural labor to the village
school. His health and morale had improved during the five years he spent
doing farm labor, and he decided to settle down there. Hence his motives in
wanting a transfer were the same as other educated commune members making
similar requests: lighter work and more reliable income. In his brigade, the
strongest male laborers, which he was not, could earn from the collective an
annual income amounting to 320 *rmb*. About 100 *rmb* would be paid in cash
and the rest in kind. But on the average, most households only earned about
half that much cash annually from the collective without their individual family sidelines. By comparison, a *minban* teacher accumulated work points worth
about 100 *rmb* in cash and kind from the team, plus a monthly cash subsidy
from the state of 12 *rmb*.[21]

Teacher Wan, on the other hand, said he had hung out at his brigade school
for five years because it was the only "happy" place around, until finally he was
allowed to teach. He admired the efforts that went into maintaining the commune school system, could not imagine what life would be like for local youth
without it, and dismissed reports of education revolution chaos everywhere:
"the newspapers always exaggerate."

Nevertheless, the two commune school systems were genuinely different in
many respects, including size, wealth, and local talent, as well as strategy and
style of local leadership. And Wan's commune had the edge on almost all
relevant points. Its smaller size of 12,000 people was not necessarily an advantage, but it was also richer and had more sources of wealth. Its agriculture was
more mechanized, and a good system of interbrigade roads had been built to
accommodate the tractors. Comparing income levels, a majority of households
in the brigade where Wan lived earned about 100 *rmb* cash annually after
deductions. The *minban* teachers, combining their work points and subsidies,
earned about 200 *rmb* cash and 100 *rmb* in kind annually. A brigade's elementary school "system," with one complete school and several small village branches,
would have about a dozen teachers total, of whom one or two would be state
salaried. The two such teachers in his brigade earned salaries of about 40 *rmb*
per month, not quite double the *minban* average.

More important than actual income levels, however, was how the two communes supported their schools. Wan did not know the origin of his commune's
arrangements, but the brigade mini-systems were already established when he

[21] In the late 1970s, 1 *rmb* = approx. U.S.$0.67.

arrived in 1972, and junior middle schools were just then being added in each brigade. His impression was that the whole complex dated back "long before" to the early 1960s. In any event, at some point the brigades had all been "empty," with no sources of income themselves, leaving the constituent small teams to foot the bill for all brigade expenditures. These included the work-point incomes of brigade leaders and the *minban* schoolteachers. To help pacify popular opinion as brigade services grew, the commune ordered the brigades to set up small-scale profit-making enterprises, and by the early 1970s each brigade was paying the work-point "salaries" of about 30 leading cadres, employees, and teachers from this source.

Also following a custom extending back to the 1960s, all students and teachers did about one afternoon of labor per week, carefully managed and supervised so as to earn money for the schools. Cash crops such as cotton, peanuts, and sesame were cultivated on these parcels of land allocated by the brigade for school use. Additionally, village schools here like those almost everywhere charged students a small study fee. The rates in Wan's brigade were 1–2 *rmb* per semester, plus another 1–2 *rmb* per student per semester for books and supplies. But these fees were not collected rigorously, and about one-third of the students never paid. Besides the *minban* teachers' subsidies, the state may have helped out in other ways, perhaps with basic construction costs and building materials. For the most part, however, the commune school system was built and maintained with local labor and funds. The schools were also properly constructed: with brick walls, tile roofs, cement floors, wooden furniture, real blackboards, and playgrounds.

As to the people responsible, at the brigade level an eight-person CCP committee made the decisions. There was no separate noncadre "poor and lower-middle peasant school management committee." Rather, a cadre with appropriate political and cultural credentials was appointed to oversee education in each brigade while the teachers ran individual schools. At the commune level, the two main people were the state-run middle school headmaster, appointed by the county education bureau, and a member of the commune CCP committee with responsibility for education. These two men were the key figures responsible for coordinating work, organizing professional activities, helping recruit salaried teachers for the brigades, approving their *minban* teacher appointments, and liaising with the county.

One final important resource was the commune's relatively large number of literates. About 90 percent of the commune population was agricultural (*nongye hukou*), but Wan estimated that perhaps one-third of the men over age 35 were literate enough to read newspapers, a rare proportion for a rural community. These older literates, who were mostly *sishu* educated, coincided with a larger than usual number of landlord, rich-peasant, and Guomindang-bureaucrat families. In most other rural localities, such families might suffer many different kinds of discrimination including the exclusion of their children from commune middle schools. Teacher Yang had recalled seeing a few such old people still going out to the fields each day "under surveillance" and recalled too that the locals "really hated them." Wan did not know why this community seemed to follow different standards for its bad-class families; he just assumed it was because there were so many of them. In any case, people from these families were the backbone of the commune's teaching staff. Of the 12 teachers in his own brigade's elementary schools, 9 were from these local families with problematic pasts; the others were resettled youth.

The commune's only "failure" was the lack of a senior middle section. Instead of demanding such an addition, commune leaders were content with a unified all-commune secondary school entrance exam which channeled the "best" students (by grades and connections) into the main commune junior middle school and/or into county-town schools. Wan estimated that there could not be many students who did not enter the first grade, but not all continued on through the fifth. Especially the girls began dropping out at the senior elementary level.[22]

By comparison, Liu's commune lacked at least two crucial ingredients, namely, managerial expertise and a supply of older literates. Its cropping patterns and sources of income were similar, and its population was larger, at 20,000. But brigades were still "empty," leaving the full burden of support to individual teams. Labor activities were organized for students with the aim of contributing to school support. But work was poorly managed and the vegetables harvested were just given to the teachers. Schools were all mud and thatch, so cold in winter that students' hands turned "white as turnips" and so damp during the rainy season that classes often could not be held. The peasants replaced their own rice-straw roofs once a year, but schools would go untended and leaking for two or three, until brigade leaders ordered teams to assign labor for the job.

The curriculum was also basic: Chinese, arithmetic, politics, and physical education. Liu recalled no direct evidence of the old *sishu* tradition, except in teaching style and content. Science or nature study (*ziran*) at the elementary level was never taught. And each day began with a 30-minute cacophony of student voices reciting aloud (*gaosheng landu*) the lessons they had memorized from the day before. Yet there were no old, retrained *sishu* teachers here and only a few ex-landlord and rich-peasant families. The *minban* teachers were primarily young recent graduates, either resettled or returned youth. They tried to maintain a program of demonstration teaching to evaluate one another's work. But when the commune education cadre instructed all brigades to organize teaching-research groups to help with course preparation, no one

[22] Interview 83/AH/8, pp. 27–29.

knew quite what to do. The work lapsed within a year – unlike in Wan's commune, where such professional activities were maintained throughout.

The problem, said Liu, was that the brigades in his commune lacked a cadre assigned specifically to oversee and coordinate education work, leaving no one between the brigade CCP committee and the teachers in charge of day-to-day school affairs. Like Tao and Yang, he blamed brigade and commune leaders. "They just appointed people with the most education to be teachers and never had anything to do with them again."

All in all, Liu's commune seemed to be about 10 years behind. Thus, the existing system that Wan saw when he arrived in his commune was only still being put together when Liu began teaching in the early 1970s. And Liu could recall quite precisely how it progressed because he had taken good notes at an all-commune teachers meeting in 1974, when leaders announced that universalizing elementary schooling could no longer be delayed. The impetus was a telegram from the State Council in Beijing, sent down via the province and county, ordering all communes that had not already done so to "grasp tightly" school growth. In fact, this commune already had a school in every brigade and commune leaders read out some statistics. For the county as a whole, the percentage of the age-group entering school had risen from 81 to 86 percent during 1973–1974; and for the commune, from 68 to 75 percent. At only 69 percent, Liu's own brigade was among the lowest and so they set to work.

The teachers themselves vetoed the idea of running extra, irregular classes on grounds they were already too busy. They also vetoed the much publicized method of allowing poor children with many younger siblings to bring them to class – as did most schools everywhere after an initial trial period. A brief experiment with a poor and lower-middle peasants committee, used in some places to mobilize attendance, also came to nothing here. But an extra village branch school was set up, and teachers began a systematic schedule of home visits, targeting families with school-age children still not enrolled. Attendance thereafter grew rapidly. Soon the main brigade school had to be expanded, which was done with some state help, and a junior middle section was added to take pressure off the main commune school, which in turn began planning for a senior-level annex.

Liu himself had made home visits, and he could say for certain that in his own team of 40 households with 220 people, only two school-age girls failed to attend at all: due to poverty, a sick mother, and too many younger siblings. He calculated that all children studied for three or four years, when dropouts then began, and that such was the communewide norm by the late 1970s, although unfortunately he had failed to keep his notes from all other meetings. The one class of students that he taught consecutively for five years had 32 students at the start in 1973, of whom only about 16 graduated in 1977. But he admitted that part of the blame lay with him, because he, more than other teachers, had insisted on failing two or three of the worst students each year and making them repeat the grade, which caused dropouts as well as extra years in school. The commune had no enforcement mechanism such as threatening to withhold parents' work points, a rare practice in any case. Localities everywhere reported resistance to such means of compulsion on grounds that they would have aroused undue popular resentment. Nevertheless, even in this culturally deprived commune, virtually every child, if provided with a school, would attend it. The real difficulty here was providing the school.

Yet Teacher Liu remained unimpressed. His lack of enthusiasm seemed to derive from his own assumptions about the purpose of schooling and the uncertain arrangements laid on by local leaders. In his view, the demand from below was only induced, not genuine. Everyone was responding to directives from above and fear of criticism: "If they did not obey, then the commune would criticize the brigade cadres, who would in turn criticize the teachers, who would then go out and do the mobilization work." His argument only weakened somewhat in trying to explain why the peasants responded by sending their children if they were not actually forced to do so. "They only send their children for face, because everyone else does, and because they want a bit of culture." But they knew it was of "no use," he said, because they knew they could never use their education for anything but becoming *minban* teachers in their village schools.[23]

The Koreans

If Teacher Liu's commune seemed 10 years behind Wan's, the Koreans could be counted 10 years ahead. Actually, they seemed in a class by themselves, and Teacher Guan insisted on telling their story because of that difference. A resettled youth from Shanghai, he was one of the few whose memories of the experience remained primarily positive. In the Northeast, a state farm was the preferred assignment, but he drew the Yanbian Korean Autonomous Prefecture, a six-county region on the border with North Korea, where he spent 10 years.

Of the Koreans' history Guan knew little, except that the older people had all been educated under Japanese rule during the Occupation, which had begun earlier in Manchuria than in China proper, and earlier still on the Korean Peninsula. But whatever the reason, Guan concluded that the educational differences between Chinese and Koreans began with assumptions about the aims of schooling. Chinese typically regarded those aims in pragmatic terms, he said, as a means to a specific end: a way out of agriculture or a better

[23] Interview 83/AH/22, pp. 11–24, 44–47, 62–75.

job or a college education. The Koreans, by contrast, seemed to accept education unquestioningly as a kind of basic human need, essential for everyone regardless of who they were or what work they did, mental or manual, urban or rural.

Guan, too, had labored for about five years before being tapped to teach in the local schools. His various job assignments had reflected the main sources of commune wealth: forestry, mining, and grain. He lived with a dozen other resettled youth in a "collective household," the only such unit in a production team of 21 ordinary Korean families totaling 150 people. About 70 resettled Shanghai youth were living in the brigade with 800 Koreans. His team's highest annual cash income in the early 1970s was 90 *rmb* for a full-time male worker. The brigades ran few enterprises, teams had few collective sidelines, and agricultural work-point incomes were declining at this time of recollectivization after a period of individual-household contracting in the 1960s. The commune ran several small factories, however, and competition for the jobs therein was keen even though pay was still in work points.

The commune itself was small, with just under 10,000 people, almost all Korean. Most local leaders were also Korean, and the serious conflicts that sometimes marred Chinese–minority relations were absent here. Landlord and rich-peasant families had long since fled, and evidently as a concession to frontier stability, the richest of the families remaining had been reclassified down a notch or two. Hence, the standard "we are all poor peasants here" line was misleading as an indicator of past or present status. In any case, economics and social composition seemed unrelated to mass education since virtually the entire commune population was literate, regardless of age or sex. Guan insisted that all school-age commune children graduated from its elementary schools except the severely handicapped, for whom no special facilities existed. Virtually everyone completed junior middle as well, after which most girls dropped out, leaving 70–80 percent of the boys to complete the course. Since no one could continue directly to college in those days, all senior middle graduates then became "returned youth" and joined the agricultural labor force in their villages.

All brigades in the commune already had their own complete elementary schools in 1970. Distances were not great, but winter snows could mean one hour's walking time for some children, which was not regarded as an excuse for nonattendance. However, local road customs decreed that students on foot must be given a lift by anyone passing on wheels. Everything was well managed and self-supporting. All teachers in brigade schools were locals, and all earned unsubsidized work-point incomes. But all were guaranteed a fixed portion in cash each year, which could not necessarily be done for all households. In lieu of tuition, students worked at most one day per week on land allocated for that purpose, with all profits returned to the school. School buildings were the strongest and sturdiest in the brigades, with all the necessary furnishings and fittings. Peasants still lived in thatched-roof houses here, but their schools were all red brick and tile. Guan did not know how much state money might have gone into the system initially, and he knew of no "overseas" contributions comparable to those in Fujian. From what he could see and calculate, all recurrent expenditures, including teachers' pay, were borne locally.

Guan also did not know how old the elementary schools were. But the expansion of secondary schooling, following directives from Beijing, coincided with his arrival in the commune and culminated with the opening of the new commune middle school in 1974. He was not allowed to join the new school as a teacher, however, until he had completed a half-year refresher course at the local teacher training school in town. Everywhere else, even much larger communes, began their new middle schools with only a few hundred students. Here the new school serving only this one commune opened with 800 students at the junior level, transferred in from the brigade classes, and 100 senior students. By 1976, the senior section had grown to 300.

The commune education officer's functions here were performed by a culture and education group (*wenjiaozu*). All three members were teacher training college graduates and were also actively involved in running the middle school. Each brigade school, too, was led by a three-person group composed of the brigade CCP secretary, a school leader, and a poor or lower-middle peasant representative. In Guan's brigade, the Party secretary was a sterling sort of incorruptible character, and the school's responsible person was a woman, the most senior of the seven teachers. The peasant representative, far from being illiterate, a common complaint elsewhere, was a junior middle graduate whose job was to manage the school's land and teach students how to cultivate it.

Guan's appreciation for the Koreans' differing assumptions grew gradually as he was inducted into their school system. He proceeded quite self-consciously in his analysis, distinguishing the Koreans on the one hand from resettled youth, younger students then in Shanghai schools, and ordinary Chinese peasants. Guan made periodic visits home to Shanghai, keeping up with developments there and swapping stories with his contemporaries teaching in communes elsewhere. He also noticed differences between the current crop of Korean students he was teaching and their elders. The Chinese, whoever they were, shared at least two assumptions which seemed alien to these Koreans. The assumptions concerned the practical utility of education as a means of self-promotion and the relation between quantity and quality. He concluded that the unusually smooth-working arrangements for school management in the region followed from these differing assumptions.

The quantity–quality dilemma was essentially nonexistent for the Koreans, who pursued both aims without any of the usual Chinese inhibitions. Commune schools retained the pre-1966 six-year curricula at both levels. But they gave open-book exams and did not follow the old promotion and punishment systems. All children entered elementary school, and all who began together usually graduated together. There were no repeaters or no dropouts, and girls still made up half the sixth-grade classes. A simple all-commune entrance exam ensured that everyone could continue on to junior middle school. In a neat twist, teachers there referred to the slower students as "the key-point section" and targeted them for special key-point tutoring (*zhongdian buxi*). Hence "quality" was not as good as in the pre-1966 key schools Guan had attended in Shanghai. Still, the Koreans were satisfied and felt the quality of their students was "not bad."

During the seven years he lived in his brigade, only two boys dropped out of school, from the junior middle level, creating something of a local scandal. The boys then joined the agricultural work force, but everyone "treated them like juvenile delinquents." Resettled youth, for their part, sympathized with them and thought all local students "very pitiful" because at the time, 1973, the senior middle school was not yet operating and so most could not continue their studies.

The outsiders could not understand why many more did not drop out and tended, like Teacher Liu, to regard education for such peasants as "useless." The resettled youth were always complaining (*falaosao*) about their own fate in these same terms, and the younger generation back home in Shanghai was no different. Because the promotion and punishment systems were broken, students just continued on from year to year and so did not study, because they did not have to. Then, whatever their grades, they had nothing to look forward to but a labor assignment, so study was doubly useless.

Such views were actually beginning to infect Korean students as well by the time Guan became a teacher in the mid-1970s. But the adults were always there to remonstrate. Guan recalled they had done the same to him when he lamented the loss of his college education and the consequent waste of all that had gone before. Whenever older Koreans heard such talk, they always countered with homilies about the general use of knowledge and reminded their own that emphasizing education was their custom. So young people carried on the tradition, explaining that everyone would "look down" on them if they did not.

The only discordant note in this tale as Guan remembered it was introduced by the resettled youth themselves, especially as morale deteriorated in the early 1970s. They knew their welcome had worn out when carters started passing them by on the road. The Koreans began recommending them in greater proportions than their own children for jobs in town when various work units came recruiting. As an extra precaution, the elders also fixed new rules: without a senior middle graduation certificate, no local youth could be recommended for nonagricultural jobs even in the commune-run factories. "They were," concluded Teacher Guan, "not at all like ordinary peasants."[24]

The beneficiaries

Calculating actual numbers of students in school was beyond the capability of most interviewees. The best that could be expected were estimates of age-group and dropout percentages by those who had themselves resided in a brigade or taught in a rural elementary school during the 1970s. Altogether 46 interviewees were in a position to venture such rough rule-of-thumb estimates, and only 6 estimated fewer than 90 percent of all children entering elementary school. Of those 6, 5 were from ethnic minority areas, and the other was a resettled youth who estimated about 80 percent for the brigade he left in 1973. In general, mobilization efforts really were not necessary to enroll most young-sters into the first grade. The problem was to keep everyone in class thereafter. Dropouts, with girls taking the lead, were commonly reported after two or three years of schooling. Sometimes such students would return and some-times not. The junior elementary expedient also seemed to have the same terminal effect as in earlier decades.

Interviewee estimates were therefore compatible with the official national figure (shown in Table 16.2) claiming 96 percent of the age-group in school, so long as that figure was interpreted to mean the numbers entering elementary school rather than completing it. The pre-1949 pattern of only a few years'

---

[24] Interview 83/JL/24, pp. 1–59. Teacher Guan's account of the Koreans' high cultural level is borne out by the 1982 national census, which showed them outperforming by far all others, including the majority Hans, on all the educational criteria measured, e.g., literacy and propor-tion of college graduates. See Zhang Tianlu, "Population Development and Changes of China's Minority Nationalities," in Li Chengrui et al., eds., *A Census of One Billion People* (Hong Kong: Economic Information and Agency, 1987), pp. 445–451.

Professor Chae-Jin Lee, in his survey of Korean minority education, adopted the conven-tional "10-year calamity" interpretation of the Cultural Revolution, focusing on the initial Red Guard violence, damage to quality, and enforced ethnic assimilation during the early 1970s, when Korean-language teaching and separate schooling were discouraged. See his *China's Ko-rean Minority: The Politics of Ethnic Education* (Boulder: Westview Press, 1986), pp. 88–95.

Confined as his experience was to the commune level, Teacher Guan did not try to comment on damage to quality elsewhere, i.e., in towns and at the local university. The language of instruction throughout his commune's school system was Korean, although a Chinese-language class was compulsory for all Korean students from the first grade onward. At the commune middle school, only about 20 percent of the students were Chinese. They were taught in separate classes and did not have to study Korean as a second language. Guan was assigned to teach math and he did so in Korean, but his command of the language was not adequate to allow him to teach other subjects, which required a more extensive vocabulary, or to serve as a head teacher. Most commune leaders were Korean as were all the middle school's leaders and a majority of its teachers. Relations between Korean and Chinese teachers were "alright," but Guan recalled friction between the two groups of students, although they always held meetings and sports events together. He recalled that although Han–Korean relations were not marred by serious conflict, the two did not entertain particularly flattering views of one another overall.

basic literacy training at the mass level was thus being reproduced, except that the numbers involved were vastly different from those shown, for example, in John Lossing Buck's rural survey from the 1930s. He had found that 45 percent of the males and 2 percent of the females received some schooling, with over 60 percent of those males averaging four years in a *sishu* only.[25]

Within commune schools

Trying to calculate whose children were benefiting most from the quantitative expansion was even more difficult. In the most generalized terms, interviewees reported a reversal of fortunes whereby new revolutionary local elites had replaced the old landlord–rich-peasant base. Especially, local cadres' offspring dominated commune and county-town secondary schools while the access of bad-class children was restricted, if not curtailed altogether.

Yet the realities surrounding this "new wine in old bottles" formula were never so simple even allowing for the usual exceptions and exemptions. The generalized picture could be elaborated on at least three dimensions: the flexible supply-and-demand principles governing school enrollment practices for bad-class students; the continuity represented by teachers themselves with their pre-1949 predecessors; and rapid upward mobility, of which brigade and team cadres, middle or poor peasants all, were the prime examples.

The flexible supply-and-demand principles governing access to rural schooling for children from the five problematic family categories (landlords, rich peasants, counterrevolutionaries, bad–criminal, rightist) were evident in most of the 37 commune and state farm schools for which interviewees could volunteer relevant firsthand observations. Accordingly, if the supply of school places was adequate, children from such families could attend; if not, they were likely to be excluded. Official policy promoted attendance by good-class youth disadvantaged in the old society. There were evidently no formal bans prohibiting school attendance for others: it just worked out that way in local practice. The conditions governing access for the places available also varied depending on (1) the severity of the parents' problem, (2) the student's own academic standing, and (3) family connections with the powers that be. All interviewees did not necessarily articulate these conditions in quite so straightforward a manner, but the individual local variations almost always conformed to these rules.

Because elementary schooling was universalized and the aim was to educate every child at that level, all children were admitted. No one reported even a

---

[25] Cited in chap. 4, n. 42, above. Definitions of achievement or basic literacy at this level have nevertheless long bedeviled debate. Hence these proportions could be used both to confirm and to refute the post-Mao proposition that there was very little improvement in China's school-age and adult literacy between 1949 and 1979. See, e.g., Vilma Seeberg, *Literacy in China: The Effect of the National Development Context and Policy on Literacy Levels, 1949–1979* (Bochum: Brockmeyer, 1990).

single contradictory case, although different kinds of discriminatory practices were noted. At the junior middle level, however, access was no longer automatic. Localities which reported universal or near universal schooling or enough seats to meet demand at that level also reported that family background was not in itself a condition for admission. By contrast, Teacher Yang's isolated school with far greater demand than it could meet refused to admit students with bad-class backgrounds, as did other schools in comparable circumstances.

Of the 26 interviewees who had some direct knowledge of admission practices at the senior level of their commune and state farm middle schools, 11 reported that students with problematic family backgrounds were usually not admitted, and 15 claimed they usually were, conditional upon their own grades, behavior, and the nature of the family situation. Given the drastic reduction of college student numbers in the early 1970s, these flexible principles would probably have meant virtually no bad-class enrollments at the tertiary level had a national ruling not stipulated that a certain small representation must be maintained.

Teachers and local cadres, on the other hand, represented studies in continuity and change as the dominant figures in local education. Rural schoolteachers in the 1970s were of diverse origins, with resettled and reassigned outsiders always in the minority. The rest included an assortment of locals such as the retrained *sishu* teachers; others of comparable vintage with some kind of modern small-town secondary schooling; dependents of people returned to their native villages due to political problems; wives of state-salaried teachers assigned to the new commune schools; wives of army men stationed in each county's garrison unit; and younger recent graduates from local schools. These teachers, together with the commune's medical personnel, were the best educated people in a commune and referred to themselves together as the only resident intellectuals. Nor was the basic dividing line within this group between state salaried and locally hired enough to erase altogether the distinction between them and everyone else.

Typically, the main commune seat school complex would be staffed primarily by state-salaried teachers, and the brigade schools primarily by *minban* teachers plus perhaps one or two better-educated, salaried "backbone elements." When brigade schools had such *gongban* teachers, they would usually be the brigade's sole salaried income earners. But whatever their status and whether first generation educated or not, none would allow their own children to sink back into illiteracy. Hence their children began moving through the commune school system.

Top commune-level leaders, including the commune Communist Party secretaries and their deputies, were subject to frequent transfer around the county and usually maintained their families elsewhere, if not in the county town then in their own home villages. But just beneath these leaders were a large number of functionaries whose families were typically commune residents. Such people's children also began moving through the commune school systems.

According to official figures, each commune had on the average only 20 "state-salaried employees" in the late 1970s.[26] But definitions varied as to what constituted commune-level state-salaried employees or "cadres." If the term was taken in its broadest sense as interviewees used it to distinguish among their students' family backgrounds, a considerably larger number fell into the category of "commune cadre," or cadres resident in communes. In formal usage, teachers and doctors, too, were state cadres, being duly ranked and salaried. But in defining the local universe in which they had lived, interviewees quite consistently referred to teachers and doctors as "intellectuals," which they distinguished in turn from cadres and from ordinary peasants who earned their livelihood through manual labor.

Following informal everyday usage, then, "commune cadre" was a catchall category for everyone besides teachers and doctors earning a state salary whose occupation was not based on manual labor. Commune enterprises and services sometimes did hire salaried workers (*gongren*). But these were never confused with accountants, clerks, and other low-ranking functionaries, who were always referred to as "cadres," since their jobs did not entail manual labor.

Commune cadre ranks therefore included a commune's leadership personnel, its Communist Party secretary and deputies, varying numbers of cadres with specific responsibility for economics, education, culture, health, etc.; the militia (*wuzhuang*) head, his communications officer, and the police (*gongan*) chief; enterprise managers; heads of tractor and power stations; those in charge of storehouses, marketing, grain processing, the movie team, the wired broadcasting network; employees of county services with local branches such as the bank and post office; and the heads of mass organizations, especially the Women's Association and the Youth League. Applying this definition, only in small communes with populations under 10,000, maintaining few non-agricultural enterprises, and with few county branch services were there no more than 20 "state-salaried employees." In larger communes with a full range of production units and services, the number of such cadres was several times greater.

Finally, between the commune-level cadres and ordinary commune members were the production brigade and team cadres. At the brigade level, those responsible for administration and production included the Party secretary and brigade chief plus their deputies, a women's cadre, militia head, security cadres, poor and lower-middle peasant representative, etc. Production team leaders numbered seven or eight per team (e.g., head, deputy, accountant, cashier, security, women's representative, poor peasant representative). These

---

[26] *China: Socialist Economic Development*, 2:37.

brigade and team leaders, or basic-level rural cadres (*nongcun jiceng ganbu*), all earned work points, and most continued to participate in agricultural labor.[27]

In the eyes of outsiders, these basic-level leaders did not deserve the designation "cadre," although they were referred to locally as such since their responsibilities and positions set them apart even if their means of remuneration did not. But only a minority would actually be CCP members, and most would have had minimal formal schooling. However much a locality might have tinkered with its class designations, these basic-level leaders were virtually all from families which had been middle or poor peasants at the time of land reform. Certainly, they had not been landlords and rich peasants, whose families had the most education in a rural locale. Interviewees moreover attested to the low literacy level of such leaders because teachers and resettled youth were regularly called upon to double as readers and writers of documents for local cadres. As part of their responsibilities, however, all were expected to set an example by sending their children to school, and by all accounts they did.

Thus, even within the microcosm of a village school at the heart of Mao's education revolution, there was being reproduced quite naturally the same association of interests between old educated and new political elites that had emerged most prominently in the key-school development of the 1960s. Such, in any case, was the image of village schools that interviewees drew in discussing whose children performed better or worse academically and whose children were most likely to proceed upward through the new commune school systems. These are not very satisfactory means of determining who benefited most from all the new schools, but they were among the few relevant and quantifiable questions that could be used given the nature of the interview accounts.

Interviewees actually had very strong opinions about such matters. According to the most frequently cited views: children of educated parents did best academically, along with those from economically secure families, relative security being seen as a necessary, if not sufficient, condition for intellectual achievement. Bad-class children performed well out of necessity, unless they lived in a locale that shut them out entirely, in which case they just gave up. The children of illiterate and impoverished parents, and agricultural laborers generally, were least successful as students. Cadres' children tended to flaunt their parents' positions and did not necessarily make the best students, because they knew their futures depended more on their parents' connections than on their own academic achievements. On the other hand, some cadre parents "who had no education themselves" were inclined to imitate intellectual lifestyles by making "special demands" on their children, forcing them to study, requesting extra tutorials for them, and so on.

[27] For a fuller outline of commune organizational structure, see John P. Burns, *Political Participation in Rural China* (Berkeley: University of California Press, 1988), pp. 43–56.

Tables 16.8 and 16.9 attempt a more systematic presentation of such recollections, and in assessing these tables, the basic proportions of a commune's political, administrative, and intellectual establishment should be kept in mind. The example is a rural south Fujian commune of 25,000 people with a senior middle school capping a full commune network, plus a good assortment of enterprises and sidelines. Using the broadest possible definitions, its work-point team and brigade cadres numbered at least 1,500 and its salaried commune-level personnel of all ranks and responsibilities (cadres) totaled 100 more or less. Additionally, teachers numbered about 130, with slightly more locally hired than salaried.[28]

According to interviewees, most cadres and teachers whose families resided within the commune sent their children to its schools once these were established. Only the top few commune leaders did not, since they usually maintained their families somewhere else. But conversely, each commune was also likely to be the native place of other people's cadres. Such families were a common feature of any local population, often with the cadre father working outside the commune while wife and children maintained an "agricultural household" within. The children were always calculated and considered by interviewees as cadres', rather than peasants', offspring, regardless of their immediate guardian's formal designation. The families of state-salaried teachers also sometimes resided elsewhere. This was especially true of those transferred down in the late 1960s. But the locals also might not be native to the commune, and their children might be living with grandparents or relatives in the hometown or native village.

Table 16.8 records the few best and worst students in terms of academic performance only, for whom interviewees could also recall the family particulars, in classes interviewees had themselves taught. The results suggest a further elaboration of their generalized opinions. The children of ordinary farm laborers do turn up in the worst position, and virtually no intellectual children can be found there. But in assessing the best, ordinary farm laborers' children appear in quite respectable proportions, and interviewees were able to recall further that some of these students were first generation formally educated, as were some of the local cadres' children. Also surprising was the strong showing of state-salaried cadres' children, who did far better than their intellectual-background classmates. The former stand out, especially considering that there

---

[28] As a rough guide, this commune probably had an above average number of state-salaried personnel due to its many enterprises and an above average number of *gongban* teachers due to the relatively well educated south Fujian population. Otherwise, the overall proportion of teachers to cadres was about standard. Additionally, each of the commune's 14 brigades had two or three barefoot doctors or health workers, but the size of the commune clinic staff was not known. By contrast, a small Shaanxi commune with about 5,000 people could boast perhaps 20 state-salaried cadres. But the total commune teaching contingent in the mid-1970s, with no senior middle section, numbered 70 (15 salaried and 55 *minban*).

Table 16.8. *Academic performance of rural (commune and state farm) students by relevant family background*

	Agricultural work-point income (main income earner, immediate family)				Nonagricultural salaried (at least one immediate family member)				
	Problematic past	Manual laborer: worker, peasant	Local cadre: team, brigade	*Minban* teacher, barefoot doctor	Teacher, doctor	State cadre	Worker	Service trades	Problematic past
The "best," or top 10%, of the class	3	27 (8 f)	9 (2 f)	1	7 (2 f)	25 (12 f)	5 (2 f)	1	5 (3 f)
The "worst" students, drop-outs, etc.	4 (1 f)	39 (10 f)	2 (1 f)	1	—	9 (2 f)	5	1 (f)	—

Sources: The recollections of 17 interviewee teachers from 14 commune and 3 state farm schools (including 6 elementary and 11 secondary). By province: GD, 2; FJ, 1; JS, 2; AH, 2; YN, 4; SX, 1; GS, 1; XJ, 1; JL, 1; HLJ, 2 (see Appendix for provincial abbreviations). All but 3 of the 17 teachers were outsiders, transplanted from big cities.

Note: f = females among total number. Family background categories used in the tables derive from the standard mix of class, occupations, and political labels used officially to differentiate Chinese citizens during the first three decades of CCP rule. Those most commonly affecting the lives of students and educators have been introduced in earlier chapters. These tables, however, reflect the more specific application of the standard red, white, and middling categories to rural life. Thus, for almost every formal category, rural designations were further complicated by the two different forms of ownership (state and collective) and their respective methods of remuneration. Family circumstances were differentiated not only by the conventional class/occupation/political categories but also by the position of members on either side of the economic dividing line. State-salaried personnel – regardless of occupation, political standing, CCP membership, or administrative rank – were seen as the beneficiaries of higher incomes and living standards. Hence the conventional categories were always further divided into two: commune state-salaried cadres or local work-point brigade and team cadres; salaried or *minban* teachers; regular commune clinic doctors or village barefoot health workers (as illustrated on the tables). These tables, in other words, use categories that seemed most relevant, as described by interviewees, in differentiating students' actual family circumstances rather than in recording either their own or their parents' formal class status. Further on the categories:

452

"Poor and lower-middle peasant" was the officially favored rural red class during the Cultural Revolution years. This class designation overlapped with occupational categories, including both agricultural laborer and local cadre. But class designation referred to how the family earned its living at the time of land reform. The others indicated whether the family still lived mainly by the sweat of its collective brow or whether it had at least one adult member supplementing the family's labors in some other way, e.g., as a local cadre. A common condition of such local cadre families was their "mixed" nature, with some members still engaged primarily in agricultural labor but benefiting economically and in other ways from the upward mobility of an immediate relative who might or might not also continue to engage in part-time agricultural labor. Hence, the formal class designation does not appear on the tables in deference to the more immediately relevant occupational status.

CCP membership usually overlapped with cadre status but was almost never identified as a separate category by interviewees. In rural areas, production brigade leaders were typically Party members, but the lower-level team leaders were not necessarily. All of these are nevertheless calculated together as "local cadres," which was the chief mark of distinction rather than Party membership itself. Similarly, "commune cadres" could be divided into leadership (also CCP members) and administrative or managerial staff (not necessarily Party members). Even the commune's culture and education cadre(s) might not be Party members. But all were state salaried, the most basic mark of distinction in local eyes. The category "state cadre" as used here therefore refers to all such commune employees, including both leadership (e.g., the commune Party secretary) and administrative (the head of the tractor station). "Salaried worker" refers to the ordinary worker in the tractor station or perhaps a worker in a nearby state-owned mining operation that had recruited locally. In a commune setting, families with one state-salaried member, whether worker or cadre, might also have some members (often the wife) still earning work points for agricultural labor performed. Such families are classified here as being from cadre or worker families rather than ordinary peasant households. On the other hand, interviewees were also inclined to identify a near relation as being of cadre status in cases where the parents were not and the relative was known to have facilitated a student's access to schooling. Such a relative, even though "relevant," does not figure on the tables, which record only the main income earner of the immediate family.

Members of the old exploiting classes could also be further distinguished by their current occupational status. Thus, members of landlord and rich-peasant families, long since expropriated but still resident in the village, worked its lands along with everyone else and may have actually lived as poor agricultural laborers while continuing to suffer various forms of discrimination due to the class label. By contrast, other members of the same families no longer resident in their native villages could claim current status as teachers, doctors, or whatever, and sometimes even successfully obscured their origins. In any case, "problematic past" as used here refers to all those with formal bad-category labels (landlord, rich peasant, counterrevolutionary, bad-criminal, rightist) whose bearers and their families were consequently subjected to discrimination whatever their occupations. A person in this category might actually be a teacher, cadre, worker, etc., but would not be recorded as such on the table. No one is recorded more than once. Intellectuals per se did not fall into the problematic categories and are not calculated as such here, nor were they so described by interviewees. Overseas Chinese were sometimes stigmatized as a separate group during the 1970s and are therefore recorded on the tables as described.

453

Table 16.9. *Student classroom cadres by relevant family background (county town, commune, state farm)*

	Agricultural work-point income (main income earner, immediate family)				Nonagricultural salaried (at least one immediate family member)				
Problematic past	Manual laborer: worker, peasant	Local cadre: team, brigade	*Minban* teacher, barefoot doctor		Teacher, doctor	State cadre	Worker	Service trades	Problematic past
1	5 (1 f)	11 (4 f)	1 (f)		1	17 (5 f)		2	2 (1 f)

Note: f = females among total number.

Sources: The recollections of 12 interviewee teachers from 13 schools: 2 county town, 9 commune, 2 state farm, including 5 elementary and 8 secondary schools. By province: FJ, 2; JS, 3; AH, 2; YN, 2; SN, 1; GS, 1; XJ, 1; JL, 1 (see Appendix for provincial abbreviations). All but 1 of the 12 teachers were outsiders, transplanted from big cities.

were usually more teachers and doctors of all kinds combined within a commune than state-salaried cadres (although probably more state-salaried cadres' families than those of state-salaried teachers alone).

Underscoring further the dominant role cadre children had assumed in the rural school milieu, one interviewee belatedly raised a strong opinion against the tendency of rural teachers to appoint such students as classroom cadres. He claimed the motive was to curry favor with their parents. In rural schools, each class might have only one or two student cadres, who would be nominated by the head teacher at least for the earliest grades. Varying degrees of democracy governed the selection thereafter as natural leaders developed among the students. Unfortunately, only the last group of 1983 interviewees could be asked this question, but the results (shown in Table 16.9) seem compatible with the assertion – except that none of those responding to the question agreed with the interviewee who raised it. Instead, they said that cadres' children tended to inherit (by observation and imitation) their parents' social skills or that classmates tended to defer to them automatically or that as head teachers they had selected students with the best grades whoever they were. Yet cadres' children seemed to have it all ways, whatever the motives for selection.

The conflicting answers to these questions seemed a subtle reflection of the interviewees' own unusual in-between role as conventional educators conscripted for service on the rural front lines. Received educators' wisdom told them that the children of educated parents must excel. Yet they had little choice but to begin inducting new generations of illiterate peasants into the world of learning. In the process, educators and cadres, as the resident basic-level intellectuals and power holders, inevitably reproduced the ancient community of interests in modern guise regardless of class backgrounds and political inclinations.

Study as the way out

Still, the "us" versus "them" stance of the revolutionary present, whereby intellectuals were usually "neither red nor white" and cadres usually all red, lingered close to the surface. If rural cadres and intellectuals out of necessity came together as creators and beneficiaries of the new commune school systems, they parted ways again soon thereafter over the new college enrollment procedures designed as the education revolution's ultimate means for intellectualizing workers and peasants. Interviewees uniformly portrayed cadres' children as the chief beneficiaries at this stage.

For resettled youth especially, this question evoked the bitterest memories. Socially disadvantaged they may have been in their rural assignments, but among interviewees most had still been able to anticipate college careers and were preparing for them via the competitive academic norms of the pre-1966 system. Now, they found themselves on alien turf in the early 1970s, when college enrollment resumed with new rules and a host of new competitors – educated rural youth – they knew to be their academic inferiors. There were few alternatives. The wait for a town job might be indefinite for resettled youth without family connections. Otherwise, there were only long visits home or worse, drifting into the aimless existence of an illegal returnee.

For rural youth, perhaps the greatest advantage of having a cadre father, no matter how low ranking, was the enhanced connections that came with such jobs. Favors done for others were regarded as an "investment" since they meant favors owed in return. But for most children, the most that could be arranged was a move from the hardest, most thankless agricultural labor to something easier. The easier jobs were those of *minban* teacher, barefoot doctor, work-point recorder, tractor driver, army recruit, brigade enterprise worker, and so on – the kinds of jobs that team and brigade leaders could arrange for their functionally literate children. Due to the absence of nonintellectuals or true peasants among interviewees, it seems unfair to let them answer for rural parents in explaining why they sent their children to school. Nevertheless, the most frequent response interviewees gave as to why rural youth continued their studies was the local expectation that extra years of schooling would qualify students for these marginally better rural jobs.

Actually leaving the agricultural world, however, meant changing one's household registration from rural to urban, moving to salaries from work points, and becoming a consumer of commercial, rather than self-sufficiency, grain. Such opportunities were few and far between in the 1970s. Sometimes state-owned mining operations would recruit a small proportion of workers locally, and commune enterprises would have a few salaried workers' jobs as well. A stint in the army was also usually rewarded with salaried or at least nonagricultural work after demobilization. But moving into a cadre slot was a rare privilege, and for young people especially, there was only one way: going to college or a specialized middle school. Students in both, regardless of their origins, moved into the ranks of state cadres (*guojia ganbu*) upon graduation, complete with salaried incomes and urban household registrations. Nor did the Cultural Revolution seriously challenge this route out despite all the efforts aimed at devaluing a college education and changing methods of access to it.

In such an environment, the question of who benefited from the new college enrollment procedures assumed an intensity which rendered all but irrelevant idealistic notions about intellectualizing peasants and ruralizing intellectuals. And within this environment, the added dimension that emerged from the interview accounts was, once again, not so much who benefited as who was seen to benefit. A key consideration in this respect was who made what decision, and the greatest power lay always with the local cadres.

The college enrollment plans were still drawn up nationally and by province as before, with all the time-honored principles of population balance, needs, and equity built in. Hence Teacher Liu's 1973–1974 notebook contained the following entry from an all-commune meeting in June 1973. According to the plan, Anhui would enroll a total of 5,600 first-year college students in the fall of 1973, including 3,600 who would attend institutions within the province and 2,000 who would attend institutions in other provinces. Additionally, about 10,000 Anhui students would be enrolled in specialized secondary schools (*zhongzhuan*).

Up to this point, the plan was the same as before. But now it also specified quite precisely the numbers of both local youth and resettled outsiders in Anhui and the numbers of each down to the county level. His own county's quotas were 51 college students (one-third of whom had to be resettled outsiders, reflecting their relatively large numbers within the county) and 116 for specialized middle schools (two-thirds of whom had to be resettled youth). The county enrollment committee, led by the county's government and education bureau, then divided up the quota between town and communes. Because of its low educational level, Liu's commune was allocated only a handful of seats. The commune was instructed to recommend to the county no more than two to three times the number of places allocated. And herein lay the greatest difference. With the national unified college entrance exams abolished, the communes and brigades themselves would nominate the candidates.

The commune meeting had actually continued for three days with all teachers and brigade leaders present, since they would be responsible for preliminary selection. Candidates had to be at least junior middle school graduates, unmarried, about 20 years of age, with a good two-year labor record. The last was an especially sensitive point since the "absenteeism" of resettled youth was a common problem. Women had to be selected as well as men, but no quotas were recommended. The labor records of bad-class applicants had to be formally verified by brigade leaders in a manner not required for others. Finally, mass meetings must be called at both team and brigade levels, with minutes recorded, to allow the masses to raise opinions publicly concerning all applicants. Given the requirements, teachers and cadres were advised that the commune had approximately 500 potential candidates, about equally divided between resettled outsiders and local junior middle graduates.

Teacher Liu could only speak for his own brigade, but he recalled that they had done it by the book, with team meetings to evaluate each applicant, where he himself recorded the minutes. Ultimately, the commune sent up about 20 names for its college quota; candidates gathered in the county town for a simple written and oral exam; colleges and universities assigned to provide the county's 51 seats as part of the prearranged plan sent their inspectors down to look the candidates over; and the commune's quota of 6 or 7 seats was finally filled.[29]

Such were the textbook procedures designed to fulfill the education revolution's aims. Candidates entered college as "worker–peasant–soldier" students, a new designation coined to mark the merger of mental and manual labor while blurring the urban–rural distinction. Resettled youth upon entering college were thereafter referred to as members of the first generation of peasant students to enter university, a claim that obscured both their own origins and the "real" peasants that were also among them.

These new college enrollment rules, impinging as they did on the professional educators' most sacrosanct domain, returned interviewees to the "worst of times" perspective. Their negative opinions were manifold: the junior middle academic level of the candidates made a travesty of college education; the procedures were open to flagrant abuse; brigade and commune cadres were the chief arbiters of what should have been a professional decision; political activism and labor skills counted more than academic achievement; cadres' children were the chief beneficiaries.

For every textbook operation such as Liu recounted, there was one just the opposite with stories about corruption and influence peddling of all kinds at all levels. Nor was there any apparent correlation between localities that had mastered the art of mass schooling and those with well-managed college admissions procedures. Seemingly a land of extremes in all seasons, the best and worst stories came from the Fujian coast. Its commitment to schooling proved no safeguard against corruption, factional rivalries, and violent clan feuds, all of which intruded into the selection process once the competitive discipline of the unified examinations was removed.

Perhaps most striking, however, was the contrast between the two Anhui communes of Teachers Liu and Wan. Thus, the same people responsible for the textbook operation in 1973 were, in Liu's eyes, also to blame for the commune's poorly led, underfinanced, and dilapidated schools. But only a few counties distant, the same cadres who tended the commune system Teacher Wan so admired presided over one of the least "democratic" operations described anywhere.

In Wan's commune, the process was "internal" and secret, with no public announcement of quotas, requirements, or procedures. Mass meetings were called only after brigade leaders had selected the candidates, to rubber-stamp their decisions. About 1975, an examination was included, but its purpose was never explained since only brigade nominees took it and all went on to college afterward. The cadres ran a tight ship, to be sure, but they also controlled everything within it. Nor were they immune from the cargo cult practices most

[29] Interview 83/AH/22, pp. 77–84.

commonly reported among youth from Shanghai, famous for its well-stocked shops and manufactured goods. In Wan's commune, the cadres traded favors, including college nominations, not for personal gifts but for hard-to-procure production equipment and supplies.[30]

Even worse was Teacher Shao's confession from Zhejiang, where he revealed that school construction materials were not the only things bartered and begged with a present here and a favor there. So well versed in these arts was young Shao that ordinary commune members came to know of his selection for a two-year course at Hangzhou University only after he had begun his studies there. He had resorted to this method after discovering the whereabouts of others who had similarly disappeared before him. With the help of a family friend, he learned how it was all arranged by brigade and commune leaders among themselves entirely in secret. With the help of the same friend, he also learned when the next quotas came down and built up his connections (*guanxi*) accordingly.[31]

Yet whether the selection was open, secret, or corrupt, on one point there was near universal agreement: the overriding power of local cadres in the process. College enrollment inspectors had final say. Sometimes they went beyond reading the candidates' files prepared by the county and traveled down to the commune seat for face-to-face interviews. But by that time, as in Liu's commune, some 500 potential candidates had been reduced to only 20, and it was almost always the brigade and commune leaders or some combination thereof who narrowed the numbers from a mass of recommended names to the manageable few. In only one case of all the many recounted did a brigade's mass meetings alone actually select the students sent to college in its name.[32]

Once again, however, the generally articulated theme took on added dimensions when interviewees were asked to recall the particulars of individuals who had actually gone to college. As shown on Tables 16.10 and 16.11, resettled youth were well represented. And of all the different abuses reported, no one ever mentioned local cadres usurping resettled-youth quotas. These were always issued separately and apparently filled separately as well. Nor was it true that resettled youth, who all entered college as worker–peasant–soldier students, usurped the new-won opportunities of rural youth. Among the latter alone, as shown on Table 16.12, cadres' children did appear as the main beneficiaries. Yet ordinary peasants' children were also well represented as they continued their unheralded passage through the new school systems. Finally, whether the success of cadres' children was due solely to favors and favoritism, or to some other combination of factors which might also explain their showing on Tables 16.8 and 16.9, and after the Cultural Revolution as well (compare Table 16.14), was a question easier debated than answered.

[30] Interview 83/AH/8, pp. 100–107.
[31] Interview 83/ZJ/16, pp. 65–67.
[32] Interview 82/FJ/3, pp. 62–71.

Table 16.10. *Urban resettled (xiaxiang) and rural educated (huixiang)*
youth from communes and state farms going on to college and specialized
secondary schools, 1969–1976

	Male	Female	Destination	
			College	Specialized secondary
City and county-town resettled youth (386)	39	44	151	30
Rural educated youth (235)	105	38	185	36

Source: Recollections of 41 interviewees; firsthand knowledge of successful candidates selected from communes and state farms while interviewees were themselves resident there. Interviewees often knew that a given number had gone away to study without knowing all the particulars, which accounts for the different sets of numbers for sex, destinations, and overall totals on Tables 16.10 and 16.11. The reference is to "regular" (for that time) two- or three-year college courses, but not including short refresher courses, political study, etc.

Table 16.11. *Destinations of college students: urban resettled (xiaxiang) and*
rural educated (huixiang) youth by college level, 1969–1976

Destination	Resettled	Rural
National universities	25	21
Provincial colleges	78	83
Junior colleges (*dazhuan*)	1	11

Source: Recollections of 40 interviewees; firsthand knowledge of college destinations of successful candidates from communes and state farms while interviewees were themselves resident there. Interviewees often knew that a given number had gone away to study without knowing all the particulars, which accounts for the different sets of numbers for sex, destinations, and overall totals on Tables 16.10 and 16.11. The reference is to "regular" (for that time) two- or three-year college courses, but not including short refresher courses, political study, etc.

Among the successful candidates whose family particulars the interviewees knew personally were cadres' children whose parents had refused to help them and cadres' children who really had been recommended by the masses for being conscientious in study and labor. This was also the question that had genuinely angered loyalist Teacher Liao. He readily admitted showing special concern for his brigade secretary's children because he admired the father's leadership, identified with his poor-peasant origins, was proud of the boys'

Table 16.12. *Rural (huixiang) college students by relevant family background, 1969–1976*

Agricultural work-point incomes (main income earner, immediate family)					Nonagricultural salaried (at least one member, immediate family)					
Prob. past[a]	Middling[b]	Man. lab.: worker, peasant[c]	Local cadre: team, brigade	Minban teacher, barefoot doctor	Teacher, doctor	State cadre	Worker	Middling[d]	Prob. past[a]	Overseas Chinese
2	6	45	31	—	1	23	5	1	1	1

[a] Problematic pasts: "hidden" landlord, 1; rich peasant, 1; rightist brother, 1.

[b] Middling, agricultural: middle-peasant class but laborer by occupation, 4; rural sideline laborers, 2. The rural sideline trades (e.g., carpentry, stonemason, bricklayer, metalworker, plasterer), although part of the agricultural collective, were inherently difficult to control due to their itinerant nature. Sideline artisans thus sometimes found themselves in trouble as the "tails of capitalism."

[c] Ordinary work-point laborers were usually poor or lower-middle peasants by class designation.

[d] Middling, nonagricultural: services, e.g., barber, mortician, stockbreeders, small merchants, peddlers, "entrepreneurs." Such people in a rural setting obviously overlapped with the rural sideline laborers and worked in varying degrees of detachment from the collective.

Source: Recollections of 36 interviewees; firsthand knowledge of family particulars of rural educated youth selected to attend college from communes while interviewees were themselves resident there; plus, similar firsthand knowledge of two classrooms of college students. The reference is to regular (for that time) two- or three-year college courses, not including short refresher courses, political study, etc.

progress as the first generation formally educated, and prouder still when they entered college after the national entrance examinations were restored in the late 1970s.

Others pointed out that basic-level cadres strengthened their children's prospects in more subtle ways, for example, by easing them into the *minban* teacher and barefoot doctor jobs. Eligibility was thus enhanced through practical experience in two specialties for which rural areas were always allocated a greater proportion of college seats (see Table 16.13 on candidates' own work experience).

Ultimately, however, most who discussed the question of cadre preeminence were content to leave it be, convinced at least that an age-old association was reproducing itself even in this most unlikely of circumstances. The CCP's early generations of village leaders were obviously learning, as many first-generation political establishments had before them, how to use their new power to enhance family prospects through the schooling of their children while changing the nature of their political and social status in the process. Except that now, for the first time, that process had also to a certain extent been transformed by its extension down to the village level in every rural community throughout the land. And the absence of teachers' children among rural college students served to highlight the nature of that transformation.

Interviewees replied uniformly that there were no bans against intellectuals' children per se at any level. Nor did interviewees provide any examples of rural teachers' children denied access to school or college because of their parents' occupation. Yet such children appeared in plausible numbers only once the unified college entrance examinations were restored (compare Tables 16.12 and 16.14). Interviewees offered a cluster of indirect explanations. Like intellectuals generally, rural teachers' families too were more likely to be those with problematic pasts. Hence the added political constraints of the Cultural Revolution era combined against them. Also, even without a political handicap, their children were at a disadvantage when competing against positively "red" cadre and laboring-peasant youth with competitive academic credentials. This resulted inevitably from the requirements and procedures: when corrupted, these gave cadres' children the advantage of their parents' connections, but when not, they emphasized political activism and labor ability.

Labor especially was said to be the chief component of the rural candidate's own "behavior" criterion and a key consideration whenever rural mass opinion was consulted, which it often was. But even *minban* teachers' children were thereby placed at a disadvantage since an educated family, according to interviewees, was more likely to emphasize intellectual pursuits to the neglect of labor skills in all aspects of life, including the upbringing of its children. Salaried teachers, by definition those with more formal education, were even more separated from rural life in this respect, and the distance always seemed

Table 16.13. *Rural (huixiang) college students by their own qualifications, 1969–1976*

			Individual's Own Occupation				
State cadre	Local cadre[a]	Minban teacher, barefoot doctor	Service trades, shop clerk	Factory work	Agric. labor	Demob. army	None[b]
5	19	29	3	2	17	5	4

Formal Educational Level		
Elementary	Jr. middle[c]	Sr. middle[c]
4	32	65

[a] Local work-point cadre jobs, e.g., militia member, stenographer, accountant.

[b] There were scattered reports throughout the period of individuals in certain fields, especially foreign languages and the performing arts, still going directly to college without doing any manual labor. The four such individuals shown here were all from 1976, after a new rule authorizing more exemptions was issued.

[c] Not necessarily graduates.

Source: Recollections of 30 interviewees; firsthand knowledge of qualifications of rural educated youth selected to attend college from communes while interviewees were themselves living there.

Table 16.14. *Rural youth admitted to college by relevant family background 1977–1982 (65 males, 25 females)*

Agricultural work-point incomes (main income earner, immediate family)					Nonagricultural salaried (at least one member, immediate family)					
Prob. past[a]	Middle peasant[b]	Man. lab.: worker, peasant	Local cadre: team, brigade	*Minban* teacher, barefoot doctor	Teacher, doctor	State cadre	Worker	Middling	Prob. past old and new[c]	Overseas Chinese
5	7	17	9	2	10	36	9	1	5	5

[a] Problematic past, agricultural: includes three with teacher or doctor parents.

[b] For an explanation of the relevant class designations, see Table 16.8.

[c] "New" problematic past refers to individuals whose admission to college was temporarily suspended pending investigation of parents, as a new generation of "reds" became "black" overnight after 1976. The five listed include three old and two new.

Source: Recollections of 23 interviewees; firsthand knowledge of family particulars for rural commune youth who were admitted to regular college courses after the national unified entrance examinations were restored in 1977.

to be passed on to their children as well. Interviewees argued quite insistently that even if all other class and political factors could be neutralized, once labor was introduced as a major criterion, teachers' children became noncompetitive in a rural community. Evidently, it would take more than massive doses of extracurricular labor assignments and proletarian propaganda to obliterate the disparate inheritances that mental and manual laborers were still bequeathing to their children.

17

The Cultural Revolution negated

Local cadres and educators worked to fulfill the terms of their new revolutionary contract, but the contract itself was far from static. School growth and all the details of daily management proceeded, especially in rural communities, with a routine logic belying both the 1966–1968 explosion itself and the continuing turbulence within the Beijing center. The mass movement may have achieved its purpose in creating a new political leadership and a new agenda of revolutionary policy objectives. But no sooner did the new order begin to take shape than the "forces of opposition" it was intended to replace also began to regroup as the sequential laws of the mass movement proceeded through its consolidation phase.

Ensuing controversies in the early 1970s were portrayed officially as part of the "two-line struggle," which was now a contest between the victorious Maoist mainstream and remnants of a defeated enemy. Overall, the struggle was registered in the manner of an ongoing series of post-1968 aftershocks, still radiating outward from Beijing but in a circle of ever diminishing intensity which might pass with barely a tremor through entire counties.

At the time, observers were inclined to dismiss the ongoing campaigns and controversies as symptoms of some unprincipled power play. Certainly, no one could believe the shrill charges that there were still enemies within the CCP bent on "walking the capitalist road." In retrospect, of course, the polemics of the early 1970s anticipated the beginning of the revolutionary end far more accurately than anyone knew. Still, it was only in death that Mao finally lost command of the mass movement. Then, for the first time in his revolutionary career, the defeated enemy rose up to overturn his verdict and change the rules of the game.

The "two-line struggle" on the education front

Education remained at the forefront of this power play, serving, in Zhang Chunqiao's words, as the "barometer" of class struggle overall.[1] During those

---

[1] Zhongyang jiaoyu kexue yanjiusuo, ed., *Zhonghua renmin gongheguo jiaoyu dashiji, 1949–1982* (Chronicle of Education in the People's Republic of China, 1949–1982) (Beijing: Jiaoyu kexue chubanshe, 1983), p. 487.

years it was possible to gauge the nature of the emerging internal opposition simply by following the controversies in this sector. Their "inner" history has yet to be revealed, but we need only note the main features here to conclude our story.

The education establishment's fortunes reached their lowest ebb between 1969 and 1971, but by 1975, it was poised on the threshold of a comeback victory. Symbolizing this progression, all Education Ministry personnel, totaling some 1,200 people, were sent down en masse to its May Seventh Cadre School located in the central heartland of Fengyang County, Chu Prefecture, Anhui. Everyone remained from October 1969 until 1971. Gradually over the next four years, people were returned to work and the school closed in 1975, the same year that the ministry was formally reestablished.[2]

Marking the first steps back, a new Science and Education Group (*kejiaozu*; hereafter, SEG) was created in 1970, under the central government State Council. The first class of worker–peasant–soldier college students, 42,000 strong, was enrolled that same year.[3] And the first national education work conference met for three months in mid-1971, coinciding with the onset of a return "from the field" for ministry personnel and college faculties generally. The aim of the conference was not to promote a return to the status quo ante but to institutionalize the experiments under way since 1968. Led by Zhang Chunqiao and Chi Qun, the conference reaffirmed the Cultural Revolution's legacy in a formula endorsed by Mao himself. Known as the "two assessments," this formula defined the first 17 years of education work (1949–1966) as being bourgeois dominated and decreed that the great majority of intellectuals were capitalist in their world outlook. The latter point formally established Mao's "internal" conclusions of 15 years previously.[4]

The struggle seemed to develop quite naturally, in trial-and-error fashion, with participants not very much clearer than observers as to where the limits of the new revolutionary order would be drawn. Nevertheless, two basic variations were evident: one occurring within the spirit of central guidelines and

---

[2] Ibid., pp. 428, 472.

[3] Ouyang Zhang, ed., *Chengren jiaoyu dashiji, 1949–1986* (Chronicle of Adult Education, 1949–1986) (Beijing: Beijing chubanshe, 1987), p. 289. The SEG's new leaders were Li Siguang, Liu Xiyao, and Chi Qun. Li died in 1971, leaving Liu and Chi the leading responsible members of this group.

[4] Ibid., pp. 290–291. Interview 79/BJ/6, p. 11. "Quanguo jiaoyu gongzuo huiyi jiyao" (Summary of the National Education Work Conference), 27 July 1971, in Yuan Zhenguo, ed., *Zhongguo dangdai jiaoyu sichao, 1949–1989* (Trends of Thought in Contemporary Chinese Education, 1949–1989) (Shanghai: Sanlian shudian chubanshe, 1991), pp. 227–236. Central Party leader Zhang Chunqiao, responsible for culture and art within the Cultural Revolution Small Group, seemed to inherit the ailing Kang Sheng's mantle as ranking promoter of radical education causes. That role was taken up in turn by Mao's wife, Jiang Qing, during the 1973–1976 campaigns against retrogression. Within the SEG itself, Chi Qun was the leading cultural revolutionary until 1976. A military man, he was also chairman of Qinghua University's Revolutionary Committee in the early 1970s.

one beyond, while pressure to extend their limits continued throughout. The main pressure points derived from the tertiary level. According to interviewees, permission was sought and received from the SEG to exempt a few students in a few fields (e.g., foreign languages, sports, the performing arts) from the manual labor prerequisite for college admission. Scattered accounts suggest that individual schools worked out their own arrangements, but that the practice remained dependent on local political protection until more exemptions were formally authorized by the newly restored Education Ministry in 1975.[5]

The new college students' "uneven" quality served as another pretext for compromise. Tertiary-level educators sought and received permission from the SEG in 1972 to add half a year of remedial training to the shortened courses.[6] Also that year, Premier Zhou Enlai lent his name to the pressure for qualitative improvement by endorsing the opinion of Chinese American Nobel Laureate Yang Zhenning on strengthening theoretical study and scientific research. Zhou also personally recommended this opinion to the vice-chairman of Beijing University, Zhou Peiyuan, whose argument for higher standards was accorded prominent press coverage.[7] And in mid-1973, according to interviewees, "the center" (presumably the SEG) instructed that locally administered examinations should be used to assess candidates' educational levels for college admission.

These 1972–1973 developments in higher education seemed to be hastened by the disappearance of Lin Biao, Mao's anointed successor, in September 1971, followed by the rehabilitation of the Cultural Revolution's penultimate target, Deng Xiaoping. Liu Shaoqi had died in the interim, but Deng returned as vice-premier of the State Council in March 1973. Yet Deng's return also seemed entirely compatible with the "implementation of policy" (luoshi zhengce) under way since 1969, as cases were cleared paving the way for leading cadres and headmasters alike to resume work within the new Maoist-dominated order.

The demise of military chief Lin Biao also seemed unrelated to the gradual withdrawal of the military representatives from middle schools which was occurring about the same time, in the early 1970s. Interviewees uniformly interpreted the military withdrawal as a natural consequence of consolidation and as having no apparent link to Lin's disgrace. With the central authorization for

---

[5] Interviews: 77/HB/2, pp. 3–5; 78/GD/1, p. 8; 78/BJ/3, pp. 10–11; 79/BJ/2, p. 13; trip notes, Beijing Middle School Number 26, Oct. 1975.

[6] Chengren jiaoyu, p. 292.

[7] Jiaoyu dashiji, pp. 443–444. Yang Zhenning visited China during the summer (Renmin ribao, 2 July 1972), and Zhou Peiyuan's argument appeared in the fall (Guangming ribao, 6 Oct. 1972). See also Renmin ribao, 17 Sept. and 15 Oct. 1972, on raising the level of science and technology, and the teaching of basic knowledge and theory. Yang Zhenning was received by Mao the following summer (e.g., Renmin ribao and Liaoning ribao, both 18 July 1973).

college entrance examinations, however, radical arbiters decided that the limits of consolidation had been breached. In fact, they had taken up this gauntlet a few months earlier, about the same time the decision on examinations was being readied, and examinations per se were not the main cause for radical alarm.

A report from the SEG in May 1973 reviewed the internal debate in progress for "more than half a year" on how to evaluate Lin Biao. But his fall was being used as pretext (and, indeed, had probably been precipitated as a consolidation-phase stratagem) by Cultural Revolution opponents to regroup. Hence, the debate over how Lin should be judged had turned into a wide-ranging critique of the Cultural Revolution itself, including the low quality of education and of the worker–peasant–soldier college students, the excessive reform of intellectuals, and the two assessments from 1971. All were being reinterpreted by critics as part of Lin Biao's ultraleft legacy. The 1973 report officially rejected their arguments. Lin was then coupled with a most unlikely partner in the campaign to "criticize Lin Biao and Confucius" (*piLin, piKong*), deliberately rephrased to counter the challenge emerging from the "right."[8]

Going against the tide

Ultimately, the campaign had little to do with either Lin or Confucius. Arcane polemics used the dead not just as surrogates for power plays among the living but also to mobilize public opinion one last time in support of Mao's grand radical visions. Zhang Tiesheng became one of several pawns in this last-ditch struggle. His July letter of protest against the entrance examinations in 1973 was used to launch what would become the Cultural Revolution's last hurrah in a vain attempt to stem the "reverse current" (*hui chao*) rising around it.[9]

There followed a series of similar incidents on the education front, of young people protesting various points along the retreat back toward regularity. All were orchestrated with the same aim and for the same maximum publicity effect under the new Maoist call to "go against the tide" (*fan chaoliu*), meaning to oppose the tide of retrogression.[10] The slogan introduced in praise of Zhang Tiesheng was written into the CCP's new constitution and seemed designed to institutionalize, for post-mobilization-phase use in all sectors, the original 1966 rallying cry: "rebellion is justified." Students, workers, and the masses at large

---

[8] *Chengren jiaoyu*, p. 294; *Jiaoyu dashiji*, pp. 451, 460. The campaign to criticize Lin and Confucius together began during the latter half of 1973 and continued throughout 1974 (e.g., *Hongqi*, issues for 1973 and 1974).

[9] As a conscientious resettled youth who had remained at his work post, Zhang Tiesheng protested as unfair the new exam requirement, for which he was unprepared (originally in *Liaoning ribao*, 19 July 1973, and *Renmin ribao*, 10 Aug. 1973); see also *Renmin ribao*, 10, 22 Sept. 1973, 7 Jan. and 10 May 1974.

[10] The slogan was introduced in *Renmin ribao*, 16 Aug. 1973; see also ibid., 7 Nov. 1973.

were once again empowered to seize the initiative, but targets were now contained and confined to specific symptoms of restoration. Thus, following regularity's comeback under cover of consolidation in 1972–1973, rebellion revived in 1973–1974.

Suddenly, newspaper columns were filled with testimonials and copycat stories of students everywhere going against the tide. Besides the Zhang Tiesheng example, two others received maximum coverage and attention from the national education revolution leadership. Beijing student Huang Shuai became the elementary school heroine of the year, celebrated for daring to challenge the authority of her teacher. The SEG instructed all provincial education bureaus to organize teachers and students everywhere to study the Huang Shuai case materials.[11]

The Mazhenfu commune incident in Henan was similarly commended to the nation's schools for study. China's opening to the noncommunist outside world added a major new ingredient to the Cultural Revolution equation. The early 1970s brought the first American visitors since 1949, including President Richard Nixon of the U.S. Chinese students began to go abroad for the first time since 1966, and foreign students returned to China. Mao himself endorsed this strategic reopening to the West, and as an indicator of the new direction, Jiang Qing even told her life story to a young American scholar.[12] English became the foreign language of choice, and if a teacher was available to introduce the subject, schools everywhere tried to include it in their curricula.

The Mazhenfu commune junior middle school had such a course, and student Zhang Yuqin turned in a blank paper for her final exam in July 1973, just a few days after Zhang Tiesheng had done the same with his physics and chemistry questions on the college entrance examination in Liaoning. Zhang Yuqin also penned a rebellious note, declaring that she was Chinese and could be a good revolutionary without learning her ABC's. Publicly reprimanded at a school assembly, she committed suicide soon thereafter. Both the head teacher and school headmaster were then arrested, and the case was transformed into a national cause célèbre for the antirestorationist cause.[13] But the case also illustrated, as did Yang Zhenning's intervention, the clashing aims and values that would have to be mediated if the cultural revolutionaries really intended to interact on their own terms with the Western capitalist world.

Some defects among the "new things" (*xinsheng shiwu*) born of the Cultural

---

[11] E.g., ibid., 28 Dec. 1973; 12 Jan., 11, 13 Feb. and 14, 22 Apr. 1974.

[12] The U.S. Ping-Pong team and the Committee of Concerned Asian Scholars group visited China in 1971, and Nixon followed in 1972. Roxanne Witke's interviews with Jiang Qing took place during the summer of 1972 (Witke, *Comrade Chiang Ch'ing*). In 1972, 36 Chinese students were sent to England and France, the first such group to study abroad since 1966, and in 1973 China began receiving foreign students, also for the first time since 1966 (*Jiaoyu dashiji*, pp. 447, 452).

[13] *Jiaoyu dashiji*, pp. 460–461; *Renmin ribao*, 28 May 1974; *Henan ribao*, Zhengzhou, 19, 23 Feb., 2, 10 Mar., and 4 June 1974.

Revolution era were also targeted, as if to put the revolutionary house in order. Abuse of the new college enrollment procedures was subjected briefly to the glare of official publicity and condemnation with the Zhong Zhimin case. Student Zhong withdrew from Nanjing University after confessing that he had entered "through the backdoor" and his father's connections.[14]

A Fujian elementary school teacher, Li Qinglin, became famous after he wrote a protest letter to Chairman Mao. Li had complained that on his teacher's salary he could barely make ends meet, let alone continue to support a rusticated son who was unable to sustain himself through his agricultural labors. Mao sent a sympathetic reply, reportedly enclosing a sum of money as well to help out, and acknowledged that many such problems within the resettlement program were awaiting solution. Li's letter and Mao's response together with Zhang Tiesheng's protest and related commentaries were all included in the 1974 editions of middle school textbooks as living study materials on the correct political line.[15]

Interviewees recalled these going-against-the-tide personalities in the then official style of tapping revolutionary models among all generations. Huang Shuai represented children, and Zhang Tiesheng youth. Li Qinglin became the middle-aged activist and, like Zhang, threw himself into campaign activities, giving talks and interviews and traveling about rendering judgments against local examples of retrogression. Both were also immediately rewarded with "helicopter" promotions, ascending directly from their humble grassroots level into the stratosphere of high official positions. Representing the older generation was Professor Yang Rongguo of Zhongshan University in Guangzhou. He was a longtime CCP member famous in earlier years as a historian and philosopher and in 1974 for his polemical contributions to the "criticize Lin Biao and Confucius" campaign.[16] With the exception of Professor Yang, long known as naturally "red" by inclination, all the national models were reputed to be, like Jiang Qing's foreign biographer, ordinary people in ordinary circumstances until caught by the sharp eye of political campaign promoters.

Undoubtedly sensing the need for something more positive than going against a rising tide, cultural revolutionaries went on the offensive in 1975 and advanced a new set of theoretical arguments on proletarian dictatorship and

---

[14] *Renmin ribao*, 18, 25 Jan. 1974.

[15] *Jiaoyu dashiji*, pp. 453, 463; interviews: 80/GD/1, p. 6; 80/ZJ/10, p. 49; 82/BJ/17, p. 34. Despite his complaint, Li was quickly recruited as a going-against-the-tide personality. See, e.g., Li Qinglin, "Tan fan chaoliu" (On Going against the Tide), *Hongqi*, no. 11 (1973), pp. 65–67.

[16] His keynote anti-Confucius essay appeared in *Renmin ribao*, 7 Aug. 1973; see also "Pilin pikong yu zhishi fenzi de jinbu" (On Criticizing Lin Biao and Confucius and the Intellectuals' Progress), *Hongqi*, no. 10 (1974), pp. 46–50. Articles by Yang, Zhang Tiesheng, and Li Qinglin are reprinted in *Yao ganyu fan chaoliu* (Daring to Go against the Tide) (Beijing: Renmin chubanshe, 1974).

restriction of bourgeois rights. At this eleventh hour, the Chaoyang Agricultural College in Liaoning was unveiled as a new "tool for proletarian dictatorship" and flagship for revolutionary higher education. Its focus was rural and its aim was to create a fail-safe model against restoration.

Publicity to the contrary notwithstanding, most of the new "regular" worker–peasant–soldier students were graduating into state cadre jobs in town just like all their predecessors. Chaoyang students would therefore have to return to their communes upon graduation. The new college also decreed an "open-door" format to enforce manual labor and practical-learning requirements. The format was an adaptation of the Jiangxi Communist Labor University work–study model whereby students would spend part of each year as ordinary laboring peasants in their production teams.[17]

In 1975, a wave of "learning from Chaoyang Agricultural College" swept through urban middle schools and colleges, which included semester-long stints of open-door education at rural branches and school farms. Following the Chaoyang example, a new kind of "returning to the commune" (*shelai shequ*) enrollment and job assignment plan was introduced for rural students. Those admitted to college under this plan knew from the start that upon graduation they would receive state salaries (although somewhat lower than "regular" graduates) but would be obligated to work in the countryside.[18]

The tide continues to rise

Still the tide could not be stopped. The Education Ministry was formally reestablished in early 1975, Zhou Rongxin was named minister, and quality-enhancing instructions continued.[19] At the same time, however, an intense media campaign was launched to defend the education revolution against its critics. These were not initially named, but leaks and subsequent disclosures all pointed to the very top, with Zhou Enlai and Deng Xiaoping serving as

[17] The Chaoyang experience was introduced in late 1973 (*Guangming ribao*, 28 Nov. 1973), and the emulation campaign developed thereafter. E.g., "Xuexiao yingdang chengwei wuchanjieji zhuanzheng de gongju" (Schools Must Become Tools for the Dictatorship of the Proletariat), *Hongqi*, no. 5 (1975), pp. 64–69; Nonglinbu kejiaoju, ed., *Chaoyang nongxueyuan zai douzhengzhong qianjin* (Chaoyang Agricultural College Advancing in Struggle) (Beijing: Nongye chubanshe, 1976); "Comrade Mao Yuan-hsin's Talks at the 'On-the-Spot Conference for Learning the Experience of Revolution in Education of Ch'aoyang Agricultural College in Liaoning,'" 23 Dec. 1974, *Issues and Studies*, Taibei, Sept. 1976, pp. 111–133; research notes, Jiangxi Communist Labor University, Oct. 1980; interview 82/NC/20, p. 70.
[18] Interviews: 83/FJ/25, pp. 61–62; 83/FJ/26, pp. 303–305. Altogether 102,000 *shelai shequ* students were enrolled in 1975 and 1976, or 19 percent and 30 percent of the total freshmen for those two years respectively (*Jiaoyu dashiji*, p. 502).
[19] On the 1975 instructions, see Teacher Pei's account below. Authorization for more exemptions to the work requirement between middle school and college was also issued by the Education Ministry prior to the 1975–1976 academic year (trip notes, Beijing Middle School Number 26, Oct. 1975).

high-level backstage backers and Zhou Rongxin as ranking spokesman. Rivers of rhetoric against "those in authority going the capitalist road" on all fronts distracted attention from the substantive issues at stake. But specific points of accusation indicated that the effort to turn back the rising tide in education had been an exercise in futility. The internal post–Lin Biao critique of 1972–1973 remained unchanged by the winter of 1975–1976, except for having strengthened in the interim.

Unnamed critics were accused of "strange sayings" aimed at "negating the education revolution." For example, good students should move directly from middle school to college. The new worker–peasant college students were inferior to their pre-1966 predecessors. Labor and practical learning (i.e., open-door education) were a waste of time. Knowledge and quality should supersede politics and class struggle. Science and technology should be led by professionals and experts, not Party secretaries and worker propaganda teams.[20]

Subsequently, Beijing wall posters revealed that Education Minister Zhou Rongxin himself had made all these same points and more in a series of internal speeches during 1975.[21] Full authority, however, lay even higher. After Zhou Enlai's death in January 1976, Deng Xiaoping was held responsible for the tide of dissent, which culminated in the first Tiananmen Square incident that spring. Again he lost all his posts. Now named for complicity in the "right deviationist wind" to reverse the Cultural Revolution's correct verdicts, Deng's reports and remarks from 1975 were circulated internally for criticism as the "three poisonous weeds." These revealed that if, as alleged, he had promised before resuming office in 1973 not to reverse the verdicts, then he must have changed his mind or his interpretation soon thereafter. Education, science, technology, and learning from the outside world were only part of his overall "General Program on Work Measures for Party and Country."[22]

Interview accounts corroborated the above interpretation, which is based on the progression of official events between 1971 and 1976. These events in turn reinforced the rationale for the 1966–1968 upheaval itself as a mobilization-

---

[20] From *Hongqi*: Beijing daxue, Qinghua daxue da pipanzu, "Gonggu he fazhan wenhua dageming de chengguo: jiaoyu geming de fangxiang bu rong cuangai" (Consolidate and Develop the Cultural Revolution's Achievements: The Direction of the Education Revolution Must Not Be Distorted), no. 12 (1975), pp. 5–12; Zhongguo gongchandang chaoyang nongxueyuan weiyuanhui, "Dashidafei wenti yiding yao bianlun qingchu" (Great Matters of Right and Wrong Must Be Clearly Debated), no. 1 (1976), pp. 38–43; "Huiji kejijie de youqing fanan feng" (Counterattack the Right Deviationist Wind to Overturn Verdicts in Science and Technology), no. 2 (1976), pp. 3–11. See also *Renmin ribao*, 6 Jan. and 13, 14, 18, 29 Feb. 1976.

[21] John Gardner, "Chou Jung-hsin and Chinese Education," *Current Scene*, Hong Kong (U.S. Consulate-General), vol. 15, nos. 11–12 (Dec. 1977), pp. 1–14; Zhou Rongxin, "Jiaoyu yao shiying sige xiandaihua de xuyao" (Education Must Meet the Requirements of the Four Modernizations), 20 Oct. 1975, in *Zhongguo dangdai jiaoyu sichao*, pp. 256–259.

[22] Reprinted in *Sirenbang shijian tansuo* (Explorations of the Gang of Four Incident) (Hong Kong: Qishi niandai zazhi she, 1977), pp. 133–200.

phase strategy designed to promote Mao's long-term revolutionary aims. The 1973–1976 antirestoration campaigns were thus limited to defending those aims rather than to igniting another 1966-style uprising against all power holders. Interviewees also confirmed, however, that the education revolution's practices were being challenged everywhere in the early 1970s. No one was closer than hearsay distance to the Beijing power center, and from their grass-roots vantage points, interviewees were never clear as to whether the influential lobbyists and their political allies were already maneuvering to negate the education revolution totally in 1972 or only to moderate its excesses. The latter effort, on the other hand, was ubiquitous from the start.

As with the initial 1966–1968 events themselves, the rural areas remained relatively insulated from the mid-1970s campaigns, with small-town middle schools usually marking the furthest extension of their influence. But for commune schools, physical distance was not the only relevant variable. Interviewees recalled instead how rural locales had deliberately exploited their isolation as a protective shield. Teacher Gao best summarized the results as relevant directives and documents had proceeded outward from the center. "If a force 10 typhoon is blowing in Beijing, it will only be force 8 by the time it reaches the provinces, and so on down the line until, in the production brigades, there will be no wind at all."

Hence, the mid-1970s campaigns had little impact on Gao's county in Shaanxi Province, and virtually none in his commune. Their education cadre did pass on all the relevant documents and materials, and all teachers in the commune read them. Some materials on Jiangxi Communist Labor University also reached them, and they all saw the movie *Clean Break* (*Juelie*) about its experience. But since they were not running a work–study university there, they decided the model did not apply to them. They let the Zhang Tiesheng and Huang Shuai episodes pass them by as well. Finally, during the campaign to criticize Lin Biao and Confucius, they did hold a few meetings, and students wrote some criticism essays (*pipan wenzhang*). But the teaching plans were only rarely interrupted in commune schools between 1974 and 1976, and never to allow time for campaign activities.

No one outside the education network, that is, the county education bureau, the commune education cadre, and the commune schoolteachers, was held responsible for any of these campaigns, and the education network handled them in its own way. No one ever came to investigate, "because there were too many documents coming down, and no one could keep track of them all." "The teachers and school leaders could just decide among themselves to ignore any particular document if they wanted to." In any event, the various "winds" that swept through city schools in the mid-1970s – breaking windows and wrecking school property – never even reached the county town. Rural people there, concluded Teacher Gao, "were basically different from city folk."

Parents would only complain if they felt a child had been disciplined unfairly. But being largely unschooled themselves, they wanted education for their children and so respected the teachers.[23]

The mid-1970s campaigns were similarly contained in Teacher Mei's Jiangsu commune. All teachers had to attend two struggle–study meetings a year, where all the political documents were read and discussed and individual teachers sometimes singled out for criticism. But the meetings were "internal," within the education system itself, which took care of its own. Students were not organized for any of the campaigns, which therefore had no influence on commune schools. The commune Party leaders also did not concern themselves, and since no outsiders ever came down on inspection tours, "everyone got the point." This left the commune education cadre and the head of the main commune school as the two key figures who together "had the power not to circulate something and then to report up that they had circulated it." If those two met with the brigade school leaders and all decided on a certain course of action, there was no one to oppose them. And no one wanted to, in Teacher Mei's view. Her colleagues were always talking wistfully about "the way we used to do things," so that the old ways continued to influence their thought and work.[24]

Teacher Yang was gone from her commune in a neighboring county before the campaigns peaked. But she recalled 1972 with great relish. In her view, the post-1966 resumption of classes did not really begin until that year, when they "grasped quality" once more. Teachers had to take a formal written examination, but they did not mind and in turn began giving their students quizzes every day. Still, students remained respectful and enthusiastic throughout, claimed Yang, even while preparing for the all-county unified assessment exams in Chinese and math which were given two or three times that year. All middle schools in the county were then ranked according to their students' average scores, just like in the old days. But the new emphasis did not last and was criticized in 1973, marking the onset of the antiretrogression campaigns.[25]

For city schools, defensive strategies were harder to arrange. In Shantou Prefecture, Guangdong, Teacher Peng's commune remained unmoved and uninfluenced. But students at the county-town middle school even set out on "revolutionary linking" excursions trying to re-create in 1974–1975 the spirit of 1966.[26] Also in Guangdong, Teacher Song recalled how the campaign against reversing the Cultural Revolution's verdicts drew strength from the internal criticism of Deng Xiaoping during the summer and fall of 1975. The municipal CCP committee and education bureau issued joint instructions that teachers

[23] Interview 83/SX/20, pp. 27–31.
[24] Interview 83/JS/10, pp. 64–68.
[25] Interview 83/JS/9, pp. 24, 44–45.
[26] Interview 82/GD/10, p. 78.

must ask students for criticism. The teachers called this "lighting a fire to burn oneself," but they had no choice.

The most lasting memory of this period among urban teachers, however, was neither personal retribution nor intimidation, and openly abusing teachers was rare at this time, recalled Teacher Song. Twice such altercations had occurred at his school, and the public security (police) was called in to deal with the students. There were actually many stories about the new Cultural Revolution generation of teachers who were not averse to matching martial arts skills with the successor generation of student rebels. But teachers remembered instead the general renewed threat to discipline and order. "The worst problem," said Song, "was inattention in class. Some students would even sit lounging with their backs to the teacher; some might sleep; others would talk with their friends. This was what was meant by discipline being bad. The idea that studying was of no use had a strong influence."[27]

Teacher Huang agreed. In his view, the main damage came from criticizing "standards of excellence," which peaked at his Fujian school during the mid-1970s campaigns. If students studied too hard, they would be criticized for putting grades first or "studying well to become an official" (*xue er youze shi*). And if teachers gave too many tests, they would be criticized as well. So everyone said teaching and learning were "no use."

Even in the eye of the storm, Teacher Hu's verdict was much the same. His recollections, cited in chapter 15, were actually from this 1974–1976 period, when he was transferred back to an urban Beijing neighborhood. On the one hand, enrollments were being increased to unprecedented levels, and on the other, schools were suffering maximum disruption. Here, windows were again broken and furniture smashed. "Teachers could not teach, students would not listen...and many classes could not be held."

Most immediately, Teacher Hu blamed the Huang Shuai campaign: "The schools' discipline and teaching order had just been restored. They were giving open-book exams and doing open-door education, but still they were able to teach and lecture in class, and that was a step forward from what had been before. Then, with the Huang Shuai affair, the teachers' prestige was wrecked again." Of course, Jiang Qing did not mean for students to trash schools, explained Teacher Hu, "but everything combined quite naturally to produce that end result." Everyone was constantly debating and arguing about how to teach and what to teach and there were never any conclusions. There was also the new idea of "equality between teachers and students...so if they can criticize a teacher's weaknesses, then they can move to the point of challenging the teacher in class as well." The teachers with all their old-fashioned ways and

[27] Interview 80/GD/6, pp. 60–61.

means felt powerless, and the students did not understand the difference between criticizing and attacking. It was in such an environment, he said, that "a strong teacher could cope; but the weaker teachers had no way to control the students."[28]

Metaphorically midway between Teacher Gao's Shaanxi commune and the Beijing storm center lay Teacher Pei's north China county town. Located just far enough from Beijing to allow room for maneuver and just close enough to guarantee good political reception, county leaders were able to negotiate all the shifting tides and currents between 1973 and 1976 with relative ease. When Chaoyang Agricultural College was being developed as a model, in 1973, a document came down on open-door schooling, phrased in a general way without clear instructions one way or another. Naturally, "there were two opinions" about what to do, so county leaders decided to play both sides of the two-line struggle. The main county-town middle school retained its "Cultural Revolution regular" format, while a deputy secretary of the county CCP committee sponsored their Chaoyang-style experiment. The number two county-town middle school was transformed completely, with its teaching plan replaced by several practical specialties (e.g., agriculture, carpentry, public health, sports). People skilled in these endeavors, including Teacher Pei, were recruited from around the county, and all the study programs were "open door," moving back and forth between the town and countryside.

The school was actually very popular and quite a success while it lasted. But Comrade Chai, the man tapped to manage the experiment, was a gregarious and well-connected commune-level cadre who had also mastered the laws of mass movement politics. For him, the instructions sent down by the restored Education Ministry in preparation for the 1975 fall semester served as the chief warning signal. Localities were instructed to return schools to their former order and strengthen teaching schedules. Symbolizing this direction, the local education bureau restored an old practice much favored by Soviet advisors in the 1950s and not seen in the county since 1966: students were required to stand and greet the teacher each morning. These mid-1975 directives were quickly rescinded when the final campaign against Deng Xiaoping moved into high gear a few months later. But Comrade Chai understood in 1975 that the rising tide would prevail and began arranging his transfer to another, less controversial post. By the time Mao died in September 1976, Chai was safely embarked on a new career track which would soon take him out of the province altogether, thus escaping the retribution suffered by many who had made their mark during the 1973–1976 campaigns.

---

[28] Interview 82/BJ/18, pp. 19–20.

The rising tide prevails: two lines become one

The story of how Mao's education revolution was finally reversed has already been told in considerable detail.[29] To reiterate briefly, within a month of Mao's death, Jiang Qing, Zhang Chunqiao, and two other leading cultural revolutionaries were arrested in a coup d'état–style operation and rechristened the "Gang of Four." In a swift preemptive strike, their allies around the country were similarly arrested. With the Party center, army, and police secure, the mass media and propaganda apparatus were quickly subdued as well, and power was effectively seized. A new round of harsh revolutionary justice began, sustained by the combined forces of all the political and intellectual enemies Mao's Cultural Revolution had created. The appetite for polemics, investigations, arrests, and trials seemed insatiable. All outstanding cases left over from the factional wars of 1966–1968 were reviewed once more even as the fresh wave of "late Cultural Revolution" Gang of Four confederates was bolstering the ranks of counterrevolutionary suspects.

That coup leaders actually meant to overthrow completely all Mao's grand designs was still not clear, however. First to be arrested were those who had made their marks most recently and most prominently in the going-against-the-tide campaigns of 1973–1976. Such targets included Zhang Tiesheng (rechristened a "counterrevolutionary political fraud").[30] Arrested as well were Li Qinglin and Chaoyang Agricultural College leaders. It was said that Yang Rongguo escaped only because he was terminally ill, and Jiang Qing's biographer because she was a foreigner. But it also seemed that in time-honored tradition, only the redefined excesses and errors of Mao's last campaign were to be sorted out and another course correction set in motion. Initial polemics

---

[29] Post-Mao education reforms have been the subject of much research by many scholars, both Chinese and Western. The onset of these reforms marks the end of this study, however, and they are only addressed here by way of a conclusion to illustrate how the change affected people and communities already introduced. On the reversal of the education revolution as realized in post-Mao education reforms, the following (titles listed in the Select Bibliography for authors and dates indicated) represent a small selection of studies available in English: Pepper (1980, 1984, 1990, 1995); Hayhoe (1984, 1989, 1992); Rosen (1985, 1987); Shirk (1979); Montaperto and Henderson (1979); Theodore Chen (1981); Hawkins (1983); Cleverley (1985); Thøgersen (1990); Epstein (1991); Du (1992); Lin (1993); Leslie Lo (1993); Paine (1994); and selected issues for the period of *Chinese Education and Society: A Journal of Translations*, ed. Stanley Rosen and Gerard Postiglione. Interviewees' accounts are summarized in the following chapter.

[30] *Renmin ribao*, 30 Nov. 1976. Zhang was formally sentenced for counterrevolutionary incitement in 1978 and spent 15 years in prison. He was released in 1991. See *Jiaoyu dashiji*, p. 453; *South China Morning Post*, Hong Kong, 21 Jan. 1992; Guan Gengyin, "Zhang Tiesheng chuyu yao dang getihu" (After Being Released from Prison, Zhang Tiesheng Is to Go into Business for Himself), *Kaifa qu daokan* (Development News), Beijing, no. 6 (1992), pp. 61–65. The disposition of many other Cultural Revolution personalities was made less secretly, but the publicity accorded the Gang of Four's trial was unique. Among those sentenced to long prison terms in 1983 after having already been in detention for several years were central education leader Chi Qun, Red Guard rebel Kuai Dafu, and Beijing University's Nie Yuanzi (*South China Morning Post*, 20 Mar. 1983 and 4 Nov. 1983).

were designed to create such an impression, written in a style replete with denunciations of those who had presumed to distort Mao's correct line.

Hence the full extent of the restorationist tide did not become clear beyond doubt until the early 1980s. Mao's successors aimed not just to correct the excesses of his Cultural Revolution but to re-create the original early-1960s rationale for his having launched it in the first place, namely, "capitalist restoration." Virtually no feature of the communist-led revolution would be exempt save the bureaucratic control of the CCP itself. Education continued to set the pace. In this sector, all the necessary decisions had actually been made and were already being implemented by the Third Plenum of the Eleventh CCP Central Committee in December 1978, which formally inaugurated Deng Xiaoping's reform administration. For education, the reversal was swift and complete, leaving literally no stone unturned and no revolutionary decision not reversed. By 1980, not a single radical model was left intact, prompting the popular riposte of that time, "all cut with a single stroke" (*yi dao qie*), and the official reply, "not a single thing" worth saving.

In May 1977, Deng Xiaoping transposed ideas from his earlier "poisonous weeds" phase into prescriptions for the new era. "Respect knowledge, respect talent," he said. "Walk on two legs." "After rigorous examinations, select the most outstanding people and concentrate them in key-point middle schools and universities." "All work, whether mental or manual, is labor."[31] These few words of authorization anticipated all that followed. Education would revert to the specific Sinicized version of the Soviet model that had evolved between 1958 and 1966. But his rationale harked back to a much earlier era. Like the late-19th-century official reformers, Deng invoked the modernization experience of Japan's Meiji Restoration, which was already registering its first successes while China's opinion leaders argued over the same decisions. The key to modernization, declared Deng, lay in science and technology, and the key to developing these was education. Japan had succeeded because it began paying attention to all three during the Meiji Restoration. China was now 20 years behind the developed countries. China had to "catch up with the most advanced countries in the world." The first priority was economic development, and the education system had to be geared to meet those aims. The social consequences and political implications need not be acknowledged.[32]

By July, the decision to restore the national college entrance examinations had been announced internally.[33] And in August, the Cultural Revolution was

---

[31] Deng Xiaoping, "Zunzhong zhishi, zunzhong rencai" (Respect Knowledge, Respect Talent), 24 May 1977, *Deng Xiaoping wenxuan*, pp. 37–38; quoted in *Jiaoyu dashiji*, p. 493.

[32] Deng Xiaoping, "Zunzhong zhishi, zunzhong rencai," pp. 37–38; Deng Xiaoping, "Guanyu kexue he jiaoyu gongzuo de ji dian yijian" (A Few Opinions on Science and Education Work), 8 Aug. 1977, in *Deng Xiaoping wenxuan*, pp. 45–55; quoted in *Jiaoyu dashiji*, p. 494.

[33] *The Asian Wall Street Journal*, Hong Kong, 24 Aug. 1977.

declared formally concluded.[34] Also in August, Deng indicated that the two assessments of 1971 would be reversed. The first 17 years of education work had been "red," not bourgeois. Teachers and scientists were not capitalist oriented but "educational workers" who had labored successfully under CCP leadership.[35]

In September, the Education Ministry began editing new, nationally unified teaching materials for reunified national elementary and secondary school curricula. In November, the worker propaganda teams were ordered withdrawn from urban middle schools. And just in case anyone had missed the point, two huge mass rallies were sponsored by the Education Ministry in November and December to criticize the two assessments, the Mazhenfu incident, Chaoyang Agricultural College, and other such educational "crimes" perpetrated by the Gang of Four.[36]

By the end of 1977, then, all the decisions necessary to reverse the education revolution had been made and announced. A new orthodoxy had been established, and for anyone foolish enough to oppose it, the full coercive powers of the state were being used yet again to enforce the charge of counterrevolution. The two-line struggle could no longer exist, because there was now only one line. Any challenge became by definition illegitimate and therefore invisible. All that remained was to draft, promulgate, and implement the relevant directives needed to restore education to its former working order, an enterprise that continued throughout 1978 and 1979.

As the basic policy line was restored to conform to the priorities and assumptions of professional educators, so the education bureaucracy was also returned to the education establishment. Rules, regulations, teaching plans, systems, etc., were all quickly rebuilt. The precise amounts of time for political study, labor, and classroom learning were all specified in the new curricula. Open-door activities were denounced as Gang of Four aberrations and were abandoned along with all rural branches and farms set up by urban schools. Directives spelled out the conditions for concentrating all the best resources in key schools at all levels. The two-year work requirement prior to college was abandoned first and the rural resettlement program for urban youth not long thereafter.

By 1978, the pursuit of regularity could be seen intensifying to a degree unprecedented in any generation. Mass movements were also formally abandoned along with all other Maoist impedimenta. But its built-in principle about going to extremes seemed self-perpetuating as regularity was used not

---

[34] *Renmin ribao*, 23 Aug. 1977.
[35] Deng Xiaoping, "Guanyu kexue he jiaoyu gongzuo de ji dian yijian," pp. 45–46. On criticism of the two assessments, see, e.g., *Renmin ribao*, 18, 19, 20 Nov. 1977, and *Guangming ribao*, 25, 27, 31 Jan. and 1 Feb. 1978.
[36] *Jiaoyu dashiji*, pp. 501–504.

just to override revolutionary excess but to establish the new paradigm as well. Dividing students, within schools, by ability had been practiced only tentatively during the 1960s. Now this method was formally advocated as a means of "quickly reversing" the damage done to quality by the Gang of Four. Students at both elementary and secondary levels were therefore divided without any face-saving subtleties into fast, average, and slow classes.[37]

Formally restored too was the original interpretation of walking on two legs, namely, the simultaneous pursuit of key-point schools for the elite few, full-day schools for others, and the unpopular work–study schools for the undistinguished laboring masses. Most extreme by far, however, were the consequences of rehabilitating the old quantity–quality conundrum, with greatest impact registered at the secondary level. Between 1958 and 1966, the systematic development of urban-based key schools represented a compromise between Maoist demands for rapid expansion and professional educators' demands for a reprieve from the egalitarian strictures of Soviet pedagogy as practiced in the 1950s. The key-point stream had therefore developed as an island of quality amid continuing quantitative growth. After 1976, this pattern was re-created only during the 1976–1978 interregnum. From 1978, key-point quality building continued while the previous decade's quantitative gains at the secondary level were slashed.

In 1977, according to interviewees, the Education Ministry began circulating internally the recommended reduced proportions of elementary and junior middle graduates who should be allowed to pass on to the level above. These controlled pass rates were preparatory to implementing the more important decision to curtail rural senior secondary schooling and drastically reduce enrollments at that level in urban areas as well. The relevant directives were never published, and the quantitative reductions were too controversial at the time to risk a major publicity campaign, but official statistics did record the results (see especially Tables 17.3, 17.5, and 17.6). By 1982, when the contraction was essentially complete, promotion rates from elementary to junior middle school had been cut from 94 percent to 66 percent; and from junior to senior middle school, from 71 percent to 32 percent. At the senior middle level, over 60 percent of all schools nationwide had been closed, and enrollments were similarly down by just over 60 percent, while the junior middle sections attached to elementary schools had virtually disappeared.

Such reductions were acknowledged and explained only in general terms as part of the overall need for secondary school "restructuring." Officially, it was said that quantitative growth had spread financial resources too thinly, aggravated the shortage of qualified teachers, undermined quality, and produced an excessive proportion of senior middle graduates in relation to college freshmen.

[37] Ibid., p. 517.

Table 17.1. *Elementary schools and enrollments, 1975–1988*

Year	No. of schools	No. of students in school (millions)
1975	—	151
1976	1,044,300	150
1977	—	146
1978	—	146
1979	923,500	147
1980	—	146
1981	894,074	143
1982	880,516	140
1983	862,165	136
1984	853,740	136
1985	832,309	134
1986	820,846	132
1987	807,406[a]	128[b]
1988		125

[a] Six-year schools: 458,671; five-year schools: 348,735.
[b] Students in six-year schools: 75 million; and in five-year schools: 53 million.
Sources: Number of schools from 1975 to 1979 – *Zhongguo baike nianjian, 1980*, p. 535.
   Number of students from 1975 to 1980 – *Zhongguo tongji nianjian, 1981*, p. 441.
   1981–1987 – *Zhongguo tongji nianjian, 1988*, pp. 873, 876.
   1987 – *Zhongguo jiaoyu tongji nianjian, 1987*, pp. 78–79.
   1988 – State Statistical Bureau communiqué for 1988, in *Renmin ribao*, 1 Mar. 1989.

The Cultural Revolution's "unitary" (*danyihua*) structure had also resulted in the expansion of general, rather than specialized and vocational, secondary education, leading to a system inappropriate for the needs of the national economy. By contrast, the 1960s were recalled as a "golden age" when the ratio of regular to vocational secondary schooling was one-to-one, when state-run, rather then *minban*, schools predominated, when county education bureaus ran middle schools, when senior middles were concentrated in county towns rather than one in every commune, and when junior middle schools were run only in rural locales where conditions were adequate instead of having one in every brigade. Quality was high and the structure of secondary schooling "appropriate" for China's level of economic development.[38]

[38] E.g., Lu Xingwei, "Gaige zhongdeng jiaoyu jiegou shizai bixing" (Reforming the Structure of Secondary Education Is Essential), and Liaoningsheng jiaoyu ju, "Juban gezhong menlei de zhongdeng zhiye jiaoyu" (Run Various Kinds of Secondary Vocational Education), both in *Renmin jiaoyu*, no. 7 (1979), pp. 42–43, 44–46, respectively; *Guangming ribao*, 20 May and 16 Aug. 1979; Xinhua-English, Beijing, 17 Aug. 1979, in *Xinhua News Bulletin*, Hong Kong, 18 Aug. 1979.

Table 17.2. *School-age children enrolled at the elementary level, 1949–1987*

Year	National elem. school-age cohorts (millions)	No. of school-age children who have entered elem. school (millions)	% of school-age children entering elem. school
1949	—	—	25.0
1965	116.03	98.29	84.7
1976	121.94	118.39	96.0
1977	121.01	116.79	95.5
1978	121.31	115.85	94.0
1979	123.23	115.80	93.0
1980	122.20	114.78	93.0
1981	120.18	111.75	93.0
1982	117.63	109.58	93.2
1983	112.51	105.78	94.0
1984	106.69	101.70	95.3
1985	103.62	99.43	95.9
1986	100.67	97.02	96.4
1987	97.51	94.77	97.2

Sources: Zhongguo tongji nianjian, 1988, p. 889. The 1949 figure only is from *China: Socialist Economic Development*, 3:134.

Later, after such restructuring was complete, the implications of the initial 1978–1979 argument were clearer. It had in fact been an introduction to the new "line," and it was implemented with a finality that brooked no dissent. The aim at the senior secondary level had indeed been to re-create the proportions of the "golden age" 1960s. These were approximated, if not achieved, through the dual adjustment whereby secondary school reductions occurred in tandem with a rapid increase at the tertiary level – which was in turn designed to bring the proportion of college-trained personnel in line with international development standards (see Table 17.7 on tertiary enrollments).[39] Meanwhile, the key-point college-preparatory stream was progressively whittled down during the early 1980s until it was producing some 600,000 senior middle graduates each year, about the same number being enrolled in the nation's colleges.[40]

Simultaneously, the greatest reduction in senior secondary schooling was occurring at the commune level (see Table 17.5). The provincial educator who had startled his foreign visitor with the comment that rural youth did not need to attend middle school could be faulted only for excessive candor. The

[39] *China: Socialist Economic Development* (Washington, D.C.: World Bank, 1983), 3:192–193.
[40] *Zhongguo jiaoyu tongji nianjian, 1987* (Yearbook of China's Educational Statistics, 1987) (Beijing: Gongye daxue chubanshe, 1988), pp. 58–59, 65, 110. See Table 17.6 (col. 3) showing similar pass rates into college in 1965 and 1985 relative to the 1970s.

Table 17.3. *Secondary schools and students: general secondary*
(including key points), 1975–1987

Year	No. of schools	No. of students (millions)
1975		44.66
1976	192,152	58.36; jr.: 43.53; sr.: 14.84
1977		67.80
1978		65.48
1979	144,233	59.05; jr.: 46.13; sr.: 12.92
	(5,200)	(5.20)
1980		55.08
1981	106,718	48.60; jr.: 41.45; sr.: 7.15
1982	101,649	45.28; jr.: 38.88; sr.: 6.40
1983	96,474	43.98
1984	93,714	45.54
1985	93,221	47.06
1986	92,967	48.90
1987	92,857	49.48; jr.: 41.74; sr.: 7.74
	(2,243)	(3.08)

Note: Key-point schools are included in the category of general, or ordinary
(*putong*), schools. All in this category, whether key or non-key, are distinguished by
being academic, rather than technical or vocational, in orientation. Separate figures
for key-point schools are shown here in parentheses for the years 1979 and 1987
only.
Sources: Schools – *Zhongguo baike nianjian, 1980*, p. 535; *Zhongguo baike nianjian,
1982*, p. 568; *Zhongguo tongji nianjian, 1988*, p. 873. The pre-1980 figures do not
agree with those given in other sources, e.g., *Zhongguo jingji nianjian, 1981*,
pp. IV-205, 206, and *China: Socialist Economic Development*, 3:134.
 Students – *Zhongguo baike nianjian, 1980*, p. 536; *Zhongguo baike nianjian, 1982*,
p. 568; *Zhongguo tongji nianjian, 1988*, p. 876.
 Key-point schools and students – Figures in parentheses, for 1979 and 1987 only,
from *Zhongguo baike nianjian, 1980*, p. 541; *Zhongguo jiaoyu tongji nianjian, 1987*,
pp. 58–59, 65.

comment was an otherwise accurate expression of the rationale for school closures then under way which was repeated by many interviewees.
 Outside observers were not just startled but perplexed by such a reversal in
official line and rhetoric. Relegating quantitative gains and rural development
alike to the realm of Gang of Four "wrecking" seemed like a vengeful backlash
against too many years of Maoist omnipotence rather than serious prescriptions for educational modernization. But most contemporary observers also
lacked the perspective of decades past and of the old controversies which had
long since been incorporated within the two-line struggle. Hence, rehabilitated

Table 17.4. *Secondary schools and students: specialized and vocational, 1949–1987*

Year	Professional (*zhuanye*): technical (*jishu*) and teacher training (*shifan*)		Vocational (*zhiye*) and agricultural (*nongye*)	
	Schools	*Students*	*Schools*	*Students*
1949	1,171	229,000	—	—
1957	1,320	778,000	—	—
1965	1,265	547,000	61,626	4,433,000
1976	2,443	690,000	—	—
1979	3,033	1,199,000	—	—
1980	3,069	1,243,000	3,314	453,600
			(390 vocational	133,600)
			(2,924 agricultural	320,000)
1981	3,132	1,069,000	2,655	480,900
			(561 vocational	213,100)
			(2,094 agricultural	267,800)
1982	3,076	1,039,000	3,104	704,000
1983	3,090	1,143,000	5,481	—
1984	3,301	1,322,000	7,002	—
1985	3,557	1,571,000	8,070	2,295,000
1986	3,782	1,757,000	8,187	—
1987	3,913	1,874,000	8,381	2,676,000

Sources: 1949–1979 – *Zhongguo baike nianjian, 1980*, pp. 535–536. 1980 – *Zhongguo jingji nianjian, 1981*, pp. IV–205, 206. 1981 – *Zhongguo baike nianjian, 1982*, p. 568. *1982–1987* – *Zhongguo tongji nianjian, 1988*, pp. 873, 876.

along with the authority of teachers were their old-fashioned assumptions about the means and ends of education and how to produce a quality product. Those assumptions therefore reemerged, not just as some curious anachronism that would disappear once the novelty of challenging everything Mao had directed wore off, but rather as an essential ingredient over which the conflict between Mao and China's education establishment had been waged.

Among the clearest indicators of this endemic conflict were the detailed directives that had been drafted by leftist educators bent on regularizing Yan'an's embryonic school system between 1938 and 1942. These old directives were published in the early 1980s (see chap. 6), evidently to serve as an authoritative historical precedent for the post-1976 regularization drive. They also provide the answer for anyone wondering how the Chinese system could have reversed itself so quickly in 1977 after a decade of revolutionary upheaval.

Table 17.5. *Urban–rural, general secondary schools and enrollments, 1963–1981*

Year	Junior middle only			Senior middle and complete middle[a]		
	Cities	County towns	Rural/communes	Cities	County towns	Rural/communes
Number of schools:						
1963	2,594	2,899	9,797	1,414	2,408	481
1973	1,927	2,174	63,858	5,139	4,301	19,925
1975	1,809	2,450	80,126	6,170	5,015	27,935
1976	1,941	3,670	126,006	7,008	5,734	47,793
1977	1,883	3,217	131,265	7,610	6,377	50,916
1978	2,699	3,328	107,103	7,106	6,106	36,003
1981	3,395	3,442	75,434	6,069	5,951	12,427
Number of students in school (millions)						
1963	2.49	1.75	2.14	0.54	0.60	0.09
1973	5.50	2.50	17.23	2.74	1.89	4.61
1975	5.91	3.34	23.77	3.24	2.12	6.28
1976	6.76	4.02	32.75	3.37	2.22	9.25
1977	7.02	4.20	38.58	3.54	2.57	11.90
1978	6.76	4.48	38.72	3.43	2.60	9.49
1981	5.58	4.63	31.23	1.96	2.16	3.02

[a] Figures for number of schools are for senior middle and complete middle; figures for number of students are for senior middle only.
Source: *Zhongguo jiaoyu nianjian, 1949–1981*, p. 1005.

Table 17.6. *Promotion rates, the college-preparatory stream, 1965–1985*

Year	(1) Elementary grads. entering general jr. middle (%)	(2) Jr. middle grads. entering general sr. middle (%)	(3) Sr. middle grads. entering college (%)
1965	44.9	26.4	45.6
1973	84.4	40.0	4.3
1975	90.6	60.4	4.3
1976	94.1	71.4	4.2
1977	92.0	63.7	4.7
1980	75.9	43.1	4.6
1982	66.2	32.3	
1985	68.4	39.4	31.5

Sources: 1965–1977 – Zhongguo jiaoyu nianjian, 1949–1981, calculated from pp. 1001, 1021 (col. 1); p. 1001 (col. 2); pp. 969, 1001 (col. 3).
1980–1985 – Zhongguo tongji nianjian, 1988, p. 889 (cols. 1 and 2); pp. 878, 881 (col. 3).

Table 17.7. *Tertiary institutions and students, 1965–1988*

Year	Institutions	Students
1965	434	674,000
1977	404	625,000
1985	1,016	1,703,000
1988	—	2,066,000

Sources: Zhongguo tongji nianjian, 1986, pp. 723, 726; *Renmin ribao*, 1 Mar. 1989.

Even though the old directives were all designed for a much "younger" system, that is, one where elementary education was the main focus of concern, they could still have served as a prototype for the return to regularity after October 1976. Item by item and point for point, these directives had established all the rules, regulations, and systems necessary to purge Yan'an elementary schools of their irregular–rural features. Resources had been reconcentrated in a few good schools, others were closed, and enrollments were deliberately reduced. In this realm of the professional educator, no school was better than an irregular one, low standards were sufficient justification for shutting down operations, and guaranteeing "quality" was a legitimate reason for restricting enrollments. Cultural revolution and class struggle had been elaborated later to produce the education revolution of 1968–1976. But at its center lay the old conflict between professional Chinese educators and advocates of radical rural-based reform.

Finally, besides the regularization drive in education, Deng Xiaoping's victory meant that several other key intra-Party disputes which had fueled Mao's crusade against "capitalist restoration" would now be settled posthumously against him as well. At least four such adjustments would have varying degrees of impact on the education sector, and all were introduced during the formative 1978–1979 years of the Deng Xiaoping administration:

(1) Decollectivizing agriculture. The first step was to introduce the household responsibility system, which replaced the collective cultivation of village lands. Each family would henceforth be responsible for its own profits and losses. Simultaneously, a new move was launched to "reduce the peasants' collective burdens." This meant among other things that unremunerated peasant labor could no longer be mobilized by brigades to support local endeavors such as schooling, health care, transport, etc.[41] The impact on rural education was twofold, deriving from the changes in family and village finances respectively. Families were given more incentives and more opportunities to make money, while their economic survival suddenly depended solely on their own resources. The advantages of nonattendance at school and early dropouts therefore increased as the contribution of all family members became even more essential to the well-being of the unit as a whole. At the same time, the demise of collective financial arrangements for local schools left rural elementary school funding in a state of uncertainty that would continue throughout the 1980s as decollectivization was completed, the commune system itself dismantled, and land divided up among individual households. These changes in the rural political economy were responsible for the declining proportion of the age-group in school at the elementary level (see Table 17.2). Regularization, which included the massive closure of commune senior middle schools and attached junior middle sections, plus decollectivization thus dealt combined major blows to the cause of rural education.

(2) End of the class line. Deng Xiaoping's liberation of intellectuals from the stigma of their bourgeois orientations was soon followed by new regulations stipulating that family background was no longer to be used as a formal criterion, either positively or negatively, in the allocation of life's benefits. In the competitive access to schooling, all were to be "equal before marks." The main categories that had served as the basis for discrimination were also abolished. The designation "rightist" was canceled while landlord and rich-peasant class categories were eliminated. The practice of discriminating against the children of people who had been so designated in matters such as admission to school,

---

[41] This move was advertised nationally in 1978 as the "Xiangxiang County experience" after the Hunan locality that pioneered it (e.g., *Jiaoyu dashiji*, p. 521).

job assignments, and joining the army, Party, and Youth League was denounced as an "abnormality" and an "imperfection" in the socialist system to be firmly corrected.[42]

The practice of collective family responsibility was not banned outright, however, since even as all remaining counterrevolutionaries from past political wars were being investigated and (usually) cleared of all charges, new counter-revolutionary categories for "late Cultural Revolution" rebels and close Gang of Four confederates were being created. Family members were still discriminated against; in 1977 and 1978, for example, if parents were being investigated and therefore under suspicion for such activities, their children were unable to enter college. Hence the formal class designations that had distinguished people by the major source of family income as of 1949 were formally abrogated, but the "counterrevolutionary" label remained for application to a variety of political offenses, with variable consequences for both offenders and family members.

(3) Reintegrating intellectual and bureaucratic power. The new demand for a "younger, better educated, and more specialized" leadership cadre followed from Deng Xiaoping's emphasis on education and expertise as prerequisites for modernization. According to the plan finalized in 1983, a college education would by 1990 be a prerequisite for all leading cadres down to the county level.[43] The historic significance of this plan went unheralded. But for the first time since the early years of the century when official reformers tried briefly to create equivalents between modern school graduates and old-style examination degrees as prerequisites for public office, the two realms of learning and bureaucratic power were being formally linked once more.

Evidently, one of the great post-1911 intellectual laments – about the usurpation of China's government by alien (military and political) forces – was now scheduled for redress at last. The 1983 plan spoke of links between specialized or professional degrees and the particular bureaucratic post rather than literary generalist learning. But the categoric Confucian association between knowledge and bureaucratic office had been formally rehabilitated. Struck down in the process was one of the education revolution's most basic charges against modern Chinese education's inheritance from its Confucian past: "studying to

---

[42] E.g., *Renmin ribao*, 26 Apr. and 17 Nov. 1978, 2, 29, 30 Jan. and 15 Feb. 1979.

[43] Deng Xiaoping, "Lao ganbu diyiwei de renwu shi xuanba zhongqingnian ganbu" (The Number One Task of Old Cadres Is the Selection of Middle-Aged and Young Cadres), 2 July 1981, in *Deng Xiaoping wenxuan*, pp. 339–343; "Notice of the Organization Department of the Central Committee," appendix 1, trans. in Burns, *The Chinese Communist Party's Nomenklatura System*, pp. 51–59. College-level training requirements were also introduced for military officers; see, e.g., Deng Xiaoping, "Jundui yao ba jiaoyu xunlian tigao dao zhanlue diwei" (The Army Should Elevate Education and Training to a Position of Strategic Importance), 23 Aug. 1977, in *Deng Xiaoping wenxuan*, pp. 56–62; Monte R. Bullard, *China's Political–Military Evolution: The Party and the Military in the PRC, 1960–1984* (Boulder: Westview Press, 1985), pp. 25–32.

become an official" and its pragmatic corollary claim, studying is "useless" otherwise.

(4) Reopening to the capitalist West. Pursuant to his demand that China catch up with advanced nations forthwith, Deng was said to have personally ordered the Education Ministry in 1978 to send 10,000 students to the U.S. as quickly as possible.[44] He was also said to have ordered all leading cadres to make at least one trip abroad. Everyone would soon discover that his objective was not just to give them a glimpse of the outside world or even to import Western capital and technology. What Mao had started on his terms, Deng would carry forward on his. Mao had presumably sought a controlled opening to the West while continuing to make his case against capitalist restoration. But Deng's aim was to graft the ways and means of capitalism onto China's socialist system in the hope of making it work more effectively. In education, China's institutions of higher learning would be thrust into the forefront of this reopening to the West. More than any other sector of Chinese society, they would be required to absorb during the 1980s ongoing waves of academic, economic, and administrative reform, all designed to apply lessons learned from the West and especially from the U.S., as its leading representative.

Clearly, education was but a single indicator in the intra-Party debate over capitalist restoration that extended back at least to the early 1960s, when CCP leaders were trying to absorb the lessons of the Great Leap Forward's collapse. Mao had wedded the concept of cultural revolution taken from past Soviet practice to his own Party's experience in mass movement politics and produced one last upheaval in a vain attempt to stave off the threat to his revolutionary legacy. Now, with Mao's power finally broken in death, Deng Xiaoping meant to change fundamentally the rules of the revolutionary game. The mass movement method of policy implementation and class-based political struggle would give way, promised the late-1970s polemics, to a new era of socialist legality and bureaucratic respectability.

[44] According to U.S. Liaison Office personnel, Beijing, Oct. 1978.

18

The mixed triumph of regularity

Contemplating the momentous events of the post-1976 years, interviewees were reserved in their expressions of liberation, relief, and revenge. A major reason for the caution was that in the late 1970s and even into the early 1980s, no one expected Deng Xiaoping's era either to last as long as it did or to continue without a major Maoist backlash. It was said, for example, that Education Minister Liu Xiyao – a moderate post-1976 holdover from the Science and Education Group – bowed out after only a short period in office, not because he opposed the new line and policies, but because he feared the consequences of implementing them. Interviewees were similarly fearful. And all were aware that the new orthodoxy was as uncompromising in demands for loyalty as its predecessor had been, while education remained a "front-line" issue. Circumspection therefore derived from a range of cross-pressures and contradictory emotions.

By and large, interviewees were nevertheless consistent in greeting post-1976 changes with the same mixed reviews they had bestowed upon the education revolution itself, albeit in reverse. Just as disruption, class discrimination, and rural assignments had been deplored, so a return to regularity in all systems, their own return to town or regular career tracks, and an end to institutionalized class conflict appeared to be welcomed without reservation by all. Nor did anyone have a single kind word for Jiang Qing. And Zhang Tiesheng fared no better, even though all accepted his original letter of protest as a spontaneous gesture like many thousands of others provoked by the 1973 examinations. Interviewees seemed to speak genuinely with one voice in upholding the harsh rules of counterrevolutionary justice which decreed long prison terms for even such relatively minor political offenses as those committed during the 1973–1976 campaigns. But beneath the plane of popular retribution – always invoked at the end against those responsible for excesses as a mass movement neared its inevitable conclusion – lurked the old familiar ambivalence between regularity and radical education reform. Hence interviewees could and did deplore the mass movement's excesses without necessarily rejecting all the mass-oriented ideals incorporated within.

The ongoing commitment to various radical reform principles was articulated on several counts. And the ambivalence, as in earlier decades, was so pervasive as to be evident in some degree at all academic levels, in all settings, both urban and rural, among different generations, classes, and factional affiliations, and even sometimes within individuals themselves. The most common points of reference in this respect were the reconcentration of resources in key schools, tracking students by ability, the new materialism, and especially the quantitative declines at the secondary level. Some interviewees were even embarrassed by the latter, or unwilling to say too much, evidently taking their cues from official press accounts which acknowledged the cutbacks but rarely any opposition to them.

For the most part, interviewees seemed unaware that they were reproducing the ambivalence of earlier generations toward radical education reform. Few seemed to know about its origins in the 1920s and 1930s, having come by their own commitments during the Maoist era of cultural revolution and class struggle. In any case, their views were now tied not to any romanticized reform ideals but to the decidedly unromantic facts of their own recent work experience. Sometimes in spite of themselves, these former teachers had acquired mass-line commitments during their revolutionary line of duty that now placed them at odds with the renewed surge of regularity being decreed from Beijing.

Instructor Li, from Guangzhou, inadvertently provided the clearest illustration of how this ambivalence was being carried forward from one political era to the next. He also illustrated how such mixed sympathies were able to transcend, as they always had, the barriers of age, educational level, and class background. His own personal experience was rich and varied, dating back to the anti-Guomindang student movement of the late 1940s. But except for a brief period in the early 1950s when he had participated as a young intellectual in land reform, expropriating and redistributing rural landholdings, Li's adult life had been confined to tertiary education. Evidently, his leftist leanings had allowed him to move more or less unscathed through the 1949–1966 years, despite his family's overseas capitalist connections. Nor did the Cultural Revolution bring him much harm. But by 1976, he was more than ready to embrace the cause of regularity, if for no other reason than to restore tertiary-level standards to university teaching and research. Merciless in his ridicule of the worker–peasant–soldier students, he gleefully contemplated their disgrace as repeated attempts to regularize their status after 1976 were rebuffed by the Education Ministry.

Still, Instructor Li could contain his enthusiasm for the competitive hustle into which his own children were thrown as they tried to adapt to all the new tracks and streams at the secondary level in Guangzhou. By 1980, the best teachers had already been reconcentrated in the key schools along with students scoring highest on the reunified secondary school entrance exams. Admission to these schools had therefore become an absolute necessity for all with college aspirations. But since junior middle schooling was universal in city schools, unprecedented numbers were now vying for admission to the few key points, making competition far more intense than before 1966.

Instructor Li's ambivalence was greatest with respect to rural schooling, however. Initially at a loss to answer such questions due to his admitted lack of firsthand experience, Li responded with some perfunctory remarks based on official accounts and conventional urban teachers' wisdom. Later, he paid a visit to his schoolteacher relatives in suburban Guangzhou, whom he had not seen for several years, and felt duty bound to return with an update on his earlier remarks.

Originally, he had presented the conventional and official argument for closing rural middle schools. Given their low quality and the new college entrance exams, rural students could not hope to attend college. Perhaps they could at least aspire to better, nonagricultural jobs. But since "most peasants are very shortsighted and cannot see that far . . . , so they ask themselves what is the point of continuing on in school." True, junior middle education had been universalized in many rural locales, but that had been a "false" achievement because it was based on the junior middle sections attached to elementary schools and most of their teachers lacked the qualifications to teach higher grades. Such schools must therefore be closed.

As luck would have it, one of Li's country cousins taught in just such an attached school. She was also its ranking teacher, with over 30 years' experience, had presided over the growth of the section grade by grade, and made short work of his received wisdom. When she arrived at this village elementary school in 1965, it had a six-year curriculum with one class of students per grade. After 1968, it became a five-year school like most in Guangdong, but then in the early 1970s, it added a two-year junior middle section. In 1977, a third year was added to make an integrated eight-year school with two classes per grade. Virtually all children in the production brigade entered first grade, and at least 80 percent of the elementary-level graduates continued their studies.

When instructions came down to close the junior middle section, commune and village authorities procrastinated on grounds their youth needed the extra years of schooling. For most students there was no alternative since the main commune school was five-hours' round-trip from the brigade. Li refused to abandon his original hallowed argument that "even if rural children study in middle school, they still have to cultivate the land, so the majority do not study diligently, because it is of no use." But he had revised his opinion that secondary schooling was of no use *at all* for such students and changed his mind about closing their schools as well. "Since the villages are so dispersed and transport is so inconvenient, if students cannot attend school near their homes, then it will be impossible to meet the needs of the peasants and develop education."[1]

---

[1] Interview 80/GD/1, pp. 83–93.

In moving one step closer to his rural relations, of course, Li's new insights took him one step away from the new Education Ministry line. Teacher Dai recalled how this came down almost immediately, in 1977. He first learned of it in the form of a restricted-circulation Guangdong provincial directive which reached his county education bureau in Shaoguan Prefecture within a year of Mao's death. Dai had just been transferred from his commune school, joining the great movement of teachers back to towns and key points from rural and ordinary schools, which also began immediately. He thus came to know the specifics of the new directive, which his former colleagues only learned about through hearsay and secondhand accounts.

According to Dai's recollection, the new directive stipulated that localities should not run schools indiscriminately and fixed precise conditions. No more than 66 percent of all elementary graduates should be allowed to continue their studies, and the proportion of junior secondary graduates continuing on should not exceed 33 percent. Too provocative to be publicized at the time or later, this directive explicitly overturned the education revolution's most sacrosanct aim by exonerating the traditional divisions between mental and manual labor, long before this restoration culminated in the 1983 directive linking college degrees and bureaucratic posts. The 1977 directive argued that schooling was unnecessary for many different occupations and that universalizing secondary education at the mass level was too expensive – hence the decision to restrict enrollments.

The new ratios were issued only "in principle," however, and when Dai left the county in early 1979, promotion rates were being maintained throughout at about 80 percent and 60 percent for the two levels, respectively. Still using the old logic, local authorities had decided the new rules should not apply to them since their county was "such a backward place" in the mountains, with minority communities as well, which was why they had especially "concentrated on developing education and running more schools." By the new logic, they would soon be running fewer schools for precisely the same reason. Dai also recalled that the restrictions had been introduced as the basis for future state expenditures, to be budgeted for the planned numbers of students and staff necessary to teach them. The reduced enrollments were also to be enforced uniformly in cities and countryside.[2] In any case, by the time secondary school restructuring was complete in the early 1980s, nationwide promotion rates had been reduced to more or less exactly the 66 percent and 33 percent limits, respectively (see Table 17.6), that Teacher Dai had recalled from the original, 1977 directive.

Between 1977 and 1982 lay years of heated arguments and angry scenes as schools and districts everywhere at first disbelieved, then tried to negotiate,

[2] Interview 80/GD/2, pp. 8, 24–25.

and finally had to submit. Only then did the full impact of "restoration" finally become apparent. In the meantime, the delayed-action sequence and "eyes only" internal explanations contributed much to the confused responses of both some interviewees and the localities they described. Throughout all the polemical arguments, no one except perhaps those in topmost Party circles seemed to take literally the allegations against those in authority bent on "walking the capitalist road." Embellishment and exaggeration were the stock-in-trade of any good rhetorician, as everyone knew. And the basic tenets of socialism seemed well established in what was after all a Marxist–Leninist party. Even the 1971 conference had prefaced its assessment of teachers' "basically bourgeois worldview" by acknowledging that "the great majority support socialism and are willing to serve the people."[3] Hence it was with genuine surprise, recalled rebel Teacher Cheng, that after years of lambasting Deng Xiaoping for walking the capitalist road, they found out it was "really true!"

One can only fantasize, then, about what a different course the Cultural Revolution might have taken had polemics been banned and the accusations spelled out for all to see ahead of time in well-researched briefing papers. Instead, when the line changed after October 1976, but at first only to the extent of denouncing those who had presumed to usurp Mao's correct revolutionary line, the tendency was to welcome an end to Maoist excess and assume all other points would be negotiable. Local authorities could therefore decide initially that the new rules restricting enrollments did not apply to them, as was their custom when instructions came down with which they disagreed "in principle." Interviewees recalled the sequence of such local responses as principles turned into absolutes and compliance was mandated through budgetary and administrative fiat.

Meanwhile, the "regular" assumptions of Chinese pedagogy were officially rehabilitated to justify the controversial consequences, free of all Soviet and Maoist constraints for the first time since 1949. The late 1970s thus witnessed the revival of ideas and assumptions kept alive after 1949, first as a foil for Soviet-style remodeling, then as part of the 1958–1966 Sino-Soviet compromise version, and finally as targets of revolutionary wrath. Now, stripped of all such disguises, the old assumptions of professional Chinese educators about how to turn out a quality product reemerged as quaint reflections of an earlier age strangely out of place in the service of Deng Xiaoping's quest for modernization and advanced world standards.

According to the old arguments, reflected in Instructor Li's original remarks, quantity and quality were not two sides of the same coin but contradictory demands that could only be met each at the expense of the other. The quantitative gains of the Cultural Revolution decade were therefore "false" and

---

[3] "Quanguo jiaoyu gongzuo huiyi jiyao," *Zhongguo dangdai jiaoyu sichao, 1949–1989*, p. 233.

did not deserve to exist, because they had been achieved through irregular schools or those without all the proper rules and regulations and systems. Such schools, by regularity's definition, were not really schools. And no schools were better than inferior ones. Peasants, in any case, did not need schooling and preferred work to study, or at least could not excel in academic pursuits because they had to labor. Education was therefore of "no use" for them – an ancient line of reasoning that pushed the parity principle to its antithetical limit.

In this manner, the new educational line was enforced, demonstrating finally what the two-line argument had been all about. But by then it seemed as if central decision makers must indeed be the sole guardians and promoters of the two lines, which were designed in ideal-type forms too pure for most ordinary mortals to accept. Hence no single interviewee could have been categorized (at least not by the time of the interview) as an unqualified adherent of Mao's radical education reform. But very few, perhaps no more than four or five, could recount without flinching all the consequences of implementing the new line. Just as in pre-1949 decades, educators seemed to fall not at one or the other ends of the regular–irregular spectrum but somewhere in between.

Old assumptions were thus used to rationalize the overthrow of Mao's line, which for its part had incorporated old radical ideals in the service of his Cultural Revolution. Both lines deliberately invoked these precedents from their past. But the ambivalent response of interviewees also suggested that regularity and populist concerns, however changed in contemporary form, remained as two opposites destined to move in an adverse relationship, each pursuing the other into an indefinite future.

Such conclusions were inescapable from interviewees' accounts of the post-Mao years and their reactions to them. It was also impossible at this point to distinguish between their own reactions and those of the communities they were describing, since the former obviously derived as much from the latter as from prior conceptions or ideological convictions. These accounts can therefore be used to illustrate both how the education revolution ended and how its populist concerns were reproduced quite naturally in a new generation of educators who had inherited such sympathies via the Cultural Revolution but now seemed destined to perpetuate them by some other means.

Reaffirming the urban–rural divide:
a place for everyone and everyone in their place

Teacher Wang disapproved of the decline in secondary-level enrollments elsewhere. But he insisted this had not yet occurred in his suburban Shanghai county in 1979 when he left, and he refused to believe it ever would. Half-educated teenagers had been "sent out into society" in the early 1960s, he said, "but they would be very bitter about doing that now." He estimated complete universalization through junior middle school among town dwellers in the county and at least 90 percent of the age-group among rural householders. Nor had dropouts increased due to the new agricultural responsibility system, of which he also disapproved nonetheless. Communes were well run and rich in suburban Shanghai, so he failed to see the advantage of breaking them up.[4]

Teacher Lei from Guangdong similarly could not believe the reports and rumors about closing attached junior middle sections. His large commune in Xunde County had relied entirely on these sections at the junior secondary level. Lei expressed something akin to the north Fujian view of rural people as distracted from learning by other paths to prosperity. "The way out for Xunde people is through commerce," he said; "they do not emphasize culture." Yet Lei and others from the county also described a rural community where mass education through the senior secondary level was firmly rooted.

Universal elementary schooling was the norm by the mid-1970s. All brigades also had well-attended junior middle sections, and a few even added an extra two years of senior schooling as well. Collective and household sidelines were common, and older students would sometimes work their own way through school, assuming individual responsibility for some sideline to earn the few dollars (*rmb*) charged for tuition and books each semester. Such student independence from what was usually a family responsibility was reported nowhere else.

This was also the only county to produce an eyewitness account of living *sishu* remnants. Three women in another commune gave private first-grade instruction in Chinese language only, combining modern textbooks with traditional methods, including chanting, memorization, and foot-rule discipline. Every year, much to the regular teachers' amusement, these women submitted their textbook purchase orders written in the old style complete with classical words of praise for Chairman Mao. Each teacher had 20 or so students, and parents paid two or three times the usual brigade school tuition rates to give their children a "proper" first-year grounding in Chinese characters. The custom had persisted through the mid-1960s, when there were still not enough elementary schools for all, and continued by popular demand into the mid-1970s because some still felt the old way of learning characters better than the new.[5]

Teacher Lei's main commune school – which had itself grown from humble origins as an attached junior middle section created in 1958 – had senior-level classes only, serving about 500 students in 1978. He left that same year, when the school was just in the first stages of "grasping quality." Everyone was already exasperated at the ensuing drive to increase pass rates into college. In

[4] Interview 80/S/4, pp. 13–15.
[5] Interview 78/GD/6, pp. 19–20.

1966, the number one mobilizing issue for the county had been these very same "capitalist" methods, and the bitter struggles against them were still fresh in everyone's memory. "The headmaster at first did not dare return to the capitalist line after the Gang of Four fell. He was afraid. But after a time, if the school wanted anything, it had to get more students into college. . . . So they are now all at it again, pushing the students on. And they do not worry about the future, because they must fear the present. People will criticize you now if your students don't get into college."

Caution was then thrown to the winds and all the old methods were revived, including some never dared before. Of about 300 graduating seniors in 1978, 100 were selected for key-point instruction, and then 20 of the best were selected for instruction during the final two months prior to the college entrance examinations. Teachers could see that only 10 had a chance of passing and did not want to waste time on the others, but the only deference made to past sensitivities was to leave the final cram class at 20 students. Ultimately, 3 were successful.

At the same time, however, the county was moving forward to the next phase of quality building. This meant not just encouraging the best students and teachers to transfer into the main county-town key point but introducing unified all-county examinations and enrollment. The highest-scoring students from each commune would then be automatically channeled into the main county school. At this point, exasperation grew into defiance, and the commune schools refused to participate in the proposed new arrangements. The issue had produced a "great contradiction" in county education circles, with argument "heated" and the situation "complex." The commune schools challenged the county education bureau's proposal: "How can you have schools competing to be first and have an all-county rank order if all the good students, the best conditions, and best teachers have already been concentrated in only one school?"[6]

This question, of course, pointed logically to the final solution. Commune senior middle schools were in the process of being redefined out of existence, although in 1978 that end had not yet been spelled out in so many words. According to the new rationale, secondary schooling was not an end in itself and peasants in any case did not need it. Senior middle schools should be college preparatory, and commune middle school graduates could not compete in cost-effective numbers with their urban counterparts.

Other interviewees recalled how the orders finally came down, between 1979 and 1981, to begin closing the schools themselves. Just as the aim was to recreate proportions from the mid-1960s, so school closures followed the same pattern. As a rough rule of thumb, schools established between 1966 and 1976, both in the city and in the countryside, were ordered to stop enrolling new students, graduate those already in the pipeline, and then cease operations. For rural communities, the goal really was to approximate the earlier "golden age" when county towns had only one or two complete middle schools and each commune area was served by only one single junior section. As indicated in Tables 17.5 and 17.6, the pattern was only approximated, not actually duplicated, but the consequences were traumatic enough.

In a neighboring Shaoguan county, Teacher Tang was able to witness the onset of implementation that Dai had missed. So far as students and teachers in the commune middle school were concerned, there had been no advance warning, prior consultations, or any opportunity to express opinions afterward. One day during the spring semester 1979, the headmaster and commune education cadre went into town for a meeting. They returned to announce that there would be no freshman class at the senior level in the autumn nor in any autumn thereafter. The decision was announced to the students at their weekly assembly, and the deed was done. About half the commune senior middle schools in the county were similarly closed that year, on a "last-opened, first-closed" basis. Although "low quality" was given as the reason, all the schools targeted had been opened during the preceding 10 years, and the closure orders disregarded differences of quality as measured by promotion rates.

Even though Tang still regarded himself as the "sacrificial victim of factionalism" because of his assignment to this far-off hill district and had already applied to emigrate as his means of escape, he nevertheless sympathized with the local people. "Of course, the peasants had opinions," he recalled, only they were given no chance to voice them. They knew their children had little hope of going to college but had set their sights on this lesser goal. There were over 80 students graduating that year from the junior level, and in previous years most would have continued on. Only about 30 passed the new, unified all-county entrance exams, however, and only a few of the 30 actually entered senior middle school, due to the distance and expense involved in going outside the commune to school. "At least they used to have the poor and lower-middle peasants' representative," said Tang. "Now, the intellectuals and education bureaus just run everything."[7]

By contrast, Teacher Hong was one of the oldest interviewees and also one of the few who could be categorized as hard-line intellectual–bureaucrat on this issue. Guangdong's provincial education bureau had decreed the return of secondary schooling to its antebellum state, he said, leaving counties and prefectures to argue over the details. By 1981, his county in southern Zhanjiang Prefecture had completed the task, allowing by his calculation a net gain of

---

[7] Interview 82/GD/9, pp. 82–84.

only two senior middle schools. After 1966, he knew of six commune junior middles that had added senior sections to approximate the standard one complete school per commune. Four of the six were then closed, along with most of the junior middle caps. These latter had been sufficient to offer places to all who wanted them at that level in town and countryside alike.

Hong also recalled quotas having been sent down from the provincial education bureau directing localities to return to the pre-1966 pass rates of about 60 percent from elementary into junior middle school and 30 percent between the junior and senior levels. Numbers must be controlled in order to "control quality," he explained, embracing the official rationale without reservation. Commune residents had "many opinions," to be sure, and the resurrection of the work–study agricultural middle school was uniformly rejected by the target population. They wanted their own ordinary commune-level schools. But "they do not understand that there is no point in an education that is of such low quality."[8]

Teacher Hong was rare in expressing himself so frankly, however. He was joined by Teachers Liu and Mei, already cited for their categoric rejection of rural education. In Teacher Fang's case, it was not quite clear whether he himself belonged in this category or was only describing the views and actions of others who did. Although relatively prosperous, his north Fujian county was a world apart from the south coast communities. Before 1966, its sole middle school had never sent more than four students per year to college. Worker–peasant–soldier students were more numerous. But in 1977, 1978, and 1979, the old pattern resumed even though most of the 13 communes in the county now had complete middle schools located within their boundaries. The entire county of nearly 300,000 people produced fewer than 10 successful candidates combined during those three years. The education bureau therefore proclaimed the "failure" of rural education and began closing commune schools while raising requirements for those remaining.

All of this produced a "great opinion" among rural residents, recalled Fang. But they "accept that the reason their children are not getting into senior middle schools is because they are too stupid to pass the entrance exams. Of course, it is not put quite in that way. . . . If it was, the peasants would surely start a fight. . . . Instead, the school just says that a child's grades were not good enough. The entrance exams mark the gate. Those who pass can go to senior middle school. This is accepted." In Fang's view, work–study agricultural middle schools were the only answer for rural youth.[9]

The new regularity nevertheless imposed its uniform logic regardless of local demands and circumstances. But if rural communities in northern Fujian

[8] Interview 82/GD/8, pp. 10, 17.
[9] Interview 83/FJ/25, pp. 21–24, 63–70.

really did give up without much of a fight, the same could never be said of the South. Multiple pressures contributed to the tensions there. As noted, Luo Sulan and many others were arrested in 1976, and investigations continued through the 1970s against August Twenty-ninth Faction members. But in Jinjiang County, retribution was especially severe. A number of commune cadres were executed for associated counterrevolutionary crimes, and several others fled to Hong Kong in fear for their lives. The purge swept through educational circles as well. Rebel Teacher Lin spent a frightened 40 days and nights incommunicado in his commune's 1977 summer struggle–study class for interrogation and criticism. He emerged chastened but otherwise absolved of his past factional sins. Many were not so lucky. There were more suicides. Some commune education cadres received prison sentences. Rebel Teacher Guo was implicated in one such case. Still, the political turmoil did not hinder the onset of regularity.

All the coast schools that had perfected Wang Yugeng's methods and then ignited the Cultural Revolution by rebelling against them now returned to the starting line. They revived all the old regimens with unexpected speed and success, taking top national honors on the college entrance examinations of 1977 and 1978. Then, while they were still basking in the national limelight, directives began to come down. Talent must be concentrated. There must be no more "selfish" competition among schools for top students such as had marred key-point symmetry and wasted resources in the early 1960s. Commune middle schools must be closed and enrollments restricted.

Initially, brigades refused to close their junior middle classes, and communes refused to give up their senior middle schools. One group of reassigned key-point teachers even refused to return to town. Then, in deliberate defiance, they vowed to apply Fujian's best-kept secret (that, with the right methods, even ordinary schools could excel) and prepped their commune students to distinction on the college entrance examinations. Rather than risk an immediate Shaoguan-style ultimatum, however, Jinjiang County authorities applied the strategy used in cities and more educationally developed locales. This strategy was based on the assumption that if first deprived of all their best talents and therefore any hope of sending students to college, ordinary schools would accept the futility of their existence and collapse more easily when ordered to do so.

Before 1966, all five of the county's complete middle schools had vied for the best students and teachers. Now, resources were more systematically concentrated in the two town-based key schools. Students whose entrance exam scores fell within their grade-point range were denied admission elsewhere in the county. The two key schools in town were also ordered to revert to a full six-year curriculum, but all other schools were forbidden to do the same. Finally, commune senior middle schools were ordered closed in the early

1980s. The three surviving complete non-key schools, which served small towns and surrounding commune catchment areas, were ordered to become vocational or agricultural middle schools.

Teacher Huang recalled how everyone had continued to protest every step of the way. At one school, teachers challenged the headmaster and local cadres to be more "daring" and add the sixth year on their own. But they did not dare. Alumni complained that in the old days, half the school's graduates went on to college and now not even one could pass. Overseas benefactors, stumbling upon the controversy unawares, volunteered a large sum to expand a now overflowing commune school they had helped establish in the early 1960s. But instead of adding more classrooms, the education bureau ordered the money spent for other purposes, not daring to explain that the school was scheduled for "restructuring."

Vocationalization was the unkindest cut of all because, by this time, a few vocational courses had already been appended to some schools and they had all immediately "failed." The most famous case was a cloth-cutting course intended to train students for work in garment factories – which were nonexistent in the area. The classic defects of vocational schooling immediately manifested themselves for all to see, in the form of overly narrow specialties and the difficulty of matching these with available jobs.

Teachers, for their part, had welcomed regularity because it allowed them to enforce discipline by, among other things, proclaiming a direct link between classroom performance and life's prospects. Vocational education severed the link and made school again of "no use." All the graduates were equipped for, said Teacher Huang, was factory work in Hong Kong. If parents sent children through middle school, it was to prepare them for better lives and jobs. To deprive some but not all of that chance arbitrarily in this fashion was resented as unfair, the more so after 1976, when the value of such opportunities was being so greatly enhanced. And to close schools under regularity's rationale on the one hand while trying to vocationalize on the other seemed like regularity's perverse revenge.

The parity principle usually thrived under such conditions, and sure enough, it could be seen at work governing everyone's demands for fair access to the opportunities available. The interlocking doctrines of regularity then pointed to the same final antithetical solution for everyone. Education that was "no use" did not deserve to exist. "Better no school than an inferior one," said the professional educator. "Better no school than a vocational one" was the popular response.

"The masses, peasants, and cadres all have opinions," said Huang. "They want to know why." They were never told why, at least not in language that made sense to them. But he and his friends had deduced the reason: to enforce the urban–rural distinction. "What else could it be?" he wondered aloud. Only the two urban schools were now sending students to college while all rural schools in the county, whatever their actual quality, had been redesigned so as to make that end impossible. If all Jinjiang County schools had been allowed to compete, he reasoned, "rural students in college would outnumber urban. . . . Then, when they graduated, they would not want to return to the countryside, and there are not enough jobs for city people as it is." Nevertheless, rural educated youth were especially dissatisfied over this "unfair" treatment, he said. And Huang could not but sympathize, for he had crossed the rural-to-urban divide himself in the mid-1960s, by way of this very same Jinjiang County rural-school-to-college route that had just been closed.[10]

One question that did not intrude in this phase of Fujian's two-line education struggle, however, was factionalism. Members of the August Twenty-ninth Faction were being finally sorted out at this time, and their opponents had finally emerged victorious to enforce the ban against all faction-based activity. Hence, "factionalism has nothing to do with reactions to closing senior middle schools," declared Teacher Guo. This was in any case a "dangerous" question, he said, because it concerned the "line" and because factional activity was now impossible. Therefore, to oppose the current policy line for education as a factional cause risked the charge of counterrevolution, and he should not even be discussing such a possibility.[11]

Guo's disavowal of links between line and faction also seemed to be borne out by the four south Fujian interviewees who discussed related concerns. If any conclusions can be drawn from so small a number, the individual's own rural or urban origins were probably more relevant than rebel or conservative associations. Teacher Lin, urban born and raised, was an active August Twenty-ninth sympathizer. But he took the most "regular" stand against commune schools even though "his" faction had been dominant in his commune during the period of their greatest growth and he had personally benefited in many ways as a result of his association. Still, he claimed to be unconcerned about closing commune senior middle schools, a prospect that was only just being broached at the time he emigrated. By contrast, Teachers Guo (rebel), Huang (conservative), and Liao (conservative) were all sympathetic to rural populist causes, and all were rural or "partly rural" natives of Jinjiang Prefecture.

Teacher Liao especially seemed to have internalized the conflicting aims of radical reform and regularity. On the one hand, Liao blamed August Twenty-ninth rebels as Gang of Four allies for his wrecked teaching systems and Headmaster Chen's brush with death, and he disliked Jiangxi Gongda as well. On the other hand, his attachment to the new commune middle school he helped build and to its Maoist priorities placed him on a collision course with the post-1976 line.

[10] Interview 82/FJ/4, pp. 63–83, 106–110, 120, 137; also, on Jinjiang County at this time, interviews 80/FJ/8 and 82/FJ/11.
[11] Interview 82/FJ/11, p. 29.

Liao's adoptive commune lay outside the overseas Chinese district, was entirely rural, and had no middle school at all before 1966. But having conspired with like-minded conservative commune leaders to run as regular an operation as possible, Liao was proud of their achievements, which included the first-ever students from the commune area to attend college, both before and after 1977, when the national entrance examinations were restored. He also recalled some of the practical-learning projects he had organized, such as soil analysis and electrical machine repair, which his students later turned to profitable ends. Delighted at the return to regularity, he and his colleagues began laying plans to upgrade their "scientific basis" in light of the commune's various sidelines, its proximity to the south coast, and all the new economic opportunities. Construction had also just been completed on a new classroom building when orders came down in 1981 to end senior middle instruction. Here, too, the aim of the plan as announced was to cut back to 1966 levels.

Local opinion was "immediate and very great" among commune leaders and residents alike. The commune lodged a formal protest with the county education bureau, which responded that the new standards required middle school teachers to be college graduates and there were not enough of these to go around. The commune countered that it could find the teachers and pay them from its own enterprise earnings. Opinion among teachers was, as usual, divided: some hoped for transfers into town and so supported the cutback. Others, including Teacher Liao, sided with commune members in their protest. He recalled the debate they had waged with the county education bureau. The latter argued the case for regularity, comparing the main county-town key school's pass rates with those of the commune school: in 1978, 50 to college and 100 to specialized secondaries versus only 3 and 11 successful candidates, respectively.

The commune built its case not on pass rates but on its needs and resources. It wanted to upgrade the level of technical expertise in its enterprises in order to compete more effectively under the new economic and open-door policies. As to resources, there was no dearth of experienced teachers in the southern counties, and over 100 new post-secondary teacher training school graduates were being assigned annually to county schools. But the new post-1976 generation of students was now mostly of urban origin and unwilling to accept jobs at the commune level. By the mid-1970s, on the other hand, the new commune school had been turning out about 100 senior middle graduates per year and most remained at home. By building upon this base and strengthening the commune school, it could produce its own talent and would not need to wait for the uncertain favors of urban graduates. Instead of 100 new graduates per year, fewer than half that number were going off to school in the county town after 1981, and they would not necessarily return. As of 1983, however, the commune senior middle section remained closed, and its request to resume enrollments had not been approved.[12]

Of all the protest stories recounted, only two had partially successful outcomes. One such account was told by Teacher Shao from a county in Ningbo Prefecture, Zhejiang. This locality was also notable in that the decisions were managed far more "democratically" overall than elsewhere. Shao knew the story well as a resettled youth who had worked in a commune just adjacent to his hometown, gone off to college through the "backdoor," and returned as a salaried teacher in that same commune's middle school. This was a region like southern Fujian with a relatively dense population and many well-attended schools. But conditions and traditions were very different. Shao's county was rich and relied on its own resources rather than overseas remittances. Both individuals and collectives here were known for their entrepreneurial skills, which took them far and wide in search of contracts and markets. Nor had clipping such wings been treated as a prerequisite for political purity even in Maoist times, according to Shao and others.

Counties were divided into districts with many medium-sized communes averaging about 10,000–15,000 people each. Elementary schooling was common before 1966, but Shao's county, with over half a million people (1964 population), had only three complete and four junior middle schools, located one to a district. By 1980, every brigade school had a junior middle section. About 45 of some 60 communes had small senior middle schools as well, usually with one class of 30–50 students per grade in each school. So this was a community that, although predominately rural and inward looking, had nevertheless progressed well beyond the illiterate-peasant stage.

In 1981, the county education bureau called a meeting of over a thousand people, with representatives from all brigades and communes, including both cadres and teachers. The bureau chief addressed the meeting, which went on for three days. He spoke of the demands from above for quality, praised everyone's past activism, but said that education could no longer be run as before. Now there must be planning and better coordination. The order to close junior middle sections had come down earlier. This meeting was called to explain the closure of commune senior middle schools. Teachers would be given examinations. Those who scored highest would be retained; other work would be arranged for everyone else. Similar meetings were then held in each commune, to bring the message home.

The meeting in Teacher Shao's commune lasted for two days, with close to a hundred people attending, including leading cadres from all the brigades and most of the commune's contingent of about 80 teachers. Shao recalled how the commune Party secretary explained the situation: "He held up his hand, first

[12] Interview 83/FJ/26, pp. 40–41, 123, 135, 162, 259.

spreading out all five fingers, then doubling it up into a fist. If I hit a person with my fist, it is better, he explained, because then I can concentrate my strength to hit the person harder. . . . Similarly, we should concentrate our strength in fewer schools." There were two opinions. But here, the teachers had no objection to the new line. Brigade cadres and masses, on the other hand, refused to accept it. According to Shao's version of the story: "They said, we are running our schools well. If we were running too many schools, why didn't you say so before? . . . They also argued that to run a middle school is glorious; the cadres and masses all felt that way. . . . The main opinion of the poor and lower-middle peasants was that if schools were closed, then the road to school would be too long for their children to travel."

After two days, commune cadres ended with the inevitable ultimatum: "The higher levels have stipulated. There is no other way." But among themselves, they had already worked out a compromise, which they announced in conclusion. In fact, the compromise within the commune over junior middle sections was similar to that worked out between the county and the communes for senior middle schooling. Within Shao's commune, 3 of the 10 brigade junior middle schools were allowed to continue as "key points." For the county as a whole, about 20 percent of the communes retained their senior-level classes, albeit only with restricted enrollments. Shao's commune had been included in the 20 percent, he said, by reason of its proximity to the county town and the consequent close "connections" maintained between commune and county leaders. But he assumed the compromise they had all worked out internally among themselves was only an interim solution and would not be allowed to continue indefinitely. Here, too, only the main school in the county seat was authorized to resume the six-year curriculum, and only that school did so.

Still, young Teacher Shao could not let the story end without paying his respects to regularity. A rebel he may have been in his Red Guard days, but 15 years separated that time from the early 1980s. By then he was a teacher and had he not said all the teachers accepted the decision? To have only 20 students in a junior middle classroom was a waste, he declared. Buildings could be put to better use by the brigade and money saved. Similarly, when teachers' educational levels were not sufficiently high, they only wasted their own time and "harmed the younger generation" as well. He therefore felt, along with his colleagues, that "it is better to close down schools."[13]

In between the most culturally advanced and the most culturally depressed rural communities lay a Shandong county town (population about 20,000) where, quite by accident, Teacher Diao found himself a witness to the same course of events as Shao described. Here, local authorities tried first to introduce two new vocational programs. But as Diao recalled, "without students,

---

[13] Interview 83/ZJ/16, pp. 44–48; also, on patterns of development in neighboring prefectures, interviews 80/ZJ/10 and 82/ZJ/1.

you can't run schools." Both closed after only a few semesters. This county's communes had not done so well in meeting contemporary goals. Only about one-third had senior middle classes and all were closed, to a mixed reception by commune residents. About half the 5,000 secondary-level students attending the county town's five regular complete middle schools were boarders in from the countryside, however. Then it was announced that two of the five must be closed down entirely, with a net loss of 2,000 students.

Opinion was not divided, because everyone was against the plan. Diao had attended the three meetings held to pacify parents: one to explain, the second for small group discussions, and the third to "summarize." He remembered them as rowdy affairs with red faces contorted in anger and people openly cursing in "rude" northern style. Some never accepted it but others ultimately agreed with the official argument and professed themselves "willing to sacrifice this generation's right to attend school for the quality of future generations."[14]

In Shaanxi, Teacher Gao had missed such scenes. When he left in 1978, his commune's school system had been developing steadily, schools were well attended, mobilization was essentially unnecessary, and the request to run senior middle classes had already been sent up. When he heard reports of closing schools, he had assumed these referred to poorly managed schools someplace else. But when he returned for a visit in the early 1980s, he discovered that much of his generation's work had been undone. Even the commune seat junior middle school had been closed. The practice of recruiting a few rural residents for factory jobs in town had also stopped. Begun initially to offer resettled youth a way out and then extended to local residents as well, Gao thought of this as one of his generation's contributions to the region's progress, along with teaching in its schools. The small county of about 90,000 people (1982 population) had lapsed back into an earlier state, with only elementary schools in the rural areas and one complete middle school in the county seat.

When Gao asked why so many schools had been closed, his former colleagues only answered that certain absolute standards were now in force, and most local schools had been unable to meet them. The percentage of new illiterates was also growing. Gao himself had done the survey in his brigade before he left and recalled that over 95 percent of all school-age youngsters were entering elementary school in the mid-1970s. When he returned in the early 1980s, the figure was only about 90 percent, and dropout rates had also increased because students were quitting school earlier to help their parents "earn money." But quality had improved: students were spending less time doing manual labor; schools were using the nationally unified materials; better-qualified teachers had been assigned; and salaries had increased.[15]

---

[14] Interview 82/SD/14, p. 10.
[15] Interview 83/SX/20, pp. 89–98.

Reaffirming the elite–mass divide

The main roads may have all been rerouted back to town, but everything was changing there as well. From Shanghai, Teacher Rao now proudly proclaimed himself to have been part of the resistance all along. As he told it, they had "shouted Maoist slogans" by day while plotting subversive stratagems by night to keep Shanghai's schools as regular as possible. But he had accepted the quantitative gains and was also proud of what had been built upon them. He estimated that only about one-third of all urban Shanghai middle schools were complete as of 1966. By 1976, 10-year schooling had been universalized throughout the city. Then, between 1979 and 1982, Shanghai also tried to turn the clock back to 1966 by closing down about two-thirds of its senior-level middle schools. Students, teachers, and parents all opposed the move, recalled Rao, but to no avail.

In cutting so uniform a swath through town and countryside alike, the reduced enrollments followed time-honored custom by maintaining at least the appearance of equity while reaffirming its opposite. The uniformly declining national percentages therefore obscured not only the reaffirmed urban–rural divide but the elite–mass differentiation occurring simultaneously as well. Closing commune senior middle schools was but an extension of the latter, in any case, since those schools ranked at the lowest end of the elite–mass spectrum. Teachers Hu and Lang, both from Beijing, explained the impact of these renewed distinctions on schools, students, and teaching.

Teacher Hu, cited above for his unusually objective account of open-door education, was more or less consistent in his approach to post-1976 changes. He insisted that major reductions had not yet been enforced in Beijing when he left his post in mid-1980, and he too refused to believe the reports and rumors. "Social pressure is very great. If they tried to rule that 70 percent of all junior middle graduates could not go on with their studies, that would contradict the development of society . . . there would be rebellion [zaofan]." Nevertheless, the process of key-point concentration – whereby ordinary senior middle schools were being redefined out of existence without the participants actually realizing it – was already well advanced.

Hu had been transferred back to town in the mid-1970s, and his new school in northeastern Beijing at that time served a diverse population of vegetable farmers and industrial workers. By the time he left, the school's catchment area had been redrawn to separate the two communities, and all the best students had been channeled into key schools. These two trends together guaranteed that the school retaining mostly farmers' children would be sending not a single student to college in 1980. And for all his populist sympathies, Hu was not above repeating the conventional rationale for this development even when it concerned agricultural households living within Beijing's city limits: "The parents do not care. Their children just go home to work. Peasants there are earning twice as much as the average Beijing worker. . . . So now peasants do not need to go to college. They just need junior middle schooling, or even elementary education is enough for them. First, they can improve their economic status and then raise up their educational level later."

In deference to the new national unified curriculum, his school had streamed students into key, ordinary, and slow classes. The best students and teachers were concentrated in the key class, which was the only one able to keep up with the new curriculum. "Before, experimentation was the rule," and only the strongest teachers could cope. "Now, all is fixed from above," but still only the strongest teachers could follow the new teaching plans. As for the end result, "they are only grasping pass rates onto the higher level, and most students cannot keep up. This way is not good. It ignores whether students can absorb what they are being taught."

In 1980, his school had eight classes of students at the junior middle three level. Two classes, for whatever reason, did not even try to continue. Most of the top, key class did well enough on the all-city unified entrance exams to transfer to a key school; four average classes stayed on; the lowest scorers were admitted as probationary students. On four subjects tested, all earning 320 points or above could transfer to a key school. By contrast, his school's pass rate was only 120 points. Some in the probationary class had not achieved even this level, but under orders from the district education bureau, they were enrolled anyway at the senior middle level. It was because of this practice, begun when Beijing achieved universal five-year secondary schooling in the mid-1970s and still being honored in 1980, that Hu assumed some such compromise would be maintained between past quantitative aims and present qualitative restructuring.[16]

Teacher Lang had remained two years longer at his post across town and so witnessed the full course of regularization. No one was more bitter over its impact on schools and teaching, although he was not past joking about the central guardians seemingly locked into their perpetual search for an ideal reform model: "If the Education Ministry did not keep changing policies back and forth all the time, how would its employees have jobs to do and food to eat!" Lang's entire working life had been spent in northwestern Beijing, home to the nation's top universities and leading intellectuals, as well as suburban rural residents, "lower-middle" office workers, and descendants of Beijing's pre-1949 lumpen proletariat. Lang had taught in elementary and middle schools serving all the district's communities during a career that spanned two decades.

In the mid-1960s, about one-third of the students graduating from his old elementary school were continuing their studies, and urban residents among

---

[16] Interview 82/BJ/18, pp. 26–35.

them sometimes entered key schools. But only a handful of farmworkers' children entered ordinary middle schools nearby and even then "could not hold up their heads" in competition with their classmates. The Cultural Revolution he characterized as a period of "great contradiction between wrecking and expansion." Ten-year schooling had been universalized, and the distinctions separating various student bodies in district schools had been blurred somewhat. Neighborhood boundaries were strictly drawn, and everyone living within attended the same school regardless of who their parents were. Now everyone could even attend middle schools previously attached to the nearby universities, maintained originally for the children of university personnel. Teacher Lang had also transferred to one such school and then on to a new middle school in the mid-1970s. He recalled 1977 and 1978 as the best years, when regular teaching routines were being restored and the curriculum was being upgraded, but before other changes had been imposed. As these took hold, Lang's world began to unravel once more. By 1982, he was happy to leave the district, its schools, and its students.

There was "chaos" (*luan*) everywhere and no one wanted to teach. He cited two reasons: lingering Cultural Revolution influence and the revived key-point system. Communism's claims to infallibility had been destroyed by the Cultural Revolution and its negation. Students now believed in nothing and everything. They were looking everywhere for answers, to anarchism, capitalism, liberalism, and rebellion. "They have an answer for everything; the teachers can tell them nothing." His own political inclinations were not much different, but he could only lament the impact on teaching and learning. Discipline was impossible to maintain. Yet he could not decide which was more responsible: politics or the key-point factor.

Key schools grasped quality for top-scoring students but seemed to demoralize all else around them. Ordinary schools raised "great opinions" arguing that "their promotion rates are being achieved with our students" as the brightest were being reconcentrated in key points. Teaching also became more difficult in schools deprived of all the best students: "The brightest are very useful in a classroom. They answer questions and other students learn from them. When the best are gone, there is no one left to perform this function."

Unlike popular opinion against reduced secondary enrollments, that aroused by key schools was acknowledged in the official press – briefly in late 1981.[17] The Education Ministry then actually reversed itself to the point of recommending neighborhood, rather than key-point, enrollment for elementary schools. This was only the second example recounted by interviewees where protest among the public concerned had any direct result in the late 1970s. "The

---

[17] E.g., *Renmin ribao*, 12, 15, 17 Nov. 1981; *Guangming ribao*, 7, 16 Nov. and 5 Dec. 1981; *Beijing ribao*, 12, 25 Dec. 1981 and 3 Jan. 1982.

reason for the reversal," said Lang, "was that ordinary schools raised too great an opinion." But the recommendation was not enforced. "In responding to pressure from the masses, they just said they would do away with key points; but then they did not actually take action." The newly re-created key schools retained their facilities and teachers. And they continued to concentrate the "best" talent in various ways. At the elementary level these usually included an assessment of the child's intelligence as well as of parents' intellectual and social standing. The ministry also refused to extend its recommendation to include key-point enrollment at the secondary level.[18]

Meanwhile, regularity's seductive message soon provided the final solution, precisely as policymakers had intended it should: "The only students who have any hope of getting into college are those who can enter the key schools. Ordinary middle school students have no hope, no hope at all. So they just relax and do not try in school. They feel that it is no use to go to school. . . . Of course, the teachers tell students not once, but repeatedly, that the purpose of schooling is not to go to college but to improve themselves and their own abilities. But it is no use. They will not listen." Regularity's self-fulfilling prophecy thus triumphed in Beijing as it had everywhere else, with increasing dropout rates and ultimately the closure of ordinary senior middle schools as well. Teacher Lang's school stopped enrolling at the senior secondary level in 1982.[19]

---

[18] The controversy over key schools continued through the 1980s, however, and the ministry did eventually rule against them at the junior middle level (see Pepper, *China's Education Reform in the 1980s*, chap. 6).

[19] Interview 83/BJ/3, pp. 45–46, 83–94.

19

Chinese radicalism and education development

Answers to questions raised at the outset can now be summarized in relatively simple terms considering the complexity of issues intervening. Those questions had multiple dimensions extending over space and backward in time while nevertheless focusing on more contemporary Chinese realities. The spatial dimension involved external perceptions, or how the international development community could have anointed China's early-1970s experience as worthy of worldwide attention and emulation when the Chinese themselves would soon declare that same experience to be devoid of even a single redeeming virtue. Confronting that question required a systematic assessment of China's early-1970s experience with educational development, which then raised additional questions about where the Chinese formula of that time came from and where it might be going.

From international dependent to Third World model

To begin with the outside world's perception, a number of hypothetical possibilities presented themselves. Most obvious was that the West had, in time-honored tradition, projected its own needs upon an idealized version of Chinese realities. The international development community's needs in this instance, however, were neither trivial nor contrived. They had evolved during a quarter century of conscious effort after World War II, building upon a prewar history extending back at least as long. Their origins seem to lay at an unrecorded point of confluence between democracy and socialism, lost somewhere in early-20th-century time. But if the issues were not new to the 1960s and 1970s, they were at least different in degree, reemerging as a series of crises and contradictions which quickly eroded the promise of new postwar and postcolonial beginnings.

The aim had been to close the gap between rich and poor nations, and education was conceived as an integral part of that endeavor. But as the United Nations First Development Decade (1960–1970) ended, the search was intensifying for more refined definitions and strategies to accommodate a changing emphasis from the wealth of nations to the realities of life within them. Priorities were shifting from urban to rural, from industry to agriculture, and from economic growth to essential human needs. The last included ways to guarantee employment, income, nutrition, health care, and schooling for those left out and left behind. Rural needs naturally emerged as a major concern in this evolving equation since they were usually greatest, most difficult to meet, and concerned the largest number of people.

Along with the new priorities finally came a growing conviction that they could not be realized without redistributing existing economic and political power. By the early 1970s, the balance of opinion within the international development community was clearly moving leftward in favor of such a socialist-style prescription for failings that the initial formulas seemed powerless to prevent or surmount.

For education specifically, the challenge entailed a series of interrelated failings. Even universal elementary schooling had proved an elusive goal. The number of illiterates in Third World countries thus continued to rise, although education systems were expanding at an unprecedented rate. It had also proved easier to build new schools than to provide comparable employment opportunities for their graduates within developing Third World economies. The disruptive potential of ensuing unfulfilled expectations prompted the initial round of serious second thoughts about the enterprise that had been launched with such high hopes only a few years previously.

Yet the kinds of adjustments that seemed necessary to ease such dysfunctions often provoked resistance too great to surmount. What was at first seen as a simple matter of quantitative growth led to demands for relevance and dilution of standards which typically conflicted in turn with inherited assumptions among providers as well as consumers about what to teach and how. Such conflicting demands also anticipated conflicts of interest associated with the most intractable of all dilemmas, namely, those concerning equity and fair access. Having proclaimed education a basic human right, societies now had to find ways whereby that right might be universally claimed by all.

The externally generated dependency principle contributed further to these dilemmas as Third World education systems sought to continue ties established during the colonial era with dominant Western nations. The aim was to maintain international standards, but the consequences were decried by critics (at home and abroad) as a form of cultural alienation, or the need to copy everything from technology to values and lifestyles. For education, both the standards and the copying were relatively easy to sustain in small colonial-style systems, but they were much more difficult to perpetuate as quantitative gains took hold. A dual "two separate worlds" solution commonly evolved, with one high-quality form of schooling up to international standard for elites and something less or nothing at all for everyone else.

Naturally, given the interrelated and conflicting nature of the concerns, there were no ideal solutions. Governments could only devise strategies that balanced costs and benefits in ways their societies would accept and their economies could afford. But it was at this point, in the early 1970s, when optimism was long gone and the reasons were being widely acknowledged, that China's new education revolution made its international debut. By a seeming coincidence of circumstances, the Chinese had encountered the same dilemmas and had designed solutions compatible in almost all respects with the new perspectives taking shape internationally.

Half the answer as to how the development community could have been so taken with the Chinese model thus lay in the eyes of the beholders themselves – already primed by two decades of frustrating experience with alternative solutions. But the other half of the answer concerned the specific Chinese solutions, which in concept and design were all but unique in providing the outside world with a real test case for its evolving hypotheses.

Internationally, China had cut its ties with the dominant powers of both the capitalist West and the communist East. Free of external obligations and the need to compete or approximate advanced world standards, the Chinese appeared set on an independent course, beholden to no one. They seemed to have emerged from the Red Guard inaugural phase of the Cultural Revolution bent on reviving the promises of an almost forgotten socialist tradition – confirming the all-or-nothing case being made for a redistribution of economic and political power as the chief prerequisite for effective strategies of action. Measures to equalize incomes further were being promoted in both Chinese industry and agriculture. The same course was also being followed in other areas of social policy. And especially in education, the dominant thrust was in the direction of a more egalitarian distribution of resources and outcomes.

Then, as the line changed after Mao's death in 1976, everyone quickly immersed themselves in another new beginning. The earlier years began to retreat into a past which everyone for their own reasons was trying to forget, deny, or negate. In such a political climate, the old Hong Kong interview technique that had proved so useful in the absence of alternative research materials became the only means of capturing memories before they receded further. The results suggest that perhaps the single greatest fault of polemical claims before and after 1976 was that each denied the validity of the other. However destructive the conflict between them had been, China's education system was in fact the net achievement of neither one nor the other but of both.

Universal elementary schooling had been actively promoted by the central government and basically achieved for rural people as well as urban (ethnic minorities exclusive). The state had assumed responsibility for this burden in cities, but in the countryside it had been achieved through the combined efforts of the collective support network and individual village communities applying the principle of local self-reliance, with minimal state assistance. The formula was able to realize the proclaimed goal of providing a school in every village or the near equivalent and also of mobilizing, short of outright compulsion, almost all children to attend.

Unified enrollment and work assignment plans, in place since the 1950s, had coordinated the supply of college graduates with the number and kinds of jobs available, including those jobs college graduates were conventionally loath to enter. Then, in the late 1960s, the Third World problem of rural–urban migration had actually been reversed, with urban youth being recruited for resettlement in the countryside. The movement was orchestrated as a political imperative but was also implemented to transfer urban youth, whose numbers exceeded the openings on their local job markets.

In terms of content and quality, education was integrated with labor or productive work at all levels. The role of examinations in school life and as entrance requirements was reduced if not actually eliminated. Chinese educators were no longer allowed to use their hallowed quality–quantity argument either to inhibit growth or to concentrate resources. And to ensure consistency, academic secondary education, as well as the tertiary level generally, was deliberately downgraded as a focus of development while major effort was concentrated on building a nationwide system of mass education through the secondary level.

Finally, what international observers lauded as egalitarian aims the Chinese themselves advertised in Marxist terms as measures designed to reduce urban–rural and mental–manual distinctions. However styled, the Chinese record in addressing this category of concerns was more ambiguous than others. A major "failure" given the declared aims was the difference between state and collective ownership and consequent forms of remuneration. This difference coincided with the urban–rural divide and marked a major distinction, adding to all the other negative features of rural life, in an economy where the great majority still derived their livelihood from agriculture. Effective curbs had also been placed on rural–urban migration in order at least to maintain the promise of urban state ownership while confining rural people indefinitely to the position they had acquired at birth on the nether side of that all-important divide. What one egalitarian socialist hand gave in terms of redistributing wealth and power the other hand took away in the half-fulfilled Chinese world of part-state, part-collective ownership. The criteria whereby urban people were transferred "downward" also reinforced the negative associations of rural life since the losers by any standard, whether politics, class, or whatever, always seemed more likely to draw the rural assignment.

Yet within the confines of those basic dividing lines, the Chinese had undertaken many specific measures aimed at reducing economic and social disparities, as well as income differentials between mental and manual laborers within both the state and collective sectors. In addition, substantial political capital had been invested with the aim of reversing the order of popular prestige between and among the various dimensions at issue. A revolutionary regime that identified directly with "poor and lower-middle peasants" was at least not obliged to make undue concessions to the old educated and social elites. Rather than sources of political power and support, these became targets for transformation and status reversal while the resources previously concentrated in their interest were redistributed more widely than ever before.

Most impressive from the outsiders' perspective, however, were the changes introduced specifically within the education system itself. These were clear and unambiguous – especially since there was no evidence of any external reference points save for an idealized revival of the old Marxist goals. Responding otherwise only to internal pressures, including those from below (the popular rejection of inferior *minban* and agricultural middle schools) and above (the Maoist assault on elites), all the arguments over two legs and two systems were laid to rest. The education revolution cut across all the social divides and barriers: urban–rural, mental–manual, elite–mass. Gone were the distinctions between regular and irregular, vocational and academic, self-supporting half-work, half-study and state-financed full-time, key and non-key.

In cities, the distinction between state and *minban*, or collective neighborhood-financed schools, also disappeared as the latter were absorbed within regular public school systems. The fundamental divide remained in the countryside between state and collective ownership, but to ensure quantitative rural expansion, the state had assumed responsibility for running a middle school in every commune and authorizing "state assistance" however minimal for collectively financed elementary schools and junior middle classes down to the village level.

Contributing further to the success of this endeavor was the commune structure itself, which served as the basic unit of local government coordinating the work of its constituent production brigades. This particular mix of public management and local collective ownership allowed the *minban* versus state-run distinction to merge, in administrative and financial fact as well as in name, within a single commune-coordinated school system.

Whether this application of the parity principle was consciously designed in deference to the popular rejection of inferior alternatives cannot be verified. But interviewees confirmed that Chinese educators had recognized and articulated the general urban and rural rejection of the two-legged solution promoted between 1958 and 1966, or at least the inferior leg thereof. Nor was the rejection of inferior expedients even by rural parents a new phenomenon. Jiang Longji's report on rural school administration from the mid-1940s, written to vindicate the success of the newfound *minban* solution, nevertheless acknowledged the local pressures for upgrading such schools to "proper" state-run status. And he had cautioned also about maintaining a quality-oriented edge in order to keep up morale as a prerequisite for maintaining local support. Once expectations had been aroused, inferior irregular expedients could not succeed in direct competition with a regular alternative. The design introduced during the 1968–1976 Cultural Revolution years acknowledged this lesson by attempting, in effect, to institutionalize irregularity as the unified norm.

On this basis, a uniform work-oriented system aimed also to equalize access across the urban–rural divide. Consistent with that aim, student enrollment plans for the restructured tertiary level contained specific quotas for rural-born youth and urbanites resident in the countryside. These quotas guaranteed places for each category while all alike were subjected to the labor requirement prior to admission.

But if neither the outside world's interest nor the Chinese reality was contrived, and if for the first time in its modern era China was not following in the wake of "world trends" but actually helping to establish them, why then did Mao's successors turn in such a fury to negate the experience that could boast such achievements? The answer lies, of course, in the outside world's readiness to "leave to one side the explicitly political" while concentrating on the "eminently sensible" Chinese approach to educational improvement.

Such a perspective was not necessarily a bad thing, of course. It had allowed China to shift its status from international dependent to Third World model. And people borrow ideas all the time without absorbing the sum total of all related parts. Indeed, such attempts at mechanical copying had long been identified as a major pitfall in the international transfer of ideas and institutions, leading China itself, when the shoe was on the other foot, to inappropriate imitation rather than creative adaptation. But in this case, to have disregarded the political imperatives surrounding China's early-1970s education revolution – and especially the 1966–1968 mobilization phase which launched it – would prove a fatal error. Accordingly, international champions were deprived of both the hindsight necessary to understand where the revolution had come from and by extension the foresight needed to anticipate its possible future course. As a further consequence, they were also robbed of their own primary reference point. Having been elevated to a unique status among Third World nations, the Chinese model was transformed overnight from asset to liability when China changed course to embrace the very priorities it had been lauded for successfully challenging.

In its role as international reference point, the Chinese model then seemed to play out one last act upon the world development stage, assuming a transitional vanguard function. China's shift in any case coincided with an abrupt halt to the bandwagon momentum for human needs priorities and socialist-style perspectives that had rolled out of the 1960s. China seemed to set the pace as world trends did an about-face to embrace capitalist alternatives once more. Old values revived in favor of privatization, free markets, cities, and industry. Rather than redistributing wealth and power, their concentration would be approved in the name of an emergent middle class, posited as the ultimate, ideal solvent for all problems. Among the latter, moreover, growing inequality was justified as an inevitable consequence of modernization to be tolerated for an uncertain period of indefinite duration.

The rise and fall of China's education revolution

Yet to note the outside world's failure to anticipate such an eventuality is not to explain China's total rejection of its education revolution: costs, benefits, international model, and all. Here, the "explicitly political" causes must be identified more directly as those associated with China's 20th-century critique of modern education and Mao Zedong's concept of cultural revolution, which finally forced that critique upon the entire school system. In an ironic ending, the final set of political-economy conditions to which development experts were turning as the course of last resort, and the conditions they saw vindicated in China's achievement, became a major pretext for its negation. The revolutionary redistribution of power culminating in the 1966–1976 Cultural Revolution was not, however, the only cause.

Given the extremes and excesses involved, either one or the other of the two forces – either systemwide radical education reform *or* the class-based cultural revolution which launched it, rationalized it, and provided the concentrated political power necessary to achieve it – would have been sufficient to provoke a mighty backlash. The two together ensured that all the enemies Mao had made in the process would unite to demolish his grand design whatever its actual achievements.

In searching for its roots, however, China's education revolution also emerged from the exercise as no accidental hero of latter-day development concerns, even though the earlier Chinese experience played no role whatever in the international community's later efforts. Yet Chinese reformers had been self-consciously exploring the same concerns or their clearly identifiable antecedents for at least half a century, making the Chinese case well equipped to serve as a model for illustrating both the issues at stake and the difficulty of their solution.

China's 1970s experience should therefore be seen as the culmination of an evolving critique almost as old as China's modern school system itself. And that experience epitomized in turn the long-standing controversies associated with introducing Western education systems into non-Western societies, especially those with large, preponderantly illiterate rural populations. The controversies were firmly grounded in 20th-century educational history, both socialist and otherwise. They were then easily transmitted across the development-conscious political time zones of pre- and post-1949 China, where they served as authoritative precedents of inspiration for the ongoing reform of its modern schooling.

The pre-1949 past

Under the old regime, Confucian learning, imperial power, and bureaucratic authority were bound together in a mutually sustaining relationship that had dominated Chinese intellectual, political, and social life for centuries. Personifying that relationship were the literati–officials and scholar–gentry, whose monopoly over both formal bureaucratic position and informal social influence derived from the examinations they had passed and the degrees they had earned. The traditional relationship between learning, power, and influence ended with the abolition of the civil service examinations in 1905 and the overthrow of the imperial system itself six years later. Observers were referring in the early 1930s to that old relationship when they noted the coherence of the traditional order by contrast with its still unreconstructed modern successor.

Perhaps because of the traditional association, political and educational reform remained closely bound in the modern era. So close were the links, in fact, that educational issues became an accurate barometer, reflecting more sensitive internal controversies within the political arena. These continued while successive generations struggled to complete the task of national reconstruction, which would remain unfinished even as the century neared its end, with a new societywide consensus yet to be formed over the necessary institutions, values, and arrangements.

Some distinguishing marks of the early modern school system that was built upon the wreckage of the imperial past were the assumption that Western learning would bring China wealth and power in a modern world where China's Confucian heritage was of little value; the assumption that study abroad and foreign degrees could be substituted for classical learning and the old examination system as a source of personal position and influence; a consequent voluntary dependence on foreign education systems as models for development; and the paradox of the reform mentality, or constant change as one of the few constants in a society struggling to reconstruct itself but unable to agree on what course to take. Consequently, students returning home with their foreign degrees superimposed a succession of foreign models upon the new education system – firm in the belief that following the dominant world trend of the day in this manner was a key to China's modern regeneration.

The modern system came to be characterized by these features as it absorbed the successive reform models and then evolved into an increasingly centralized, officially authorized, "Chinese-style" amalgam of tradition and modernity. Yet even as the system developed in this manner, it simultaneously inspired an ongoing antithetical rebuttal. The ensuing demands for more radical reform grew initially from a complex self-critical reaction that set in among intellectuals after 4 May 1919. They were reacting partly against the new Western learning, which they themselves were importing, and partly from the perspective of that learning against continuing features of Chinese tradition, which they were also perpetuating. Thus, like everything else in Chinese society of that time, including the modern school system itself, the critics' motives also were a mix of old and new. According to this new critical assessment of progress to date, however, that system was suddenly derided as a "hybrid," a "head with no base," and the "worst of both worlds."

Specific points in the new radical critique were the creation by modern schooling of an urban-oriented elite divorced from Chinese realities and especially from rural realities; the mechanical adherence of that elite to Western models; and the formalistic nature of these models whatever their national origin when transplanted into Chinese soil. Meanwhile, the new intellectuals were like the old in their aversion to manual labor, their aspiration to become public officials, and their separation from the masses. Intellectuals stood accused of maintaining the ancient pretensions of the Confucian past and transmitting them from one generation to the next while abandoning their traditional informal leadership roles as rural scholar–gentry for the lure of modern city life.

The critique thus drew strength from the major social and economic divisions that modernization also stood accused of intensifying. Those divisions were especially between town and countryside – or a way of life that was more outward-oriented, wealthier, and more intellectually advanced, by contrast with the inward-looking, technologically backward, economically deprived, and semiliterate existence of China's rural majority.

In its origins, then, this was a critique of and by the intellectuals. It concerned the changing nature of education and the design of institutions that would prepare successor generations for their new places in a modernizing society. And these concerns placed China's pre-1949 critics many decades ahead of postcolonial dependency theorists in worrying about the dysfunctional coexistence of separate forms of schooling: one for elites tied to external realities and one tied to the grassroots concerns of everyone else.

But for China itself, the pre-1949 critique also heralded a specific pattern of response to the all-important Western intrusion that would extend well beyond the education sector. Having held out for some four decades longer than the Japanese when similarly challenged, the Chinese then jettisoned their empire and their Confucian classical learning with unseemly haste for so unyielding a tradition. Perhaps because the tradition had been so self-confident and the rush to learn from the outside world so unaccustomed an exercise, selective superficial copying became the rule and dislocations the inevitable result, followed by individual and social self-doubt.

The critique of Western learning that matured after 1919 was only the first such major reassessment following the first rush to overthrow the past, which culminated in the 1911 revolution. But the pattern was set: rushing to embrace the outside world in hopes of finding solutions to problems its intrusion had precipitated, and then reacting adversely when the solutions failed to materialize. Nor did it matter that the copies were always selective and partial aspects of the foreign experience as seen through Chinese eyes. Reflecting the still unfinished tasks of national reconstruction which initially set it in motion, the pattern of attraction and reaction would also still be evident, albeit on a diminishing scale, even in the final decade of the century.

Chinese intellectual and political leaders would never again abandon outright their sensitivity to foreign influence. Hence, they could be seen tilting in succession for inspiration toward Japan, America, Germany, Russia, France, and then dividing their loyalties between the emerging mid-20th-century superpowers – as each in turn epitomized the dominant "world trend" of the day. The habit could be seen at work almost continuously, appearing both in grander, more overt and in lesser, indirect versions. But from at least 1919 onward, the preoccupation with world trends rarely continued for long unchallenged by the antithetical charges of mechanical copying, dependency, national inferiority complex, etc. And whenever the borrowing was indiscriminate enough to produce clearly identifiable negative consequences too great to be contained, co-opted, or absorbed in the traditional manner, some such self-critical antiforeign backlash would be sure to follow. It was as if the 19th century's resistance had evolved into a 20th-century interim solution for checking and balancing foreign influence that served as a defense mechanism against the intrusive outside world until such time as China's modern reconstruction could be successfully accomplished and the nation's self-esteem restored.

During the 1920s and 1930s, education reform projects inspired by the new ideals came and went. Even if most individual reform projects failed, however, the critique itself lived on and sharpened into a critical consensus. All intellectuals everywhere were not necessarily in agreement, and those who were did not necessarily place equal weight on all the associated points. But adherents could be found all along the political spectrum, and their arguments had grown so popular that almost everyone seemed at least to be paying lip service to them.

Yet despite this common denominator of agreement, the regular education system defied the challenge and remained impervious to reform along the lines being advocated. Reform projects failed for reasons that could usually be traced to some immediate political or military intervention. But the interests and commitments of professional educators and intellectuals were also responsible. Typically, so little tolerance existed within the regular school system for reform experiments that such projects had to be set up outside the system, where, without protection, they fell easy prey to myriad enemies.

By an accident of circumstances, the stark landscape of northern Shaanxi provided the clearest pre-1949 illustration of just how "established" the critique of regular schooling had become. Yet clearly indicated as well was the gulf that separated the critical ideals from regular schooling and how that gulf would be reinforced under communist rule. Literacy rates in the Shaanxi–Gansu–Ningxia Border Region were among the lowest anywhere when the region became the CCP's new headquarters, and there was no formal modern education to speak of until Long March veterans began promoting basic elementary schooling. But leftist refugee intellectuals, who arrived in ever greater numbers from Japanese-occupied China after 1937, soon took over the CCP-led education department in Yan'an. The results were immediately apparent as they began transforming the haphazard rural-oriented development they found into a conventional pattern identical in form and structure to that developing elsewhere in China.

Accordingly, the new system created in Yan'an between 1938 and 1942 was distinguished by its preoccupation with "quality" and the pursuit of "regularity" deemed essential to achieve it. Item by item and directive by directive, these definitions were imposed upon the border region's schools. Quality could only be guaranteed via fixed, uniform standards governed in turn by fixed "systems" of rules and regulations for all aspects of school life. Quality also could only be guaranteed by concentrating resources in a few centers of strength. And quantity had to be sacrificed for quality even to the point of closing down existing schools. This could be justified by citing a lack of demand among illiterates, plus ensuing obstacles so great that "a hundred years" would be needed to surmount them.

Equally explicit, however, were the reform directives of 1944 which reversed the regularization drive. Citing Marx, Lenin, and China's own experience, the new line stopped quantitative decline in favor of a more practical kind of education based, at the elementary level, on an updated government-assisted version of the old *sishu* tradition with its ad hoc financial arrangements and teaching methods to match. Following this logic, the only way there could be a school in every village, and by extension universal elementary education, was through such irregular expedients wherein uniform standards, fixed systems, and quality control were impossible to maintain.

This dual reform exercise in Yan'an was pivotal to China's educational development on several counts. One was the manner in which the differences between the regular system and its critics were reinforced by the two sets of reform proposals. Each followed consecutively at the immediate and clearly apparent expense of the other, based on antithetical definitions of quality and quantity. Schools had to be closed and enrollments reduced if the 1938–1942 regularization drive could achieve its purpose. Subsequently, it was claimed, the only way there could be a school in every village was by not worrying too much about regularity's prerequisites.

The 1938–1942 regularization drive thus showed most clearly what could only be deduced from earlier and later data, namely, that poverty and lack of "demand" among illiterates were not the only obstacles to mass education. The priorities of professional educators, with their assumptions about the need for quality and how to structure a system so as to produce it, were also responsible for pre-1949 China's poor record in eradicating illiteracy. The decision to reduce enrollments throughout the Shaan–Gan–Ning region illustrates this point. So too does the respective use of traditional private tutor schools. The regular system ignored them as a spent resource, while the emerging irregular alternative began to recycle them as the only means of achieving universal elementary schooling.

The latter solution was, of course, still slow to evolve by comparison with Japan's efficiency in tapping the potential of its own similar *terakoya* tradition. But even though they were then looking to the Japanese for inspiration, China's early modernizers essentially ignored Japan's mass-level achievement together with the leadership, funding, and administrative arrangements necessary to accomplish it.

Instead, Chinese educational leaders proclaimed the same aims but seemed to remain tied to their own much stronger intellectual bureaucratic tradition and assumed that the new learning should be used as a formal substitute for the old. They therefore turned the old facilities for preparing candidates to take the civil service examinations into modern schools while encouraging them to rely on the same administrative and financial arrangements as their predecessors. The new modern schools were then advertised as foreign inspired, and for better or worse, the entire society regarded them as such. But they were designed and managed to reproduce formalistic definitions of quality education that owed as much to China's own tradition of learning and examinations for elite selection as to any foreign inspiration.

Consequently, the masses continued to be educated in unreformed *sishu*, memorizing their Confucian primers or nothing at all for half a century after educated elites had shifted to regular modern schools. Hence the critics complained about a widening divide between elites and masses precipitated by the new modern schools. Hence also the critics maintained that even with the existing handicaps represented by a large, preponderantly illiterate, impoverished, rural population, China's educational leaders were themselves at fault for the ineffective use of existing resources in developing a modern system of mass education.

That at least some understood the complexities of the task was demonstrated in the mid-1940s Yan'an reform documents, which detailed quite precisely the checklist of prerequisites for creating a viable system of mass education especially in a rural setting. These included the impetus provided by higher authority via an overall public policy with adequate enforcement mechanisms; plus, at the grassroots level, leadership, funding, clientele support, and parity sufficient to sustain local interest. But understanding the task and performing it universally were two separate features of the same reality that were never effectively joined in pre-1949 China – kept apart by the same considerations that separated advocates of regular-schooling from their reform-minded critics.

Reflecting and reinforcing that separation, moreover, was the means whereby irregular alternatives were imposed in Yan'an: as part of a major rectification drive designed to strengthen CCP leadership via imposed political and intellectual conformity. In this way, the Yan'an experience played an important adaptive function between past and future. Integrating the decades-old critique of China's modern education within the theory and practice of Chinese communism allowed the old reform ideals to become part of a policymaking precedent within a new political establishment that was about to win national power. Yet the experience presumed to close the gap between lip service and action via rectification, or enforced obedience. And it was the Yan'an solution as a whole that would later be invoked as precedent rather than the more benignly ineffective critique contained within it.

Nor did the Yan'an solution have to be invoked directly in so many words. Thereafter, whenever education reform aimed to implement key elements of the old critique on a major scale, interests of the regular educational establishment were inevitably threatened, and the resistance it inevitably posed was overridden by CCP dictate. The essence of the precedent then became enforced political and intellectual obedience as a prerequisite for radical education reform.

Learning from the Soviet Union

Inexplicably, the CCP then set aside one of the most basic lessons from its Yan'an experience in deference to a foreign precedent. Perhaps intimidated by the burden of national power, Mao and his Party sought authoritative foreign reference points in a manner comparable to the initial turn-of-the-century rush to learn from the outside world. Perhaps the CCP was also daunted by the enormity of its commitment to overthrow both existing forms of economic ownership and the social-class structure based upon them. Popular enthusiasm generated by a national mass movement to learn from Soviet big brother could serve as a useful expedient in neutralizing some of the resistance a socioeconomic revolution of such magnitude would create.

Nevertheless, the Party paid a heavy price for its initial decision to emulate the Soviet Union in all things great and small. Costs were calculated in many currencies: political, economic, and social. But from the CCP's perspective, a most basic miscalculation in "mechanically" transplanting the Soviet model was its status as the end product of Stalin's adventure in revolutionary and economic development when the CCP was only just embarking upon that course. Then, compounding the basic miscalculation, no sooner had decisions been made and all necessary plans had begun to take shape than Stalin died. His passing in 1953 precipitated important changes within the Soviet bloc and for Soviet education, as well as for China and Chinese education.

Hence, it was only after the intervening embarrassment of de-Stalinization in the Soviet Union began to compromise their new foreign copy that CCP leaders shifted gears in the mid-1950s to pick up where they left off a decade earlier when civil war interrupted rural-oriented mass-line reform. Not surprisingly, editorial writers and intellectual critics needed little prompting to revive the old "mechanical copying" theme. Premier Zhou Enlai himself had to stand before the nation's intellectual community in 1956 and perform the CCP's mea culpa as he proclaimed the changes necessary to break China's dependency on the Soviet Union.

In the meantime, Chinese educators and the system over which they presided had been making their own accommodations with the Soviet import. These were accommodations of the lesser sort, when a major antiforeign backlash was not possible or necessary, but which were endemic in the presence of a foreign intrusion and netted much the same result, in the long run, through absorption. Despite initial objections, restructuring Chinese higher education to emphasize science and technology was accepted, along with the dispersal of tertiary-level training away from a few major urban centers into every province. This historic adjustment in the career structure of higher-level Chinese intellectuals held and was undoubtedly assisted by being tied so firmly to the state plans for economic development. It guaranteed "cadre," or official, careers and status within the new system of material rewards and social prestige. But not accepted were the egalitarian prerequisites of Soviet pedagogy and various irregular remnants also remaining from the Soviet Union's own past. On these points, co-optation set in almost at once between the Soviet transplant and its host environment as Chinese educators demanded appropriate adaptation to "Chinese conditions." Many such adjustments occurred, always at the expense of the Soviet model in deference to its regular Chinese counterpart.

By 1956, the points of adjustment already included the demise of shortened five-year elementary schooling, the demise of worker–peasant short-course middle schools, authorization to create key-point schools, the pattern of quantitative decline associated with qualitative reorganization at the elementary level, the use of unified examinations to rank schools, and the introduction of a unified national college entrance examination. After de-Stalinization in the Soviet Union precipitated the "hundred-flowers" liberalization in China and mechanical copying was officially approved as a subject for criticism, the ensuing debates suggested just how much further the regular education system might have gone, if allowed, in rejecting the Soviet transplant.

At the same time, *minban* schools, junior middle caps, ad hoc teacher training courses, and anti-illiteracy work were all residual features from the CCP's own "irregular" rural past that suffered setbacks as regularization proceeded in the form of a genuine Sino-Soviet compromise. In all the "necessary systems" relied upon by Chinese educators to maintain order, discipline, and daily routines, as well as in their ambivalent approach to manual labor and practical training, it was often difficult to see where regular Chinese modes stopped and those of Soviet educators began.

A conventional urban-oriented college-preparatory system had been deemed essential to meet demands for trained personnel once planned Soviet-style heavy industry was accepted as the basis of Chinese modernization. The Soviet model thus provided a ready opportunity for Chinese educators to reassert inherited assumptions about how to produce a quality product. And on that basis, they were by the mid-1950s already well on their way to taking over the Soviet import.

That a newly victorious CCP would not be able to live with the contradictions inherent in such a system, whatever its mix of regular Soviet and Chinese features, should have been anticipated but evidently was not. In effect, the CCP's most basic challenge at this juncture was its inability to reconcile or ignore the conflicting demands created by Soviet-style industrialization, Chinese socioeconomic realities, and the CCP's own revolutionary commitments.

The new education system continued to rest upon a base of mass illiteracy which it could offer little hope of eliminating in the foreseeable future. The demand to improve quality as needed for Soviet-style modernization and as defined by Chinese educators could only be achieved at the cost of reducing numbers and the rate at which teachers were trained to teach them. The goal of universal elementary schooling would recede even further into the future under a rigorous application of the Sino-Soviet convergence model.

At the same time, the unprecedented growth of elementary and secondary schools that had occurred meant increasing numbers of graduates for whom there were no places available at the next higher level. Another potentially disruptive symptom of development was therefore looming in the form of young people whose aspirations for more schooling and/or employment commensurate with their new education could not be immediately met.

Because of the great need for development personnel, most secondary school graduates in the years after 1949 had been able to continue on to college. But expansion at the tertiary level could not continue indefinitely to match that of secondary enrollments. An increasing number of elementary- and secondary-level graduates would therefore have to reconcile themselves to "productive labor" in agriculture and industry, and forms of secondary schooling would have to be designed that would be college preparatory for some but terminal and work oriented for the majority. Far from safeguarding China against these typical development dilemmas, the Soviet model seemed to compound them, and by the mid-1950s, China was already searching for alternatives.

The CCP was also looking for a model better able to meet its conflicting commitments overall since it remained bent upon fulfilling the terms of its self-proclaimed revolutionary mandate to eliminate private ownership and overthrow the existing class structure. Yet the need for trained personnel meant that the existing educated elite would perpetuate itself into the indefinite future, especially after the Party's early hopes for high worker–peasant college enrollments disappeared under the weight of Sino-Soviet regularization. And the educated elite was not only bourgeois by reason of its birth but, according to Mao's reckoning, remained essentially unchanged in its concerns and commitments, which were being passed on to the younger generation as well.

After the CCP inaugurated its class-based land revolution in Jiangxi during the 1930s, Mao had declared that discriminating against bourgeois teachers had been detrimental to its complementary goal of educating peasant children. Class warfare was then temporarily set aside in deference to the anti-Japanese united front. Party rectification in Yan'an had proceeded without the class-struggle imperative. Hence it was not until over a decade later, in 1957, that Party rectification and the antirightist campaign began the final step of combining radical education reform with the full force of China's social revolution.

Cultural Revolution

The struggle between regular education and its radical antithesis would, of course, not culminate until the 1966–1976 Cultural Revolution. Meanwhile, the CCP continued its search between 1957 and 1966 for a more appropriate Chinese route to socialism, which also culminated in the 1966–1976 experience. Undoubtedly not foreordained in 1957, that experience was the end result of an eclectic trial-and-error approach which proceeded from the demise of the Soviet model, through the Great Leap Forward, severe economic recession, and ensuing disagreements among CCP leaders over what to do next.

To say that the outside world's praise for China's independent course was not unfounded in the early 1970s, however, is not to say the same for Maoist claims to original inspiration. Particularly at the start, when China had to begin looking for another way, the 20th-century habit of seeking reassurance from authoritative foreign precedents was probably still operative. Politically embarrassed by their inappropriate Soviet copy, CCP leaders conducted their search more discreetly thereafter. But all the circumstantial evidence points to continuing Soviet influence, with the Chinese simply looking backward to a point in time when the Russian revolution was at a stage of development more comparable to that of China in the late 1950s.

The clues in this line of argument began with the education reforms of 1958 introduced by Stalin's successor to correct certain formalistic features of Soviet schooling. China launched a similar set of reforms at the same time, albeit without acknowledging the debt of foreign inspiration. Instead, the reforms were proclaimed as the cultural component of China's Great Leap Forward then under way. Meanwhile, Khrushchev for his part was invoking precedents from his own youth during a radical period in the late 1920s that Stalin had soon repudiated. The Chinese were warned repeatedly from 1949 onward that they should benefit by coming later and avoid such rash adventures as had occurred in Russia at that time. But after Stalin's death, details of the earlier period were selectively liberated from the dustbin of Soviet history with the publication of Stalin's *Works* covering the period and Khrushchev's partial exoneration of it. Assessing in retrospect the main features of China's Great Leap Forward, all could be found in some recognizable form within the earlier Russian episode. And a key rationale uniting both was the concept of cultural revolution in the superstructure as a safeguard against bourgeois restoration overall.

Both featured the general line for socialist construction, or high-speed in-dustrial and agricultural growth as a corollary of socializing economic owner-ship. As a further corollary, since it was the very moment when the "roots of capitalism" were being extracted, both also feared a bourgeois restoration led by dissident rightist intellectual forces. Both therefore redefined cultural revo-lution to include, besides conventional cultural and educational development, more or less militant versions of class struggle within the superstructure. Both treated conventional planners as "hopeless bureaucrats." Both championed mass action and mass movements to promote their aims from below as well as above. Both designed educational reforms to produce "red and expert" intel-lectuals who could succeed their bourgeois counterparts as leaders in education and industry. In this earlier incarnation, then, Stalin bore little resemblance to the commander of the regimented industrial model with its classless new elite of bureaucrats and technicians that would stand as his sole legacy. By contrast, the earlier Stalin had everything in common with Mao as of 1958. The main difference was that Stalin would soon repudiate his mass-line image, declaring its job done while he dispatched remaining enemies by other means, whereas Mao would reaffirm that image in an effort to continue the revolution and preserve its original goals.

Mao also had every incentive and opportunity to abandon the adventure. Overall high-speed economic growth collapsed into economic recession, and goals for agrarian communism – as the CCP's ultimate answer for China's 20th-century preoccupation with rural reconstruction – had to be drastically scaled down as well. For education, the original 1958 reforms were in any case an eclectic mix and might have been allowed to continue in that vein unchal-lenged by further revolutionary disruptions. Evidently, CCP leaders, who had been united behind the Great Leap in 1958, were now divided, with some ready to call it a day and move on to more conventional "revisionist" formulas.

Instead, Mao consolidated his forces and tried again with the Great Proletarian Cultural Revolution. The contradictions built into the original 1958 education reform package were therefore addressed from the radical "left" rather than the bureaucratic "right."

If China initially copied from the Soviet Union due to inexperience, however, Chinese leaders were still not very experienced when they struck off on their own in 1958. This inexperience showed not only in the apparent continuing need to adapt (if not copy) foreign precedents but also in the unviable combinations that more astute social designers might have avoided. Since Mao's critics never even hinted that in this instance (unlike the 1957 blooming, contending, and antirightist sequence) he meant to lay a trap for professional educators, it must be assumed that the contradictions of 1958 derived from genuine miscalculations about how to combine conflicting goals.

One major contradiction was created with the authorization of quality-oriented key-point schools in the midst of a developing cultural revolution already being defined as a safeguard against bourgeois restoration. A second major miscalculation was to promote irregular inferior alternatives for the masses while key-point-led regularity was being established as the system's standard-bearer. Designers seemed initially oblivious to the bizarre nature of the structures and functions they had thrown together in this two-legged solution.

For the irregular mass end of the spectrum, education policymakers in 1958 seemed not yet able to grasp the implications of their modernizing efforts to date, which would soon be acknowledged elsewhere as the revolution of rising expectations and pressures for parity generated thereby. Probably because ordinary folk had seemed content with their *sishu* and the *minban* version adopted in Yan'an, so policymakers in applying the 1958 formula seemed genuinely unprepared for the change that had overtaken their mass base during little more than a decade's time. But the story was the same everywhere, in city and countryside alike, with the targeted clientele rejecting agricultural and *minban* alternatives as inferior versions of "real" regular state-run schools.

For the elite end of the spectrum, designers seemed equally oblivious of the restorationist tendencies key schools would advance. Khrushchev's initial reform proposals for the Soviet Union also contained a provision for such special schools, to serve as islands of quality in an expanding mass system. But the elitist implications proved still too controversial and were formally dropped. In China, they were retained, evidently as a gesture of compromise with professional educators, who had chafed and grumbled throughout the 1950s under the egalitarian strictures of Soviet pedagogy.

Yet given the state of its developing revolution, the CCP could not have sanctioned a more inappropriate course since it not only legitimized all the convictions of Chinese educators about regularity but actually strengthened them by reviving associated ways and means that had lain dormant for decades.

China's key-point hierarchies were thus systematically established only after 1958. And they were unique in trying to adapt for nationwide use principles of regional representation and educational achievement inherited from the imperial past, when carefully controlled proportions of candidates were maintained at every level and in every region.

It was as though China, unified in fact as well as in name for the first time since the end of the imperial era, was now moving instinctively to re-create nationally unified educational structures and practices for elite selection that had also not been seen since the fall of that same empire. The formula would have been anachronistic in any modern setting but was especially incongruous for China between 1958 and 1966. The organizational strength of a communist state was being used to re-create educational forms and functions modeled directly on those of the imperial bureaucratic past – even as CCP leaders were formulating the rationale for continuing the revolution to prevent a bourgeois restoration in the superstructure!

The warning signals began in 1962, with the increasing emphasis on politics and class or family background as admissions criteria. Favored family backgrounds were revolutionary reds: workers, peasants, and cadres. Yet ordinary worker and peasant youth reputedly could not hold their own, especially in key schools, where academic achievement was measured on competitive examinations. Hence the common response among headmasters was to relax admissions standards for those among them most able to compete, namely, cadres' children, while compensating them further with special tutorials to help them on their way. In this manner, the 1958 formula was also restoring another time-honored function of the imperial bureaucratic tradition by inducting the children of a newly empowered "outsider" political establishment into the rarified world of China's intellectual elite.

For China's intellectuals, then, the post-1958 construction of key-point hierarchies and all that went with them, including the assumptions of professional educators about how to produce "quality" via examination success, epitomized the central contradiction that Mao had long ago perceived between the prerequisites for revolution and those for development. The CCP had done its best to discredit the "old" intellectuals for their bourgeois orientations and, in 1957, to expropriate any of their remaining independent political influence. Yet the Party had also reaffirmed their authority over the education sector, even encouraging them for the sake of Chinese national independence and modernization to exercise that authority through the most traditional of means.

In any event, had Mao set out to create a target against which to mobilize his last great revolutionary upsurge, he could have done no better than the Chinese education system created from the 1958 reform package he authorized. The end result suited his purposes perfectly as he first activated the successor generation of cadres' and intellectuals' offspring to rise up and overthrow the system that benefited them first and foremost, and then manipulated the aroused energy to challenge their parents' generation for his continuing revolution. In this way, the possibility of suppressing the education establishment's influence and redesigning the entire system would finally be realized. And it was this unprecedented endeavor that caught the world's attention in the early 1970s. But the contradictions inherent in such a course would also ultimately leave the old radical reform ideals contained within it exposed to dangers as great, relative to scale, as those suffered at the outset by the isolated reform experiments in their original pre-1949 variations.

Incorporating the old ideals within Mao's definition of Chinese communism brought official political protection never previously enjoyed. It also risked rejection should Mao's definitions themselves be overthrown. Such an eventuality might have been preempted at any one of several points along the way after the education system's designers commenced their work in 1949. Instead, the assumptions of professional educators about quality and regularity, about how to achieve it, and whose children were best situated to produce it were actually strengthened during the 1950s and 1960s. Then, once those assumptions were tied to the all-encompassing finality of the two-line struggle in 1966, and once the lives and careers of all China's top leaders were jeopardized by that struggle as well, the end result was a foregone conclusion. The logic of extremes Mao had manipulated to such spectacular advantage was finally turned against him in death to negate his ultimate goal of safeguarding the revolution for posterity.

The post–Cultural Revolution future

Radical education reform under CCP rule was always associated with the conformity enforced by a rectification-style campaign.[1] But the education establishment seemed to emerge stronger in its convictions after each assault, displaying the same resilience after 1949 as before. All the old defining documents and directives from the 1930s were thus reissued after 1976, including both the GMD originals and the 1938–1942 Yan'an version. These served as authoritative precedents for the post-Mao course. And despite all that had happened in the interim, the restored system was also essentially the same in form and philosophy as that which professional educators had tried to develop in the Shaan–Gan–Ning Border Region between 1938 and 1942, when they sought to purge the nascent education system there of its irregular, rural features. The alternatives included: "regular" systems for everything; a preoccupation with

---

[1] This concluding section is based on a survey of education reform in the 1980s, as outlined in Pepper, *China's Education Reform in the 1980s*, pt. 2; and an update covering the early 1990s, in Pepper, "Regaining the Initiative for Education Reform and Development." For other sources on this period, see chap. 17, n. 29.

fixed, uniform standards; concentrating resources in a few elite schools; closing others to promote quality; relegating any remaining "irregular" solutions to a separate inferior status; and all the rest.

Accordingly, the professional Chinese educator's assumptions about whose children did best in school and whose children needed schooling were rehabilitated as well, while lack of demand, interest, ability, and other obstacles among the rural masses were cited to justify closing schools and sending students home to work. Also rehabilitated was learning directly from the experience of the capitalist West, which was entirely familiar to educators in 1938 but had not been permitted in so overt a manner since 1949. Deng Xiaoping himself promoted the revival of corollary assumptions, namely, that China could catch up quickly with advanced-world standards and that science, technology, and education were the keys to national wealth and power.

Beyond these pre-1949 precedents, however, the system restored after 1976 was the same as had evolved from those precedents in its mid-1960s format, complete with all the same policies, structures, names, and symbols. Included was the nationwide hierarchy of urban-based key schools and, at its pinnacle, the nationally unified college entrance examinations. Simultaneously, the regular system's incompatible radical companions from the mid-1960s disappeared completely. The Maoist legacy of class struggle, mass movements, and cultural revolution as a safeguard against capitalist restoration was repudiated and all enemies targeted thereby were exonerated. Gone as well were both negative discrimination against all the old enemies and positive discrimination in favor of the formerly disadvantaged blue-collar classes, leaving the children of cadres and intellectuals to reconcentrate unobstructed within the revived urban key-point stream.

Finally, pushing the trends a step further, new regulations were introduced in the early 1980s making tertiary-level education a prerequisite for official bureaucratic positions down to and including those at the county level – reestablishing the ancient link between academic degrees and public office. From there, it was only a few more steps to the postulates of some power holders and intellectuals in the 1980s. These included theories about "new authoritarianism" and tutelage-based democracy, the idea that their superior learning qualified higher-level intellectuals for political leadership, and the demand that they be designated a separate class or stratum – formulations all more reminiscent of the imperial past than of Mao's much feared capitalist restoration.

Some had evidently concluded that a "new" consensus for national 20th-century reconstruction was emerging based upon a reconcentration of intellectual, political, and bureaucratic resources within China's educated elite. But it was, after all, the late 20th century rather than a hundred years earlier, and in between lay the mass-based concerns that had come together during the early decades of the century to create the ongoing critique of China's early modern school system. Yet the logic of the political struggle had removed those concerns more effectively from the field of educational controversy than at any time since they were first raised more than 50 years earlier. In the late 1970s, all such concerns related to foreign borrowing, urban–rural disparities, and elite–mass distinctions were in effect banned not only from the realm of official policy but from public discourse as well.

The regular education system re-created after 1976 would therefore have appeared curiously disembodied were it not for ongoing indications that the old issues had not disappeared but only retreated inward. Had those concerns actually been eliminated or solved with the passage of time, they might have been safely consigned to the pages of history. Instead, it was only the public controversy that was, for a time, more or less effectively suppressed. Meanwhile, the regularization drive strengthened related tensions until they emerged once again, in a manner similar to their pre-1949 antecedents, when everyone acknowledged them but lacked the will or wherewithal to enforce genuine solutions.

By the early 1980s, tensions were already such that they could no longer be ignored or dismissed as interventions of recalcitrant Maoist sympathizers. Without actually admitting that the faults lay within the newly restored system itself, education authorities nevertheless began acknowledging the critical "opinions in society" which it had provoked. A stream of supplementary adjustments and reforms within reforms then continued throughout the 1980s, for every educational level, addressing various "opinions" and "interests" while carefully avoiding any direct mention of the more basic challenge they represented to the urban-based, elite-dominated regular system.

The most serious of those tensions as registered in the continuous undercurrent of pressures for adjustment throughout the 1980s were the demoralized state of rural schooling and the need for reliable sources of rural school financing; restricted enrollments overall at the secondary level; the many faults of the key-point system; the attempt to reimpose clear-cut vocational tracks and elitist streams; college students all drawn from the same urban key-point middle school source; the reluctance of such graduates even from smaller county-town key points to accept positions at the "basic" rural levels, where by the late 1980s they were most needed; and sending more students abroad to be educated in accordance with advanced world standards than could be similarly accommodated upon their return home.

In similar vein, the then minister of culture and former "rightist," Wang Meng, penned a dissenting rebuttal that flowed directly from the post-1919 reform tradition. But he was writing in 1987, with student activism already mounting over the multiple economic and political issues building within the post-Mao order. Sparring left and right, he deplored continuing evidence of the "line struggle as the key link" with political adversaries, who applied rhetoric over reason. But he also declaimed against the then popular tendency to look to the West for solutions. "During the past century of China's history, there were often people of the so-called modern school and the false foreign devils who learned a few superficial things from the West. But they ended up isolated and pitiful, with not a thing achieved."[2]

Midway through the decade, however, the old Education Ministry was upgraded to become the seemingly more powerful Education Commission. This mark of official recognition for the importance of its enterprise was in reality a kind of symbolic high point drawn even as the power of the central education bureaucracy, painstakingly accumulated over so many political generations, began to recede once more.

Demands for administrative and financial autonomy had grown along with the modern education system itself as its professional guardians sought means of safeguarding their sphere of endeavor from the political and economic uncertainties of the early republican era. But they eventually realized, as did their professional adversaries who criticized the regular system's deficiencies, that because education was a public endeavor, they needed a larger public authority to serve as protector, provider, and guarantor. Hence the demand of professional educators was not so much for local autonomy as for functional autonomy within a centralizing government bureaucracy. This demand could be seen at many points: in the successful lobbying efforts of provincial education associations during the mid-1910s for autonomous education bureaus within the provincial governments; in the abortive University Council system of the late 1920s; and subsequently in the national codification of an emerging "Chinese-style" system.[3]

Under communist rule, the centralizing trend strengthened but so too did nonprofessional and political interference. So thoroughly were their interests overridden in this manner that by the time education administration was decentralized during the 1968–1976 years, professional educators could do little more than hatch subversive schemes and reminisce about "the way things used to be."

Then, liberated from the dictates of Maoist rule, all the centralizing authority of a communist state was used to re-create the education system in regular form – until about the mid-1980s, which marked another "new" departure. In fact, it emerged gradually as the post-Mao market-oriented economic reforms were applied to schools in the form of increasing student fees, rising costs, and decentralized financing. The last, announced in 1984 but not fully operational until the early 1990s, in effect separated urban and rural funding. City school systems retained more reliable sources of public support while rural counties,

---

[2] *Renmin ribao*, Beijing (national domestic ed.), 8 Sept. 1987.
[3] Chauncey, *Schoolhouse Politicians*, p. 100; and chap. 4, above.

townships, and villages were left to rely on their own resources, without any higher-level public assistance.[4]

The result turned the clock back many decades as an economic crisis swept the nation's education system in 1993. Hardest hit was rural school financing, not yet reconstructed after the demise of collective agriculture and the support system that had been built around it. The phenomenon of unpaid teachers' salaries, a familiar problem before 1949, was reported from almost every province and acknowledged by Education Minister Zhu Kaixuan to be "unprecedented in amount, duration, and extent" since 1949.[5] Yet remedial measures were only partially successful. By mid-1994, just five provinces and three cities had cleared fully all their teachers' back pay, and some provinces were still unwilling to report their relevant statistics to the Education Commission in Beijing.[6] Nor did the center have the power to enforce compliance. Thus, the post-Mao education establishment had won a professional right to legislate for its own sphere against the intrusions of Cultural Revolution radicalism. But at the same time, mandated sources of funding for that sector were dissolving under the impact of economic decentralization.

The "fault," as always, was not one or the other but variable combinations of politics, economics, and professional assumptions about how to design and manage a modern school system. And, as always, this latest crisis unfolded *within* the regular system while the old tensions that had sustained the radical critique *against* it remained clearly in evidence. Urban incomes had grown to more than double those in agriculture, and some very old sounding concerns began to be voiced about the gap between coastal and hinterland development as well as about the potential danger of growing disparities between town and countryside.

Epitomizing these concerns for education specifically was the issue of private schooling advocated by the Education Commission as one of several expedients. The consequences immediately reflected the realities of Chinese life in the 1990s – and provoked a conventionally ambivalent response. For the new rich, ostentatiously advertised elite schools (*guizu xuexiao*) immediately appeared, charging thousands of *rmb* in deposits, tuition, and boarding fees. So ill-timed was this publicity in the midst of the 1993 crisis over public school funding, and so adverse was the public reaction, that central authorities promptly issued an official criticism of such pretensions.[7] In deference to popular sensibilities,

[4] Zhou Daping, "Tuoqian jiaoshi gongzi: yige bixu zhuajin jiejue de wenti" (Defaulted Teachers Wages: A Problem That Must Be Firmly Resolved), *Liaowang zhoukan* (Outlook Weekly), Beijing (domestic ed.), no. 42 (18 Oct. 1993), pp. 8–11.

[5] Quoted in ibid., p. 8.

[6] Liu Bin, "Guanyu shenhua nongcun jiaoyu zonghe gaige de jige wenti" (Some Problems on Deepening the Comprehensive Reform of Rural Education), *Renmin jiaoyu*, no. 12 (1994), p. 7.

[7] E.g., *Renmin ribao*, Beijing (domestic ed.), 4 Aug. 1993 (article by Zhu Kaixuan, minister of the State Education Commission).

all private schooling was rechristened as *minban*, or run by the people. Beneath the humble *minban* umbrella, however, grew another new sign of the times. Those with long enough memories may not have believed their eyes, but private-tutor classes had also revived after a hiatus of 40 years. They were being acknowledged, along with the name *sishu*, as the only means of providing low-cost elementary instruction for poor rural children whose parents could otherwise not afford the ever-rising fees charged by regular public schools even in rural locales.[8]

In time, the disruptive impact of such contrasts must wind down, since there is no indication of demand from any quarter to revive the class-based extremes of the communist revolution which galvanized popular sensitivities. But in the early 1990s, there was every indication that the old divisive concerns, which predated that revolution and helped define it, were still drawing strength from all the same unresolved contradictions of modernizing Chinese society that captured the attention of Chinese reformers during the 1920s.

The traumas that had shattered the coherence of China's old order and continued throughout the 20th century thus seemed certain to persist into the 21st. But eventually the measure of their ultimate resolution would be a new national consensus as strong as the old but incorporating the endemic modern concerns related to urban–rural disparities, elite–mass distinctions, and foreign borrowing. Accordingly, the paradox of the reform mentality would also moderate, and the nation's schools would be among the institutions reconstructed to withstand change and dissent instead of opening, closing, and re-creating themselves at every shift of the political wind.

[8] *Guangming ribao*, 16 Oct. 1994.

Appendix

The Hong Kong interviews

Part III of this study is based largely on data collected through interviews conducted in Hong Kong with former residents of China. The use of such émigré interviews as source material for academic research developed primarily among American scholars during the 1960s and 1970s to satisfy growing interest at a time when the state of diplomatic relations between the two countries precluded any kind of research in China itself. With published Chinese materials both restricted and ever more polemical in content after 1958, the émigré interview became an increasingly useful approach, whether as a substitute for survey research or as an oral history supplement for documentary studies. Most interviewing was done at the old Universities Service Centre on Argyle Street. The centre was set up originally, in the early 1960s, to facilitate independent scholarly research based on published materials from China, which were more easily collected at that time in Hong Kong than elsewhere. But the centre also maintained just the right combination of run-down academic respectability and detached anonymity necessary to accommodate interviewing, which became in later years its most important function.

As a latter-day convert to the method, I began interviewing sporadically in the late 1970s to supplement information gleaned during brief trips to China in 1975, 1977, and 1978, which in turn were providing bits and pieces of data for journal articles on changes in education policy. The Hong Kong interviews were also begun in hopeful preparation for a more systematic study in China itself to ask the same kinds of education development questions about the costs and benefits of Cultural Revolution policies implemented during the early 1970s.

The window of opportunity that seemed to be opening up in 1977 and 1978 did not materialize for this particular topic, however, due to the negative verdict soon imposed upon the entire 1966–1976 Cultural Revolution episode. My proposal to conduct a few months of interviews with university administrators under the new national United States–China scholar exchange program (administered by the Committee on Scholarly Communication with the People's Republic of China) was approved by the Chinese Education Ministry in 1980 on condition that questions be confined to post-1976 reforms only. Hence I decided to proceed more systematically with the oral history approach in Hong Kong, which I did during three summers in 1980, 1982, and 1983. By 1980, with the political trends of the post-Mao era already in place explicitly reversing all the same policies and programs that had earlier attracted the international community's attention – and with all the powerful opinion makers on this question, both political and intellectual, following suit – it seemed imperative to capture recollections as quickly as possible.

Following upon the interview-based research of Chan, Rosen, Shirk, and Unger (see Select Bibliography), who had all worked primarily with former secondary school students from the nearby city of Guangzhou, I decided to focus on small towns and rural areas and to tap the increasing numbers of immigrants entering Hong Kong from provinces other than neighboring Guangdong. My aim was not only to build upon the earlier education research but also to explore the reach of earlier polemical Chinese claims for Cultural Revolution education policies. These had made much of quantitative growth for everyone and explicitly of trying to reduce urban–rural differences. The reality of the Cultural Revolution's anti-elitist egalitarian claims was evident in cities everywhere as the regular system hastened to show off its reconcentrating resources. But simultaneously in the late 1970s, official statements announced across-the-board quantitative cutbacks and indicated a new posture of benign neglect for rural education in particular – suggesting that the preceding Maoist administration had followed different priorities to some substantive end. These were the more obscure undocumented and unresearched developments of the Cultural Revolution era and their subsequent reversal that I hoped to explore through the interview alternative.

I therefore returned from the 1980 China research trip to expand and modify my questions specifically to accommodate a rural focus, with three sections: one for elementary schooling, another for secondary, and a third for enrollment beyond and work assignments. I also adjusted the questions further to accommodate primarily those with the most extensive firsthand experience in education, that is, adults (teachers and administrators) rather than students. After 1980, I discouraged interviewees whose experience was limited to the tertiary level.

The interviews themselves were only semistructured in that I followed the topic outlines but encouraged interviewees to expand beyond whenever possible. Personal questions were asked only about each interviewee's own education and employment experience. I did not raise direct questions about their individual political attitudes, reasons for leaving China, or family class and political history – unless the conversation seemed to be heading in that direction. With so many potential topics, conversations could theoretically continue for weeks and sometimes did, depending on the experience and disposition of the interviewee, although the average interview lasted 13 hours (1,041 hours total for 82 interviewees).

In the late 1970s, I had experimented with different venues and methods, for example, interviewing in people's homes or in restaurants, having a research assistant present, or having a research assistant conduct the interview without my being present. But none of these proved satisfactory, due primarily to distractions and lack of control over essential follow-up argument. Accordingly, I conducted almost all the interviews alone in an office at the USC. The language used was Mandarin Chinese (*putonghua*) in all but two or three cases where the interviewee spoke in English. I took verbatim notes and typed them up as soon as possible afterward. The transcripts total 4,381 single-spaced typed pages. I also followed the conventions that had developed around such interviewing at the USC in not using a tape recorder and in giving a small "research assistance fee." In the late 1970s, the customary rate was H.K.$15 (U.S.$3.30) per hour, and in the early 1980s, H.K.$20 (U.S.$4.40) per hour. Small grants from the Ford

Foundation in 1979 and the American Association of University Women in 1982 helped defray these expenses.

By 1980, however, such interviewing had to adjust to some marked changes in supply and demand. Most American scholars were already going or planning to go directly to China. With fewer people interviewing in Hong Kong, the pool of informal contacts previously relied upon for introductions began to shrink. Those of us still in the business had no choice but to place advertisements in the classified sections of local Chinese-language newspapers. I placed several such ads beginning in 1980, all reading something like: "American scholar studying Chinese rural education seeks experienced people from China for interview research." For my topic at least, this means of tapping the supply proved a blessing in disguise since the old informal contacts were inadequate for producing so many people with the particular specialized experience desired from a range of localities.

Also in 1980, however, the Hong Kong government for various reasons abandoned its tolerant approach toward illegal immigrants from China. Thus, what one hand gave with the new recruiting approach in terms of greater selection and quality the other took away by limiting the pool of interviewees to a single type of individual, namely, the legal immigrant. The legal immigrant was defined by Chinese government regulations as an individual with overseas Chinese relations, that is, close family ties or business interests either in Hong Kong or elsewhere outside China. Only such individuals were permitted to emigrate legally from China by the Chinese government when it relaxed restrictions in 1972, according to interviewees.

In the 1960s before the onset of the Cultural Revolution, legal emigration from China to Hong Kong was governed by an unwritten agreement which aimed to keep numbers at an average of 50 per day. After 1966, the number of legals dwindled, and the Hong Kong government adopted a more lenient approach toward others. But from 1972, the number of both categories rose sharply until another informal agreement in 1979 limited legals to 75 per day. The 1980 decision then banned illegals altogether. In fact, new legal arrivals still remained well in excess of the revised quota figures through 1982, according to Hong Kong government statistics. These show about 480,000 new legal arrivals between 1972 and 1982.[1]

Neither Hong Kong nor China distinguished between those planning to join families in Hong Kong and those whose families were elsewhere. But since other countries maintained much stricter immigration policies toward this group, it was assumed that most would remain in Hong Kong indefinitely. As shown in Table A.l, my interviewees were drawn almost entirely from this pool of legal immigrants who arrived in Hong Kong during the 10-year period from 1972.

Overall, the legal–illegal distinction probably had little net impact since my questions

---

[1] The total is from a compilation of Hong Kong government Immigration Department statistics cited in John P. Burns, "Immigration from China and the Future of Hong Kong," *Asian Survey*, no. 6 (June 1987), p. 664; and also in Norman Miners, *The Government and Politics of Hong Kong* (Hong Kong: Oxford University Press, 1981), p. 305 n. 10. The 1979 agreement of 75 per day was not publicized at the time but was frequently referred to as the basic minimum standard into the early 1990s (e.g., *Hong Kong Standard*, 30 Sept. 1992; *Wenhuibao*, Hong Kong, 24 Dec. 1992). The daily quota was increased from 75 to 105 in late 1993, and from 105 to 150 in mid-1995 (*South China Morning Post*, 14 June 1995).

were already drawing me away from students to older interviewees with longer educational experience, most of whom even in the 1970s were already legal immigrants. But the uniformity imposed by the single overseas Chinese criterion served to highlight problems of bias and selectivity always cited as the main drawbacks to using such interview data for academic research. According to the argument, people well integrated within a society would not leave and should therefore be expected to bring a negative bias to their recollections of it. Moreover, being self-selected in coming forward of their own accord, they are likely to be people with an ax to grind, more willing than the average citizen to articulate grievances for the outside world's consumption. Nor, under the circumstances of their selection, can they be representative of any given group or region except perhaps the disaffected immigrant community itself. Such considerations also seemed more important in a political–educational history such as this than in the work, for example, of William Parish and Martin Whyte, whose joint studies on urban and rural life (see Select Bibliography) were the most methodologically rigorous of all those based on Hong Kong interview material. Since my choices were limited either to using such material or to abandoning the topic, however, it seemed essential to recognize the problems, work with them, and try to qualify conclusions accordingly.

By the early 1990s, of course, old questions about the general political bias against communist China within the Hong Kong émigré community seemed largely irrelevant. On the contrary, international events had turned that negative bias into an overall plus by recasting earlier generations who had "voted with their feet" as people ahead of their time in the overall worldwide rejection of communist rule. But to consider more carefully the significance of the overseas Chinese criterion, most interviewees shared by reason thereof a common negative experience directly relevant to the subject about which I was soliciting information, namely, education and the rural focus in particular. Indeed, this particular group of people found themselves standing quite literally astride the social and political fault lines that converged in Mao's 1966–1976 Cultural Revolution.

Overseas Chinese are perpetuators of the centuries-old tradition whereby people of the coastal areas, especially Guangdong and Fujian but also Zhejiang, Jiangsu, and other southern provinces, migrated overseas first to Taiwan and the Philippines, then to Southeast Asia, and finally to the American West and Australia. Those who live outside the boundaries of China or Taiwan are called overseas Chinese (*Huaqiao*); Hong Kong and Macau compatriots are distinguished as a separate subcategory. Overseas, the communities they built were typically urban, and their livelihoods were derived from commerce. As a group, they seemed unlikely members of the CCP's constituency, but leftist sympathies were strong in many communities before 1949. Even stronger were ties of loyalty and patriotism, retained through several generations abroad, both to their individual hometowns and villages and to the national homeland.

Hence many thousands returned with their families in the 1950s, drawn by the prospect of a newly reunified China after close to a century of civil war and foreign intervention. They were also attracted by the CCP's "united front" appeals welcoming everyone home regardless of political affiliation. These were called "returned overseas Chinese" (*guiguo Huaqiao*). Relatives and dependents in China of those living abroad are called *qiaojuan*. The links between those inside and outside China were typically reinforced by regular cash remittances to poorer family members in China as well as by contributions to schools, temples, clan halls, and other charitable ends in their native localities. My interviewees were drawn from among these two categories of "returned overseas Chinese" (those choosing to resume their lives overseas) and *qiaojuan* (dependents in China setting out for the first time) since only such people qualified to emigrate.[2]

Although they represented more of an economic than an intellectual elite, overseas Chinese naturally stood in the forefront of the urbanized outward-looking orientation that differentiated itself during the early decades of the century. That orientation was further reinforced by the commercial success and capitalist economic interests of overseas Chinese communities generally. Hence their families in China found themselves in an increasingly uncertain position during the 1960s as cultural revolutionary concerns developed. Chapter 14 suggests the vulnerability of those with "overseas connections" (*haiwai guanxi*), especially during the 1966–1968 mobilization years, when all manifestations of capitalist thought and action were fair game for Red Guard investigators. People were not necessarily targeted just for the overseas connection, but more often than not, that connection coincided with bourgeois class status. And in any case a host of associated potential charges existed, such as conspicuous consumption if presents from overseas had been too openly flaunted, colluding with China's enemies abroad, spying, sharing national secrets if too much overseas correspondence had been observed coming and going, and so forth.

---

[2] Reliable statistics are not available, but conventional wisdom has it that most of those who returned to China from overseas in the 1950s and 1960s departed in the post-1972 exodus. One interviewee with more than hearsay knowledge of overseas Chinese affairs since the early 1950s questioned the reliability of the published official Chinese figures shown below, since they have always represented a sensitive area in China's relations with the host countries. In his view, the actual 1963 figure for returnees was probably much higher, perhaps by as much as 50 percent, and the 1983 figure probably included Chinese from Vietnam, who were not regarded as overseas Chinese and not allowed to return during the years when North Vietnam was a fraternal socialist country. More than 200,000 ethnic-Chinese fled to China from Vietnam after relations between the two countries deteriorated in the late 1970s (e.g., *South China Morning Post*, 8 Jan. 1993). Definitions of *huaqiao* and *qiaojuan* also varied in practice. Sometimes one year's residence in a private nonstudent capacity abroad was sufficient to earn overseas Chinese status, whereas five years was the more conventional standard. Also, officially, only the closest relatives (parents, spouses, offspring) were regarded as *qiaojuan*, but many others might claim relationship or not depending on the costs and benefits at different periods. Presumably, the 1983 figure of one million returnees represented the total number who had returned rather than the number still living in China.

Category	1963	1983	1989
Returnees, overseas Chinese in China (*guiguo huaqiao*)	400,000	1 million	—
Relatives in China (*qiaojuan*)	10 million	20 million	—
Returnee and relatives combined			30 million

Sources: Fang Fang, "Zai guiqiao, qiaojuan, guiqiao xuesheng zhong shuli gengduo de hongqi biaobing" (Establish Ever More Red Flag Models among the Returned Overseas Chinese, Overseas Chinese Relatives, and Returned Overseas Chinese Students), *Qiaown bao* (Overseas Chinese Affairs News), Beijing, no. 5 (1963), p. 3; Liao Chengzhi, in *Hua sheng bao* (Overseas Chinese Voice), Beijing, 9 Jan. 1983; *Guanyu qiaolian gaige de jidian sikao* (A Few Reflections on the Reform of the Overseas Chinese Association) (Beijing: Zhongguo huaquiao chuban gongsi, 1989), p. 91.

Yet even before 1966, those with overseas connections were aware of subtle distinctions being drawn against them regardless of their actual economic circumstances or political commitments. In retrospect, they said they were never treated as equals but rather as "united front objects": those who could unite in revolution with the red classes but never on a par with them. In Yan'an days, the fear of spies and enemy agents was the excuse. During the Korean War as casualties mounted, young men with overseas connections were welcomed into the army, but the welcome quickly cooled once the war ended. A small number who made the extra effort to qualify were admitted into the CCP, and many joined the less restrictive Communist Youth league as students. But for most, the question of loyalty to the revolution remained forever open (see Table A.10, on interviewees' family backgrounds).

The consequence of their intermediate status that most concerns us here was the tendency to channel them into less popular teaching careers and more specifically into the least desirable small-town and rural schools as well. Thus one of the distinctions awaiting unsuspecting returned overseas Chinese involved the combination of academic achievement plus class and political criteria governing admission to middle school and college. At the tertiary level, this automatically excluded them from all defense-related specialties as potential "revolutionary security risks." Off-limits to them, for example, was Beijing's Aeronautics Institute, famous as a bastion of loyalist leadership during the Cultural Revolution, with its student body dominated by naturally red, higher-level cadres' children. Especially those who had themselves returned from overseas were also usually of a "lower cultural level" due to weaker grounding in the Chinese language. These candidates were granted preference within a 10-point range in dual recognition of their patriotism and their disadvantage. But their patriotism could never outweigh their potentially questionable revolutionary loyalty. As a rule, then, the handicaps of people with overseas connections tended to exclude them from the top universities, leaving the less prestigious teacher training colleges and post-secondary courses as common alternatives.

Since the "sample" here is made up mainly of middle school teachers, who are usually trained in such lower-ranking institutions, we cannot conclude that the large number of graduates among them from these types of schools is actually representative of all those with overseas connections. Nevertheless, 45 of the 82 interviewees had studied at the tertiary level before, during, or after the Cultural Revolution decade (1966–1976). And they produced a collective college career profile generally consistent with conventional wisdom about people who had handicaps such as those deriving from the overseas Chinese connection (see Table A.3).

Similarly, regular state-salaried teachers assigned to rural schools during the Cultural Revolution decade often spoke resentfully, blaming the rural assignment on their intermediate class/political status, of which the overseas connection was one component. Younger middle school students resettled in the countryside and then hired locally as *minban* teachers spoke of their status in similar terms, although in such cases the teaching position itself was seen as a step up from manual labor.

As a further indicator of their "second-class" status, I began to notice that only teachers were answering my ad. Yet I had deliberately retained throughout the phrase "people with experience in rural education," hoping to attract a mix of teachers, administrators, and relevant "others." When asked why this might be, interviewees were amused that I was so slow to catch on. They claimed that people with overseas connections were generally excluded from the top leadership positions in schools and within the government education bureaucracy, even down to the most basic commune and county levels.

There is no way to prove this claim and there might conceivably be other explanations. For instance, people in more responsible positions might be less likely to want to emigrate or they might not be granted permission to emigrate (a reason volunteered by one interviewee) or they might be less willing to come forward as interviewees. But whatever the reason, most were teachers. Of the 82 individuals interviewed, 62 had been teachers (6 tertiary, 41 secondary, 15 elementary); 13 were students; and 7 were otherwise occupied. All 62 teachers began their careers as such, and only 3 went on to assume at some time the lower-level leadership role of supervisor (*jiaodaozhuren*) within individual schools. Additionally, 1 became headmaster (and later a revolutionary committee member) of a rural school, and 6 others spent short periods working in temporary capacities within local government education bureaus but not in permanent positions of authority therein. One young rebel teacher served briefly as a deputy head of his school's revolutionary committee.

The economic reasons (better employment prospects) given for leaving China, as shown in Table A.11, may therefore be somewhat deceptive. The restricted opportunities in China were probably compounded by the factor of intermediate sociopolitical status, one component of which was the overseas connection. Interestingly, no one mentioned discrimination against teachers or intellectuals per se or Cultural Revolution disruption as reasons for leaving. Almost all abandoned their teaching careers in coming to Hong Kong, where Chinese credentials were not then recognized. Only one was working on a temporary contract basis as a teacher in one of Hong Kong's few "left-wing" schools.

In any event, without more information, we cannot claim that those with overseas connections were more likely than others to receive rural work assignments. Nor do we have any idea if others would have been equally resentful upon receiving such an assignment, although the unpopularity of the assignment suggests such a possibility. All we can say for certain is that all of the legal immigrant interviewees had overseas connections; that the professional experience of most was confined to teaching; that there was an alleged tendency to channel people of intermediate social and/or educational standing such as that associated with overseas connections into the less prestigious and less popular teaching profession; and that the teacher interviewees shared the professional Chinese educator's conventional urban bias by regarding a rural position as the most restricted of all possible prospects. The prejudicial circumstances of interviewees' rural assignments which compounded resentment are discussed more fully in chapter 15.

Ultimately, however, as the historic dimensions of their experience took shape within the study, it seemed reasonable to conclude that the handicaps of negativism and bias the interviewees brought to their role as observers were balanced by the other role they had played as participants in urban–rural transfer. Far from being atypical outsiders and conscripted urbanites suitable only for opening methodologically sanitized windows on an otherwise "internal" subject, they could be seen taking their rightful places within the subject itself. There they epitomized the outward-looking urban orientation of

Chinese society and the clash of urban–rural concerns that had become a leitmotif of China's 20th-century modernization.

Within the specific conditions fixed by the interviewees' overseas-connected and legal-immigrant status, moreover, they emerged as people not only caught in the middle but of the middle. Their middle-of-the-road status was evident on several counts, including both political and professional, and they approached the interviews in a similarly cautious, conventional manner. As noted in chapter 18, no one expressed confidence that there would not be some sort of backlash to the post-1976 order, given its drastic departure from the recent Maoist past. Consistent with this cautious forecast, interviewees said they had proceeded with their applications to emigrate, which often remained in the pipeline for several years and could have been withdrawn at any time, because they felt economic and political conditions, and their own intermediate status, would not register any marked improvement. All who spoke of these matters still claimed to be operating on this same set of assumptions when interviewed.

Also in line with this cautious approach, almost everyone was sensitive to the unorthodox step they had taken in agreeing to be interviewed. Most came via the classifieds, looking for contacts in a new city and more permanent employment. The first 20–30 minutes with each person was always spent explaining the project, and invariably everyone demanded to know what my purpose (*mudi*) was. Most agreed to participate only after satisfying themselves that my aim was academic and not political, that they would be contributing "raw materials" for scholarly research only, and that their own and their schools' anonymity would be guaranteed. Some were curious as to what it was about their experience that foreigners found worth studying. Others were just homesick and welcomed an excuse to talk. Still others mentioned the Chinese intellectual's sense of mission, seen in this case as a duty to help correct misconceptions, including both positive and negative, about China.

Three interviewees did declare that they had specific agendas of their own, namely, to inform the outside world negatively about communist China. One was past caring and is the one "dedicated anticommunist" shown among the political indicators in Table A.11. He alone was willing to be quoted by name for publication and said he did not care if his family, still in China, suffered as a consequence. But in adopting so extreme a position, he placed himself beyond the pale by comparison with the conventional stance of everyone else. This group of interviewees had selected itself to answer questions about educational development following the sense of the advertisement and generally wanted to keep to its terms of reference. Nor did interviewees introduced informally respond much differently. National honor and family privacy always constituted the unspoken areas of self-constraint although definitions varied. Related to concerns about national honor, for example, were questions concerning Cultural Revolution violence, which some were willing to describe in firsthand, eyewitness terms but most were not.

The self-imposed constraints also created problems at another relevant point, namely, in going beyond the overseas connection and trying to understand the impact of additional family background and class status criteria on interviewees' own careers and perspectives. I did not ask such questions directly, but since most volunteered some information, it was possible to compile the data shown in Table A.10. The data are organized according to standards generally obtaining as of 1966 – after family background criteria had become more important but before their use accelerated during the 1966–1968 mobilization years. The table follows the then conventional mix of class, occupation, political, and criminal criteria according to which people were categorized. Thus, good or red meant workers, peasants, and revolutionary cadres. Bad meant landlords, rich peasants, counterrevolutionaries, bad elements (criminals), and rightists. Capitalists per se were not included in the bad categories before 1966. Middling meant everyone else, or everyone who was "neither red nor white."

Distinguishing interviewees, especially between middling and bad backgrounds, presented difficulties, however, since actual, as opposed to formal, class status always depended on a mix, even more complex and subjective, of inherited family economics and the political history of dominant male members – which usually extended into the realm of family privacy. Borderline cases, for example, were "overseas Chinese capitalist with no political problems" or a father who was a "county-level administrative cadre, CCP member, capitalist class, with distant overseas relations." Even more difficult was "provincial-level technical cadre, almost a rightist, and with close relatives in America." The family political particulars in such cases would have made all the difference in determining actual status and consequences, whether good, bad, or middling.

A few interviewees did provide enough information, volunteering that the family status was categorically bad by reason of a "reactionary landlord" or an "active counterrevolutionary" father, and by revealing career profiles of their own consistent with such a bad-class background. Ultimately, I categorized 17 interviewees as bad class on the basis of information provided; arbitrary decisions were made in a few borderline cases. Of the 17, 9 also expressed views which placed them within the three negative or dissident political orientations shown in the table of political indicators (Table A.11). Otherwise, the majority claimed to be from white-collar and other middling categories and had career profiles to match. Most also remained safely noncommittal in articulating political views.

Similarly intermediate was the experience of this group during the Cultural Revolution decade. With the heightened class consciousness of those years, political pressures increased for everyone with overseas connections. But the heightened potential for danger did not materialize equally for all. Indeed, at least two interviewees joined the CCP in the early 1970s. And many were also enthusiastic participants in the mobilization phase, following its course of development, outlined in chapter 14. As noted therein, family background, including the overseas connection, had varying impact on the participants at different stages of the movement. For victims and targets, of course, the connection compounded their difficulties.

During the 1968–1976 years, everyone was then caught somewhere between the official evenhanded class-line pronouncements being issued from Beijing and the realities of heightened class consciousness, which varied in implementation from one work unit to the next. One interviewee, for example, was not allowed to teach elementary school on a northeastern state farm because his origins were overseas Chinese capitalist, while another of similar background in the same area was forced to teach because no one else wanted the job. Such anomalies abounded even for members of the same family – with one sibling admitted to college and another unable to continue on to senior middle school, allegedly due to the overseas connection.

In the overall balance of personal resources, the overseas connection and even the more important class standing itself were not absolute. If the other sibling had been an outstanding student or had some special talent, family connections would have weighed less heavily. The potential for the latter considerations to wreak havoc with personal aspirations was greatly enhanced during the 1968–1976 period for this group of interviewees as a whole in comparison with earlier years. But individual fates actually depended on many external factors as well, such as the number of people in a work unit with overseas connections, extent of the competition for coveted work and study assignments, bias of local leaders in interpreting central policy, etc.

Professionally, too, the interviewees were of middling status, perhaps best summarized as just above average. Their relevant personal and professional characteristics are shown in Tables A.2–A.5. Most had a tertiary education and a few had attended leading national and regional institutions, including Beijing, Xiamen, and Zhongshan Universities, in the 1950s and 1960s. But a majority were graduates of teacher training colleges and went on to become middle school teachers. Most were also in their thirties, making them overwhelmingly the "Red Guard" generation of secondary and college students. But most were also regular, professionally trained teachers rather than the locally hired *minban* variety, and a majority had five years or more on-the-job experience.

Even the rural localities and schools to which they were assigned were middling or just above average. From 1980, my aim was to interview people with personal firsthand experience in formal rural educational institutions during the 1970s. I turned away several "applicants" from big city suburbs, county towns, state farms, and national minority areas on grounds that they were not representative of rural education (usually to a barrage of arguments about why they were). My aim was to keep down the numbers from such schools while continuing the search for those who had experience in genuinely rural areas at the commune and village levels. My aim further was to interview people who had taught in schools serving the agricultural population. Within such a population, a majority of people are from households engaged in agricultural pursuits (*nongye hukou*) rather than in nonagricultural urban occupations (*jumin hukou*). Even so, several "unwanted" interviewees (fortunately) slipped through my preliminary filtering procedure. After 1980, I also drew the line against people from Guangdong, and in 1982, against people from the south coast or overseas Chinese districts of Fujian as well. The resulting provincial distribution is shown in Tables A.8 and A.9. Table A.6 shows the extent of my failure to avoid the unrepresentative, unwanted categories. Nevertheless, one dimension was impossible to guard against, namely, the upward bias in the economic and educational levels of the rural localities and schools themselves.

Most but not all interviewees who taught in rural schools were outsiders, nonnative to the area, and most were also relatively well qualified given their tertiary training. But interviewees said that such teachers even during the height of the Cultural Revolution were usually not assigned to teach in the poorest areas and most backward schools. (This refers to the teaching assignment, not to temporary periods of obligatory manual labor, the circumstances of which varied widely.) Nor were rusticated city youth, that is, urban middle school graduates sent to work in the countryside (the main source of those listed as *minban* teachers), assigned to the most economically depressed localities. So that although a college graduate from Shanghai might consider assignment to a north Fujian county town as intellectual exile, such a teacher was not likely to have been sent to the poorer west Fujian counties.

It must therefore be assumed that interviewees were probably not discussing educational developments in the poorest and most backward rural areas. Indeed, everything seemed to conspire in producing the same results: for example, the overrepresentation of Guangdong, a relatively rich and educationally well-developed province; the lack of any interviewees from the reputedly poorest western and central Fujian counties; and the overrepresentation of richer counties for both Anhui and Jiangsu. Also, three relatively prosperous state farms and two similarly well-off counties comprised the Northeast rural "sample." Even the four Xinjiang and Gansu interviewees had all, by their own admission, been assigned to relatively well-off localities although they had drawn those distant and unpopular destinations by reason of problematic family backgrounds.

Thus, despite the biases deriving from the interviewees' common "overseas Chinese experience," which contrived to make all of them to some degree outsiders in their native land and contributed to their collective decision to leave it, the group was best characterized as middle-of-the-road on most dimensions relevant for this study. The dominant political bias was neither red nor white, and professional status was neither the highest nor the lowest. Most interviewees had post-secondary training, but few were educated in top-ranking institutions of higher learning, and the localities in which they were assigned to work were neither especially rich and advanced nor especially poor and backward. Additionally, most interviewees were born and educated in China and worked there as full participating members of their communities. And although they may have come forward as self-selected interviewees in an unorthodox Hong Kong research setting, they nevertheless contributed in-depth firsthand accounts for an extensive random selection of schools and localities that would have been impossible to duplicate in any other way.

Some notes on the use of the interview material

(1) In order to preserve anonymity, I identify each interview in most cases only by the location of the *main academic experience* described. Thus, a citation to interview 80/ GD/1 indicates the first interview conducted in 1980, with Guangdong as the location of the main educational experience described, even though that particular individual also described a teaching job he held for several years outside Guangdong. I have also used this standard in compiling the statistical summaries of interviewees' relevant characteristics and, of course, in designating the status of each interviewee to yield the breakdown: 62 teachers, 13 students, and 7 others. In this regard, each interviewee was counted only once, regardless of the number or quality of additional educational experiences described and presented in this study. However, interviewees were often able to describe their firsthand experiences in more than one school, including those recalled from their own student days. Thus, Table A.7 records all *firsthand accounts* by work unit (school) described, yielding considerably more schools (149) than interviewees (82). Tables A.8 and A.9 show the geographic distribution of these accounts.

(2) In analyzing the interview material, it was also useful to distinguish first- and secondhand accounts from hearsay. "Firsthand" refers to the direct first-person experience of the interviewee; "secondhand" refers to information the interviewee received from someone directly involved. "Hearsay," the least reliable of all, refers to general information, gossip, etc., for which the interviewee did not know the source. The

assessment of secondhand information, so identified at a number of points in this study, was largely subjective on my part but became possible with experience in listening to many accounts.

Thus, if someone claimed to have taught middle school in a particular county for 10 years from 1962 to 1972 and could speak in detailed and consistent terms about secondary education in that county, such a person could plausibly know that "every commune in the county had set up an agricultural middle school in 1958" and that "only two remained by 1966." This was because the number of middle schools in a rural county was usually not great, and the circulation of information and people on a professional basis within a county middle school "system" was considerable, in the form of regular semester or annual report meetings and political study sessions in the county town. By contrast, the professional world of a village elementary school teacher was more limited. Hence, unless the circumstances were explained, such a teacher could not claim more than hearsay knowledge of agricultural middle schools in an entire county. My estimate of the number of schools for which interviewees had some reliable secondhand knowledge, in contrast with their principal, firsthand accounts, was calculated in this manner as a means of summarizing approximately the data at hand. Calculating totals overall, interviewees were able to provide firsthand and plausible secondhand information for 525 communes and state farms and for 760 production brigades or equivalent units (see Table A.9). Typically, rural secondary school teachers could provide at least basic information on the number and type of schools in neighboring communes and often could do so for an entire county, whereas elementary school teachers could usually provide such information for most of the production brigades in a single commune. See chapter 16 on the varying sizes of communes, their production brigade subdivisions, and the state farm equivalents.

(3) All personal names used in the narrative with reference to the interview material are, of couse, fictitious. To reduce confusion, each surname used has been assigned to only one person, so that there is only one Li, one Liu, etc.

(4) The abbreviations used in the interview file numbers are as follows:

AH – Anhui	HB – Hebei	S – Shanghai
BJ – Beijing	HLJ – Heilongjiang	SD – Shandong
FJ – Fujian	HN – Henan	SHN – Shanxi
GD – Guangdong	HUB – Hubei	SN – Sichuan
GS – Gansu	HUN – Hunan	SX – Shaanxi
GX – Guangxi	JL – Jilin	XJ – Xinjiang
GZ – Guizhou	JS – Jiangsu	YN – Yunnan
		ZJ – Zhejiang

Six interviewees did not want their accounts to be cited even by province and for them I use two catchall regions: NC (north China, north of the Yangzi River) and SC (south of the river). When describing individual accounts in the text, I followed the interviewee's wishes concerning the level to be identified by name and the degree of anonymity preferred. In a few cases such as Baoan County and others adjacent to Hong Kong or Jinjiang County in the heart of Fujian's overseas Chinese district, interviewees were unconcerned about citing the county by name. But usually the prefecture, an administrative configuration of several counties, was the lowest unit to be cited for publication.

Once satisfied that their anonymity would be maintained, however, virtually everyone provided more than enough local place-names and population estimates to permit corroboration of the county they were describing and its size in Zhonghua renmin gongheguo minzhengbu, *Zhonghua renmin gongheguo xianji yishang xingzhengqu huayange* (The Evolution of the Administrative Divisions at the County Level and above within the People's Republic of China), 3 vols. (n.p.: Cehui chubanshe, 1986–1988); and Guojia tongjiju renkou tongjisi and Gonganbu sanju, eds., *Zhonghua renmin gongheguo renkou tongji ziliao huibian, 1949–1985* (Compilation of Population Statistical Materials for the People's Republic of China) (n.p.: Zhongguo caizheng jingji chubanshe, 1988).

Table A.1. *Interview and immigration data for the 82 interviewees*

	No. of interviewees
Year interviewed:	
1977	4
1978	13[a]
1979	7
1980	10[b]
1982	21
1983	27
Date of leaving China:	
1972–1975	16
1976–1979	31
1980–1983	31
N.A.	4
Time between Hong Kong interview and interviewee's last association with main Chinese work unit described:	
6 months or less	11
1 year	12
2 years	10
3 years	9
4 years	12
5 years	10
6 years or more	17
N.A.	1

[a] Six of the 13 were illegal immigrants to Hong Kong.
[b] One of the 10 was an illegal immigrant.
Note: N.A. = information not available.

Table A.2. *Personal characteristics of interviewees*

	No. of interviewees
Age when interviewed:	
Twenties	13
Thirties	44
Forties	18
Fifties	5
60 or over	2
Sex:	
Female	26
Male	56

Table A.3. *Profile of interviewees' own college education (45)*

Type of institution	1949–1966	1969–1976	1977–1979
National or regional leading institutions (8)	7	1	—
Provincial universities (9)	6	1	2
Teacher training (19)	16	1	2
Post-secondary (teacher training not included) (6)	4	2	—

Note: One interviewee studied overseas, dates not available. Dates and type of institution attended not available for two of the interviewees with college education.

Table A.4. *The level of formal education attained by the 62 teachers*

Type of teacher and level of education	No. of teachers
College teachers (6):	
Graduate training	4
College graduate	2
Secondary school teachers (41):	
College graduate (4- to 5-year courses)	19
Post-secondary (2- to 3-year courses)[a]	11
Regular or specialized senior secondary[b]	10
Regular junior secondary	1
Elementary school teachers (15):	
Regular senior secondary graduate[c]	8
Regular junior secondary graduate[d]	7

[a] Including regular courses (4); courses cut short by the Cultural Revolution in 1966 (5); and shortened cultural revolution courses (2).
[b] Including course cut short by 1 year with the suspension of schooling in 1966 (1).
[c] Lost 1 year, 1966–1967 (3); shortened cultural revolution course (1).
[d] Lost 1 year (3).

Table A.5. *The 62 teachers by seniority*

Years on the job	No. of teachers
Two years or less	5
3–5 years	22
6–10 years	10
11–20 years	21
Over 20 years	4

Table A.6. *Interviewees by location of main education or employment experience described*

	Urban	County town	Suburban, rural	State farm, rural	National minority area, rural	Rural
All interviewees (82)	26	5	9	5	7	30
Guangdong interviewees only (20)	6	2	1	1	1	9

Table A.7. *Number of schools, firsthand accounts (149) (based on interviewees' own personal experience)*

Type of school	No. of schools
Tertiary	12
Secondary:	
Specialized senior middle	2
Urban (cities, county towns)	37
Rural (all rural locales)	36
Rural (junior middle attached to elementary)	10
Rural (agricultural middle)	4
Elementary:	
Urban	12
Rural	36

Table A.8. *Geographic distribution of firsthand interview accounts*
(no. of interviewees)

	Main work/study experience (all interviewees)	Their own schooling (all interviewees)	Main work experience (teachers only)	Their own schooling (teachers only)
Beijing	9	11	6	7
Shanghai	5	17	5	14
Guangdong	20	18	15	14
Guangxi	1	2	1	2
Fujian	7	7	6	6
Jiangxi	0	1	0	0
Anhui	5	2	3	1
Jiangsu	3	3	3	3
Zhejiang	5	5	4	4
Yunnan	5	3	5	3
Guizhou	2	1	1	0
Sichuan	2	2	1	1
Hebei	1	2	1	2
Henan	2	0	1	0
Shandong	1	0	1	0
Hubei	1	2	1	2
Hunan	1	1	0	0
Shanxi	2	0	2	0
Shaanxi	1	0	1	0
Gansu	2	0	2	0
Xinjiang	2	0	1	0
Heilongjiang	3	1	1	1
Jilin	2	1	1	0
Overseas	0	3	0	2
Total	82	82	62	62

Table A.9. *Geographic distribution of interview accounts*

	Origins of all firsthand accounts (*no. of localities*)		Origins of firsthand and secondhand rural accounts (*no. of work units*)	
	Cities, including prefectural seats	Counties, including county seats	Communes and state farms	Production brigades and equivalents
Beijing and suburbs	1	0	2	21
Shanghai and suburbs	1	2	19	24
Guangdong	3	12	115	119
Guangxi	0	1	1	8
Fujian	1	4	73	335
Anhui	1	5	8	35
Jiangsu	0	3	37	21
Zhejiang	1	5	136	49
Yunnan	1	5	15	19
Guizhou	2	2	2	3
Sichuan	0	2	2	11
Hebei	1	0	0	0
Henan	2	0	0	0
Shandong	0	1	11	11
Hubei	0	1	23	8
Hunan	1	0	0	0
Shanxi	1	1	28	0
Shaanxi	0	1	11	18
Gansu	1	2	16	4
Xinjiang	0	2	4	24
Heilongjiang	1	4	14	41
Jilin	1	1	8	9
Total	19	54	525	760

Table A.10. *Family class/political background, as of 1966*

Background	No. of interviewees
Red (1):	
Father a revolutionary cadre	1
Neither red nor white (47):	
Father/mother:	
White collar	33
Overseas Chinese capitalist/no other problem	8
Overseas Chinese small merchant	3
Poor peasant	2
Overseas Chinese worker	1
White (17):	
Father:	
Big capitalist/landlord	9
Political problem/counterrevolutionary	6
Rightist	1
Self:	
Rightist	1
Information not available (17)	17
Nature of the overseas Chinese connection:	
Self[a]	14
Parents	14
By marriage	6
Other	32
None	6[b]
Information not available	10

[a] Those born overseas who returned to China after 1949.

[b] Five of the 6 were illegal immigrants.

Table A.11. *Some political indicators*

Indicator	Number of interviewees
Conventional participation in China (14):	
CCP members	3
Communist Youth League members	8
Army	3
Participation during the Cultural Revolution in China (31):[a]	
As teachers	12
As students	19
Political views articulated in Hong Kong (37):	
Dedicated anticommunist	1
Dissident, critical of CCP rule	10
Selectively critical	14
Partially positive	5
Generally positive	6
Committed procommunist	1
Stated reasons for leaving China (62):	
Political:	
To escape CCP rule	6
To escape official retribution against Cultural Revolution rebels	2
To escape discrimination against overseas Chinese	5
Economic:	
Greener pastures generally	23
To escape a rural work assignment specifically	11
Personal:	
Family obligations	13
Wanderlust	2

[a] See chapter 14 for definitions of Cultural Revolution participation.

Select bibliography

References are arranged in alphabetical order by author and then in chronological order for more than one work by the same author or the same combination of authors. *Pinyin* is used for transliterating all Chinese-language sources, but original spellings are retained in the English-language works, which contain a variety of styles.

As with the book itself, the emphasis in this bibliography is on the pre-1980 years. It also excludes most newspaper and news magazine articles cited in the text. Nor has every article cited therein from the main official education journal, *Renmin jiaoyu*, been selected for inclusion here. Reference must be made to the footnotes for these citations, and to the footnotes as well as to the Appendix for all information pertaining to the interview material. The Chinese-language periodicals and translation services cited most frequently in the text are the following:

Guangming ribao (Enlightenment Daily), Beijing
Hongqi (Red Flag), Beijing
Jiaoshibao (Teachers News), Beijing
Jiaoyu yanjiu (Education Research), Beijing
Renmin jiaoyu (People's Education), Beijing
Renmin ribao (People's Daily), Beijing
Xinhua banyue kan (New China Semimonthly), Beijing
Xinhua yuebao (New China Monthly), Beijing
Xuexi (Study), Beijing
Zhongguo qingnian (Chinese Youth), Beijing
Chinese Education and Society: A Journal of Translations (formerly, *Chinese Education*), New York, Stanley Rosen and Gerard Postiglione, eds.
Current Background (*CB*), U.S. Consulate General, Hong Kong; topical translations.
Extracts from China Mainland Magazines (*ECMM*), U.S. Consulate General, Hong Kong; magazine translations (1950s).
Joint Publications Research Service (JPRS), Washington, D.C.; research materials translations.
Selections from China Mainland Magazines (*SCMM*), U.S. Consulate General, Hong Kong; magazine translations (1960s).
Selections from China Mainland Magazines – Supplement (*SCMM-S*), U.S. Consulate General, Hong Kong; originally internal Chinese magazine translations, restricted access.
Survey of China Mainland Press (*SCMP*), U.S. Consulate General, Hong Kong; newspaper translations.

Survey of China Mainland Press – Supplement (SCMP-S), U.S. Consulate General, Hong Kong; originally internal Chinese newspaper translations, restricted access.
In 1974, "People's Republic of China" was substituted for "China Mainland" in the Hong Kong translation services, which were terminated in 1977. Their functions were ultimately taken over by the surviving Foreign Broadcast Information Service (FBIS) *Daily Report* series for China and by the Joint Publications Research Service topical series.

Chinese-language references

An Ziwen. "Gongchandang nenggou lingdao kexue, wenhua he jiaoyu gongzuo" (The CCP Can Lead Science, Culture, and Education Work). *Zhongguo qingnian*, no. 13 (1 July 1957), pp. 5–6.

Bao Xiaying, Tao Duanyu, et al. *Nongcun banxue jingyan* (The Experience of Running Schools in the Countryside). Beijing: Sanlian, 1949–1950.

Beidahuang fengyun lu (Recollections from a Time in the Great Northern Wilderness), Beijing: Zhongguo qingnian chubanshe, 1990.

Beijing daxue, Qinghua daxue da pipanzu. "Gonggu he fazhan wenhua dageming de chengguo: jiaoyu geming de fangxiang bu rong cuangai" (Consolidate and Develop the Cultural Revolution's Achievements: The Direction of the Education Revolution Must Not Be Distorted). *Hongqi*, no. 12 (1975), pp. 5–12.

Cai Xiaoqian. *Jiangxi suqu, hongjun xi chan huiyi* (Recollections of the Jiangxi Soviet District, and the Westward Flight of the Red Army). Hong Kong: Da zhonghua chubanshe, 1970.

Cai Yuanpei. *Cai Yuanpei quanji* (Complete Works of Cai Yuanpei). 7 vols. Beijing: Zhonghua shuju, 1984–1989.

Chen Boda. "Zai Mao Zedong tongzhi de qizhi xia" (Under the Banner of Comrade Mao Zedong). *Hongqi*, no. 4 (1958), pp. 1–12.

Chen Guang. "Jiangsusheng nongye zhongxue chuangban qizhounian" (Seven Full Years of Agricultural Middle Schools in Jiangsu Province). *Hongqi*, no. 4 (1965), pp. 36–47.

Chen Guisheng. "Mao Zedong tongzhi zai diyici guonei geming zhanzheng shiqi dui jiaoyu de gongxian" (Comrade Mao Zedong's Contribution to Education during the First Revolutionary Civil War Period). *Jiaoyu yanjiu*, no. 11 (1983), pp. 2–7.

Chen Qingzhi. *Zhongguo jiaoyu shi* (A History of China's Education). Taibei: Shangwu yinshuguan, 1978. Originally published in Shanghai, 1936.

Chen Tiejian. *Qu Qiubai zhuan* (A Biography of Qu Qiubai). Shanghai: Shanghai renmin chubanshe, 1986.

Chen Xuanshan. "Banianlai gaodeng shifan jiaoyu de juda chengjiu bu rong mosha" (The Great Achievements in Higher Teachers Training during the Past Eight Years Must Not Be Written Off). *Renmin jiaoyu*, Oct. 1957, pp. 11–14.

Chen Yuanhui, Qu Xingui, and Zou Guangwei (of the Zhongyang jiaoyu kexue yanjiusuo), eds. *Laojiefangqu jiaoyu ziliao (1): tudi geming zhanzheng shiqi* (Materials on Education in the Old Liberated Areas, vol. 1: The Period of the Agrarian Revolutionary War). Beijing: Jiaoyu kexue chubanshe, 1981. (See Zhongyang jiaoyu kexue yanjiusuo, ed., for vol. 2, pts. 1 and 2 of this series.)

Chen Yuanhui, Qu Xingui, and Zou Guangwei, eds. *Laojiefangqu jiaoyu jianshi* (A Short History of Education in the Old Liberated Areas). Beijing: Jiaoyu kexue chubanshe, 1982.

Chen Zenggu. "Fu Su fangwen kaocha de jingguo he shouhuo: 2 yue 8 ri zai jiaoyubu di 40 ci buwu huiyi shang de baogao" (The Course and Results of an Inspection Visit to the Soviet Union: Report to the 40th Ministry of Education Affairs Meeting on February 8). *Renmin jiaoyu*, Mar. 1956, pp. 7–10.

———. "Guanyu fu Su fangwen kaocha de zong baogao" (General Report on an Investigation Visit to the Soviet Union). *Renmin jiaoyu*, Apr. 1956, pp. 9–22.

Chen Zhiming. *Xu Teli zhuan* (A Biography of Xu Teli). Changsha: Hunan renmin chubanshe, 1984.

Cheng Jieming. *Zhongguo jiaoyu gaige* (China's Education Reform). Hong Kong: Shangwu yinshuguan, 1992.

Chi Liaozhou. "Wenhua jiaoyu gongzuo de zhandou gangling" (A Militant Program for Cultural and Educational Work). *Zhongguo qingnian*, no. 12 (1960), pp. 2–3.

Dai Botao, ed. *Jiefang zhanzheng chuqi suwan bianqu jiaoyu* (Education in the Jiangsu–Anhui Border Region during the Early Period of the Liberation War). N.p.: Renmin jiaoyu chubanshe, 1982.

Dai Shuren. "Cong jige sheng, shi kan jinnian jiaoyu shiye de fazhan" (The Development of This Year's Education Enterprise as Seen from Various Provinces and Cities). *Renmin jiaoyu*, Jan. 1957, pp. 13–15.

Dangqian jiaoyu jianshe de fangzhen (The Present Policy of Educational Construction). Guangzhou: Xinhua shudian, 1950.

Deng Xiaoping. *Deng Xiaoping wenxuan* (Deng Xiaoping's Selected Works). Beijing: Renmin chubanshe, 1983.

Deng Zihui. "Xiang nongcun qingnian he zhongxiao xuesheng jinyiyan" (A Word to Rural Youth and Secondary and Elementary School Students). *Zhongguo qingnian*, no. 10 (16 May 1957), pp. 5–8.

"Disici quanguo jiaoyu xingzheng huiyi de chengguo" (The Results of the Fourth National Education Administration Conference). *Renmin jiaoyu* (May 1958), p. 20.

Diyici guonei geming zhanzheng shiqi de nongmin yundong ziliao (Materials on the Peasant Movement during the Period of the First Revolutionary Civil War). Beijing: Renmin chubanshe, 1983.

"Diyici quanguo zhongdeng jiaoyu huiyi jingguo" (The Convention of the First National Secondary Education Conference). *Xinhua yuebao*, vol. 4, no. 1 (25 May 1951), pp. 174–175.

Fang Junfu. "Zhongxue jiaoyu youmeiyou chengji, chengji zai nali" (Have There Been Accomplishments in Secondary Education and If So What Are They?). *Renmin jiaoyu*, Oct. 1957, pp. 14–18.

Feng Youlan. "Guanyu *Wu Xun zhuan* de pipan" (On the Criticism of *The Story of Wu Xun*). *Xuexi*, vol. 4, no. 5 (16 June 1951), pp. 24–25.

Gansusheng shehui kexue yuan lishi yanjiusuo, ed. *Shaan–Gan–Ning geming genjudi shiliao xuanji (disiji)* (Selection of Historical Materials from the Shaanxi–Gansu–Ningxia Revolutionary Base [vol. 4]). Lanzhou: Gansu renmin chubanshe, 1985.

Gao Qi, ed. *Zhongguo xiandai jiaoyu shi* (A History of China's Modern Education). Beijing: Beijing shifan daxue chubanshe, 1985.

Guan Gengyin. "Zhang Tiesheng chuyu yao dang getihu" (After Being Released from Prison, Zhang Tiesheng Is to Go into Business for Himself). *Kaifa qu daokan* (Development News), Beijing, no. 6 (1992), pp. 61–65.

Guanyu qiaolian gaige de jidian sikao (A Few Reflections on the Reform of the Overseas Chinese Association). Beijing: Zhongguo huaqiao chuban gongsi, 1989.

Guo Lin. "Bu xu dongyao jiaoyu xiang gongnong kaimen de fangzhen" (The Policy of Opening the Doors of Education for Workers and Peasants Should Not Waiver). *Renmin jiaoyu*, Sept. 1957, pp. 11–12.

Guo Moruo. "Guanyu wenhua jiaoyu gongzuo de baogao" (Report on Culture and Education Work). *Xuexi*, vol. 5, no. 2 (16 Nov. 1951), p. 17.

Guojia tongjiju renkou tongjisi and Gonganbu sanju, eds. *Zhonghua renmin gongheguo renkou tongji ziliao huibian, 1949–1985* (Compilation of Population Statistical Materials for the People's Republic of China, 1949–1985). N.p.: Zhongguo caizheng jingji chubanshe, 1988.

He Hongchen et al. "Beijing jingshan xuexiao jiaogai shiyan ershiwu nian" (The 25-Year Experiment in Education Reform by Beijing's Jingshan School). *Jiaoyu yanjiu*, no. 12 (1985), pp. 27–35.

Hongri zhao zheng cheng: ji Jiangxi gongchanzhuyi laodong daxue (Arduous Journey under a Brilliant Red Sun: Commemorating Jiangxi Communist Labor University). Shanghai: Shanghai jiaoyu chubanshe, 1977.

Hongweibing ziliao (Red Guard Publications). 20 vols. Washington, D.C.: Center for Chinese Research Materials, Association of Research Libraries, 1975. *Supplement*. 8 vols. 1980.

Huabei renmin zhengfu jiaoyubu, ed. *Shifan xuexiao shiyong: xiaoxue jiaoyu lilun yu shiji cankao ziliao* (Reference Materials on the Theory and Practice of Elementary Education for Use in Teacher Training Schools). Beijing: Xinhua shudian, 1950.

Huadong shifan daxue, jiaoyuxi, jiaokesuo, ed. *Zhongguo xiandai jiaoyu shi* (A History of Modern Education in China). Shanghai: Huadong shifan daxue chubanshe, 1983.

Huang Fujin. "Ji diyici quanguo gongnong jiaoyu huiyi" (A Record of the First National Conference on Worker–Peasant Education). *Renmin jiaoyu*, Nov. 1950, pp. 49–51.

Huang Yanpei. *Huang Yanpei jiaoyu wenxuan* (Selections from Huang Yanpei on Education). Shanghai: Shanghai jiaoyu chubanshe, 1985.

"Huiji kejijie de youqing fanan feng" (Counterattack the Right Deviationist Wind to Overturn Verdicts in Science and Technology). *Hongqi*, no. 2 (1976), pp. 3–11.

Hunan diyi shifan xiaoshi, 1903–1949 (The History of the First Hunan Provincial Normal School, 1903–1949). Shanghai: Shanghai jiaoyu chubanshe, 1983.

Jiang Nanxiang. "Luelun gaodeng xuexiao de quanmian fazhan de jiaoyu fangzhen" (A Brief Discussion of the Educational Policy of Overall Development for Institutions of Higher Learning). *Zhongguo qingnian*, no. 20 (16 Oct. 1956), pp. 9–12.

"Jiaoshi tan jiaoyu gongzuo neibu maodun" (Teachers Discuss Contradictions within Education Work). *Renmin jiaoyu*, June 1957, pp. 6–13.

Jiaoyu gaige zhongyao wenxian xuanbian (A Selection of Important Documents on Education Reform). Beijing: Renmin jiaoyu chubanshe, 1986.

Jiaoyu kexue yanjiusuo choubei chu, ed. *Laojiefangqu jiaoyu ziliao xuanbian* (Selected Materials on Education in the Old Liberated Areas). Beijing: Renmin jiaoyu chubanshe, 1959–1983.

Jiaoyu shinian (Ten Years of Education). Beijing: Renmin jiaoyu chubanshe, 1960.

"Jiaoyu zhiliang shibushi 'jin bu ru xi'? Beijing shida jiaoshou chi youpai fenzi dui jiaoyu zhiliang de wumie" (Is It True That Educational Quality Today Cannot Compare with the Past? Beijing Teacher Training University Professors Denounce the Rightists' Slander of Educational Quality). *Renmin jiaoyu*, Sept. 1957, pp. 30–36.

"Jinianlai woguo jiaoyu shiye de fazhan gaikuang" (A Survey of Our Country's Educational Development in Recent Years). *Tongji gongzuo tongxun* (Statistical Work Bulletin), no. 20 (1956). Reprinted in *Xinhua banyue kan*, no. 24 (1956), pp. 93–94.

Jin Zhong. "Dayuejin e si ren de xin ziliao: Zhonggong guanfang renkou tongji yanjiu" (New Data on Starvation Deaths during the Great Leap Forward: Research on Official CCP Population Statistics). *Kaifang zazhi* (Open Magazine), Hong Kong, Jan. 1994, pp. 49–53.

Kai-luo-fu, Yi. An. "Guanyu gaijin he tigao Sulian putong xuexiao de jiaoyu zhiliang wenti" (On the Problems of Improving and Raising Educational Quality in the Soviet Union's Ordinary Schools). *Renmin jiaoyu*, Mar. 1957, pp. 4–9.

Ke Lan. *Mingyun zhi mi – Xu Teli zhuan* (An Enigmatic Fate – The Biography of Xu Teli). Beijing: Jiaoyu kexue chubanshe, 1989.

Lai Zhikui. "Guanyu suqu jiaoyu yanjiu zhong de jige lilun wenti" (Some Theoretical Problems in Research on Education in the Soviet District). *Jiaoyu yanjiu*, Oct. 1984, pp. 56–61.

Laojiefangqu jiaoyu gongzuo huiyilu (Recollections of Education Work in the Old Liberated Areas). Shanghai: Shanghai jiaoyu chubanshe, 1979.

Laojiefangqu jiaoyu gongzuo jingyan pianduan (Selections on Education Work Experience in the Old Liberated Areas). Shanghai: Shanghai jiaoyu chubanshe, 1979.

Li Qinglin. "Tan fan chaoliu" (On Going against the Tide). *Hongqi*, no. 11 (1973), pp. 65–67.

Li Rui. *Mao Zedong tongzhi de chuqi geming huodong* (The Early Revolutionary Activities of Comrade Mao Zedong). Beijing: Zhongguo qingnian chubanshe, 1957.

Li Shaoxian, ed. *Zhongguo jiaoyu mingren zhuanlue* (Biographical Sketches of Famous Chinese Educators). Shenyang: Liaoning daxue chubanshe, 1985.

Li Xin et al., eds. *Zhongguo xinminzhuzhuyi geming shiqi tongshi* (A Comprehensive History of China's New Democratic Revolutionary Period). 4 vols. Beijing: Renmin chubanshe, 1962. Reprint, 1980–1981.

Liaoningsheng jiaoyuju. "Juban gezhong menlei de zhongdeng zhiye jiaoyu" (Run Various Kinds of Secondary Vocational Education). *Renmin jiaoyu*, no. 7 (1979), pp. 44–46.

Lin Qingshan. *Pohai kuang – Kang Sheng* (Kang Sheng – The Persecutor). Tianjin: Baihua wenyi chubanshe, 1989.

Liu Bin. "Guanyu shenhua nongcun jiaoyu zonghe gaige de jige wenti" (Some Problems on Deepening the Comprehensive Reform of Rural Education). *Renmin jiaoyu*, no. 12 (1994), pp. 7–9.

Liu Shaoqi. *Liu Shaoqi xuanji* (Liu Shaoqi's Selected Works). 2 vols. Beijing: Renmin chubanshe, 1981–1985.

Liu Songtao. "Ban xiaoxue de liangtiao luxian" (The Two Lines for Running Elementary Schools). *Renmin jiaoyu*, June 1957, pp. 14–18.

Lu Dingyi. "Jiaoyu bixu yu shengchan laodong xiangjiehe" (Education Must Be Combined with Productive Labor). *Hongqi*, no. 7 (1958), pp. 1–12.

———. "Nongye zhongxue chuangban erzhounian" (Two Full Years of Agricultural Middle Schools). *Renmin jiaoyu*, no. 2 (1960). Reprinted in *Xinhua banyuekan*, no. 5 (1960), pp. 83–84.

Lu Sima. *Qu Qiubai zhuan* (A Biography of Qu Qiubai). Hong Kong: Zilian chubanshe, 1962.

Lu Xingwei. "Gaige zhongdeng jiaoyu jiegou shizai bixing" (Reforming the Structure of Secondary Education Is Essential). *Renmin jiaoyu*, no. 7 (1979), pp. 42–43.

Lu Xun. *Lu Xun quanji* (Complete Works of Lu Xun). 16 vols. Beijing: Renmin wenxue chubanshe, 1981.

Lun you hong you zhuan (On Being Both Red and Expert). Beijing: Zhongguo qingnian chubanshe, 1958.

Ma-er-gu-she-wei-qi. "Guanyu Sulian putong xuexiao shishi zonghe jishu jiaoyu de jige wenti" (On Some Problems of Carrying out Comprehensive Technical Education in the Soviet Union's Ordinary Schools). *Renmin jiaoyu*, June 1956, pp. 7–15.

Ma Xulun. "Diyici quanguo zhongdeng jishu jiaoyu huiyi kaimuci" (Opening Statement at the First National Secondary Technical Education Conference). *Renmin jiaoyu*, Aug. 1951, p. 23.

———. "Gaodeng jiaoyu de fangzhen, renwu wenti" (Questions on the Policy and Tasks of Higher Education). *Renmin jiaoyu*, Apr. 1953, pp. 13–14.

Mao Lirui, ed. *Zhongguo jiaoyu shi jianbian* (A Concise History of Chinese Education). Beijing: Jiaoyu kexue chubanshe, 1984.

Mao Lirui and Shen Guanqun, eds. *Zhongguo jiaoyu tongshi* (A Comprehensive History of Chinese Education). Vol. 5. Jinan: Shandong jiaoyu chubanshe, 1988.

Mao Zedong. *Mao Zedong xuanji* (Selected Works of Mao Zedong). 5 vols. Beijing: Renmin chubanshe, 1951–1977.

———. *Mao zhuxi shicha xuexiao* (Chairman Mao Inspects Schools). Beijing: Zhongguo shaonian ertong chubanshe, 1959.

———. *Mao zhuxi jiaoyu yulu* (Quotations from Chairman Mao on Education). ed. Hongdaihui, zuozhanbu doupigai bangongshi. Beijing: Beijing dianji xuexiao, dongfanghong gongshe, 1967.

———. *Mao Zedong sixiang wansui* (Long Live the Thought of Mao Zedong). 2 vols. N.p., 1967–1969.

———. *Mao Zedong ji* (Collected Works of Mao Zedong). 10 vols. Hong Kong: Jindai shiliao gongying she, 1975.

———. *Jianguo yilai Mao Zedong wengao* (Mao Zedong's Manuscripts since Liberation). 8 vols. Beijing: Zhongyang wenxian chubanshe, 1987–1993.

Mo-luo-zi-ang. "Sugong diershici daibiao dahui de jueyi he Sulian xuexiao de renwu" (The Decisions of the Soviet Union's 20th Communist Party Congress and the Tasks of the Soviet Union's Schools). *Renmin jiaoyu*, July 1956, pp. 15–19.

Na-wu-mo-fu, Xie. "Genju Sulian gongchandang diershici daibiao dahui jueyi de jingshen: tan Sulian guomin jiaoyu de jixiang renwu" (In Accordance with the Spirit of the Resolutions of the Soviet Union's 20th Communist Party Representative Congress: A Discussion of the Various Tasks of the Soviet Union's National Education). *Renmin jiaoyu*, Jan. 1957, pp. 7–12.

Nonglinbu kejiaoju, ed. *Chaoyang nongxueyuan zai douzhengzhong qianjin* (Chaoyang Agricultural College Advancing in Struggle). Beijing: Nongye chubanshe, 1976.

Ouyang Zhang, ed. *Chengren jiaoyu dashiji, 1949–1986* (Chronicle of Adult Education, 1949–1986). Beijing: Beijing chubanshe, 1987.

Qian Junrui. "Wei tigao gongnong de wenhua shuiping, manzu gongnong ganbu de wenhua yaoqiu er fendou" (Struggle to Raise the Cultural Level of Workers and Peasants, and Satisfy the Cultural Demands of Worker–Peasant Cadres). *Renmin jiaoyu*, May 1951, pp. 12–16.

——. "Cong taolun Wu Xun wenti women xuedao xie shenma" (What We Have Learned from the Discussion of Wu Xun's Problems). *Renmin jiaoyu*, Sept. 1951, pp. 11–13.

——. "Gaodeng jiaoyu gaige de guanjian" (The Key to Reforming Higher Education). *Xuexi*, vol. 5, no. 1 (1 Nov. 1951), pp. 10–11.

Qingong jianxue xuexi ziliao (Study Materials on Diligent Work and Frugal Study). Hangzhou: Zhejiang renmin chubanshe, 1958.

Qu Qiubai. *Qu Qiubai shige qianshi* (A Simple Selection of Qu Qiubai's Poems and Songs). Nanning: Guangxi renmin chubanshe, 1981.

——. *Qu Qiubai wenji* (Qu Qiubai Collected Works). 6 vols. Beijing: Renmin wenxue chubanshe, 1985–1988.

Qu Shipei. *Kangri zhanzheng shiqi jiefangqu gaodeng jiaoyu* (Higher Education in the Liberated Areas in the Period of the War of Resistance against Japan). Beijing: Beijing daxue chubanshe, 1985.

"Quanguo geji xuexiao xuesheng renshu de fazhan jiyu jiefangqian de bijiao" (The Development of National Student Enrollments at the Various Levels of Schooling and a Comparison with before Liberation). *Renmin jiaoyu*, Oct. 1954, pp. 34–36.

Renmin chubanshe, ed. *Pipan "Wu Xun zhuan"* (Criticizing "The Story of Wu Xun"). 2 vols. Beijing: Renmin chubanshe, 1951.

Shaan–Gan–Ning bianqu jiaoyu fangzhen (The Education Policy of the Shaanxi–Gansu–Ningxia Border Region). N.p.: Shaan–Gan–Ning bianqu zhengfu bangongting, July 1944.

Shehuizhuyi jiaoyu jianshe gaochao (High Tide of Socialist Education Construction). Beijing: Renmin jiaoyu chubanshe, 1958.

Shen Shengdu. "Xuexi Mao Zedong tongzhi zai geming genjudi de banxue sixiang" (Studying Comrade Mao Zedong's Thought on Running Schools in the Revolutionary Base Areas). *Jiaoyu yanjiu*, no. 12 (1983), pp. 7–8, 73.

Shinian hou de pingshuo – "wenhua da geming" shi lun ji (A Critique 10 Years Later – Collection of Essays on the History of the "Great Cultural Revolution"). Beijing: Zhonggong dangshi ziliao chubanshe, 1987.

Shi-teng-hui-xiu [Saneto Keishu]. *Zhongguoren liuxue riben shi* (A History of Chinese Studying in Japan). Trans. Tan Ruqian and Lin Qiyan. Beijing: Sanlian, 1983.

Shu Ming. "Lun jiaoyu gongzuo de tongyixing he difangxing" (On the Unified and Local Natures of Education Work). *Renmin jiaoyu*, May 1957, pp. 6–9.

Shu Xincheng, ed. *Zhongguo jindai jiaoyu shi ziliao* (Materials on the History of China's Modern Education). 3 vols. Beijing: Renmin jiaoyu chubanshe, 1980. Originally published in Shanghai, 1928.

Sidalin [Stalin, Joseph]. *Sidalin quanji* (Stalin's Collected Works). 13 vols. Beijing: Renmin chubanshe, 1953–1958.

Sirenbang shijian tansuo (Explorations of the Gang of Four Incident). Hong Kong: Qishi niandai zashi she, 1977.

Su Ren. "Zhong, xiaoxue jiaoyu fazhan wenti de wojian" (My Views on the Developmental Problems of Secondary and Elementary Education). *Renmin jiaoyu*, May 1957, pp. 9–11.

Sun Si. "Tantan jinnian gaodeng xuexiao zhaosheng gongzuo zhong de jige wenti" (Discussing a Few Questions about This Year's College Enrollment Work). *Zhongguo qingnian*, no. 13 (July 1958), pp. 19–21.

Sun Zongrong. "Dangqian jiaoyu gemingzhong de jige wenti: xuexi Shaoqi, Kang Sheng tongzhi lai benxiao shicha shi suo zuo tanhua de jidian tihui" (Some Problems in the Current Education Revolution: Study a Few Points of Experience from What Was Said by Comrades Shaoqi and Kang Sheng When They Came to Our Schools on an Inspection Visit). *Zhongguo qingnian*, no. 2. (1959), pp. 7–9.

Tao Xingzhi. *Tao Xingzhi nianpu gao* (Chronicle of the Life of Tao Xingzhi). Beijing: Jiaoyu kexue chubanshe, 1982.

——. *Tao Xingzhi quanji* (The Complete Works of Tao Xingzhi). 6 vols. Changsha: Hunan jiaoyu chubanshe, 1983–1985.

——. *Tao Xingzhi nianpu* (Chronicle of the Life of Tao Xingzhi). Hefei: Anhui jiaoyu chubanshe, 1985.

——. *Tao Xingzhi yanjiu* (Tao Xingzhi Research). Changsha: Hunan jiaoyu chubanshe, 1986.

Tao Zhixing (Xingzhi), *Zhongguo jiaoyu gaizao* (China's Education Reform). Shanghai: Yadong tushuguan, 1928.

Tian Jiagu, ed. *Kangzhan jiaoyu zai Shaanbei* (Education in North Shaanxi during the War of Resistance against Japan). Hankou: Mingri chubanshe, 1938.

Tianjin shi xiaoxue jiaodao yanjiuhui, ed. *Xiang Sulian xuexi* (Learning from the Soviet Union). Beijing and Tianjin: Dazhong shudian, 1951.

Wang Bingzhao et al. *Jianming Zhongguo jiaoyu shi* (A Concise History of Chinese Education). Beijing: Beijing shifan daxue chubanshe, 1985.

Wang Jianmin. *Zhongguo gongchandang shigao* (History of the Chinese Communist Party). 3 vols. Taibei: Zhongyang wenwu gongyingshe, 1965.

Wang Tie. *Zhongguo jiaoyu fangzhen de yanjiu: xin minzhuzhuyi jiaoyu fangzhen de lilun yu shijian* (A Study of China's Education Policy: The Theory and Practice of the New Democratic Education Policies). Beijing: Jiaoyu kexue chubanshe, 1982.

Wei Chunyi. "Guanyu xuesheng he gongnong jiehe de wenti" (On the Question of Unity between Students and Workers and Peasants). *Zhongguo qingnian*, no. 23 (1 Dec. 1955), pp. 3–5.

Wu Heng, ed. *Kangri zhanzheng shiqi jiefangqu kexue jishu zhan shi ziliao* (Historical Materials on the Development of Science and Technology during the Period of the War of Resistance against Japan). 2 vols. Beijing: Zhongguo xueshu chubanshe, 1983–1984.

Wu Yanyin. "Beijingshi xiaoxue shiyan wunian yiguanzhi liangnianlai de chubu jingyan" (The Preliminary Experience of Experimenting with the Five-Year Integrated Elementary School during the Past Two Years in Beijing). *Renmin jiaoyu*, Dec. 1952, pp. 4–16.

Xiaoxue jiaoyu de lilun yu shijian (The Theory and Practice of Elementary School Education). Hong Kong: Xin minzhu chubanshe, n.d.

Xu Teli. *Xu Teli wenji* (Xu Teli's Collected Works). Changsha: Hunan renmin chubanshe, 1980.

———. *Xu Teli jiaoyu wenji* (Xu Teli's Collected Works on Education). Rev. ed. Beijing: Renmin jiaoyu chubanshe, 1986.

Xu Zongyuan. *Tao Xingzhi*. Beijing: Renmin chubanshe, 1988.

"Xuexi Beijingshi tigao zhong xiaoxue jiaoyu zhiliang de cuoshi" (Study Beijing's Measures for Raising the Quality of Middle and Elementary School Education). *Renmin jiaoyu*, Aug. 1954, pp. 5–6.

Xuexi chaoyang nongxueyuan de xinxian jingyan (Study the New Experience of the Chaoyang Agricultural College). Beijing: Renmin chubanshe, 1975.

Yan Jiaqi and Gao Gao. *"Wen ge" shi nian shi* (A History of Ten Years of "Cultural Revolution"). Hong Kong: Wannianqing chubanshe, 1989.

Yan Yangchu. *Yan Yangchu quanji, 1919–1937* (Complete Works of Yan Yangchu, 1919–1937). Changsha: Hunan jiaoyu chubanshe, 1989.

Yang Rongguo. "Pilin pikong yu zhishi fenzi de jinbu" (On Criticizing Lin Biao and Confucius and the Intellectuals' Progress). *Hongqi*, no. 10 (1974), pp. 46–50.

Yang Zhihong. "Yaoqiu xuesheng 'men men wu fen' dui ma" (Is It Correct to Demand "Five Points in Every Subject" of Students?). *Renmin jiaoyu*, Feb. 1957, p. 26.

Yao ganyu fan chaoliu (Daring to Go against the Tide). Beijing: Renmin chubanshe, 1974.

Yuan Zhenguo, ed. *Zhongguo dangdai jiaoyu sichao, 1949–1989* (Trends of Thought in Contemporary Chinese Education, 1949–1989). Shanghai: Sanlian shudian chubanshe, 1991.

Zeng Zhaolun. "Sannianlai gaodeng jiaoyu de gaijin" (Improvements in Higher Education during the Past Three Years). *Renmin jiaoyu*, Jan. 1953, pp. 11–12.

Zhang Jian. "Luetan gaodeng xuexiao xuexi Sulian xianjin jingyan de chengjiu he wenti" (A Brief Discussion of the Accomplishments and Problems of Tertiary Institutions Learning from the Advanced Experience of the Soviet Union). *Renmin jiaoyu*, Feb. 1955, pp. 12–15.

———. "Xuexi Sulian jingyan de chengji bushi zhuyao de me" (Have Not the Achievements Been the Main Thing in Learning from the Soviet Experience?). *Renmin jiaoyu*, Aug. 1957, pp. 12, 16–18.

———. "Woguo de gaodeng jiaoyu shi yueban yuehao le" (Our Country's Higher Education Is Being Run Better and Better). *Renmin jiaoyu*, Oct. 1957, pp. 6–10.

Zhang Jichun. "Gengkuai genghao di fazhan wo guo de jiaoyu shiye" (Develop Our Country's Educational Enterprise Faster and Better). *Hongqi*, no. 3 (1960), pp. 10–16.

Zhang Xiruo. "Muqian guomin jiaoyu fangmian de qingkuang he wenti" (Present Situation and Problems of National Education). *Renmin jiaoyu*, July 1956, pp. 8–11. Also in *Xinhua banyue kan*, no. 14 (1956), pp. 75–77.

Zhang Yeming. "He Jiang Nanxiang tongzhi shangque jiaoyu fangzhen wenti" (Discussing Questions of Education Policy with Comrade Jiang Nanxiang). *Renmin jiaoyu*, Dec. 1956, pp. 5–8.

Zhang Zhidong. *Zhang Wenxiang gong quanji* (The Complete Works of Zhang Zhidong). 6 vols. ed. Wang Shutong. Taibei: Wenhai chubanshe, 1963.

Zhejiang "wenge" jishi, 1966.5–1976.10 (Record of the "Cultural Revolution" in Zhejiang, May 1966 to October 1976). N.p.: "Zhejiang fangzhi" bianjibu, 1989.

Zhonggong renming lu (Biographies of Chinese Communists). Taibei: Zhonghua minguo guoji guanxi yanjiusuo, 1967.

Zhongguo baike nianjian, 1980 (China Encyclopedic Yearbook, 1980). Beijing: Zhongguo dabaike quanshu chubanshe, 1980.

Zhongguo baike nianjian, 1981 (China Encyclopedic Yearbook, 1981). Beijing: Zhongguo dabaike quanshu chubanshe, 1981.

Zhongguo baike nianjian, 1982 (China Encyclopedic Yearbook, 1982). Beijing: Zhongguo dabaike quanshu chubanshe, 1982.

Zhongguo dabaike quanshu: jiaoyu (Chinese Encyclopedia: Education). Beijing and Shanghai: Zhongguo dabaike quanshu chubanshe, 1985.

Zhongguo geming genjudi jiaoyu jishi, 1927.8–1949.9 (Record of Education in China's Revolutionary Bases, August 1927 to September 1949). Beijing: Jiaoyu kexue chubanshe, 1989.

Zhongguo gongchandang chaoyang nongxueyuan weiyuanhui. "Dashidafei wenti yiding yao bianlun qingchu" (Great Matters of Right and Wrong Must Be Clearly Debated). *Hongqi*, no. 1 (1976), pp. 38–43.

Zhongguo gongchandang lici zhongyao huiyiji (An Anthology of the Various Important Meetings of the Chinese Communist Party). Shanghai: Shanghai renmin chubanshe, 1982.

Zhongguo gongchandang zhongyang, Huanan fenju xuanquanbu, ed. *Gaoxiao he chuzhong biyesheng congshi laodong shengchan xuanquan jianghua* (Propaganda Talk on Senior Elementary and Junior Middle School Graduates Engaging in Labor Production). Guangzhou: Huanan renmin chubanshe, 1954.

Zhongguo jiaoyu chengjiu tongji ziliao, 1980–1985 (Achievement of Education in China, Statistics, 1980–1985). Department of Planning, State Education Commission. Beijing: Renmin jiaoyu chubanshe, 1986.

Zhongguo jiaoyu nianjian, 1949–1981 (China Education Yearbook, 1949–1981). Beijing: Zhongguo dabaike quanshu chubanshe, 1984.

Zhongguo jiaoyu nianjian, 1949–1984: difang jiaoyu (China Education Yearbook, 1949–1984: Local Education). Changsha: Hunan jiaoyu chubanshe, 1986.

Zhongguo jiaoyu tongji nianjian, 1987 (Yearbook of China's Educational Statistics, 1987), Beijing: Gongye daxue chubanshe, 1988.

Zhongguo jingji nianjian, 1981 (Almanac of China's Economy, 1981). Beijing: Jingji guanli zazhi she, 1981.

Zhongguo jingji nianjian, 1983 (Almanac of China's Economy, 1983). Xianggang: Zhongguo jingji nianjian youxian gongsi, 1983.

Zhongguo qingnian yundong liushi nian, 1919–1979 (Sixty Years of the Chinese Youth Movement, 1919–1979). Beijing: Zhongguo qingnian chubanshe, 1990.

Zhongguo tongji nianjian, 1981 (Statistical Yearbook of China, 1981). Beijing: Zhongguo tongji chubanshe, 1981.

Zhongguo tongji nianjian, 1983 (Statistical Yearbook of China, 1983). Xianggang: Jingji daobao she, 1983.

Zhongguo tongji nianjian, 1986 (Statistical Yearbook of China, 1986). Beijing: Zhongguo tongji chubanshe, 1986.

Zhongguo tongji nianjian, 1988 (Statistical Yearbook of China, 1988). Beijing: Zhongguo tongji chubanshe, 1988.

Zhongguo xinminzhuzhuyi geming shiqi genjudi fazhi wenxian xuanbian (Collected Legal Documents from the Base Areas for the Period of China's New Democratic Revolution). 4 vols. N.p.: Zhongguo shehui kexue chubanshe, 1981–1984.

Zhonghua renmin gongheguo fagui huibian, 1958 7 yue–12 yue (Compilation of Laws and Regulations of the People's Republic of China, July–December 1958). N.p.: Falu chubanshe, 1959, 1982.

Zhonghua renmin gongheguo fagui huibian, 1959 1 yue–6 yue (Compilation of Laws and Regulations of the People's Republic of China, January–June 1959). N.p.: Falu chubanshe, 1959–1982.

Zhonghua renmin gongheguo guojia tongjiju. *Guanyu 1955 niandu guomin jingji jihua zhixing jieguo de gongbao* (Report on the Results of the National Economic Plan for 1955). Beijing: Tongji chubanshe, 1956.

Zhonghua renmin gongheguo minzhengbu. *Zhonghua renmin gongheguo xianji yishang xingzhengqu huayange* (The Evolution of the Administrative Divisions at the County Level and above within the People's Republic of China). 3 vols. N.p.: Cehui chubanshe, 1986–1988.

Zhonghua suweiai gongheguo falu wenjian xuanbian (Compilation of Legal Documents from the Chinese Soviet Republic). Comp. and ed. Xiamen University Law Department and Fujian Provincial Archives. Nanchang: Jiangxi renmin chubanshe, 1984.

Zhongyang geming genjudi shiliao xuanbian (A Selection of Historical Materials on the Central Revolutionary Base). 3 vols. Comp. and ed. Jiangxi Provincial Archives and the Party History Teaching and Research Office of the Party School of the Jiangxi Provincial CCP Committee. Nanchang: Jiangxi renmin chubanshe, 1982.

Zhongyang jiaoyu kexue yanjiusuo, ed. *Zhonghua renmin gongheguo jiaoyu dashiji, 1949–1982* (Chronicle of Education in the People's Republic of China, 1949–1982). Beijing: Jiaoyu kexue chubanshe, 1983.

———. *Zhou Enlai jiaoyu wenxuan* (Selections from Zhou Enlai on Education). Beijing: Jiaoyu kexue chubanshe, 1984.

———. *Laojiefangqu jiaoyu ziliao (2): kangri zhanzheng shiqi (shang)* (Materials on Education in the Old Liberated Areas [vol. 2]: The Anti-Japanese War Period [pt. 1]). Beijing: Jiaoyu kexue chubanshe, 1986. (See Chen Yuanhui, Qu Xingui, and Zou Guangwei, eds., for vol. 1 of this series.)

———. *Laojiefangqu jiaoyu ziliao (2): kangri zhanzheng shiqi (xia)* (Materials on Education in the Old Liberated Areas [vol. 2]: The Anti-Japanese War Period [pt. 2]). Beijing: Jiaoyu kexue chubanshe, 1986. (See Chen Yuanhui, Qu Xingui, and Zou Guangwei, eds. for vol. 1 of this series.)

———. *Zhongguo xiandai jiaoyu dashiji, 1919–1949* (Chronicle of Major Events in Modern Chinese Education, 1919–1949). Beijing: Jiaoyu kexue chubanshe, 1988.

Zhongyang jiaoyu kexue yanjiusuo jiaoyu shi yanjiushi, ed. *Zhonghua minguo jiaoyu fagui xuanbian, 1912–1949* (A Selection of Laws and Regulations on Education from the Chinese Republic, 1912–1949). Nanjing: Jiangsu jiaoyu chubanshe, 1990.

Zhongyang jiaoyubu gongnong sucheng zhongxue jiaoyuchu. "Wunianlai de gongnong sucheng zhongxue" (Worker–Peasant Short-Course Secondary Schools during the Past Five Years). *Renmin jiaoyu*, Nov. 1954, pp. 34–35.

Zhongyang jiaoyubu zhongxue jiaoyusi. "Diyici quanguo gongnong sucheng zhongxue gongzuo huiyi zongjie zhaiyao" (Summary of the First National Conference on Worker–Peasant Short-Course Middle School Work). *Renmin jiaoyu*, Feb. 1952, pp. 11–14.

Zhou Daping. "Tuoqian jiaoshi gongzi: yige bixu zhuajin jiejue de wenti" (Defaulted Teachers' Wages: A Problem That Must Be Firmly Resolved). *Liaowang zhoukan* (Outlook Weekly), Beijing (domestic ed.), no. 42 (18 Oct. 1993), pp. 8–11.

Zhou Tiandu. *Cai Yuanpei zhuan* (A Biography of Cai Yuanpei). Beijing: Renmin chubanshe, 1984.

English-language references

Abe, Hiroshi. "Borrowing from Japan: China's First Modern Educational System." In Hayhoe and Bastid, *China's Education and the Industrialized World.*

Ahn, Byung-joon. *Chinese Politics and the Cultural Revolution: Dynamics of Policy Processes.* Seattle: University of Washington Press, 1976.

Alitto, Guy S. *The Last Confucian: Liang Shu-ming and the Chinese Dilemma of Modernity.* Berkeley: University of California Press, 1979.

Altbach, Philip G. *Higher Education in the Third World.* Singapore: Maruzen Asia, 1982.

Altbach, Philip G., and Gail P. Kelly, eds. *Education and Colonialism.* New York and London: Longman, 1978.

Anderson, C. Arnold. "Access to Higher Education and Economic Development." In Halsey, Floud, and Anderson, *Education, Economy, and Society.*

——. "Economic Development and Post-primary Education." In Piper and Cole, *Post-primary Education and Political and Economic Development.*

Anderson, C. Arnold, and Mary Jean Bowman, eds. *Education and Economic Development.* Chicago: Aldine, 1965.

Austin, Alvyn J. *Saving China: Canadian Missionaries in the Middle Kingdom, 1888–1959.* Toronto: University of Toronto Press, 1986.

Averill, Stephen C. "The New Life in Action: The Nationalist Government in South Jiangxi, 1934–37." *China Quarterly*, no. 88 (Dec. 1981), pp. 594–628.

——. "Party, Society, and Local Elite in the Jiangxi Communist Movement." *Journal of Asian Studies*, vol. 46, no. 2 (May 1987), pp. 279–303.

Ayers, William. *Chang Chih-tung and Educational Reform in China.* Cambridge: Harvard University Press, 1971.

Bailey, Paul J. "The Chinese Work–Study Movement in France." *China Quarterly*, no. 115 (Sept. 1988), pp. 441–461.

——. *Reform the People: Changing Attitudes towards Popular Education in Early Twentieth-Century China.* Vancouver: University of British Columbia Press, 1990.

Bairoch, Paul. *Urban Unemployment in Developing Countries.* Geneva: International Labour Office, 1973.

Barendsen, Robert D. "The 1960 Educational Reform." *China Quarterly*, no. 4 (Oct./ Dec. 1960), pp. 55–65.

————. "The Agricultural Middle School in Communist China." *China Quarterly*, no. 8 (Oct./Dec. 1961), pp. 106–134.

————. *Half-Work Half-Study Schools in Communist China: Recent Experiments with Self-Supporting Educational Institutions*. Washington, D.C.: U.S. Department of Health, Education, and Welfare, 1964.

————. *Education in the People's Republic of China: A Selective Annotated Bibliography of Materials Published in the English Language, 1971–1976*. Washington, D.C.: U.S. Department of Education, 1981.

Bastid, Marianne. "Economic Necessity and Political Ideals in Educational Reform during the Cultural Revolution." *China Quarterly*, no. 42 (Apr./June 1970), pp. 16–45.

————. "Chinese Educational Policies in the 1980s and Economic Development." *China Quarterly*, no. 98 (June 1984), pp. 189–219.

————. *Educational Reform in Early Twentieth-Century China*. Trans. Paul J. Bailey. Ann Arbor: Center for Chinese Studies, University of Michigan, 1988.

Baum, Richard. *Prelude to Revolution: Mao, the Party, and the Peasant Question, 1962–1966*. New York: Columbia University Press, 1975.

Baum, Richard, and Frederick C. Teiwes. *Ssu-Ch'ing: The Socialist Education Movement of 1962–1966*. China Research Monographs, no. 2. Berkeley: University of California, 1968.

Bays, Daniel H. *China Enters the Twentieth Century: Chang Chih-tung and the Issues of a New Age, 1895–1909*. Ann Arbor: University of Michigan Press, 1978.

Beeby, C. E. *The Quality of Education in Developing Countries*. Cambridge: Harvard University Press, 1966.

Bell, Daniel. *The Coming of Post-industrial Society: A Venture in Social Forecasting*. 2d ed. New York: Basic Books, 1976. Originally published in 1973.

Bennett, Gordon A., and Ronald N. Montaperto. *Red Guard: The Political Biography of Dai Hsiao-ai*. Garden City, N.Y.: Doubleday, 1971.

Bereday, George Z. F., William W. Brickman, and Gerald H. Read, eds. *The Changing Soviet School*. Boston: Houghton Mifflin, 1960.

Bernstein, Thomas P. *Up to the Mountains and Down to the Villages: The Transfer of Youth from Urban to Rural China*. New Haven: Yale University Press, 1977.

Bettelheim, Charles. *Class Struggles in the USSR, Second Period: 1923–1930*. New York: Monthly Review Press, 1978.

Biggerstaff, Knight. *The Earliest Modern Government Schools in China*. Ithaca: Cornell University Press, 1961.

Blaug, Mark. *An Introduction to the Economics of Education*. London: Allen Lane, Penguin, 1970.

————. *Education and the Employment Problem in Developing Countries*. Geneva: International Labour Office, 1973.

Borthwick, Sally. *Education and Social Change in China: The Beginnings of the Modern Era*. Stanford: Hoover Institution, 1983.

Boudon, Raymond. *Education, Opportunity, and Social Inequality: Changing Prospects in Western Society*. New York: John Wiley, 1974.

Bourdieu, Pierre, and Jean-Claude Passeron. *Reproduction in Education, Society and Culture*. Trans. Richard Nice. London and Beverly Hills: Sage, 1977.

Bowie, Robert R., and John K. Fairbank, eds. *Communist China, 1955–1959: Policy Documents with Analysis*. Cambridge: Harvard University Press, 1962.

Bowles, Samuel. "Education, Class Conflict, and Uneven Development." In Simmons, *The Education Dilemma*.

Bowles, Samuel, and Herbert Gintis. *Schooling in Capitalist America: Educational Reform and the Contradictions of Economic Life*. New York: Basic Books, 1976.

Bowman, Mary Jean, and C. Arnold Anderson. "Concerning the Role of Education in Development." In Geertz, *Old Societies and New States*.

Brandt, Conrad, Benjamin Schwartz, and John K. Fairbank, eds. *A Documentary History of Chinese Communism*. London: George Allen and Unwin, 1952.

Bratton, Dale. "University Admissions Policies in China, 1970–1978." *Asian Survey*, vol. 19, no. 10 (Oct. 1979), pp. 1008–1022.

Braun, Otto. *A Comintern Agent in China, 1932–1939*. London: C. Hurst, 1982.

Brown, Hubert O. "Primary Schooling and the Rural Responsibility System in the People's Republic of China." *Comparative Education Review*, vol. 30, no. 3 (Aug. 1986), pp. 373–387.

———. "American Progressivism in Chinese Education: The Case of Tao Xingzhi." In Hayhoe and Bastid, *China's Education and the Industrialized World*.

Buck, David D. "Educational Modernization in Tsinan, 1899–1937." In Elvin and Skinner, *The Chinese City between Two Worlds*.

———. *Urban Change in China: Politics and Development in Tsinan, Shantung, 1890–1949*. Madison: University of Wisconsin Press, 1978.

Buck, John Lossing. *Land Utilization in China*. London: Oxford University Press, 1937.

Buck, Pearl S. *Tell the People: Talks with James Yen about the Mass Education Movement*. New York: International Institute of Rural Reconstruction, 1959.

Buck, Peter. *American Science and Modern China, 1876–1936*. Cambridge: Cambridge University Press, 1980.

Bullard, Monte R. *China's Political–Military Evolution: The Party and the Military in the PRC, 1960–1984*. Boulder: Westview, 1985.

Bullock, Mary Brown. *An American Transplant: The Rockefeller Foundation and Peking Union Medical College*. Berkeley: University of California Press, 1980.

Burns, John P. "Immigration from China and the Future of Hong Kong." *Asian Survey*, vol. 27, no. 6 (June 1987), pp. 661–682.

———. *Political Participation in Rural China*. Berkeley: University of California Press, 1988.

———, ed. *The Chinese Communist Party's Nomenklatura System*. Armonk, N.Y.: M. E. Sharpe, 1989.

Byron, John, and Robert Pack. *The Claws of the Dragon: Kang Sheng – The Evil Genius behind Mao – And His Legacy of Terror in People's China*. New York: Simon and Schuster, 1992.

Carnoy, Martin. *Education as Cultural Imperialism*. New York: David McKay, 1974.

———. *The State and Political Theory*. Princeton: Princeton University Press, 1984.

Carnoy, Martin, and Henry M. Levin. *The Limits of Educational Reform*. New York: David McKay, 1976.

———. *Schooling and Work in the Democratic State*. Stanford: Stanford University Press, 1985.

Carnoy, Martin, Henry M. Levin, and Kenneth King. *Education, Work and Employment*. Vol. 2. Paris: Unesco International Institute for Educational Planning, 1980.

Castle, E. B. *Education for Self-Help*. New York and London: Oxford University Press, 1972.

CCP Documents of the Great Proletarian Cultural Revolution, 1966–1967. Hong Kong: Union Research Institute, 1968.

Chaffee, John W. *The Thorny Gates of Learning in Sung China: A Social History of Examinations*. Cambridge: Cambridge University Press, 1985.

Chan, Anita. "Images of China's Social Structure: The Changing Perspectives of Canton Students." *World Politics* (Apr. 1982), pp. 295–323.

——. *Children of Mao: Personality Development and Political Activism in the Red Guard Generation*. London: Macmillan, 1985.

Chan, Anita, Richard Madsen, and Jonathan Unger. *Chen Village: The Recent History of a Peasant Community in Mao's China*. Berkeley: University of California Press, 1984.

Chan, Anita, Stanley Rosen, and Jonathan Unger. "Students and Class Warfare: The Social Roots of the Red Guard Conflict in Guangzhou." *China Quarterly*, no. 83 (Sept. 1980), pp. 397–446.

Chang, Chung-li. *The Chinese Gentry: Studies on Their Role in Nineteenth-Century Chinese Society*. Seattle: University of Washington Press, 1955.

——. *The Income of the Chinese Gentry*. Seattle: University of Washington Press, 1962.

Chang, Jen-chi. *Pre-Communist China's Rural School and Community*. Boston: Christopher Publishing House, 1960.

Chauncey, Helen R. *Schoolhouse Politicians: Locality and State during the Chinese Republic*. Honolulu: University of Hawaii Press, 1992.

Ch'en, Jerome. *Mao and the Chinese Revolution*. London: Oxford University Press, 1970.

——. *Yuan Shih-k'ai*. 2d ed. Stanford: Stanford University Press, 1972.

——, ed. *Mao Papers: Anthology and Bibliography*. London: Oxford University Press, 1970.

Chen, Theodore H. E. *Thought Reform of the Chinese Intellectuals*. Hong Kong: Hong Kong University Press, 1960.

Chen, Theodore Hsi-en. *The Maoist Educational Revolution*. New York: Praeger, 1974.

——. *Chinese Education since 1949: Academic and Revolutionary Models*. New York: Pergamon, 1981.

Cheng, Chu-yuan. *Scientific and Engineering Manpower in Communist China, 1949–1963*. Washington, D.C.: National Science Foundation, 1965.

Cheng, Joseph Yu-shek, and Maurice Brosseau, eds. *China Review, 1993*. Hong Kong: Chinese University Press, 1993.

Cheng, Nien. *Life and Death in Shanghai*. London: Grafton Books, 1986.

Cheng, Ronald Yu Soong. *The Financing of Public Education in China: A Factual Analysis of Its Major Problems of Reconstruction*. Shanghai: Commercial Press, 1935.

Chiang, Monlin. *Chinese Culture and Education: A Historical and Comparative Survey*. Taipei: World Book Co., 1963. Originally published as *A Study in Chinese Principles of Education* (Shanghai: Commercial Press, 1918–1924).

China Handbook, 1937–1944. Chungking: Chinese Ministry of Information, 1944.

China: Issues and Prospects in Education. Washington, D.C.: World Bank, 1985.

China: Socialist Economic Development. 3 vols. Washington, D.C.: World Bank, 1983.

Chinese National Association for the Advancement of Education. *Bulletins on Chinese Education, 1923.* 2d ed. Shanghai: Commercial Press, 1925. Originally published individually.

Chow Tse-tsung. *The May Fourth Movement: Intellectual Revolution in Modern China.* Cambridge: Harvard University Press, 1960.

Christian Education in China: The Report of the China Educational Commission of 1921–1922. Shanghai: Commercial Press, 1922.

Ch'ü T'ung-tsu. *Local Government in China under the Ch'ing.* Stanford: Stanford University Press, 1962.

Cleverley, John. *The Schooling of China.* London: George Allen and Unwin, 1985.

Cohen, Paul A. *China and Christianity: The Missionary Movement and the Growth of Chinese Anti-foreignism, 1860–1870.* Cambridge: Harvard University Press, 1963.

Cohen, Paul A., and John E. Schrecker, eds. *Reform in Nineteenth-Century China.* Cambridge: East Asian Research Center, Harvard University, 1976.

Coleman, James S[amuel]., et al. *Equality of Educational Opportunity.* Washington, D.C.: U.S. Government Printing Office, 1966.

Coleman, James S[moot]., ed. *Education and Political Development.* Princeton: Princeton University Press, 1965.

Committee of Concerned Asian Scholars. *China! Inside the People's Republic.* New York: Bantam, 1972.

Compton, Boyd. Introduction to *Mao's China: Party Reform Documents, 1942–44*, trans. Boyd Compton. Seattle: University of Washington, 1952.

Comrade Mao Tse-tung on Educational Work. Trans. in *Chinese Education: A Journal of Translations*, vol. 2, nos. 1–3 (spring–fall 1969). Originally published in Beijing: People's Education Publishing House, 1958.

"Comrade Mao Yuan-hsin's Talks at the 'On-the-Spot Conference for Learning the Experience of Revolution in Education of Ch'aoyang Agricultural College in Liaoning.'" *Issues and Studies*, Taipei (Sept. 1976), pp. 111–133.

Coombs, Philip H. *The World Educational Crisis: A Systems Analysis.* New York: Oxford University Press, 1968.

——. *The World Crisis in Education: The View from the Eighties.* New York: Oxford University Press, 1985.

Coombs, Philip H., and Manzoor Ahmed. *Attacking Rural Poverty: How Nonformal Education Can Help.* Baltimore and London: Johns Hopkins University Press, 1974.

Coombs, Philip H., and Jacques Hallak. *Managing Educational Costs.* New York: Oxford University Press, 1972.

Cremin, Lawrence A. *The Transformation of the School: Progressivism in American Education, 1876–1957.* New York: Alfred A. Knopf, 1962.

Crook, David. "Recollections of an English Teacher in China – from the Liberated Areas to the Fall of the Gang of Four." *Monsoon*, Hong Kong (Apr.–May 1979), pp. 12–23.

Culp, Robert J. "Elite Association and Local Politics in Republican China: Educational Institutions in Jiashan and Lanqi Counties, Zhejiang, 1911–1937." *Modern China*, vol. 20, no. 4 (Oct. 1994), pp. 446–477.

Curle, Adam. *Educational Strategy for Developing Societies: A Study of Educational and Social Factors in Relation to Economic Growth*. London: Tavistock, 1963.

———. *Education for Liberation*. London: Tavistock, 1973.

Dale, Roger, et al., eds. *School and Capitalism: A Sociological Reader*. London: Routledge and Kegan Paul; Henley: Open University Press, 1976.

Daubier, Jean. *A History of the Chinese Cultural Revolution*. Trans. Richard Seaver. New York: Vintage, 1974.

De Witt, Nicholas. *Education and Professional Employment in the U.S.S.R.* Washington, D.C.: National Science Foundation, 1961.

Deutscher, Isaac. *Stalin: A Political Biography*. New York: Vintage, 1960.

Dewey, John. *John Dewey's Impressions of Soviet Russia and the Revolutionary World: Mexico – China – Turkey, 1929*. New York: Teachers College, Columbia University, 1964. Originally published in *New Republic*, 1929.

———. *John Dewey: Lectures in China, 1919–1920*. Trans. Robert W. Clopton and Tsuin-chen Ou. Honolulu: University Press of Hawaii, 1973.

Dirlik, Arif. "The Ideological Foundations of the New Life Movement: A Study in Counter-revolution." *Journal of Asian Studies*, vol. 34, no. 4 (Aug. 1975), pp. 945–980.

Djung, Lu-dzai. *A History of Democratic Education in Modern China*. Shanghai: Commercial Press, 1934.

Dobson, Richard B. "Social Status and Inequality of Access to Higher Education in the USSR." In Karabel and Halsey, *Power and Ideology in Education*.

Dore, R. P. *Education in Tokugawa Japan*. Berkeley: University of California Press, 1965.

Dore, Ronald. *The Diploma Disease: Education, Qualification and Development*. London: George Allen and Unwin, 1976.

Du, Ruiqing. *Chinese Higher Education: A Decade of Reform and Development (1978–1988)*. London: Macmillan, 1992.

Duiker, William J. *Ts'ai Yüan-p'ei: Educator of Modern China*. University Park: Pennsylvania State University Press, 1977.

Durkheim, Emile. *The Evolution of Educational Thought: Lectures on the Formation and Development of Secondary Education in France*. Trans. Peter Collins. London: Routledge and Kegan Paul, 1977.

Eastman, Lloyd. *The Abortive Revolution: China under Nationalist Rule, 1927–1937*. Cambridge: Harvard University Press, 1974.

Economic and Social Commission for Asia and the Pacific, Secretariat. *Economic and Social Survey of Asia and the Pacific, 1978: Biennial Review and Appraisal at the Regional Level of the International Development Strategy for the Second United Nations Development Decade* (draft). Manila: United Nations Economic and Social Council, 1979.

Education: Sector Working Paper. Washington, D.C.: World Bank, 1974.

Eisenstadt, S. N. "Education and Political Development." In Piper and Cole, *Postprimary Education and Political and Economic Development*.

Elman, Benjamin A. "Political, Social, and Cultural Reproduction via Civil Service Examinations in Late Imperial China." *Journal of Asian Studies*, vol. 50, no. 1 (Feb. 1991), pp. 7–28.

Elvin, Mark, and G. William Skinner, eds. *The Chinese City between Two Worlds*. Stanford: Stanford University Press, 1974.

Emerson, John Philip. *Administrative and Technical Manpower in the People's Republic of China*. Washington, D.C.: U.S. Department of Commerce, 1973.

Epstein, Irving, ed. *Chinese Education: Problems, Policies, and Prospects*. New York: Garland, 1991.

Esherick, Joseph W. *Reform and Revolution in China: The 1911 Revolution in Hunan and Hubei*. Berkeley: University of California Press, 1976.

———. *The Origins of the Boxer Uprising*. Berkeley: University of California Press, 1987.

Fainsod, Merle. *Smolensk under Soviet Rule*. London: Macmillan, 1958.

Fairbank, John K., ed. *Chinese Thought and Institutions*. Chicago: University of Chicago Press, 1957.

Faure, David, James Hayes, and Alan Birch, eds. *From Village to City: Studies in the Traditional Roots of Hong Kong Society*. Hong Kong: Centre of Asian Studies, University of Hong Kong 1984.

Faure, Edgar, et al. *Learning to Be: The World of Education Today and Tomorrow*. Paris: United Nations Educational, Scientific, and Cultural Organization, 1972.

Fei, Hsiao-tung. *Peasant Life in China: A Field Study of Country Life in the Yangtze Valley*. London: Routledge and Kegan Paul, 1939.

Fenn, William Purviance. *Christian Higher Education in Changing China, 1880–1950*. Grand Rapids, Mich.: William B. Eerdmans, 1976.

Fincher, John H. *Chinese Democracy: The Self-Government Movement in Local, Provincial and National Politics, 1905–1914*. London: Croom Helm, 1981.

———. *Chinese Democracy: Statist Reform, the Self-Government Movement, and Republican Revolution*. Tokyo: Institute for the Study of Languages and Cultures of Asia and Africa, 1989.

Fingar, Thomas, ed. *Higher Education in the People's Republic of China: Report of the Stanford University Delegation, May 22–June 11, 1980*. Stanford: Stanford University, 1980.

Fitzpatrick, Sheila. *The Commissariat of Enlightenment: Soviet Organization of Education and the Arts under Lunacharsky, October 1917–1921*. Cambridge: Cambridge University Press, 1970.

———. *Education and Social Mobility in the Soviet Union, 1921–1934*. Cambridge: Cambridge University Press, 1979.

———, ed. *Cultural Revolution in Russia, 1928–1931*. Bloomington: Indiana University Press, 1978.

Forster, Keith. *Rebellion and Factionalism in a Chinese Province: Zhejiang, 1966–1976*. Armonk, N.Y.: M. E. Sharpe, 1990.

Foster, Philip. *Education and Social Change in Ghana*. London: Routledge and Kegan Paul, 1965.

Foster, Philip J. "The Vocational School Fallacy in Development Planning." In Anderson and Bowman, *Education and Economic Development*.

Franke, Wolfgang. *The Reform and Abolition of the Traditional Chinese Examination System*. Cambridge: East Asian Research Center, Harvard University, 1960.

Fraser, Stewart, ed. *Chinese Communist Education: Records of the First Decade*. New York: John Wiley, 1965.

Fraser, Stewart E., ed. *Education and Communism in China: An Anthology of Commentary and Documents*. Hong Kong: International Studies Group, 1969.

Freire, Paulo. *Pedagogy of the Oppressed*. Trans. Myra Bergman Ramos, New York: Herder and Herder, 1970.

Fried, Morton H. *Fabric of Chinese Society: A Study of the Social Life of a Chinese County Seat*. New York: Octagon, 1974.

Friedman, Edward, Paul G. Pickowicz, and Mark Selden, with Kay Ann Johnson. *Chinese Village, Socialist State*. New Haven: Yale University Press, 1991.

Frolic, B. Michael. "A Visit to Peking University – What the Cultural Revolution Was All About." *New York Times Magazine*, 24 Oct. 1971, pp. 29, 115–129.

———. *Mao's People: Sixteen Portraits of Life in Revolutionary China*. Cambridge: Harvard University Press, 1980.

Furnivall, J. S. *Colonial Policy and Practice: A Comparative Study of Burma and Netherlands India*. 2d ed. New York: New York University Press, 1956. Originally published in 1948.

Furth, Charlotte, ed. *The Limits of Change: Essays on Conservative Alternatives in Republican China*. Cambridge: Harvard University Press, 1976.

Gamble, Sidney D. *Ting Hsien: A North China Rural Community*. New York: Institute of Pacific Relations, 1954.

Gardner, John. "Educated Youth and Urban–Rural Inequalities, 1958–66." In Lewis, *The City in Communist China*.

———. "Chou Jung-hsin and Chinese Education." *Current Scene*, Hong Kong (U.S. Consulate General), vol. 15, nos. 11–12 (Dec. 1977), pp. 1–14.

Garrett, Shirley S. *Social Reformers in Urban China: The Chinese Y.M.C.A., 1895–1926*. Cambridge: Harvard University Press, 1970.

Geertz, Clifford, ed. *Old Societies and New States: The Quest for Modernity in Asia and Africa*. New York: Free Press, 1963.

Gillin, Donald G. *Warlord: Yen Hsi-shan in Shansi Province, 1911–1949*. Princeton: Princeton University Press, 1967.

Gintis, Herbert. "Towards a Political Economy of Education." *Harvard Educational Review*, vol. 42, no. 1 (1972), pp. 70–96.

Glassman, Joel. "Change and Continuity in Chinese Communist Education Policy: 'Two-Line Struggle' versus Incremental Trends." *Contemporary China* (Columbia University), vol. 2, no. 2 (summer 1978), pp. 51–70.

Goldman, Merle. *Literary Dissent in Communist China*. Cambridge: Harvard University Press, 1967.

———. *China's Intellectuals: Advise and Dissent*. Cambridge: Harvard University Press, 1981.

Goldman, Rene. "Peking University Today." *China Quarterly*, no. 7 (July/Sept. 1961), pp. 101–111.

———. "The Rectification Campaign at Peking University: May–June 1957." *China Quarterly*, no. 12 (Oct./Dec. 1962), pp. 138–153.

Gould, Sidney H. *Sciences in Communist China*. Washington, D.C.: American Association for the Advancement of Science, 1961.

Grant, Nigel. *Soviet Education*. 4th ed. New York: Penguin, 1979.

Grieder, Jerome B. *Hu Shih and the Chinese Renaissance: Liberalism in the Chinese Revolution, 1917–1937*. Cambridge: Harvard University Press, 1970.

——. *Intellectuals and the State in Modern China: A Narrative History.* New York: Free Press, 1981.

Griffiths, V. L. *The Problems of Rural Education.* Paris: Unesco International Institute for Educational Planning, 1968.

Grimm, Tilemann. "Academies and Urban Systems in Kwangtung." In Skinner, *The City in Late Imperial China.*

Guldin, Gregory Elliott. "'Overseas' at Home: The Fujianese of Hong Kong." Ph.D. diss. University of Wisconsin – Madison, 1977.

Hallak, Jacques. *Planning the Location of Schools: An Instrument of Educational Policy.* Paris: Unesco International Institute for Educational Planning, 1977.

Halsey, A. H., Jean Floud, and C. Arnold Anderson, eds. *Education, Economy, and Society: A Reader in the Sociology of Education.* New York: Free Press, 1961.

Hamrin, Carol Lee, and Timothy Cheek. *China's Establishment Intellectuals.* Armonk, N.Y.: M. E. Sharpe, 1986.

Harrison, James Pinckney. *The Long March to Power: A History of the Chinese Communist Party, 1921–72.* New York: Praeger, 1972.

Hawkins, John N. *Mao Tse-tung and Education: His Thoughts and Teachings.* Hamden, Conn.: Shoe String Press, 1974.

——, ed. *Education and Social Change in the People's Republic of China.* New York: Praeger, 1983.

Hayford, Charles W. *To the People: James Yen and Village China.* New York: Columbia University Press, 1990.

Hayhoe, Ruth. "Catholics and Socialists: The Paradox of French Educational Interaction with China." In Hayhoe and Bastid, *China's Education and the Industrialized World.*

——. *China's Universities and the Open Door.* Armonk, N.Y.: M. E. Sharpe, 1989.

——, ed. *Contemporary Chinese Education.* London: Croom Helm, 1984.

——. *Education and Modernization: The Chinese Experience.* Oxford: Pergamon, 1992.

Hayhoe, Ruth, and Marianne Bastid, eds. *China's Education and the Industrialized World: Studies in Cultural Transfer.* Armonk, N.Y.: M. E. Sharpe, 1987.

Hayter, Teresa. *Aid as Imperialism.* Baltimore: Penguin, 1971.

Henze, Jürgen. "Developments in Vocational Education since 1976." *Comparative Education*, vol. 20, no. 1 (1984), pp. 117–140.

Hinton, William. *Hundred Day War: The Cultural Revolution at Tsinghua University.* New York: Monthly Review Press, 1972.

——. *Shenfan: The Continuing Revolution in a Chinese Village.* New York: Vintage, 1984.

Ho, Kan-chih. *A History of the Modern Chinese Revolution.* Peking: Foreign Languages Press, 1959.

Ho, Ping-ti. *The Ladder of Success in Imperial China: Aspects of Social Mobility, 1368–1911.* New York: Columbia University Press, 1962.

Hsiao, Kung-chuan. *Rural China: Imperial Control in the Nineteenth Century.* Seattle: University of Washington Press, 1960.

Hsiao, Theodore E. *The History of Modern Education in China.* Shanghai: Commercial Press, 1935.

Hsiao, Tso-liang. *Power Relations within the Chinese Communist Movement, 1930–1934: A Study of Documents.* Seattle: University of Washington Press, 1961.

——. *Power Relations within the Chinese Communist Movement, 1930–1934: The Chinese Documents.* Seattle: University of Washington Press, 1967.

——. *The Land Revolution in China, 1930–1934: A Study of Documents.* Seattle: University of Washington Press, 1969.

——. *Chinese Communism in 1927: City vs. Countryside.* Hong Kong: Chinese University of Hong Kong Press, 1970.

Hu, Chang-ho Jiugow. "A General Outline on the Reorganization of the Chinese Educational System." Doctor of Pedagogy diss., New York University, 1916.

Hu, Chang-tu, ed. *Chinese Education under Communism.* New York: Bureau of Publications, Teachers College, Columbia University, 1962.

Huang, Philip C. *Liang Ch'i-ch'ao and Modern Chinese Liberalism.* Seattle: University of Washington Press, 1972.

Huang, Philip C. C., Lynda Schaefer Bell, and Kathy Lemons Walker. *Chinese Communists and Rural Society, 1927–1934.* China Research Monographs, no. 13. Berkeley: University of California, 1978.

Hunter, Edward. *Brain-washing in Red China.* New York: Vanguard, 1953.

Hunter, Neale. *Shanghai Journal: An Eyewitness Account of the Cultural Revolution.* Boston: Beacon, 1969.

Huntington, Samuel P. "Political Development and Political Decay." *World Politics*, no. 3 (Apr. 1965), pp. 386–430.

——. *Political Order in Changing Societies.* New Haven: Yale University Press, 1968.

Ichiko, Chuzo. "The Role of the Gentry: An Hypothesis." In Wright, *China in Revolution.*

Israel, John. *Student Nationalism in China, 1927–1937.* Stanford: Hoover Institution, 1966.

Ivory, Paul E., and William R. Lavely. "Rustication, Demographic Change, and Development in Shanghai." *Asian Survey*, vol. 17, no. 5 (May 1977), pp. 440–455.

Japan. Ministry of Education, Science, and Culture. Minister's Secretariat. Research and Statistics Division. *Japan's Modern Educational System: A History of the First Hundred Years.* Tokyo: Ministry of Finance, 1980.

Jencks, Christopher, et al. *Inequality: A Reassessment of the Effect of Family and Schooling in America.* New York: Basic Books, 1972.

——. *Who Gets Ahead? The Determinants of Economic Success in America.* New York: Basic Books, 1979.

Johnson, David. "Communication, Class, and Consciousness in Late Imperial China." In Johnson, Nathan, and Rawski, *Popular Culture in Late Imperial China.*

Johnson, David, Andrew J. Nathan, and Evelyn S. Rawski, eds. *Popular Culture in Late Imperial China.* Berkeley: University of California Press, 1985.

Joint Publications Research Service, trans. *Compendium of Laws and Regulations of the People's Republic of China.* General Series: 14, 346 (2 July 1962).

Jones, Phillip W. *International Policies for Third World Education: UNESCO, Literacy, and Development.* London and New York: Routledge, 1988.

Joseph, William A., ed. *China Briefing, 1994.* Boulder: Westview Press, 1994.

Joseph, William A., Christine P. W. Wong, and David Zweig, eds. *New Perspectives on the Cultural Revolution.* Contemporary China Series, no. 8. Cambridge: Harvard University, 1991.

Kan, David. *The Impact of the Cultural Revolution on Chinese Higher Education.* Hong Kong: Union Research Institute, 1971.

Karabel, Jerome, and A. H. Halsey. "Educational Research: A Review and an Interpretation." In Karabel and Halsey, *Power and Ideology in Education*.

——, eds. *Power and Ideology in Education*. New York: Oxford University Press, 1977.

Katz, Michael B. *The Irony of Early School Reform: Educational Innovation in Mid-19th Century Massachusetts*. Cambridge: Harvard University Press, 1968.

——. *Class, Bureaucracy, and Schools: The Illusion of Educational Change in America*. Expanded ed. New York: Praeger, 1975.

Kau, Michael Ying-mao, and Susan H. Marsh, eds. *China in the Era of Deng Xiaoping: A Decade of Reform*. Armonk, N.Y.: M. E. Sharpe, 1993.

Keenan, Barry C. "Educational Reform and Politics in Early Republican China." *Journal of Asian Studies*, vol. 33, no. 2 (Feb. 1974), pp. 225–237.

——. *The Dewey Experiment in China: Educational Reform and Political Power in the Early Republic*. Cambridge: Harvard University Press, 1977.

Kerr, Clark, John S. Service, et al. *Observations on the Relations between Education and Work in the People's Republic of China: Report of a Study Group, April 25 to May 15, 1978*. Berkeley: Carnegie Council on Policy Studies in Higher Education, 1978.

Khrushchev, Nikita. *Khrushchev Remembers*. Trans. Strobe Talbott. London: André Deutsch, 1971.

Kim Ilpyong J. *The Politics of Chinese Communism: Kiangsi under the Soviets*. Berkeley: University of California Press, 1973.

Klochko, Mikhail A. *Soviet Scientist in Red China*. Trans. Andrew MacAndrew. New York: Praeger, 1964.

Korol, Alexander G. *Soviet Education for Science and Technology*. Cambridge: Massachusetts Institute of Technology; New York: John Wiley and Sons, 1957.

Kracke, Edward A., Jr. "Region, Family, and Individual in the Chinese Examination System." In Fairbank, *Chinese Thought and Institutions*.

——. *Civil Service in Early Sung China, 960–1067*. Cambridge: Harvard University Press, 1968.

Kraus, Richard Curt. *Class Conflict in Chinese Socialism*. New York: Columbia University Press, 1981.

Kuhn, Philip A. *Tao Hsing-chih, 1891–1946, an Educational Reformer*. Papers on China, 13. Cambridge: Harvard University, Dec. 1954.

Kuo, Ping Wen. *The Chinese System of Public Education*. New York: Teachers College, Columbia University, 1915.

Kuo, Warren. *Analytical History of the Chinese Communist Party*. 4 vols. Taipei: Institute of International Relations, 1968–1971.

Kwok, D. W. Y. *Scientism in Chinese Thought, 1900–1950*. New Haven: Yale University Press, 1965.

Kwong, Julia. *Chinese Education in Transition: Prelude to the Cultural Revolution*. Montreal: McGill–Queen's University Press, 1979.

——. "The Educational Experiment of the Great Leap Forward, 1958–1959: Its Inherent Contradictions." *Comparative Education Review*, vol. 23, no. 3 (Oct. 1979), pp. 443–455.

——. *Cultural Revolution in China's Schools, May 1966–April 1969*. Stanford: Hoover Institution, 1988.

Kwong, Luke S. K. *A Mosaic of the Hundred Days: Personalities, Politics, and Ideas of 1898*. Cambridge: Harvard University Press, 1984.

La Fargue, Thomas E. *China's First Hundred*. Pullman: State College of Washington, 1942.

Lampton, David M., ed. *Policy Implementation in Post-Mao China*. Berkeley: University of California Press, 1987.

Lapidus, Gail Warshofsky. "Educational Strategies and Cultural Revolution: The Politics of Soviet Development." In Fitzpatrick, *Cultural Revolution in Russia*.

Latourette, Kenneth Scott. *A History of Christian Missions in China*. Taipei: Ch'eng-wen Publishing Co., 1966. Originally published in London: Society for Promoting Christian Knowledge, 1929.

Lauglo, Jon, and Kevin Lillis, eds. *Vocationalizing Education: An International Perspective*. Oxford and New York: Pergamon, 1988.

Lauglo, Jon, and Martin McLean, eds. *The Control of Education: International Perspectives on the Centralization–Decentralization Debate*. London: Heinemann, 1985.

League of Nations' Mission of Educational Experts. *The Reorganisation of Education in China*. Paris: League of Nations' Institute of Intellectual Co-operation, 1932.

Lee, Chae-jin. *China's Korean Minority: The Politics of Ethnic Education*. Boulder: Westview, 1986.

Lee, Hong Yung. *The Politics of the Chinese Cultural Revolution*. Berkeley: University of California Press, 1978.

Lee, Thomas H. C. *Government Education and Examinations in Sung China*. Hong Kong: Chinese University Press, 1985.

Lerner, Daniel. "Toward a Communications Theory of Modernization." In Pye, *Communications and Political Development*.

Levine, Marilyn A. *The Found Generation: Chinese Communists in Europe during the Twenties*. Seattle: University of Washington Press, 1993.

Lewis, John Wilson, ed. *The City in Communist China*. Stanford: Stanford University Press, 1971.

Li Chengrui et al., eds. *A Census of One Billion People*. Hong Kong: Economic Information and Agency, 1987.

Li, Jui. *The Early Revolutionary Activities of Comrade Mao Tse-tung*. Trans. Anthony W. Sariti. White Plains, N.Y.: M. E. Sharpe, 1977.

Liang, Heng, and Judith Shapiro. *Son of the Revolution*. New York: Vintage, 1984.

Liao T'ai-ch'u. "Rural Education in Transition: A Study of Old-fashioned Schools (Szu Shu) in Shantung and Szechuan." *Yenching Journal of Social Studies*, no. 2 (1949), pp. 19–67.

Lifton, Robert Jay. *Thought Reform and the Psychology of Totalism: A Study of "Brainwashing" in China*. New York: W. W. Norton, 1963.

Lin, Jing. *Education in Post-Mao China*. Westport, Conn., and London: Praeger, 1993.

Lindbeck, John M. H. "Organization and Development of Science." In Gould, *Sciences in Communist China*.

Linden, Allen B. "Politics and Education in Nationalist China: The Case of the University Council, 1927–1928." *Journal of Asian Studies*, vol. 27, no. 4 (Aug. 1968), pp. 763–776.

Lindsay, Michael. *Notes on Educational Problems in Communist China, 1941–47*. New York: Institute of Pacific Relations, 1950.

Ling, Ken. *The Revenge of Heaven.* New York: Putnam, 1972. The British edition appeared under the title *Red Guard: From Schoolboy to "Little General" in Mao's China* (London: MacDonald, 1972).

Lipset, Seymour Martin. "Research Problems in the Comparative Analysis of Mobility and Development." *International Social Science Journal,* vol. 16, no. 1 (1964), pp. 35–48.

Liu, Kwang-ching. "Politics, Intellectual Outlook, and Reform: The T'ung-wen Kuan Controversy of 1867." In Cohen and Schrecker, *Reform in Nineteenth-Century China.*

Lo, Chi Kin, Suzanne Pepper, and Tsui Kai Yuen, eds. *China Review, 1995.* Hong Kong: Chinese University Press, 1995.

Lo, Leslie Nai-kwai. "The Changing Educational System: Dilemma of Disparity." In Cheng and Brosseau, *China Review, 1993.*

Lo, Ruth Earnshaw, and Katharine S. Kinderman. *In the Eye of the Typhoon: An American Woman Shares in the Upheavals of China's Cultural Revolution, 1966–1978.* New York: Harcourt Brace Jovanovich, 1980.

Löfstedt, Jan-Ingvar. *Chinese Educational Policy: Changes and Contradictions, 1949–79.* Stockholm: Almqvist and Wiksell International, 1980.

Lotveit, Trygve. *Chinese Communism, 1931–1934: Experience in Civil Government.* Scandinavian Institute of Asian Studies, Monograph Series, no. 16. 1973.

Luk, Bernard H. K. "Lu Tzu-chün and Ch'en Jung-kun: Two Exemplary Figures in the *Ssu-shu* Education of Pre-war Urban Hong Kong." In Faure, Hayes, and Birch, *From Village to City.*

Lutz, Jessie Gregory. *China and the Christian Colleges, 1850–1950.* Ithaca: Cornell University Press, 1971.

MacFarquhar, Roderick. *The Origins of the Cultural Revolution.* 2 vols. New York: Columbia University Press, 1974–1983.

——, ed. *The Hundred Flowers Campaign and the Chinese Intellectuals.* New York: Praeger, 1960.

MacFarquhar, Roderick, Timothy Cheek, and Eugene Wu, eds. *The Secret Speeches of Chairman Mao: From the Hundred Flowers to the Great Leap Forward.* Cambridge: Council on East Asian Studies/Harvard University, 1989.

MacFarquhar, Roderick, and John K. Fairbank, eds. *The Cambridge History of China. Vol. 14, The People's Republic.* Pt. 1, *The Emergence of Revolutionary China, 1949–1965.* Cambridge: Cambridge University Press, 1987.

——. *The Cambridge History of China. Vol. 15, The People's Republic.* Pt. 2, *Revolutions within the Chinese Revolution, 1966–1982.* Cambridge: Cambridge University Press, 1991.

MacKinnon, Stephen R. *Power and Politics in Late Imperial China: Yuan Shi-kai in Beijing and Tianjin, 1901–1908.* Berkeley: University of California Press, 1980.

Madsen, Richard. *Morality and Power in a Chinese Village.* Berkeley: University of California Press, 1984.

Malassis, Louis. *The Rural World: Education and Development.* London and Paris: Croom Helm and Unesco, 1976.

Mao Tse-tung. *Selected Works.* 4 vols. Peking: Foreign Languages Press, 1961–1965.

Mao Tsetung. *A Critique of Soviet Economics.* Trans. Moss Roberts and Richard Levy. New York: Monthly Review Press, 1977.

Mao Zedong. *Mao Zedong: Report from Xunwu*. Trans. Roger R. Thompson. Stanford: Stanford University Press, 1990.

Marks, Robert. *Rural Revolution in South China: Peasants and the Making of History in Haifeng County, 1570–1930*. Madison: University of Wisconsin Press, 1984.

Martin, W. A. P. *The Awakening of China*. New York: Doubleday, Page and Co., 1907.

Matthews, Mervyn. *Privilege in the Soviet Union: A Study of Elite Life-Styles under Communism*. London: George Allen and Unwin, 1978.

——. *Education in the Soviet Union: Policies and Institutions since Stalin*. London: George Allen and Unwin, 1982.

Mauger, Peter, et al. *Education in China*. London: Anglo-Chinese Educational Institute, 1974.

McCormick, Robert, ed. *Tanzania: Education for Self-Reliance*. Rev. Ed. Milton Keynes: Open University Press, 1979.

McDonald, Angus W., Jr. *The Urban Origins of Rural Revolution: Elites and the Masses in Hunan Province, China, 1911–1927*. Berkeley: University of California Press, 1978.

McDougall, Bonnie S. *Mao Zedong's "Talks at the Yan'an Conference on Literature and Art": A Translation of the 1943 Text with Commentary*. Papers in Chinese Studies, no. 39. Ann Arbor: University of Michigan, 1980.

McNamara, Robert S. *One Hundred Countries, Two Billion People: The Dimensions of Development*. New York: Praeger, 1973.

Meisner, Maurice. *Li Ta-chao and the Origins of Chinese Marxism*. Cambridge: Harvard University Press, 1967.

Menzel, Johanna M., ed. *The Chinese Civil Service: Career Open to Talent?* Boston: D.C. Heath, 1963.

Meskill, John. *Academies in Ming China: A Historical Essay*. Tucson: University of Arizona Press, 1982.

Metzger, Thomas A. *Escape from Predicament: Neo-Confucianism and China's Evolving Political Culture*. New York: Columbia University Press, 1977.

Milton, David, and Nancy Dall Milton. *The Wind Will Not Subside: Years in Revolutionary China, 1964–1969*. New York: Pantheon, 1976.

Miners, Norman. *The Government and Politics of Hong Kong*. Hong Kong: Oxford University Press, 1981.

Miyazaki, Ichisada. *China's Examination Hell: The Civil Service Examinations of Imperial China*. Trans. Conrad Schirokauer. New Haven: Yale University Press, 1981.

Monroe, Paul. *China: A Nation in Evolution*. New York: Macmillan, 1928.

Montaperto, Ronald N., and Jay Henderson, eds. *China's Schools in Flux*. White Plains, N.Y.: M. E. Sharpe, 1979.

Mosher, Steven W. *Broken Earth: The Rural Chinese*. New York: Free Press, 1983.

Mu Fu-sheng. *The Wilting of the Hundred Flowers: The Chinese Intelligentsia under Mao*. New York: Praeger, 1963.

Munro, Donald J. *The Concept of Man in Contemporary China*. Ann Arbor: University of Michigan Press, 1977.

Nakayama, Shigeru. *Academic and Scientific Traditions in China, Japan, and the West*. Trans. Jerry Dusenbury. Tokyo: University of Tokyo Press, 1984.

Nee, Victor. *The Cultural Revolution at Peking University*. New York: Monthly Review Press, 1969.

Ng, Alice Ngai-ha Lun. "Village Education in the New Territories Region under the Ch'ing." In Faure, Hayes, and Birch, *From Village to City.*

Ng, Lun Ngai-ha. "Village Education in Transition: The Case of Sheung Shui." *Journal of the Hong Kong Branch of the Royal Asiatic Society,* vol. 22 (1982), pp. 252–270.

Nivison, David S. "Protest against Conventions and Conventions of Protest." In Wright, *The Confucian Persuasion.*

Nyerere, J. K. *Education for Self-reliance.* Dar-es-Salaam: Government Printer, 1967.

Oi, Jean C. *State and Peasant in Contemporary China: The Political Economy of Village Government.* Berkeley: University of California Press, 1989.

Orb, Richard A. "Chihli Academies and Other Schools in the Late Ch'ing: An Institutional Survey." In Cohen and Schrecker, *Reform in Nineteenth-Century China.*

Orleans, Leo A. *Professional Manpower and Education in Communist China.* Washington, D.C.: National Science Foundation, 1960.

——, ed. *Science in Contemporary China.* Stanford: Stanford University Press, 1980.

Oxenham, John, ed. *Education versus Qualifications?* London: George Allen and Unwin, 1984.

Paine, Lynn Webster. "Progress and Problems in China's Educational Reform." In Joseph, *China Briefing, 1994.*

P'an Kuang-tan and Fei Hsiao-t'ung. "City and Village: The Inequality of Opportunity." In Menzel, *The Chinese Civil Service.* Originally published as "K'e-chü yü she-hui liu-tung" (The Examination System and Social Mobility), *She-hui k'e-hsüeh* (Social Science), vol. 4 (1947), pp. 1–21.

Parish, William L., and Martin King Whyte. *Village and Family in Contemporary China.* Chicago: University of Chicago Press, 1978.

Peake, Cyrus H. *Nationalism and Education in Modern China.* New York: Howard Fertig, 1970. Originally published by Columbia University Press, 1932.

Pennar, Jaan, Ivan I. Bakalo, and George Z. F. Bereday. *Modernization and Diversity in Soviet Education.* New York: Praeger, 1971.

Pepper, Suzanne. "Education and Political Development in Communist China." *Studies in Comparative Communism,* vol. 3, nos. 3–4 (July/Oct. 1970), pp. 132–157.

——. *Civil War in China: The Political Struggle, 1945–1949.* Berkeley: University of California Press, 1978.

——. "Education and Revolution: The 'Chinese Model' Revisited." *Asian Survey,* vol. 18, no. 9 (Sept. 1978), pp. 847–890.

——. "Chinese Education after Mao: Two Steps Forward, Two Steps Back and Begin Again?" *China Quarterly,* no. 81 (Mar. 1980), pp. 1–65.

——. "China's Universities: New Experiments in Socialist Democracy and Administrative Reform – A Research Report." *Modern China,* vol. 8, no. 2 (Apr. 1982), pp. 147–204.

——. *China's Universities: Post-Mao Enrollment Policies and Their Impact on the Structure of Secondary Education: A Research Report.* Monographs in Chinese Studies, no. 46. Ann Arbor: University of Michigan, 1984.

——. "Education for the New Order" and "New Directions in Education." Chaps. 4 and 9 in MacFarquhar and Fairbank, *The Cambridge History of China,* vol. 14, pt. 1.

——. *China's Education Reform in the 1980s: Policies, Issues, and Historical Perspectives.* China Research Monograph, no. 36. Berkeley: University of California, 1990.

———. "Education," chap. 7 in MacFarquhar and Fairbank, *The Cambridge History of China*, vol. 15, pt. 2.

———. "Post-Mao Reforms in Chinese Education: Can the Ghosts of the Past Be Laid to Rest?" In Epstein, *Chinese Education*.

———. "Educational Reform in the 1980s: A Retrospective on the Maoist Era." In Kau and Marsh, *China in the Era of Deng Xiaoping*.

———. Introduction to "Rural Education (I)." *Chinese Education and Society: A Journal of Translations*, vol. 27, no. 5 (Sept.–Oct. 1994), pp. 5–22.

———. "Regaining the Initiative for Education Reform and Development." In Lo, Pepper, and Tsui, *China Review, 1995*.

Peterson, Glen. "State Literacy Ideologies and the Transformation of Rural China." *Australian Journal of Chinese Affairs*, no. 32 (July 1994), pp. 95–120.

Phillips, H. M. *Planning Educational Assistance for the Second Development Decade*. Paris: Unesco International Institute for Educational Planning, 1973.

Pickowicz, Paul G. *Marxist Literary Thought in China: The Influence of Ch'ü Ch'iu-pai*. Berkeley: University of California Press, 1981.

Piper, Don C., and Taylor Cole, eds. *Post-primary Education and Political and Economic Development*. Durham, N.C.: Duke University Press; London: Cambridge University Press, 1964.

Potter, Sulamith Heins, and Jack M. Potter. *China's Peasants: The Anthropology of a Revolution*. Cambridge: Cambridge University Press, 1990.

Price, Jane L. *Cadres, Commanders, and Commissars: The Training of the Chinese Communist Leadership, 1920–45*. Boulder: Westview, 1976.

Price, Ronald F. *Education in Communist China*. London: Routledge and Kegan Paul, 1970.

———. *Marx and Education in Russia and China*. London: Croom Helm, 1977.

———. "Labour and Education." *Comparative Education*, vol. 20, no. 1 (1984), pp. 81–91.

———. "Convergence or Copying: China and the Soviet Union." In Hayhoe and Bastid, *China's Education and the Industrialized World*.

Psacharopoulos, George, and Keith Hinchliffe. *Returns to Education: An International Comparison*. San Francisco: Jossey-Bass, 1973.

Psacharopoulos, George, and William Loxley. *Diversified Secondary Education and Development: Evidence from Colombia and Tanzania*. Baltimore and London: Johns Hopkins University Press, 1985.

Psacharopoulos, George, and Maureen Woodhall. *Education for Development: An Analysis of Investment Choices*. New York: Oxford University Press, 1985.

Purcell, Victor. *Problems of Chinese Education*. London: Kegan Paul, Trench, Trubner and Co., 1936.

Pye, Lucian W., ed. *Communications and Political Development*. Princeton: Princeton University Press, 1963.

Raddock, David. *Political Behavior of Adolescents in China: The Cultural Revolution in Kwangchow (Canton)*. Tucson: University of Arizona Press, 1977.

Rankin, Mary Backus. *Early Chinese Revolutionaries: Radical Intellectuals in Shanghai and Chekiang, 1902–1911*. Cambridge: Harvard University Press, 1971.

———. *Elite Activism and Political Transformation in China: Zhejiang Province, 1865–1911*. Stanford: Stanford University Press, 1986.

Rawls, John. *A Theory of Justice*. London and New York: Oxford University Press, 1972.

Rawski, Evelyn Sakakida. *Education and Popular Literacy in Ch'ing China*. Ann Arbor: University of Michigan Press, 1979.

Reese, William J. *Power and the Promise of School Reform: Grassroots Movements during the Progressive Era*. Boston and London: Routledge and Kegan Paul, 1986.

Rickett, Allyn, and Adele Rickett. *Prisoners of Liberation*. Garden City, N.Y.: Anchor/ Doubleday, 1973.

Robinson, Jean C. "Decentralization, Money, and Power: The Case of People-run Schools in China." *Comparative Education Review*, vol. 30, no. 1 (Feb. 1986), pp. 73–88.

Roethlisberger, F. J., and W. J. Dickson. *Management and the Worker*. Cambridge: Harvard University Press, 1939.

Rosen, Stanley. *The Role of Sent-down Youth in the Chinese Cultural Revolution: The Case of Guangzhou*. China Research Monograph, no. 19. Berkeley: University of California, 1981.

——. *Red Guard Factionalism and the Cultural Revolution in Guangzhou (Canton)*. Boulder: Westview, 1982.

——. "Recentralization, Decentralization, and Rationalization: Deng Xiaoping's Bifurcated Educational Policy." *Modern China*, vol. 11, no. 3 (July 1985), pp. 301–346.

——. "Restoring Key Secondary Schools in Post-Mao China: The Politics of Competition and Educational Quality." In Lampton, *Policy Implementation in Post-Mao China* (1987).

Rozman, Gilbert. *A Mirror for Socialism: Soviet Criticisms of China*. Princeton: Princeton University Press, 1985.

Rue, John E. *Mao Tse-tung in Opposition, 1927–1935*. Stanford: Hoover Institution, 1966.

Schoenhals, Michael. "Unofficial and Official Histories of the Cultural Revolution – A Review Article." *Journal of Asian Studies*, vol. 48, no. 3 (Aug. 1989), pp. 563–572.

Schoppa, R. Keith. *Chinese Elites and Political Change: Zhejiang Province in the Early Twentieth Century*. Cambridge: Harvard University Press, 1982.

Schram, Stuart R. *The Political Thought of Mao Tse-tung*. New York: Praeger, 1963.

——. *Mao Tse-tung*. Baltimore: Penguin, 1966.

——, ed. *Mao Tse-tung Unrehearsed, Talks and Letters: 1956–71*. Harmondsworth: Penguin, 1974.

Schwarcz, Vera. *The Chinese Enlightenment: Intellectuals and the Legacy of the May Fourth Movement of 1919*. Berkeley: University of California Press, 1986.

Schwartz, Benjamin I. *Chinese Communism and the Rise of Mao*. Cambridge: Harvard University Press, 1958.

Science and Technology in the People's Republic of China. Paris: Organisation for Economic Co-operation and Development, 1977.

Seeberg, Vilma. *Literacy in China: The Effect of the National Development Context and Policy on Literacy Levels, 1949–1979*. Bochum: Brockmeyer, 1990.

Selden, Mark. *The Yenan Way in Revolutionary China*. Cambridge: Harvard University Press, 1971.

Seybolt, Peter J. "The Yenan Revolution in Mass Education." *China Quarterly*, no. 48 (Oct./Dec. 1971), pp. 641–669.

——. "Terror and Conformity: Counter-espionage Campaigns, Rectification, and Mass Movements, 1942–1943." *Modern China*, vol. 12, no. 1 (Jan. 1986), pp. 39–73.

——, ed. *Revolutionary Education in China: Documents and Commentary*. White Plains, N.Y.: International Arts and Sciences Press, 1973.

——. *The Rustication of Urban Youth in China: A Social Experiment*. New York: M. E. Sharpe, 1977.

Shaffer, Lynda. *Mao and the Workers: The Hunan Labor Movement, 1920–1923*. Armonk, N.Y.: M. E. Sharpe, 1982.

Sheringham, Michael. "Popularisation Policies in Chinese Education from the 1950s to the 1970s." *Comparative Education*, vol. 20, no. 1 (1984), pp. 73–80.

Shirk, Susan L. "The 1963 Temporary Work Regulations for Full-time Middle and Primary Schools: Commentary and Translation." *China Quarterly*, no. 55 (July/ Sept. 1973), pp. 511–546.

——. "Educational Reform and Political Backlash: Recent Changes in Chinese Educational Policy." *Comparative Education Review*, vol. 23, no. 2 (June 1979), pp. 183–217.

——. *Competitive Comrades: Career Incentives and Student Strategies in China*. Berkeley: University of California Press, 1982.

Simkins, Tim. *Non-formal Education and Development: Some Critical Issues*. Manchester Monographs, no. 8. Manchester: University of Manchester, 1976.

Simmons, John. "Retention of Cognitive Skills Acquired in Primary School." *Comparative Education Review*, vol. 20, no. 1 (Feb. 1976), pp. 79–93.

——, ed. *The Education Dilemma: Policy Issues for Developing Countries in the 1980s*. New York: Pergamon, 1980.

Singer, Martin. *Educated Youth and the Cultural Revolution in China*. Papers in Chinese Studies, no. 10. Ann Arbor: University of Michigan, 1971.

Skinner, G. William, ed. *The City in Late Imperial China*. Stanford: Stanford University Press, 1977.

Snow, Edgar. *Red Star over China*. New York: Grove Press, 1961.

Socialist Upsurge in China's Countryside. Peking: Foreign Languages Press, 1978.

Spence, Jonathan. *To Change China: Western Advisers in China, 1620–1960*. New York: Penguin, 1980.

Stalin, J. V. *Works*. 13 vols. Moscow: Foreign Languages Publishing House, 1952–1955.

State Statistical Bureau. *Ten Great Years*. Peking: Foreign Languages Press, 1960.

Statistical Yearbook of China, 1983. Hong Kong: Economic Information and Agency, 1983.

Street, Brian V. *Literacy in Theory and Practice*. Cambridge: Cambridge University Press, 1984.

Suttmeier, Richard P. *Science, Technology, and China's Drive for Modernization*. Stanford: Hoover Institution, 1980.

Suttmeier, Richard P., and Genevieve Dean. "The Institutionalisation of Science." In *Science and Technology in the People's Republic of China*.

Sutton, Antony C. *Western Technology and Soviet Economic Development, 1917–1930*. Stanford: Hoover Institution, 1968.

Swetz, Frank. *Mathematics Education in China: Its Growth and Development*. Cambridge: MIT Press, 1974.

Tawney, R. H. *Land and Labour in China*. London: George Allen and Unwin, 1932.
——. *The Radical Tradition*. London: George Allen and Unwin, 1964.
Taylor, Robert. *Education and University Enrolment Policies in China, 1949–1971*. Canberra: Australian National University Press, 1973.
Teng, Ssu-yü, and John K. Fairbank, eds. *China's Response to the West: A Documentary Survey, 1839–1923*. Cambridge: Harvard University Press, 1961.
Thøgersen, Stig. "China's Senior Middle Schools in a Social Perspective: A Survey of Yantai District, Shandong Province." *China Quarterly*, no. 109 (Mar. 1987), pp. 72–100.
——. *Secondary Education in China after Mao: Reform and Social Conflict*. Aarhus, Denmark: Aarhus University Press, 1990.
Thomson, James C., Jr. *While China Faced West: American Reformers in Nationalist China, 1928–1937*. Cambridge: Harvard University Press, 1969.
Thurston, Anne F. *Enemies of the People: The Ordeal of the Intellectuals in China's Great Cultural Revolution*. Cambridge: Harvard University Press, 1988.
Todaro, Michael P. *Internal Migration in Developing Countries: A Review of Theory, Evidence, Methodology and Research Priorities*. Geneva: International Labour Office, 1976.
Townsend, James R. *The Revolutionization of Chinese Youth*. China Research Monographs, no. 1. Berkeley: University of California, 1967.
Turnham, David, and Ingelies Jaeger. *The Employment Problem in Less Developed Countries: A Review of Evidence*. Paris: Development Centre of the Organisation for Economic Cooperation and Development, 1971.
Twiss, George Ransom. *Science and Education in China: A Survey of the Present Status and a Program for Progressive Improvement*. Shanghai: Commercial Press, 1925.
Unger, Jonathan. "China's Troubled Down-to-the-Countryside Campaign." *Contemporary China* (Columbia University), vol. 3, no. 2 (1979), pp. 79–92.
——. "The Chinese Controversy over Higher Education." *Pacific Affairs*, vol. 53, no. 1 (spring 1980), pp. 29–47.
——. "Bending the School Ladder: The Failure of Chinese Educational Reform in the 1960s." *Comparative Education Review*, vol. 24, no. 2, pt. 1 (June 1980), pp. 221–237.
——. *Education under Mao: Class and Competition in Canton Schools, 1960–1980*. New York: Columbia University Press, 1982.
Vaizey, John. *Education in the Modern World*. London: Weidenfeld and Nicolson, 1975.
Varg, Paul A. *Missionaries, Chinese, and Diplomats*. Princeton: Princeton University Press, 1958.
Vladimirov, Peter. *The Vladimirov Diaries: Yenan, China, 1942–1945*. Garden City, N.Y.: Doubleday, 1975.
Waller, Derek J. *The Kiangsi Soviet Republic: Mao and the National Congresses of 1931 and 1934*. China Research Monographs, no. 10. Berkeley: University of California, 1973.
Wang, Y. C. *Chinese Intellectuals and the West, 1872–1949*. Chapel Hill: University of North Carolina Press, 1966.
Ward, F. Champion, ed. *Education and Development Reconsidered: The Bellagio Conference Papers*. New York: Praeger, 1974.

Watson, Andrew, ed. *Mao Zedong and the Political Economy of the Border Region.* Cambridge: Cambridge University Press, 1980.

Watson, Keith, ed. *Dependence and Interdependence in Education: International Perspectives.* London: Croom Helm, 1984.

Weiler, Hans N. "Education and Development: From the Age of Innocence to the Age of Scepticism." *Comparative Education*, vol. 14, no. 3 (Oct. 1978), pp. 179–198.

West, Philip. *Yenching University and Sino-Western Relations, 1916–1952.* Cambridge: Harvard University Press, 1976.

White, D. Gordon. "The Politics of *Hsia-hsiang* Youth." *China Quarterly*, no. 59 (July/Sept. 1974), pp. 491–517.

White, Gordon. *The Politics of Class and Class Origin: The Case of the Cultural Revolution.* Canberra: Contemporary China Centre, Australian National University, 1976.

Who's Who in Communist China. 2 vols. Hong Kong: Union Research Institute, 1969–1970.

Whyte, Martin K. "Educational Reform: China in the 1970s and Russia in the 1920s." *Comparative Education Review*, vol. 18, no. 1 (Feb. 1974), pp. 112–128.

Whyte, Martin King, and William L. Parish. *Urban Life in Contemporary China.* Chicago: University of Chicago Press, 1984.

Williams, Peter, ed. *Prescription for Progress? A Commentary on the Education Policy of the World Bank.* London: University of London, Institute of Education, 1976.

Wilson, Dick. *Mao: The People's Emperor.* London: Hutchinson, 1979.

——, ed. *Mao Tse-tung in the Scales of History.* Cambridge: Cambridge University Press, 1977.

Witke, Roxane. *Comrade Chiang Ch'ing.* Boston: Little, Brown and Co., 1977.

Woodhead, H. G. W., ed. *The China Year Book, 1934.* Shanghai: North-China Daily News and Herald, 1934.

Woodside, Alexander. "Some Mid-Qing Theorists of Popular Schools: Their Innovations, Inhibitions, and Attitudes toward the Poor." *Modern China*, vol. 9, no. 1 (Jan. 1983), pp. 3–35.

——. "Real and Imagined Continuities in the Chinese Struggle for Literacy." In Hayhoe, *Education and Modernization.*

Wright, Arthur F. *The Confucian Persuasion.* Stanford: Stanford University Press, 1960.

Wright, Mary Clabaugh. *The Last Stand of Chinese Conservatism: The T'ung-Chih Restoration, 1862–1874.* Stanford: Stanford University Press, 1962.

——, ed. *China in Revolution: The First Phase, 1900–1913.* New Haven: Yale University Press, 1968.

Wylie, Raymond F. *The Emergence of Maoism: Mao Tse-tung, Ch'en Po-ta, and the Search for Chinese Theory, 1935–1945.* Stanford: Stanford University Press, 1980.

Yang Jung-kuo. "Confucius – A Thinker Who Stubbornly Supported the Slave System." In *Selected Articles Criticizing Lin Piao and Confucius.* Peking: Foreign Languages Press, 1974.

Yung, Wing. *My Life in China and America.* New York: H. Holt, 1909.

Zweig, David. *Agrarian Radicalism in China, 1968–1981.* Cambridge: Harvard University Press, 1989.

Index

post-1976 repudiation, 532
targeting school authorities, 358–64
Ma Xulun, 169, 181–4, 207
May Fourth (1919) Movement, 89, 107
Ma Yinchu, 72–3
Mazhenfu commune incident, 470
mechanical copying
criticism of, 64, 240–2, 251–2, 525
end of (1958), 259
Mao's accusations of, 138–9
of Soviet education system, 191,
524–5
medical training, 384, 394–5, 408–10
Mei, Teacher
on sent-down youth, 395–6
on two-line struggle, 475
military representatives in schools, 370,
373, 468
Min, Comrade, 399
minban (run by the people) schools
border regions (1944), 144–9
contribution of, 154
in education revolution (1958), 281
incorporation in state-financed system,
386
limitations on and revival of (1952),
194, 196–7
within national education system, 345
private schools as (1990s), 536
role in rural universal elementary
schooling, 220–1, 225
in Shanghai during regularization,
334–5
unpopularity of, 345
used interchangeably with *gongban*,
427–8
Ming dynasty (1368–1644), 47, 338
missionaries, foreign
campaign against (1950s), 164, 172
Christian missionaries in rural
rehabilitation, 105–6
missionary schools, Christian, 38, 54, 115
modernization
Deng's education reform, 479
with Great Leap Forward, 287–8
idea of educational, 60
prerequisites under Deng's reforms, 489
return to ideas of professional
educators, 495–6
in students' expectations, 307–8

Nanjing Higher Teachers Training
School, 75
nationalism
antiforeign demonstrations (1919 and
after), 94
of May Fourth period, 88–90
sources of, 114
Nationalist government (1928–49)
See also Chiang Kai-shek
anticommunist purges, 94, 112, 122
education system under, 62–4,
109–17
effect of Sino-Japanese War on, 128
government service training program,
111
rural education–reconstruction project,
105–7, 118
National Secondary Education
Conference (1951), 205, 209
National Southeastern University, 75
New Culture Movement (1910s), 94
See also May Fourth (1919)
Movement
education sector within, 90–1
sources and assumptions of, 88–9, 112
undermining of, 109–10
New Education Movement, republican
era, 91–4
Nie Yuanzi, 355, 357, 371
Niu, Doctor
on rural health work, 395
Nixon, Richard, 470

overseas Chinese, 369, 431–3, 539,
540–3, 545–7

Parish, William, 540
parity concept, regional
in Chinese education system, 516
in designation of key-point schools,
323–5, 346
with reduction in school access, 502
parity principle, 27, 308, 324
peasant movement, Hunan (Mao's
report), 100–1, 124, 360–1
peasant problem, 95
peasants
college admission priorities, 282
in educational reform, 147
education policy related to, 209